ORGANIZING FOR EVANGELISM

lanning an effective program for witnessing

by Alvin C. Rueter

Augsburg Publishing House

Minneapolis

ADMINISTRATION SERIES FOR CHURCHES

Topics in this series are grouped in seven major areas: Theology of Administration; Organization Development; Finance, Accounting and Cash Control; Program Planning and Evaluation; Personnel and Office Policies; Property and Insurance; Communications. Each publication in this series will have been field-tested in congregations and presented by authoritative writers. Topic suggestions and comments are sought from all readers.

John R. Dewey
Division for Life and Mission in the Congregation
The American Lutheran Church

ORGANIZING FOR EVANGELISM
planning an effective program for witnessing

International Standard Book No. 0-8066-2026-9.

Manufactured in the United States of America

Contents

Preface

So you're on the evangelism committee. Congratulations! Not everyone would compliment you, and in Chapter Two we'll talk about that. I congratulate you because you have responsibility for a ministry that people need. So many people think they've heard the gospel, but it's clear they haven't found out yet what it means to live forgiven. And you and your colleagues in the ministry of evangelism can show them.

This is not a big book, but it touches on a number of aspects about organizing for evangelism. One of its functions is to introduce you to the excellent books listed in Additional Resources. These books provide significant information on a range of topics, so many, perhaps, that the size of the job could get you down. Don't fret. Evangelism is urgent, but it's also worth doing well. You and your committee may need some time to digest what's offered here and to analyze where you are, where you want to go, and how you'll get there. You probably won't achieve all your goals this year; you may want to work out a three-year plan, or a five-year plan. Paul wrote to Corinthians, "We work with you for your joy" (2 Corinthians 1:24). By taking a thoughtful and systematic approach, you and your committee can indeed have joy in the ministry of evangelism.

God's blessings as you study and then plan and then administer the program of evangelism in your congregation!

Alvin C. Rueter

Chapter 1

Why We Do Evangelism

> **Witnessing is one beggar telling another beggar where to find bread.**
> **—D. T. Niles**

Old Christ Church used to have two services every Sunday; now it has one, and even then the pews are half-empty. The congregation has had to let the secretary and the janitor go, filling the gap with volunteer help. The bills are piling up. Will the members need to make the pastor part-time next?

Young Grace Church financed its building with denominational funding for the first few years at below-market rates. According to agreement, it then refinanced the mortgage to release church funds for starting another mission. Now it's paying 15% on its debt.

For Christ Church one answer to the question, "Why do we do evangelism?" would be "To keep the doors open." For Grace Church it would be "To pay off the debt."

No one denies the realism behind those motives. But that would be membership recruitment, not evangelism. For an evangelism committee looking for a reason for its existence, there must be something more. Suppose both congregations found enough new members to meet their financial obligations. Would their mission to evangelize be finished?

Some people would point out: "Our Lord said, 'Go therefore and make disciples of all nations, baptizing them in the name of the Father and of the Son and of the Holy Spirit.' Until that is done completely, we must spread the Word."

Others would answer, "Certainly not. We have the gospel of Christ and people would be lost without it. We owe it to them." This reply surely rings true to the sound of Romans chapter 1 where Paul writes: "I am under obligation both to Greeks and to barbarians, both to the wise and to the foolish: so I am eager to preach the gospel to you also who are in Rome" (vv. 14-15).

We'll suggest in this manual that Christians are "under obligation" to evangelize, that we have received a pearl of great price without our deserving it, that our faith in Christ has meant so much to us it would be selfish to hoard it for our benefit alone.

In the possessing of this gift of faith there can be temptation to haughtiness. The witness of some Christians bears a trace of snobbery—although perhaps it's entirely unintended. These well-meaning folks somehow project an image that they think they're better than the people to whom they're witnessing. "We go to church every Sunday, and you really should be going, too," they say. The objects of their concern then either tune them out or jam the channel of communication with comments like: "Oh yeah? I'm as good as any of you hypocrites!" When the witnesser knows that he or she is saved only by grace—God's undeserved love in Christ—then the self-righteousness disappears.

Why do we do evangelism? Because we beggars have found where to find bread. We want to share the good news.

Chapter 2

Evangelism We Don't Do

Stories abound of old, historic, tradition-bound, "declining" congregations which suddenly, almost miraculously "come to life" because at least some of the members learned to listen well, to "hear," to shape answers and solutions with care and compassion, and, as a result, to help set their church community—and their ministry—on a new path.[1]

Trinity Church had its annual meeting last Sunday. According to its constitution the newly elected officers and the incumbents must meet within a week to organize themselves into a church council. The various committee chair positions are up for grabs. Experienced members speak up quickly for property and stewardship and finance. Before long education and worship and youth are also taken. One slot is left. The unwary new officer finds himself or herself as the new chairperson of evangelism. The rest count themselves lucky for having escaped that fate. Some congregations have a history of rapid turnover in evangelism; few persons last more than one year and often regard that year as something like a prison term, experiencing great relief upon release. *Why is this?*

Of several possible reasons, two stand out: they didn't know what the job was (which is difficult enough); and they couldn't measure the results (if any—and which is probably even more difficult to determine).

Repairing Leaks

Suppose the church roof is leaking. You can see the puddles on the floor and the stains on the plaster. The property committee gets estimates on what it will take to undo the damage. A member of the stewardship committee gives a "temple talk" during services, telling of a special offering for this urgent cause. The money is raised. The contracts are let and fulfilled. The property committee knows to the penny how much it cost, and the stewardship committee knows to the penny how much the offering was. Now the two chairpersons can make their reports: "We saw what was to be done and we did it."

I live in St. Paul, Minnesota. At the beginning of winter I usually build a skating rink in our backyard. After making the base out of snow sprayed into slush and frozen, I've found that it works best to put down one layer of water at a time. Perhaps on my day off I'll plan to build up the ice with several layers, one every hour or so. I may go out at, say, 8:00 a.m. to sprinkle the rink, only to come out again at 9:00 a.m. to find every drop of the first sprinkling has escaped! There is obviously a pinhole leak somewhere. I can't see it, but it took away all my water.

The frustration I feel over my skating rink is something with which the evangelism chairperson can identify. Where is the leak that drained off three of every four of this congregation's youth? Why were there twice as many members lost last year as were gained? The frustration only mounts when the evangelism chairperson sees statistics showing how pinhole leaks from many congregations issue into a flood. For example, during the decade of the 1970s the American Lutheran Church lost members equal to more than 40% of its total membership, the equivalent of three of its largest districts.[2] The net loss, of course, was much less because of new members gained.

With so many removals from membership rolls through inactivity, no wonder those assigned to oversee the congregation's ministry of evangelism too often yearn to be delivered from this responsibility. But Paul told the Corinthians that his function was to work with them for their joy. How do the rest of us work with the evangelism chairperson so that we may help him or her to have joy? And how does the evangelism chairperson work with the committee so that they too may have fun in their ministry?

But we're not quite ready yet to struggle with answers to those questions. There are still more difficulties to be identified.

Removing Barriers

Our church buildings provide opportunities for many good things to happen to many persons. But we're beginning to see that the stairs up to the entrance and up to the altar and down to the rest rooms are obstacles of no small consequence to a substantial number of people—obstacles we didn't intend, but obstacles, nevertheless.

It's clear that structural barriers in the church building are barriers to evangelism. Installing ramps and elevators will be expensive. But if the barriers are physical, a committee can see the problem and usually can move the congregation to act. It can then publish its report: "We saw what was to be done and we did it."

Not so evident are other barriers to evangelism, barriers probably more troublesome to remove than stairways. Again, these obstacles may not be intended, but they *are* obstacles, nevertheless.

One is the barrier of **labels.** "Active" members tend to view "inactives" as delinquents. "Inactives" tend to view "actives" as hypocrites. Only God knows how many "delinquents" may have wanted to return to the fellowship but were prevented by their fear of hearing a stalwart member jest, "Well, look who's here! Watch out, the roof's going to cave in!" Whether or not anyone would be that insensitive may not be the issue; the "inactive" *fears* this will happen.

Another is the barrier of **social coolness.** Sometimes we get scolded for being unfriendly at church. In a way that's an unfair criticism. Nobody has meant it to be so. When we come to worship and study, what could be better than to chat with relatives and friends? Or what could be more efficient than to visit with a fellow officer and help some cogs in the congregation's machinery turn more smoothly? Meanwhile, strangers have come in and strangers have gone out. We've been aware of our negligence; so we've delegated the welcoming business to official greeters, even listing their names in the service bulletin. Strangers may well appreciate the smile and the handshake of these designated friends, but if the rest of the community of believers shuts itself off, they'll sense that our cordiality is shallow.

Another barrier to evangelism is that of **unfamiliar cultural forms.** Some people reared outside the Roman Catholic tradition might hesitate to venture into a Mass because they have heard of holy water and genuflecting. They say to themselves, "I'm not going to embarrass myself. I'll be the only person there who doesn't know what to do next." In the same way, those reared outside the Lutheran tradition may find its music and liturgy difficult to enjoy. Just picking their way through the liturgy may put them off. Then there are those who aren't accustomed to singing—or who just can't sing—for whom music of any sort is a barrier. Dale Trautman, Director for Evangelism, The American Lutheran Church, points out that cultural forms are not limited to music or liturgy: "A person doesn't need to enjoy lutefisk or have a short hair style to be part of the people of God. This realization is particularly important when considering the responses of young people. . . . The reason they give most often for inactivity is that they cannot identify with the lifestyle of the congregation."[3]

There are also barriers of **class.** One year I was enrolled in the Center for Urban Encounter, where I was introduced to a variety of challenges to the church in Minneapolis/St. Paul. On one weekend I took "the plunge": I dressed myself as a street person, paid 75¢ for a bed at a mission, and lived on the streets and in the bars. On Sunday I went to worship at a cathedral where no one paid any attention to me. Later that morning I went to a rather chic Protestant church. Here the ushers greeted me, showed me where to hang my coat, gave me a service bulletin, and took me to a pew. After the service a person sitting in front of me made sure I shook hands with a pastor, and commented, "He really sang the hymns!" Then he took me over to the guest register to have me sign my name. I give this congregation a lot of credit. No doubt I embarrassed them, but, because of my attire, I was probably more embarrassed than they were! Yet I learned from that experience just how difficult it can be for someone who doesn't "fit in" even to *try*.

Homogeneity or Diversity?

There are some people who advocate a policy of "homogenized" churches, where everybody talks and dresses and votes nearly the same. The idea is: "If you see to it that no 'misfits' find their way into the fellowship, your churches stand a better chance of growing." This strategy may help bring in members of a given level, but what about a man like Zacchaeus who was out of place almost everywhere. But when he climbed into a sycamore tree to see the Lord, Jesus invited himself to his house (Luke 19:1-10).

There was also a Greek woman, a Syrophoenician by birth, who—it seemed—was so out of place she was even being put off by Jesus. He told her, "I was sent only to the lost sheep of the house of Israel." When she then pleaded, "Lord, help me," again it seemed Jesus was closing the door. But apparently he was only drawing her out. He said, "It is not fair to take the children's bread and throw it to the dogs"; to which she replied, "Yes, Lord, yet even the dogs eat the crumbs that fall from their master's table." Jesus immediately took her into the family of faith (Matthew 15:21-28; Mark 7:24-30).

A Combination

Perhaps there's a way of taking advantage of the attraction of being with your own kind while also building relationships through small groups. We may find identification by age in youth and senior citizen fellowships or by gender in men's and women's societies. In some urban congregations it may be feasible to have associations by trade or vocation: building crafts, education, investments, sales, computers, medicine, law, management, automobiles, travel, unions, secretaries, communications. They can meet to knit bonds of fellowship and explore how they express their life in Christ in their daily work. Important, too, are caring groups that show their Christian faith by their prayers and by willing service to help others.

In the East Harlem Parish, New York City, there are Bible study groups meeting in the various apartment buildings where the members live, groups in which people discuss the text for the coming Sunday's sermon. They may invite neighbors and friends without needing to confront them with unfamiliar cultural forms in hymns and liturgy.

Southern Baptist congregations have a place for everyone in their Sunday schools by age and gender, adults included. In some congregations you can be in a class where everyone is within six months of your age. Small homogeneous groups can be the bridge to the larger diverse fellowship when all the small groups come together for common worship. The friends within the small groups introduce the newcomers to the unfamiliar cultural forms and help them adjust to the outward differences in those with whom they are one in Christ.

While the homogenized small group ought to be the vehicle bringing people into the larger fellowship of diversity, it can also become a roadblock. It's great when the members of a youth group or a women's circle become so supportive of one another they even remember each other's birthdays, but this intimacy may unintentionally shut outsiders out. The newcomer soon tires of asking (or more likely never gets the courage for asking), "What are you talking about?" In such a case, an evangelism committee has the function not of telling the group what its business is but asking, "What is your attitude toward strangers, and how does it contribute to our common ministry of evangelism?"

Overcoming the Tyranny of Numbers

As if repairing leaks and removing barriers weren't enough, there's also the deceptive and disconcerting tyranny of numbers.

Years ago I would have been tempted to say that it's easy to measure results in evangelism. Just look at the statistics. How many new members did you bring into the fellowship last year? How many members did you lose? What was your net gain? What was your increase in average weekly attendance at worship? How many new pupils did you add to your church schools? How does this year's attendance in the church schools compare with last year's? How many adults were baptized and how many confirmed?

I began to come up against the tyranny of numbers in 1954 when I accepted a call to form a mission congregation in Tulsa, Oklahoma, in a culture where Lutherans and ex-Lutherans are scarce. There was not one person in the entire county that had asked my family and me to come there. Unlike some parts of the U.S.A., here no rural congregations were sending their young people to the church in our city. Knowing there were thousands of people in Tulsa outside the church had seemed reason enough to begin a church there. Now we found that some of them had been "inoculated" to Christianity with one or more brands of denominationalism in their childhood.

We further discovered that more than a few people were suspicious of the Lutheran church as an ethnic group. They were staying away from all churches, but they were staying away from the Lutheran church the most. I recruited, instructed, and confirmed a nucleus of individuals who then became my co-workers in finding others.

Along with parish workers and parish mission builders, as we called them, this young congregation and I made over 4,000 calls a year. Going house to house in the summers, some days we obtained no other positive result than that someone offered us a drink of water. I instructed and confirmed two-thirds of all the people received into membership, and one-third of the membership moved out of town every year, mostly because the oil companies had transferred them to another part of the world.

After five years, when we had about 175 members, I heard an official at a convention tell of the wonderful things happening in Minnesota, where new congregations were being started with as many as 300 charter members. It took me a while to climb out of the pit into which this statistic threw me. I ask: Were those new congregations in Minnesota doing more evangelism than we were in Oklahoma? Maybe. Maybe not.

What if your congregation is rural? When the farms keep getting larger, the farmers keep becoming fewer. Is evangelism going on in your parish? Maybe. Maybe not. You can't always tell by looking only at the numbers.

What if your congregation is in the inner city? Your pastor is probably conducting two, three, or four funerals a month. With some of your fellow members, your pastor may be visiting nursing homes and cancer hospices weekly, getting people ready to live or die. Few of these patients ever join your congregation or brighten up your statistics with attendance or money. Perhaps the widows in your neighborhood are renting out rooms to young people just in from rural areas. Your pastor and your evangelism colleagues may have sought out these newcomers and made them welcome at church, but when these young people change jobs, or even just change their minds, they'll pack a few boxes and move to the other side of town.

The seemingly fruitless effort of ministering to rootless young adults—how do you measure that kind of effort in an annual report? Since the inner city is a "point of entry," families with children are also in transit; as soon as they can get on their feet, they move to the home of their dreams. Even at that, the rate of growth of inner-city churches is often higher than that of suburban churches. Statistical forms do provide a place to record the transfers out of your congregation. A real ministry for the inner-city congregation is to build up the suburban church—but we don't give much credit for such achievements. Transfers out are listed under losses. Is evangelism going on in the inner-city congregations? Maybe. Maybe not. You can't tell just by looking at the numbers.

With all the agents of discouragement working to prevent us from doing evangelism—the pinhole leaks that become floods, the barriers that are shadowy but substantial, the numbers that both deceive and defeat—how can organizers of evangelism find joy in their assignment? How do we devise a plan of action that is as satisfying as repairing a leak in the roof?

Attainable, Measurable, and Meaningful Goals

I suggest that the best plan is to set goals that are attainable, measurable, and meaningful. Churches need to decide to do *something*. They need a focus.

Suppose that your congregation decided it was time to conduct a door-to-door survey of the neighborhood around your church building. This goal could be attainable. You could estimate how many dwelling units there are, how many people you could reach in an hour, and how many callers it would take over how long a period of time. You could even guess how many residents might not be home and how many follow-up calls by telephone might be required.

You could then set aside three months when all the energies of the congregation would be directed toward reaching this goal—a goal which is not only attainable but measurable. Afterwards you can *see* all the cards your workers filled out; you can *count* them; you can even *weigh* them if you like. The trouble, however, is that there are just too many of them. Who will follow through?

The entire congregation was wrapped up in this project and got it done, but now everybody's tired. And so the cards remain in their boxes, and in a year or two, someone either stows them away in the attic or tosses them into the trash barrel. It was not a meaningful goal. The evangelism committee may report, "We saw what needed to be done and we did it," but they will be plagued by the guilt of seeing the follow-up work that isn't being done. The project did not issue into joy. Attainable, measurable, but not meaningful.

What kind of goal meets all three requirements? I find an example in the plan a friend used for a personal project. He discovered that his house needed painting about every four years. To cover it all at one time was a bigger job than he cared to tackle. So he did one side every summer. Attainable, measurable, and meaningful.

Apply this principle to the matter of conducting a survey in your neighborhood. Suppose your analysis suggests that the turnover of population requires a survey every three years. Divide up your territory into thirds and survey a third each year. Better yet, divide each third into tenths and recruit a small group to survey that tenth-of-a-third each month, giving them two months a year off.

What you're doing is turning up cards for follow-up calling at a pace you can manage, making it more likely the follow-up calls will be made.

But there are still some other drawbacks that could be eliminated. When a congregation sets itself to the task of surveying its whole territory in one grand effort, it usually has to decree that the energies of every available person be harnessed toward meeting this goal. The result: The workhorses become worn out. What's more, for three months all other congregational work has been left undone. All this frustration can be avoided if survey-callers are recruited from the ranks of those who might otherwise be overlooked: high school youth for going door-to-door and senior citizens for using the telephone.

Young and Old

There are excellent reasons for inviting high school youth to make survey calls. People sometimes resent door-to-door salespersons and evangelists, but they generally like to see the faces of fresh and eager young people. Besides, I've found that young people are more likely to follow instructions than some adults. The evangelism committee may have gone to the trouble of designing a special survey form, with questions for a specific purpose. Some adults tend to regard this or that question as irrelevant and won't ask it, depriving your committee of desirable information. Your youth are more likely to do the whole job.

Senior citizens, on the other hand, are good recruits for survey work done by telephone. But why use the telephone at all? Not everyone will be home when your survey callers go door-to-door, and some apartment buildings are locked and door-to-door persons won't be able to get in. There are telephone directories available listing phone numbers by address; you may be able to obtain access to one from a businessperson or from the library.

Why invite senior citizens to do the telephoning? Many older adults enjoy visiting by telephone. Such an assignment also provides them with a way to participate in the church's ministry without having to leave their homes. Another consideration: At least some of these calls will need to be made at night, and since single senior citizens often find evenings to be the loneliest time of the day, you'll be offering them a fruitful way to spend hours that might otherwise be dull and empty.

Notice that you're preventing burnout in these people because you're asking them to do a job with limits, one that's attainable, measurable, and meaningful. These people do surveying only. They don't have to feel responsible for what happens to the cards they produce. They've done their part well; they have a right to feel good.

Follow-Up

So who will do the follow-up work? Other people. But not *everyone* will try to do *all* of it. Here again, you need to define the task so that it becomes attainable. "Follow-up" is just too broad and hazy an assignment. It can mean many things. If someone blindly agrees to do "follow-up" without knowing what the limits are, you have another person looking for the nearest exist, trying to escape from the guilt of an unfinished and impossible task. The evangelism committee is well advised to consider exactly what is involved in follow-up and to explore the possibility of dividing the process into stages, with certain people recruited for each stage.

One stage of follow-up is to lead a person from outside the faith into a relationship with Christ. We might think that every Christian should be able to share the gospel. The evangelism committee may even have this objective as part of its vision for the congregation. But in the real world, evangelism recruiters will hear Christians saying, "Oh, I could *never* do that!" In Paul's letter to the Ephesians we learn that there are indeed a variety of gifts from the Holy Spirit, and that while not everyone has them all, some people have the special gift to be evangelists (Ephesians 4:11). So the evangelism committee will pray for the gift of discerning which people are best suited to the work of leading others to faith in Christ, and will recruit and train these persons specifically for this work.

For those members who feel that leading a person into the faith is not an attainable goal for them, you ask them to do something they believe they can do. You ask, "Would you be willing to go with another person to visit people just to make them feel welcome? to cultivate their good will? to prepare the way so somebody else can invite them to make a commitment to Christ and join the church? Would you be willing to make four such calls a month, 10 months a year?" There's a fair chance they'll respond, "I guess I could do that."

You're helping people be witnesses, people who aren't ready or able to be evangelists. You ask them to do a job with limits, one that's attainable, measurable, and meaningful. At the end of the year, these callers can count up the visits they made and measure whether their goal was reached. And if it was, they can say, "We did what we were asked to do. We did it well, and we feel good."

In later chapters we'll discuss the division of labor in more detail. Here we're simply illustrating the principle of helping the organizers of evangelism to have joy in their ministry by setting goals that are attainable, measurable, and meaningful. At the end of the year, the evangelism committee can look back and say, "We set a goal of completing this many survey calls and this many cultivation calls. We recruited enough people to make the calls; they did their job and we did ours. We all feel good about it."

Why haven't we been doing evangelism? Why has this ministry of the congregation too often been regarded as a dreary kind of service? Because the task is so vast and the potential discouragements are so heavy. How do we bring the job down to size so we can do it and can even find joy in it? Set goals that are attainable, measurable, and meaningful.

---

1. Elten A. Zerby and Ralph H. Quere, *An Evangel for Everyone* (Minneapolis: Augsburg Publishing House, 1981), p. 5.

2. Dale C. Trautman, *An Investigation of Inactivity in The American Lutheran Church: Its Causes and Cures* (Minneapolis: Augsburg Publishing House, 1982), pp. 2-3.

3. Ibid., p. 16.

Chapter 3

How We Look to Others

Many of the nonchurched say that people who are members of congregations are phonies.[4]

Somewhere in the United States there's a church where the front doors are always locked—even on Sunday morning. How does anyone get in? Through the kitchen door, of course—that's the entry closest to the parking lot. Everybody knows that.

Somewhere in the United States there's a church where the women's rest room can easily be found, but the men's room is at the far end of the basement. There are no signs giving directions. Every man and boy knows where it is anyway.

Though cultivation of group solidarity is a legitimate concern also in the church, the spirit of exclusiveness or clannishness, which easily results from group solidarity, is not wholesome. We need to follow Jesus in seeking out those who need the gospel.

In the previous chapter we thought about the things that have been preventing us from *doing* evangelism. Now we want to consider what may be preventing others from *accepting* our invitation. This is only part of the story, but it's not an unimportant part—that sometimes even those who have shown signs of interest are put off by our self-centeredness. Paul wrote: "Let each of you look not only to his own interests, but also to the interests of others" (Philippians 2:4). It's not easy to change your way of thinking so that in regard to everything that comes along you ask yourself: "How does this look to others? How do we legitimately adapt ourselves—without compromising—to other people's points of view? How do we frame our appeal so that it meets their self-interest?"

Just for fun, some Sunday go to a church where nobody knows you. My wife and I have done that occasionally and have been amused and depressed. One congregation may have greeters and ushers; we can tell by their badges. But they're so busy chatting with each other they hardly give us a glance. We almost have to beg a bulletin from them.

In another church it seems the organist has never learned to count, throwing the congregation off its rhythm. The organist then turns up the volume to move the singers along because it seems as though they're dragging. Well, they are.

In a third place the readers of the lessons are mumbling; they're mispronouncing words and putting the emphasis in the wrong places, seeming to have little sense of what they're reading. When the pastor reads the Gospel, it's not much better. He makes the good news sound dull. And his preaching is from long ago and far away and only gets to our concerns in the latter minutes when we may not be listening anymore.

Admittedly, these examples illustrate the dark side of the picture, but you do wonder how some of these congregations stay alive, why the members keep coming. "Well, it's *always* been our church." And of course, when it's *our* church—and not intended to be *anybody else's* church—then it makes little difference when only insiders know how to get into the building.

Image Survey

If you think your congregation can take it, hire a couple of graduate students in sociology to conduct an "image survey" of your congregation. We had one done in one parish I served. We didn't come off too well, however, myself included. But once we knew how we looked to others, we could tailor our evangelism program to fit people's needs.

There was a time when I wondered whether we should bother about how we look to others. Shouldn't we just proclaim the gospel, take it or leave it? Isn't it unbiblical to shape our proposal to meet the interests of others?

I soon found all kinds of biblical models using this very appeal. The Old Testament abounds in them: "Honor your father and your mother, that your days may be long in the land which the Lord your God gives you" (Exodus 20:12); and "Blessed is the man who walks not in the counsel of the wicked . . . but his delight is in the law of the Lord" (Psalm 1).

But surely the New Testament wouldn't use an appeal to self-interest, would it? Certainly not Jesus! In the Sermon on the Mount, Jesus teaches a selfless love: "If anyone strikes you on the right cheek, turn to him the other also" (Matthew 5:39). But Jesus goes on to say: "Every one who hears these words of mine and does them will be like a wise man who built his house upon the rock" (Matthew 7:24). This was an eye-opener for me, that in order to move me to practice selflessness, Jesus was inviting me to consider my self-interest.

Another biblical communicator who appealed to the common drive for self-respect was Paul. When he was raising his famine-relief offering, he wrote to the Corinthians that he'd been boasting to the Macedonians about how well the Corinthians had been giving and that their zeal had stirred up most of them. But Paul was taking no chances; he was sending a delegation to Corinth to make sure they actually were performing up to the level he'd been bragging about, "lest if some Macedonians come with me and find that you are not ready, we be humiliated—to say nothing of you—for being so confident" (2 Corinthians 9:1-4).

The appeal to self-interest is scriptural but risky. Each effort must be tested against the gospel and the golden rule: Is it consistent with bearing one's cross for Christ? Does it show just as much love for my neighbor as it does for me?

In considering "How We Look to Others," one of the first things to influence the outsider is the appearance of the church property. Are there weeds in the cracks of the sidewalk? Are the letters on the outdoor sign presentable, and are they readable from a passing car? Are the doors inviting? Is the building accessible to persons with disabilities? Can newcomers find their way easily to the church office, the library, the meeting rooms, the rest rooms? Do new pupils for the church school know where to go to enroll? Are the rest rooms clean? Is the basement musty? If there is anything in the condition of the property that hinders your congregation's outreach, your committee needs to have a discussion with the property committee. Your proposal will have a better chance of getting through if you can find a way to link it to the property committee's self-interest.

Property Appearance Checklist

	In Good Shape	So-So	Needs Work
1. Exterior paint			
2. Lawn			
3. Flower beds			
4. Outdoor signs			
5. Parking lot			
6. Interior signs			
7. Sidewalks			
8. Trees			
9. Interior paint			
10. Rest rooms			
11. Stairways			
12. Narthex			
13. Basement			
14. Classrooms			
15. Nave			
16. Carpets			
17. Floors			
18. Entrance			
19. Bulletin boards			
20. Windows			

From the Mailbox to the Wastebasket

Your newsletter may need careful scrutiny: How does it rate from the viewpoint of the people you're trying to reach? It may be true that people are counting the hours until the next issue appears so they can memorize every word. Just in case they aren't, might it not be better to consider that your parish publication has to do its job on the way from the mailbox to the wastebasket?

To accomplish this task, the editor should construct headlines that grab attention. He or she should also break up the longer articles; one way would be to sprinkle the pages with subheadings that sum up the gist of the articles so that those who only take a glance will still get the main points. To capture the interest of those less interested, the newsletter should be as brief as possible, uncluttered and uncrowded, neat and attractive.

What is the general *tone* of your newsletter? Is it positive or is it whining? Not that it should cover up what's unpleasant—both Christian morality and constructive public relations require telling the truth—but our stance is "speaking the truth in love" (Ephesians 4:15). Besides, scolding people in print is cold—and probably unproductive.

Does your congregation broadcast its services on radio or television? How we look and sound to others may not be as crucial an item as we'd like to think. Media ratings don't give much attention to Sunday mornings, but surveys we do have indicate that broadcasts of church services reach mostly the church's own. That's not bad. The broadcasts can be an effective ministry to those prevented from assembling in the sanctuary. For some others who happen to tune in, the liturgy may be a puzzle. For them, and even for the church's own, there could be an announcer both describing and interpreting what's going on.

Self-Interest in Classroom and Pulpit

Do the church school teachers follow the biblical model in applying the lesson to the self-interest of their pupils? A helpful exercise for a teacher's meeting would be to ask those present to develop a lesson plan on the commandment, "Remember the Sabbath day, to keep it holy." The teachers' self-interest is to have pupils who attend regularly, because when they take in every lesson they're easier to teach. Their pupils may not see it that way, however. Some teachers need to take a turn of 180 degrees before they can look at their lessons from the viewpoint of their students.

If the sermons in your congregation are biblical but not interesting to the people, perhaps the staff support group or a comparable committee can approach the preacher(s) to discuss the matter. (Or do the job yourself.) One remedy would be for your pastor(s) to enroll in a communications course in a college or university speech department. Linking your proposal with the self-interest of the preacher(s), you and your spokesperson could point out:

1. The congregation still reaches more people through preaching than by any other means;

2. Preaching is a demanding art, and it isn't fair to the preacher's spouse that he or she be the only one giving constructive feedback;

3. A communications course affords the preacher(s) competent, ongoing, and inexpensive coaching in this crucial aspect of ministry;

4. The evangelism committee loves the preacher(s) and admires him or her for many reasons, such as . . .

We haven't taken up all the possible hindrances to a congregation's outreach, but it's hoped these examples are enough to point the alert committee to other areas in parish life that may also need patient attention.

Looking to the interests of others, studying who the people are and what their interests might be, will give the evangelism committee focus. An image sometimes used is the "target." You analyze the audience to know who the target is. That way you may hit the bull's-eye more consistently.

There is a parallel to this analogy in the world of business. It's not uncommon for a company to find out what the public needs before it creates the product to meet that demand. That way the product is unlikely to miss. In the church we establish adult Bible classes because everyone should know the Bible better. The need is there, but it's not targeted, so usually only a few take part. Would it work better to analyze the potential audience and design Bible classes that do hit the target? For some people the targeted need might be: "Law and Gospel in Rearing Children"; for others, "Law and Gospel in Resolving Disputes"; or perhaps, "Law and Gospel in Building a Better Self-Image."

The ministry of Word and Sacrament is basic to every congregation. Yet we can't deny that the setting for such a ministry varies with the makeup of every parish and with the community in which it is placed. The same shoe doesn't fit everyone. The organizers of the evangelism program will want to analyze both the congregation and its unique missionary responsibilities and then aim at specific targets.

A parish in the inner city founded by German immigrants has a natural ministry to the descendants of those immigrants, who by now may be scattered to the suburbs but still come back "home." But while the congregation still has strength, it needs to reach out also to other people in the neighborhood of the church building. Potato pancake suppers may not attract blacks and Hispanics. What kind of program can the evangelism committee devise that will draw both commuters and locals? Is advocacy the right role?

In surveying the interests of their potential constituencies, some evangelism committees in inner-city parishes have invited members of the congregation to be tutors to the children and youth living near the church—providing a ministry of caring and a bridge to the neighbor.

A congregation whose building is off the main traffic arteries should think about placing signs in strategic places and opening up its meeting rooms to the public to allow as many community meetings as feasible, putting their church's name and location more firmly in the public's mind. A congregation in a place experiencing an outflow of people may consider making coalitions with other congregations and community groups to explore causes and remedies. Are families moving away because the schools are poor? Are people leaving for lack of jobs? or too low a price for their crops?

It may seem that problems like these are beyond the scope of even a coalition; maybe so. But who can say what could happen with imagination, determination, and prayer? "Ask, and it will be given you; seek, and you will find; knock, and it will be opened to you" (Matthew 7:7). There may be resources you haven't dreamed of. The many eyes of all the people in the coalition multiply your ability to seek, and together you may find a solution you didn't know was there.

Looking to the interests of others may draw you into coalitions for other reasons. Perhaps public transportation is inadequate on Sundays. Your congregation could send a van to its own designated area and pick up worshipers for all the churches. The other parishes would do the same for their designated areas. Or hunger might be the problem; the churches could cooperate in a feeding program. Ecumenical efforts offer many advantages. You might cooperate on use of a subsidized-rent high-rise apartment complex in the neighborhood. Your area may need some kind of community center, providing listening ears and survival information on clinics, food shelves, and counseling. The building's management may provide the space if church members living in the high-rise will do the staffing, supported by church members living elsewhere.

Ministry of Service

There's good reason to claim that the mark of a church is not only its ministry of Word and Sacrament but also its ministry of service. The first officers of the first church were appointed as deacons, ministers of service, to oversee the congregation's program of caring (Acts 6:1-6).

Analyzing the congregation and its potential constituency may cause an evangelism committee somewhere to suggest to the proper authorities that they institute some kind of training in worship for children, perhaps a choir school or some other weekday education. (Additional Resources suggests a possible curriculum.) Another evangelism committee may plant the idea of building a gymnasium with enough funding in the budget to staff it for a program of outreach, nurture, and recreation. Having choirs or other programs for children and youth might make your congregation just that much more attractive.

In many places a youth program is in order, but the community doesn't need another gym. Instead, the evangelism committee could consider learning from an organization like Young Life, which puts its workers where the youth are, in the schools, at the games, and the other special "hangouts," building trust and developing relationships that can either bring the youth into the faith or restore them in it.

Another evangelism committee, from a congregation whose church is in a business area, seeing the bars down the street, might ask itself some probing questions: "Why does there seem to be more fellowship at the bars than in our church?" "Why do people go to the bars?" "Who is helping the hurts of the people in the bars?" "How is it that Jesus was always attracting people whom others looked down on?" "Where did he find his 'publicans and sinners'?" "How do we help our congregation serve the same kinds of people in our neighborhood?"

Up to now the purpose of this book has been to deal with **the attitude for evangelism.** Under this heading we've thought about *guarding against defeatism* (by establishing goals that are attainable, measurable, and meaningful). We've also sought to strengthen the attitude of *thinking from the other person's point of view* (helping the entire congregation to practice this policy and to design an evangelism ministry to fit the concerns of its potential constituency). Next we'll examine what is involved in **making evangelism happen.**

---

4. *A Handbook for Parish Callers,* Frank W. Klos, ed. (Minneapolis: Augsburg Publishing House; Philadelphia: Fortress Press, 1977), p. 43.

Chapter 4

Every Member a Witness

He came to this world and became a man in order to spread to other men the kind of life He has—by what I call "good infection." Every Christian is to become a little Christ.[5]

Suppose a friend, neighbor, or relative caught what C. S. Lewis calls "the good infection" from you. Would you be happy to have that new Christian exposed to more carriers of the faith? Of course. Would you be happy to have that new Christian exposed to the members of a "contagious" congregation?

It's clear that the spirit of the congregation is significant to your ministry of outreach; it can attract and nourish or it can repel and deaden. Is your congregation accepting of people or is it judgmental? Is it bubbling with enthusiasm for the kingdom of God or is it cranky? If your committee were to announce a five-year goal, "Every Member a Witness," you might frighten some folks who'd protest, "I just couldn't find the words to witness." You could help them understand that being a witness means contributing to the infectiousness of a contagious community alive with enthusiasm for Christ.

The contagious community *intends* to bear witness to Christ. A clannish congregation does not intend to disturb the way things are; it does not intend to encourage "foreigners" to intrude.

The intention to witness comes from relationship to Christ. That's what was driving Paul: "Woe to me if I do not preach the gospel!" (1 Corinthians 9:16). The contagious congregation has caught the compassion of Christ for the throngs who are "like sheep without a shepherd" (Matthew 9:36, Mark 6:34). People today are still harassed and helpless because of problems of human relationships, personal esteem, health, ethics, and guilt. Members of a contagious congregation keep praying for opportunities to do what is called for in 1 Peter 3:15: "Always be prepared to make a defense to any one who calls you to account for the hope that is in you." Even those who are less bold in spreading the good news can still be carriers of "the good infection." They too can contribute—consciously or unconsciously—to the climate of openness and supportiveness so helpful to evangelism.

If your congregation needs some improvement in its attitude toward those who are outside the fellowship, what strategy will you follow to warm up your fellow members? Again we find a helpful pattern in the apostle Paul. Paul was upset over an issue that bothered him. In Acts 17 we read that when he was in

Athens, "his spirit was provoked within him as he saw that the city was full of idols" (v. 16).

Common Ground

For a Hebrew and a former Pharisee, this false worship was an outrage. When the Epicurean and Stoic philosophers challenged him to explain his point of view, how did Paul begin his remarks? "Men of Athens, I perceive that in every way you are very religious" (v. 22). Intent upon winning friends for Christ, Paul was establishing all the common ground he could find. As you read the rest of this remarkable sermon (Acts 17:22-31), you'll detect several ways by which Paul established more common ground.

He had noticed one idol with the inscription, "To an unknown god." Perhaps the Athenians were afraid they might have overlooked one of the deities and hoped they could quench the anger of the offended one this way. So Paul used the inscription as his text: "What therefore you worship as unknown, this I proclaim to you" (Acts 17:23). Instead of reviewing the history of Abraham (as he would have done in establishing common ground with a Jewish audience), he quoted a Greek poet who said that we are God's offspring. He argued that God cannot be an idol because—"being then God's offspring"—we're not made of gold or stone.

Paul didn't win many converts that day, but he did win some—under circumstances none too favorable.

As wrought up as he was about their idolatry, Paul could have fallen into using a sledgehammer on the philosophers. Since he didn't, we'll never know what the outcome would have been. But we can assume that establishing common ground was more productive. In the same way, as you and your colleagues go about the business of persuading fellow members to be open and supportive to strangers and new members, you'll want to mark out common ground, one square inch at a time if necessary.

Common Ground Possibilities

Faith in God	Neighborhood
Respect for the Bible	Background
Desire for friendship	Recreational interests
Search for useful service	Desire to grow spiritually
Children	Confidence in God's grace
Local school, club, hobby	Mutual acquaintances

Your congregation respects the Bible; so does the one to whom you are witnessing. That's common ground. Your church teaches that we're saved only by grace through faith. Again, that may be common ground. You could further appeal to Ephesians 2:11-22, showing that in the early church Jews and Gentiles could have formed separate churches, but that God's intention in Christ was to make them into one body, "no longer strangers." Since many of us are Gentiles, we could have been excluded from salvation if it hadn't been for Christ. Or you could develop your common ground on the basis of Romans 15:7-13, that it's only through God's doing that we Gentiles have any place whatsoever in his kingdom. The only proper action, then, is to do as Paul urges: "Welcome one another, therefore, as Christ has welcomed you, for the glory of God" (Rom. 15:7).

In recent years congregations have faced a special problem when trying to plant the newcomer where he or she will get the proper sun, moisture, and nourishment. That difficulty has arisen from the way we've been living, with the generations shut off from each other. Some parishes have hardly anyone attending except the elderly. Others have hardly anyone in the pews but parents and children. Retired farmers have moved to town, and younger couples have moved to the city—or more likely, to the suburbs. The inner city is left to widows, widowers, and young singles who for economic reasons gravitate toward the areas where senior citizens are living.

Attract and Support

Older people and young singles thrown together by economic forces often don't see themselves as having anything in common. And though the suburbs may have largely people below 50, they also have some above 50. So how does a congregation serving chiefly one age bracket of the population make itself congenial to other ages? The evangelism committee has work to do. Creating the contagious community—one that will attract and support various generations—may come slowly.

We start with the assumption that the generation *difference* need not be a generation *gap:* senior citizens and their grandchildren often have a close relationship. Of course the parents, seeing how relaxed their own parents are with the grandchildren, shake their heads and mutter, "Mom and Dad never let *us* get by with anything like that." Grandpa and Grandma have an advantage: They don't have primary responsibility for these children. But they've been through the mill already. They can have the longer view. So they take it easy with the younger generation. Then too, grandparents often have more time than parents; some of them make jokes and tell stories. They may even have a good ear for listening.

I'm describing conditions that do exist, but not everywhere. Why not? Well, some elderly people are bitter. There may be many reasons for bitterness, but one of them surely has to be this, that if you had to look at four walls days and night with no one else around to soften your outlook, it would be easy to think that no one cares and that you have no reason for living.

As for youngsters getting to enjoy their grandparents, 37% of Americans are deprived of this blessing because Grandma and Grandpa live somewhere else.

How might the congregation help both generations? Why not try a foster grandparent program? The congregation affords several opportunities for bringing senior citizens and young people together, especially through the church school. Although some senior citizens may not care to have full care of a class, they could be teacher's aides—with a chance to shower the children with love and attention. Senior citizens could also be resource persons. For example, when confirmation pupils are studying church history, and come to the history of your congregation, what better way to learn that history than from someone who's been a member for 50 years! Senior citizens could also be employers of children and youth—for tending yards and windows and performing other chores. Some parishes have a "Rent-A-Kid" program—to serve both generations and to promote interaction between them. Above all, meaningful sharing around the study of the Word in Bible class and receiving the Sacrament together create the tie that binds.

These suggestions don't exhaust the possibilities. When an evangelism committee intends that its congregation be a contagious community, it will find ways to brings this about. Here again, the committee will ensure satisfaction for itself by establishing goals that are attainable, measurable, and meaningful.

"Every Christian Is to Become a Little Christ"

Concerning the long-term goal, "Every Member a Witness":

- The goal has already been achieved: Every baptized member *is* a witness.
- Being a witness and being an evangelist are not necessarily the same.
- Most of the church's growth (75-80%) results from the invitation of friends and relatives, ordinary witnesses, nonevangelist types.[6]

So what's left to do? Even the objective, "Every Christian is to become a little Christ," is already met. When we are justified by grace through faith, Christ takes our place and we take his. God looks at us and sees Jesus. Baptized in him, we are "little Christs."

Has the entire business of growth as Christians already been accomplished? No. All of us are aware of how far we still have to go. But being justified by grace through faith tends to shape all programs of Christian nurture in a distinctive style. That spirit means we don't develop commandments for pounding people into line; rather, we help those who are baptized to become *what they are* by God's grace, free and fruitful. It means renewal; for to proceed on the assumption, "Every member is already a witness," or, "Every Christian is already a little Christ," is not wishful thinking but an amazing reality!

How does the evangelism committee help members of the church become what they are? Above all, by *declaring* the fact: "You are a witness; you are a little Christ." Committee members declare it themselves, and they remind the preacher(s) and teachers to keep declaring this fact whenever the opportunity occurs.

The evangelism committee also helps fellow Christians become what they are by *explaining* their role as witnesses. The committee makes it clear that to be a witness is something that belongs to *all* who are baptized, but that to be an evangelist is for those who are gifted by the Holy Spirit for that specific ministry (Ephesians 4:11). The committee explains that a witness is "one who has personal knowledge of something," and that since they have personal knowledge of being in relationship with Christ, they are witnesses.

Training Programs

The evangelism committee further helps members of the congregation become what they are by giving them *practice* in witnessing. Both the American Lutheran Church and the Lutheran Church in America have developed excellent training programs.

If one is in the process of becoming, then one has not yet become. That a beginner should be able to witness is not unthinkable, but it doesn't happen too often, probably because we haven't intended it to happen. Even so, when you intend for a child to learn to swim, you don't row to the middle of the lake and dump the youngster overboard and slip away. A swimming coach shows the beginner how to blow bubbles in the water, how to float, how to kick, how to move the arms, and then how to put all these skills together.

Becoming the witness you are can be taught the same way. Additional Resources lists learning materials that don't expect witnesses to be born full-grown. They are meant to give beginners practice in talking the gospel in a safe environment, step-by-step. The trainees will first put into words—just for their own benefit—why they believe in Christ and why they go to church; then they'll practice sharing that witness with other members. Only then will they venture into the waters of witnessing to a friend or associate or stranger outside the church.

By no means will all members of a church be eager to embark on such training. So it is important to set attainable goals annually and then work to reach them. It is also good to have various strategems for reaching different groups with some form of training for evangelism.

As for the young generation of Christians coming up in your congregation, why not train them also as witnesses? You could ask the education committee to encourage the teaching staff to study the materials you're using for coaching adults in witnessing. You could suggest that the teachers adapt this same approach to use with their pupils, giving them similar step-by-step exercises as part of their regular class work.

Is it feasible for the evangelism committee to train every member of the congregation in witnessing? Such a goal may be attainable—or it may not, even over a period of years. One option would be choosing to reach a substantial percentage of the membership. Your committee will have to decide. Make your goal big enough to challenge you, but keep it realistic.

Meanwhile, as this training program is in progress, the evangelism committee can be providing other stimuli to baptized members to become the witnesses they are.

Scheduling Special Events

One way is to **schedule special events,** making them entry points for the relatives, friends, neighbors, and co-workers of the baptized people of God. From the pastor in Tulsa I learned a practical lesson in setting a goal that's attainable, measurable, and meaningful. When there was an opportunity to invite others to a special worship event, his committee would put up a chart showing each pew, inviting members to put their names on the pew or pews they promised to fill.

Special events vary. They could be mission festivals or preaching missions or music concerts or youth services or laity Sundays. They could even be homecomings, which take various forms, such as the "Memorial Day cemetery picnic," a community pig roast, or lutefisk dinner. Carl S. Dudley has an important observation:

> After visiting many homecoming events in small congregations, and larger churches as well, I believe that this kind of annual event provides a useful index for the future of the church. Some congregations have relatively large numbers of people to return, but I believe that these congregations will die. Some may not have as many, but they will be sustained and might even grow. The difference is not in the numbers of people who return, but in the way that some congregations expand the event to include the new members in their preparations. The new member who has helped in the annual event is really adopted into the family.[7]

More examples of special events: the vacation church school has its closing program during the Sunday service, or a Sunday church school completes a unit and summarizes its studies in a program during a Sunday service, with parents, grandparents, aunts, uncles, and neighbors attending. In a community where everybody knows everyone, it might seem awkward to invite a nonchurchgoer for a regular Sunday worship, but often it's easier to invite them when Susie or Scottie is assisting in the service. A guest speaker on an unusual topic may provide the special reason to invite some whom relatives and friends would otherwise hesitate to ask.

Special Events as Entry Points

Event	Annual Date (if any)	Date Last Used	Future Date Scheduled
Christmas Eve Service			
Easter Sunrise Service			
Good Friday Tenebrae			
Mother's Day			
Mission Speaker			
Vacation Church School			
Ecumenical Event			
Church Picnic			
Choir Concert			
Organ Recital			
Fellowship Evening			
Organization's Special Event			
Youth Service			
Folk Service			
Open House			

In my own experience I have found it useful to plan a special series of sermons for September and October. It gave us a focus for our advertising in kicking off the new season, and it gave the witnesses another opportunity to invite others. Some years I'd prepare for the fall series by circulating questionnaires during the Easter season, either submitting a list of potential topics and asking people to mark which ones would be of the most interest, or asking them to submit a "life-situation" on which they'd like guidance from the Scriptures.

I always insisted that the suggestions be made anonymously, and I always pledged that the material submitted would be generalized so that no one could possibly decipher who had submitted the "life-situation." During the several years I did this, only twice did I know the source of the problem turned in. In each case it was only because these two individuals came to me afterwards and identified themselves. This exercise forced me to address real needs of real people in my preaching, and it gave the baptized people of God another occasion to become the witnesses they are by inviting others to come with them.

Celebrating Victories

A second stimulus for members to become the witnesses they are is to **celebrate the victories,** large or little. If the youth of your church visit the homebound or conduct a door-to-door survey, that's important in itself. Perhaps just as important is telling the congregation that they're doing it. When your committee reaches one of its goals—recruiting 10 pairs of people to make two cultivation calls a month for the next 10 months—you ought to celebrate that somehow. But you should let the congregation celebrate it, too!

If you received 20, 50, or 100 new members during the past year, that's a victory that should be savored. In a couple of parishes I served, one Sunday a year we had a reunion of all new members received during the previous 12 months; they were reintroduced to the congregation and posed for a group picture. A logical time for this might be the Seventh Sunday of Easter (the Sunday after Ascension Day). Just before Jesus ascended, he said, "You shall be my witnesses." This Sunday could become a natural time for celebrating the victories and for encouraging the people of God toward becoming witnesses even more intentionally.

The celebration of victories need not be limited to what's going on in your own parish. News of the nationwide and worldwide mission of your church also encourages the contagious community to keep on being carriers of the faith. If no one else in the congregation is fueling the interest in missions, the evangelism committee will find this challenge right in line with its purpose: to encourage all fellow members to spread the good infection.

Encouraging Creativity

Still a third stimulus is to **encourage creativity** as a way of influencing our culture for the gospel. What would it mean if you spotted someone with talent in your congregation and fanned the spark, someone who has a gift for writing, someone who could create plays or novels? someone who could show the world how the gospel works in real life?

Jesus promised that those who follow him can expect abuse and ridicule—and the movies, stage, and television often fulfill his predictions. Many writers either ignore Christianity or caricature it, perhaps because they've never met the real thing. It takes talent, training, and work to become an effective writer. The Roman Catholic church has produced a few. Maybe your congregation could do it, too.

According to the Lutheran doctrine of vocation, we serve God and our neighbor in our daily work. Being a carpenter or a typist—working at any honest trade or job—these all fit into God's grand scheme of caring for his creation. We don't exalt one vocation over another. But we're thinking here about the privilege of witnessing, about communicating the faith. The evangelism committee should be on the lookout for those members with special gifts in communication.

There is a place for witnessing to the faith in the larger society where artists, journalists, columnists, public relations specialists, film-makers, photographers, songwriters, actors, directors, composers, poets, dancers, performing musicians, and others have the opportunity to influence the way the whole country thinks. They are all "Monday ministers." At least once a year, the evangelism committee might ask itself, "Have we discovered anyone with talent for communicating the gospel to the larger society? If so, how can we nurture that gift? Might we sponsor an 'Art Festival' or a 'Talent Search'?"

As you consider ways to motivate members to spread the good contagion, look again at your congregation's mission statement, at its constitutional paragraph that states its purpose. It's likely there will be a clear announcement that witnessing is indeed the business of this congregation and of every member. Use whatever you find in your congregation's official documents to establish common ground with other members, urging them to share in your common ministry to those outside the church.

Most of the church's growth (75-80%) results from the invitation of friends and relatives, but because of special circumstances, your congregation may have grown for other reasons; there are always exceptions. But the norm seems to be that substantial growth of a congregation results from witnessing by the general membership. This is not to say that format of the services, quality of preaching, music, teaching, or the ministry of caring are unimportant—to be sure, if these are deficient, the baptized people of God will be slower to issue the invitation. But if the majority of the church's growth comes through the initiative of friends and relatives, the evangelism committee has an asset worthy of further development.

Summary of Committee Tasks

1. Choose an evangelism strategy
2. Consider economic factors
3. Bridge generations
4. Give practice in witnessing
5. Teach children to witness
6. Schedule special events
7. Publicize sermons
8. Celebrate victories
9. Develop talent

---

5. C. S. Lewis, *Beyond Personality* (New York: Macmillan Co., 1945), pp. 23-24.

6. Charles (Win) Arn, "How Do People Come into Church Membership?" Institute for Church Growth, Pasadena, Calif.

7. Carl S. Dudley, *Making the Small Church Effective* (Nashville: Abingdon, 1978), pp. 112-113.

Chapter 5

Organizing the Calling Process

And God has appointed in the church . . . administrators (1 Cor. 12:28).

So far we've thought about **the attitude for evangelism:** guarding against defeatism and also thinking from the other person's point of view. We've begun the other major section of this manual, **making evangelism happen,** discussing the objective, "Every Member a Witness." So far we haven't said a thing about the evangelism committee itself making any calls. We've seen the committee setting goals and carrying them out. We've seen the committee in the roles of motivators, recruiters, and trainers. But isn't its main job to make the calls? Not usually.

You may be good at visiting. That's probably why you were chosen for this committee. But you will serve your congregation better if you concentrate on *administering* the program, organizing people to make evangelism not just your personal effort but a ministry by many in your church. In this respect you'll identify with the expert teacher who's been made principal, or the crack salesperson who's been appointed sales manager. They—and you—were recognized for excellence by being "promoted" to administration. But *doing* the thing and *managing* the thing are not the same. Some people may have the gift for both. Many don't. The Holy Spirit has dispensed a variety of talents, all of them vital. The organizer and the evangelist need one another. As Paul says, the church is like a human body: the foot, the ear, and the eye all work together (1 Corinthians 12:14-31). An evangelism caller is no more or less important than an evangelism committee person. If your heart isn't in the work of administration, perhaps you should find a replacement for yourself on the committee, someone with interest and talent for organizing. Then you can return to making the visits yourself.

Organizers of evangelism are people who can spot various kinds of talent. As administrators you can guard against defeatism by defining the types of calling to be done. The survey callers make survey calls; they know the limits of their assignment; they can measure what they've done and feel good about it. We've noted that those who follow up the survey callers may also have limits: cultivating friendship is a work for some people, while gaining commitments (or recommitments) to Christ and his church may be a work for others. There's a place for those who like to use the telephone. There are opportunities for ministry in a number of administrative positions. An effective committee member has the ability to size up people, to recognize their potential, and then to fit them with an assignment that challenges that potential.

If we can agree that the role of the evangelism committee is not to *be* the machinery but to *run* it, then we'll need to analyze what's required to make the wheels turn. I've chosen to designate six operations:

Preevangelism	Commitment
Identification	Naturalization
Cultivation	Reclamation

Three ways of organizing these six operations are:

1. **Nongeographic,** with different groups of people serving your entire territory;
2. **Geographic,** with a leader for a given number of members living in the same area who do all the kinds of evangelism ministry within that area;
3. **Combination,** nongeographic for some operations, geographic for others.

Another way might be to organize around target groups: singles, minority groups, apartment dwellers, new residents, or teenagers. In succeeding chapters, we'll look at various operations and show some of the possibilities for running the machinery in your congregation.

Chapter 6

Getting Ready for Evangelism

I have become all things to all men, that I might by all means save some (1 Corinthians 9:22).

Suppose your committee decides to have an image survey of your congregation done to find out what the barriers to evangelism might be. Let's also suppose your church building is located in a town of 15,000 people. The image survey reveals that in your community your church is seen as mainly a congregation of farmers. Your committee likes farmers, but it would also like to include other unchurched folks in town.

One congregation faced with this situation made a conscious effort to remove this barrier. It knew it had members from town, and it knew the community didn't realize it, so the evangelism committee planned a series of advertisements in the local newspaper. One week the advertisement would carry a picture of a member who was a druggist, the next week a picture of a member who was a music teacher, another week a picture of a member who was a service station operator—and so on. With each picture there was a statement by that person telling why he or she belonged to that church.

When I began a mission congregation in Tulsa, Oklahoma, I was faced with the general opinion there that "Lutheranism is an off-brand form of Christianity." I've always felt that to invite people to consider the blessings of the gospel is exciting. But when the people don't hear you because they see you as strange or eccentric, you have to take account of their perceptions and find a way to break through their misunderstanding. I decided to try to start overcoming this barrier by using the radio.

I reasoned that people who would tune out a preacher might be attracted to easy-listening, high-quality, well-performed music of the church. My goal was to adapt the message of the gospel to the idiom of radio, to be a friendly voice with music, saying as little as possible between recordings. To get the most impact out of what I did say, I tried to keep both the music and commentary on one theme. Music selected illustrated the appointed lessons for the day, with the hope this would help break down some of the cultural resistance to a liturgical church. The program was well received and is now broadcast on more than 325 stations weekly.

How much effect this radio program had in forming that one congregation would be hard to prove. Our growth was a combined effort. I'm just trying to illustrate what preevangelism, getting ready for evangelism, is. No matter what form it takes, it's always hard to say how much good all this effort does. Yet the obstacles to evangelism are there. We need to identify them and then go about trying to remove these hindrances as intelligently and purposefully as we know how.

My definition of preevangelism—a conscious effort to break down the barriers—is something like what is often called public relations. If you have a public relations committee in your church, you might want to discuss this chapter with them and see how your two committees help each other. If you don't have such a group, then this part of running the evangelism machinery is all up to you.

What these barriers to evangelism might be vary from place to place. Some form of audience analysis is required to discover what they are. You might feel you know what the barriers are already. Your intuition may be sound, but it could be incomplete. The barriers you perceive might indeed be there—but how do you know whether you've sensed them all?

We've already considered the need for removing barriers. Next we'll look at the various means available to churches for the practice of public relations or preevangelism. We've already had examples of some of the means. Taking stock is one of them. Using the mass media is another. Enough has been said about the former; more needs to be said about the latter.

Being Drowned Out

In using the mass media, how do you make the church's voice heard above the din of other sounds?

Back in the years when the church was at the crossroads of the community, the church bell might have been preevangelism enough. Nowadays with television sets going full blast in some households six hours a day or more and with radios you can wear while jogging, small wonder that many churches don't have bells anymore.

When the church does try to make use of the mass media, it has to vie with all the other sounds clamoring for attention. One survey discovered that 89% of the people interviewed never read the church page—and especially the church ads—in the newspaper.[8] Radio and TV stations usually limit their broadcast of religious services to Sunday mornings—and generally only to the earliest hours at that—afraid they'll lose their audiences to competing programs.

Being Heard

We need to find ways to rise above the din without becoming noisy. Some of those who don't read the church page do read the letters to the editor. A thoughtful, balanced, calm letter from your church council on an issue of importance to your church will be noticed. And it might show that the gospel has relevance to life, beyond the announcement of a rummage sale on the church page.

Studying the public relations manuals listed in Additional Resources will give you ideas on how to tell your story through the mass media, so that it could be printed on page five or even on page one and broadcast on the 6:00 p.m. news. What your church is doing to feed and clothe the needy or help the unemployed are examples of news that ring the bell with editors.

Tell the print and broadcast editors when the bishop comes to your church, and they might assign a reporter to do an interview, especially if the bishop has a special concern or achievement that's newsworthy. See if you can schedule your guest speakers wherever there's already an established audience, such as on a talk show or at a civic club luncheon.

When a convention or any other special meeting is to be held in your church, tell the print and broadcast media about the issues or actions that deal with the public's self-interest—and if a fire or a robbery doesn't crowd out your story, it could make the news that day.

Being heard without being noisy means finding ways to serve the needs of the mass media. The American Lutheran Church's weekly program SCAN adapts itself to the idiom of rock radio. It plays music by rock artists, music that ties in with the theme under discussion: child abuse, prisons, peace and war, hunger, chemical addiction, and so on. Between recordings there are interviews with people who know about the subject, either as experts or as victims.

Because SCAN puts its concerns into a format rock stations can use, SCAN is broadcast weekly on hundreds of stations on public service time. How do programs like SCAN or JOY or other national broadcasts benefit your evangelism or public relations committee?

As an asset to exploit
To identify your congregation with a broadcast, you might consider buying 60 seconds of time following the program. In the case of SCAN, for example, you could refer to similar types of discussions going on in your congregation.

As an example to follow
If you're developing your own radio program, fit it into the format of the station. For example, you could imitate SCAN's practice of developing the topic by means of interviews. Radio and television like to give the audience the feeling of overhearing a conversation.

Another radio format that has possibilities for the church is the call-in show. Schedule your guest speaker on such a program if you can, especially if he or she is involved with some issue of general interest. Or develop your own call-in show.

For a while I hosted such a program at midnight once a week. I was impressed with the fact that being on the air in the wee hours is not as pointless as one might think. People who couldn't sleep were calling in. Why weren't they sleeping? Some of them were just getting home from work and weren't ready for bed yet. Others were awake because they were hurting. Since callers didn't have to identify themselves, they were free to talk about their hurts if they wanted to. What an opportunity for the church! How often we wish we could be on the spot when people are in need—the late-night broadcast offers that possibility.

Is it really true that 89% of the people never read the church page of the newspaper? Some excellent church pages must surely make the readership higher, but whatever the percentage, we probably won't deny that more people read the comics and the sports than the church announcements.

Some radio and television stations make five minutes a day available to the churches of the community on a rotating basis for a devotional message. How many people listen? Not as many as to a ball game. Should we then abandon the church page and devotions on the air? Not at all!

Even if the audience is only 11%, chances are it's still more people than assemble under your roof on Sundays. The point is, let's do our job as well as possible. Carol Burnett has caricatured "Sermonette," the two-minute close of the broadcast day. She has a right to imply that it's dreary, because too often that's what it is.

Some station personnel are willing to give preachers counsel on how best to use their medium. If not, there are consultants available in metropolitan areas. Preachers are expected to do so many things already that they need not be embarrassed to work with a coach to gain more skills in communicating on the air. If a consultant is out of reach, either in location or in cost, look for assistance in the speech or broadcasting department of your nearest college.

Being represented on the church page can also be done with distinction. Remember the church that had the image of being for farmers only? When it ran its series of ads picturing members who lived in town and represented non-farming vocations, giving their reasons for attending that church, those ads were noticed and talked about.

See Additional Resources for sources of advertisements for the local congregation, ads with space for your imprint, ads that are out of the ordinary and will attract readership. Another way to advertise with distinction is to hire an agency to create and to place your ads. If a member of your congregation is a copywriter, he or she may be willing to contribute this service.

Preevangelism Tools

Television (regular)	Broadcast interviews
Television (cable)	Community events
Radio	Church signs
Newspaper ads	Bulletin boards
Newspaper articles	Publicity brochures
Image survey	Calling cards
Bus cards (advertisements)	Leaflets
Bumper stickers	Direct Mail

Preevangelism—breaking down the barriers and creating a climate favorable to your witness—is an ongoing operation in running the machinery of evangelism. If no other group in your congregation is in charge of this already, at least one person on your committee might have this as a primary responsibility.

---

8. *Religious Public Relations Handbook: For Local Congregations of All Denominations,* 2nd ed. (New York: Religious Public Relations Council, 1976), p. 19.

Chapter 7

We Owe the Gospel

Abdul	**Gronouski**	**Kim**	**Nielsen**	**Renault**	**Thorfinnson**
Dubois	**Johnson**	**MacDowell**	**Nkrumah**	**Smythe**	**Yang**
Goldberg	**Juarez**	**Monteverdi**	**Rashad**	**Schmidt**	**Yellowbird**

Which of the names above belong in the membership directory of a Lutheran congregation?

In the 19th and early 20th centuries, when immigrants from Lutheran areas of Europe were swarming into the New World, door-to-door surveys were conducted asking only one question, "*Wird hier Deutsch gesprochen?*" ("Is German spoken here?") I suppose Lutherans of Scandinavian heritage can report similar stories. Probably their ethnic congregations gathered in only their own kind also. Various church schools were probably meant to preserve the mother tongue as much as anything else.

The challenge of reaching these immigrants was immense, perhaps overwhelming early members of the church. It's hard to estimate, but they probably brought only one-third to one-half of their homeland's immigrants into Lutheran congregations. To whom did they owe the gospel? To all the Johnsons, Nielsens, Schmidts, and Thorfinnsons they could find.

Let it not be forgotten that some immigrants had a vision of evangelizing Indian Americans as well. For example, colonists sent out by Pastor Wilhelm Loehe of Neuendettelsau, Germany, to Saginaw County, Michigan, were to demonstrate to the native Americans the way of practical Christian living while their pastors labored for their conversion. There were some baptisms, but the project soon failed.

From our vantage point, it looks as though these earnest colonists failed to do their audience analysis. They were expecting the native Americans to stay put on a certain plot of ground as they themselves were doing, while the native Americans thought of the land as belonging to the people as a whole, not to individuals, and so they moved around. That's probably why the strategy conceived in Neuendettelsau couldn't work.

Before we criticize the early pioneers too much, let's remember that our own record could be better. Though our membership rosters do list some names from places other than Northern Europe, we're still failing to reach many who consider themselves Lutherans. When we add up the statistics of all Lutheran church bodies in the United States, we arrive at a total of about 8.5 million members. But the Gallup Poll records 14.5 million Americans who consider themselves Lutherans.[9] Where are those extra 6 million? Some live in your neighborhood.

Your committee can aim to find them. It can also locate others outside the church who've never claimed to be Lutheran. Your committee can take courage from knowing something else Mr. Gallup has learned: There is among the unchurched in America a feeling of goodwill toward the church and toward Christ. Among those presently outside the fellowship, 75% want their children to be in Sunday school; 52% say they could see themselves being active in a church now; only 13% claim they see no future for themselves in the church.[10]

Identifying those to whom we owe the gospel—that's one of the operations in running the machinery of evangelism.

The easiest ones to identify are also the most likely prospects for membership: those who visit your services. How did they happen to attend? They were invited or they came on their own. Either reason is an advantage to your committee. If they appeared at your church through the inducement of a friend or relative (as 75-80% of our new members usually do), then you have the ties of affection and family pulling for you.

It would be too bad if these people lost interest because they were neglected by your committee. What about those who came on their own? Yes, they may have seen your ad in the Yellow Pages, or they may have driven by your building and were attracted by its appearance—contributing factors, of course—but these people did show up at your service without previous human contact from your congregation. They *wanted* to come and they *did*. These new friends are worthy of high consideration.

Follow-up

How soon should you follow up on a visitor? Some congregations have so many nonmembers attending that they don't try to make contact until someone has come twice. I'm sympathetic to their situation and glad they have so many visitors. My inclination has always been that local visitors should be reached before the next Sunday.

Suppose you didn't make your contact until two weeks had elapsed, and suppose the visitors hadn't come back that second Sunday. No matter what you say or how you say it, your reaching them at this point tends to make you into something like a truant officer.

But what if you can't get around to every visitor in person before the next Sunday? In-person house calls are no doubt to be desired. But if that can't be done, recruit a telephone committee to do the welcoming. (As noted before, senior citizens are prime candidates for this kind of ministry.) The telephoners can express their happiness that these people attended your church, and out of the conversation will flow the kind of information your committee needs: first of all, does this household presently have an active church connection in this community? If it does, then your responsibility here is finished. If it doesn't, your responsibility has just begun.

The people making the first contact, whether by telephone or in person, should seek to gain as much additional information as possible without prying, in order to make the cultivation of this household's friendship more effective, information like:

- Is anyone home during the day?
- What other people live in this household?
- What are the ages of the children, if any?
- Do they have an active church connection in this community?
- What occupations are represented in this household?

Often, much of this information comes up without asking for it. When talking with people who have visited your church, you should ask three things:

1. How long have you lived here?
2. Where did you come from?
3. What church did you attend there?

These questions start with the general and narrow down to the specific—the reason for your call. By listening carefully and picking up on how the new friend responds, the caller generally will gain all the information desired for the cultivation calls.

First Contact Canvass Card

Ask:	Answer:
Address: ________________	
Date: ________ **Caller:** ________	
Does this household attend any particular church?	________
How many people live at this address?	________
Would you be interested in receiving our mailings?	________
Do you know the location of our church?	________
Would you spell the family name(s)?	________
Comments:	

If a specific local church is named in answer to the first question, make an encouraging comment and leave. If no local church is indicated, proceed with the other questions. Discover also whether the household includes children.

How does your committee obtain the names of visitors? The greeters may steer newcomers to the guest book. The problem is, however, that while the greeter is standing with one guest another may slip by. Or you can provide visitor cards in the pew racks. Some visitors comply with the request to fill them out; many don't bother. Why not? Who knows? What seems to work best is the every-worshiper-registration at every service. At a designated point in the order of worship, the pastor refers to the pad in each pew and asks every worshiper to give name and address and then pass it on. When the pad reaches the end of the pew, it is to come back to the place of beginning. In that way everyone can see the names of all who are in the pew, taking special notice of those who live close to them and greeting everyone after the service. Since all the worshipers give their names and addresses, visitors are likely to give theirs as well.

Another group of people to identify in your missionary outreach are those persons outside the membership who have received your congregation's pastoral ministry. At weddings, baptisms, and funerals—whether everyone affected is a member or not—the pastor has made use of the opportunity to counsel those involved and to apply the gospel as it relates to their situation. Since the first contacts have been made by the pastor(s), the evangelism committee's role in the identification phase is clerical, making sure these names get into the responsibility file. Likewise, the names of new enrollees in Sunday school and vacation church school should be carefully listed for follow-up if the parents are not members of the church.

Hospital Contacts

Hospitals often have a file for clergy listing patients by congregation. In some hospitals those patients who don't have a congregation—or don't want to state which one they belong to—will still be listed by denomination. Since many people have hospital insurance, the names of some of those 6 million unattached Lutherans may be located in those hospital files. However, untrained and insensitive pastors or other callers have abused the privileges given them by these files and have made their way unwanted into hospital rooms, invading the patient's privacy. In recent years some hospitals have posted a "Patient's Bill of Rights," which includes being protected against unwelcome purveyors of religion.

If the caller is intent only on gaining another "soul," then his or her attitude will betray that, and the patient may resent it. But when the caller goes to the hospital bed with a sense of caring for the whole person, that attitude will also come through. In my years of calling on nonmembers in the hospitals, I can remember being asked to leave only rarely. Sometimes I left rather soon on my own, especially when the patient was weak. I've been a patient myself and I've suffered from well-meaning, misguided visitors who stayed too long and prayed too long.

In my ministry I have tried to be aware of how nonmember patients might feel toward the church. To offer myself as a resource without intruding on their privacy, I have worked out this introduction: "I'm ______________________ from ______________________ Church at ______________________. I saw your name in our files here at the hospital. Since you live in our general area, I thought I'd ask if you have anyone from any church calling on you; if not, I'll be glad to do that." I can point to any number of people who have been brought closer to the Lord through such a contact.

Hospital chaplains paid by the hospital as part of its healing team go to every patient, offering an ear and a heart. Sometimes these chaplains will send your church the names of unattached Lutherans from your neighborhood. Chaplains from Lutheran Social Service or your council of churches may direct your attention to people they've found in hospitals, through the courts, or in prisons.

Church School Calls

Another group of high priority, people to whom your congregation owes the gospel, is the families of pupils in your church schools. A husband and wife may have drifted away from the church; but now their firstborn is three years old, and they—like the 75% of the unchurched that Gallup and Poling tell us about—want their youngster in Sunday school. It's also likely that some of the good Lord's youngsters have persuaded a friend to come along to their classes and outings, new pupils who are the only ones of their household to be connected to any church. The church schools are a rich resource for the evangelism committee. You surely want to have a good working relationship with the education committee, so that either you'll have ready access to its files, or the church school secretaries (vacation church school, Sunday school, day school, nursery) will supply you with the names and addresses of the families of pupils having no church affiliation.

Some congregations have no central file of church school pupils. Those persons in charge have reasoned that since each teacher has an attendance book, that's enough. "Paperwork" is the bane of nearly everyone's existence. We applaud all efforts to bring it to a minimum. But what is likely to happen when the only record of pupils is in the teacher's attendance book?

Names will get lost. Let's say a pupil is absent for a while. The teacher may or may not follow up. The pupil keeps staying away. The teacher is discouraged in seeing the string of absences, so the teacher solves the problem by crossing off the pupil's name. The next time the attendance books are made out, that pupil's name is left out. Since there is no other record, that name is lost.

Information will be incomplete. If the teacher has the only record of who is in the class, then the teacher is responsible for enrolling new pupils. But teachers are hard pressed to finish the lesson within the time allotted. So the teacher cannot take time during the class period to gain all the information desired and may not take the time after class either. I have seen teachers' attendance books in which the new pupil is represented only by the first name, with no address or phone number listed.

It would be in the self-interest of the evangelism committee if the church school files provided:

1. Full name of pupil
2. Date enrolled
3. Address and phone number
4. Age and/or grade
5. Father's name and his church
6. Mother's name and her church

If you get no more than the name, address, and phone number, then your telephone committee can obtain the rest of the desired information, as when making contact with visitors to the church service. It's more likely you'll at least get this minimum of information if the church schools have a central file, a central place where pupils enroll, and signs directing new pupils to that central place.

Why make an issue of not losing the names of pupils who've been absent? One year my congregation was able to recruit 22 more pupils for the confirmation classes by combing the inactive section of our church school records. It's part of the function of your committee to see to it that pupils who have become inactive are identified and not lost to the records.

Inactive Members

The congregation has adult inactive members, too. Its constitution probably defines who they are. It may stipulate that a person who has been absent from worship for one year may be removed from the active membership list. There may be some reference to a lack of financial contributions during that year. But the evangelism committee can't afford to wait for a year before becoming concerned:

> **Studies indicate that once a person has been inactive for a period of six to eight weeks, it is extremely difficult to reverse his/her direction and restore him/her to the congregation's life. . . . People who consider leaving the church think that no one will miss them if they do leave; they test their assumption by leaving for a time and discover that they were right all along—no one does miss them.**[11]

So here's another use for the registration of every worshiper at every service. Early warning signals can be given by a clerical force (that records the attendance of members) whenever someone misses church for more than four weeks.

But we're really not talking here about how to bring inactive ones back to the classes and to the church services; we leave that to the chapter on reclamation. This chapter is about identifying those to whom we owe the gospel. The registration practice makes it easier to note visitors who may be seeking a church home.

Registration serves other uses also. Though it's likely more specific care is needed for members who move away, the same principle applies. It alerts the committee to the need for action. If people miss church for six to eight weeks through moving, the chances become poorer that they'll keep their connection with the body of Christ. So before they leave—if at all possible—the evangelism committee will plan a service of farewell, to thank them for the part they have played in the congregation and to wish them every blessing in their new home and new congregation.

It will take some doing to establish this practice, to make it known that the service of "Farewell and Godspeed" (as listed in *Occasional Services*) is not only for the "prominent" members but for all.

Your pastor(s) and teachers can help your committee instruct the congregation in a "Theology of Church Membership": that the church is more than the "home church." Loyalty to the "home church" ought to mean remaining with the body of Christ no matter where we move. We need the "assembling of ourselves together" for our own nurturing in the faith (Hebrews 10:25). We're "blessed to be a blessing" (Genesis 12:1-3). When a church member moves, it's as natural to inform the church as it is to advise the newspaper carrier—and much more important. The church wants to send members off with a decent expression of gratitude and goodwill.

If your members receive the national church magazine, then you may have an assistant in your ministry to those who move. Some magazine staffs will send a notice to a congregation near the new address, encouraging that parish to invite members who have moved. Since not every congregation has a strong evangelism program, that notice may not always be enough. A personal letter from your committee to the new congregation would show concern and could be the spark that touches off the action you want.

Your students away from home should be referred to the campus ministry personnel at their schools. In many congregations the secretary of the women's organization takes care of this; if no one is responsible for making this connection, then your committee should find a way to keep in touch with your students at this critical point in their lives. Keep them on the list for receiving the church newsletter, for one thing.

Define Territory

So far we've been considering those who come to your church—or formerly came. Your committee will also want to identify other people to whom you also owe the gospel. When Paul was writing to the Romans, he said he was eager to come to their city not only to win converts there (1:13) but to be helped by them to go on to Spain, where he also wanted to carry on his work of evangelism (15:22-29). He wasn't working only with those who came to him. He'd received a treasure he hadn't earned, something everyone else ought to have, and so he wrote: "I have an obligation to all peoples, to the civilized and to the savage, to the educated and to the ignorant" (1:14, TEV).

We'd say we're under obligation to those 6 million unattached Lutherans and to the many more millions of unattached anybodies in the United States and everywhere else. Though we feel this sense of debt to the masses, to avoid defeatism your committee should set a limit that's attainable, measurable, and meaningful. Define your territory, the area around your church building for which you take special responsibility. Some congregations have a mission to the entire metropolitan community, but they'll also find it prudent to be accountable for a specific area, a place where their ministry can make a particular witness.

Everyone in your territory who's without a current and local connection with the body of Christ is someone to whom your congregation owes the gospel. But even if you do your surveying on a three-year cycle, one-third of your territory each year, what about those who move in in-between? There are a number of resources available to help you locate the newcomers:

The Welcome Wagon. The hostess visits newcomers bringing information about the community. For a fee, she'll put your congregation's brochure in the packet she leaves at each home and send you the names of the Lutherans she discovers.

The Utility Companies. Not all, but some, will provide you with a list of their new customers.

The Council of Churches. In some communities, the council of churches collates the reports from the Welcome Wagon and the utility companies and passes on its findings to the congregations.

Real Estate Firms. Advertisements for houses often say, "near schools, churches, and shopping." How much do the salespersons know about your church? Your committee could send them a letter containing some information. Perhaps you could ask whoever controls the mailing list to put these firms on it for your newsletter, to give them continuing information.

Your Fellow Members. Motivate them to be alert to the moving vans in their neighborhoods. They may issue the invitation to your church themselves, or they can pass on the news to your committee.

The Post Office. In your parish newsletter, just a couple of spaces below your congregation's return address, print "Address Correction Requested." Your letter carrier will then bring you the changes of address for a fee. Along with keeping your mailing list up to date, that postal notice has another function: it tells you that someone else is likely moving in at the former address.

Identification and Follow-up Assignments

Persons to be contacted	Name of caller	Caller notified by	Caller reports to
Visitors			
(those affected by) Official Acts			
Hospitalized			
Parents of Pupils			
Inactives			
Unattached			
Neighborhoods (new residents)			

---

9. George Gallup Jr. and George Poling, *The Search for America's Faith* (Nashville: Abingdon, 1980), p. 90.
10. Ibid., p. 101.
11. Trautman, pp. 13-14.

Chapter 8

Cultivating Friendship

Mechanical Bartenders?

> **. . . A firm in Virginia has invented an automatic bartender. It is a computerized machine programmed to mix and dispense 120 different drinks. . . . If these things catch on, what will happen to the fellow who settles down at the bar and says, "Bartender, my wife doesn't understand me anymore." We can envision him sitting down at home saying, "Honey, my bartender doesn't understand me anymore.[12]**

People are being ground to powder by the millstones of the institutions with which they must deal. When they have a grievance at work, one that's too big for the supervisor to handle, they must go to some nameless body in the front office who can only go by what he or she reads in the policy manuals. When they park by a meter that won't accept their coin, they come back to find a ticket on the windshield. So they trudge to a police station and explain this circumstance to some nameless body who may have too many other things to do and perhaps doesn't even hear what they're saying. When there's a mistake on their charge account, they have to present themselves to the company in the form of a 10-digit number. When they write to their U.S. representative or senator, they may get a reply that doesn't answer the question they asked.

There are just too many people for industry or business or government to deal with as persons. Our Lord must see them as he saw the crowds in Galilee, "harassed and helpless" (Matthew 9:36). When these unfortunate souls come to worship, to be fed and healed, and find that the church is impersonal too, that's a calamity. It's also a contradiction, because the church proclaims the gospel of the good shepherd, who knows his own and who calls each by name.

The people in the pews have heard the gospel; they know they are full-fledged members of the family of God. So they have a rising expectation of experiencing that family relationship even in this life. Dale Trautman observes: "It is interesting to note that ALC research indicates that the top priority of lay persons is building community. The need for solid, lasting, meaningful fellowship growing from a broadly focused congregation is a growing desire on the part of most contemporary Americans" [13] and, quoting church historian Martin Marty: "Every study shows that churches prosper only if the needed feel needed and the needy can give support to others." [14]

Dr. James Russell Hale, professor at Lutheran Theological Seminary, Gettysburg, Pennsylvania, interviewed people with no church affiliation living in six of the most nonchurched counties in the United States. Among other things, he reports that in his interviews he recognized a sense of loneliness everywhere. Many people felt that nobody knew or cared that they were there.

Establishing Relationships

Though there are many reasons why people remain outside the church, we can't do much about these problems until we establish relationships with the disaffected. That's the mission of your co-workers in the ministry of cultivation. Since the momentum of our society is more toward depersonalizing us than keeping us human, those who make the cultivation calls are in themselves demonstrations of the gospel at work.

Your evangelism committee has a vital ministry to perform, helping fellow members become healers of the disease of loneliness. Your committee and those whom you recruit must be sure to see building relationships as a ministry in itself. We tend to resent the insurance salesperson who's nice to us only because he or she wants to make a sale. When the Bible says, "God is love" (1 John 4:8), it's speaking of *agape,* selfless love. Jesus said that our heavenly Father sends sunshine and rain upon all alike, the evil and the good, whether or not he gets a response (Matthew 5:45).

Your colleagues in the ministry of cultivating friendship will keep praying that they themselves will *be* the gospel as they make contact with those outside the church. They view these people not as objects to be manipulated but as *persons,* showing them the love of Christ whether or not they ever join your congregation.

There is a tension here. We have the charge to establish relationships free of exploitation. But we're also under divine compulsion to evangelize. It's a tension given us by Jesus himself when he commanded us to "love one another" as he has loved us (John 15:12), and when he also said, "You shall be my witnesses" (Acts 1:8). Just recognizing the problem helps to alleviate it. The people being visited know that their callers are from the church. A witness is already taking place. With sanctified common sense and caring hearts, your callers can keep themselves from even the appearance of manipulation. People manipulated into the church are those most likely to leave first.

Cultivation

There are numerous ways to organize the ministry of cultivation. One would be to look through the membership roster prayerfully to select warmhearted people with the gift of making friends, invite them to take up this challenge, train them, and then send them out on a regular schedule as ambassadors-at-large. Another way would be to choose the callers according to zones, train them, and send them only to the unchurched households in their neighborhoods. Still another way would be to look to the fellowship groups within your congregation, asking them to cultivate the friendship of those unchurched who are the most amenable to their group. Your committee will then make assignments to the men's organization, the women's circles, and the youth leagues, according to the information gained from the identification callers.

Here's where you'll appreciate the specifics of what your identification callers have reported. For example, if you know the occupation(s) represented in a given household, you can try to send someone there having the same or a kindred vocation. If your church school registration form asks the father's name and the mother's name separately, also asking their church connections separately, you tend to learn certain things that might elude you otherwise: Are both parents living in the home? Are both parents of the same faith? Whatever is discovered, you'll probably have greater success if you can send callers who'll be the most sensitive to the particular situation.

If you're relying on the fellowship groups to administer your ministry of cultivation, your committee should find a way to have people appointed from each fellowship who are then made responsible to your committee. Why not ask each fellowship group to let you recruit the callers you want from their number? That way you'll have cultivation callers who will honor their commitment to you and who will also try to "naturalize" their new friends into the congregation by introducing them into their fellowship groups.

At one church I know, every Thursday—afternoon or evening—Sunday school teachers are making evangelism calls. This congregation sees the Sunday school as the best possible structure for cultivating the friendship of those who are outside. If you had a Sunday school like this one, that surely would be true.

A nonchurched family in its neighborhood can find a class for every person in the household, with the members of each class within six months in age of each other. What's more, the grade-school boy in that house will be in a class with boys. Male and female teenagers and single adults and young marrieds will have male and female together. Classes for older adults are held by age and gender. That's not all. A youngster below the age of three will have a "cradle roll visitor" assigned to bring a lesson every three months for the parents, helping them rear that tot in the faith. Suppose a nonchurched family has five members: father, mother, grade-school boy, grade-school girl, and a two-year-old. Over a period of time this household will receive visits from five different groups—four classes and the cradle roll.

The Southern Baptists list certain "laws" of evangelism when carried on through the church school:

Number of Workers
The limit is 1 worker to 10 pupils. If you increase the number of workers (teachers, secretaries, musicians, and others) to the ratio of 1 to 5, the Sunday school will grow until you have a ratio of 1 to 10.

New Units
Classes generally reach their maximum growth a few months after they start, with smaller classes gaining a higher percentage of new pupils than larger ones. So teachers are given only *half* a class plus a list of prospects. The more active congregations organize new classes each semester.

Visitation
It takes 16 calls on the average to enroll one person in Sunday school. (Note: not a *maximum* of 16 calls, but 16 calls on the *average;* sometimes it takes more.)

This mode of evangelism may give your committee guidance in meeting a new challenge. The drop in the birthrate in the United States begs for a strategy to evangelize a growing segment of society—couples who choose to remain childless. In the past when a couple of church dropouts got married, the evangelism committee could expect that in a few years a preschool tot from that home would appear in church school, eventually bringing the young parents back into the church family.

I've heard childless couples say, "We don't have time for church, and we don't miss it; we have a full life without it." My answers don't have as much clout as those of a churchgoing married couple without children would have. How can your congregation cultivate the friendship of those who are without children? If there's no group of couples without children in your parish, can you help the appropriate committee develop such a fellowship? If forming a fellowship isn't feasible, can you recruit at least one such couple for your crew of cultivation callers? As you train these married couples, ask them to probe their hearts for their own motives for staying in the church. So many of their peers have dropped out that they'll need to be able to state a "reason for the hope that is in them" (1 Peter 3:15).

Reaching Out through Day Schools

A resource for some Lutheran congregations and a possibility for others is the Christian day school. Some Christian day schools were started partly to preserve the culture of the immigrants from Northern Europe. Now in some places they have become instruments of reaching out across cultures to people of other races.

Since most parents will sacrifice almost anything to give their children a chance, some congregations with day schools find that nonchurched parents are willing to pay sizable tuition for quality education. The church is teaching the Christian faith to children outside the church, and parents are paying for it.

It should be noted that Christian day school education is not simply other subjects plus Bible study. It is learning to look at all of life from a Christian point of view. In a Christian day school, "two plus two equals four," to be sure, but it also adds up to more. Since we can see the invisible God in the things he has made (Romans 1:20), we can see him also in arithmetic. Arithmetic is dependable and precise, attributes of the good Lord.

The Christian day school can be an ally of the evangelism committee; the whole day long its pupils are soaking in Christian values and viewpoints. Before a child is enrolled, the parents usually meet with the pastor, the principal, and a member of the board of education and are told about the school's philosophy and policies. There are also PTA meetings and conferences with teachers, further opportunities to cultivate friendship around the gospel.

People in Crisis

Some congregations have made a specialty of ministering to people in crises. Converts to Mormonism uniformly testify that they became Latter Day Saints because people of that faith were there to assist them when they were in trouble. **Again, we don't help people to get something out of them, even something so sacred as church membership.** "We love, because he first loved us" (1 John 4:19). We help people in crisis situations even if they *never* join a church. Those who are unemployed, bereaved, divorced, or facing family tensions need the ministry of the gospel.

If your congregation can mediate God's grace to them through personal visits and support groups, you will be the cause of much thanksgiving rising to God from the hearts of those you help.

Much of what was said in Chapter 6 on preevangelism also applies to the ministry of cultivation. All those you are developing as friends of the congregation will be on your mailing list, if for no other reason than to keep their addresses up-to-date. Some parishes have two newsletters. One is for members, announcing circle meetings, confirmation classes, and so on. The other is for the nonmember friends, with carefully written, attractive articles addressing their concerns, inviting them into the fellowship of faith. If your congregation sends the same newsletter out to everybody, and if you feel it's necessary, you could meet with the editor to discuss what can be done to make your newsletter even more helpful in the cultivating of friends.

We've considered various ways of establishing nonexploitive relationships of trust with the people to whom your congregation owes the gospel. The good Lord has given your committee imagination so that you can adapt the ideas given here to meet your situation. Your God-given creativity can also help you to devise your own strategies for reaching out and serving with the gift of friendship.

---

12. *St. Paul Dispatch*, April 19, 1969.
13. Trautman, p. 20.
14. Ibid.

Chapter 9

Gaining Commitments

If you confess with your lips that Jesus is Lord and believe in your heart that God raised him from the dead, you will be saved (Romans 10:9).

At one place where my family lived, I planted strawberries. I followed the instructions in the gardening book and set them out just so, with plenty of space between the rows for me to walk or crawl to pick the fruit. It was a neat design. But the plants kept sending out runners and filling up the spaces where I wanted to go. The birds didn't have my difficulty; they helped themselves freely. In the course of time I also noticed raspberry plants growing among the strawberries, a gift from the robins.

We've been laying out an evangelism plan that's neat, an attempt to administer a parishwide program that utilizes a variety of talents. Some folks will make identification calls. Some will make cultivation calls. Others will make commitment calls. But what if a team of identification callers brings in somebody's request for a transfer of membership? Or what if a team of cultivation callers signs up a person for the pastor's class? That need not bother your committee a bit. There are bound to be unlooked for rewards and unanticipated excitement which the identification or cultivation team members will experience.

I *did* keep clearing out the growth between the strawberry rows, and I *did* transplant the unexpected raspberries to their own space. Neatness is not crucial, but it does make it easier to pick strawberries. The neat evangelism design also has its purpose:

- Your committee can recruit more people when you divide up the work and set limits, when you give each team goals that are attainable, measurable, and meaningful. You can enlist some people for identification calls or cultivation calls who would shrink from making commitment calls.
- Over a period of time your committee can gain new commitment callers from the ranks of the other visitors. Your committee may recognize that some people have the talent and dedication to become excellent commitment callers. These people should be personally recruited. Then give them promising visits to make so that they develop the confidence to take on more difficult calls.

Additional Resources lists current manuals on recruiting and training those who will lead people to make a commitment to Christ and his church. There is one school of thought that deems it wise simply to train callers in the art of inviting others to the pastor's class. The operating philosophy is that the pastor is the professional with the background to give thoughtful answers to the important questions of faith.

Another school of thought considers it possible and desirable to train commitment callers to be grounded sufficiently in the Bible so they can also give "a reason for the hope that is in them." These callers will still solicit enrollees for the pastor's class. Along with receiving information, the trainees gain practice in telling the good news, first to members of their group, then to others in the congregation, and only after that to people outside the parish.

In some models, the trainees go out with the pastor for a certain number of weeks, observing him or her conducting the visits. There is one plan in which those coached by the pastor will then take on two more trainees for several months, and then when these trainees are ready to go on their own, they also each take on two more trainees, and so on. This program starts slowly and solidly, but before long it starts to mushroom.

Setting a Calendar

How you decide to set up your commitment calling and how you perceive your field determine how you arrange your other activities. Training your callers primarily in the art of inviting people to the pastor's class implies a certain calendar. Training commitment callers in theology and then sending them out once a week with the pastor or another veteran may imply another kind of scheduling.

Take the first instance. Sending out callers to bring in students for the pastor's class means you have to block out the time for the class, whether it's once, twice, or several times a year. That class schedule determines the schedule for your commitment calls.

Under one approach, seven weeks before a new class begins, the evangelism committee enlists the callers. Four weeks before the class starts, the callers engage in a heavy campaign of visits, two or three nights in a row for two or three weeks. The teams may meet at 6:00 p.m. for supper, training, and assignments, go out on calls at 7:00, and then return about 9:00 to report back and to encourage one another. The supper provides the means of getting them together early enough to have a productive evening.

The supper can serve another purpose, providing others in the congregation a chance to take part, either by bringing food, by serving, or by cleaning up. With perhaps two or three pastor's classes a year, there will be two or three membership receptions a year, welcoming not only those from the class but also those joining by letter of transfer. Each membership Sunday will be accompanied by the "naturalization" (sometimes called "assimilation") practices to be discussed in the next chapter. This plan has a rhythm to it. It puts certain activities at certain times, and that means there's more of a chance these things will actually be done.

The other plan of organizing your commitment calling may call for the very same schedule of classes and membership Sundays and naturalization practices.

But when your commitment callers are going out one night every week, and the next pastor's class doesn't start for three months, they may wish their candidates didn't have so long to wait. There's a system that fits in well with the continuous calling program: a continuous pastor's class. Every week, at the same time, on the same day, 10 months a year, there's a session. If a student comes in at Lesson 3, he or she continues till the end of the course and then takes Lessons 1 and 2.

Every member can know that a friend, relative, or neighbor with questions about the Christian faith can be brought to your church on such a day at such a time any week. And your commitment callers have the advantage of being able to say, "Our pastor teaches a class in the fundamentals of the Christian faith; if he doesn't discuss your questions, you be sure to bring them up. The class meets day after tomorrow at 8:00 p.m. and runs for ____ weeks. Is that a convenient time for you?"

With a continuous pastor's class, there will be a continuous flow of people ready for membership, 3 or 4 one month, 7 or 8 the next month, 20 or 30 another month. It might even be a good idea to have monthly membership receptions. Perhaps your congregation can "naturalize" 3 or 4 new members better and more easily 10 times a year than 15 or 20 new members twice a year.

As you look over the training manuals recommended in Additional Resources, you'll find more suggestions on how to organize this part of your evangelism ministry. By analyzing your congregation and examining the styles of training offered, you'll be able to judge which pattern of commitment calling is most useful for you.

Chapter 10

Naturalization

. . . Perhaps we might better use a word like "naturalization" when we speak of incorporating a person into the church. This word carries the idea that the new person brings to the life of the congregation all of his gifts, strengths, wisdom, and history in order to share with all of the rest.[15]

Naturalization is a good term because it implies the enthusiasm a new citizen has for his or her new country. It's possible that naturalized citizens are more grateful for the liberties symbolized by a nation's flag than are those who were born into citizenship. Just so, the person naturalized into the congregation may have more zeal for the kingdom of God than do some of its charter members. Naturalization, however, does have some of the same problems as assimilation. In the way it's been used in the past, it signifies putting all the immigrants into the melting pot where they'll lose their own distinctiveness and blend into the mixture. They will be like everyone else. If that's the connotation of naturalization, then we're still looking for a better word. I'm using naturalization because I like the meaning Dale Trautman puts into it, "that the new person brings to the life of the congregation all of his gifts, strengths, wisdom, and history."

I think of a Jewish mother I baptized, with whom our congregation did badly concerning naturalization, whose "gifts, strengths, wisdom, and history" we did not value. We invited her to a women's circle meeting right away. A neighbor living on the same street was glad to bring her, and she was happy to come. But the Bible study leader that night made an issue of how the Jews had harassed Jesus. The woman never came back. We could have profited by her history to gain more insight into Jesus (a Jew), the apostles and prophets (all Jews), and to better understand our own history as adopted children of Abraham.

I think also of a science teacher I met at a conference. I'd spoken to the group concerning the doctrine of Christian vocation, about how the man who takes care of automobiles doesn't serve God only because he also sings in the choir, but that he serves God right there in his shop, making cars run well so that God's other workers can go about their business serving God and their neighbors. During the coffee break, this teacher told me, "I consider my teaching of science as a Christian vocation. I wish I could have the chance to show others in my church how science serves God, but all my church has ever asked me to do is usher."

Your evangelism committee will scarcely despise the role of an usher, the congregation's host to all worshipers and especially to the newcomers. This science teacher did take his turn as the congregation's host, not looking down on that position. He was simply lamenting the fact that his congregation was not utilizing all of his "gifts, strengths, wisdom, and history."

New Members

When we miss the mark in naturalizing our new members, everybody loses: the congregation is deprived of the blessings the new member can offer, and the new member is deprived of the blessings the congregation can give. Just how crucial the ministry of naturalization is may be seen in this comment by Trautman: "Some contend that inactivity really begins when a person first joins the congregation. If he/she hasn't found meaningful involvement in the congregation within 60-90 days, that person is already on the way toward 'dropping out.' "[16] He also tells us that "nearly 40 percent of those confirmed are inactive within two years."[17] Another relevant observation from Trautman:

> Nearly every congregation of any size and of some age could discover that approximately 10 percent of the members are alive and "on fire" for the gospel. Another 20 percent of the membership will be cold, dead, and functionally inactive. The remaining 70 percent are present but not deeply involved in the congregation.
>
> It is easy to become obsessed with the 20 percent of our membership who are not participating at all and forget to be concerned for the larger number. Yet, the remaining 70 percent are moving either toward increased activity or toward total inactivity. An important remedy for inactivity in our congregations is an attempt to arrest the movement of those who are moving toward dropping out.[18]

Who is equal to all of this? Clearly the few people on the evangelism committee can't do it all. But someone from your committee needs to administer the program. There could even be a subcommittee that has the ministry of naturalization as a distinct responsibility, overseeing and expanding the process of nurturing new members and stimulating the 70% to more love and good works. The person or subcommittee in charge of naturalization would establish networks with other committees, such as education, youth, membership, and stewardship, as well as with the auxiliaries or fellowship groups.

No matter what kind of naturalization program is used, it should boil down to one essential: Each new member should have some kind of sponsorship. There is simply no substitute for personal concern. In a choir it may take the form of having a representative from each section notice those who are present and check on those who are missing. The representative acts not as a truant officer but as one who wants to know when a fellow tenor has troubles.

Sponsors

Sponsorship for babies at baptism is part of our culture, recognized even by those outside the church, but it can become almost meaningless. That likelihood is increased by our high mobility. When people were born and lived and died in the same community, it was realistic to expect that your sponsors would be around your whole life as friends and advocates. But my family, for example, moved away from my birthplace when I was three years old, and I have never known my sponsors.

Maybe it's time for some changes. Since the child is baptized into the community of believers, and since the congregation assumes responsibility for its baptized members, the congregation could appoint a new sponsor if the baptismal sponsors are not close at hand. Especially when the youngster starts to take Communion or when the youth begins confirmation instruction would this practice be valuable.

I have observed this plan in action in connection with a system of confirmation instruction in which the pupils did their "homework" in the learning center at church, with confirmation sponsors coming every week to assist their charges with their studies. In some cases the sponsor was a parent of one of the pupils, branching out to guide one or two others as well. I saw a bond developing that lasted well beyond the date of confirmation.

It doesn't matter whether the pupil is slow or fast in learning. The important thing is to provide the opportunity for the bond to grow. When these young adults come back from college, from the military, or from working out-of-town, they'll seek out friends of their own age, of course, but don't be surprised if they look up the adults who were their friends in their teens.

Some congregations also appoint sponsors for adults who join their fellowship. The sponsors even stand with them in the rite of reception and take part with them in the new member orientation programs and classes. This practice goes back to the original form of sponsorship. When the early church was about to baptize an adult pagan and that pagan was unknown to the bishop, there had to be a Christian adult standing up with the pagan adult to vouch for him or her and to watch over that person in the instruction that followed Baptism.

Today's mobile society makes it desirable to have some organized system to integrate not only the newly baptized adult but everyone new to the fellowship. Not all congregations presently appointing sponsors for adults are satisfied with the way they're handling the program, however. Generally it seems there's a lack of understanding as to what the sponsor is supposed to do. There also appears to be a lack of follow-through by someone in charge.

Other Possibilities

Another possibility to bring people closer to one another through the church is set forth by Daniel Fuelling and Audrey Rothmaler in the booklet *Congregational Outreach and Care* (Augsburg Publishing House, 1982). It provides for mini-parish groupings under trained leaders within a congregation. Your subcommittee for naturalization or the congregation's committee on membership can dig into these possibilities, defining the nature of the problem, setting goals, and then organizing necessary workers. This group can also work out a simple system of periodic reports, so that there is accountability resulting in follow-through. The report will include what the sponsor or mini-parish leader has discovered concerning the talents, experience, and interests of the new member. This reporting might include recommendations on how best to let that new person's "gifts, strengths, wisdom, and history" be a blessing to the congregation.

What if the person selected doesn't do the job? The new member may not be naturalized, and the person assigned may become ashamed and drop out. Then you've lost two people; you're worse off than if you hadn't appointed someone. To prevent this problem you can make it known to people that if at any time they can't keep up with their assignment, they should inform the committee and let the responsibility go to someone else. With such an understanding, when it's time for a report and none has appeared, you're free to intervene. The chances are good there won't be any hard feelings.

Now, about those members of the congregation, perhaps 70%, who "are present but not deeply involved, who are moving toward dropping out." They are sometimes the ones who complain, "The only time the church comes to see us is when it wants our money." How do you manage a ministry of naturalization for these folks?

In general, there are two possible structures: ambassadors-at-large and shepherds-of-zones. Your stewardship committee may already be using one or both of these plans. In the fall of the year it may send teams of callers to every household. The committee may disperse them without regard to geography, sending those most suitable to each situation (the ambassador-at-large concept). Or the committee could deploy them largely to their own neighborhoods (the shepherding concept). A variation might be that the committee will set up cottage meetings in each zone (again, shepherding). The stewardship committee is seeking commitment from every member, and so is your evangelism committee. There is a clear overlap of interest.

To overcome the accusation, "The only time the church comes to see us is when it wants our money," your ambassadors-at-large or your shepherds-of-zones might find other occasions to call, at two or three designated seasons. Here's an overlap of interest with several other committees. The education committee may want a survey of the adults to discover what topics they'd be interested in studying and discussing. The worship committee may want to promote home devotions or attendance at midweek Lenten or Advent services. The church council may want ideas for the coming year's agenda, what the members see as needs to be met. Any of these contacts with the membership can be made either through the ambassadors-at-large or shepherds-of-zones, who also should stop in just to visit, to see how things are going.

Whom should congregations recruit to minister to the moderately active 70%? Let's say you are part of the 10% who are heavily involved already. You hesitate when another member of the 10% from another committee comes around for help. Why not look for ambassadors or shepherds among the 70%? The first time around, recruiters could focus their calling on finding ambassadors or shepherds. When a few have been found, commission them to help sign up more. When there are enough, time should be taken to train them before they are sent out.

Which plan your committee should adopt, ambassadors-at-large or shepherds-of-zones, depends on your congregation's history, its people, and the circumstances. The ambassadors-at-large machinery is relatively simple to start and keep going: you just enlist the suitable and willing, then find ways to brief them, to send them out, and to receive their reports. You do this three or four times a year. The shepherds-of-zones machinery also involves recruitment, training, and reporting, but further requires the work of defining the zones. This plan has the advantage of providing a means by which your committee can promote bonds of friendship between members living in the same neighborhoods.

Devise Strategy

If your stewardship committee has attempted cottage meetings by neighborhoods, it's probably discovered that people don't necessarily come to such a meeting just because they've been invited. Other interests and duties interfere: football on TV, bowling leagues, laundry, shopping, children, etc. Or perhaps some are bashful about meeting strangers; others are just not interested.

If you sense that cottage meetings would be difficult to pull off, don't program yourself for discouragement. Plan ahead. Devise a step-by-step strategy to break down barriers and establish ties so that people won't resist the notion of cottage meetings and may even look forward to them. How might that be done? You could promote bonds of friendship between the flock and its shepherd by giving the shepherd occasions for regular visits: ask the shepherd to deliver the devotional booklets, such as *Christ in Our Home,* as often as they come out.

Obviously the devotional booklets could reach the members' homes by some other means, perhaps even more efficiently, but they can provide the shepherd a point of contact, a way to lead to conversation and to establish a tie. If the shepherd should then later invite these people to his or her home, they'd already know the shepherd and might be more inclined to accept the invitation.

You can also make connections by a linkage system of visiting. Either choose or write a brief booklet on a subject needing congregational attention, such as evangelism, stewardship, home devotions, the liturgy, vocation, education, service, social action, etc. Identify clusters of neighbors within the membership, three to five neighbors in a cluster. On the front of the booklet draw a chain with as many links as there are members in the cluster. Write the name, address, and phone number of one household on each link. By letter invite the people named on the first link of each cluster to pick up the booklet at church on a certain Sunday, perhaps during the service. Ask them to read the booklet and then take it to the next household. That household does the same, and so on. The last household brings the booklet back to church on a certain date. Try to forestall breakdowns by sending a letter to all members, enclosing a copy of the linkage they're involved with. This notice may promote a sense of responsibility for making the project work, but if nothing else, it will alert them to the fellow members living near them.

In one parish I served, we had a program of confirmation instruction that established neighborhood networks. We used a three-year curriculum with the three years taught consecutively, not concurrently. Therefore, if a family had a youth in the first year and another in the third, both would be studying the same lesson, and the family could work on it together. We met in homes by zones, parents and children together. After the lesson there were refreshments, with the parents visiting with each other and the pupils in the basement playing table tennis or whatever else the house had to offer.

Several families with children of confirmation age joined the congregation during the time we had this program and were naturalized into the fellowship wholeheartedly. These neighborhood meetings had a purpose that met the self-interest of the families concerned, and so they worked.

I know of one parish organized by zones for the purpose of meeting to study the coming Sunday's scripture readings. The pastor visits each zone in turn, one or two zones per week, not to teach but to listen, to learn what the questions and concerns of his people are, so that his coming sermon might come closer to meeting their needs. This program didn't develop overnight, however. The pastor and his people had a long-range goal; they worked toward it by stages that were attainable, measurable, and meaningful.

Whatever system of naturalization and continuing nurture your committee adopts, you can be sure it will be a blessing to many. You'll be filling what is often a large gap in a congregation's ministry. In this connection, one final passage from Trautman pertains:

> One of the frequent complaints of inactive members is that they had a need and the church was inadequate to meet that need. . . . Changes in lifestyle (including inactivity) are most likely during high periods of stress. Congregations should be aware of pain and hurt among their people. Systems should be developed to respond quietly and fully to real need.[19]

Your imagination and persistence can bring those "systems" into being.

---

15. Ibid., p. 16.
16. Ibid., p. 15.
17. Ibid.
18. Ibid., pp. 12-13.
19. Ibid., pp. 19-20.

Chapter 11

Reclamation

What man of you, having a hundred sheep, if he has lost one of them, does not leave the ninety-nine in the wilderness, and go after the one which is lost, until he finds it? (Luke 15:4)

I have heard several pastors say something like, "I can get more results working with new people than with inactive members." From 33 years in the parish ministry, I know this to be true. Calling on strangers has elements of freshness and excitement. They don't know your failings, and there's a chance for a new start. New people bring new zeal and new ideas. To deal with inactive members is to listen to complaints. And if their complaint is against you, then they're not the only ones who are suffering.

Since "evangelism . . . is forgiven people practicing the forgiveness they have received,"[20] we can't go on without looking for healing. As Jesus said, "If you are offering your gift at the altar, and there remember that your brother has something against you, leave your gift there before the altar and go; first be reconciled to your brother, and then come and offer your gift" (Matthew 5:23-24).

Because of the pain we fear may come from facing up to a problem, we tend to avoid such confrontations. But out of the pain there can come the joy of reconciliation when people who were at odds have found peace with each other. The expectation of this joy fortifies us and moves us to take the first step.

If the complaint is not against you, then there is still the prospect of the joy of the shepherd who, when he has found his lost sheep, calls together his friends and neighbors for a celebration (Luke 15:6).

We're motivated not only by the joy that comes from the ministry of reclamation but also by the need. Previously in this manual we've noted the following figures:

- During the decade of the 1970s, the American Lutheran Church lost more than 40% of its members (not counting new members gained).
- There is a gap of 6 million between the number of members U.S. Lutheran churches have on their rolls and the number whom the Gallop Poll has found claiming to be Lutherans.

Figures so huge, instead of motivating us to act, might rather depress us so much we fail to act. That need not be. There is good reason for encouragement.

Programs of reclamation initiated by a United Methodist pastor, Dr. John Savage, and carried on by a United Presbyterian pastor, the Rev. Mark Dowdy, as well as by an American Lutheran Church pastor, the Rev. Gerhard Knutson, prove that the lost sheep can not only be found but carried home. A visitation program in 1978 in Indianapolis on behalf of nine Christian churches had 34 persons forming teams and visiting 186 persons. The return rate overall was 42.5%. Those who were visited fell into two groups:

Group A—people in the process of leaving the church, but not having dropped out completely

Group B—people completely inactive in the church

The return rate for Group A was 63% and for Group B 28%. Statistics show the wisdom of getting to people before they have completely dropped out, since the chances for bringing them back are twice as good then as otherwise.[21]

But you say, "I'm not thinking of the numbers nationwide. Just here in our own church we have so many inactives that we can never get them all." What is that proverb, a journey of a thousand miles begins with the first step? The Rev. Mark Dowdy is quoted as saying:

> **Two people as a team can make four calls in one month. . . . Four calls is not too much to ask of people in the local parish. Say they take the summer off and it's only 10 months. It's still 40 calls. If you have three teams of two callers each who have been trained, you get into the homes of 120 families in a year's time.**[22]

Look for the Lost Sheep

There's another objection, perhaps not what you'd say but it's what you might hear from others as you set about establishing a ministry of reclamation: "These people made promises when they were confirmed and when they transferred into our congregation. They've been instructed; they know better. If they don't keep their word, it's not our problem."

I suppose we could answer that the lost sheep should have known better, too, but that the shepherd still went out looking for it. But what also stirs me is the research on *why* people drop out of church: it reveals that sometimes the fault is with the congregation. Some inactives are "burned out," having been overloaded with congregational work. Others have the opposite complaint; they were ignored. Some find the congregation's teaching, preaching, and worship services inadequate (irrelevant, shallow, dull, or not in their language). Some complain about what they see as unwise spending by church leaders. And others say the congregation is too much taken with preserving itself, detached from the community, neglecting the uniqueness of Christ and his mission in the world. Still others complain they had a crisis (sickness, death, divorce, unemployment) and the church forgot them.

I'll admit that with some of the inactives I've known, the basic problem seemed to be something else: perhaps they'd bought a boat and that boat took them out of town every weekend possible. Or if it wasn't a boat, it was a snowmobile or a set of golf clubs. But I also need to admit that the church hasn't always dealt with such dropouts in a loving way. I speak of the letter—sometimes even a mimeographed letter—that came to these people notifying them they'd been dropped from the roll for lack of attendance at worship. I've found that the hurt of that rejection is sometimes so deep that even though the letter had been received years ago, they still had it and got it out of the drawer and showed it to me. Yes, the inactives may well bear responsibility for being inactive, but we who are active may also bear at least part of the blame. So we go to them.

Additional Resources lists some excellent manuals on how to minister to inactives. With one voice they urge on us the need to be good listeners, to let the old wounds get opened up—to let all the "garbage" spill out so that the healing may begin.

What kind of people do you recruit and train for the ministry of reclamation? Gerhard Knutson has some wise counsel:

> **The recruitment process involves looking for people who have gifts in relating to, and caring about, others. The "flashiest" and most talkative persons do not necessarily make the best listening witnesses. But rather, look for those people with the gifts of sensitivity, faithfulness, attentiveness, and genuine caring for other human beings. They may not all possess confidence, but that can be built up through training and encouragement.**[23]

It's true—your committee can probably make a better record for itself by concentrating on new people and paying no attention to the inactives. But I've found satisfaction in calling on dropouts. And I don't think the Lord minds it at all that bringing them back was fun for me.

> **And when he has found it, he lays it on his shoulders, rejoicing. And when he comes home, he calls together his friends and his neighbors, saying to them, "Rejoice with me, for I have found my sheep which was lost" (Luke 15:5-6).**

---

20. Gerhard Knutson, *Ministry to Inactives* (Minneapolis: Augsburg Publishing House, 1979), p. 5.

21. Ray Ruppert, religion ed., "Presbyterians Map Out Game," *Seattle Times*, August 2, 1980.

22. Ibid.

23. Knutson, p. 35.

Chapter 12

Sorting Things Out

> **Evangelism is urgent, but it's also worth doing well. You and your committee may need some time to digest what's offered here and to analyze where you are, where you need to go, and how you'll get there. You probably won't achieve all your goals this year** (from the Preface).

At this point are you all by yourself, the chairperson who's supposed to recruit and train a committee? You might reread Chapter 5, "Organizing the Calling Process." Then go through the congregation's membership roster to list the persons you judge to have the gift of organizing. Seek advice from the pastor(s) and officers. Set a deadline, a date by which you'll have your committee assembled. Then program yourself for success: do your recruiting in person.

The telephone is helpful, of course; you'll want to use it to set up appointments for your in-person visits. But to ask someone over the telephone to take part in such an important mission is to downplay it and to make it too easy for the other person to refuse without considering the value and urgency of the task. It may work better not to ask your potential colleagues for an answer on the spot; you could even leave a copy of this manual and then get back to them in a week for their response.

When you have your committee lined up, then you study and plan. I think it would be worthwhile if you took as many as five meetings to read and discuss the chapters on this schedule:

1. Chapters 1 and 2
2. Chapters 3 and 4
3. Chapters 5, 6, and 7
4. Chapter 8 and 9
5. Chapters 10, 11, and 12

These meetings could be monthly or weekly. If weekly, you could meet during Sunday school. Or you could discuss this manual in two sessions under the main headings:

I. The Attitude for Evangelism
   Chapters 1, 2, and 3

II. Making Evangelism Happen
   A. Every Member a Witness, Chapter 4
   B. Running the Machinery, Chapters 5 through 12

A three-session course would be like the two-session one, except that you could devote one session to Chapter 4.

It might be workable to have the committee members read the entire manual all at once and then discuss it in one session. But whatever course you take, follow it with a session on setting goals. Here you will consider what you're already doing and whether it needs any adjustment. Then you'll discover what you're not doing. Decide what needs to be worked on and in what order and how soon. You may sketch out a plan for the next several years.

At the end of your congregation's fiscal year, your committee will review its progress toward its goals and make a report to the congregation. At the beginning of the new fiscal year, the committee will break in any new members and then set new goals.

Interrelationship

One more thing. You may have noticed a theme running through the other chapters: Your committee should have good relationships with the other committees and groups in the congregation. Related to that is the assumption that the evangelism committee stimulates all other parts of the parish to do evangelism.

It might be useful for you to review each chapter and to make a list of the various items that affect each of the other committees and fellowship groups, in order to get a picture of how evangelism reaches into all facets of congregational life. Wouldn't it be good if each committee and group drafted a goal each year that showed how its specific ministry could contribute to the ministry of evangelism? Can you lay the groundwork this year for that practice to begin next year? Tell them that the goal is to be attainable, measurable, and meaningful.

Ask them to give your committee a copy of their goal after their second meeting of the year. At the end of the year, ask them to give a report on how they fared in their goal on evangelism. If any of them ask you for suggestions on what kind of goal to set, rejoice! This is just the kind of opening you want.

I doubt that the evangelism teams of Paul and Barnabas or Paul and Silas or anyone else in the early church had a manual on organizing for evangelism. But they surely did evangelize. There is no claim that the plan of action outlined in this book is the only way to do it. This little book, however, does grow out of some biblical principles:

- The gospel makes us debtors to those who don't have the gospel (Romans 1:14-15).
- All who are baptized into the people of God are witnesses (1 Peter 2:9-10).
- Some have the gift of being evangelists (Ephesians 4:11).
- Some have the gift of being administrators (1 Corinthians 11:28).
- We look to the interest of others (Philippians 2:4) and find ways to connect our offer of the gospel to their self-interest (1 Corinthians 9:19-23).

Take what you want from this manual; expand on it; revise it; improve it; adapt it; but *do* evangelize. And do find ways to support your fellow members in this ministry—not forgetting to show them your appreciation for their efforts—so that both in organizing and in evangelizing they may find joy.

Additional Resources

Bible Study

Proclaim Curriculum. Augsburg Publishing House. A general Sunday church school curriculum starting with home nursery (infants and toddlers) and continuing through grade 9, establishing mission as a priority for the people of God. Many of the auxiliary pieces have a strong witness orientation.

SEARCH. Augsburg Publishing House. A laity-led small group Bible study with a mission focus, undergirding the evangelism effort of the church.

Word and Witness. Fortress Press. A Bible overview course looking at the Scriptures from the viewpoint of evangelism.

Motivation

Believers Incorporated. Walter R. Wietzke, Augsburg Publishing House, 1977.

Go Make Disciples. Rolf A. Syrdal, Augsburg Publishing House, 1977.

Go with the Gospel. David W. Preus, Augsburg Publishing House, 1977.

We Are Ambassadors. Rolf A. Syrdal, Augsburg Publishing House, 1976.

Training for Outreach

An Evangel for Everyone: A training course for those sharing the Gospel. Elten A. Zerby and Ralph H. Quere, Augsburg Publishing House, 1981. An in-depth, 15-session study of the theology and practice of evangelism; supervised calling, with the pastor accompanying the trainees.

Share the Word. Kevin E. Ruffcorn, Augsburg Publishing House, 1982. A popularly written book on the theology of evangelism from a Lutheran perspective.

Training Parish Callers. Donn Rosenauer and Frank W. Klos, Augsburg Publishing House and Fortress Press, 1977. Five teaching sessions and two supervised visiting experiences. Useful in training for other kinds of calling, too, such as to the sick, shut-in, bereaved, as well as for making stewardship calls.

Witnesses for Christ: Training for Intentional Witnessing. Edward F. Markquart, Augsburg Publishing House, 1981. Applies to "Every Member a Witness." Helps people to verbalize the faith within already existing natural relationships.

Training for Ministry to Inactives

An Investigation of Inactivity in The American Lutheran Church: Its Causes and Cures. Dale C. Trautman and the Congregational Life/Dynamics Task Force, Augsburg Publishing House, 1982. A study presented to the Church Council, The American Lutheran Church.

Ministry to Inactives. Gerhard Knutson, Augsburg Publishing House, 1979. Utilizes the insights of research done by John Savage and others, giving a practical plan for a local congregation.

Witness Across Cultures and to Other Specific Audiences

My Witness Series (pamphlets). Augsburg Publishing House, 1982.

My Witness to Those of Another Culture
My Witness to a Contrary Witness
My Witness in the Face of Hostility
My Witness in Crisis Situations
My Witness to Those Close to Me
My Witness to the Electronic Christian
My Witness in Everyday Situations
My Witness to Humanists

Our Neighbors in Hiding. Augsburg Publishing House. A 4-session study guide sensitizing church members to the plight of undocumented aliens in the United States.

The *Unchurched: Who They Are and Why They Stay Away.* James Russell Hale, Harper and Row, 1980.

Evangelism in Small Churches

Making the Small Church Effective. Carl S. Dudley, Abingdon, 1978.

Small Congregations in Rural Settings: Aspects of Christian Presence and Ministry. Lou Accola, Division for Life and Mission in the Congregation, The American Lutheran Church, 1982.

The Small Town Church. Peter J. Surrey, Abingdon, 1981.

"Preevangelism" or Public Relations for the Church

Religious Public Relations Handbook: For Local Congregations of all Denominations. 1969, First Edition; 1976, Second Edition; 1982, Third Edition. Produced by professionals of the Religious Public Relations Council, Room 1031, 475 Riverside Drive, New York, NY 10027.

Words Ring Louder than Bells: How to Produce Better Parish Newsletters. Raymond H. Wilson, The Center for Parish Communication, PO Box 627, Whitefish, MT 59937.

Choir School Curriculum

Alleluia Series. Augsburg Publishing House. Featuring basic fundamentals of reading music, Bible learning, worship, creative activities such as art, crafts, movement and drama, fellowship, in a three-year cycle.

Organizing the Shepherding Program

Congregational Outreach and Care: a manual for mini-parish leadership. Daniel Fuelling and Audrey Rothmaler, Augsburg Publishing House, 1982. Practical helps for congregational leaders of small groups organized for outreach.

The Shepherding Program (Life and Growth Plan, Zone Plan, Undershepherd Program). Division for Life and Mission in the Congregation, The American Lutheran Church, 422 South Fifth Street, Minneapolis, MN 55415.

Evangelism in the Sunday School

Parish Education Helps for Reaching Out through the Church School. Paul Pallmeyer, Division for Life and Mission in the Congregation, The American Lutheran Church, 422 South Fifth Street, Minneapolis, MN 55415.

Leaflet Ministry (Augsburg Publishing House)

An Invitation to Parents

How to Move without Getting Lost

Keep Your Eyes on Christ

Mormonism: Is this the Church of Jesus Christ?

Saying and Doing the Gospel

The ABC's of Life

The Lutheran Church Teaches

The Powerful Partnership

The Ten Steps of Effective Christian Witnessing

Use and Misuse of the Bible

What's Your Gift? Encourages members to recognize their gifts for witnessing to Christ.

Why Baptize Infants?

Worship and Witness Go Together. Encourages Christians to praise God openly and to reach out to others.

On Setting Goals, Parishwide

Shared Vision. Augsburg Publishing House. A congregational self-study instrument and interpretation guide to aid congregations in their planning for mission and ministry and in setting priorities.

Parish Evangelists

Clergy and lay persons trained to be consultants to the local congregation, advising them in evangelism. Congregations seeking this form of evangelism support should contact their district office or: Director for Witness, Division for Life and Mission in the Congregation, The American Lutheran Church, 422 South Fifth Street, Minneapolis, MN 55415.

Crisis Support Groups

Caring Community Project. A plan to develop within the congregation an intergenerational community of 35-70 people meeting weekly for six to nine months, seeking to recapture what life together was like in the early church. For information contact: Division for Life and Mission in the Congregation, The American Lutheran Church, 422 South Fifth Street, Minneapolis, MN 55415.

Newspaper Advertisements for the Church

Contact: Office of Communication and Mission Support, The American Lutheran Church, 422 South Fifth Street, Minneapolis, MN 55415.

Preaching through the Press. International Lutheran Laymen's League, 2185 Hampton Avenue, St. Louis, MO 63139.

National Radio Broadcasts

Church World News. Fifteen-minute weekly broadcast reviewing church news around the world. Media Services Center, The American Lutheran Church, 1568 Eustis Street, St. Paul, MN 55108.

JOY. Thirty-minute weekly program of easy-listening, high-quality music of the church, related to the scripture Lessons for the Day. KFUO Lutheran Radio, 801 DeMun, St. Louis, MO 63105.

SCAN. Thirty-minute weekly program with interviews on live issues, geared for a rock music station but usable on other formats. Media Services Center, The American Lutheran Church, 1568 Eustis Street, St. Paul, MN 55108.

(*Church World News, JOY,* and *SCAN* are available only on "Public Service Time," that is, they come free to the stations and the stations broadcast them without charge.)

Lutheran Vespers. Thirty-minute weekly program of preaching and singing. The program comes free to the stations but Lutheran Vespers pays for the broadcast time. Lutheran Vespers, 421 South Fourth Street, Minneapolis, MN 55415.

Evangelism through the Christian Day School

For information contact: Dr. Donald A. Vetter, Director for Christian Day Schools, The American Lutheran Church, Wartburg College, Waverly, IA 50677.

Cellular and Molecular Mechanisms Underlying Higher Neural Functions

Goal of this Dahlem Workshop:

to apply new cellular and molecular concepts to
the understanding of plasticity in synapses, cells, local circuits,
and defined systems in the mature brain

Life Sciences Research Report LS 54

Held and published on behalf of the
Freie Universität Berlin

Sponsored by:
Senat der Stadt Berlin

Cellular and Molecular Mechanisms Underlying Higher Neural Functions

Edited by

A.I. SELVERSTON and P. ASCHER

Report of the Dahlem Workshop on
Cellular and Molecular Mechanisms
Underlying Higher Neural Functions
held in Berlin 1993, February 28 – March 5

Program Advisory Committee:
A.I. Selverston and P. Ascher, Chairpersons
J.S. Altman, P. Andersen, M.B. Kennedy, P.H. Seeburg, W. Singer

JOHN WILEY & SONS
Chichester • New York • Brisbane • Toronto • Singapore

Telephone (+44) 243 779777

Library of Congress Cataloging-in-Publication Data

Dahlem Workshop on Cellular and Molecular Mechanisms Underlying Higher Neural Functions (1993 : Berlin, Germany)
Cellular and molecular mechanisms : report of the Dahlem Workshop on Cellular and Molecular Mechanisms Underlying Higher Neural Functions, Berlin, 1993, February 28–March 5 / edited by A.I. Selverston and P. Ascher.
p. cm. — (Life sciences research report ; 54) (Dahlem workshop reports)
Includes bibliographical references and index.
ISBN 0-471-94304-5 (cased)
1. Molecular neurophysiology—Congresses. I. Selverston, Allen I. II. Ascher, P. (Philippe) III. Title. IV. Series. V. Series : Dahlem workshop reports.
QP356.2.D34 1993
612.8—dc20 93–46293
CIP

British Library Cataloguing in Publication Data

A catalogue record for this book is available from the British Library

ISBN 0-471-94304-5

Dahlem Editorial Staff: J. Lupp, C. Rued-Engel, G. Custance
Typeset in 10/12pt Times from editor's disks by Text Processing Department, John Wiley & Sons Ltd, Chichester
Printed and bound in Great Britain by Biddles Ltd, Guildford, Surrey

Contents

The Dahlem Konferenzen

In 1974, the Stifterverband für Deutsche Wissenschaft[1] in cooperation with the Deutsche Forschungsgemeinschaft[2] founded the *Dahlem Konferenzen*. It was created to promote an interdisciplinary exchange of scientific ideas as well as to stimulate cooperation in research among international scientists. Dahlem Konferenzen proved itself to be an invaluable tool for communication in science, and so, to secure its long-term future, it was integrated into the Freie Universität Berlin in January, 1990.

As has been evident over recent years, scientific research has become highly interdisciplinary. Now, before real progress can be made in any one field, the concepts, methods, and strategies of related fields must be understood and able to be applied. Coordinated research efforts, scientific cooperation, and basic communication between the disciplines and the scientists themselves must be promoted in order for science to advance.

To meet these demands, Dahlem Konferenzen created a special type of forum for communication, now internationally recognized as the *Dahlem Workshop Model*. These workshops are the framework in which coherent discussions between the disciplines take place and are focused around a topic of high priority interest to the disciplines concerned. At a Dahlem Workshop, scientists are able to pose questions and solicit alternative opinions on contentious issues from colleagues of related fields. The overall goal of a workshop is not necessarily to reach a consensus, but rather to identify gaps in knowledge, to find new ways of approaching controversial issues, and to define priorities for future research. This philosophy is implemented at every stage of a workshop: from the selection of the theme to its breakdown in the discussion groups, from the writing of the background papers to the composition of the group reports.

Workshop topics are proposed by leading scientists and are approved by a scientific board, which is advised by qualified referees. Once a topic has been approved, a Program Advisory Committee of scientists meets approximately one year before the workshop to delineate the scientific parameters of the meeting, select participants, and

---

1 The Donors Association for the Promotion of Sciences and Humanities, a foundation created in 1921 in Berlin and supported by German trade and industry to fund basic research in the sciences

2 German Science Foundation

assign them their tasks. Participants are invited on the basis of their scientific standing alone.

Every workshop is organized around four key questions, each of which is addressed by a discussion group consisting of approximately ten participants. Lectures or formal presentations are tabu at Dahlem. Instead, concentrated discussion—within a group and between groups—is the means by which maximum communication is achieved. To facilitate this discussion, participants prepare the workshop theme prior to the meeting through the "background papers," the themes and authors of which are chosen by the Program Advisory Committee. These papers specifically review a particular aspect of the group's discussion topic as well as function as a springboard to the group discussion, by introducing controversies or unresolved problem areas.

During the workshop week, each group sets its own agenda to cover the discussion topic. Cross-fertilization between groups is both stressed and encouraged. By the end of the week, in a collective effort, each group has prepared a report reflecting the ideas, opinions, and contentious issues of the group as well as identifying directions for future research and problem areas still in need of resolution.

A Dahlem Workshop initiates and facilitates discussion between a certain number—necessarily restricted—of scientists. Because it is imperative that the discussion and communication should continue after a workshop, we present the results to the scientific community at large in the form of this published volume. In it you will find the revised background papers and group reports, as well as an introduction to the workshop theme itself.

We sincerely hope that the spirit of this workshop as well as the ideas and/or controversies raised will stimulate you in your work and future endeavors.

Prof. Dr. Klaus Roth, Director
Dahlem Konferenzen der Freien Universität Berlin
Rothenburgstr. 33, 12165 Berlin, F.R. Germany

List of Participants with Fields of Research

JENNIFER S. ALTMAN Flat D, 37 Lordship Park, GB–London N16 5UN, U.K.

Higher-order control of motor outputs and behavior in invertebrates; modeling decision-making processes and temporal organization

PER ANDERSEN Institute of Neurophysiology, University of Oslo, P.O. Box 1104, Blindern, N–0317 Oslo, Norway

Relation between long-term potentiation and learning properties of individual hippocampal synapses

ALAIN ARTOLA Max-Planck-Institut für Hirnforschung, Deutschordenstr. 46, Postfach 71 06 62, D–60528 Frankfurt am Main, F.R. Germany

Mechanisms of use-dependent synaptic plasticity in the neocortex; long-term depression and long-term potentiation of excitatory synaptic transmission in the rat's visual cortex (slices)

PHILIPPE ASCHER Laboratoire de Neurobiologie, Ecole Normale Supérieure, 46, rue d'Ulm, F–75005 Paris, France

Glutamate receptors

ATTILA BARANYI Department of Comparative Physiology, Jozsef Attila University of Szeged, Kozepfasor 52, H–Szeged, 6726, Hungary

In vivo *intracellular recording and voltage clamp studies on long-term potentiation and long-term depression induced in different cell types of the motor cortex and visual cortex of cats*

CAROL A. BARNES Arizona Research Laboratories, Division of Neural Systems, Memory, and Aging, University of Arizona, 384 Life Sciences North Building, Tucson, AZ 85724, U.S.A.

Neurophysiological and cognitive changes with age; biological basis of learning and memory

PAUL R. BENJAMIN Sussex Centre for Neuroscience, School of Biology, University of Sussex, Falmer, Brighton, GB–E. Sussex BN1 9QG, U.K.

Molecular and physiological analysis of multiple peptide expression arising from a single gene; modulation of central pattern generating circuits

LYNN J. BINDMAN Department of Physiology, University College London, Gower Street, GB–London WC1E 6BT, U.K.

Postsynaptic activity-dependent induction of long-term depression in hippocampal area CA1; nitric oxide synthesis required for induction of long-term potentiation in frontal cerebral cortex

JOËL BOCKAERT CCIPE (INSERM CNRS), Rue de la Cardonille, F–34094 Montpellier Cedex 05, France

Molecular neurobiology, receptor research, second messenger in synaptic plasticity (CAMP, NO, IP_3, Ca^{2+}), G proteins, excitatory amino acid receptors, metabotropic and serotonin receptors

TOBIAS BONHOEFFER Max-Planck-Institut für Psychiatrie, Am Klopferspitz 18a, D–82152 München-Martinsried, F.R. Germany

Mechanisms underlying synaptic plasticity in the hippocampus and the neocortex; development of functional maps in the mammalian (visual) cortex

WILLIAM A. CATTERALL Department of Pharmacology, SJ–30, University of Washington, Seattle, WA, 98195, U.S.A.

Ion channel structure and function

GRAHAM L. COLLINGRIDGE Department of Pharmacology, Medical School, University of Birmingham, Edgbaston, GB–Birmingham B15 2TT, U.K.

Cellular mechanisms of long-term potentiation

TOM CURRAN Department of Molecular Oncology and Virology 102/5, Roche Institute of Molecular Biology, Nutley, NJ 07110, U.S.A.

Molecular oncology; transcription regulation; immediate early genes in neurons

YADIN DUDAI Department of Neurobiology, The Weizmann Institute of Science, Rehovot 76100, Israel

Molecular and cellular mechanisms of learning and memory; function of cortex in taste and odor learning; theories of learning

FRANCES A. EDWARDS Department of Pharmacology, University of Sydney, New South Wales 2006, Australia

Synaptic transmission in the mammalian central nervous system mediated by ligand-gated ion channels; methods: patch clamp recording in brain slices

YVES FRÉGNAC Institut Alfred Fessard, CNRS, Avenue de la Terrasse, F–Gif-sur-Yvette 91198, France

Visual cortical plasticity

UWE FREY Institut für Neurobiologie, Brenneckestr. 6, Postfach 1860, D–39008 Magdeburg, F.R. Germany

Mechanisms underlying later phases in long-term potentiation; protein synthesis-dependent stage of long-term potentiation

STEN GRILLNER Nobel Institute for Neurophysiology, Karolinska Institutet, P.O. Box 60400, S–104 01 Stockholm, Sweden

Cellular basis of behavior

STEVE HEINEMANN Laboratory of Molecular Neurobiology, The Salk Institute, P.O. Box 85800, La Jolla, CA 92138, U.S.A.

Glutamate receptor structure and function

SCOTT L. HOOPER Department of Biological Sciences, Ohio University College of Osteopathic Medicine, Irvine Hall, Athens, OH 45701, U.S.A.

Mechanisms underlying neural network multifunctionality

HANS R. HULTBORN Institute of Neurophysiology, Blegdamsvej 3C, DK–2200 Copenhagen N, Denmark

Spinal generation of locomotion in mammals

MASAO ITO Frontier Research Program, Institute of Physical and Chemical Research (RIKEN), Wako, Saitama 351–01, Japan

Synaptic plasticity, cerebellum

PETER JONAS Max-Planck-Institut für Medizinische Forschung, Abt. Zellphysiologie, Jahnstr. 29, D–69120 Heidelberg, F.R. Germany

Glutamate receptor channels in brain slices; synaptic transmission in hippocampus

LEONARD K. KACZMAREK Department of Pharmacology, Yale University School of Medicine, 333 Cedar St., New Haven, CT 06510, U.S.A.

Regulation of ion channels by protein kinases; regulation of potassium channel gene expression

REGIS B. KELLY Department of Biochemistry and Biophysics, University of California, San Francisco, CA 94143–0448, U.S.A.

Protein targeting; biogenesis of secretory vesicles; adhesion between signaling cells

MARY B. KENNEDY Division of Biology 216–76, California Institute of Technology, Pasadena, CA 91125, U.S.A.

Molecular structure and function of central nervous system synapses

THOMAS KNÖPFEL CIBA, Pharmaceuticals Division, K–125.6.12, CH–4002 Basel, Switzerland

Synaptic mechanisms in the cerebellum

IRWIN LEVITAN Department of Biochemistry, Brandeis University, Waltham, MA 02254, U.S.A.

Neuromodulation; cellular and molecular approaches to the understanding of ion channel properties and regulation

STEPHEN G. LISBERGER Department of Physiology, Box 0444, University of California, 513 Parnassus Ave., San Francisco, CA 94143, U.S.A.

Neural mechanisms of long-term adaptive plasticity in the vestibule-ocular reflex

ROBERT C. MALENKA Department of Psychiatry, Langley Porter Psychiatric Institute, University of California, Box 0984, San Francisco, CA 94143–0984, U.S.A.

Mechanisms of synaptic plasticity in the hippocampus

EVE MARDER Department of Biology, Brandeis University, Waltham, MA 02254, U.S.A.

Neuromodulation of oscillatory neural networks

DAVID A. MCCORMICK Section of Neurobiology, Yale University School of Medicine, SHM C303, 333 Cedar St., New Haven, CT 06510, U.S.A.

Neuroscience; cellular basis of state-dependent activity in thalamocortical networks

BRUCE L. MCNAUGHTON Arizona Research Laboratories, Division of Neural Systems, Memory, and Aging, University of Arizona, 384 Life Sciences North Building, Tucson, AZ 85724, U.S.A.

Behavioral, biophysical, and computational aspects of synaptic plasticity

HANNAH MONYER Zentrum für Molekulare Biologie, Universität Heidelberg, Im Neuenheimer Feld 282, D–69120 Heidelberg, F.R. Germany

Molecular characterization of glutamate receptor subtypes; ontogenic expression of glutamate receptor subtypes

RICHARD G.M. MORRIS Laboratory for Neuroscience, Department of Pharmacology, University of Edinburgh, 1 George Square, GB–Edinburgh EH8 9JZ, U.K.

Spatial learning; neurobiology of hippocampus; role of long-term potentiation in learning

MAURICE MOULINS Laboratoire de Neurobiologie et Physiologie Comparées, Place Peyneau, F–33120 Arcachon, France

Cellular and synaptic mechanisms implicated in the expression of neural networks of the crustacean stomatogastric nervous system

J. ANTHONY MOVSHON Howard Hughes Medical Institute, Center for Neural Science and Department of Psychology, New York University, 4 Washington Place, New York, NY 10003, U.S.A.

Function and development of central visual pathways in primates

WOLFGANG MÜLLER Pharmakologisches Institut der Universität, Universitätsstraße 22, D–91054 Erlangen, F.R. Germany

Central synaptic transmission and its long-term modulation; Ca^{2+} signaling in central neurons and neuronal networks

ROGER A. NICOLL Department of Pharmacology, University of California, P.O. Box 0450, S–1210, San Francisco, CA 94143–0450, U.S.A.

Long-term potentiation, synaptic physiology

LORNA W. ROLE Department of Anatomy and Cell Biology, College of Physicians and Surgeons of Columbia University, 630 W. 168th St., New York, NY 10032, U.S.A.

Developmental regulations of synaptic functions; relationship of diversity in primary structure to function in neuronal nicotinic ACHRs; modulation of neuronal nicotinic receptor functions

PETER H. SEEBURG Zentrum für Molekulare Biologie, Universität Heidelberg, Im Neuenheimer Feld 282, D–69120 Heidelberg, F.R. Germany

Neurotransmitter-activated ion channels: molecular biology, expression in CNS, genetic control of Ca^{2+} permeability through glutamate receptor channels

MENAHEM SEGAL Department of Neurobiology, The Weizmann Institute of Science, 76100 Rehovot, Israel

Imaging of calcium transients in cultured hippocampal neurons; second messenger regulation of neuronal reactivity to NMDA

ALLEN I. SELVERSTON Neurobiology Group, Department of Biology, 0322, University of California, San Diego, 9500 Gilman Drive, La Jolla, CA 92093–0322, U.S.A.

Mechanisms of pattern formation in neural circuits

WOLF SINGER Max-Planck-Institut für Hirnforschung, Deutschordenstr. 46, Postfach 71 06 62, D–60528 Frankfurt am Main, F.R. Germany

Use-dependent synaptic plasticity; temporal codes in sensory processing

LARRY R. SQUIRE Veterans Affairs Medical Center, (V–116A), 3350 La Jolla Village Dr., San Diego, CA 92161, U.S.A.

Structure and organization of memory; brain systems and cognition in humans and nonhuman primates

CHARLES F. STEVENS The Salk Institute, 10010 North Torrey Pines Rd., La Jolla, CA 92037, U.S.A.

Synaptic transmission and long-term potentiation

THOMAS C. SÜDHOF Howard Hughes Medical Institute Research Laboratories, University of Texas, Southwestern Medical Center at Dallas, 5323 Harry Hines Blvd., Dallas, TX 75235–9050, U.S.A.

Molecular neurobiology

1

Introduction

A.I. SELVERSTON[1] and P. ASCHER[2]
[1]Neurobiology Group, Department of Biology, University of California, San Diego, 9500 Gilman Drive, La Jolla, CA 92093–0322, U.S.A.
[2]Laboratoire de Neurobiologie, Ecole Normale Supérieure, 46 rue d'Ulm, F-75005 Paris, France

The study of the physiological mechanisms underlying higher brain function represents one of the most important ongoing research efforts of modern biology. This analysis is proceeding at all levels of organization, from the molecular to the behavioral.

Some of the most visible progress has occurred at the molecular level, where in the last ten years, methodological developments in molecular genetics, biochemistry, and electrophysiology have allowed the identification of a spectacular series of signaling molecules: messengers, receptors, ionic channels. The sheer number of these molecules, however, raises an immense problem, and we are very far from any picture integrating all these molecules into a coherent vision of neurons, synapses, or nervous systems.

At the cellular level, one of the most remarkable developments has been the possibility of analyzing central synapses at a level of precision which for many years was the privilege of peripheral synapses like the neuromuscular and ganglionic junctions. It was obviously exciting to discover that central synapses differed in many respects from the prototypic ones, in particular by the presence of some long-term plastic properties, and to find out that one could study *in vitro* processes like LTP or LTD originally described in whole brain studies. But as this enthusiasm brought a wealth of data, it became clear that a major uncertainty remained if one attempted to transfer the data obtained on *in vitro* plasticity to the understanding of behavioral plasticity.

Similarly, the *in vitro* study of small synaptic networks (most notably in invertebrates) started on the premise that some principles could be extracted to understand how individual neurons interact to produce the spatio-temporal patterns which underlie sensory coding and the sequential contraction of muscles. This was indeed a successful enterprise, but one of its limits was soon perceived when one tried to extend one of its principles (e.g., the possibility of "reconfiguring" a network) to the interpretation of higher-order behavior of the intact organism.

Cellular and Molecular Mechanisms Underlying Higher Neural Functions
Edited by A.I. Selverston and P. Ascher

Thus it seems that in the development of neurobiological studies, a major limiting factor may lie in the difficulties encountered in relating diverse levels of organization, and in particular using the data obtained at lower levels to explain higher levels of neural activity.

The workshop was centered around this question and had broad ambitions of bridging some of these gaps between levels. It was organized around four groups, the first of which probably faced the most difficult task since it was concerned with the behavioral level. To limit the extent of the problems considered, the discussion was centered on those examples of behavioral plasticity for which a claim had been made of a direct relation with some of the cellular processes studied *in vitro*.

The discussion was primed by five background papers: an examination of the role of LTP in behavior by Morris; the effects of LTD on cerebellar learning by Ito; possible sites for learning of the vestibulo-ocular reflex by Lisberger; plasticity in the mature neocortex by Singer and Artola; and how *in vivo* neuronal changes correlate with behavior by Dudai.

The three main questions we asked were: Are current preparations adequate models for explaining neural plasticity in the intact animal? Are other preparations better suited for establishing the relationships between changes in synaptic strength and changes in brain circuits? Are we overlooking entirely some of the mechanisms which may underlie learning?

As will be seen in the group report (Barnes et al.), the discussion at the meeting confirmed the extremely prudent conclusions of these five reports, showing that we are indeed very far from any direct correlation between the cellular processes of LTD and LTP and the behavioral plasticity. Nevertheless, there seems to be little alternative to the present approach of patiently correlating the many forms of memory described by experimental psychologists with the various elementary processes described *in vitro*, taking into account as much as possible all the anatomical and physiological diversity involved in each experiment.

At the next lower level, the circuit, we considered how state-dependent changes can occur under the influence of neuromodulators. The idea that neural circuits can be functionally reconfigured is now widespread, and the implications of these phenomena for understanding the brain are profound. The background papers dealt with circuits which have been shown to be modulated by metabotropic actions of neurotransmitters and neuromodulators: Dynamic changes in functional activity in the well-characterized stomatogastric system by Harris-Warrick et al.; the effect of similar changes in the more complicated lamprey system by Grillner et al.; and modulation of thalamo-cortical connectivity by McCormick. The main cellular effects involved in these modulatory effects are likely to be alterations of ionic permeabilities, which were summarized in the background paper by Kaczmarek and Perney. The goal of this group (Hooper et al.) was to try to establish how the plasticity in these circuits is controlled by modulators and what mechanisms are actually involved in altering the functional connectivity of the neurons within them. This was a more limited ambition than that of the first group, and it was therefore not too surprising that consensus could be more easily reached. Indeed, most participants would probably have agreed that it was possible to foresee the time at which a complete formal (mathematical) description of a real modulated network would be produced.

The third group (Edwards et al.) centered on the cellular level and on the question of how adequate current explanations for long-term synaptic modifications *in vitro* are. We thought it would be extremely useful to those not working on LTP to get an up-to-date assessment of some of the current issues by researchers intimately involved. The papers which establish the background for understanding some of the controversial issues include a summary of current models of LTP by Nicoll et al., biochemical and molecular models which have been suggested for studying LTP by Kennedy, and activity-induced structural changes by Greenough et al.

To the surprise of some participants, it turned out that, despite the precision of the methods used, and the wealth of data available, consensus was still lacking on some key experiments. As the discussion illustrated, the preparations used for the study of central synapses are not as simple as one would like them to be and, as a result, the characterization of central synaptic transmission has not yet reached the level of precision it has enjoyed in peripheral systems. The group tried to list both the points on which there is wide agreement, and those on which ingenuity, imagination, and hard work will have to be applied to obtain such an agreement.

Finally, at the most reductionistic level, the fourth group (Role et al.) examined the molecular mechanisms likely to be involved in plasticity; the background papers here are: The diversity of glutamate receptors by Seeburg; protein targeting requirements for plasticity by Kelly; activity-dependent control of gene transcription by Curran and Morgan; phosphorylation of channels and receptors by Catterall; and how presynaptic mechanisms might be involved in plasticity by Südhof and Jahn. The goal for this group was to try and suggest ways in which data at the molecular level might be incorporated into not only cellular mechanisms but into higher levels of organization as well.

The meeting of this group was particularly marked by the reactions of the molecular biologists, some of whom had been attracted to the meeting by the naive belief that the molecular study of learning was now at hand. They were surprised to discover how many basic questions remained to be settled in describing the physiological behavior of the simplest *in vitro* preparations (not to mention higher levels of organization) and how polemical were some of the best publicized results. This realization of the complexity of the simplest cellular models of learning did not overcome them, however, and they recovered to some fantasies of how one could make use of the nearly unlimited number of tools now available to modify a neuron, a synapse, a network, or an organism.

2

Reflections on Whether Hippocampal Long-term Potentiation Plays a Role in Certain Kinds of Learning or Memory

R.G.M. MORRIS
Laboratory for Neuroscience, Department of Pharmacology,
University of Edinburgh, 1 George Square, GB–Edinburgh EH8 9JZ, U.K.

ABSTRACT

This chapter outlines several experimental approaches that have been pursued to investigate the possible role of hippocampal long-term potentiation (LTP) in learning or memory. These include studies showing that (a) alterations of synaptic efficacy of hippocampal pathways are associated with concomitant changes in a type of learning that is artificially dependent upon those pathways; (b) drugs that block or enhance LTP affect the rate of acquisition of tasks, such as spatial learning, which require the integrity of hippocampal function; and (c) mutant animals lacking enzymes critical for the expression of LTP are also deficient in spatial learning. Efforts to impair learning by prior physiological saturation of LTP have, notwithstanding the theoretical importance of such a result, met with less success, although such studies have shown a striking correlation between physiological and behavioral plasticity within individual animals. Studies looking at whether learning itself can cause LTP-like changes have run into the problem that behavioral activity induces changes in brain temperature, which in turn affects synaptic potentials. The chapter concludes with several speculations about the kind of experiments that might be undertaken to test the "LTP and learning" hypothesis more rigorously.

INTRODUCTION

Persistent changes in synaptic efficacy have long been thought to be the neural basis of memory. Recently, there has been widespread speculation that the associative NMDA receptor-dependent form of hippocampal LTP (Bliss and Lømo 1973) engages some of the same neural mechanisms as those used normally during certain kinds of

Cellular and Molecular Mechanisms Underlying Higher Neural Functions
Edited by A.I. Selverston and P. Ascher

learning: the so-called "LTP and learning hypothesis." Fueling this speculation is the fact that several of the physiological properties of hippocampal LTP are pertinent to a candidate memory mechanism—its prominence in a brain structure involved in the formation of certain kinds of long-term memory, its persistence over time, the synapse specificity of its expression—and that its induction requires associativity between pre- and postsynaptic activity. However, while these physiological properties are suggestive, the task of establishing (a) *whether LTP occurs during and is necessary for certain kinds of learning*, and identifying (b) *what its role may be* is proving very difficult. In this chapter, I review some of the strategies that have been pursued to address these questions and ideas that have guided them. I conclude with some reflections about the kinds of experiments that need to be done.

TWO QUALIFICATIONS

I shall use the shorthand of enquiring about "the role of LTP in learning" rather than the more convoluted "whether any of the same neural mechanisms as those activated during a physiological experiment on LTP are also activated during learning." In writing the former, I do of course mean the latter (I appreciate that the high-frequency coactivation of thousands of perforant path fibers, a commonly used tetanic stimulus in experiments on LTP *in vivo*, is most unlikely to occur naturally). Second, discussion is restricted to hippocampal LTP. Clearly, LTP occurs elsewhere (Bindman et al. 1988; Artola and Singer 1990), and current preoccupation with the mechanisms and functions of hippocampal LTP may seem narrow. But we have to start somewhere.

EVIDENCE THAT HIPPOCAMPAL LTP PLAYS SOME ROLE IN CERTAIN KINDS OF LEARNING

The first published evidence supporting a role in memory was Barnes' (1979) study, which indicated that the speed of learning of a spatial task was positively correlated with the persistence of LTP. One interpretation, although surely not the only one, is that persistent changes of synaptic efficacy in the hippocampus induced "naturally" during learning are causally responsible for the information storage involved in learning the task.

This study has now been followed up by many other functionally oriented studies, capitalizing upon discoveries about the physiological properties and neuropharmacological mechanisms of LTP. The aim of this work has been largely empirical, with relatively little work addressing the conceptual issue of what LTP is doing. This state of affairs is inevitable, if intellectually unsatisfying, and reflects the continuing disagreements about the role of the hippocampus during learning as anything else. It is difficult to have a theory of the function of LTP without having or adopting a psychological theory of hippocampal function also. For example, if one believes that the hippocampus creates and consolidates declarative memories (Squire 1992), one might hold a different view about the role of LTP than if one believed it to be involved in, for example, cognitive mapping (O'Keefe and Nadel 1978).

Figure 2.1 summarizes six different ways of thinking about the role of LTP in learning: *selective augmentation and stabilization of reflex pathways, memory indexing, distributed associative memory, representation of abstract relationships, permissive coupling of cortical neurons, and two-stage model of memory*. These ideas are hardly "theories" of LTP but rather constitute the basic building blocks that might eventually be developed into formal theories.

Alterations in Synaptic Efficacy of Hippocampal Pathways Cause Changes in Learning and Retention Dependent on Those Pathways

The selective augmentation and stabilization idea (Figure 2.1A) has prompted studies that attempt to mimic enhanced signal throughput as it might occur normally in neural circuits. For example, Skelton et al. (1985) took this approach in experiments using direct stimulation of the perforant path as a conditioned stimulus (CS). Their key finding was that animals given high-frequency trains which induced LTP, learned a perforant path-shock (CS–US) association more rapidly than controls. This suggests that neural activity on the perforant path can elicit some kind of "stimulus" that, through learning, gains control over behavior, and whose degree of control can be modulated by LTP. A similar approach has been pursued by Laroche et al. (1989), with the notable exception that they used a short high-frequency train to the perforant path as the CS rather than a single stimulus. They found that the degree of learning a CS–US association was linearly correlated with the amount of LTP and was blocked by both commissural stimulation and by the NMDA antagonist, D–AP5. Doyère and Laroche (1992) have also reported that the forgetting of this simple CS–US association over time is correlated with the decay time course of LTP (Figure 2.2).

These experiments indicate that alteration of synaptic efficacy at perforant path terminals has functional consequences in learning tasks that are explicitly designed to utilize neural activity in this pathway as a stimulus. However, they seem to me to suffer from two weaknesses.

First, in many LTP experiments, Laroche's group followed the convention of adjusting stimulus intensity to obtain a comparable 1 mV population spike in all animals at the outset of training. This virtually guarantees that LTP induction and its subsequent decay are just about the only ways in which variation in dentate granule cell excitability can occur. Thus, while highly significant correlations between behavior and LTP have been obtained, these could be secondary to a relationship with granule cell firing. In fact, Skelton et al.'s (1985) data suggest that the extent of granule cell firing is a critical determinant of whether perforant path stimulation will serve as an effective stimulus. If so, other ways of modulating granule cell activity (such as via neuromodulatory transmitter activation) might also affect learning (or retention). If LTP is merely being used to boost signal strength to achieve cell firing in a particular

A. Selective augmentation and stabilization of reflex pathways

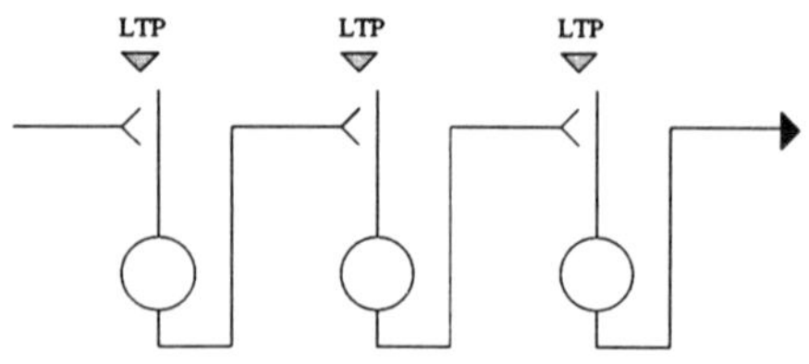

B. Memory indexing

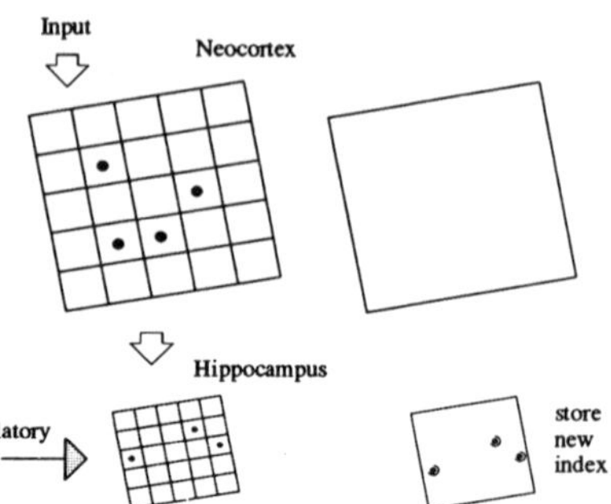

D. Representation of abstract relationships

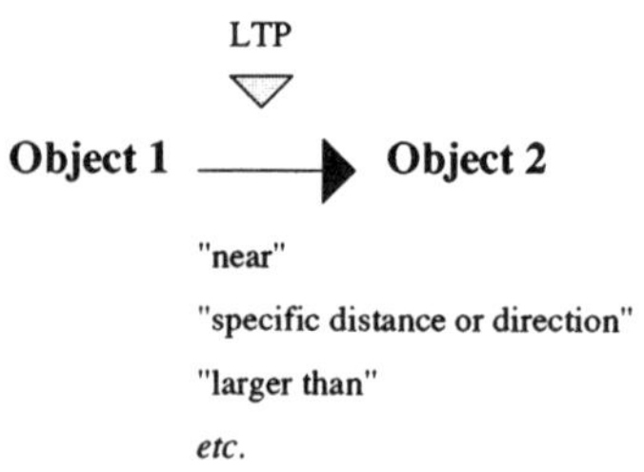

C. Distributed associative memory

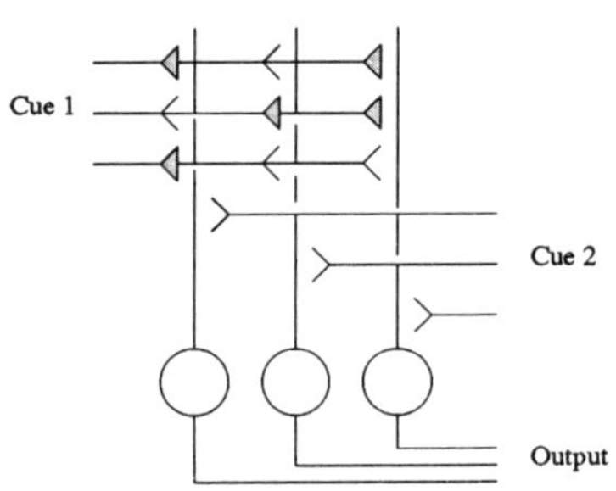

E. Permissive coupling of cortical neurons

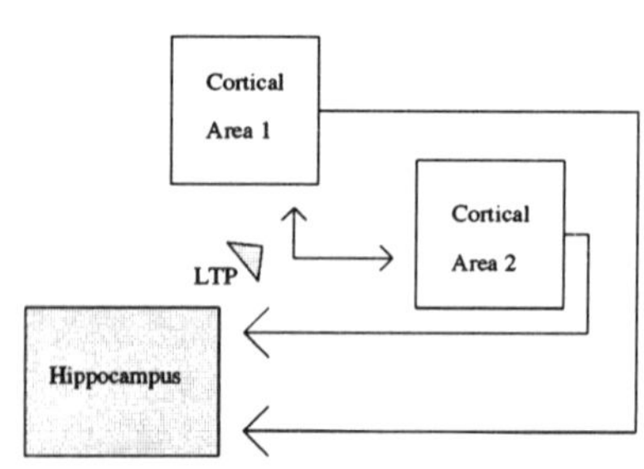

F. Two-stage model of memory

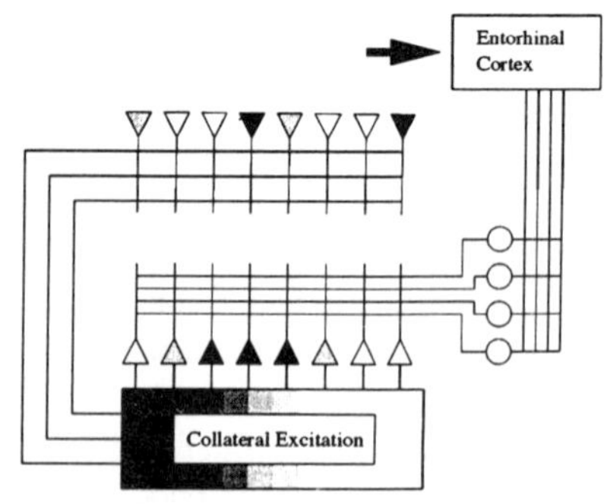

brain area, *it is not clear if these experiments are really addressing the notion of selective stabilization of neural circuits at all.*

Second, the use of LTP as a kind of "bioassay" is artificial. While these studies demonstrate that LTP induction can influence behavior by augmenting signal strength, we cannot infer, from such results, that this is what LTP does *normally*. It is essential to know the nature of the information being passed to the hippocampus before ideas about the role (if any) of selective augmentation of even the perforant pathway can be evaluated. In addition, as it is inherently unlikely that perforant path activity represents relatively unprocessed sensory information whose intensity needs to be increased to evoke a learned response, experiments in which such stimulation is used as a CS serve as a model of a putative process *whose functional status in relation to hippocampal function is extremely unclear.*

Drugs that Block or Enhance LTP Affect the Rate of Hippocampal-dependent Learning

If certain types of learning depend on LTP, blocking LTP should pharmacologically impair learning. Morris et al. (1986) examined the effects of chronic intraventricular infusion of the selective NMDA antagonist AP5 upon LTP both *in vivo* and in the learning of two distinct behavioral tasks. The drug or vehicle solution was infused continuously over two weeks into the lateral ventricle from subcutaneously implanted minipumps. The results showed that, at a drug concentration sufficient to block LTP

Figure 2.1 Models of the possible role of LTP in learning and memory. (A) Selective augmentation and stabilization of reflex pathways refers to the idea that LTP could help increase the strength of a neural signal passing along a simple reflex pathway and, in the process, stabilize and improve the reliability of that circuit (after Skelton et al. 1985). (B) Memory indexing refers to the idea that hippocampal LTP could be a form of limited storage in hippocampus that provides an index of where information about facts or events are stored in neocortex (after Teyler and Discenna 1986). (C) Distributed associative memory refers to the idea that perceptually processed information entering the hippocampus may be represented as a spatially distributed code of neural activity and that hippocampal LTP is the mechanism through which different bits of information are associated and stored in an overlaid manner in hippocampal circuitry (after McNaughton and Morris 1987). (D) Representation of abstract relationships refers to the idea that hippocampal LTP could be part of a mechanism by which the hippocampus might discover and represent abstract (e.g., spatial) relationships between different bits of information (after Morris 1990). (E) Permissive coupling refers to the idea that hippocampal LTP might provide a signal back to active neurons in distinct cortical regions enabling those initially weakly coupled neurons to become more strongly coupled such that activity in one set can subsequently evoke activity in another (after Rolls 1989; also Sejnowski, Read-Montague, and Dayan, pers. comm.). (F) Two-stage model of memory refers to the idea that the hippocampus oscillates between two phases, one encoding information in a relatively labile form during exploratory behaviour (theta activity) and the other converting this labile trace into a more long-lasting form (during hippocampal sharp waves). Only the latter phase is displayed (after Buzsaki 1989).

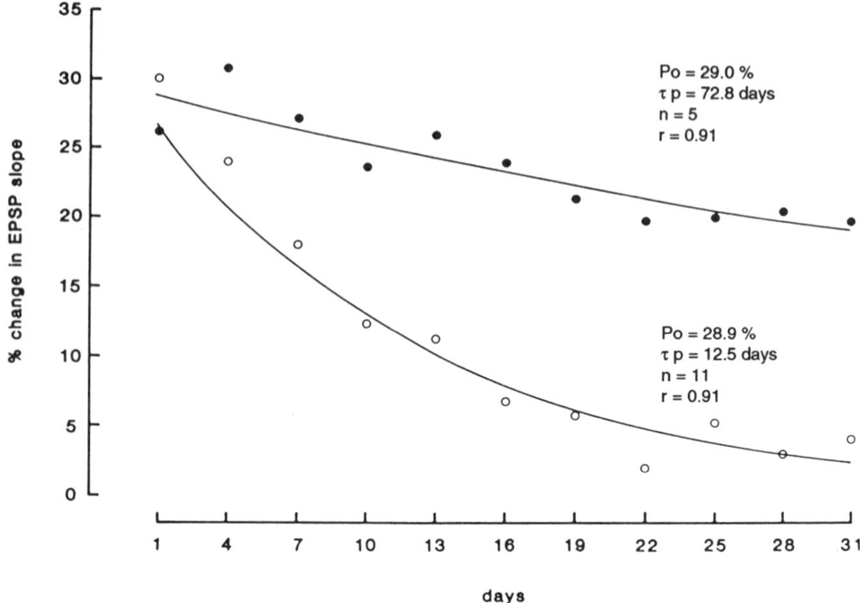

Figure 2.2 Decay time course of LTP in animals that remembered a perforant path CS–US association (filled circles) and animals that showed forgetting (open circles). From Doyère and Laroche (1992).

without effect upon dentate gyrus field potentials, spatial learning in a watermaze was impaired while acquisition of a visual discrimination in the same apparatus was unaffected. The selectivity of this impairment is important for two reasons: (a) it indicates that AP5 was not impeding behavioral performance by virtue of some gross sensorimotor disturbance, and (b) it establishes a parallel between the effects of NMDA receptor blockade and those of hippocampal lesions. Such lesions impair the spatial memory task but not the visual discrimination task. Part of the force of this striking similarity between the drug- and lesion-induced behavioral dissociation between different learning tasks stems from it not being a foregone conclusion: *AP5 might have had no effect on hippocampal-dependent learning despite causing a complete blockade of LTP. However, this did not occur.*

There are, nonetheless, numerous problems of interpretation. Goddard (1986) wondered whether differential regional drug diffusion was really at the root of behavioral dissociation. To address this query, Butcher et al. (1991) measured drug levels *in vivo* and found that they were relatively uniform. They also bilaterally infused AP5 directly into occipital area 2 (i.e., just anterior to visual cortex) and found a whole-tissue concentration of AP5 in visual cortex comparable to that which, in the hippocampus, impairs spatial learning. The visual discrimination control task was still unimpaired. The implication is that NMDA receptor-dependent plasticity in cortex is not involved in visual discrimination learning in the way that it seems to be for spatial learning in the hippocampus. This is intriguing and raises the fundamental question of *whether the synaptic plasticity underlying declarative and procedural types of learning may be different.*

An almost diametrically opposite concern has been that widespread AP5 diffusion would cause an NMDA receptor blockade all over the brain, whose functional consequences are bound to be complex. It follows that the spatial learning impairment induced by intraventricular administration of NMDA antagonists could be unrelated to the demonstrated blockade of LTP and/or due to an interruption of perceptual, attentional, or motivational processes (Mondadori et al. 1989; Keith and Rudy 1990; Daw et al. 1993). This disquiet has proved harder to address; however, a series of experiments have made it seem less likely. First, Morris et al. (1989) showed that acute intrahippocampal infusions of nanomolar quantities of AP5 are sufficient to impair spatial learning in the watermaze. Second, a dose-response analysis in conjunction with *in vivo* microdialysis (Davis et al. 1992) has established that the dose-related AP5-induced impairment of spatial learning overlaps and parallels the disruption of dentate gyrus LTP *in vivo* (Figure 2.3), and occurs across the same range of extracellular AP5 concentrations in hippocampus as those reflecting the D–AP5 blockade of LTP *in vitro*. Third, several studies have established that other hippocampal-dependent tasks (i.e., tasks impaired by hippocampal lesions) are also impaired by NMDA

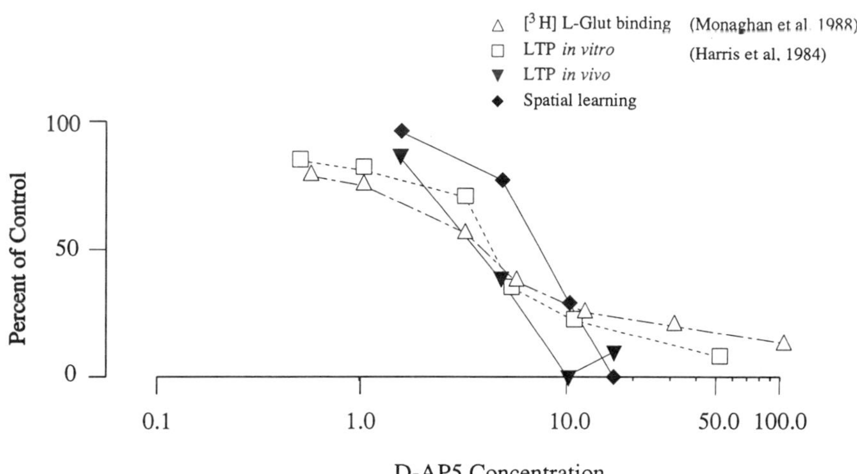

Figure 2.3 Comparison of inhibition by D–AP5 of spatial learning and LTP *in vivo* with inhibition of LTP *in vitro* and displacement of [3H]–L–glutamate binding. The D–AP5 concentrations are the estimated extracellular concentrations in hippocampus *in vivo* derived from microdialysis measurements (after Davis et al. 1992); the bath concentrations of D–AP5 in a hippocampal brain slice chamber (from Harris et al. 1984); and the concentrations of D–AP5 used in an autoradiographic binding assay. From Monaghan et al. 1988.

antagonists (e.g., Tonkiss et al. 1988; Ward et al. 1990; Shapiro and O'Connor 1992; Willner et al. 1992); the parallels are, however, not exact, and there are certain memory tasks impaired by lesions that are unaffected by NMDA antagonists—a discrepancy that is potentially of great theoretical interest. Taken together, these studies suggest that the *blockade of hippocampal NMDA receptors is a sufficient condition for impairing several of the types of learning thought to involve hippocampal processing*.

It is important to note that the AP5-induced impairment is not specific to spatial learning. Furthermore, the dissociation between spatial learning and visual discrimination in the Morris et al. (1986) study is confounded with that between declarative and procedural learning (Squire 1992). Thus, to explore Morris's (1990) idea that hippocampal LTP is concerned with learning abstract relations (Figure 2.1D) properly, it will be necessary to examine the effects of AP5 upon hippocampal-dependent tasks that involve abstract relationships: both spatial and nonspatial. No relevant experiments have, to my knowledge, been reported.

To date, the pharmacological approach has been largely restricted to drugs that *block* LTP. A complementary strategy would be to examine drugs that *improve* LTP. Two candidates are a recently developed monoclonal antibody, which enhances NMDA receptor channel activity in a glycine-like manner (B6B21), and a partial agonist at the same site (D-cycloserine). These drugs have recently been shown to cause dramatic enhancements in trace-conditioned eye-blink task learning (Thompson et al. 1992; see Figure 2.4). Pseudoconditioning controls indicated that this enhancement of performance was probably not due to sensitization alone. However, the authors are cautious about interpreting their results exclusively, with respect to LTP, in view of other findings indicating that eye-blink conditioning is associated with alterations in pyramidal cell excitability (Disterhoft et al. 1986) rather than specifically synaptic changes.

Saturation of LTP Should Impair Retrieval of Previously Learned Information and New Learning

This strategy is most closely related to the notions of memory indexing and distributed associative memory (Figure 2.1B and 2.1C). It is based on the idea that physiological saturation of LTP should disrupt existing "memory indexes" or information stored as distributed overlaid patterns as well as to disrupt new learning. It is a potentially powerful nonpharmacological technique unlikely to suffer from the same constellation of side effects that plague pharmacological experiments. Unfortunately, saturation experiments have indicated that repeated high-frequency stimulation of the perforant path does not cause retrograde amnesia (McNaughton et al. 1986). Moreover, while it has been reported to impair new spatial learning (Castro et al. 1989), others have failed to replicate this finding, and the status of this approach is now in doubt.

One problem is that unilateral high-frequency stimulation of the perforant path in rabbits has been reported to cause precisely the opposite outcome in discriminative nictitating membrane conditioning (Berger 1984). However, the apparent

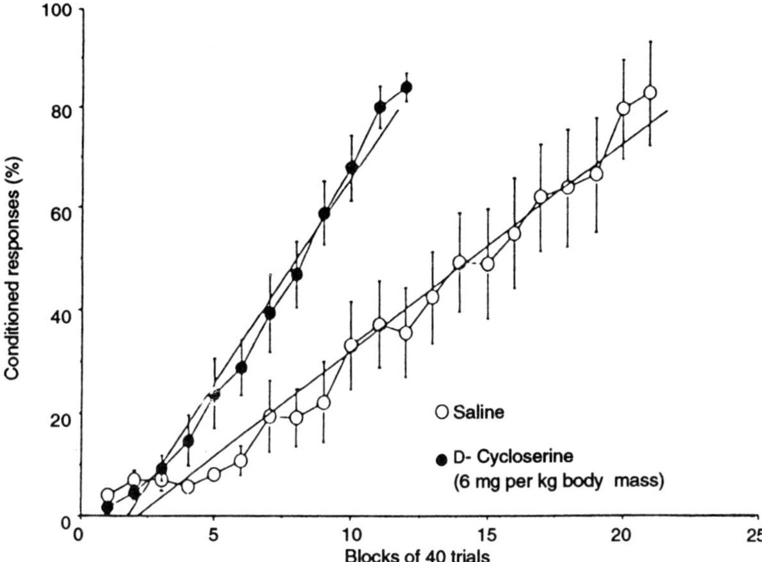

Figure 2.4 Daily treatment with D-cycloserine, a partial agonist at the glycine coagonist site of the NMDA receptor facilitates trace eye-blink conditioning in rabbits. From Thompson et al. (1992).

contradiction is not quite what it seems because, unlike spatial learning, the integrity of the hippocampus is unnecessary for nictitating membrane conditioning. For a number of reasons, not least the discovery of the role of the cerebellum in this type of conditioning (Thompson 1990), I have long adopted the conventional view that the hippocampus cannot be involved in simple conditioning because hippocampal lesions do not affect its acquisition or expression. However, matters may not be so straightforward. Logically speaking, a satisfactory lesion study establishes whether the integrity of a structure is required for a type of learning. However, the failure to see a lesion impairment does not rule out the possibility that a structure normally participates in that type of learning but that some compensatory change has occurred in other brain regions to take over the role that structure plays normally. That intracerebral infusions of glycine agonists in the vicinity of the hippocampus enhance the rate of trace-conditioned eye-blink conditioning indicates that the hippocampus has some involvement in such conditioning tasks.

A second problem is that the saturation-induced learning impairment of spatial learning has proved hard to replicate in other laboratories (Cain et al. 1993; Jeffery and Morris 1993; Korol et al. 1993; McNamara et al. 1993; Sutherland et al. 1993; see also Bliss and Richter-Levin 1993). The reasons for this irreproducibility are unclear but could include (a) unrecorded seizures in the "successful" experiments, (b) that only perforant path terminals get saturated, not the terminals of other intrinsic pathways, and (c) failure to saturate the full septo-temporal axis and molecular layer termination zone of the perforant path. With respect to the last of these possibilities, if saturation of LTP were to be restricted to a small part of the dentate gyrus, a substantial "resource" of modifiable synapses would still be available. It would not then be surprising that learning proceeds normally. Interestingly, the extent of potentiation then measured could, rather than impair learning, serve as an index of synaptic modifiability in individual animals. In this vein, while Jeffery and Morris (1993) found no difference in subsequent learning rate in each of two experiments between groups given LTP-inducing or non-LTP-inducing stimulation, they found a significant correlation within the high-frequency group between the magnitude of LTP and performance in the watermaze task. This result extends earlier *ex vivo* findings of Deupree et al. (1990) and suggests, as shown in Figure 2.5, that it is necessary to have two separate indices of the LTP displayed by individual animals: (a) Can this animal show good LTP? (b) Is the amount of LTP induced throughout the hippocampus close to the true asymptote? If an animal shows good LTP (i.e., has readily modifiable synapses)

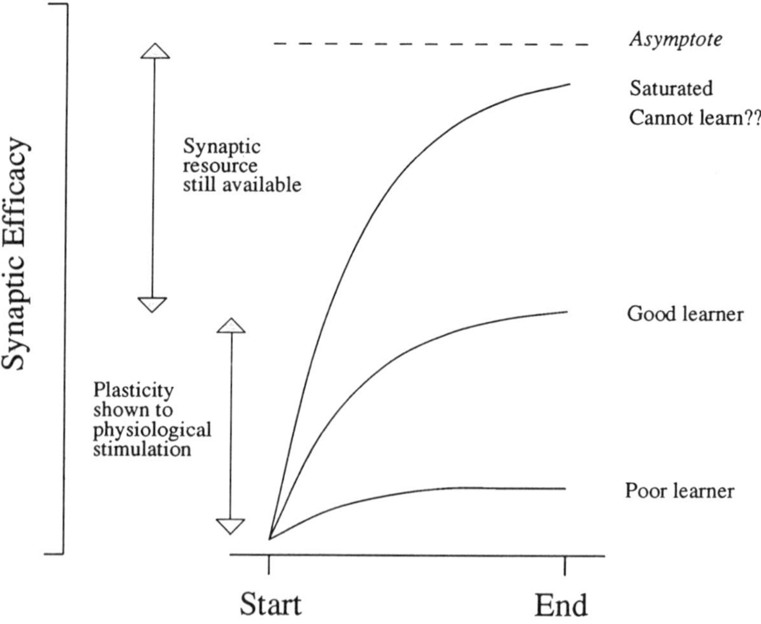

Figure 2.5 Model of how individual variation in hippocampal synaptic plasticity might predict learning rate provided the plasticity shown to physiological stimulation is only a fraction of the total synaptic resource available. If it is eventually possible to find a way of saturating synaptic efficacy on a pathway crucial for learning, the lack of synaptic plasticity near asymptote should result in poor learning.

but LTP does not approach the asymptote, then the animal should learn *well.* If either little LTP occurs or if LTP reaches a clear asymptote throughout the hippocampus, then the animal's capacity for spatial learning should be poor. Put another way, an animal's "plasticity personality" may be a good index of its capacity for learning *until, but only until, that resource has been fully used.*

Mutant Animals Engineered to Lack an Enzyme Critical for the Expression of LTP Are Deficient in Spatial Learning

A radically new approach, provided by Silva et al. (1992a, b) utilizes homologous recombination to make mutant mice deficient in the alpha subunit of Ca^{2+}/calmodulin-dependent protein kinase II (CaMKII). Hippocampal brain slices taken from such animals showed that they rarely displayed LTP (although, interestingly, a few slices did show normal LTP) and, in separate experiments, animals from this same strain of mutant mice (–/–) were impaired in learning two different spatial versions of the watermaze task. As other electrophysiological observations indicated that both AMPA and NMDA currents were normal, and as further behavioral experiments suggested that the impairment of spatial learning was not due to a lack of motivation or an inability to see distal cues, the loss of αCaMKII appears to have had a remarkably selective effect on synaptic plasticity and spatial learning.

The αCaMKII mutant is the first of a series of mutants whose electrophysiological and behavioral profile promises to illuminate the mechanisms and significance of LTP. Others include the tyrosine kinase *fyn* mutant (Grant et al. 1992), whose broadly similar phenotype (impaired LTP and spatial learning) but a different second-messenger abnormality and deletions of NMDA-receptor subunits are surely on the way (will homozygous mutants be viable?). These gene "knock-out" experiments are a considerable scientific and molecular engineering achievement but are not without their own share of difficulties.

In the case of the Silva et al. (1992a, b) studies, the alpha-rich CaMKII holoenzyme is very abundant, comprising approximately 2% of total protein in hippocampus, 1% in cortex, and a far greater proportion in postsynaptic densities. Given this abundance, it seems strange—or at least ironic—that its deletion apparently has such subtle effects. One aspect of this irony is the possibility that the learning capacity of the mutant mice may have been *under*estimated. Specifically, while the mutants were at chance in the watermaze transfer test, the wild-type controls (+/+) also did not perform particularly well, perhaps because spatial training followed random visual platform training in which all the animals had an opportunity to learn that an escape platform could be at any position in the maze. Search performance during the transfer test after hidden platform spatial training will then be less localized.

Second, it is not yet possible to delete αCaMKII in a specific region of the brain. This limitation points to the more general problem of selectivity in the application of molecular biological techniques to the analysis of neural function. It is important not to be blinded by the technology and ensure that transgenic mutants are subject to the same critical scrutiny as any other neurobiological experiment. Silva et al. are acutely aware of this obligation. Transgenesis and homologous recombination are each proving valuable in studying a wide variety of problems in neuroscience; however, "the small industrial revolution in the construction of mice with mutated neural genes" that is now upon us (Morris and Kennedy 1992) carries with it the potential to mislead as well as to illuminate. On a more positive note, the mechanisms and functional significance of LTP would be greatly illuminated by an experiment in which the capacity for LTP and for learning could somehow be restored in mutants, and such experiments are surely underway.

Does LTP Occur Naturally in the Course of Learning?

So far I have focused upon whether LTP is necessary for learning to occur. A more straightforward approach, however, might be to ask simply whether LTP occurs when learning occurs. Recordings of hippocampal field potentials (or transmitter release, postsynaptic receptor efficacy, etc) would be taken before and after a variety of different learning experiences. An increase in field potential slope would indicate that LTP had been involved during that particular type of learning. Unfortunately, although increases in neuronal excitability, transmitter release, and second messengers have each been reported, no long-lasting change in the synaptic component of field potentials has been found. Where sustained slope changes have been seen, they have occasionally been traced to modulation by behavioral state (Hargreaves et al. 1990), although there are now reasons to suspect a different explanation (see below).

The problem with the "simple" prediction that LTP should occur during learning is that changes in synaptic efficacy after an individual learning experience would surely prove very difficult to detect. If a brain structure such as the hippocampus has any significant storage capacity, why should an individual training experience be expected to cause a change in field potentials across a large array of synapses? On the contrary, if LTP is a mechanism of information storage, its physiological property of synapse specificity leads one to expect changes restricted to a subset of synapses. Pointing out this implication, McNaughton and Morris (1987) coined it the "Catch-22" problem of memory—the catch being that "if you can measure it, it probably isn't memory." I shall return to a more serious version of this argument shortly.

A short-term exploratory modulation (STEM) of field potentials has been discovered and its initial analysis suggested a possible way forward (Sharp et al. 1989; McNaughton and Barnes 1990). STEM resembles physiologically induced LTP in several respects but also shows a number of important differences (viz. STEM and LTP do not occlude each other, spike latency declines but spike amplitude does also). However, a serious complication that applies to STEM and, more generally, to the measurement of LTP in any chronic recording experiment has recently been identified. Moser et al. (1993) found that when animals are allowed to explore in the manner of STEM experiments, the forebrain warms up by as much as 2°C (measured using miniature thermistors implanted into the brain), and it cools down when they are made to swim in cold water for short periods. Simultaneous recordings of dentate field potentials indicated that the field potential slope rises in the exploratory situation but declines with swimming in cool water, while the population spike measure shows the opposite changes (Figure 2.6). Further evidence that this bidirectional pattern is largely associated with temperature came from experiments in which brain temperature was altered directly by means of a heating lamp. This also caused field potentials to change

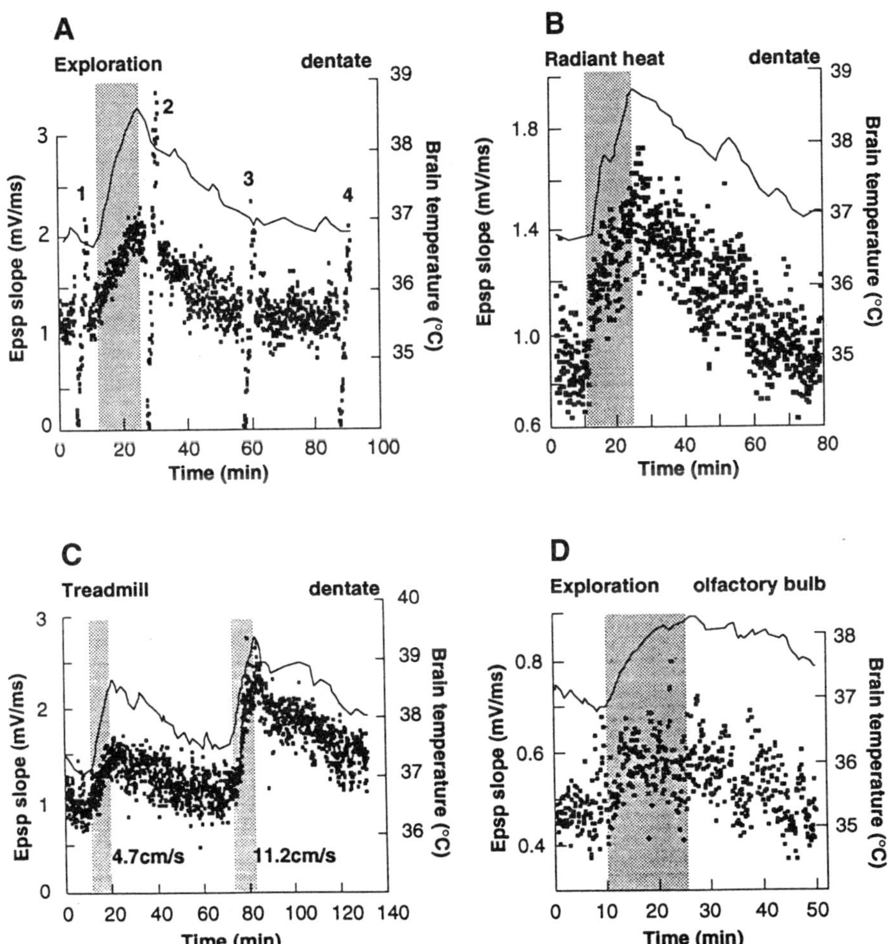

Figure 2.6 Covariation of dentate field potential slope and brain temperature in animals (A) allowed to explore, (B) in response to radiant heat, or (C) running on a treadmill. (D) Changes in field potentials in the olfactory bulb during exploration. From Moser et al. (1993).

in the appropriate direction while "temperature clamping" of the brain in experiments in which animals explored or ran on a treadmill resulted in no change in the field potentials. These findings call into question the hypothesis linking STEM to the temporary storage of information during exploration. Whether STEM is *entirely* caused by changes in brain temperature is, in my view, unlikely. However, definitive experiments investigating whether information processing and storage in the hippocampus is associated with synaptic changes will have to subtract out temperature-induced changes in field potentials by means of appropriate calibration. Moser et al.'s (1993) experiment raises numerous fascinating issues, including the question of why the brain is less homeothermic than has previously been supposed. Yet for immediate purposes, the general implication is that the intracerebral implantation of thermistors in future experiments on LTP in behaving animals is essential.

Another way of approaching the issue of learning-induced changes in field potentials is to consider why they might be so difficult to detect. There are two main reasons for the difficulty in seeing LTP following learning. First, there is the conceptual link between the synapse specificity of LTP and information storage capacity. Second, there is the possibility that LTP is accompanied by hetero- and homosynaptic depression at inactive synapses.

Let us assume, for the sake of argument, that the hippocampus is an associative memory system (Figure 2.1C). Associative synaptic conjunctions that trigger long-term increases in synaptic efficacy would, if it were operating at near optimal signal-to-noise efficiency (Willshaw and Dayan 1990), occur in proportion to the product of the probability of activity on afferent fibers (pre) and the probability of sufficient depolarization (i.e., neural activity) in their target cells (post). Assuming that a relatively sparse code is used to maximize storage capacity (i.e., that pre is small), the proportion of synapses that will potentiate following an individual learning experience will almost certainly be a very small fraction of the whole (i.e., proportional to the product pre × post). It follows that changes in population measures, such as field potentials, will prove very difficult to detect. Indeed, I will go further and assert that the failure to see LTP following learning *is not only an embarrassment to the LTP and learning hypothesis, it is actually predicted by it!*

The second reason why LTP might be difficult to detect after learning is that it is sometimes associated with heterosynaptic depression at inactive synapses (Levy and Steward 1979). There have also been reports of an associative, homosynaptic depression of afferents whose activity is out of phase with conditioning tetani (Stanton and Sejnowski 1988), although there is some question of the reliability of this observation in adult rats (Paulsen et al. 1990). In any case, if synaptic depression were to occur during learning, it is plausible that, of the afferents stimulated physiologically when probing for the existence of learning-induced LTP, one subset (n1) would be potentiated while another subset (n2) would be depressed. Long-term depression might serve (statistically if not formally) a normalizing role by ensuring that the sum of the synaptic weights on any given neuron remains roughly constant.

CONCLUDING DISCUSSION

Can LTP enhance learning to a signal involving neural activity at specific synaptic terminals? Yes. *Does selective blockade of LTP impair learning?* I am inclined to conclude with a cautious "yes" on the basis of experiments with NMDA antagonists and the recent work with mutant mice. The caution is essential, given the behavioral side effects of these drugs and the lack of regional specificity in the gene knock-out experiments. *Does saturation of LTP cause retrograde amnesia for recent information and impairments in new learning?* The weight of recent evidence is now moving against this possibility but we do not yet know why the experiment does not work. *Does enhancement of LTP improve learning?* Not enough research has yet been reported to draw any safe conclusion. *Does LTP occur naturally during learning?* According to my reading of the literature, there are simply no convincing reports that alterations in synaptic plasticity occur during learning, and the implication of Moser et al.'s (1993) observations on the temperature dependence of hippocampal field potentials is that more exacting protocols have to be developed for all chronic recording experiments in future.

I have four concluding thoughts. First, no amount of work on the question of whether LTP is necessary for learning will be persuasive enough in the absence of studies definitively establishing that LTP occurs naturally during learning. Uncomfortable as it is, we have to face up to the complications that now confront us in chronic recording experiments and devise experiments that stand a chance of revealing learning-induced alterations in synaptic efficacy. Looking for changes in the cross-correlation functions of simultaneously recorded hippocampal neurons in CA3 and CA1 might be one heroic strategy. However, progress will be slow on this front because the "right" experiments are exceedingly difficult and, to my knowledge, few laboratories have the expertise for isolated single-cell recording from two sites in hippocampus in freely moving animals.

Second, we need more work on the physiological determinants of LTP in freely moving animals. Buzsaki's (1989) theory (Figure 2.1F) suggests that sharp waves are the critical eliciting stimulus, while the work of Pavlides et al. (1988) and Otto et al. (1991) suggest that activity in phase with the hippocampal theta rhythm may be more relevant. Experiments such as Cahusac et al.'s (1991) demonstration of potentiation to natural visual patterns may also be interesting to explore.

Third, I am not yet prepared to give up on the idea that saturation of LTP should impair hippocampal-dependent learning. There are a host of reasons, beyond those highlighted above why this experiment might be difficult to carry out successfully. Working with "reduced" preparations (e.g., animals with at least unilateral hippocampal lesions and perhaps partial lesions ipsilateral to the recording site) could be one way forward, by analogy with the successful use of reduced preparations in the invertebrate field. Such a strategy would obviate the need to saturate the full septo-temporal extent of the hippocampus on both sides of the brain, but it is plagued with difficulty. One of these is that we have very few "pure" memory tasks. Paired-associate learning, as it is studied in humans (Squire 1992), is arguably the most sensitive task for examining declarative memory (e.g., R.B. was impaired on such learning), yet we still do not know how to do paired-associate learning in animals, and I frankly doubt that object-reward tasks are unambiguous analogies. The watermaze task is, to my knowledge, the most sensitive hippocampal-dependent learning task for rodents in the formal sense of minimizing the variance within and maximizing the separation between different treatment groups. However, animals with discrete ibotenate hippocampal lesions given strictly postoperative training can eventually learn to find the hidden platform well with overtraining. This may suggest that the hippocampus participates in spatial reference memory but is not ultimately required for it (cf. Figure 2.1E); more worryingly, it may reflect an ambiguity in the processing demands of the watermaze task, namely that it can be solved in a variety of ways. The general point is that a "reduced preparation" approach *runs the risk of encouraging animals to use learning strategies that are not dependent upon hippocampal function and thus do not engage hippocampal LTP*.

Fourth, while the various approaches to thinking about the role of LTP in learning summarized in Figure 2.1 are helpful, they are not formal theories and cannot easily be distinguished on the basis of the extant literature. Time and again, I find myself coming back to the fact that working out what LTP is doing presupposes that we have a satisfactory, widely agreed theory of hippocampal function. The uncomfortable truth is that we do not. It may be comforting to reflect on the possibility that studying the role of hippocampal LTP in learning will help us to realize such a theory. But, as critics of the LTP and learning hypothesis believe of the hypothesis itself, such thoughts are, in Prospero's words , "such stuff as dreams are made of."

ACKNOWLEDGEMENTS

The ideas in this chapter reflect the contributions of my colleagues in the Hippocampal Research Group in Edinburgh, particularly David Bannerman and Kate Jeffery. I am also grateful for discussions with Per Andersen, Tim Bliss, and Paul Chapman. My research is supported by the U.K. Medical Research Council, the Human Frontiers Science Panel, and the McDonnell-Pew Institute for Cognitive Neuroscience (University of Oxford).

REFERENCES

Artola, A., and W. Singer. 1990. The involvement of N-methyl-D-aspartate receptors in induction and maintenance of long-term potentiation in rat visual cortex. *Eur. J. Neurosci.* **2**:254–269.

Barnes, C.A. 1979. Memory deficits associated with senescence: A neurophysiological and behavioural study in the rat. *J. Comp. Physiol. Psychol.* **93**:74–104.

Berger, T.D. 1984. Long-term potentiation of hippocampal synaptic transmission affects rate of behavioural learning. *Science* **224**:627–630.

Bindman, L., K.P.S.J. Murphy, and S. Pockett. 1988. Postsynaptic control of the induction of long-term changes in efficacy of transmission at neocortical synapses of rat brain. *J. Neurophysiol.* **60**:1053–1065.

Bliss, T.V.P., and T. Lømo. 1973. Long-lasting potentiation of synaptic transmission in the dentate area of the anaesthetised rabbit following stimulation of the perforant path. *J. Physiol.* **232**:331–356.

Bliss, T.V.P., and G. Richter-Levin. 1993. Spatial learning and the saturation of long-term potentiation. *Hippocampus* **3**, in press.

Butcher, S.P., A. Hamberger, and R.G.M. Morris. 1991. Intracerebral distribution of D,L-2-aminophosphonopentanoic acid (AP5) and the dissociation of different types of learning. *Exp. Brain Res.* **83**:521–526.

Buzsaki, G. 1989. Two-stage model of memory trace formation: A role for noisy brain states. *Neurosci.* **31**:551–570.

Cahusac, P.M.B., E.T. Rolls, and F.H.C. Marriott. 1991. Potentiation of neuronal responses to natural visual input paired with postsynaptic activation in the hippocampus of the awake monkey. *Neurosci. Lett.* **124**:39–43.

Cain, D.P., E.L. Hargreaves, F.Boon, and Z. Dennison. 1993. An examination of the relations between hippocampal long-term potentiation, kindling, afterdischarge, and place learning in the watermaze. *Hippocampus*, in press.

Castro, C.A, L.H. Silbert, B.L. McNaughton, and C.A. Barnes. 1989. Recovery of spatial learning following decay of experimental saturation of LTP at perforant path synapses. *Nature* **342**:545–548.

Davis, S., S.P. Butcher, and R.G.M. Morris. 1992. The NMDA receptor antagonist D-2-amino-5-phosphonopentanoate (D–AP5) impairs spatial learning and LTP *in vivo* at intracerebral concentrations comparable to those that block LTP *in vitro*. *J. Neurosci.* **12**:31–34.

Daw, N.W., P.S.G. Stein, and K. Fox. 1993. The role of NMDA receptors in information processing. *Ann. Rev. Neurosci.* **16**:207–222.

Deupree, D.L., D.A. Turner, and C.L. Watters. 1990. Spatial performance correlates with *in vitro* potentiation in young and aged Fischer 344 rats. *Brain Res.* **554**:1–9.

Disterhoft, J.F., D.A. Coulter, and D.L. Alkon. 1986. Conditioning-specific changes of rabbit hippocampal neurons measured *in vitro*. *Proc. Natl. Acad. Sci. USA* **83**:2733–2737.

Doyère, V., and S. Laroche. 1992. Linear relationship between the maintenance of hippocampal long-term potentiation and retention of an associative memory. *Hippocampus* **2**:39–48.

Goddard, G.V. 1986. A step nearer a neural substrate. *Nature* **319**:721–722.

Grant, S.G.N., T.J. O'Dell, K.A. Karl, P.L. Stein, P. Soriano, and E.R. Kandel. 1992. Impaired long-term potentiation, spatial learning and hippocampus development in *fyn* mutant mice. *Science* **258:**1903–1910.

Hargreaves, E.L., D.P. Cain, and C.H. Vanderwolf. 1990. Learning and behavioural long-term potentiation. Importance of controlling for motor activity. *J. Neurosci.* **10**:1472–1478.

Harris, E.W., A.H. Ganong, and C.W. Cotman. 1984. Long term potentiation in the hippocampus involves activation of N-methyl-D-aspartate receptors. *Brain Res.* **323**:132–137.

Jeffery, K.J., and R.G.M. Morris. 1993. Cumulative long-term potentiation in the rat dentate gyrus correlates with, but does not modify, performance in the watermaze. *Hippocampus*, in press.

Keith, J.R., and J.W. Rudy. 1990. Why NMDA receptor-dependent long-term potentiation may not be a mechanism of learning and memory: Reappraisal of the NMDA receptor blockade strategy. *Psychobiol.* **18**:251–257.

Korol, D.L., T.W. Abel, L.T. Church, C.A. Barnes, and B.L. McNaughton. 1993. Hippocampal synaptic enhancement and spatial learning in the Morris swim task. *Hippocampus* **3**, in press.

Laroche, S., V. Doyère, and V. Bloch. 1989. Linear relation between the magnitude of long-term potentiation in the dentate gyrus and associative learning in the rat. A demonstration using commissural inhibition and local infusion of an NMDA receptor antagonist. *Neurosci.* **28**:375–386.

Levy, W.B., Jr., and O. Steward. 1979. Synapses as associative memory elements in the hippocampal formation. *Brain Res.* **175**:233–245.

McNamara, R.K., R.D. Kirkby, G.E. de Pape, R.W. Skelton, and M.E. Corcoran. 1993. Differential effects of kindling and kindled seizures on place learning in the Morris watermaze. *Hippocampus* **3**, in press.

McNaughton, B.L., and C.A. Barnes. 1990. From cooperative synaptic enhancement to associative memory: Bridging the abyss. *Sem. Neurosci.* **2**:403–416.

McNaughton, B.L., C.A. Barnes, G. Rao, J. Baldwin, and M. Rasmussen. 1986. Long-term enhancement of hippocampal synaptic transmission and the acquisition of spatial information. *J. Neurosci.* **6**:563–571.

McNaughton, B.L., and R.G.M. Morris. 1987. Hippocampal synaptic enhancement and information storage within a distributed memory system. *Trends Neurosci.* **10**:408–415.

Monaghan, D.T., H.J. Olverman, L. Nguyen, J.C. Watkins, and C.W. Cotman. 1988. Two classes of N-methyl-D-aspartate recognition sites: Differential distribution and differential regulation by glycine. *Proc. Natl. Acad. Sci. USA* **85**:9836–9840.

Mondadori, C., L. Weiskrantz, H. Buerki, F. Petschke, and G.E. Fagg. 1989. NMDA receptor antagonists can enhance or impair learning performance in animals. *Exp. Brain Res.* **75**:449–456.

Morris, R.G.M. 1990. Towards a representational hypothesis of the role of hippocampal synaptic plasticity in spatial and other forms of learning. *Cold Spring Harbor Symp. Quant. Biol.* **55**:161–174.

Morris, R.G.M., E. Andersen, G. Lynch, and M. Baudry. 1986. Selective impairment of learning and blockade of long-term potentiation by an N-methyl-D-aspartate receptor antagonist, AP5. *Nature* **319**:774–776.

Morris, R.G.M, R. Halliwell, and N. Bowery. 1989. Synaptic Plasticity and Learning II: Do different kinds of plasticity underly different kinds of learning? *Neuropsych.* **27**:41–59.

Morris, R.G.M., and M. Kennedy. 1992. The Pierian Spring. *Curr. Biol.* **12**:511–514.

Moser, E., I. Mathieson, and P. Andersen. 1993. Association between brain temperature and dentate field potentials in exploring and swimming rats. *Science* **259**:1324–1326.

O'Keefe, J., and L. Nadel. 1978. The Hippocampus as a Cognitive Map. Oxford: Oxford Univ. Press.

Otto, T., H. Eichenbaum, S.I. Wiener, and C.G. Wible. 1991. Learning-related patterns of CA1 spike trains parallels stimulation parameters optimal for inducing hippocampal long-term potentiation. *Hippocampus* **1**:181–192.

Paulsen, Ø., Ø. Hvalby, and P. Andersen. 1990. Failure to produce long-term depression in hippocampal synapses by an anti-correlation procedure. *Eur. J. Neurosci.* S4123.

Pavlides, C., Y.T. Greenstein, M. Grudman, and J. Winson. 1988. Long-term potentiation in the dentate gyrus is induced preferentially on the positive phase of theta rhythm. *Brain Res.* **439**:383–387.

Rolls, E.T. 1989. Parallel distributed processing in the brain: Implications of the functional architecture of neuronal networks in the hippocampus. In: Parallel Distributed Processing:

Implications for Psychology and Neurobiology, ed. R.G.M. Morris, pp. 286–307. Oxford: Clarendon.

Shapiro, M.L., and C. O'Connor. 1992. N-methyl-D-aspartate receptor antagonist MK–801 and spatial memory representation. Working-memory is impaired in an unfamiliar environment but not a familiar environment. *Behav. Neurosci.* **106**:604–612.

Sharp, P.E., B.L. McNaughton, and C.A. Barnes. 1989. Exploration-dependent modulation of evoked response in fascia dentata. Fundamental observations and time course. *Psychobiol.* **17**:257–269.

Silva, A.J., R. Paylor, J.M. Wehner, and S. Tonegawa. 1992a. Impaired spatial learning in α-calcium-calmodulin kinase II mutant mice. *Science* **257**:206–211.

Silva, A.J., C.F. Stevens, S. Tonegawa, and Y. Wang. 1992b. Deficient long-term potentiation in α-calcium-calmodulin kinase II mutant mice. *Science 257*:201–206.

Skelton, R.W., J.J. Miller, and A.G. Phillips. 1985. Long-term potentiation facilitates behavioural responding to single-pulse stimulation of the perforant path. *Behav. Neurosci.* **99**:603–620.

Squire, L.R. 1992. Memory and the Hippocampus: A synthesis from findings with rats, monkeys and humans. *Psychol. Rev.* **99**:195–231.

Stanton, P., and T.J. Sejnowski. 1989. Associative long-term depression in the hippocampus induced by Hebbian covariance. *Nature* **339**:215–218.

Sutherland, R.J., H.C. Dringenberg, and J.M. Hoesing. 1993. Induction of long-term potentiation at perforant path dentate synapses does not affect place learning or memory. *Hippocampus* **3**, in press.

Teyler, T.J., and P. Discenna. 1986. The Hippocampal Memory Indexing Theory. *Behav. Neurosci.* **100**:147–154.

Thompson, L.T., J.R. Moskal, and J.F. Disterhoft. 1992. Hippocampus-dependent learning facilitated by a monoclonal antibody or D-cycloserine. *Nature* **359**:638–641.

Thompson, R.F. 1990. Neural mechanisms of classical conditioning in mammals. *Phil. Trans. R. Soc. Lond. B.* **329**:161–170.

Tonkiss, J., R.G.M. Morris, and J.N.P. Rawlins. 1988. Intraventricular infusion of the NMDA antagonist AP5 impairs DRL performance in the rat. *Exp. Brain Res.* **73**:181–188.

Ward, L., S.E. Mason, and W.C. Abraham. 1990. Effects of the NMDA antagonists CPP and MK–801 on radial arm maze performance in rats. *Pharmacol. Biochem. Behav.* **35**:785–790.

Willner, J., M. Gallagher, P.W. Graham, and G.B. Crooks, Jr. 1992. N-methyl-D-aspartate antagonist D–APV selectively disrupts taste-potentiated odour aversion learning. *Behav. Neurosci.* **106**:315–323.

Willshaw, D.J., and P. Dayan. 1990. Optimal plasticity from matrix memories: What goes up must come down. *Neural Comp.* **2**:85–91.

3

Is Long-term Depression Associated with Learning in the Cerebellum?

M. Ito
Frontier Research Program, Institute of Physical and Chemical Research (RIKEN), Wako, Saitama 351–01, Japan

ABSTRACT

To address the question of whether long-term depression (LTD) plays a critical role in cerebellar learning, three types of tests have been developed. The first looks to see whether deprivation of LTD, by means of surgical lesioning or local application of a pharmacological agent, leads to impairment of cerebellar learning. The second attempts to find out whether behavior of Purkinje cells during cerebellar learning is explicable by LTD. The third involves the reproduction of cerebellar learning in a model of a cerebellar system with LTD incorporated. These three strategies have been applied to various model systems of cerebellar learning. Adaptation of the vestibulo-ocular reflex has been extensively examined, and evidence is accumulating to indicate that LTD plays a crucial role in this learning function.

CEREBELLAR LEARNING AND LTD

Cerebellar learning has been assumed to occur on the basis of classical neurophysiology of the functional compensation that follows partial lesioning of the cerebellum (see Dow and Moruzzi 1958). During the past two decades, various model systems of cerebellar learning (such as adaptation of vestibulo-ocular reflex [VOR], eye-blink classic conditioning, adaptation of locomotion or voluntary arm movement) have been established. These model systems give us concrete ideas of cerebellar learning and opportunities to investigate its neural mechanisms.

Under the current understanding of brain mechanisms, it is generally assumed that self-organization of a neuronal network based on synaptic plasticity such as LTD or long-term potentiation (LTP), underlies learning processes. In other words, synaptic plasticity is thought to represent a memory process required for learning. The presence of synaptic plasticity in the cerebellum was theoretically proposed around 1970 (Marr

Cellular and Molecular Mechanisms Underlying Higher Neural Functions
Edited by A.I. Selverston and P. Ascher

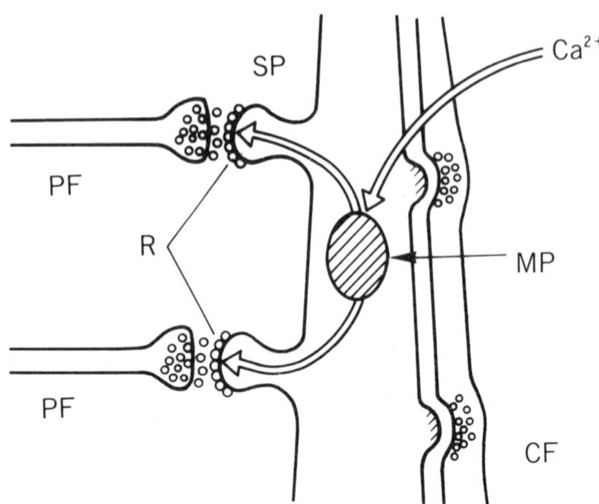

Figure 3.1 Cellular processes of long-term depression (LTD). SP: spine on a Purkinje cell dendrite; PF: parallel fiber; R: AMAPA-selective glutamate receptor; MP: messenger processes; CF: climbing fiber.

1969; Albus 1971), and accordingly, LTD was found experimentally in the 1980s (see Ito 1989). LTD is the sustained depression of synaptic efficacy that occurs in synapses supplied by parallel fibers (axons of granule cells) to Purkinje cells. LTD occurs specifically when parallel fiber synapses are repeatedly activated in conjunction with another distinct synapse supplied by climbing fibers (axons of inferior olive cells; see Figure 3.1). Recently, the signal transduction underlying LTD has been subject to extensive investigation. It has been shown to involve Ca^{2+} ions, nitric oxide, cyclic GMP, and protein kinases C and G, and eventually leads to sustained desensitization of AMPA-selective glutamate receptors mediating parallel fiber synapses (see Ito 1991; Ito and Karachot 1992; see Figure 3.2).

While LTD has been established as a characteristic form of synaptic plasticity prevailing in the cerebellar cortex, the question has been raised as to whether LTD actually plays a crucial role in cerebellar learning. A counter argument may be that a change of state in the cerebellar network, such as onset of local reverberation within cerebellar circuit, represents a memory process, as discussed in this volume. Thus, a rigorous effort has been devoted to confirm the postulated crucial role of LTD in cerebellar learning.

TESTING THE INVOLVEMENT OF LTD IN CEREBELLAR LEARNING

Three major strategies have been adopted—two experimental and one theoretical—to test the association of LTD with cerebellar learning. None of these strategies is free

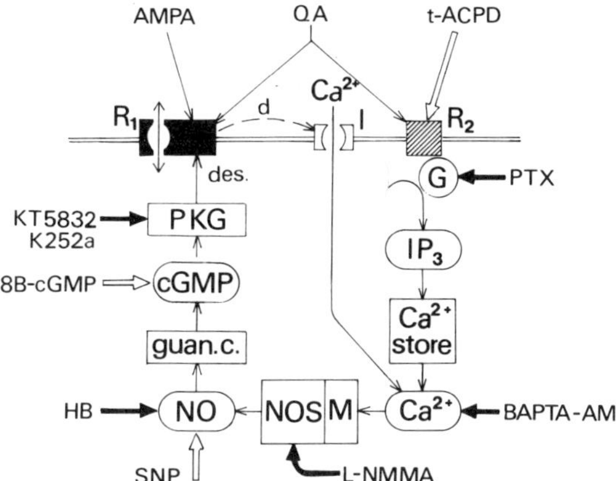

Figure 3.2 Signal transduction underlying long-term depression (LTD). Messenger reactions connecting Ca^{2+} entry to desensitization (des.) of AMPA-selective glutamate receptor (R_1). M: calmodulin; NOS: NO synthase; guan. c.: guanylate cyclase; PKG: protein kinase G; L–NMMA: inhibitor of NOS; SNP: sodium nitroprusside; KT5823: inhibitor of PKG; K252a: nonspecific inhibitor; R_2: metabotropic glutamate receptor; G: G-protein; QA: quisqualate; t–ACPD: agonist for metabotropic glutamate receptor; PTX: pertussis toxin (Ito and Karachot 1990).

of errors from various sources, and none can be sufficient by itself. Combined application of these three strategies is necessary for drawing a convincing conclusion.

Deprivation of LTD

Involvement of LTD in cerebellar learning can be indicated most directly if removal of LTD results in the impairment of cerebellar learning. As an initial step, a surgical lesion may be made on a cerebellar cortex; however, an expected complication involves retrograde degeneration, which would occur in the inferior olive. One cannot be certain if the impairment of learning is solely due to lesion of the cerebellar cortex.

As a second step, a chemical lesion using kainic acid or the transient removal of neuronal activity using xylocain or muscimol would be attempted, since these procedures do not cause retrograde degeneration. However, another complication may arise in that inactivation of a cerebellar cortical area may impair the function of a corresponding vestibular or cerebellar nuclear region through the withdrawal of Purkinje cell inhibition. Even if learning is conducted in the cerebellar nuclear region, it would be disturbed, and would most likely appear lost, under the influences of cortical dysfunction. This complication, however, could be removed if the disturbances caused by withdrawal of Purkinje cell inhibition diminish over time as a result of a homeostatic processes within the CNS.

The final step of testing requires the specific blocking of LTD without inducing any other disturbance in the cerebellar circuit. Hemoglobin seems to provide an ideal tool for such testing because it absorbs nitric oxide which plays a key role in the messenger processes underlying LTD (Nagao and Ito 1991). As our knowledge at the molecular level advances, we should be able to obtain more effective tools, e.g., the gene targeting technique could help remove LTD.

Purkinje Cell Behavior

Another experimental test has been performed by recording Purkinje cells in the cerebellar cortex, to find out if their behavior is closely correlated with learning. Correlation must be close enough to suggest causality.

In conducting such experiments, an important basis is the fine functional localization in the cerebellar cortex. The entire cerebellar cortex has been divided into seven longitudinal zones, and each zone has further been divided and segmented into numerous elongated microzones. Each microzone is connected to a small group of vestibular or cerebellar nuclear neurons and is involved in a particular function (Figure 3.3). It is notable that each microzone is as narrow as a fraction of a millimeter. Recording from Purkinje cells in relation with learning should be performed within a microzone specifically serving that function. Since a peripheral stimulus reaches a number of microzones through diverging mossy fibers, similar responses in Purkinje

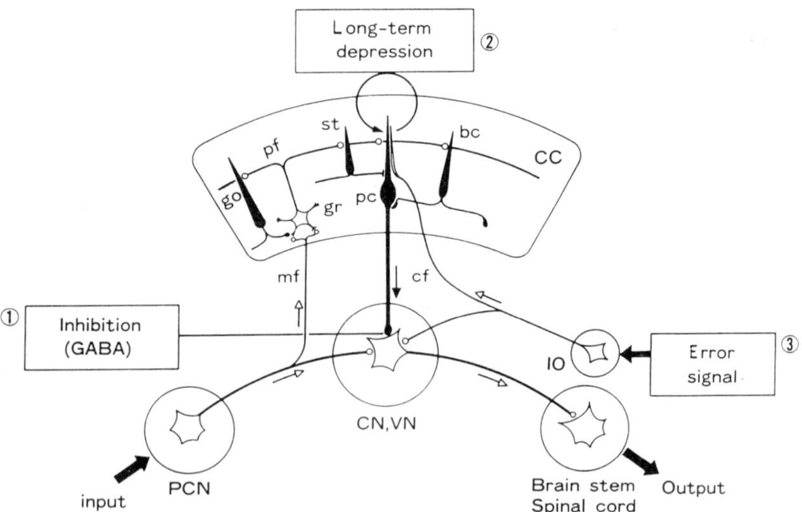

Figure 3.3 Corticonuclear microcomplex of the cerebellum. CC: microzone of the cerebellar cortex; go: Golgi cell; pf: parallel fiber; st: stellate cell; gr: granule cell; pc: Purkinje cell; bc: basket cell; mf: mossy fiber; cf: climbing fiber; IO: inferior olive; CN, VN: cerebellar and vestibular nuclei; PCN: precerebellar nuclei.

cells to a certain peripheral stimulus does not prove their belonging to the same microzone. Even climbing fiber inputs will not help to identify a microzone, since climbing fiber branches originating from the same inferior olive neuron reach cerebellar areas remote to each other. A specific relationship of a Purkinje cell to a microzone should be secured in some way in addition to the recording of responses to peripheral stimuli. Exact mapping of the cerebellar cortex under visual control may be one of these ways; however, local electrical stimulation also provides a good means, since the effect of such stimulation will be expressed through a functional system to which the stimulated microzone is connected. It is noteworthy that ignorance of microzone structure of the cerebellum has been a major source of errors in testing Purkinje cell behavior in connection with a certain function.

Modeling of Cerebellar Learning With LTD

Eventually, learning mechanisms in a given cerebellar system could be explained on the basis of its neuronal diagram, with LTD incorporated. Computer simulation of the mechanisms would reproduce learning capabilities. Errors at this stage would arise from an inaccurate neuronal diagram, in which important information could be missing.

These two experimental and one theoretical tests have been applied to various models of cerebellar learning. VOR adaptation has been most thoroughly investigated, as will be discussed below.

ADAPTATION OF VOR

VOR is a reflex that induces eye movements which compensate for head movements, so as to keep retinal images constant during head movement. VOR exhibits a distinct adaptation phenomenon. Under visual-vestibular combined stimulation, VOR gain is progressively altered, either depressed or enhanced, depending on the conditions of visual-vestibular interaction. VOR adaptation has been demonstrated in humans, rabbit, monkey, and fish through dove prism goggles (Gonshor and Melvill Jones 1976), telescopic lenses (Miles and Eighmy 1980), or by rotating a subject in various phase relationships with a screen representing visual surroundings (Ito et al. 1974). VOR is adaptively depressed with dove prism goggles or inphase rotation of turntable and screen, and enhanced with telescopic lenses or outphase rotation of turntable and screen.

Flocculus Hypothesis of VOR Control

The findings that (a) Purkinje cells in a small area of the cerebellum, the flocculus, project to relay cells of VOR in vestibular nuclei (Ito et al. 1970) and (b) the flocculus receives mossy fibers from labyrinths (Brodal and Høivik 1964) and climbing fibers from the retina via the inferior olive (Maekawa and Simpson 1973) have led to the formulation of the flocculus hypothesis of VOR control. This hypothesis states that the flocculus regulates signal flow from labyrinths to the flocculus to the relay cells of VOR, referring to error signals arising from the retina (Ito 1972, 1974, 1982, 1984). VOR is a typical feedforward control which, due to lack of feedback, is unable to perform by itself with precision. It is therefore thought that the proposed adaptive control mechanism in the flocculus is essential for the precise operation of VOR.

Testing of VOR Adaptation with Deprivation of LTD

Lesioning of the cerebellum in cats, rabbits, and monkeys abolished VOR adaptation. Chemical lesion also abolished VOR adaptation in rabbits. Therefore, it is generally agreed that the flocculus is in some way involved in VOR adaptation.

Furthermore, a crucial test was recently conducted with subdural application of hemoglobin, which blocked VOR adaptation without affecting dynamic characteristics of the oculomotor system (Nagao and Ito 1991). It may be that hemoglobin depleted a highly diffusible gas, NO, from floccular tissues, thereby blocking LTD in the flocculus.

Purkinje Cell Behavior Related to VOR Adaptation

In the flocculus of rabbits and monkeys, it is known that Purkinje cells display certain types of frequency modulation in their simple spike discharges during VOR, mainly due to mossy fiber inputs to the flocculus (Ghelarducci et al. 1975; Miles et al. 1980; see also below). Flocculus Purkinje cells also discharge complex spikes, which represent climbing fiber inputs arising from retinal errors. Further, the simple spike modulation is modified during adaptation of the VOR (Dufossé et al. 1978; Miles et al. 1980; Watanabe 1984, 1985; Nagao 1989).

Studies in rabbits have been based on the identification of the microzone structure of rabbit flocculus. Electrical stimulus mapping reveals a narrow strip in the rabbit flocculus from which horizontal eye movement in the ipsilateral direction is induced upon stimulation (Figure 3.4; Dufossé et al. 1977; Nagao et al. 1985: Simpson et al. 1992); this indicates involvement of the zone in horizontal oculomotor function. The remaining areas are related to vertical or rotatory eye movement, or even to non-oculomotor function. When data from Purkinje cells recorded in the H-zone and in other areas of rabbit flocculus were analyzed separately, their behavior during the horizontal VOR was fully consistent with the flocculus hypothesis in the H-zone group, but not in the non-H-zone group. Similarly, Watanabe (1984, 1985) specified the H-zone in monkey flocculus and confirmed that the H-zone Purkinje cells in monkeys behaved consistently with the flocculus hypothesis, as in rabbits.

Since different behavior of flocculus Purkinje cells was observed in monkeys (Miles et al. 1980), Miles and Lisberger (1981) discarded the flocculus hypothesis and proposed another hypothesis in which the modified behavior of Purkinje cells in the flocculus reflect changes of eye movements through eye velocity inputs to the

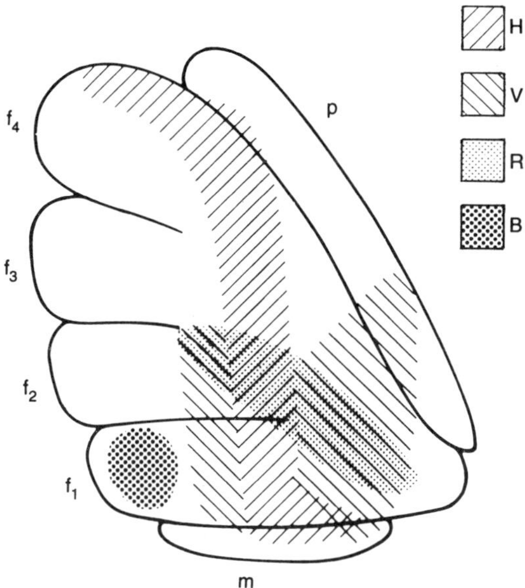

Figure 3.4 Microzone structure of rabbit flocculus as determined by electrical stimulus mapping. Five eye-related areas represented in the unfolded folia of the flocculus. H, V, R: areas from which horizontal, vertical, and rotatory eye movements were evoked, respectiviely; B: areas from which eye blink was induced (Nagao et al. 1985).

flocculus as a result of, but not as a cause for, VOR adaptation. Miles et al. (1980), however, did not specify the H-zone, and it is now apparent that their recording sites were not in the genuine flocculus (see below).

Bidirectional Behavior

When an animal is rotated sinusoidally, floccular Purkinje cells show simple spike discharges modulated sinusoidally either inphase or 180° outphase with the head velocity toward the direction ipsilateral to the flocculus under study. More strictly speaking, flocculus Purkinje cells display all varieties of phase shifts of the simple spike modulation relative to head velocity, but the amplitude of modulation is larger around 0° and 180° phase shifts. Purkinje cells showing inphase or outphase modulation are more numerous than those modulating otherwise (Figure 3.5).

The inphase and outphase modulation in flocculus Purkinje cells implies a bidirectional mechanism modifying the VOR gain. In the horizontal VOR, vestibular signals are relayed by (a) a group of excitatory vestibular nuclear cells to the medial rectus motoneurons of the ipsilateral eye and, at the same time, (b) a group of inhibitory vestibular nuclear cells to the lateral rectus motoneurons (Figure 3.6). The vestibular organ sends out signals when the head is rotated ipsilaterally, which induce contraction

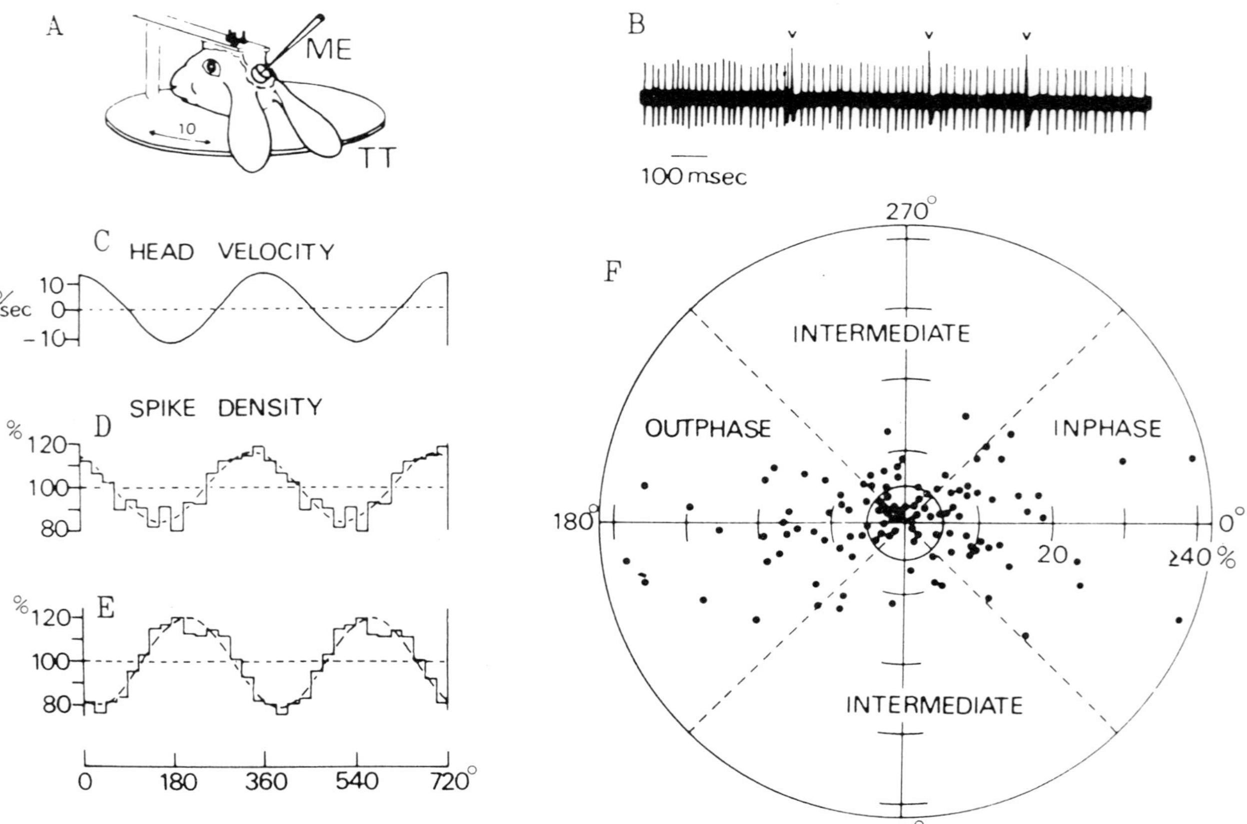

Figure 3.5 Modulation of simple spikes of flocculus Purkinje cells during VOR. (A) Experimental arrangement: the body of the rabbit is omitted for simplicity. (B) Specimen record of discharge from a Purkinje cell. Triangles mark complex spikes. (D) and (E) are two cases of spike density histogram for simple discharges. (F) is a polar diagram plotting the amplitude and phase shift for rabbit floccular Purkinje cells (Ghelarducci et al. 1975).

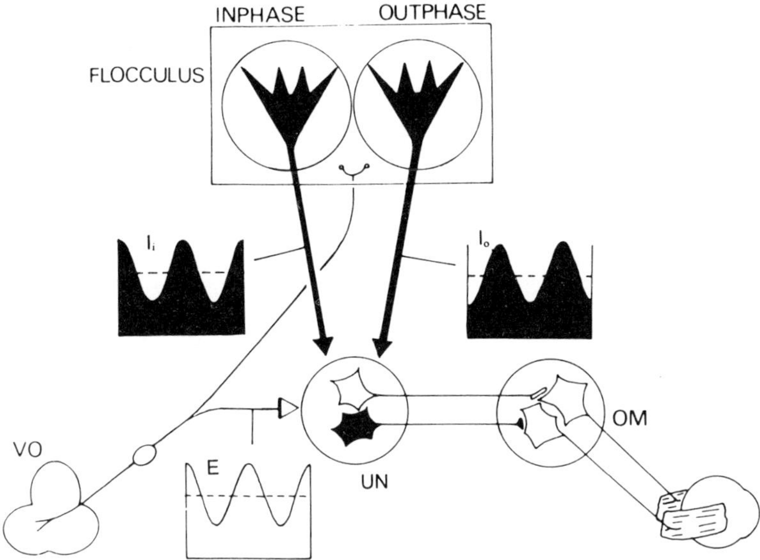

Figure 3.6 Schematic diagram illustrating the mechanism of bidirectional control of VOR by the flocculus. VO: vestibular organ; E: modulation of primary vestibular impulses during sinusoidal head rotation; UN: vestibular nuclear neurons; OM: oculomotor neurons; I_i, I_o: inphase and outphase modulating of Purkinje cell signals.

of the medial rectus and relaxation of the lateral rectus, so that the eye rotates contralaterally, inducing VOR compensating for the head movement. In this situation, relay neurons discharge inphase with head velocity. These relay neurons also receive inhibitory signals from flocculus Purkinje cells. If these Purkinje cells discharge inphase with head velocity, the inhibitory signals counteract vestibular signals so that VOR will be depressed. If they discharge outphase with head velocity, the inhibitory signals waning and waxing in opposition to vestibular signals will enhance the VOR. In this way, in flocculus Purkinje cells, inphase modulation acts to depress the VOR, while outphase modulation acts to enhance the VOR.

Changes During VOR Adaptation

As compared before and after 1 hour of continuous rotation with *inphase* or *outphase* combined rotation of turntable and screen, H-zone flocculus Purkinje cells displayed changes in the modulation pattern of their simple spike discharges (Figure 3.7). During inphase combination which adaptively depressed VOR, the inphase modulation pattern became dominant. During outphase combination, which adaptively enhanced VOR, the outphase modulation became dominant. It is concluded that the flocculus adaptively modifies VOR through changes of simple spike modulation in Purkinje cells.

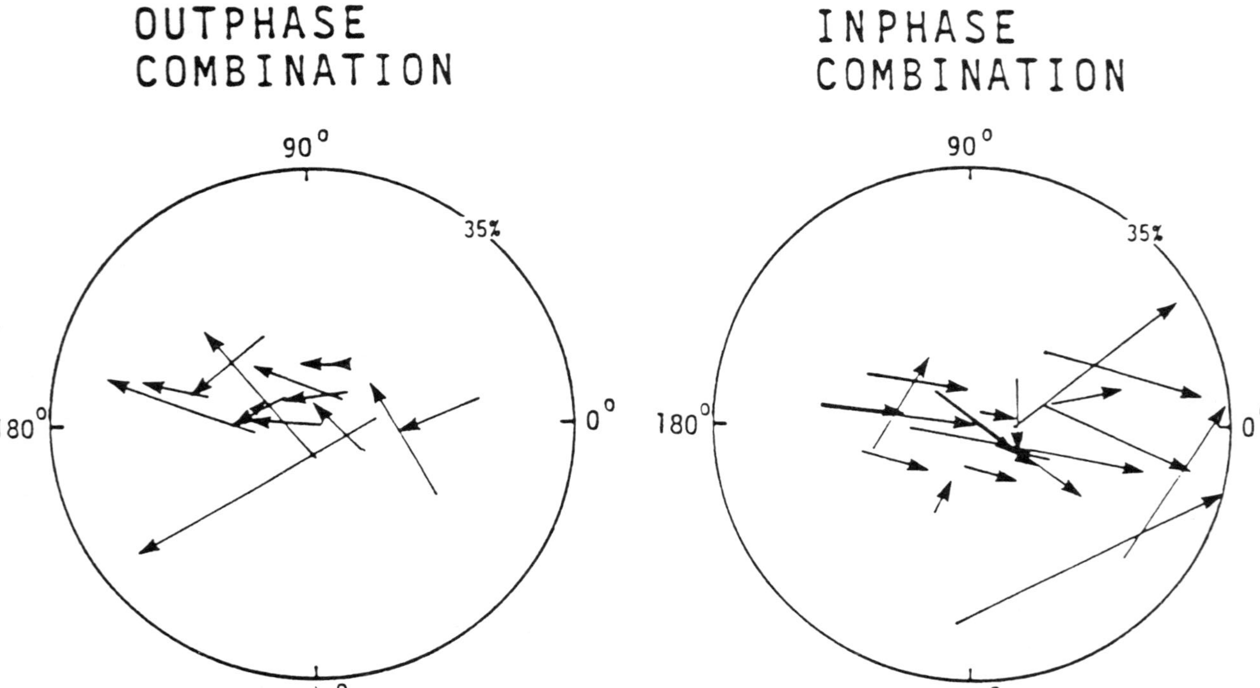

Figure 3.7 Adaptive changes of simple spike modulation in flocculus Purkinje cells of monkeys. The modulation pattern for each Purkinje cell is shown by an arrow connecting the position before and after 1 h adaptation with outphase or inphase combined rotation of turntable and screen (Watanabe 1984).

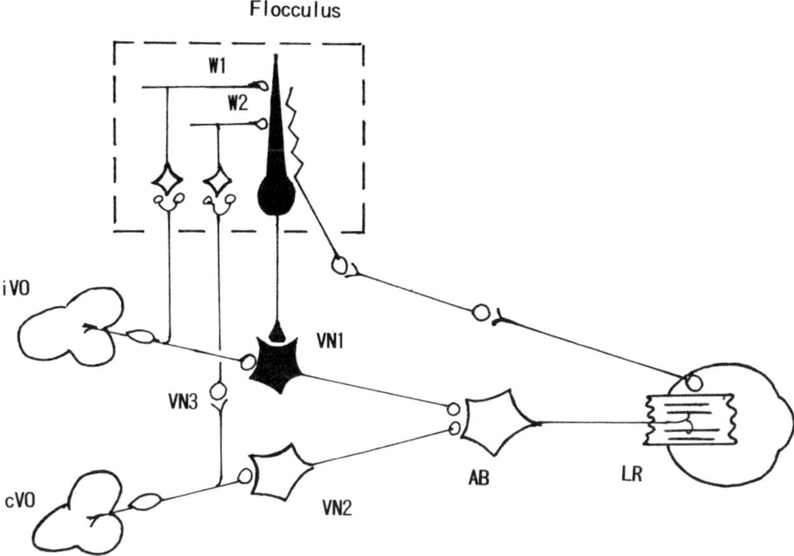

Figure 3.8 Neuronal circuit for floccular control of the VOR incorporating bilateral vestibular organs. iVO, cVO: vestibular organs ipsi- and contralateral to the side of the illustrated eye and flocculus; VN1, VN2: inhibitory and excitatory VOR relay neurons; VN3: another vestibular nuclear neuron; AB: abducens motoneuron; LR: lateral rectus muscle; W1, W2: two sets of modifiable synapses. Note that VN2 does not receive input from floccular Purkinje cells.

MODELING OF VOR ADAPTATION

Mechanism of Bidirectional Change of VOR Gain

As mentioned above, VOR can be enhanced by outphase modulating floccular Purkinje cells and depressed by inphase modulating ones. How do these two types of modulation emerge? Since a flocculus receives vestibular mossy fiber inputs from bilateral vestibular organs, it can be assumed that the inphase modulation is driven by mossy fiber signals predominantly from the ipsilateral vestibular organ, while outphase modulation is driven by signals predominantly from the contralateral vestibular organ (Figure 3.8; Ito 1982). Therefore, it is expected that VOR would be depressed through the strengthening of the ipsilateral vestibular input, while strengthening of the contralateral vestibular input would lead to enhanced VOR.

Fujita (1982) proposed a model of VOR adaptation that incorporates his adaptive filter model of the cerebellum. This model provides an additional mechanism for diversifying the phase shifts of vestibular signals. The phases of vestibular signals are shifted when passing through the filter consisted of granule cells and Golgi cells, so that a set of signals with greatly varied phase shifts will emerge in parallel fibers, including inphase and outphase signals.

Role of LTD in VOR Adaptation

Climbing fiber responses of flocculus Purkinje cells representing retinal errors exhibit strong directionality. These occur when the visual surroundings move in the contralateral direction relative to the head (forward in front of the ipsilateral eye, in the case of rabbit). Therefore, during inphase and outphase combinations of head and screen rotation, it is expected that LTD occurs in different vestibular inputs.

Inphase Combination

When the head turns ipsilaterally while the visual screen also turns ipsilaterally, one would expect the following combined activity:

ipsilateral vestibular organ (inphase modulating) ...... fires
contralateral vestibular organ (outphase modulating) ... ceases to fire
retinal error signal .... silences.

This would not bring an adaptive change in the flocculus Purkinje cells. However, when the head turns contralaterally with the screen also turning contralaterally, there would be:

ipsilateral vestibular organ (inphase modulating) ...... ceases to fire
contralateral vestibular organ (outphase modulating) ... fires
retinal error signal .... arises.

Thus, parallel fiber synapses mediating contralateral vestibular signals (W2 in Figure 3.8) will undergo LTD because of their conjunctive activation with climbing fibers. As a consequence, the outphase modulation in Purkinje cells driven by the contralateral vestibular input will become less dominant. The inphase modulation driven by the ipsilateral vestibular organ will thus dominate and act to depress VOR (Figure 3.7).

Outphase Combination

By contrast, when the screen turns contralaterally during ipsilateral head rotation:

ipsilateral vestibular organ (inphase modulating) ...... fire
contralateral vestibular organ (outphase modulating) ... ceases to fire
retinal error signal .... arises

so that parallel fiber synapses conveying ipsilateral vestibular signals (W1 in Figure 3.8) will undergo LTD, leading to relative dominance of outphase modulation of Purkinje cells and thereby to enhancement of VOR. However, when the head turns contralaterally, while the screen rotates ipsilaterally:

ipsilateral vestibular organ (inphase modulating) . . . . . . ceases to fire
contralateral vestibular organ (outphase modulating) . . fires
retinal error signal . . . . silences

so that no adaptive change will occur.

Thus, LTD occurs in W1 during outphase combination or in W2 during inphase combination, which shifts Purkinje cell behavior to dominance of outphase or inphase modulation in the flocculus (Figure 3.8). This explains satisfactorily the bidirectional VOR adaptation.

In addition to the above qualitative arguments, two elaborate neural network models consistent with the flocculus hypothesis have been proposed (Fujita 1982; Gomi and Kawato 1992). Computer simulations based on these models were able to reproduce VOR adaptation satisfactorily well.

DEFENDING THE FLOCCULUS HYPOTHESIS

Miles and Lisberger (1981) and Lisberger and Sejnowski (1992) challenged the flocculus hypothesis on the basis of mismatching between the rabbit data on which the hypothesis is based and the early monkey data by Miles et al. (1980). In these models, a major mossy fiber input to the flocculus is provided by eye velocity signals, and learning is assumed to take place in the brainstem rather than in the flocculus. This contrasts with the flocculus hypothesis, which assumes that a major mossy fiber input to the flocculus arises from the vestibular organ and that the flocculus is the major site of VOR adaptation. The flocculus hypothesis, nevertheless, can be defended in light of recent knowledge (Ito 1993).

Identification of Flocculus H-Zone in Monkeys

Gerrits and Voogd's (1989) recent thorough anatomical study of the monkey flocculus revealed that only the caudal half of the traditionally defined monkey flocculus is the genuine flocculus. The rostral half is homologous to the ventral paraflocculus. Stone and Lisberger (1990) noted that they have been recording primarily from the rostral area, which is therefore not the flocculus. Nagao (1992) recently reported that Purkinje cells in the monkey ventral paraflocculus behaved just as the horizontal gaze velocity cells defined by Miles et al. (1980), but differently from H-zone Purkinje cells described by Watanabe (1984, 1985). He suggested that these horizontal gaze velocity cells are involved in the control of smooth pursuit eye movement instead of VOR. The inconsistency of earlier monkey data with the flocculus hypothesis can now be understood as being due to the misidentification of the flocculus H-zone in the monkey cerebellum.

Eye Velocity Signals to Flocculus Purkinje Cells

The method for evaluating eye velocity input to the flocculus, employed by Miles et al. (1980), is problematic. On a turntable, a monkey would show eye movement due to VOR. This eye movement is suppressed when the monkey gazes at a light spot fixed to the turntable. Often it happens that Purkinje cells show only a little response during VOR; nonetheless, a substantial response appears when the VOR is visually suppressed. Miles et al. (1980) interpreted this as indicating that vestibular and eye velocity signals of similar size cancel each other during VOR, yielding only a small Purkinje cell response, and that when the eye velocity is nullified by visual suppression of VOR, the vestibular response is revealed. The difference between the responses during VOR and those during visual suppression is taken as an eye velocity response. However, another, more straightforward interpretation is possible: the poor response of the Purkinje cell during VOR is simply due to a weak vestibular input, while the substantial response raised during visual suppression of VOR primarily represents higher command signals arising from the cerebral cortex, which act to cancel VOR (Ito 1984). If this is so, the signals measured by Miles et al. (1980) do not reflect eye velocity but rather higher command signals. The claim that eye velocity signals are a major input to the flocculus has been made on the basis of measurements in the ventral paraflocculus Purkinje cells made via the visual cancellation method. The visual cancellation method, however, should be used judiciously.

Nagao (1992) reported that visual suppression induced a significant response in the ventral paraflocculus Purkinje cells but not in H-zone Purkinje cells of a monkey. Repeated measurements in rabbit H-zone Purkinje cells, carried out under a method different from Miles et al. (1980), consistently indicate that eye velocity is a minor input to rabbit flocculus (Nagao 1991). Thus, some eye velocity input to H-zone Purkinje cells exists but may not play a dominant role.

Synaptic Plasticity in the Brainstem Pathway

Lisberger and Sejnowski (1992) adopted an oversimplified neuronal circuit, where the vestibular mossy fiber input to the flocculus through the granule cells as a single line, as in Figure 3.3, thus implying a single function. If this important input to the Purkinje cell dendrite is represented so simplistically, it is evident that it would not be able to account for the bidirectional adaptation of the VOR, which is either enhanced or depressed depending on visual-vestibular stimulating conditions. This is one of the reasons why Lisberger and Sejnowski (1992) assumed a second VOR modulatory site in the vestibular nuclei.

In the model illustrated in Figure 3.8, however, we see that whether VOR is enhanced or depressed depends eventually upon which of the two sets of vestibular inputs to Purkinje cell dendrites is depressed by LTD. Thus, there is no need for a second modulatory site in the vestibular nuclei to account for bidirectional VOR adaptation.

Some experimental evidence in monkey and goldfish has been reported for the presence of synaptic plasticity in the brainstem VOR pathway (Lisberger 1988; Pastor et al. 1992). However, more direct evidence is needed to establish such plasticity. Since the entire process of VOR adaptation is abolished by lesioning of the cerebellum or by applying hemoglobin, a question arises as to why such brainstem synaptic plasticity does not show up in the absence of cerebellar plasticity. The postulated brainstem synaptic plasticity, if any, should develop only secondarily to the cerebellar plasticity.

COMMENTS

A central theme of neuroscience is to bridge knowledge at synaptic and behavioral levels. Studies of VOR adaptation provide an excellent example of such efforts. Causal relationship of LTD with motor learning has been proposed in terms of flocculus hypothesis and subjected to rigorous experimental examinations. Evidence supporting the flocculus hypothesis has accumulated over recent years, and the apparent conflicts with it are being removed in light of newly gained knowledge. Other model systems of cerebellar learning are also in various phases of examination and will serve to establish the mechanisms of synapse-behavior relationship.

REFERENCES

Albus, J.S. 1971. A theory of cerebellar function. *Math. Biosci.* **28**:167–171.

Brodal, A., and B. Høivik. 1964. Site and mode of termination of primary vestibulo-cerebellar fibers in the cat. An experimental study with silver impregnation methods. *Arch. Ital. Biol.* **102**:1–21.

Dow, R., and G. Moruzzi. 1958. The Physiology and Pathology of the Cerebellum. Minneapolis: Univ. of Minnesota Press.

Dufossé M., M. Ito, P.I. Jastreboff, and Y. Miyashita. 1978. A neuronal correlate in rabbit's cerebellum to adaptive modification of the vestibulo-ocular reflex. *Brain Res.* **150**:611–616.

Dufossé, M., M. Ito, and Y. Miyashita. 1977. Functional localization in the rabbit's cerebellar flocculus determined with relationship with eye movements. *Neurosci. Lett.* **5**:273–277.

Fujita, M. 1982. Simulation of adaptive modification of vestibulo-ocular reflex with an adaptive filter model of the cerebellum. *Biol. Cybern.* **45**:207–214.

Gerrits, N.M., and J. Voogd. 1989. The topographical organization of climbing and mossy fiber afferents in the flocculus and the ventral paraflocculus in rabbit, cat, and monkey. *Exp. Brain Res. Suppl.* **17**:26–29.

Ghelarducci, M., M. Ito, and N. Yagi. 1975. Impulse discharge from flocculus Purkinje cell of alert rabbits during visual stimulation combined with horizontal head rotation. *Brain Res.* **87**:66–72.

Gomi, H., and M. Kawato. 1992. Adaptive feedback control models of the vestibulo-cerebellum and spinocerebellum. *Biol. Cybern.* **68**:105–114.

Gonshor, A., and G. Melvill Jones. 1976. Extreme vestibulo-ocular adaptation induced by prolonged optical reversal of vision. *J. Physiol. Lond.* **256**:381–414.

Ito, M. 1972. Neural design of the cerebellar motor control system. *Brain Res.* **40**:81–84.

Ito, M. 1974. The control mechanisms of cerebellar motor system. In: The Neurosciences, Third Study Programs, ed. F.O. Schmitt and F.G. Worden, pp. 293–303. Boston: MIT Press.

Ito, M. 1982. Cerebellar control of the vestibulo-ocular reflex: Around the flocculus hypothesis. *Ann. Rev. Neurosci.* **5**:275–296.

Ito, M. 1984. The Cerebellum and Neural Control. New York: Raven Press.
Ito, M. 1989. Long-term depression. *Ann. Rev. Neurosci.* **12**:85–102.
Ito, M. 1991. The cellular basis of cerebellar plasticity. *Curr. Opin. Neurobiol.* **1**:616–620.
Ito, M. 1993. Cerebellar flocculus hypothesis. *Nature* **363:**24–25.
Ito, M., S.M. Highstein, and J. Fukuda. 1970. Cerebellar inhibition of the vestibulo-ocular reflex in rabbit and its blockage by picrotoxin. *Brain Res.* **17**:524–526.
Ito, M., and L. Karachot. 1990. Messengers mediating long-term desensitization in cerebellar Purkinje cells. *NeuroReport* **1**:129–132.
Ito, M., and L. Karachot. 1992. Protein kinases and phosphatase inhibitors mediating long-term desensitization of glutamate receptors in cerebellar Purkinje cells. *Neurosci. Res.* **14**:27–38.
Ito, M., T. Shiida, N. Yagi, and M. Yamamoto. 1974. The cerebellar modification of rabbit's horizontal vestibulo-ocular reflex induced by sustained head rotation combined with visual stimulation. *Proc. Jpn. Acad.* **50**:85–89.
Lisberger, S.G. 1988. The neural basis for learning of simple motor skills. *Science* **242**:728–735.
Lisberger, S.G., and T.J. Sejnowski. 1992. Motor learning in a recurrent network model based on the vestibulo-ocular reflex. *Nature* **360**:159–161.
Maekawa, K., and J.I. Simpson. 1973. Climbing fiber responses evoked in vestibulo-cerebellum of rabbit from visual system. *J. Neurophysiol.* **36**:649–666.
Marr, D. 1969. A theory of cerebellar cortex. *J. Physiol. Lond.* **202**:437–470.
Miles, F.A., D.J. Braitman, and B.M. Dow. 1980. Long-term adaptive changes in primate vestibulo-ocular reflex. IV. Electrophysiological observations in flocculus of adapted monkeys. *J. Neurophysiol.* **43**:1477–1493.
Miles, F.A., and B.B. Eighmy. 1980. Long-term adaptive changes in primate vestibulo-ocular reflex. 1. Behavioral observations. *J. Neurophysiol.* **43**:1406–1425.
Miles, F.A., and S.G. Lisberger. 1981. Plasticity in the vestibulo-ocular reflex: A new hypothesis. *Ann. Rev. Neurosci.* **4**:273–299.
Nagao, S. 1989. Behavior of floccular Purkinje cells correlated with adaptation of vestibulo-ocular reflex in pigmented rabbits. *Exp. Brain Res.* **77**:531–540.
Nagao, S. 1991. Contribution of oculomotor signals to the behavior of rabbit floccular Purkinje cells during reflex eye movements. *Neurosci. Res.* **12**:169–184.
Nagao, S. 1992. Different roles of flocculus and ventral paraflocculus for oculomotor control in the primate. *NeuroReport* **3**:13–15.
Nagao, S., and M. Ito. 1991. Subdural application of hemoglobin to the cerebellum blocks vestibuolo-ocular reflex adaptation. *NeuroReport* **2**:193–196.
Nagao, S., M. Ito, and L. Karachot. 1985. Eye field in the cerebellar flocculus of pigmented rabbits determined with local stimulation. *Neurosci. Res.* **3**:39–51.
Pastor, A.M., R.R. De la Cruz, and R. Baker. 1992. Characterization and adaptive modification of the goldfish vestibulo-ocular reflex by sinusoidal and velocity step vestibular stimulation. *J. Neurophysiol.* **68**:2003–2015.
Simpson, J.I., J. Van der Steen, and J. Tan. 1992. Reference frames of the rabbit flocculus. In: Vestibular and Brainstem Control of Eye, Head and Body Movements, ed. H. Shimazu and Y. Shinoda, pp 301–313. Tokyo.: Jpn. Sci. Soc. Press/Basel: Karger.
Stone, L.S., and S.G. Lisberger. 1990. Visual responses of Purkinje cells in the cerebellar flocculus during smooth-pursuit eye movements in monkeys. I. Simple spikes. *J. Neurophysiol.* **63**:1241–1261.
Watanabe, E. 1984. Neuronal events correlated with long-term adaptation of the horizontal vestibulo-ocular reflex in the primate flocculus. *Brain Res.* **297**:169–174.
Watanabe, E. 1985. Role of the primate flocculus in adaptation of the vestibulo-ocular reflex. *Neurosci. Res.* **3**:20–38.

4

Multiple Sites of Motor Learning in the Vestibulo-ocular Reflex

S.G. LISBERGER
Department of Physiology, Box 0444, W.M. Keck Center for Integrative Neuroscience, and Neuroscience Graduate Program, University of California, San Francisco, CA 94143–0444, U.S.A.

INTRODUCTION

The vestibulo-ocular reflex (VOR) is one of a handful of systems in which it has been possible to investigate the neural networks that mediate learning and memory in the complex brains of vertebrates, including primates. In normal monkeys, the VOR stabilizes gaze in space by generating smooth eye motion that is opposite in direction and equal in amplitude to rotatory head motion (Fuchs and Kimm 1975; Keller 1978; Miles and Eighmy 1980). As a result, images from the stationary surroundings are nearly stable on the retina and good visual acuity is preserved. Learning is induced by fitting animals with magnifying or minaturizing spectacles that require the the VOR to become either twice or one quarter as large as normal (Miles and Fuller 1974; Lisberger and Pavelko 1986). Over a time course of several days, the interaction of visual and vestibular stimuli corrects the performance of the VOR until it approaches the demands placed by the spectacles. Passive head turns in darkness then reveal that the gain of the VOR (eye speed divided by head speed) has increased or decreased to values of 1.8 or 0.25, respectively.

In this chapter, I first introduce the relevant neural network for motor learning in the VOR, along with recent questions about exactly which structures are the most important. Then, I list nine observations that must be accounted for by any hypothesis or model of motor learning in the VOR. Finally, I discuss the implications of these observations for two models of motor learning. One model, supported by Ito (1972, 1982, this volume), proposes a single site of learning in the cerebellar cortex. The other model, suggested by Miles, Braitman et al. (1980) and Miles and Lisberger (1981) and extended by Lisberger and Sejnowski (1992), proposes a site of learning in the brainstem VOR pathways as well as one or more sites in the vestibular inputs to the cerebellar cortex.

Cellular and Molecular Mechanisms Underlying Higher Neural Functions
Edited by A.I. Selverston and P. Ascher

RELEVANT NEURAL NETWORK

Figure 4.1 summarizes the basic structures that participate in the VOR in monkeys. The most direct VOR pathway involves primary vestibular afferents, VOR interneurons in the vestibular nucleus, and extraocular motoneurons (Baker et al. 1972; Fukuda et al. 1972; Highstein 1973; Ito et al. 1977). There are two groups of VOR interneurons: PVP cells, which do not receive monosynaptic inputs from Purkinje cells in the flocculus and ventral paraflocculus, and flocculus target neurons (FTNs), which do receive monosynaptic cerebellar inputs (Lisberger and Pavelko 1988). The flocculus and ventral paraflocculus receive inputs from the vestibular system, the visual system, and the oculomotor system (Miles, Fuller et al. 1980; Gerrits and Voogd 1989; Stone and Lisberger 1990) and project directly to the brainstem (Balaban et al. 1981; Langer et al. 1985).

Until recently, we treated the flocculus and ventral paraflocculus together as a single unified structure with a single function. Our understanding of the function of these structures was based primarily on recordings from a specific group of Purkinje. However, retrospective reconstruction of the sites where these Purkinje cells have been recorded reveals that they have been studied primarily (but not exclusively) in the ventral paraflocculus. Thus, there could be a different group of Purkinje cells in the flocculus, and they could play a different role in motor learning in the VOR. Available data do not resolve this issue. Therefore, my approach in this chapter is to focus on data that exist and to seek explanations for known data.

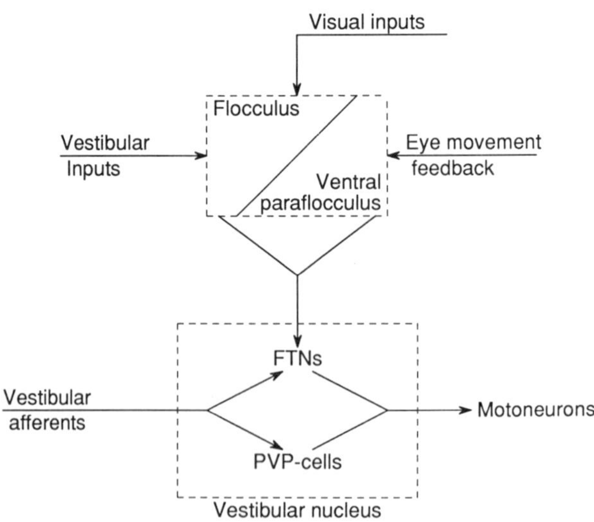

Figure 4.1 Diagram showing the basic pathways for the vestibulo-ocular reflex. Arrows show the basic flow of neural signals and the dashed boxes delimit important anatomical structures in the cerebellum (flocculus and ventral paraflocculus) and brainstem (vestibular nucleus).

OBSERVATIONS

1. The ability to undergo motor learning is abolished through bilateral ablations that include the entire cerebellar flocculus and paraflocculus in monkeys (Lisberger et al. 1984), the whole cerebellum in cats (Robinson 1976) and goldfish (Michnowitz and Bennett 1987), and the flocculus in rabbits (Nagao 1983). The use of different species and the difference in the relative sizes of the flocculus and ventral paraflocculus among the species make it impossible to deduce, at this time, whether the most important structure is the flocculus, the ventral paraflocculus, or both. These experiments demonstrate that parts of the cerebellum are required for motor learning to occur.
2. In one monkey, motor learning was retained but had a longer time course than normal after an ablation that completely removed the flocculus on both sides but spared the most rostral 3 folia of the ventral paraflocculus bilaterally (Lisberger et al. 1984). This observation shows that the ventral paraflocculus alone can support some motor learning and requires that any model of motor learning take into account the responses of the Purkinje cells recorded in the ventral paraflocculus.
3. If the relevant parts of the cerebellum are ablated after an animal has undergone learning, then the modified VOR is either partly or fully retained. In goldfish, Pastor et al. (1990) made surgical lesions of the flocculus after motor learning in the VOR and found that the transient part of the adapted VOR was remembered, but the sustained part was forgotten. In cats, Luebke and Robinson (1992) demonstrated that stimulation of the decussation of the climbing fiber pathway at 7 Hz completely inactivated the simple spikes in 95% of the Purkinje cells in the flocculus. A high or low VOR gain was remembered perfectly if this procedure was used to ablate reversibly the flocculus. These experiments demonstrate that at least some of the memory for an adapted VOR lies outside the flocculus.
4. Motor learning in the VOR is associated with clear changes in the simple spike firing of a specific group of Purkinje cells in the ventral paraflocculus and flocculus. If measured during the VOR, the changes are in the correct direction to support motor learning (Miles, Braitman et al. 1980; Watanabe 1984, 1985; Lisberger and Pavelko 1988). If measured during cancellation of the VOR, when the monkey tracks a target oscillating exactly with him, the changes are in the wrong direction to support the associated changes in the gain of the VOR (Miles, Braitman et al. 1980; Lisberger and Pavelko 1988). These data demonstrate that the output of the cerebellum supports motor learning in the VOR. This in itself creates a paradox since the changes measured during cancellation of the VOR and the changes measured during the VOR are in opposite directions and would be expected to cause contradictory changes in the gain of the VOR.
5. The Purkinje cells that express changes in their responses in association with learning include, and may be limited to, "horizontal gaze velocity Purkinje

cells" or "HGVP cells." These cells have been studied primarily in the ventral paraflocculus but have also been found in the flocculus (Lisberger and Pavelko, in prep.). Each HGVP cell has separate components of simple spike discharge related to eye and head velocity (Lisberger and Fuchs 1978a; Miles, Fuller et al. 1980; Stone and Lisberger 1990). The eye velocity component dominates P-cell firing rate during smooth pursuit eye movements with the head stationary. The head velocity component dominates the P-cell firing rate when the monkey cancels the VOR by tracking a target that moves exactly with him during head turns. The eye and head velocity components appear separately in eye movement or vestibular mossy fibers recorded in the white matter of the flocculus and ventral paraflocculus (Lisberger and Fuchs 1978b; Miles, Fuller et al. 1980). The eye velocity component of firing requires that models of the VOR include a pathway that transmits eye velocity commands as feedback to the cerebellum.

6. Motor learning in the VOR is associated with large changes in the responses of a group of brainstem neurons (FTNs) that receive monosynaptic inhibition from the flocculus and ventral paraflocculus and that are likely to be interneurons in the most direct VOR pathways (Lisberger and Pavelko 1988). The changes in the responses of FTNs are expressed during the VOR and are in the correct direction to support the associated changes in the gain of the VOR. These data identify a group of brainstem cells that plays an essential role in motor learning.
7. The VOR evoked by transient head turns starts at a latency of 14 ms after the onset of head motion. Eye movements in the first 5 ms of the response do not vary as a function of the gain of the VOR. Eye velocity traces evoked when the gain of the VOR is low, normal, and high start to separate 19 ms after the onset of head motion (Lisberger 1984). These data show that the VOR has separate modified and unmodified components and establishes that the earliest modified component is expressed 19 ms after the onset of a rapid head turn.
8. During the VOR evoked by rapid head turns, the firing rate of FTNs starts to respond at an average of 13 ms after the onset of the head motion (Lisberger and Pavelko 1988). This latency is compatible with the hypothesis that the output from FTNs is responsible for the earliest expression of motor learning in eye movements, 6 ms later. For the same stimulus conditions, the simple spike firing of HGVP cells starts to respond at an average of 23 ms after the onset of head motion (Lisberger and Pavelko 1988). This analysis shows that the responses of HGVP cells start too late after the onset of head motion to drive the shortest latency expression of the modified VOR. Therefore, there must be a site of learning outside the HGVP cells that have been studied.
9. Motor learning is expressed in the eye movements evoked by stimulation of the vestibular apparatus with single electrical pulses (Broussard et al. 1992). Eye velocity response to electrical pulses begins 5 ms after the pulse, and the eye velocity in the earliest part of the response depends on the gain of the VOR.

The short latency of these earliest eye movements does not allow enough time for vestibular inputs to be transmitted through the cerebellar cortex. Therefore, there must be a site of motor learning for the VOR that is outside the cerebellar cortex.

IMPLICATIONS FOR MODELS OF MOTOR LEARNING

Ito (1972, 1982, this volume) proposed that there is a single site of motor learning in the VOR. He suggests that learning is caused by changes in the strength of synaptic transmission between parallel fibers and Purkinje cells in the flocculus. Although the effect of motor learning on the responses of HGVP cells during the VOR is consistent with Ito's hypothesis, many of the other observations listed above contradict Ito's hypothesis. These include:

1. Motor learning in the VOR is remembered, at least partly, if the flocculus is removed after the gain of the VOR has been increased or decreased.
2. Motor learning causes changes in the responses of HGVP cells during cancellation of the VOR that are in the wrong direction to cause changes in the gain of the VOR.
3. For rapid head turns, the latency from the onset of head motion to the onset of HGVP cell responses during the VOR is too long to cause either the earliest responses of FTNs or the earliest expression of motor learning in the eye movements.
4. For electrical stimulation of the vestibular system, motor learning is expressed in the evoked eye movements only 5 ms after the stimulus, too soon to allow transmission through a site of learning in the cerebellar cortex.

Miles and Lisberger (1981) proposed a model in which there were two sites of learning for the VOR. At one site there was a change in the strength of transmission through the brainstem VOR pathways, while at the other site there was a change in the strength of the vestibular inputs to the HGVP cells. This latter site could be in the cerebellar cortex. The site of learning in the brainstem would be responsible for changing the gain of the VOR, and the site of learning in the vestibular inputs to the HGVP cells would correct cerebellar function to compensate for the changes in the brainstem. Lisberger and Sejnowski (1992) extended the model to operate on inputs that varied as a function of time and to generate outputs that varied as a function of time. In addition to the two sites of changes in the strength of transmission proposed by Miles and Lisberger (1981), Lisberger and Sejnowski (1992) found that it was possible to account for the effect of motor learning on the responses of FTNs and HGVP cells only if there were changes in the time course of the vestibular inputs to HGVP cells. In their model, changes in the time course of the cerebellar vestibular inputs work with alterations in the strength of transmission to FTNs to cause variations in the gain of the VOR, while alterations in the strength of vestibular inputs to the HGVP cells would correct cerebellar function to compensate for learning in the brainstem. All of the observations listed in the previous section are compatible with the model of Lisberger and Sejnowski (1992).

REFERENCES

Baker, R., W. Precht, and R. Llinas. 1972. Cerebellar modulatory action on the vestibulo-trochlear pathway in the cat. *Exp. Brain Res.* **15**:364–385.

Balaban, C.D., M. Ito, and E. Watanabe. 1981. Demonstration of zonal projections from the cerebellar flocculus to vestibular nuclei in monkeys (*Macaca fuscata*). *Neurosci. Lett.* **27**:101–105.

Broussard, D.M., H.M. Bronte-Stewart, and S.G. Lisberger. 1992. Expression of motor learning in the response of the primate vestibulo-ocular pathway to electrical stimulation. *J. Neurophysiol.* **67**:1493–1508.

Fuchs, A.F., and J. Kimm. 1975. Unit activity in the vestibular nucleus of the alert monkey during horizontal angular acceleration and eye movement. *J. Neurophysiol.* **38**:1140–1161.

Fukuda, J., S.M. Highstein, and M. Ito. 1972. Cerebellar inhibitory control of the vestibulo-ocular reflex investigated in rabbit IIIrd nucleus. *Exp. Brain Res.* **14**:511–526.

Gerrits, N.M., and J. Voogd. 1989. The topographical organization of climbing and mossy fiber afferents in the flocculus and the ventral paraflocculus in rabbit, cat and monkey. *Exp. Brain Res. Suppl.* **17**:26–29.

Highstein, S.M. 1973. Synaptic linkage in the vestibulo-ocular and cerebello-vestibular pathways to the VIth nucleus in the rabbit. *Exp. Brain Res.* **17**:301–314.

Ito, M. 1972. Neural design of the cerebellar motor control system. *Brain Res.* **40**:80–84.

Ito, M. 1982. Cerebellar control of the vestibulo-ocular reflex: Around the flocculus hypothesis. *Ann. Rev. Neurosci.* **5**:275–298.

Ito, M., N. Nisimaru, and M. Yamamoto. 1977. Specific patterns of neuronal connexions involved in the control of the rabbit's vestibulo-ocular reflexes by the cerebellar flocculus. *J. Physiol.* **265**:833–854.

Keller, E.L. 1978. Gain of the vestibulo-ocular reflex at high rotational frequencies. *Vision Res.* **18**:311–315.

Langer, T., A.F. Fuchs, M.C. Chubb, C.A. Scudder, and S.G. Lisberger. 1985. Floccular efferents in the rhesus macaque as revealed by autoradiography and horseradish peroxidase. *J. Comp. Neurol.* **235**:26–37.

Lisberger, S.G. 1984. The latency of pathways containing the site of motor learning in the monkey vestibulo-ocular reflex. *Science Wash. DC* **242**:74–76.

Lisberger, S.G., and A.F. Fuchs. 1978a. Role of primate flocculus during rapid behavioral modification of vestibulo-ocular reflex. I. Purkinje cell activity during visually guided horizontal smooth-pursuit eye movements and passive head rotation. *J. Neurophysiol.* **41**:733–763.

Lisberger, S.G., and A.F. Fuchs. 1978b. Role of primate flocculus during rapid behavioral modification of vestibulo-ocular reflex. II. Mossy fiber firing patterns during horizontal head rotation and eye movement. *J. Neurophysiol.* **41**:764–777.

Lisberger, S.G, F.A. Miles, and D.S. Zee. 1984. Signals used to compute errors in monkey vestibulo-ocular reflex: Possible role of flocculus. *J. Neurophysiol.* **52**:1140–1153.

Lisberger, S.G., and T.A. Pavelko. 1986. Vestibular signals carried by pathways subserving plasticity of the vestibulo-ocular reflex in monkeys. *J. Neurosci.* **6**:346–354.

Lisberger, S.G., and T.A. Pavelko. 1988. Brainstem neurons in modified pathways for motor learning in the primate vestibulo-ocular reflex. *Science* **242**:771–773.

Lisberger, S.G., and T.J. Sejnowski. 1992. Motor learning in a recurrent network model based on the vestibulo-ocular reflex. *Nature* **360**:159–161.

Luebke, A.E., and D.A. Robinson. 1992. Climbing fiber intervention blocks plasticity of the vestibulo-ocular reflex. *Ann. NY Acad. Sci.* **656**:428–431.

Michnovicz, J.J., and M.V.L. Bennett. 1987. Effects of rapid cerebellectomy on adaptive gain control of the vestibulo-ocular reflex in alert goldfish. *Exp. Brain Res.* **66**:287–294.

Miles, F.A., D.J. Braitman, and B.M. Dow. 1980. Long-term adaptive changes in primate vestibulo-ocular reflex. IV. Electrophysiological observations in flocculus of adapted monkeys. *J. Neurophysiol.* **43**:1477–1493.

Miles, F.A., and B.B. Eighmy. 1980. Long-term adaptive changes in primate vestibulo-ocular reflex. I. Behavioral observations. *J. Neurophysiol.* **43**:1406–1425.

Miles, F.A., and J.H. Fuller. 1974. Adaptive plasticity in the vestibulo-ocular responses of the rhesus monkey. *Brain Res.* **80**:512–516.

Miles , F.A., J.H. Fuller, D.J. Braitman, and B.M. Dow. 1980. Long-term adaptive changes in primate vestibulo-ocular reflex. III. Electrophysiological observations in flocculus of normal monkeys. *J. Neurophysiol.* **43**:1437–1476.

Miles, F.A., and S.G. Lisberger. 1981. Plasticity in the vestibulo-ocular reflex: A new hypothesis. *Ann. Rev. Neurosci.* **4**:273–299.

Nagao, S. 1983. Effects of vestibulo-cerebellar lesions upon dynamic characteristics and adaptation of vestibulo-ocular and optokinetic responses in pigmented rabbits. *Exp. Brain Res.* **53**:36–46.

Pastor, A.M., M. Weiser, S. McElligott, and R. Baker. 1990. Velocity step training of the goldfish vestibulo-ocular reflex suggests multiple sites are involved in gain modification. *Soc. Neurosci. Abstr.* **16**:1083.

Robinson, D.A. 1976. Adaptive gain control of the vestibulo-ocular reflex by the cerebellum. *J. Neurophysiol.* **39**:954–969.

Stone, L.S., and S.G. Lisberger. 1990. Visual responses of Purkinje cells in the cerebellar flocculus during smooth-pursuit eye movements in monkeys. I. Simple spikes. *J. Neurophysiol.* **63**:1241–1261.

Watanabe, E. 1984. Neuronal events correlated with long-term adaptation of the horizontal vestibulo-ocular reflex in the primate flocculus. *Brain Res.* **297**:169–174.

Watanabe, E. 1985. Role of the primate flocculus in adaptation of the vestibulo-ocular reflex. *Neurosci. Res.* **3**:20–38.

5

Plasticity of the Mature Neocortex

W. SINGER and A. ARTOLA
Max Planck Institute for Brain Research, Deutschordenstr. 46,
D–60528 Frankfurt/Main, F.R.Germany

ABSTRACT

During critical periods of early postnatal development, neocortical circuits are highly susceptible to use-dependent modifications. More recent evidence indicates that substantial changes of cortical maps can also be induced in the mature neocortex by manipulating the patterning of afferent activity. The developmental modifications consist of selective stabilization and disruption of axonal projections. The mechanisms underlying the reorganization in the adult have not yet been identified; however, it is likely that they include use-dependent, long-term changes in synaptic efficacy. Evidence for activity-dependent, long-term potentiation (LTP) and depression (LTD) is available from *in vitro* investigations of cortical slices. These indicate that use-dependent changes of synaptic gain are initiated through a surge of Ca^{2+} in the postsynaptic compartment. Available data are compatible with the view that large increases of intracellular [Ca^{2+}], such as those which result from the combined activation of ligand and voltage-gated Ca^{2+} conductances, lead to LTP, while smaller increases, such as those which result from, e.g., the activation of voltage-gated conductances alone, lead to LTD. In this chapter, we propose that the conversion of synaptic activity into gradual changes of postsynaptic [Ca^{2+}] could serve as a common mechanism for the initiation of use-dependent synaptic modifications, both in the developing and mature neocortex.

Most theories on the organization of memory processes in the mammalian brain are based on the assumption that engrams ultimately are engraved in the neocortex. Quite surprisingly, however, solid experimental evidence for use-dependent malleability of the mature neocortex has only been obtained rather recently. For decades, studies on use-dependent cortical plasticity have concentrated on the developmental paradigms that had been pioneered by Hubel and Wiesel in the visual system (Wiesel and Hubel 1963). These studies revealed a very high degree of activity-dependent malleability of thalamocortical and corticocortical connections, but they also indicated that this malleability declines with age and is by and large lost in the mature cortex. During the last ten years, however, new experimental procedures have been developed which allow the induction of use-dependent modifications in the mature neocortex. Since the mechanisms of synaptic plasticity identified in the mature neocortex have numerous features in common with those found in the developing cortex, the main issues of the developmental studies will be briefly recapitulated.

Cellular and Molecular Mechanisms Underlying Higher Neural Functions
Edited by A.I. Selverston and P. Ascher

PRINCIPAL RESULTS FROM DEVELOPMENTAL STUDIES

Most of the data on experience-dependent developmental plasticity come from studies of the mammalian visual cortex. As many of the principles discovered in this structure have subsequently been confirmed in other sensory cortices, data from the visual system alone are reviewed here.

In general, use-dependent developmental processes can be understood as an activity-dependent competition between converging afferents for synaptic contacts with their target cells. These selection processes occur while developmental processes, such as axonal sprouting, cell differentiation and synaptogenesis, are still active (Cragg 1972, 1975a, b) and therefore lead to modifications of the architecture of connections. The critical variable that determines the direction of a synaptic modification is the correlation between pre- and postsynaptic activity; positive correlations lead to consolidation while negative correlations result in disconnection (Rauschecker and Singer 1979, 1981; Frégnac et al. 1988; Stryker et al. 1990). These modifications have a high threshold, which is related to postsynaptic activation. *In vivo*, this threshold appears to be reached only if the noradrenergic projection from the locus coeruleus (Kasamatsu and Pettigrew 1976), the cholinergic projection from the basal forebrain (Bear and Singer 1986) and the serotonergic projection from the raphe nuclei (Gu and Singer 1991) are sufficiently active. These modulatory systems seem to facilitate use-dependent modifications in a synergistic way, since isolated lesions of either the cholinergic (Bear and Singer 1986) or the noradrenergic projections alone do not abolish cortical plasticity (Adrien et al. 1985; Daw et al. 1983, 1984, 1985a, b; for review see Gordon et al. 1988). The plasticity-enhancing effects of the modulatory projections are mediated by β receptors (Shirokawa and Kasamatsu 1986), M_1 receptors (Gu and Singer 1993), and 5-$HT_{1,2}$ receptors (Gu and Singer 1991), respectively. Another prerequisite to reach the threshold for synaptic modifications is the activation of NMDA receptors, as the blockage of these receptors prevents experience-dependent changes of functional connectivity (Kleinschmidt et al. 1987; Cline et al. 1987; Bear et al. 1990; for review see Collingridge and Singer 1990; Fox and Daw 1993). The interpretation of these results is complicated by the fact that blockage of NMDA receptors reduces neuronal responses to light stimuli (Fox et al. 1989; Miller et al. 1989). Therefore, the function of the NMDA receptor should not be considered solely in the context of use-dependent synaptic plasticity. Nevertheless, it appears as if the special properties of this receptor, its ability to evaluate the coincidence of pre- and postsynaptic activity, and its Ca^{2+} permeability are used for the gating of synaptic modifications, both during development (Fox and Daw 1993) and in the adult nervous system (see below). Accordingly, *in vivo* modifications can be facilitated by electrical activation of modulatory projections (Singer and Rauschecker 1982), through direct application of the neuromodulators acetylcholine and noradrenaline (Greuel et al. 1988), or through direct activation of postsynaptic neurons with excitatory amino acids (Greuel et al. 1988) or potassium ions (Frégnac et al. 1988). The neuromodulators could act in several ways: (a) they could reduce K^+ conductances and thereby enhance the depolarizing response of the postsynaptic neuron, (b) they could enhance the sensitivity of glutamate receptors via second messenger cascades (e.g., Markram and Segal 1992), and (c) they could directly influence the second messenger cascades that mediate use-dependent synaptic modifications (for a review, see Singer 1990). The NMDA receptors could contribute (a) by amplifying the depolarizing responses, since they contribute substantially to excitatory transmission in the neocortex (Tsumoto et al. 1987; Miller et al. 1989), and (b) by injecting Ca^{2+} ions into the cell. In conclusion, these results identify the level of postsynaptic depolarization as a crucial variable for the induction of synaptic modifications. In addition, they assign an important role to the activation of NMDA receptor-gated conductances.

Most of the developmental modifications described so far can be accounted for by assuming two rules. First, the synaptic connections that win in competition are those which succeed in activating their respective NMDA receptor-gated conductances, which requires coincidence between presynaptic activation and strong postsynaptic depolarization. Second, synapses weaken and tend to become disconnected if they are inactive and therefore cannot activate their respective NMDA receptors during episodes when the postsynaptic cell is activated by other inputs. For this "heterosynaptic" weakening of connections to occur, active inputs must generate strong postsynaptic depolarization. Under normal *in vivo* conditions, the required level of depolarization seems to be reached only if the active inputs can activate NMDA receptors and if the neuromodulators are present (for a review, see Singer 1990). A possible scenario is that the strong increase of $[Ca^{2+}]$, which occurs at postsynaptic sites of active inputs and results from the activation of both NMDA receptor- and voltage-gated Ca^{2+} channels, leads to the strengthening and consolidation of the respective synapses, while the more moderate increase of $[Ca^{2+}]$, which occurs at inactive synapses when cells are strongly depolarized and results from voltage-gated conductances and/or release from intracellular stores, causes a reduction of synaptic efficacy and eventually disconnection. This interpretation accounts well for the available *in vivo* results on experience-dependent developmental changes. The implication that synapses need not be active to undergo repression concurs with the finding that silencing completely the afferents from one eye through intraocular TTX injection does not prevent these afferents from becoming disconnected (Greuel et al. 1987). The involvement of NMDA receptors in the strengthening and consolidation of synaptic connections is suggested by the observation that blockade of NMDA receptors prevents the recovery from monocular deprivation after reverse suture (Gu et al. 1989). Finally, this scenario is also compatible with the somewhat unexpected finding that active inputs undergo depression if postsynaptic cells are silenced by application of muscimol (Reiter and Stryker 1988) or high doses of APV (Bear et al. 1990). The calcium hypothesis also agrees with Lisman's (1989) suggestion for a dual role of calcium in use-dependent synaptic plasticity and is in line with recent *in vitro* studies on synaptic modifications in mature neocortex (see below).

In conclusion, the developmental changes in connectivity that occur postnatally have features characteristic of learning processes: they are use-dependent, follow an associative correlation rule, and are gated by modulatory systems whose activity is related to arousal and attention.

USE-DEPENDENT MODIFICATIONS OF SENSORY REPRESENTATIONS IN THE MATURE NEOCORTEX

Initially, investigations of activity-dependent plasticity in the mature neocortex employed the same paradigms as the developmental studies. They exploited the notion that use-dependent rearrangements depend on competition and on the temporal correlation between the activation patterns of converging afferents. However, in agreement with Hubel and Wiesel's definition of a critical period, standard deprivation paradigms were rather ineffective in the mature visual cortex. Major modifications of cortical response properties were only observed when (a) monocular deprivation was preceded by dark rearing (Cynader and Mitchell 1980; Mower et al. 1985), (b) sensory experience was manipulated in a way which led to behaviorally aversive conflicts between retinal signals and other sensory inputs (Singer et al. 1982), or (c) visual stimulation was paired with additional pharmacological activation of cortical neurons (Greuel et al. 1988; Frégnac et al. 1988; Frégnac et al. 1992; Shulz and Frégnac 1992).

The first indications that cortical representations can also undergo major modifications in the adult have been obtained from studies of the somatosensory cortex, where patches of cortex were deprived of their normal sensory input by severing peripheral nerves or by amputating digits. Neurons in the deprived cortex became responsive to stimulation of sensory surfaces adjacent to those that had been denervated (Merzenich et al. 1983, 1984, 1990). These findings were interpreted as compatible with activity-dependent competition between afferents for representational space in the cortical sheet. Such deprivation-dependent reorganization of cortical representations can occur over surprisingly large distances: up to 3.5 mm after denervation of the volar surface of the hand (Garraghty and Kaas 1991a) and over distances of 10–12 mm after a dorsal rhizotomy that led to the denervation of the entire arm representation (Pons et al. 1991). Plasticity of sensory maps has also been documented for the tonotopic organization in the auditory cortex after pharmacological lesions of the cochlea (Schwaber et al. 1992) and for the retinotopic organization of the primary visual cortex either after (a) lesions at corresponding retinal sites in the two eyes (Heinen and Skavenski 1991; Gilbert and Wiesel 1992) or (b) local lesions in one eye and enucleation of the other (Kaas et al. 1990). Finally, comparable modifications have been found for the map of muscle representations in the motor cortex of adult rats after peripheral deafferentation of selected muscle groups (Donoghue et al. 1990).

Some of these shifts in receptive fields occur immediately after silencing the input (Calford and Tweedale 1991; Byrne and Calford 1991; Merzenich et al. 1983; Gilbert and Wiesel 1992), which makes sprouting and formation of new synapses unlikely as a mechanism for these early modifications. Possibilities are that latent excitatory inputs are unmasked by a reduction of inhibition (Jacobs and Donoghue 1991) or that synapses of previously weak connections potentiate. However, other modifications, especially those involving shifts of receptive fields over large distances, appear to occur only after prolonged periods of time (Pons et al. 1991), suggesting the possibility of anatomical rearrangements.

While in some cases these changes in cortical representations appear to reflect reorganization at subcortical levels, in others they have to be attributed to adaptive processes in the cortex; in yet others they seem to be the result of changes at several levels. Receptive field modifications similar to those described at the cortical level have been observed in subcortical relay stations after denervation, both in the somatosensory and auditory system (Rhoades et al. 1987; Garraghty and Kaas 1991b; Edeline and Weinberger 1991). Evidence for cortical processes comes from observations of long-term modifications of inhibitory mechanisms in the cortex. Glutamic acid decarboxylase (GAD) immunoreactivity has been found to decrease in the visual cortex of adult primates after monocular deprivation (Hendry and Jones 1986), in the rat somatosensory cortex after hindlimb deafferentation (Warren et al. 1989) and in the barrel cortex of the adult mouse after peripheral deprivation (Welker et al. 1989). An involvement of cortical mechanisms in the delayed modifications is also suggested by the demonstration that repetitive intracortical stimulation can entrain changes of representations (Nudo et al. 1990; Spengler et al. 1992). Finally, a cortical location of compensatory processes in somatosensory cortex is likely because of the evidence that the cholinergic projection from the basal forebrain (Juliano et al. 1991; Webster et al. 1991) and the noradrenergic input from locus coeruleus (Levin et al. 1988) have a permissive role in this type of plasticity, and that local blockade of cortical NMDA receptors prevents functional reorganization of adult cat somatosensory cortex (Kano et al. 1991). These latter findings also suggest an interesting relationship with the mechanisms subserving use-dependent reorganization of representations in the developing cerebral cortex, since these processes also depend upon the activation of NMDA receptors and receptor systems for acetylcholine and noradrenaline (see above).

Long-lasting alterations of cortical receptive field properties have also been reported after more physiological modifications of the patterning of afferent activity than is obtained with denervation. Jenkins et al. (1990) found an expansion of the representation of digit tips after these had been overstimulated, and Allard et al. (1991) observed that increasing the synchrony among the activation patterns of afferents by surgically fusing adjacent digits led to the appearance of multidigit receptive fields in the somatosensory cortex of monkeys. This latter finding emphasizes the notion that temporal patterning and, in particular, the synchrony of afferent activity are important variables for the dynamic organization of cortical functions.

Finally, there are now several reports on receptive field modifications in the auditory cortex following classical conditioning procedures. Pairing of tone blips with aversive electrical stimuli produced neurons with an increased sensitivity to the frequency of the conditioned tone, if the frequency of the conditioned tone differed from the preferred frequency of the recorded neuron (Bakin and Weinberger 1990; Scheich 1991). Similar modifications, however, have already been observed at the thalamic level (Edeline and Weinberger 1991).

Following the hypothesis that correlated firing should strengthen the coupling among coherently active neurons, Ahissar et al. (1992) recently were able to demonstrate in awake behaving monkeys, that stimulation conditions leading to contingent activation of spatially separate, simultaneously recorded neurons caused an increased coupling of these neurons, as evidenced by increased correlation of their respective activities. Conversely, decorrelating the sensory stimuli led to a decrease of coupling. These modifications were transient and lasted for 10–15 min. As in the experiments on the somatosensory cortex by Jenkins et al. (1990), these changes only occurred when the animal attended to the stimuli.

EVIDENCE FOR USE-DEPENDENT MODIFICATIONS OF SYNAPTIC EFFICACY

Long-term Potentiation

Systematic search for use-dependent long-term modifications of synaptic transmission in identified pathways of the mature cortex started only after the discovery of hippocampal LTP by Bliss and Lømo (1973), roughly a decade ago. The abundant evidence on use-dependent malleability of the developing visual cortex encouraged attempts to induce LTP in this structure with tetanic stimulation, initially *in vivo* and later also in slice preparations. The results of these early experiments were difficult to interpret because they relied on field potential recordings. In the neocortex, unlike in the hippocampus, electrical activation of afferent projections usually elicits a mixture of mono- and polysynaptic responses in virtually every layer, and these responses are further complicated by inhibitory interactions with different synaptic delays. This makes it notoriously difficult to determine whether (a) an increase in the field response, which is usually a composite response, is due to an increase of synaptic gain in mono- or polysynaptic pathways, (b) it results from increased excitability of the postsynaptic target cells, or (c) it reflects a reduction of efficacy of the multiple inhibitory pathways. Consequently, some are hesitant to equate the response enhancement that was observed after tetanic stimulation in a number of studies with LTP (Komatsu et al. 1981; Lee 1982). The first demonstration of an input-specific potentiation of a monosynaptic EPSP was obtained *in vivo* in the motor cortex of adult cats by Baranyi and Feher (1981a, b). These authors demonstrated that pairing of low-frequency stimulation of the ventrolateral nucleus with either intracellular depolarization or activation of an independent converging pathway led to long-lasting potentiation of the monosynaptic EPSP evoked from VL. Later, through *in vitro* recordings from visual cortex slices, it has been shown that tetanic stimulation of white matter afferents can lead to LTP of a monosynaptic EPSP in pyramidal cells of supragranular layers (Artola and Singer

1987). Both the AMPA and NMDA receptor-mediated EPSP components can undergo LTP, and they can do so independently (Artola and Singer 1990). The pathways responsible for this monosynaptic EPSP probably include a large fraction of cortico-cortical projections that ascend from white matter and terminate on supragranular neurons. Subsequent *in vitro* and *in vivo* studies confirmed the inducibility of LTP in the visual cortex (Perkins and Teyler 1988; Komatsu et al. 1988; Kimura et al. 1989; Kossel et al. 1990; Kirkwood et al. 1992), in the motor cortex (Iriki et al. 1989, 1991; Keller et al. 1991), in the prefrontal cortex (Sutor and Hablitz 1989, for a polysynaptic response; Hirsch and Crépel 1990), in the sensorimotor cortex (Baranyi and Szente 1987; Bindman et al. 1988; Keller et al. 1990), and in the entorhinal cortex (Sah and Nicoll 1991).

The requirements for the induction of neocortical LTP closely resemble those of hippocampal LTP: (a) presynaptic activation has to occur in conjunction with strong postsynaptic depolarization and (b) the induction of cortical LTP also requires a surge of intracellular Ca^{2+} since it is blocked by chelating intracellular Ca^{2+} (Kimura et al. 1990; Yoshimora et al. 1991; Hirsch and Crépel 1992). In the neocortex, the level of depolarization required for LTP induction is reached only if (a) GABAergic inhibition is reduced (Artola and Singer 1987, 1990; Kimura et al. 1989; Hirsch and Crépel 1990; Sah and Nicoll 1991), (b) the postsynaptic neuron is depolarized with current injection during presynaptic activation (Bindman et al. 1988; Artola et al. 1990; Kossel et al. 1990; Frégnac et al. 1990), or when (c) strong stimuli are applied very close to the recorded neuron (Kirkwood et al. 1992). However, when potentiation was induced with low-frequency pairing it tended to decay within 15–20 min. As in the hippocampus (Malinow and Miller 1986) hyperpolarization of the postsynaptic neuron prevents tetanus-induced LTP (Keller et al. 1991), and in the case of low-frequency pairing, it can even lead to depression (Frégnac et al. 1990). In most situations, induction of LTP is also abolished by pharmacologically blocking NMDA receptors (Artola and Singer 1987, 1990; Kimura et al. 1989; Sah and Nicoll 1991). This is to be expected since activation of NMDA receptors enhances not only the depolarizing responses of cortical neurons but also the increase of intracellular $[Ca^{2+}]$. With certain stimulation regimens, however, LTP can be induced even when NMDA receptors are blocked (Komatsu et al. 1991; Bear et al. 1992). These stimulation regimens and preparations have in common that they guarantee strong postsynaptic responses and/or activation of voltage-gated Ca^{2+} conductances, even when NMDA receptors do not contribute to excitatory transmission (Komatsu and Iwakiri 1992). Some of these experiments have been performed in slices of young animals in which the conditions for LTP induction appear to be more favorable (see below). Finally, in both neocortical and hippocampal LTP, the AMPA- and the NMDA receptor-mediated EPSP components can undergo LTP, whereby the induction threshold for the potentiation of the NMDA receptor-mediated EPSP is lower than that of the AMPA receptor-mediated component (Artola and Singer 1990).

Relations between neocortical LTP and developmental plasticity are suggested by two observations. First, the thresholds for the induction of synaptic modifications are lower in slices of young as opposed to adult animals (Komatsu et al. 1981; Perkins and Teyler 1988; Kato et al. 1991), whereby the period of enhanced LTP susceptibility coincides roughly with the critical period for developmental changes. Second, cholinergic and noradrenergic agonists facilitate LTP induction in the mature cortex in the same synergistic way as they facilitate developmental changes (see above and Bröcher et al. 1992a). The greater susceptibility of young cortices to undergo LTP is most likely due to the greater contribution of NMDA receptor-gated conductances to excitatory transmission in young animals (Tsumoto et al. 1987; Fox et al. 1989, 1992; Kato et al. 1991). In young animals, NMDA receptors have different gating characteristics (Hestrin 1992; Carmignoto and Vicini 1992) and are more numerous (Bode-Greuel and Singer 1989). Another contributing factor may be the higher density of voltage-gated Ca^{2+} channels in young animals (Bode-Greuel and Singer 1988). $[Ca^{2+}]$ measurements in slices of the visual cortex have revealed substantial developmental changes in stimulation-dependent Ca^{2+} fluxes from extra- to intracellular space (Bode-Greuel and Singer 1991). The facilitation of LTP by cholinergic and noradrenergic agonists is most likely due to the fact that these compounds enhance the depolarizing response to the tetanus and thereby increase the activation of NMDA receptor-gated conductances to this response (Bröcher et al. 1992a). However, one must also consider the more direct influences on second messenger cascades involved in LTP induction.

Long-term Depression

The first demonstration of a use-dependent weakening of synaptic transmission in the neocortex that fulfilled the criteria established for long-term depression (LTD), i.e., the input-specific reduction of monosynaptic EPSPs in the absence of changes in input resistance and inhibition, came from experiments on slices of adult rat visual cortex (Artola et al. 1990). In these experiments, LTD was demonstrated for the monosynaptic EPSP which occurs in supragranular cells after stimulation of white matter. LTD has also been reproduced by several groups in the visual (Kimura et al. 1990; Kirkwood et al. 1992) and prefrontal cortex (Hirsch and Crépel 1990; 1991). It was found that the induction of LTD required postsynaptic depolarization since it could be blocked by hyperpolarizing the postsynaptic neuron during the inducing tetanus. The required depolarization, however, was less than that necessary for the induction of LTP (Artola et al. 1990). Accordingly, stimulation protocols that fail to induce LTP can still induce LTD. Thus, LTD was found to be readily inducible without disinhibition (Artola et al. 1990), with low-frequency stimulation (Kirkwood et al. 1992) and even when NMDA receptors are blocked (Artola et al. 1990; Hirsch and Crépel 1991).

Interestingly, the induction of LTD is blocked by buffering intracellular calcium (Bröcher et al. 1992b; Hirsch and Crépel 1992; but see Kimura et al. 1990; Yoshimura et al. 1991), which indicates that it requires a surge of intracellular $[Ca^{2+}]$ just as is the case for LTP. This is supported by the recent finding that high extracellular Ca^{2+} facilitates tetanus-induced LTD. High frequency subthreshold activation of a presynaptic input, which by itself is not sufficient to induce LTD, caused input-specific depression when applied during high Ca^{2+} (Artola et al. 1992). But the increase of $[Ca^{2+}]_i$ required for LTD appears to be smaller than that necessary for LTP. This is suggested by the finding that partial buffering of intracellular calcium prevents induction of LTP but not of LTD (Bröcher et al. 1992b). The recently published result that calcium buffering leads to the induction of LTD does not contradict this result, because there are reasons to believe that Ca^{2+} buffering was incomplete in these experiments (Kimura et al. 1990; Yoshimura et al. 1991). The assumption that induction of LTD requires a less pronounced increase of intracellular Ca^{2+} than induction of LTP also concurs with the observations that LTD is inducible with less depolarization than LTD, and even after blockade of NMDA receptor-gated Ca^{2+} conductances, which are particularly effective in raising intracellular Ca^{2+} (MacDermott et al. 1986).

LTD can also be induced without synaptic activation by exposing slices of the rat visual cortex transiently to high extracellular calcium concentrations (4 mM) (Artola et al. 1992). After return to normal calcium levels, monosynaptic excitatory EPSPs are depressed in the absence of changes in membrane potential and input resistance. This Ca^{2+}-induced depression can be prevented by hyperpolarizing the cells during the Ca^{2+} pulse, excluding direct effects of high calcium on presynaptic mechanisms as a cause for the depression. Hence, the depression appears to be initiated by a calcium-dependent process in the postsynaptic neuron. This Ca^{2+}-induced depression is apparently due to similar mechanisms as the tetanus-induced homosynaptic depression, because it occludes the latter (Artola et al. 1992).

The notion that cortical synapses can undergo LTD irrespective of whether they are active or inactive if $[Ca^{2+}]$ in the postsynaptic compartment reaches a critical level accounts also for the phenomenon of heterosynaptic depression. In the motor cortex (Bindman et al. 1988), prefrontal cortex (Hirsch et al. 1992), and visual cortex (Artola, in prep.), strong activation of an input can depress other inputs converging on the same neuron. This heterosynaptic form of depression resembles the heterosynaptic depression that has been demonstrated in the hippocampus after similar activation conditions (for a review, see Artola and Singer 1993).

Taken together, these results suggest that a moderate increase of calcium concentration in the postsynaptic cell leads to a depression of synaptic transmission. It seems to be irrelevant whether the increase of calcium is caused by activity of the input that undergoes depression (homosynaptic LTD) or by other conditions (heterosynaptic LTD). In the former case, the depression is input specific; in the latter it is not.

THE RELATIONSHIP BETWEEN LTP AND LTD

It is now possible to relate the initial finding of two different voltage-dependent thresholds for LTD and LTP (Artola et al. 1990) to corresponding changes of intracellular calcium. The inductions of LTD and LTP both require an increase of intracellular calcium; at least part of the calcium surge appears to result from calcium influx. For the induction of LTP, very high calcium concentrations have to be reached, and for most stimulation protocols this requires activation of NMDA receptor-gated calcium conductances. By contrast, LTD appears to be readily inducible with calcium increases that can be obtained in the absence of NMDA receptor activation and result, most likely, from influx through voltage-gated calcium channels and/or from release by intracellular stores. Since ligand-gated calcium conductances are usually not required to reach the calcium concentrations necessary for LTD, depression can readily occur at inactive synapses as, for example, in heterosynaptic depression. In this case, it is likely that either voltage-gated calcium channels are activated in the vicinity of the synapses which get depressed or that calcium concentrations increase due to propagating calcium waves. However, calcium entering through NMDA receptor-gated channels can also contribute to the induction of LTD. In the visual cortex, homosynaptic LTD can be induced with very low stimulation frequencies and, in this case, LTD induction is prevented by blockade of NMDA receptors (Kirkwood et al. 1992). Thus, it is the *level* rather than the *origin* of the calcium surge in the vicinity of the modifiable synapse that appears to be the critical variable determining whether the synapse potentiates or depresses. This is further supported by evidence from the hippocampus that LTP can also be induced in the absence of NMDA receptor-activation by raising intracellular Ca^{2+} (see Nicoll et al., this volume). In the neocortex, it has proven difficult so far to induce LTP with high Ca^{2+} alone; this is in line with the evidence that it is more difficult to reach the LTP threshold in the cortex than in the hippocampus.

These considerations, however, do not imply that the origin of Ca^{2+} is also irrelevant under physiological activation conditions. The NMDA receptor-gated channels, the voltage-controlled calcium channels, and the intracellular release sites are associated with different cellular compartments and are probably not distributed homogeneously. Thus, if what matters is the absolute concentration of Ca^{2+} at a particular effector enzyme, the effect of the various Ca^{2+} sources will depend very much upon the relative locations of release and effector sites. All available evidence, both from the hippocampus and neocortex, indicates that NMDA receptor-gated Ca^{2+} conductances are the most effective source for the Ca^{2+} surge required for LTP induction. Consequently, the induction threshold for LTP has often been related to the activation threshold of NMDA receptors. Moreover, activation of NMDA receptors tends to override the effects of Ca^{2+} provided by other sources, thereby protecting synapses from becoming depressed. As mentioned before, transient exposure to high Ca^{2+} leads to depression of inputs to cells if these are sufficiently depolarized. However, if during the Ca^{2+} pulse a subset of inputs is additionally activated with a weak tetanus, these inputs do not undergo depression; they remain unchanged or may even get potentiated (Artola et al. 1992). The most likely explanation is that synaptic activation led to additional calcium entry at the activated synapses, both through voltage- and NMDA receptor-gated calcium channels, and that this additional rise of calcium reached the threshold of the LTP mechanism, thereby antagonizing the development of LTD. A mechanism by which different Ca^{2+} concentrations could exert opposite effects on synaptic efficacy has been proposed by Lisman (1989). He suggested that low $[Ca^{2+}]_i$ could lead to selective activation of enzyme systems with high Ca^{2+} affinity while high $[Ca^{2+}]_i$ could preferentially activate enzymes with low affinity.

In summary, the available evidence on cortical LTP and LTD suggests that both modifications require a surge of postsynaptic Ca^{2+} and that the amplitude of the surge rather than its cause determines the sign of the synaptic change. This predicts that all the signaling systems which can influence ligand- and voltage-gated Ca^{2+} conductances and the release of intracellular calcium should contribute to the regulation of the thresholds for LTD and LTP induction. These signaling systems include both excitatory and inhibitory synaptic inputs as well as a host of modulatory transmitter systems, but none appear to be specific for the induction of either LTP or LTD. Depending on their relative efficacy to contribute to the Ca^{2+} surge, some signaling cascades may actually turn out to be more effective for the induction of LTP, such as the NMDA receptor, while others, such as voltage-gated Ca^{2+} channels, may be more suitable for the induction of LTD.

CONCLUDING REMARKS

The results reviewed in this chapter reveal a high degree of use-dependent plasticity in the mature neocortex. This agrees with the commonly accepted notion that the neocortex serves functions such as memory and learning and that corticalization is one of the major reasons for the increase of adaptivity in highly developed organisms. However, it was quite unexpected to find such a high degree of plasticity already at the level of primary sensory areas. For a long time it has been held that these areas are malleable only during early development and do not support adaptive functions such as learning in the adult. It is only recently that models on cortical processing no longer consider primary sensory cortices as relay stations with fixed properties but emphasize the distributed nature of cortical operations, the importance of reciprocal bottom-up and top-down interactions, and assign similar functions to all cortical areas. Hence, use-dependent long-term modifications of synaptic transmission should also occur at the level of primary sensory cortices.

This postulate agrees with recent psychophysical evidence, which suggests that forms of perceptual learning occur as early as in the primary visual cortex (Poggio et al. 1992; Karni and Sagi 1991). The time course of these modifications was very slow, several days of training being required before perceptual changes became manifest. Thus, if they occur under natural conditions, LTP and LTD might be more closely related to sensory adaptation phenomena, which are rapidly induced and reversible. It is also conceivable that LTP and LTD only represent the first step in the transformation of electrical activity to lasting changes of synaptic gain, and that only the later steps in the cascade of events lead to modifications in transmission large enough to be measurable with behavioral techniques.

The *in vitro* analysis of use-dependent synaptic modifications in the visual cortex has revealed the coexistence of mechanisms for homosynaptic LTD and LTP in the same neuron and probably in the same synapses. Postsynaptic depolarization and $[Ca^{2+}]$ have been identified as the most important control parameters for the direction of the gain change. These variables depend on the state of other converging excitatory and inhibitory inputs and, because of the involvement of the NMDA receptor, also on the temporal coincidence between pre- and postsynaptic activation. Modifications are, therefore, associative and depend on the cooperativity of converging inputs. They differ substantially, however, in their effect from modifications predicted by the classical Hebb rule, in that they include a negative term (see Figure 5.1). Recently, the conditions identified by Artola et al. (1990) for the induction of LTD and LTP have been formalized and implemented as a synaptic modification rule (the ABS rule) in an associative neuronal network (Hancock et al. 1991). These simulations revealed that the ABS rule is more powerful than previously implemented rules for synaptic modification because it allows for error correction, for the learning of exceptions, and for a very effective orthogonalization of representations in associative neuronal networks. As reviewed elsewhere (Collingridge and Singer 1990; Singer 1990) this

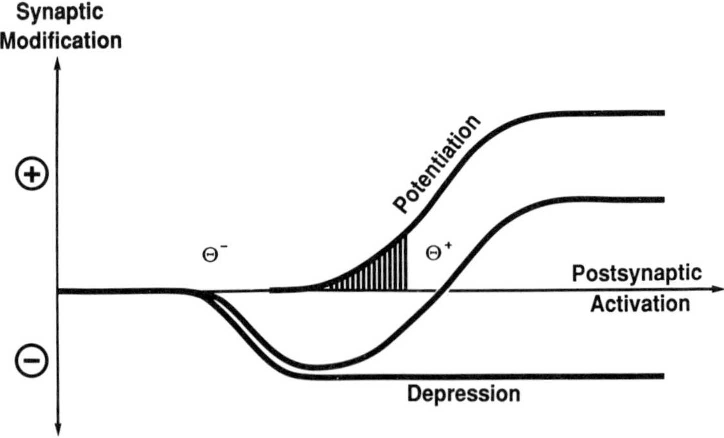

Figure 5.1 Schematic representation of the two different voltage-dependent thresholds (Θ^- and Θ^+) for the induction of homosynaptic LTD and LTP. The ordinate indicates the direction of the synaptic gain change and the abscissa the membrane potential level of the postsynaptic neuron that is maintained during presynaptic activation. If the first threshold, Θ^-, is reached a mechanism is activated which leads to a long-lasting depression of synaptic efficacy. If the second threshold, Θ^+, is reached, another process is triggered that leads to the potentiation of the synapse.

rule accounts also for most of the experience-dependent changes of cortical functions that have been observed during early development. Considering the numerous similarities between the mechanisms of developmental and adult plasticity, it appears likely that homosynaptic LTD and LTP and heterosynaptic LTD (Figure 5.2) actually constitute the initial steps in a chain of events that eventually leads to the experience-dependent modifications of the functional architecture of neocortex during development. On theoretical grounds, Bienenstock et al. (1982) postulated a synaptic modification rule, the BCM rule, to account for experience-dependent developmental changes in the visual cortex. This rule closely resembles the ABS rule in that it also assumes weakening of synapses with weak and strengthening of synapses with strong activation; however, it differs from the ABS rule in that it does not assume a threshold for LTD and uses, as the activation parameter, the product of presynaptic and postsynaptic activity which excludes changes at inactive synapses. Recent simulation studies that were based on rather realistic biological assumptions confirmed that this rule can also account for a large number of use-dependent developmental modifications in the visual cortex (Clothiaux et al. 1991).

Because of the associative nature of cortical LTP and LTD it is also likely that these use-dependent synaptic modifications are the substrate for the experience-dependent modifications of response properties observed in the mature neocortex *in vivo* (see above). The evidence that both LTP *in vitro* and the receptive field modifications *in vivo* are facilitated by the neuromodulators noradrenaline and acetylcholine and by activation of NMDA receptors supports this conjecture.

As to the processes that follow the increase of intracellular calcium and eventually lead to LTD and LTP, much less is known for the neocortex than for the hippocampus and cerebellum. As far as they are known, the conditions for the induction of neocortical LTP and LTD resemble closely those of the corresponding modifications in hippocampus and cerebellum, suggesting similarities of mechanisms. However, the expression of these mechanisms apparently differs in different cell types and structures as, e.g., LTP does not seem to be inducible in Purkinjie cells in the same way as it is in the cortex and hippocampus, and LTD is less easily induced in hippocampus than in neocortex.

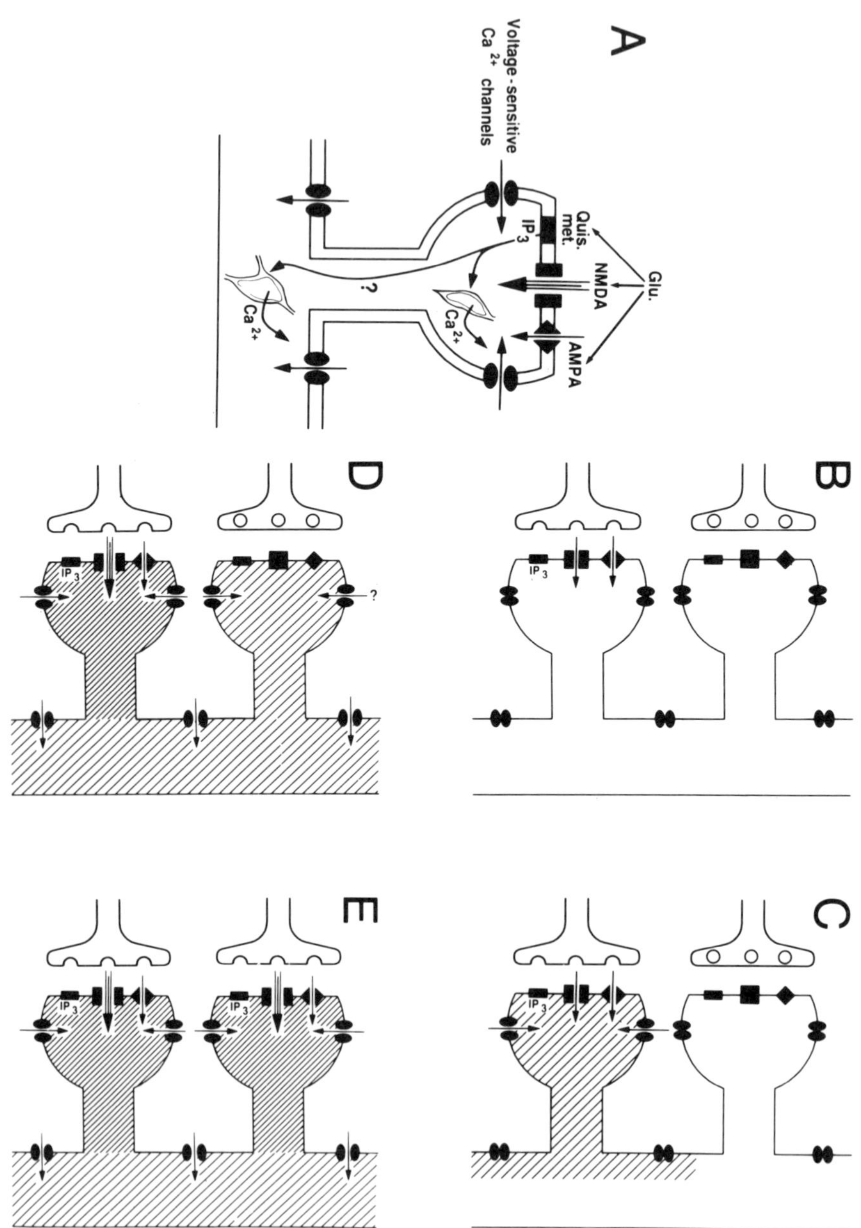
A
Glu.
Quis.
met.
NMDA
AMPA
IP3
Voltage-sensitive
Ca 2+ channels
Ca 2+
Ca 2+
?
B
IP3
C
IP3
D
IP3
?
E
IP3
IP3

REFERENCES

Adrien, J., G. Blanc, P. Buisseret, Y. Frégnac, E. Gary-Bobo, M. Imbert, J.P. Tasson, and Y. Trotter. 1985. Noradrenaline and functional plasticity in kitten visual cortex: A reexamination. *J. Physiol.* **367**:73–98.

Ahissar, E., E. Vaadia, M. Ahissar, H. Bergman, A. Arieli, and M. Abeles. 1992. Dependence of cortical plasticity on correlated activity of single neurons and on behavioral context. *Science* **257**:1412–1415.

Allard, T., S.A. Clark, W.M. Jenkins, and M.M. Merzenich. 1991. Reorganization of somatosensory area 3b representations in adult owl monkeys after digital syndactyly. *J. Neurophysiol.* **66**:1048–1058.

Artola, A., S. Bröcher, and W. Singer. 1990. Different voltage-dependent thresholds for inducing long-term depression and long-term potentiation in slices of rat visual cortex. *Nature* **347**:69–72.

Artola, A., T. Hensch, and W. Singer. 1992. A rise of [Ca^{2+}] in the postsynaptic cell is necessary and sufficient for the induction of long-term depression (LTD) in neocortex. *Soc. Neurosci. Abstr.* **18**:567.30.

Figure 5.2 Schematic representation of the suggested role of intracellular calcium in use-dependent synaptic modifications. (A) Summary of ligand- and voltage-gated mechanisms that modulate calcium concentration in the postsynaptic dendritic compartment. (B) to (E): Homo- and heterosynaptic modifications of synaptic transmission for two inputs terminating on spines of the same dendritic segment. Mechanisms influencing intracellular calcium concentration are indicated by symbols as in A. Arrows indicate calcium fluxes and their number the amplitude of the flux. The density of the hatching in the postsynaptic compartment is meant to reflect the expected concentration increase of intracellular calcium. In (B) to (D), only the lower input is assumed to be active while in (E) both inputs are simultaneously active. The four conditions differ in addition by the amplitude of the depolarizing responses of the postsynaptic dendrite. It is assumed that this amplitude is determined both by the activity of the modifiable synapses and by the state of the many other excitatory, inhibitory, and modulatory inputs to the same dendritic compartment (not shown). (B) AMPA, NMDA, and metabotropic quisqualate receptors are only moderately activated, voltage-gated calcium conductances are inactive. There is no substantial rise of intracellular calcium and no lasting modification of synaptic transmission at the active synapse. (C) In addition to the activation condition in (B), voltage-gated calcium conductances in the dendritic spine are also activated. Postsynaptic calcium rises to an intermediate level and induces LTD of the active synapse. There is only little spread of calcium from the active spine to other dendritic compartments. (D) Activation causes more postsynaptic depolarization than in (B) and (C); accordingly, NMDA receptor-gated conductances and voltage-gated calcium channels are strongly activated. The massive increase of calcium in the activated spine leads to LTP. Moreover, depolarization spreads to other compartments of the dendrite where it activates voltage-gated conductances. This leads to an intermediate rise of calcium also at the postsynasptic side of the inactive synapse which therefore undergoes heterosynaptic depression. (E) The second input is now activated as well. It no longer undergoes LTD but becomes potentiated as well because the rise of calcium in the postsynaptic compartment is now sufficient for the induction of LTP.

Artola, A., and W. Singer. 1987. Long-term potentiation and NMDA receptors in rat visual cortex. *Nature* **330**:649–652.

Artola, A., and W. Singer. 1990. The involvement of N-methyl-D-aspartate receptors in induction and maintenance of long-term potentiation in rat visual cortex. *Eur. J. Neurosci.* **2**:254–269.

Artola, A., and W. Singer. 1993. Long-term depression in the mammalian central nervous system: A reappraisal. *Trends Neurosci.*, in press.

Bakin, J.S., and N.M. Weinberger. 1990. Classical conditioning induces CS-specific receptive field plasticity in the auditory cortex of the guinea pig. *Brain Res.* **536**:271–286.

Baranyi, A., and O. Feher. 1981a. Long-term facilitation of excitatory synaptic transmission in single motor cortical neurones of the cat produced by repetitive pairing of synaptic potentials and action potentials following intracellular stimulation. *Neurosci. Lett.* **23**:303–308.

Baranyi, A., and O. Feher. 1981b. Synaptic facilitation requires paired activation of convergent pathways in the neocortex. *Nature* **290**:413–415.

Baranyi, A., and M.B. Szente. 1987. Long-lasting potentiation of synaptic transmission requires postsynaptic modifications in the neocortex. *Brain Res.* **423**:378–384.

Bear, M.F., A. Kleinschmidt, Q. Gu, and W. Singer. 1990. Disruption of experience-dependent synaptic modifications in striate cortex by infusion of an NMDA receptor antagonist. *J. Neurosci.* **10**:909–925.

Bear, M.F., W.A. Press, and B.W. Connors. 1992. Long-term potentiation in slices of kitten visual cortex and the effects of NMDA receptor blockade. *J. Neurophysiol.* **67**:841–851.

Bear, M.F., and W. Singer. 1986. Modulation of visual cortical plasticity by acetylcholine and noradrenaline. *Nature* **320**:172–176.

Bienenstock, E.L., L.N. Cooper, and P.W. Munro. 1982. Theory for the development of neuron selectivity: Orientation specificity and binocular interaction in visual cortex. *J. Neurosci.* **2**:32–48.

Bindman, L.J., K.P.S.J. Murphy, and S. Pockett. 1988. Postsynaptic control of the induction of long-term changes in efficacy of transmission at neocortical synapses in slices of rat brain. *J. Neurophysiol.* **60**:1053–1065.

Bliss, T.V.P., and T. Lømo. 1973. Long-lasting potentiation of synaptic transmission in the dentate area of the anaesthetized rabbit following stimulation of the perforant path. *J. Physiol.* **232**:331–356.

Bode-Greuel, K.M., and W. Singer. 1988. Developmental changes of the distribution of binding sites for organic Ca^{2+}-channel blockers in cat visual cortex. *Exp. Brain Res.* **70**:266–275.

Bode-Greuel, K.M., and W. Singer. 1989. The development of N-methyl-D-aspartate receptors in cat visual cortex. *Devel. Brain Res.* **46**:197–204.

Bode-Greuel, K.M., and Singer, W. 1991. Developmental changes of calcium currents in the visual cortex of the cat. *Exp. Brain Res.* **84**:311–318.

Bröcher, S., A. Artola, and W. Singer. 1992a. Agonists of cholinergic and noradrenergic receptors facilitate synergistically the induction of long-term potentiation in slices of rat visual cortex. *Brain Res.* **573**:27–36.

Bröcher, S., A. Artola, and W. Singer. 1992b. Intracellular injection of Ca^{2+} chelators blocks induction of long-term depression in rat visual cortex. *Proc. Natl. Acad. Sci. USA* **89**:123–127.

Byrne, J.A., and M.B. Calford. 1991. Short-term expansion of receptive fields in rat primary somatosensory cortex after hindpaw digit denervation. *Brain Res.* **565**:218–224.

Calford, M.B., and R. Tweedale. 1991. Immediate expansion of receptive fields of neurons in area 3b of macaque monkeys after digit denervation. *Somatosens. Motor Res.* **8**:249–260.

Carmignoto, G., and S. Vicini. 1992. Activity-dependent decrease in NMDA receptor responses during development of the visual cortex. *Science* **258**:1007–1011.

Cline, H.T., E.A. Debski, and M. Constantine-Paton. 1987. N-methyl-D-aspartate receptor antagonist desegregates eye-specific stripes. *Proc. Natl. Acad. Sci. USA* **84**:4332–4335.

Clothiaux, E.E., M.F. Bear, and L.M. Cooper. 1991. Synaptic plasticity in visual cortex: Comparison of theory with experiment. *J. Neurophysiol.* **66**:1785–1804.

Collingridge, G.L., and W. Singer. 1990. Excitatory amino acid receptors and synaptic plasticity. *Trends Pharmacol. Sci.* **11**:290–296.

Cragg, B.G. 1972. The development of synapses in cat visual cortex. *Invest. Ophth.* **11**:377–385.

Cragg, B.G. 1975a. The development of synapses in kitten visual cortex during visual deprivation. *Exp. Neurol.* **46**:445–451.

Cragg, B.G. 1975b. The development of synapses in the visual system of the cat. *J. Comp. Neurol.* **160**:147–166.

Cynader, M., and D.E. Mitchell. 1980. Prolonged sensitivity to monocular deprivation in dark-reared cats. *J. Neurophysiol.* **43**:1026–1054.

Daw, N.W., R.K. Rader, T.W. Robertson, and M. Ariel. 1983. Effects of 6-hydroxydopamine on visual deprivation in the kitten striate cortex. *J. Neurosci.* **3**:907–914.

Daw, N.W., T.W. Robertson, R.K. Rader, T.O. Videen, and C.J. Coscia. 1984. Substantial reduction of noradrenaline by lesions of adrenergic pathway does not prevent effects of monocular deprivation. *J. Neurosci.* **4**:1354–1360.

Daw, N.W., T.O. Videen, D. Parkinson, and R.K. Rader. 1985a. DSP–4 depletes noradrenaline in kitten visual cortex without altering the effects of monocular deprivation. *J. Neurosci.* **5**:1925–1933.

Daw, N.W., T.O. Videen, R.K. Rader, T.W. Robertson, and C.J. Coscia. 1985b. Substantial reduction of noradrenaline in kitten visual cortex by intraventricular injections of 6-hydroxydopamine does not always prevent ocular dominance shifts after monocular deprivation. *Exp. Brain Res.* **59**:30–35.

Donoghue, J.P., S. Suner, and J.N. Sanes. 1990. Dynamic organization of primary motor cortex output to target muscles in adult rats. II. Rapid reorganization following motor nerve lesions *Exp. Brain Res.* **79**:492–503.

Edeline, J.M., and N.M. Weinberger. 1991. Thalamic short-term plasticity in the auditory system: Associative retuning of receptive fields in the ventral medial geniculate body. *Behav. Neurosci.* **105**:618–639.

Fox, K., and N.W. Daw. 1993. Do NMDA receptors have a critical function in visual cortical plasticity? *Trends Neurosci.* **16**:116–122.

Fox, K., N. Daw, H. Sato, and D. Czepita. 1992. The effect of visual experience on development of NMDA receptor synaptic transmission in kitten visual cortex. *J. Neurosci.* **12**:2672–2684.

Fox, K., Sato, H., and N. Daw. 1989. The location and function of NMDA receptors in cat and kitten visual cortex. *J. Neurosci.* **9**:2443–2454.

Frégnac, Y., D. Shulz, E. Bienenstock, and S. Thorpe. 1992. Cellular analogs of visual cortical epigenesis. I. Plasticity of orientation selectivity. *J. Neurosci.* **12**:1280–1300.

Frégnac, Y., D. Shulz, S. Thorpe, and E. Bienenstock. 1988. A cellular analogue of visual cortical plasticity. *Nature* **333**:367–370.

Frégnac, Y., D. Smith, and M.J. Friedlander. 1990. Postsynaptic membrane potential regulates synaptic potentiation and depression in visual cortical neurons. *Soc. Neurosci. Abstr.* **16**:798.

Garraghty, P.E., and J.H. Kaas. 1991a. Functional reorganization in adult monkey thalamus after peripheral nerve injury. *NeuroReport* **2**:747–750.

Garraghty, P.E., and J.H. Kaas. 1991b. Large scale functional reorganization in adult monkey cortex after peripheral nerve injury. *Proc. Natl. Acad. Sci. USA* **88**:6976–6980.

Gilbert, C.D., and T.N. Wiesel. 1992. Receptive field dynamics in adult primary visual cortex. *Nature* **356**:150–152.

Gordon, B., E.E. Allen, and P.Q. Trombey. 1988. The role of norepinephrine in plasticity of visual cortex. *Prog. Neurobiol.* **30**:171–191.

Greuel, J.M., H.J. Luhmann, and W. Singer. 1987. Evidence for a threshold in experience-dependent long-term changes of kitten visual cortex. *Devel. Brain Res.* **34**:141–149.

Greuel, J.M., H.J. Luhmann, and W. Singer. 1988. Pharmacological induction of use-dependent receptive field modifications in the visual cortex. *Science* **242**:74–77.

Gu, Q., M.F. Bear, and W. Singer. 1989. Blockade of NMDA receptors prevents ocularity changes in kitten visual cortex after reversed monocular deprivation. *Devel. Brain Res.* **47**:281–288.

Gu, Q., and W. Singer. 1991. Involvement of serotonin in neuronal plasticity of kitten visual cortex. *IBRO Abstr.* **3**:47.7.

Gu, Q., and W. Singer. 1993. Effects of intracortical infusion of anticholinergic drugs on neuronal plasticity in kitten striate cortex. *Eur. J. Neurosci.* **5**:475–485.

Hancock, P.J.B., L.S. Smith, and W.A. Phillips. 1991. A biologically supported error correcting learning rule. *Neural Comp.* **3**:201–212.

Heinen, S.J., and A.A. Skavenski. 1991. Recovery of visual responses in foveal V1 neurons following bilateral foveal lesions in adult monkey. *Exp. Brain Res.* **83**:670–674.

Hendry, S.H.C., and E.G. Jones. 1986. Reduction in a number of immunostained GABAergic neurones in deprived-eye dominance columns in monkey area 17. *Nature* **320**:750–753.

Hestrin, S. 1992. Developmental regulation of NMDA receptor-mediated synaptic currents at a central synapse. *Nature* **357**:686–689.

Hirsch, J.C., G. Barrionuevo, and F. Crépel. 1992. Homo- and heterosynaptic changes in efficacy are expressed in prefrontal neurons: An *in vitro* study in the rat. *Synapse* **12**:82–85.

Hirsch, J.C., and F. Crépel. 1990. Use-dependent changes in synaptic efficacy in rat prefrontal neurons *in vitro*. *J. Physiol.* **427**:31–49.

Hirsch, J.C., and F. Crépel. 1991. Blockade of NMDA receptors unmasks a long-term depression in synaptic efficacy in rat prefrontal neurons *in vitro*. *Exp. Brain Res.* **85**:621–624.

Hirsch, J.C., and F. Crépel. 1992. Postsynaptic calcium is necessary for the induction of LTP and LTD of monosynaptic EPSPs in prefrontal neurons. An *in vitro* study in rat. *Synapse* **10**:173–175.

Iriki, A., C. Pavlides, A. Keller, and H. Asanuma. 1989. Long-term potentiation in the motor cortex. *Science* **245**:1385–1387.

Iriki, A., C. Pavlides, A. Keller, and H. Asanuma. 1991. Long-term potentiation of thalamic input to the motor cortex induced by coactivation of thalamocortical and corticocortical afferents. *J. Neurophysiol.* **65**:1435–1441.

Jacobs, K.M., and J.P. Donoghue. 1991. Reshaping the cortical motor map by unmasking latent intracortical connections. *Science* **251**:944–947.

Jenkins, W.M., M.M. Merzenich, M.T. Ochs, T. Allard, and E. Guic-Robles. 1990. Functional reorganization of primary somatosensory cortex in adult owl monkeys after behaviorally controlled tactile stimulation. *J. Neurophysiol.* **63**:82–104.

Juliano, S.I., W. Ma, and D. Eslin. 1991. Cholinergic depletion prevents expansion of topographic maps in somatosensory cortex. *Proc. Natl. Acad. Sci. USA* **88**:780–784.

Kaas, J.H., L.A. Krubitzer, Y.M. Chino, A.I. Langston, E.H. Polley, and N. Blair. 1990. Reorganization of retinotopic cortical maps in adult mammals after lesions of the retina. *Science* **248**:229–231.

Kano, M., K. Iino, and M. Kano. 1991. Functional reorganization of adult cat somatosensory cortex is dependent on NMDA receptors. *NeuroReport* **2**:77–80.

Karni, A., and D. Sagi. 1991. Where practice makes it perfect in texture discriminations: Evidence for primary visual cortex plasticity. *Proc. Natl. Acad. Sci. USA* **88**:4966–4970.

Kasamatsu, T., and J. Pettigrew. 1976. Depletion of brain catecholamines: Failure of ocular dominance shift after monocular occlusion in kittens. *Science* **194**:206–209.

Kato, N., A. Artola, and W. Singer. 1991. Developmental changes in the susceptibility to long-term potentiation of neurones in rat visual cortex slices. *Devel. Brain Res.* **60**:43–50.

Keller, A., E. Miyashita, and H. Asanuma. 1991. Minimal stimulus parameters and the effects of hyperpolarization on the induction of long-term potentiation in the cat motor cortex. *Exp. Brain Res.* **87**:295–302.

Keller, A., C. Pavlides, and H. Asanuma. 1990. Long-term potentiation in the cat somatosensory cortex. *NeuroReport* **1**:49–52.

Kimura, F., A. Nishigori, T. Shirokawa, and T. Tsumoto. 1989. Long-term potentiation and N-methyl-D-aspartate receptors in the visual cortex of young rats. *J. Physiol.* **414**:125–144.

Kimura, F., T. Tsumoto, A. Nishigori, and Y. Yoshimura. 1990. Long-term depression but not potentiation is induced in Ca^{2+}-chelated visual cortex neurons. *NeuroReport* **1**:65–68.

Kirkwood, A., C.D. Aizemann, and M.F. Bear. 1992. Common forms of plasticity in hippocampus and visual cortex *in vitro*. *Soc. Neurosci. Abstr.* **18**:628.33.

Kleinschmidt, A., M.F. Bear, and W. Singer. 1987. Blockade of “NMDA” receptors disrupts experience-dependent plasticity of kitten striate cortex. *Science* **238**:355–358.

Komatsu, Y., K. Fujii, J. Maeda, H. Sakaguchi, and K. Toyama. 1988. Long-term potentiation of synaptic transmission in kitten visual cortex. *J. Neurophysiol.* **59**:124–141.

Komatsu, Y., and M. Iwakiri. 1992. Low-threshold Ca^{2+} channels mediate induction of long-term potentiation in kitten visual cortex. *J. Neurophysiol.* **67**:401–410.

Komatsu, Y., S. Narajima, and K. Toyama. 1991. Induction of long-term potentiation without the participation of N-methyl-D-aspartate receptors in kitten visual cortex. *J. Neurophysiol.* **65**:20–32.

Komatsu, Y., K. Toyama, J. Maeda, and H. Sakaguchi. 1981. Long-term potentiation investigated in a slice preparation of striate cortex of young kittens. *Neurosci. Lett.* **26**:269–274.

Kossel, A., T. Bonhoeffer, and J. Bolz. 1990. Non-Hebbian synapses in rat visual cortex. *NeuroReport* **1**:115–118.

Lee, K.S. 1982. Sustained enhancement of evoked potentials following brief, high-frequency stimulation of the cerebral cortex *in vitro*. *Brain Res.* **239**:617–623.

Levin, B.E., R.I. Craik, and P.J. Hand. 1988. The role of norepinephrine in adult rat somatosensory (sml) cortical metabolism and plasticity. *Brain Res.* **443**:261–271.

Lisman, J. 1989. A mechanism for the Hebb and the anti-Hebb processes underlying learning and memory. *Proc. Natl. Acad. Sci. USA* **86**:9574–9578.

MacDermott, A.B., M.L. Mayer, G.L. Westbrook, S.J. Smith, and J.L. Barker. 1986. NMDA receptor activation increases cytoplasmic calcium concentration in cultured spinal cord neurones. *Nature* **321**:519–522.

Malinow, R., and J.P. Miller. 1986. Postsynaptic hyperpolarization during conditioning reversibly blocks induction of long-term potentiation. *Nature* **320**:529–530.

Markram, H., and M. Segal. 1992. The inositol 1,4,5-trisphosphate pathway mediates cholinergic potentiation of rat hippocampal neuronal responses to NMDA. *J. Physiol.* **447**:513–533.

Merzenich, M.M., J.H. Kaas, J.T. Wall, M. Sur, R.J. Nelson, and D.J. Felleman. 1983. Progression of change following median nerve section in the cortical representation of the hand in areas 3b and 1 in adult owl and squirrel monkeys. *Neurosci.* **10**:639–665.

Merzenich, M.M., R.J. Nelson, M.P. Stryker, M.S. Cynader, A. Schoppmann, and J.M. Zook. 1984. Somatosensory cortical map changes following digit amputation in adult monkeys. *J. Comp. Neurol.* **224**:591–605.

Merzenich, M.M., G.H. Recanzone, W.M. Jenkins, and K.A. Grajski. 1990. Adaptive mechanisms in cortical networks underlying cortical contributions to learning and nondeclarative memory. *Cold Spring Harbor Symp. Quant. Biol.* **55**:873–887.

Miller, K.D., B. Chapman, and M.P. Stryker. 1989. Visual responses in adult cat visual cortex depend on N-methyl-D-aspartate receptors. *Proc. Natl. Acad. Sci. USA* **86**:5183–5187.

Mower, G.D., C.J. Caplan, W.G. Christen, and F.H. Duffy. 1985. Dark rearing prolongs physiological but not anatomical plasticity of the cat visual cortex. *J. Comp. Neurol.* **235**:448–466.

Nudo, R.J., W.M. Jenkins, and M.M. Merzenich. 1990. Repetitive microstimulation alters the cortical representation of movements in adult rats. *Somatosens. Motor Res.* **7**:463–483.

Perkins, A.T.,IV, and T.J. Teyler. 1988. A critical period for long-term potentiation in the developing rat visual cortex. *Brain Res.* **439**:222–229.

Poggio, T., M. Fahle, and S. Edelman. 1992. Fast perceptual learning in visual hyperacuity. *Science* **256**:1018–1021.

Pons, T.P., P.E. Garraghty, A.K. Ommaya, J.H. Kaas, E. Taub, and M. Mishkin. 1991. Massive cortical reorganization after sensory deafferentation in adult macaques. *Science* **252**:1857–1860.

Rauschecker, J.P., and W. Singer. 1979. Changes in the circuitry of the kitten visual cortex are gated by postsynaptic activity. *Nature* **280**:58–60.

Rauschecker, J.P., and W. Singer. 1981. The effects of early visual experience on the cat's visual cortex and their possible explanation by Hebb synapses. *J. Physiol.* **310**:215–239.

Reiter, M.O., and M.P. Stryker. 1988. Neural plasticity without postsynaptic action potentials: Less active inputs become dominant when kitten visual cortical cells are pharmacologically inhibited. *Proc. Natl. Acad. Sci. USA* **85**:3623–3627.

Rhoades, R.W., G.R. Belford, and H.P. Killakey. 1987. Receptive-field properties of rat ventral posterior medial neurons before and after selective kainic acid lesions of the trigeminal brainstem complex. *J. Neurophysiol.* **57**:1577–1600.

Sah, P., and R.A. Nicoll. 1991. Mechanisms underlying potentiation of synaptic transmission in rat anterior cingulate cortex *in vitro*. *J. Physiol.* **233**:615–630.

Scheich, H. 1991. Comparative aspects of maps and plasticity. *Curr. Opin. Neurobiol.* **1**:236–247.

Schwaber, M.K., P.E. Garraghty, A. Morel, and J.H. Kaas. 1992. Neuroplasticity of the adult primate auditory cortex following cochlear hearing loss. *J. Otol.* **107**:787–791.

Shirokawa, T., and T. Kasamatsu. 1986. Concentration-dependent suppression by beta-adrenergic antagonists of the shift in ocular dominance following monocular deprivation in kitten visual cortex. *Neurosci.* **18**:1035–1046.

Shulz, D., and Y. Frégnac. 1992. Cellular analogs of visual cortical epigenesis. II. Plasticity of binocular integration. *J. Neurosci.* **12**:1301–1318.

Singer, W. 1990. The formation of cooperative cell assemblies in the visual cortex. *J. Exp. Biol.* **153**:177–197.

Singer, W., and J.P. Rauschecker. 1982. Central core control of developmental plasticity in the kitten visual cortex: II. Electrical activation of mesencephalic and diencephalic projections. *Exp. Brain Res.* **47**:223–233.

Singer, W., F. Tretter, and U. Yinon. 1982. Evidence for long-term functional plasticity in the visual cortex of adult cats. *J. Physiol.* **324**:239–248.

Spengler, F., B. Godde, and H.R. Dinse. 1992. Emergence of new cortical representations of skin fields in somatosensory cortex of rats induced by intracortical microstimulation. In: Rhythmogenesis in Neurons and Networks. Proceedings of the 20th Göttingen Neurobiology Conference, ed. N. Elsner and D.W. Richter. Abstr. 130.

Stryker, M.P., B. Chapman, K.D. Miller, and K.R. Zahs. 1990. Orientation columns in visual cortex. *Cold Spring Harbor Symp. Quant. Biol.* **55**:939–952.

Sutor, B., and J.J. Hablitz. 1989. Long-term potentiation in frontal cortex: Role of NMDA-modulated polysynaptic excitatory pathways. *Neurosci. Lett.* **97**:111–117.

Tsumoto, T., K. Hagihara, H. Sato, and Y. Hata. 1987. NMDA receptors in the visual cortex of young kittens are more effective than those of adult cats. *Nature* **327**:513–514.

Warren, R., N. Tremblay, and R.W. Dykes. 1989. Quantitative study of glutamic acid decarboxylase-immunoreactive neurons and cytochrome oxidase activity in normal and partially deafferented rat hindlimb somatosensory cortex. *J. Comp. Neurol.* **288**:583–592.

Welker, E., E. Soriano, and H. van der Loos. 1989. Plasticity in the barrel cortex of the adult mouse: Effects of peripheral deprivation on GAD-immunoreactivity. *Exp. Brain Res.* **74**:441–452.

Webster, H.H., U.-K. Hanisch, R.W. Dykes, and D. Biesold. 1991. Basal forebrain lesions with or without reserpine injection inhibit cortical reorganization in rat hindpaw primary somatosensory cortex following sciatic nerve section. *Somatosens. Motor Res.* **8**:327–346.

Wiesel, T.N., and D.H. Hubel. 1963. Single-cell responses in striate cortex of kittens deprived of vision in one eye. *J. Neurophysiol.* **26**:1003–1017.

Yoshimura, Y., T. Tsumoto, and A. Nishigori. 1991. Input-specific induction of long-term depression in Ca^{2+}-chelated visual cortex neurons. *NeuroReport* **2**:393–396.

6

On the Relevance of *in Vivo* Neurobiological Observations to Learning and Memory

Y. DUDAI
Department of Neurobiology, Weizmann Institute of Science,
Rehovot 76100, Israel

ABSTRACT

Neurobiologists investigating learning and memory should be ready to defend the relevance of their findings to the *in vivo* mechanisms of these phenomena. Yet scrutiny of such relevance is sometimes circumscribed or even ignored. Here I argue that:

- Assessment of the relevance of neurobiological data to the mechanisms of memory requires a distinction between information storage mechanisms that *subserve* memory and specific encoding of particular items in the brain which *is* memory. Information storage mechanisms are neuronal syntactic operations, whereas memories are tokens of neuronal semantics.
- Assessing the relevance of neurobiological data to memory requires deciphering the representational and computational codes in the neural system under investigation.
- Current neurobiological data usually unveil information storage mechanisms rather than instantiation of memory.
- The relevance of *in vivo* observations to the mechanisms of both information storage and memory should be assessed by a set of rigorous criteria listed below. Current data on neuronal information storage fulfill at most only part of these criteria.

REPRESENTATIONS, OR NEURONAL SEMANTICS

Learning and memory are classically defined as experience-dependent modifications in behavior resulting from individual experience (for a review of definitions see Dudai 1992). This definition does not explicitly refer to the brain, does not guide us to brain

Cellular and Molecular Mechanisms Underlying Higher Neural Functions
Edited by A.I. Selverston and P. Ascher

properties essential for memory, and does not yield criteria to assess the relevance of neurobiological observations to memory. Reconsideration of learning and memory in neuronally relevant terms should be helpful.

The information encoded in the brain about the world can be formally treated in terms of event spaces encoded in neuronal spaces (Anderson and Rosenfeld 1988), or "internal representations," i.e., neuronally encoded versions of the world that could potentially guide behavior (Dudai 1989). Internal representations are an essential property of all nervous systems and vary tremendously in their complexity. The common denominators of them all are: (a) they are encoded in the activity and connectivity of neuronal systems, (b) they result from the interaction of sensory information with intrinsic neuronal activity, (c) they are capable of controlling behavior; and (d) they have finite behaviorally relevant states. Hence, when altered, internal representations modify behavior or the potential to behave.

Learning can thus be defined as *the experience-dependent generation or modification of enduring internal representations*. (The effect of rigid developmental programs and pathology is conventionally excluded.) Memory is *the retention of experience-dependent internal representations over time* (Dudai 1989). The representational treatment of learning and memory emphasizes that memory is a semantic token in the neuronal language of the brain and clearly tags the neuronal alterations that instantiate the memory, namely, those that alter representational properties of the system.

SEMANTICS, HENCE MEMORY, IS IN THE CONTEXT, HENCE THE CIRCUIT

The representational nature of memory provides a theoretical guideline to deal with the issue of relevancy expressed in the title of this chapter; whenever changes are identified in a neuronal system that subserves memory, the relevance of these changes to memory should be judged by a clear-cut criterion—the contribution of these changes to modification of the representation encoded in the system. Alas, we do not yet know the representational codes of most neuronal systems. The reason for that is anchored in the level of analysis in which neuronal semantics is expected to emerge.

"Level" denotes a position on a complexity scale. In brain research, an acceptable, parsimonious division into levels is: molecular, cellular, circuit, brain, behavior. "Circuit" is here taken to denote a general term, encompassing networks that share a discrete function. A critical issue is the delineation of functions performed at each level. The behavioral is the global input and output level. The circuit level is expected to encode specific representations and to perform molar computations on these representations. The ability of individual neurons within a network to encode independently meaningful chunks of information is still a matter of dispute; however, most experts propose that the representational information encoded in a single node of a neuronal network must be weighed only in the context of the network.[1] Accordingly, the view presented here is that investigation of a few or single neurons out of their *in vivo* context, and clearly that of individual synapses and molecular complexes, can not disclose neuronal semantics.

A caveat is appropriate here. Semantics and syntax are level-dependent notions. Levels can often be treated as nearly independent entities, with each level requiring for proper operation only limited access (if at all) to processes within other levels (Whyte et al. 1969). Therefore, although operations in any level follow sets of rules and result in meaningful statements at that level, those same statements only contribute to general, syntactic statements in a higher level. For example, suppose a neurotransmitter activates receptor(s) in a neuronal membrane. The metabolic cascade follows molecular syntax, from transmitter-binding to cellular substrate modification. The identity of the specific substrates so modified, determined by the identity of the transmitter and by the spatial and temporal molecular context in that neuron, conveys a specific meaning to the cellular operation, e.g., phosphorylation and blockade of a specific ion channel equates to a characteristic increase in the excitability of a specific dendrite. In isolation, however, this whole molecular cascade generates only a syntactic operation in the circuit level, i.e., altered resistance in a node, which may or may not contribute to a significant change in circuit semantics, depending on the context within the circuit. For the present discussion, "semantics" thus refers to meaning in the molar level. Examples of neuronal syntax and semantics are provided in Table 6.1.

Unveiling neuronal semantics thus requires unveiling representational and computational codes by analyzing coherent circuit activity. Much work is being carried out toward that end, but progress is slow (for references see Dudai 1992). High resolution multicellular recording and imaging techniques, and the appropriate analytical tools to handle the data so obtained, are definitely required (e.g., Lieke et al. 1989; Belliveau et al. 1991). Yet the lack of appropriate research tools at this point in time must not tarnish the criteria and the goal, and should not blur the distinction between information storage mechanisms and memory.

CRITERIA FOR RELEVANCE

It is appropriate at this point to construe the title of this chapter as enquiring into the relevance of neurobiological observations to mechanisms that subserve memory rather than to embodiment of memory. Several criteria are delineated below.

1. Is the observation correlated with learning and memory? Much of the data used to construct proposals for *in vivo* learning and memory mechanisms are derived

---

[1] The crux of the argument is the criticality of the context rather than the number of units that represent the token. This argument does not contradict the ability to correlate activity of single units with discrete stimuli or behavioral acts, or to activate behaviors via unit stimulation (e.g., Newsome et al. 1989; Gross 1992; Salzman et al. 1992).

Table 6.1 Simplified examples of neural syntax and semantics[1] (adapted from Dudai 1992; see references therein).

Operation	Level	Realized In
Syntax		
"and" gate	Molecular, synaptic	NMDA receptor, Ca^{2+}/calmodulin-activated adenylate cyclase
Conditional "and"	Molecular, synaptic	NMDA receptor modulated by, e.g., glycine, acetylcholine
Altered efficacy, $w_{i,j}(t+1) = w_{i,j}(t) + \Delta w_{i,j}(t)$, where $\Delta w_{i,j}(t) = f[a_i(t), a_j(t)]$*	Synaptic	Hebbian synapse
Place code = f(Time code)	Circuit	Delay lines and coincidence detectors; phase-locked loops
A coherent brain state** = $f[S_i(t-k)]$, $k = 0...25$ msec	Assemblies	Coherent oscillations
Semantics		
Pressure P on skin = muscle retraction R	Circuit	Efficacy of transmission in circuit subserving Aplysia withdrawal reflex
Pressure P on skin = facilitated muscle retraction $R+\Delta R$	Circuit	Efficacy of transmission in circuit subserving sensitized *Aplysia* withdrawal reflex
Neurons N_i fire optimally = interaural time difference is tμsec	Circuit	Opposite delay lines and coincidence detectors in brainstem of barn owl
This is a banana	Assemblies	Primate brain, realization not yet known

[1] *Semantics* is used here to denote molar information capable of guiding behavior. For futher discussion, see text.

* $w_{i,j}$ is the weight of the connection from presynaptic unit u_j to postsynaptic unit u_i; $a_j(t)$ and $a_i(t)$ are measures of pre- and postsynaptic activity; $\Delta w_{i,j}(t)$ is the change in synaptic efficacy.

** This is a postulated conjunction operator, revealed in intrinsic cortical oscillations; t = 25 msec is a representative value. S_i are states of the oscillating assemblies. Discrete modes of oscillations may also have semantic value.

from investigations in which observations are *correlated* with acquisition, consolidation, and retention of memory. Correlation may be of the first order, i.e., of the observed change with learning and memory, or of higher order, i.e., of the observed change with a physiological phenomenon that itself was correlated with learning and memory. Examples of a first-order correlation are the presynaptic facilitation in a sensory-to-motor synapse correlated with sensitization of defensive reflexes in *Aplysia* (Kandel and Schwartz 1982), or the increase in glutamate release and in phosphoinositide turnover detected in the dentate gyrus after classical conditioning in the rat (Laroche et al. 1991). An example of a higher-order correlation is the modulation of *Aplysia* cell adhesion molecules (apCAM) by application of serotonin to sensory neurons in culture; this molecular change is indirectly correlated with long-term sensitization, since the structural changes in the synaptic connections between the sensory neurons and their target cells are correlated with long-term sensitization and can be induced *in vitro* by serotonin (Mayford et al. 1992). Another example is the proposal that in rat brain, Ca^{2+}/calmodulin-sensitive adenylate cyclase is important for learning, because in *Drosophila*, a mutation in the gene encoding this enzyme disrupts learning (see below), while in rat, the mRNA for this enzyme is expressed in brain areas implicated in learning and memory (Xia et al. 1991).

Correlation is a popular and rather permissive criterion. The pitfalls of unveiling incidental or linked but noncausally related processes should be kept in mind. Correlation can serve as guideline for models and for design of experiments intended to probe necessity and sufficiency (see below).

2. Does the mechanism bear similarity to properties of learning and memory? Research on long-term potentiation (LTP) can serve as an example for exercising this criterion. Many authors substantiate the claim that LTP plays a role in memory because it displays properties expected from memory, such as persistence following brief stimuli, associativity, order-dependency in associativity, and occurrence in brain regions critical for memory (reviewed in Dudai 1989). Such similarity is appealing, but may be misleading. Furthermore, there is no reason to expect that parts should display the properties of the whole and *vice versa*, hence that molecular and cellular devices should display the phenomenology of behavior (e.g., Bechtel 1982).
3. Is the mechanism useful for generation and retention of memory? If this is the case, it may suggest that the mechanism functions *in situ*. There are two versions to this criterion. The first involves pragmatical usefulness, i.e., is the process experimentally useful in inducing learning-related alterations? This may be tested in experiments that also aim to establish correlation (above) or sufficiency (below). For example, serotonin is useful in inducing presynaptic facilitation in *Aplysia* (Mayford et al. 1992); β-adrenergic activation is useful in triggering plasticity changes in the hippocampus (Dunwiddie et al. 1992); and stimulation protocols similar to those eliciting LTP are useful in conditioning the piriform cortex and hippocampus in rats (Laroche et al. 1991; Staubli 1992). The second version of this criterion is conceptual usefulness, i.e., can the implicated mechanism be integrated into models of learning and memory, thus forming a coherent picture of available data, capable of generating testable hypothesis (e.g., Friedrich 1990)? Pragmatical usefulness of course does not prove that the mechanism is

recruited *in vivo.* Conceptual usefulness, either explicit or implicit, is instrumental in integrating data and guiding research.

4. Is the mechanism necessary for memory? The approach here is to infer function from dysfunction, by testing the effect of anatomical, genetic, or metabolic lesions on learning and memory. Examples are provided by the studies that implicate hippocampus in memory because hippocampal lesions abolish facets of memory (Squire 1992), NMDA receptors in learning because antagonists to these receptors block learning (Morris 1989), and the cAMP cascade in memory because mutations in genes that encode specific components of that cascade result in organisms with feeble memory (Dudai 1989). Lesion experiments immediately raise issues of specificity: is the site of lesion well circumscribed (e.g., see the interpretation of the effect of amygdala lesions on memory in monkeys; Zola-Morgan et al. 1989)? Multiple, partially overlapping lesions might be informative in this respect but are rarely performed (Glassman 1978). In addition, is the effect on learning and memory clear-cut (e.g., how specific is the effect of gene knockout in mice on physiology and behavior; Silva et al. 1992)?

   Function-from-dysfunction arguments are widely employed. They present candidate loci and mechanisms for biological processes but do not provide proof that these loci and mechanisms are functional *in vivo*. Two caveats are appropriate here. First, it can not be assumed a priori that a lesioned system simply behaves as the intact one minus the disabled component because adaptability may involve recruitment of parallel processes and generation of shunts. Second, though Occam's razor is recommended in interpretation, in reality the role of the lesioned part may be much more complex or remote from straightforward interpretations. Here modeling (3 above) might be helpful.

5. Does the mechanism suffice for memory formation? This criterion is far more difficult to fulfill. The methodology is similar to that employed in attempts to fulfill criterion 3 above, namely mimicry experiments, only that the claim and interpretation are more pretentious and *in vivo* causality is assumed. Some of the experiments that claim to demonstrate that LTP-like stimulation in identified pathways can substitute for an associated stimulus in conditioning, might be interpreted as attempting to show that LTP in a given pathway is sufficient to encode behaviorally relevant information in that pathway *in vivo* (for a critical discussion see Laroche et al. 1991; Staubli 1992). An attempt to demonstrate sufficiency and causality is illustrated in the report by Farley et al. (1983), which states that membrane changes in a single photoreceptor cause associative learning in a conditioned phototaxis paradigm in *Hermissenda*. Currently none of the aforementioned experiments is generally interpreted as demonstrating sufficiency. A more recent and intriguing example of the use of mimicry in determining the role of an identified brain system in guiding action is provided by the analysis of the effect of brain microstimulation on visually guided behavior (Salzman et al. 1992).

6. Is the mechanism exclusive? This is the most demanding criterion, as the claim is made not only for *in vivo* usage and causality but also for *in vivo* exclusiveness. Such a claim cannot be currently made for any candidate mechanism in learning. Moreover, the question can be raised whether exclusiveness can be expected at all, since multiplicity of mechanisms and parallel pathways appear to be the rule in learning (reviewed in Dudai 1989).

CONCLUSION

We should clearly distinguish between general information-storage mechanisms that realize memory (neuronal syntax) and encoding of information about specific items in memory (neuronal semantics). We are currently capable of elucidating facets of neuronal syntax at the molecular and cellular level.[2] However, we do not yet have satisfactory tools and concepts to tackle the problem of internal representations in circuits which is the key to understanding memory. Therefore, instead of enquiring what is the relevance of neurobiological data to memory, we can currently deal only with the question: what is the relevance of such data to neuronal information storage mechanisms?

Several criteria, differing in stringency, can be formulated for the assessment of the aforementioned relevance. Current data propose correlation, similarity, and sometimes necessity of certain neuronal mechanisms in realization of learning and memory. It appears that the molecular and cellular principles involved in this facet of neuronal plasticity are not markedly different from those employed in other types of cells in response to stimuli. Experiments that claim to demonstrate necessity must be scrutinized for the specificity of the effect. This is important in pharmacological experiments and in manipulations of genes that are not cell-type specific or developmentally regulated. Sufficiency and exclusiveness of mechanisms of information storage are not yet demonstrated, and the latter may not even be feasible. The criteria listed here should also be useful in assessing the relevance of neurobiological data to memory when the tools to decipher specific representations and their experience-dependent change become available.

ACKNOWLEDGMENTS

I am grateful to Ehud Ahissar, Rafi Malach, and Rina Schul for comments, and to the Whitehall Foundation, Florida, and the Grodetsky Center for Brain Research, Weizmann Institute of Science, for support.

---

2 Faithful to the title of this meeting, the focus here is on the molecular and cellular levels. Investigations at the anatomical and brain-organ level implicate discrete brain areas in flowchart models of learning and memory (see 4 above) and in general operations performed in specific types of learning and memory, e.g., hippocampus in spatial learning, amygdala in fear learning (Davis 1992; Squire 1992).

REFERENCES

Anderson, J.A., and E. Rosenfeld, eds. 1988. Neurocomputing. Cambridge, MA: MIT Press.

Bechtel, W. 1982. Two common errors in explaining biological and psychological phenomena. *Philosoph. Sci.* **49**:549–574.

Belliveau, J.W., D.N. Kennedy, R.C. McKinstry, B.R. Buchbinder, R.M. Weisskoff, M.S. Cohen, J.M. Vevea, T.J. Brady, and B.R. Rosen. 1991. Functional mapping of human visual cortex by magnetic resonance imaging. *Science* **254**:716–719.

Davis, M. 1992. The role of the amygdala in fear and anxiety. *Ann. Rev. Neurosci.* **15**:353–375.

Dudai, Y. 1989. The Neurobiology of Memory. Oxford: Oxford Univ. Press.

Dudai, Y. 1992. Why "learning" and "memory" should be redefined (or, an agenda for focused reductionism). *Concepts Neurosci.* **3**:99–121.

Dunwiddie, T.V., M. Taylor, L.R. Heginbotham, and W.R.Proctor. 1992. Long-term increases in excitability in the CA1 region of rat hippocampus induced by β-adrenergic stimulation: Possible mediation by cAMP. *J. Neurosci.* **12**:506–517.

Farley, J.M., W.G. Richards, L.J. Ling, E. Liman, and D.L. Alkon. 1983. Membrane changes in a single photoreceptor cause associative learning in *Hermissenda*. *Science* **221**:1201–1203.

Friedrich, P. 1990. Protein structure: The primary substrate for memory. *Neurosci.* **35**:1–7.

Glassman, R.B. 1978. The logic of the lesion experiment and its role in the neural sciences. In: Recovery from Brain Damage, ed. S. Finger, pp. 3–31. New York: Plenum.

Gross, C.G. 1992. Representation of visual stimuli in inferior temporal cortex. *Phil. Trans. R. Soc. Lond. B* **335**:3–10.

Kandel, E.R., and J.H. Schwartz. 1982. Molecular biology of learning: Modulation of transmitter release. *Science* **218**:433–443.

Laroche, S., V. Doyere, and C.R. Del Negro. 1991. What role for long-term potentiation in learning and in the maintenance of memories? In: Long-term Potentiation, a Debate of Current Issues, ed. M. Baudry and J.L. Davis, pp. 301–316. Cambridge, MA: MIT Press.

Lieke, E.E., R.D. Frostig, A. Arieli, D.Y. Ts'o, R. Hildesheim, and A. Grinvald. 1989. Optical imaging of cortical activity: Real-time imaging using extrinsic dye-signals and high resolution imaging based on slow intrinsic-signals. *Ann. Rev. Physiol.* **51**:543–559.

Mayford, M., A. Barzilai, F. Keller, S. Schacher, and E.R. Kandel. 1992. Modulation of an NCAM-related adhesion molecule with long-term synaptic plasticity in *Aplysia*. *Science* **256**:638–644.

Morris, R.G.M. 1989. Synaptic plasticity and learning: Selective impairment of learning in rats and blockade of long-term potentiation *in vivo* by the N-methyl-D-asparte antagonist AP5. *J. Neurosci.* **9**:3040–3057.

Newsome, W.T., K.H. Britten, and J.A. Movshon. 1989. Neuronal correlates of a perceptual decision. *Nature* **341**:52–54.

Salzman, C.D., C.M. Murasugi, K.H. Britten, and W.T. Newsome. 1992. Microstimulation in visual area MT: Effects on direction discrimination performance. *J. Neurosci.* **12**:2331–2355.

Silva, A.J., R. Paylor, J.M. Wehner, and S. Tonegawa. 1992. Impaired spatial learning in alpha-calcium-calmodulin kinase II mutant mice. *Science* **257**:206–211.

Squire, L.R. 1992. Memory and the hippocampus: A synthesis from findings with rats, monkeys, and humans. *Psychol. Rev.* **99**:195–231.

Staubli, U. 1992. Parallel properties of LTP and memory. In: Neural Mechanisms of Plasticity, ed. J.L. McGaugh. New York: Oxford, in press.

Whyte, L.L., A.G. Wilson, and D. Wilson, eds. 1969. Hierarchical Structures. New York: American Elsevier.

Xia, Z., C.D. Refsdal, K.M. Merchant, D.M. Dorsa, and D.R. Storm. 1991. Distribution of mRNA for the calmodulin-sensitive adenylate cyclase in rat brain: Expression in areas associated with learning and memory. *Neuron* **6**:431–443.

Zola-Morgan, S., L.R. Squire, D.G. Amaral, and W.A. Suzuki. 1989. Lesions of perirhinal and parahippocampal cortex that spare the amygdala and hippocampal formation produce severe memory impairment. *J. Neurosci.* **9**:4355–4370.

Standing, left to right:
Masao Ito, Tony Movshon, Yadin Dudai, Richard Morris, Steve Lisberger, Wolf Singer, Yves Frégnac, Attila Baranyi
Seated, left to right:
Carol Barnes, Larry Squire, Lynn Bindman, Maurice Moulins
Not present:
Thomas Knöpfel

7

Group Report: Relating Activity-dependent Modifications of Neuronal Function to Changes in Neural Systems and Behavior

C.A. BARNES, Rapporteur

A. BARANYI, L.J. BINDMAN, Y. DUDAI,
Y. FRÉGNAC, M. ITO, T. KNÖPFEL,
S.G. LISBERGER, R.G.M. MORRIS, M. MOULINS,
J.A. MOVSHON, W. SINGER, L.R. SQUIRE

CONCEPTUALIZING THE NEURAL BASIS OF LEARNING AND MEMORY

What Are the Kinds of Long-term Memory for which Mechanistic Explanations Are Needed?

Studies of human amnesic patients and brain-lesioned animals suggest that there are at least two main types of long-term memory storage. Prominent among these is one memory system referred to in varying contexts as *declarative*, *explicit*, *episodic and semantic*, *cognitive*, or *representational*. The other major category has been characterized as nondeclarative, implicit, or procedural. Broadly speaking, the declarative memory system involves memory for facts and events, is typically fast and flexible, and is very efficient at storing information rapidly and permanently. The nondeclarative category probably consists of more than one system (including memory for skills and habits, simple conditioning, and priming) and often takes a greater number of repetitions for effective storage. Although the emphasis in the past has indicated that the hippocampus, either alone or together with the amygdala, is involved in the former memory system and structures such as cerebellum, neostriatum, and neocortex in the latter, a number of recent experiments involving lesions of these structures have

Cellular and Molecular Mechanisms Underlying Higher Neural Functions
Edited by A.I. Selverston and P. Ascher

refined our understanding of the neural components that contribute to the former memory system.

It is now clear that the hippocampus proper is part of a larger *medial temporal lobe memory system*, a finding that has raised the possibility that each component of the system may contribute in different ways to flexible encoding of new information. Recent methods have allowed individual assessment of selective damage to the amygdala, hippocampus proper, perirhinal, parahippocampal, and entorhinal cortical structures. These new results suggest, for example, that the amygdala is critical for attaching an appropriate affect in the formation of memories in monkeys, and thus may contribute this independent function to the medial temporal lobe memory system (Zola-Morgan et al. 1989a, b; Gaffan and Murray 1990; Murray 1992). On the other hand, selective lesions of the hippocampal region (Angelie et al. 1993) or bilateral fornix lesions (Gaffan and Harrison 1989) in monkeys indicate that impairment consistently occurs on tasks that have a spatial component. This may also be true in humans with right temporal lobe excisions that include large hippocampal removal (Pigott and Milner 1993). Thus, as in rats, a very consistent way in which to observe deficits following hippocampal damage in primates is to use tasks in which the spatial domain is important. Other declarative (nonspatial) tasks appear to be affected, to a greater extent, when damage is extended to include other medial temporal lobe neocortical structures (e.g., Horel et al. 1987; Gaffan and Murray 1992; Zola-Morgan et al. 1993). Therefore, an important issue is to determine whether spatial memory is a special function of the hippocampus (O'Keefe and Nadel 1978), or whether the acquisition of spatial memory is simply a good example of the computational job that is accomplished by this brain system (Squire 1992).

The consensus in our group was that with the new information gained from lesion studies, combined with perspectives from neural networks, the idea of multiple memory systems has validity at the psychological and brain system levels. We also agreed, however, that this division does not necessarily predict that the implementation of these memories should necessarily occur through wholly different neural systems, or that the cellular and molecular mechanisms will necessarily turn out to be long-term potentiation (LTP) or long-term depression (LTD). Nevertheless, on theoretical grounds, it is tempting to imagine that slower learning systems may be dependent upon a balance between LTP and LTD, possibly implemented as small gradual changes in the individual circuit elements contributing to the storage process; faster learning systems may, on the other hand, rely most heavily on rapid, robust modifications using LTP mechanisms.

Seeking the Best Paradigms for Analyzing Learning and Memory Systems

Several properties need to be considered in choosing an experimental system to investigate learning and memory. It would be advantageous to use paradigms in which:

- learning is very fast (e.g., one-trial learning), so that molecular and cellular alterations could be identified and followed within a brief and well-defined time window;
- the stored memory is robust and long-lasting, so that various phases of memory formation, including consolidation and long-term retention and retrieval, could be conveniently quantified;
- the learned stimulus is well-controlled and preferably unimodal to facilitate localization of changes in circumscribed brain region(s);
- the anatomical system subserving processing and memory of the sensory input is well-defined; and the experimental organism is amenable to scrutiny at different levels of analysis and using a battery of different experimental techniques, from behavior, anatomy, electrophysiology, and molecular biological analysis;
- the behavioral context (i.e., the computational and representational functions of the neuronal system) is preserved as much as possible throughout all levels of analysis to permit assessment of the relevance of the changes observed to learning and memory.

In practice, however, experimenters must compromise, as no single experimental system combines all these desirable features (see Dudai, this volume). The consensus was that as long as assumptions are made explicit as to how a given paradigm might illuminate the set of processes and mechanisms of interest, then that procedure could be used until proven inadequate. There are considerable practical reasons for being conservative, both within and between laboratories, about the protocols followed in any one learning task (e.g., with respect to replicability and the need for comparisons between succeeding studies). These pressures, however, should not be so great as to inhibit imaginative ideas about new tasks that could help fractionate dissociable memory processes. It should always be borne in mind that learning tasks are a means to an end, not an end unto themselves, and an aid to understand learning processes and mechanisms. A compilation of a number of major systems and paradigms used in contemporary memory research is given in Table 7.1.

What Biological Mechanisms Can We Use to Understand Behavioral Plasticity?

When considering possible relationships between behavioral plasticity and LTP- and LTD-like mechanisms, it is necessary to consider (a) the range of possible neurobiological implementations of plastic changes and (b) the possibility that synaptic plasticity might serve many functions in the nervous system other than those associated with learning and memory.

For many, LTP and LTD come to mind when thinking about learning and memory. These plastic phenomena have a correlational structure useful for models (like most contemporary implementations of "neural networks") that require changing synaptic weights to modify the behavior of the system. The consensus view, however, was that

Table 7.1 Examples of learning and memory paradigms that have been widely used to investigate long-term memory.

Paradigm	Species	Comment
Habituation and sensitization	*Aplysia*	One of the few cases in which there has been work at many levels (behavioral, physiological, molecular).
Priming	Humans	Good example of implicit learning.
Perceptual aftereffects	Humans, higher vertebrates	Can be surprisingly long-lasting, provided that subject is not exposed to test stimuli in retention interval.
Reflexive classical conditioning (e.g., withdrawal reflexes, eye-blink, monosynaptic spinal reflexes, fear-potentiated startle)	Invertebrates, vertebrates	Paradigmatic example of associative learning in which a stimulus comes to invoke a behavioral response as a result of conditioning that it did not evoke at the outset of training.
Sensory-reward conditioning (e.g., taste conditioning)	Vertebrates	Can be very rapid (e.g., 1 trial) and may occur despite long CS–US intervals.
Passive and active avoidance conditioning	Rats, mice	Rapid and durable, often used in conjunction with pharmacological agents to dissect memory components.
Stimulus-response conditioning (limb-withdrawal inhibitory avoidance, etc.)	Invertebrates, vertebrates	Classic example of instrumental or operant conditioning in which an animal's response is rewarded or punished in a particular stimulus situation. Habit learning. Typically slow and does not depend on memory of individual training trials.
Motor learning	Vertebrates	Learning of precise motor skills.
Vestibular-ocular reflex adaptation	Rabbit, monkey	Well-developed paradigm for which the relevant anatomical circuit is well enough understood for formal neural models to be evaluated. Controversy about relationship between models and empirical evidence.

continues

Table 7.1 *continued*

Paradigm	Species	Comment
Recognition memory (e.g., delayed nonmatching to sample)	Humans, monkeys, rats	Very widely used task to explore anatomical basis of declarative memory. Extensive body of literature with common protocols enabling detailed comparisons between studies.
Spatial learning	Mainly rats but also other vertebrates	Very fast (can be 1 trial). Several paradigms (radial maze, circular platform, water task) widely used to investigate the representation of spatial information and behavioral navigation.
Object discrimination learning and retention	Monkeys, rats	Another declarative task in which animals appear to learn the fact that an object is specifically associated with reward rather than just acquire value as in sensory-reward conditioning.
Context-specific and configural conditioning	Rats, rabbits	Paradigm in which ambiguous stimulus-reward relationships can be explored. Instance of complex type of associative conditioning.
Imprinting	Young birds and other young vertebrates	Rapid learning restricted to a critical period shortly after birth.
Bird-song	Song birds	The learning of songs is sometimes separated in time from their performance.

it would be premature to assert that the family of LTP- and LTD-like processes are *the* only mechanisms to be considered for plastic changes in the nervous system. There are many ways in which one could obtain alterations in the system that could depend little or not at all on synaptic weight changes. Possibilities here include (a) the regulation of dendritic excitability by local postsynaptic control of voltage-dependent channels; (b) regulation of overall neuronal excitability, by one of several possible forms of neuromodulation; or (c) modulation of the state of multistable neuronal circuits by brief external perturbations. At the network, cellular, and synaptic levels, these and other possible mechanisms might be implemented in forms that have little in common with LTP and LTD as we presently conceive them; for example, changes in synaptic weights might be achieved by modifications of synaptic structure, and changes in network dynamics may depend on modulatory influences in neural networks (e.g., Marder and Selverston 1992; see Hooper et al., this volume). Indeed, appropriately configured neural networks can have multiple stable states, as is often the case for nonlinear dynamic systems. In this case, a particular input configuration can induce a pattern of activation that is stabilized by dynamic interactions and maintained until erased or modified by subsequent inputs. In such multistable systems, changes between states can be supported by, but do not require, any modification in the coupling between, or integration properties of, the contributing elements. It may be doubted that such networks can assume enough stable states to store a large number of permanent memories efficiently; however, their potential utility as a short-term working store is clear.

Just as memories may be stored by mechanisms very different from LTP and LTD, it must be recalled that LTP- and LTD-like mechanisms may well have a role in regulating a variety of cellular and network properties that are unrelated to behavioral plasticity but may instead have homeostatic functions in regulating system behavior. Indeed, the prevalence of LTP in sites that are unlikely to be involved in memory (e.g., the lateral geniculate nucleus; Scharfman et al. 1991) suggests that this process must subserve other functions than memory storage. Thus it may be that synaptic and behavioral plasticity are as closely related as some might hope, but it is also plausible that these apparently analogous processes might be more strongly related to other and very different mechanisms.

These caveats must be kept in mind when examining synaptic changes as potential learning processes. Most of the group agreed, however, that the synapse is likely to be a good place for information storage to occur, largely because such mechanisms potentially have higher information storage capacity than mechanisms that involve entire cells or larger cellular components. If it is agreed that it is useful to examine changes that occur at the synapse, then it is equally true that we must look to molecular biological approaches to understand mechanisms of learning. Some argued that until we understand more about the organizational properties of neuronal memory networks, molecular details of the storage mechanism will not be of major utility. For example, most agreed that calcium is important in determining whether one gets LTP or LTD; the addition of more detailed molecular information concerning this may not help us understand the dynamic properties of the system any better. As one participant put it, "the study of molecular mechanisms of learning may be rather like trying to understand Shakespeare by understanding the paper on which he wrote." On the other hand, others had the intuition that an understanding at all levels is going to be necessary to understand truly the circuits important for learning and memory. A member of another group suggested that "trying to understand plasticity without understanding its molecular basis may be like trying to read Shakespeare without being able to understand English."

TESTS OF THE HYPOTHESIS THAT LTP AND LTD ARE RELATED TO LEARNING AND MEMORY

What Is LTP?

It was difficult to come to a consensus on the definition of the phenomenon of LTP; however, most agreed that it was an associatively induced increase in the monosynaptic EPSP which lasts at least an hour (excluding CA3). Most felt that similar mechanisms were involved in hippocampal (fascia dentata, CA1) and neocortical LTP. Another view expressed—although not universally endorsed—was that the term LTP should only be applied to those synapses in which it was first discovered (the perforant path-granule cell synapse). It was the group's opinion that LTP was best defined as a set of phenomena, since the mechanisms supporting the underlying synaptic changes remain unclear in detail. The general issue of defining LTP was also considered by other groups, for whom the matter of mechanism was more critical than the simple presence of the phenomenon (see Edwards et al., this volume).

What Is LTD?

LTD is an activity-dependent, long-lasting (greater than 60 min) decrease in a monosynaptic EPSP. There is general agreement that associative LTD can be induced in cerebellar slices *in vitro* and *in vivo* at the parallel fiber-Purkinje cell synapse. At this synapse, LTD is induced when parallel fiber activity is associated with strong postsynaptic depolarization of Purkinje cells produced by climbing fiber inputs or postsynaptic depolarization (e.g., Ito 1984, 1989; Crépel and Krupa 1990; Crépel and Jaillard 1991). There appears to be agreement concerning its existence, induction methods, and time course in the cerebellum. It was also agreed that LTD could be found in the hippocampus and neocortex but that the conditions under which it can be obtained are less well-defined in the hippocampus than in the neocortex. Because the coexistence of LTD and LTP is of considerable significance to theories of hippocampal memory function, the discussion here is confined to the LTD found in the hippocampus.

Does LTD Occur in the Hippocampus?

There is evidence for both homosynaptic and heterosynaptic LTD in the dentate gyrus of hippocampus *in vivo* and in CA1 *in vitro*. Homosynaptic LTD could be induced at the perforant path to granule cell synapse by a 15 Hz tetanus (one train of 100 stimulus pulses); LTP was induced in an equal number of cases (Bramham and Srebro 1987). Heterosynaptic LTD has been found between components of the entorhinal cortical projection to the granule cells of the fascia dentata (Abraham and Goddard 1983; Abraham and Wickens 1991; Christie and Abraham 1992a; Colbert et al. 1992; Levy and Steward 1979, 1983). Within CA1 in slices, homosynaptic LTD can be induced by low-frequency (e.g., 1 Hz) stimulation in the Schaffer collateral pathway, where the postsynaptic depolarization it induces is inadequate to produce LTP (Mulkey and Malenka 1992; Dudek and Bear 1992). There have also been reports of a homosynaptic associative LTD where the test input occurs immediately following a heterosynaptic depolarization or during postsynaptic hyperpolarizing current (Stanton and Sejnowski 1989; Chattarji et al. 1989; Stanton et al. 1991); others, however, have not been able to produce LTD using this induction procedure (e.g., Paulsen et al. 1990; Kerr and Abraham 1993). Christie and Abraham (1992b) found a priming dependency (using theta frequency stimulation) of this associative induction procedure in the lateral perforant path to the dentate granule cells. This priming effect lasted at least 2 hours. Heterosynaptic LTD in CA1 has also been produced, but somewhat unreliably (Andersen et al. 1977; Lynch et al. 1977; cf. Alger et al. 1978). Postsynaptic induction of nonassociative LTD, which experimentally bypasses the conditioning input pathway, can, however, be reliably induced in inactive inputs (i.e., heterosynaptic LTD) when evoked synaptic transmission during the conditioning procedure is either blocked or reduced pharmacologically (Pockett et al. 1990; Christofi et al. 1993; Bindman et al. 1993).

Mechanisms and a Possible Functional Role of LTD

Using insights obtained from the visual cortex (Artola and Singer 1990), where the level of postsynaptic depolarization determines whether no effect, LTD, or LTP results in a test pathway following tetanic stimulation of this input, one can infer that the precise level of intracellular calcium concentration at the test synapses would determine the sign of the plastic change. Other experiments in neocortex, using intracellular calcium-chelating agents, have supported this suggestion (Baranyi and Szente 1987; Artola et al. 1990; Kimura et al. 1990; Yoshimura et al. 1991; Hirsch and Crépel 1992).

Measurements of activity-dependent increases in calcium concentration in the soma have been made under various experimental conditions that gave rise to postsynaptic induction of nonassociative, heterosynaptic LTD, or have failed to induce LTD (Christofi et al. 1993). These measurements suggest that there are four ranges of activity-dependent calcium change:

1. the lowest level, in which no change in synaptic efficacy is observed (e.g., when extracellular calcium is reduced experimentally during conditioning);
2. at a second level, where LTD is reliably produced (e.g., when evoked synaptic activity is blocked by a raised magnesium concentration during conditioning);
3. at a third, still higher, level neither LTD nor LTP can be produced (e.g., when the postsynaptic conditioning occurs with no drugs present in the bathing medium during conditioning); this situation was described by Bindman et al. (1993) and is also discussed by Edwards et al. (this volume);
4. finally, it is plausible to suppose that LTP is induced when the activity-dependent rise in intracellular calcium concentration reaches a fourth, and highest, level.

One view of the possible role of nonassociative LTD processes in neocortex or hippocampus would be to sculpt on the dendrites of a single cell, conditions that are analogous to surround inhibition in a network, but over a longer time scale. Associative LTD, on the other hand, might theoretically have an impact on the ability to assist with orthogonalization of representations in a given set of inputs. It might, for example, be an effective mechanism for learning about exceptions or a means by which synapses might be "punished" for being active in the wrong context. Although it is conceivable that LTP is the critical mechanism used for storing information (see below), and that LTD may exist simply to reset LTP (Fujii et al. 1991), it must be noted that it is also conceivable for the converse to be true. One possible network role for LTD might be to renormalize synaptic weights that have been altered by LTP. If the system has built-in passive decay, then such LTD might not be necessary. If it does not, then such LTD may be needed to keep plastic circuits from saturating.

Links between Hippocampal LTP and Memory

The possible relationship between hippocampal LTP and memory has been one of the most active areas of research at the interface between behavioral and cellular neuroscience because of the very attractive possibility that a tight relationship could be drawn between processes defined at the synaptic and systems levels. The interest in the possibility that LTP might play a role in learning and memory has led to a number of experimental approaches designed to test this hypothesis, or at least to explore possible experimental support for it. None of the approaches taken to date has been completely satisfactory by itself. Four kinds of approach can be considered. The first is to obtain *correlational evidence* between parameters of learning, such as rate of acquisition or strength of retention, with LTP parameters (such as its magnitude or persistence) in individual animals. Early evidence of this sort came from Barnes (1979) and subsequently from recent studies discussed at this meeting by Morris (Jeffery and Morris 1993).

Beyond the correlational approach, there are three general classes of possible experiments involving disruption of LTP, each of which leads to a specific set of predictions. In principle, LTP may be *blocked*, the capacity for LTP may be *saturated*, or LTP might be reversed or *erased*. Under ideal circumstances the first type of disruption predicts a deficit of acquisition of new information with no effect on established memory (see details in Morris, this volume). Interpretation of the outcome of saturation experiments depends to some degree upon the theoretical model under consideration. In general, its logic is that if memory is encoded as a specific distribution of synaptic strengths, then saturation of this distribution towards the maximal possible value at a large fraction of the relevant synapses should both impair new acquisition and obliterate any information in the distribution. In the case of the hippocampus, this retrograde disruption might exhibit a temporal gradient like that seen following damage to the hippocampus. Finally, the ability to erase LTP selectively should result in the abolition of stored information (again possibly with a temporally limited gradient), with either no effect or a possible facilitation in the acquisition of new information.

Evidence from experiments in the first two categories (correlational and blocking experiments) is considered in detail by Morris (this volume). While pharmacological studies have established that drugs (like AP5) which block NMDA-receptor dependent LTP also appear to impair certain types of memory (e.g., spatial memory), there is still doubt whether adequate controls have been conducted to distinguish drug-induced deficits in learning from likely changes in other kinds of performance that could be associated with NMDA-receptor blockade.

We also discussed the possible technical and theoretical reasons why saturation experiments might be difficult (and hence why they have been somewhat unreliable in practice). In particular, theories concerning the storage capacity of distributed associative memories predict a sigmoidal relation between the degree of "LTP saturation" (i.e., how many synapses are used up) and memory disruption. Given that it is known that bilateral LTP "saturation" in these experiments involved primarily the dorsal hippocampus, the possibility exists that the range of saturation achievable may lie near the bottom of the region of the theoretical curve in which memory storage would begin to be severely disrupted. Hence, considerable variability might be expected.

Besides ensuring, perhaps with multiple electrode sites, that saturation occurs over the entire hippocampus, other behavioral tasks might also be effectively administered. It should at least be considered that tasks other than those used to date may be more sensitive to hippocampal disruption and would provide other methodological advantages. This might include serial position experiments similar to those that have been conducted in rats (Kesner et al. 1988) or in humans (Wright et al. 1990), in which decisions are made about items in a list. Compared to memory for the middle items on the list, there is better memory for the most recent items (based on short-term memory, the *recency* component) and also better memory for the first items (which are longer-lasting and based on long-term memory, the *primacy* component). We know that medial temporal lobe lesions affect the primacy component of serial position curves (i.e., memory for the early items in the list) without effect on the recency component, in spite of equivalent attention to both kinds of items. The structure of the data typically obtained from this kind of task makes it particularly straightforward to separate memory components from those simply related to performance deficits that might attend a particular manipulation. Manipulations which block or saturate LTP would be expected preferentially to affect the primacy component of the serial position curve, while any general performance deficits would lack this specificity.

Finally, conduct of erasure experiments has been impeded by the lack of any known pharmacological intervention capable of selective reversal of LTP. If such a technique could be found and implemented selectively in the neural structure of choice, then it would be possible to conduct a critical behavioral test of the hypothesis that LTP is related to long-term memory.

Another idea for relating LTP to memory is to find a way to observe synaptic changes while animals are learning. As outlined in the background paper by Morris, short-term exploratory modulation, or STEM, was originally hypothesized to offer this situation (Sharp et al. 1989; Green et al. 1990). It was the group's consensus, however, that the weight of evidence suggests that the primary effect of STEM on the perforant path-granule cell EPSP was on local brain temperature (Moser et al. 1993). An issue that presently awaits resolution is whether there is any residual synaptic change left after the temperature effect is removed. Because it is unlikely that more than 10% of the change observed during STEM could be related to information storage, it appears that the hypothesis that STEM is primarily related to this function must be abandoned. The consensus was that the evidence suggested that the electrophysiological changes observed as a result of thermal modulation during STEM were not likely to be of functional significance, but a minority argued that these effects could indicate a modulatory role for STEM in information storage, and that there is insufficient empirical evidence at this time to distinguish between these alternatives. Laroche (1993) recently reported differential changes in perforant path evoked field potentials in conditioned and pseudoconditioned rats in a tone-shock fear-conditioning paradigm. This is an interesting observation; however, it is not possible to know whether these conditioning protocols were associated with changes in brain temperature—different aspects of the results argue both in favor and against this possibility.

The opinion was expressed that one of the main reasons it may be so difficult to see changes in the brain that reflect information storage, is that the actual structure of the representation may not be accessible with currently available technology. It was predicted, however, that within the next decade, as parallel recording methods are improved, that the examination of the interactions of many cells recorded simultaneously, during well-defined behaviors, may lead to insights about these elusive representations. Furthermore, approaches that are currently available, but under-used, include those exemplified by the Kim and Fanselow (1992) study, in which the consolidation gradient for a context-specific fear response was tracked, with lesion methods, across a 4-week period. This approach could help us understand the dynamics of the interactions between medial temporal lobe structures and neocortex during the formation of long-term memory.

Computational Requirements and the Relative Expression of LTP and LTD

In developing hypotheses about the possible significance of one or another plasticity mechanism, it will be important to consider both the anatomical context (network architecture) in which it is expressed and what computational task is required of the network. Recent concepts from neural network theory may help focus thinking on this issue. Broadly speaking, there are two classes of learning in neural nets: one which can capture information rapidly in a single trial (e.g., Marr 1971), but makes rather inefficient use of storage elements, and one which optimizes storage and representational efficiency, but requires a lengthy process of repeated presentation of all of the items to be stored with gradual adjustments of synaptic strengths (Mazzoni et al. 1991). The former systems preserve differences among individual events. The latter systems are well suited to complex mapping and classification problems in which smooth generalizations over the problem domain are required.

The former "rapid learning" systems typically make use of very sparse encoding and large positive changes (e.g., large LTP) to the connections, whereas the latter "slow learning" systems work better with more distributed encoding and small changes whose sign may be positive or negative (weak LTP or LTD) depending on some error function. The key point is that optimization of the synaptic weight distribution in the "slow learning system" (at least in currently studied models) requires access to all of the data to be stored so that the representation of each item can be optimized with respect to the rest. Attempts to store new data after the optimization has been performed leads to catastrophic interference (McCloskey and Cohen 1989). The difficulty is that for many kinds of learning problems the world does not provide the luxury of repeated trials over the whole problem domain. It has been suggested (McClelland et al. 1992) that this difficulty could be overcome by having two different memory systems: a fast but temporary one, possibly the hippocampus, and a slow but more permanent one, possibly the neocortex. The hippocampus could then act as a teacher for the cortex, providing the opportunity for repeated learning trials within the context of the information whose stored representations have already been optimized. This theory at least accounts for the apparent slowness of the memory consolidation process and predicts that hippocampal synapses should exhibit robust LTP but weak LTD whereas cortex might exhibit both processes equally, but only in small amounts under normal levels of activation.

CHARACTERISTICS AND POSSIBLE FUNCTIONS OF ACTIVITY-DEPENDENT SYNAPTIC CHANGES IN THE NEOCORTEX

Although LTP and LTD were first described in other parts of the brain, both forms of synaptic plasticity have now been described in a number of areas of the neocortex. The prevalence of these processes outside traditional "memory" areas leads to a variety of hypotheses concerning their functional role in other parts of the brain.

Associative Procedures Used to Induce LTP and LTD in the Cortex

Both tetanus of afferent input and pairing (electrical or sensory evoked) induced methods have been used to obtain changes in synaptic gain in a variety of regions of cortex. In visual, sensorimotor, motor, and frontal neocortex, homosynaptic LTP and heterosynaptic and homosynaptic LTD have been observed. The time course of these effects has been measured in slices, acutely anesthetized preparations and awake animals (Baranyi, Szente et al. 1991). Depending on the experimental induction conditions, increases in synaptic strength can occur for up to 2 hours undiminished for monosynaptic responses (i.e., until the recording session was terminated). This is comparable to the LTP duration usually observed in the hippocampus. Furthermore, decreases in synaptic efficacy can be induced that last for approximately the same time course, again, with little decrement out to 2 hours in some cases. Functional changes *in vivo*, in which the duration and sign parallel that of synaptic changes, have been reported also (Frégnac et al. 1988, 1992). Changes lasting less than one hour have been observed, which might reflect short-term processes (STP and STD) like those found elsewhere. Like Group 3, the group discussed, but did not reach consensus on the question of whether these short-term changes represented some reduced form of the long-term process or reflected instead the action of some different process or processes.

In the neocortex, LTP and LTD have been studied by a relatively small number of groups, and their data seem to be in good general agreement with one another. Some of our group were concerned that this congenial state might disappear as more researchers started to work in the neocortex: in the spirit of a comment made by a member of the group, "the more doctors we have, the more ill people we have." A certain amount of discussion was therefore devoted to a number of interesting technical points concerning the study of these processes in the neocortex. Particular mention was made of some of the difficulties of recording from cortical slices, which may be of benefit to those contemplating entering the field. First of all, the state of the postsynaptic neuron will be critical in determining the effect of the test responses and conditioning stimulation. At the single cell level during intracellular recordings, the basic membrane parameters (such as the resting potential, input resistance, spike properties, I–V relationships, spike threshold, and parameters of available synaptic responses, etc.) can be very different, both under *in vivo* versus *in vitro* conditions and also among different cell types in the same experiment. When measuring the synaptic change in the neocortex, the consensus was that it is impossible to interpret field potential recordings because the exact basis for the different, very complicated components is not understood. In particular, sources and sinks of EPSPs (and other events) are intermingled. Second, spike firing, EPSPs, and IPSPs overlap in time during the field potential responses; the cortex' ubiquitous disynaptic inhibition may on occasion even occur rapidly enough to obscure the monosynaptic EPSP. Even when assessing the intracellular EPSP in the neocortex, it is important to measure only the initial slope, in order to reduce contamination by IPSPs that may occur very early in the wave form. Studies of pure EPSPs cannot, however, be achieved, since there seems to be a ceiling level of bicuculline (1–1.2 μM) above which epileptiform activity will occur. Another perspective might be derived not from attempting to isolate individual synaptic components but by measuring the overall amplitude of the response to extract an average gain from the system or measure of "effective" connectivity (Aertsen et al. 1988). This approach does not allow one to determine the separate components of the processes contributing to the network but may capture important overall organizational and network features of the response that cannot be assigned to particular synaptic components.

Another consideration is that when stimulating cortical slices, it is simply not possible to stimulate specific afferent axons, because the white matter also contains association fibers and efferent axons with recurrent collaterals. Indeed, the vast majority of the fibers in white matter are not thalamocortical, and so the response evoked by this stimulus in cortex is quite different from that elicited by selective stimulation of specific afferents. Moreover, most recordings in the slice are from layer 2–3 or layer 5 pyramidal cells, which do not receive thalamic afferents. Regular-spiking cells, bursting cells, and fast-spiking (presumed inhibitory) neurons can be modified. In the motor cortex of anesthetized and nonanesthetized cats, during intracellular recordings *in vivo*, it is possible to induce LTP (and LTD) without bicuculline at resting potentials around –67 mV in anesthetized and –64 mV in awake cats (Baranyi, Szente et al. 1991). Similar data are available from the *in vivo* visual cortex (Baranyi, Debanne et al. 1991; Frégnac et al. 1993). Other evidence indicates that NMDA-dependent and independent forms of LTP can be induced in the neocortex (Komatsu et al. 1991). The relationships between cell type and induction conditions or other properties of synaptic plasticity, seem to be critical and have to be interpreted more fully in the neocortex. In addition to these technical issues, it must be recalled that the circuit properties of the cortex appear to be quite different from those of the hippocampus. It seems to be much more difficult to obtain a lasting effect in the cortex *in vivo* under natural physiological conditions, perhaps because of the greater amount of inhibition in cortical circuits. It was nonetheless the consensus of the group that there was no reason to suppose, on the basis of currently available data that there are important variations in at least the potential for plasticity across different cortical cell types or areas. It may be that every neuron in neocortex is capable of expressing LTP and LTD.

Functional Roles of LTP and LTD in Cortical Plasticity

As yet there is no direct evidence that LTP and LTD are related to the developmental changes involved in the establishment of cortical function. There are, however, a number of correlative observations that make the hypothesis attractive, i.e., that the processes involved in the induction of LTP and LTD also serve as initial steps in experience-dependent rearrangements of cortical connectivity during development. The latter consists essentially of consolidation of connections, exhibiting a high degree of correlated activity with the postsynaptic target cells, and of disconnection of connections that are often inactive while the postsynaptic cell is strongly activated by other inputs. The first change resembles homosynaptic potentiation and the second heterosynaptic depression. The hypothesis derived from *in vitro* studies on LTP and LTD suggests that the former requires a strong surge of Ca^{2+} in the postsynaptic dendrite, as is normally obtained only with NMDA receptor activation, while the latter requires smaller Ca^{2+} rises, such as can be obtained with activation of voltage-gated Ca^{2+} channels. Thus, both LTP and consolidation of synapses will normally require NMDA receptor activation and hence coincidence of presynaptic activity with strong postsynaptic depolarization, while LTD and disconnection only require strong post-synaptic activations. To attain the level of depolarization required to depress inactive inputs, it is normally required that the activating inputs can use the NMDA mechanism to enhance postsynaptic depolarization. This accounts for similarities between requirements for the induction of developmental modification and LTP and LTD, such as their dependence on NMDA receptors, the differentiating role of correlated activity, and the facilitating action of neuromodulators such as acetylcholine and norepinephrine. In conclusion, the conversion of electrical signals into graded changes of postsynaptic Ca^{2+} concentrations could serve as a first step for the initiation of the processes that lead to changes in circuitry during development and LTP and LTD throughout life (see Singer and Artola, this volume).

LTP and presumably also LTD are more easily induced during early development because of reduced inhibition, expression of NMDA receptors with prolonged opening kinetics, and a variety of other factors including redistribution of voltage-gated Ca^{2+} channels, Ca^{2+} buffering mechanisms, and modulatory systems. None of these developmental changes actually seem to be limiting factors for the critical period, rather the decline of the system's susceptibility to undergo changes of circuitry appears to be associated with the decline of genuine developmental processes such as sprouting, synaptogenesis, and retractions of transiently formed synaptic contacts. The fact that these developmental processes seem to be influenced by the same activity-dependent mechanisms that are also involved in the induction of LTP and LTD suggests that in both cases the conversion of electrical activity into molecular signaling cascades depends upon the same trigger mechanism. This explains why synaptic modification rules initially developed to explain experience-dependent map formations, like the BCM or the Hebb/Stent rule, resemble closely those derived from *in vitro* studies of LTP and LTD in the adult cortex (see below). Unfortunately, however, very little is known to date about the mechanism downstream of the differential changes of Ca^{2+}, either with respect to the developmental processes or in the context of LTP and LTD. In the former case, the search will have to include mechanisms involved in structural consolidation of synapses and hence will have to concentrate also on an analysis of cell-recognition molecules and structural proteins.

Cortical maps can also be modified in adult animals following modification of sensory input either by experimental rearrangement or by training (Merzenich et al. 1983, 1984; Kaas et al. 1990; Gilbert et al. 1990; Reccanzone et al. 1992). While some of these modifications may reflect reorganizations in subcortical structures, there are certainly cases in which changes in cortical circuits must be involved. At present there is no direct evidence that the cortical component of these map changes is mediated by LTP or LTD (although there is a single report suggesting that the changes are dependent upon signals relayed through the NMDA receptor (Kano et al. 1991). Map changes may require the unmasking of latent excitatory connections, perhaps carried by the well-known system of horizontal intracortical connections (Gilbert et al. 1990). Such unmasking might best be understood in terms of alterations in the balance of cortical excitation and inhibition; however, due to the involvement of basal forebrain cholinergic input, the requirement for attention and the possible dependence on NMDA receptor activation, the participation of cortical mechanisms related to developmental plasticity and/or LTP and LTD seems a likely possibility (see Singer and Artola, this volume).

Computational Rules of Synaptic Plasticity

Different models have been proposed to predict the amplitude and sign of the synaptic change as a function of pre- and postsynaptic activity. These models can usefully be seen as extensions of the original proposal of Hebb (1949) for strengthening appropriately correlated synaptic connections. Figure 7.1 illustrates hypothetical rules of

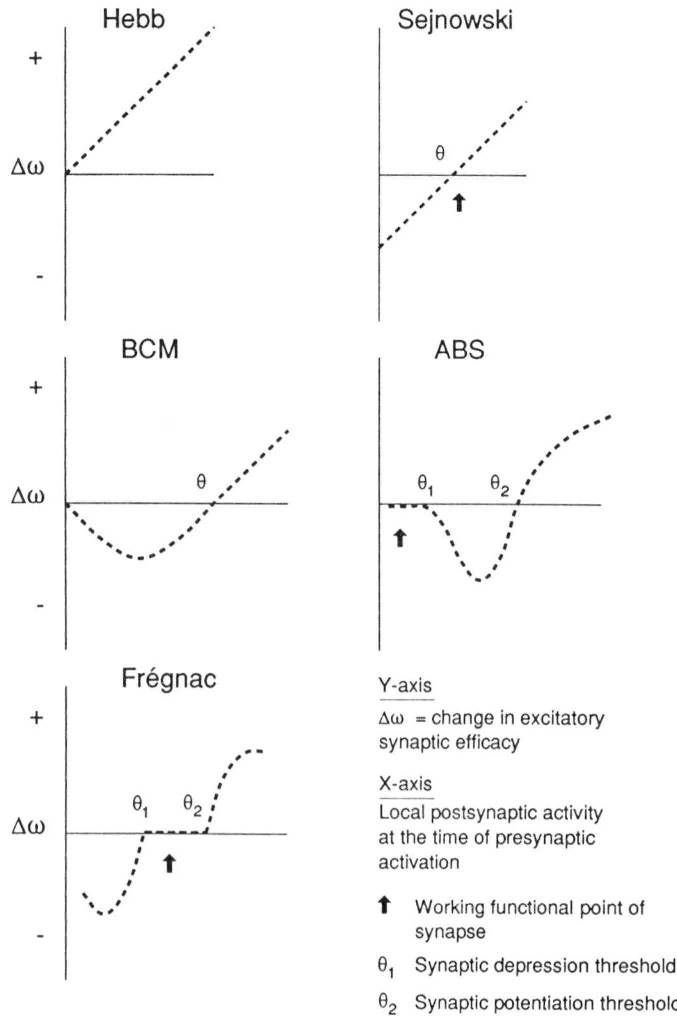

homosynaptic plasticity that have been put forward in cerebellum (Figure 7.1B) and visual cortex (Figure 7.1C–E), and which might be related to the classical Hebb-like schemes of synaptic plasticity (regrettably, time constraints prevented extension of this discussion to consideration of heterosynaptic plasticity). It should be made clear that to devise more stringent requirements in experimental tests of these models, the relevant postsynaptic variables are neither measured (most recordings are current clamp somatic intracellular recordings) nor unequivocally defined (membrane potential, change in calcium level, etc.). It could be that the apparent contradiction between the various schemes may simply reflect differences in the experimental approaches that are known to affect the functioning point of the synapse in response to the test input. This should be kept in mind, especially when one compares the *in vitro* and *in vivo* situations in which the mean level of activity is completely different. In spite of these remarks, agreement was reached concerning the blockade of the induction of LTD and LTP in totally calcium-chelated neocortical neurons (Baranyi and Szente 1987; Bröcher et al. 1992; Hirsch and Crépel 1992). However, the observation that tetanus-induced LTD in partially chelated neurons (Figure 3 in Bröcher et al. 1992; Kimura et al. 1990; Yoshimura et al. 1991) makes one wonder how the rise in free intracellular calcium evoked postsynaptically by test synaptic activity in the chelated

---

Figure 7.1 Comparison of the predictions of different rules of changes in excitatory synaptic efficacy (+: potentiation; –: depression) in an active pathway as a function of concomitant postsynaptic activity (given by either the firing state of the neuron (A–C) or by more local variables, such as the postsynaptic membrane potential at the synapse, the calcium level in the spine, etc.).

(A) Hebb's postulate (1949) predicts only positive changes in synaptic efficacy, which increase linearly with postsynaptic activity, the slope being proportional to presynaptic activity.

(B) Sejnowski's hypothesis in the cerebellum (1977) predicts both an increase and decrease in synaptic efficacy, which reflect in their sign and amplitude that of the covariance between pre- and postsynaptic activity. Only one postsynaptic plasticity threshold is defined, below and above which, respectively, synaptic depression and potentiation can occur.

(C) Bienenstock et al. (1982) introduced the hypothesis of a floating threshold depending on the past synaptic activity of the cell. The lower the average past activity, the faster the threshold would move to the left, and the more easily synaptic potentiation will be induced .

(D) Artola and colleagues (1990) proposed the existence of two sliding thresholds. A progressive depolarization from the resting membrane potential predicts the successive crossing of a low threshold above which depression occurs, before a second higher threshold is reached, above which synaptic potentiation is obtained. Two distinct ranges of membrane potential are proposed for which no synaptic changes are expected.

(E) Frégnac and collaborators (Frégnac et al. 1990; Baranyi, Debanne et al. 1991) observed *in vitro* and *in vivo* potentiation of compound PSPs when paired with intracellular depolarization, and depression of the same PSP when paired with hyperpolarization. They propose the existence of a unique "read-only" state (see arrow) representing the admissible range of potential at the synapse which still allows sensory neurons to transmit reliably visual information.

The vertical arrow corresponds to the normal functioning state of the synapse reached at the time of activation of the test input.

neurons compares with that evoked during normal control synaptic transmission. Defining preparations in which such measurements could be made appears to be an important experimental goal.

For an extensive presentation of possible cellular mechanisms implied in LTP and LTD in the neocortex, the reader is referred to the chapter by Singer and Artola (this volume). Nonetheless, a number of independent experiments suggest that homosynaptic depression can be induced when (a) test input activation is paired with hyperpolarization of the target cell (Stanton and Sejnowski 1989; Frégnac et al. 1990; Baranyi, Debanne et al. 1991), (b) when afferent activity *in vivo* is associated with blockade of postsynaptic activity by iontophoretic means (Frégnac et al. 1988, 1992), or (c) via $GABA_A$ agonist application (Reiter and Stryker 1988). Although they depart from the classical view that hyperpolarization blocks the induction of synaptic changes, these observations can be compared phenomenologically with the recent cross-correlation studies in the behaving monkey by Ahissar et al. (1992), discussed below. These authors observed significant short-lasting reduction in the effective coupling between the two neurons recorded simultaneously, following the imposition of a reduced correlation between their activity during the attentional phase of the behavioral task. These different results obtained in a variety of experimental situations (*in vitro*, *in vivo* anesthetized, *in vivo* behaving) leave open the possibility that repetitive failure in synaptic transmission caused by postsynaptic factors, which interfere with the normal input-output processing of the neuron, could result in a down regulation of synaptic gain or at least functional coupling.

A Homeostatic Function for LTP and LTD?

LTP was first described in the hippocampus, while LTD was first described in the cerebellum. These two structures have long been associated with theories of memory and learning, and it was perhaps natural to imagine that the synaptic plasticity found there represented the cellular foundations of memory and learning function. Inconveniently, LTP and LTD are now known to be prevalent throughout the neocortex (see preceding section) and possibly also in thalamus as well (Scharfman et al. 1991). Although we concentrated on considering the role of LTP and LTD in plasticity, it is also clear that an argument can be made that LTP and LTD in some structures serve to *defeat* plasticity by playing a stabilizing or homeostatic role in neural processing.

There is certainly a need for such homeostatic mechanisms. Sensory and motor processes in the neocortex and thalamus often depend upon achieving a precise balance between opposing input signals or on precisely regulating the dependence of responses on afferent inputs (e.g., Movshon et al. 1978). It is difficult to imagine that all this neural machinery can remain precisely and perfectly calibrated under all the trials and perturbations that the brain must experience in the course of everyday life, and it is therefore very attractive to imagine that synaptic plasticity could serve to *maintain* the function of neural circuits in the face of changes in input signal strength or reliability. Indeed, it may be that the cortical map reorganization discussed above, and some of the short-term gain changes discussed below, reflect the action of neocortical LTP and LTD processes that are acting to stabilize cortical function in the face of perturbed afferent input. It is attractive and possibly correct to think of synaptic plasticity as a mechanism of change (= learning, memory). It is also appealing to imagine it as a mechanism that resists change when change is not wanted.

PLASTIC NEURAL CIRCUITS FOR FUTURE EXPLORATION

In this final section, we consider a number of interesting and important examples of plastic neural systems in the cerebellum and neocortex whose cellular and molecular foundations are not yet known, but which may be important targets for future work aimed at linking the cellular and systems levels of explanation.

Plasticity of the Vestibulo-ocular Reflex (VOR)

Of the examples in this section, the VOR is the simplest and most completely worked out. Interestingly, it is also an area of long-standing and principled disagreement between two major research groups, and thus it offers an important set of insights and cautions. The views of these two groups are articulated by Ito and Lisberger (both this volume), so that this section concentrates on the points of difference between the two.

When the head moves, even in darkness, the eyes move in the opposite direction to compensate and maintain visual stabilization. The "flocculus hypothesis" described by Ito (this volume) gives an explanation for the anatomy and behavior of cells involved in the adaptation of the VOR that could account for this reflex. As outlined by Lisberger (this volume), there is another point of view concerning the operation and anatomy of the VOR. There are a number of issues on which these two points of view diverge:

1. Ito contends that Lisberger does not have good anatomical control over the cells from which he records, suggesting that Lisberger has recorded from the wrong Purkinje cells in the wrong part of the cerebellum. Ito uses microstimulation to prove localization in the H-zone of the flocculus or ventral paraflocculus and argues that this control is necessary to be certain of the type of cells recorded from. Lisberger cites histological evidence that he has recorded from parts of the flocculus and ventral paraflocculus that overlap with the areas studied by Ito's group (although not the most caudal 3 folia). This issue cannot be resolved at present because Lisberger typically does not use this microstimulation method, and Ito typically does not identify the cells he uses in testing conditions comparable to Lisberger's.
2. Lisberger cites two studies (Luebke and Robinson 1992; Paster et al. 1990) in which changes in the gain of the VOR were at least partially remembered if the animal was first adapted and the flocculus then ablated, suggesting that part of

the memory may reside outside the cerebellar cortex. Ito quoted Robinson's 1976 paper, where there was no such memory after lesion of the cerebellum. Ito and Lisberger agree that the new data must be evaluated critically before this issue can be resolved.

3. Another experiment by Collewijn and Grootendorst (1979) suggests that it is possible to obtain motor learning in the VOR without providing any vestibular stimulation, which would suggest a nonvestibular input to the flocculus. Ito agrees that there is crosstalk between VOR learning and optokinetic reflex adaptation and explained how this crosstalk could still happen within the flocculus.
4. Ito asserts that previous recordings of the vestibular responses of Purkinje cells used techniques that were inappropriate for measuring the strength of their vestibular inputs. Lisberger, Miles, and others have relied on recordings from cells in monkeys who tracked a target which moved in synchrony with the monkey during head rotation, cancelling the VOR. Ito suggested that the cell firing under these conditions reflects input from a separate signal that is a higher motor command for smooth pursuit eye movements; this signal is used both to generate smooth eye movements when the head is still and to counteract the VOR when the target moves with the head. Lisberger replied by citing evidence that there are separate head velocity and eye velocity inputs in the mossy fibers recorded in the flocculus and ventral paraflocculus. He argued that these two inputs sum to determine Purkinje cell firing, so that the head velocity input alone determines the Purkinje cell firing during cancellation of the VOR. There was no consensus on this issue, but both Ito and Lisberger agreed that it could be resolved with a better understanding of the mechanisms of the generation of smooth pursuit eye movements and of visual cancellation of the VOR.
5. Lisberger cites Broussard et al. (1992) as having demonstrated that motor learning in the VOR can be expressed in the eye movements evoked 5 msec after the application of a single electrical pulse to the vestibular apparatus, an interval too brief to allow transmission through the flocculus. Lisberger also has data to suggest that brainstem neurons can express learning at latencies of 12 msec after the onset of a rapid head turn, while Purkinje cells do not respond until later. Ito again cites disagreement about whether Lisberger has recorded from the relevant group of Purkinje cells and would like to see further experiments performed to resolve this issue.
6. In computational models, Lisberger incorporates two sites of learning in his model to allow the model to regulate both stability of the VOR and the gain of the VOR. Ito's models, by making different assumptions about the relative importance of the various pathways that mediate the VOR, are able to achieve stable performance with one site of modification within the cerebellar cortex. Both investigators' models give good independent fits to the data the individuals believe to be true about the VOR system.

Finally, there were two main points of agreement between Ito and Lisberger. First, both accept a potential role for LTD at parallel fiber-Purkinje cell synapses in the cerebellum for motor learning in the VOR, although it must be stressed that Lisberger's model admits but does not require this. Second, perhaps a more important point of agreement, concerns the need to record more Purkinje cells from regions of the flocculus that participate in the horizontal VOR so that their data can be compared more readily. As to the second question of whether VOR adaptation involves plasticity in the brainstem as well as in the flocculus, as proposed by Lisberger in his 1988 model, Ito suggested that while he does not accept the computational reasoning in that model, he leaves open the possibility (given strong experimental evidence) that plasticity may occur elsewhere than in the cerebellum. Ito argues, however, that such plasticity would be subsidiary to plasticity in the cerebellar cortex.

Paradigms for Studying Neocortical Plasticity

A number of different experiments were discussed that illustrate a variety of ways in which cortical plasticity can be examined in animals. One of particular interest was that done by Ahissar et al. (1992), who recorded from auditory cortical cells during a vigilance task, in which animals had to depress a lever until a change in tone was detected. The cross-correlations between cells were determined in the period before conditioning occurred. During the conditioning procedure, in which the animal's attention to the auditory stimulus was also elicited, each time one cell fired, an auditory stimulus was presented that activated the other cell. This altered the correlation between the firing of the pre- and postsynaptic cells, usually increasing the correlation. This in turn led, in the space of a few minutes, to stronger coupling in the cross-correlation function between the pairs of cells measured in the *absence* of the auditory stimulus. This increased coupling was generally brief but could last up to 20 minutes. Interestingly, in those cases where the effect of the auditory stimulus was to decrease the correlation between the two cells, the coupling was also decreased. Therefore, this paradigm is capable of revealing changes in neuronal association in both directions, suggesting that it might provoke the joint action of processes like LTP and LTD.

In another approach, Woody and his colleagues used classical conditioning and intracellular recording techniques to study the cellular correlates of the conditioned eye-blink reflex in the motor cortex of awake cats (Woody 1982; Woody et al. 1991; Aou et al. 1992a, b). Although changes in synaptic responses to the conditioned auditory stimulus were not studied in detail, the electrophysiological properties of neurons measured intracellularly before and after conditioning in the same animal showed postsynaptic excitability changes, suggesting that synaptic plasticity might be involved. Synaptic changes have also been observed following classical α-conditioning of a CS (stimulation of the nucleus interpositus) and a US (footshock) in the awake cat (Rispal-Padel and Meftah 1993).

A related but little-known experiment performed in the 1960s by Dumenko (1961) was discussed, in which EEG recordings were performed in dogs following Pavlovian conditioning to either visual or auditory stimuli. Dumenko reported that the establishment of a tone- or light-conditioned paw withdrawal reflex led to the emergence of ~40 Hz oscillatory response components that were synchronized in the cortical areas involved in the conditioning paradigms (cf. von der Malsburg and Singer 1988; Singer 1990). Thus coherent oscillations occurred over the visual cortex and the front-paw representation in the motor cortex when front-paw withdrawal was conditioned to visual stimuli; when the conditioning stimulus was auditory, or rear-paw withdrawal was conditioned, the synchronous cortical activity shifted appropriately. The coherent oscillations thus outlasted the actual conditioning and were specific to the areas that were relevant to the conditioning paradigm. The results suggest that plastic changes in the strength of cortico-cortical connections may be associated with classical conditioning, although again without providing any hint about the underlying cellular mechanism.

Another potentially very exciting experiment that may tap into properties of cells involved in lasting memories that may be medial temporal lobe-dependent was recently reported by Sakai and Miyashita (1991). Monkeys learned to recognize pair associations across a 5-second delay in a set of 12 pairs of arbitrary visual patterns in such a way that two patterns were always paired (i.e., if pattern A was presented, the monkey chose B; if B was presented, the monkey chose A). After an extended learning period, recording in anteroventral temporal cortex (probably perirhinal or possibly area TE) revealed a substantially increased proportion of cells responding to subsets of the 24 "trained" patterns. Moreover, they found two interesting types of cells: *pair-responsive* neurons that responded to members of each pair with increased firing and *pair-recall* neurons that showed increased firing after presentation of a cue stimulus, in neuronal "expectation" of the stimulus with which the first stimulus had been paired during training. That is, these neurons increased their firing to a stimulus belonging to a previously learned pair, during the 5-second interval between presentations. The interest in this type of approach was that it might be possible to watch the development of a representation in the neocortex at the cellular level. The main caveat is that the task was apparently very difficult to learn, taking many months, and it remains to be established if it is dependent upon the medial temporal lobe memory structures. Also, very few neurons exhibited these properties. It is important to note that the strategies adopted by monkeys (especially in tasks on which they have been "overtrained" in the interests of obtaining asymptotically reliable performance) can often be quite different from those expected or intended by experimenters.

A case in point is the recent reinterpretation of data on "working memory" cells described by Miller and Desimone (pers. comm.). These investigators originally reported that cells in the anteroventral cortex of monkeys functioned as "adaptive memory filters," whose response was a joint product of the current stimulus and stored memory traces. In monkeys trained to recognize the second appearance of a cued item in a list (i.e., A–B–C–D–A, where A is the cue), cells in this cortex showed a reduced response to the second presentation of A (Miller et al. 1991, 1993), as though the specific memory of the cue was retained in the cortex. By changing the procedure to include repeated distractor stimuli, they discovered that the monkey was not doing the recognition task intended but was instead responding to simple pair-repetition (i.e., in the sequence A–B–C–C–A, the monkey responded not to the second A, but to the second C, which occurred before the final A). Likewise, the cells in question showed reduced responses to the repeated C as well as to the final A, indicating that their response was also determined by simple repetition. When the monkey was retrained to oblige it to perform the intended task, the cells in temporal cortex actually *increased* their firing rates (the opposite of the result obtained previously), and this increase was specific to the one stimulus that matched the cued item. Therefore, the new task uncovered a neuronal property that may actually be a basis for working memory which coexists with other mechanisms that may underlie the recognition of repetition or recency. These data have important implications for an accurate interpretation of cellular behavior in a wide range of experimental situations.

Other forms of plasticity in the neocortex are evident in a variety of phenomena, whose time course usually varies in the range of seconds to minutes. These changes are expressed in the visual cortex through the action of mechanisms that serve to regulate the gain and sensitivity of cortical neurons, in response to variations in the average intensity of ongoing stimulation, and are reflected in visual perception in the form of several aftereffects. These aftereffects can produce a variety of changes in the perception of motion (waterfall effect), form (tilt aftereffect, figural aftereffect, spatially selective elevation of contrast thresholds, etc.), and other aspects of the visual scene. Interestingly, these aftereffects often show a phenomenon known as *storage*, in which an aftereffect that would be expected to decay in seconds or minutes can be "preserved" and affect perception many hours after the adaptation period. The best-known example of this kind is the McCollough effect (McCollough 1965; a contingent color-orientation effect), which has been reported to persist for many days after prolonged induction (Skowbo et al. 1974; Thompson and Movshon 1978).

Some of these aftereffects are known to depend on adaptive changes in the response properties of cortical neurons (e.g., Maffei and Fiorentini 1973; Vautin and Berkley 1977; Ohzawa et al. 1985). Interestingly, these effects cannot be explained by simple regulation of the gain of cortical neurons, because responses of a single neuron to the adapting target are usually more affected than responses to other targets of equivalent effectiveness (Movshon and Lennie 1979). It is often assumed, but has not been formally shown, that the long-lasting "stored" aftereffects are also caused by changes in the characteristics of cortical networks in primary, or low-order, sensory areas.

The relevance of these effects to other cortical areas is not known. It seems reasonable, however, to assume that the plastic changes in visual cortex, following adaptation, reflect the use of mechanisms present and functional in all parts of neocortex. Certainly, the feedback control of local gain seems likely to be a feature of many kinds of cortical processing, and computational models suggest that these changes can be mediated by cortical circuits that are certainly not unique to the visual cortex (e.g., Heeger 1992).

How Are Cortical Long-term Memory Representations Established?

Although the medial temporal lobe memory system is essential for the creation of new long-term memories, it has long been known that after a time, these memories reside in, and can be retrieved from, the neocortex alone. Two extreme views as to how permanent memories are set up in the neocortex can be delineated. The first is that all long-term memory is initially stored in medial temporal lobe structures, and that there is no fast-onset plasticity of a permanent nature in neocortex, and that permanent memories are gradually transferred to the neocortex through some incremental process that adjusts synaptic weights. The second view is that all long-term information storage takes place immediately in the neocortex, but that the cortex cannot make use of it without the participation of medial temporal lobe structures. According to this view, the neocortex holds the permanent memories and the medial temporal lobe structures assist in binding together these memories into meaningful and retrievable ensembles. These views are, of course, extreme, and there is a range of intermediate possibilities as well.

At present there are essentially no data that would definitively support one or the other view. Many in the group favored the second view (neocortical storage from the outset) because of possible limitations in the storage capacity of medial temporal lobe memory system structures. On the other hand, physiological studies of LTP and LTD in the cortex (described above) do not permit a definitive answer to the question of whether the cortex possesses the ability for rapidly induced long-lasting plasticity; it may be that the inhibitory properties of cortical circuits make it difficult to generalize from the long-lasting plastic changes seen *in vitro*.

An experimental test of these two ideas might become possible if techniques for erasing LTP at different times after learning become available. Upon first view, such manipulations would only be effective in the period immediately after learning in the medial temporal lobe memory system structures; the second view would suggest that such a manipulation would be effective both in the neocortex and medial temporal areas.

CONCLUSIONS

Although we could not agree on a single approach or experiment that would resolve the broad question of how long-term memories are established in the brain, there were both conceptual and experimental points of consensus that are important to reiterate. First, it is clear that there are multiple long-term memory systems. A more precise delineation of these systems will, at the very least, require an understanding both of the behavioral process that is being measured by the task of choice (i.e., see example from Miller and Desimone [pers. comm.]), as well as the precision with which damage can be constrained to single structures of interest (i.e., see examples from Zola-Morgan et al. 1989a, b). Given some anatomical constraints on storage of specific types of long-term memory, the relative roles that medial temporal lobe structures play versus other neo- and subcortical regions becomes central. Presumably, if methods become available that allow selective, timed, erasure of memory events, the extent to which traces are laid down in multiple structures may become known, along with the ways in which these systems act in synchrony to produce lasting memories.

While most were prepared to entertain the hypothesis that the expression of LTP- and LTD-like processes (dependent upon postsynaptic calcium levels) at neocortical and hippocampal synapses may be utilized to implement information storage, all agreed that this hypothesis remains to be substantiated or refuted. Nevertheless, the fact that LTP and LTD can be found in structures known to be important for memory has inspired an exploration of the implications of how different learning rules might be implemented to bring about persistent modifications that could be used by the neural circuits under study. It is expected that critical assessment of the advantages of various computational approaches will help to create both new theoretical frameworks and new experimental tests to sharpen our hypotheses concerning long-term memory. Some of the important experimental approaches to take in the future will certainly include strategies aimed at discovering specific modification events while memories are being laid down, either by assessing individual or multiple synaptic events or by monitoring the dynamic interaction among large groups of simultaneously recorded cells. This may allow assessment of whether the rules of synaptic modification now under consideration are useful for understanding the richness of our enduring recollections of experience.

REFERENCES

Abraham, W.C., and G.V. Goddard. 1983. Asymmetric relationships between homosynaptic long-term potentiation and heterosynaptic long-term depression. *Nature* **305**:717–719.

Abraham, W.C., and J.R. Wickens. 1991. Heterosynaptic long-term depression is facilitated by blockade of inhibition in area CA1 of the hippocampus. *Brain Res.* **546**:336–340.

Aertsen, A.M.H., G.L. Gerstein, M. Habib, and G. Palm. 1988. Dynamics of neuronal firing correlation: Modulation of "effective" connectivity. *J. Neurophysiol.* **61**:900–917.

Ahissar, E., E. Vaadia, M. Ahissar, H. Bergman, A. Arieli, and M. Abeles. 1992. Dependence of cortical plasticity on correlated activity of single neurons and on behavioral context. *Science* **257**:1412–1415.

Alger, B.E., A.L. Megela, and T.J. Teyler. 1978. Transient heterosynaptic depression in the hippocampal slice. *Brain Res.* **3**:181–184.

Andersen, P., S.H. Sundberg, O. Sveen, and H. Wigstrom. 1977. Specific long-lasting potentiation of synaptic transmission in hippocampal slices. *Nature* **266**:736–737.

Angelie, S.J., E.A. Murray, and M. Mishkin. 1993. Hippocampectomized monkeys can remember one place but not two. *Neuropsych.*, in press.

Aou, S, C.D. Woody, and D. Birt. 1992a. Changes in the activity of units of the cat motor cortex with rapid conditioning and extinction of a compound eye blink movement. *J. Neurosci.* **12**:549–559.

Aou, S., C.D. Woody, and D. Birt. 1992b. Increases in excitability of neurons of the motor cortex of cats after rapid acquisition of eye blink conditioning. *J. Neurosci.* **12**:560–569.

Artola, A., S. Brocher, and W. Singer. 1990. Different voltage-dependent thresholds for inducing long-term depression and long-term potentiation in slices of rat visual cortex. *Nature* **347**:69–72.

Artola, A., and W. Singer. 1990. The involvement of N-methyl-D-aspartate receptors in induction and maintenance of long-term potentiation in rat visual cortex. *Eur. J. Neurosci.* **2**:254–269.

Baranyi, A., D. Debanne, D. Shulz, and Y. Frégnac. 1991. Potentiation and depression of visual responses induced *in vivo* by low frequency pairings in intracellularly recorded kitten visual cortical neurons. *Soc. Neurosci. Abstr.* **17**:1470.

Baranyi, A., and M.D Szente. 1987. Long-lasting potentiation of synaptic transmission requires postsynaptic modifications in the neocortex. *Brain Res.* **423**:378–384.

Baranyi, A., M. Szente, and C.D. Woody. 1991. Properties of association long-lasting potentiation induced by cellular conditioning in the motor cortex of conscious cats. *Neurosci.* **42**:321–334.

Barnes, C.A. 1979. Memory deficits associated with senescence: A neurophysiological and behavioral study in the rat. *J. Comp. Physiol. Psychol.* **93**:74–104.

Bienenstock, E., L.N. Cooper, and P. Munro. 1982. Theory for the development of neurone selectivity: Orientation specificity and binocular interaction in visual cortex. *J. Neurosci.* **2**:23–48.

Bindman, L.J., G. Christofi, S.R. Bolsover, and A.V. Nowicky. 1993. Postsynaptic induction of long-term depression (LTD) of synaptic transmission in the hippocampal slice. In: Long-Term Potentiation: A Debate of Current Issues, vol. 2, ed. M. Baudry and J. Davis. Cambridge, MA: MIT Press, in press.

Brahman, C.R., and B. Srebro. 1987. Induction of long-term depression and potentiation by low- and high-frequency stimulation in the dentate area of the anesthetized rat: Magnitude, time course and EEG. *Brain Res.* **405**:100–107.

Bröcher, S., A. Artola, and W. Singer. 1992. Intracellular injection of Ca^{++} chelators blocks induction of long-term depression in rat visual cortex. *Proc. Natl. Acad. Sci. USA* **89**:123–127.

Broussard, D.M., H.M. Bronte-Stewart, and S.G. Lisberger. 1992. Expression of motor learning in the response of the primate vestibulo-ocular reflex pathway to electrical stimulation. *J. Neurophysiol.* **67**:1493–1508.

Chattarji, S., P.K. Stanton, and T.J. Sejnowski. 1989. Commissural synapses, but not mossy fibre synapses, in the hippocampal field CA3 exhibit associative long-term potentiation an depression. *Brain Res.* **495**:145–150.

Christie, B.R., and W.C. Abraham. 1992a. NMDA-dependent heterosynaptic long-term depression in the dentate gyrus of anaesthetized rats. *Synapse* **10**:1–6.

Christie, B.R., and W.C. Abraham. 1992b. Priming of associative long-term depression in the dentate gyrus by theta frequency synaptic activity. *Neuron* **9**:79–84.

Christofi, G., A.V. Nowicky, S.R. Bolsover, and L.J. Bindman. 1993. The postsynaptic induction of non-associative long-term depression (LTD) of excitatory synaptic transmission in rat hippocampal slices. *J. Neurophysiol.* **69**:219–229.

Colbert, C.M., B.S. Burger, and W.B. Levy. 1992. Longevity of synaptic depression in the hippocampal dentate gyrus. *Brain Res.* **571**:159–161.

Collewijn, H., and A.F. Grootendorst. 1979. Adaptation of optokinetic and vestibulo-ocular reflexes to modified visual input in the rat. In: Reflex Control of Posture and Movement, Progress in Brain Research, ed. R. Granit and O. Pompeiano, pp. 772–781. Amsterdam: Elsevier.

Crépel, F., and D. Jaillard. 1991. Pairing of pre- and postsynaptic activities in cerebellar Purkinje cells induces long-term changes in synaptic efficacy *in vitro*. *J. Physiol. Lond.* **432**:123–141.

Crépel, F., and M. Krupa. 1990. Modulation of the responsiveness of cerebellar purkinje cells to excitatory amino acids. In: Excitatory Amino Acids and Neuronal Plasticity, ed. Y. Ben-Ari, pp. 323–329. New York: Plenum.

Dudek, S.M., and M.F. Bear. 1992. Homosynaptic long-term depression in area CA1 of hippocampus and effects of N-methyl-D-aspartate receptor blockade. *Proc. Natl. Acad. Sci. USA* **89**:4363–4367.

Dumenko, W.N. 1961. Veränderungen der elektrischen Rindenaktivität bei Hunden bei der Bildung eines Sterotyps motorisch bedingter Reflexe. *Pavlov Zeitschr. höhere Nerventätigkeit* **11(2)**:184–191.

Frégnac, Y., D. Debanne, D. Shulz, and A. Baranyi. 1993. Does postsynaptic membrane potential regulate functional plasticity in kitten visual cortex? In: LTP/LTD: A Debate of Current Issues, ed. M. Baudry and J. Davis. Boston: MIT Press, in press.

Frégnac, Y., D. Shulz, E. Bienenstock, and S. Thorpe. 1992. Cellular analogs of visual cortical epigenesis. I. Plasticity of orientation selectivity. *J. Neurosci.* **12**:1280–1300.

Frégnac, Y., D. Shulz, S. Thorpe, and E. Bienenstock. 1988. A cellular analogue of visual cortical plasticity. *Nature* **333**:367–370.

Frégnac, Y., D. Smith, and M. Friedlander. 1990. Postsynaptic membrane potential regulates synaptic potentiation and depression in visual cortical neurones. *Soc. Neurosci. Abstr.* **16**:798.

Fujii, S., K. Saito, H. Miyakaua, K. Ito, and M. Kato. 1991. Reversal of long-term potentiation (depotentiation) induced by tetanus stimulation of the input to CA1 neurons of guinea-pig hippocampal slices. *Brain Res.* **555**:112–122.

Gaffan, D., and S. Harrison. 1989. Place memory and scene memory: Effects of fornix transection in the monkey. *Exp. Brain Res.* **74**:202–212.

Gaffan, D., and E.A. Murray. 1990. Amygdalar interaction with the mediodorsal nucleus of the thalamus and the ventromedial prefrontal cortex in stimulus-reward associative learning in the monkey. *J. Neurosci.* **10**:3479–3493.

Gaffan, D., and E.A. Murray. 1992. Monkeys with rhinal cortex lesions succeed in object discrimination learning despite 24-hour intertrial intervals and fail at matching to sample despite double sample presentations. *Behav. Neurosci.* **106**:30–38.

Gilbert, C.D., J.A. Hirsch, and T.N. Wiesel. 1990. Lateral interactions in visual cortex. *Cold Spring Harbor Symp. Quant. Biol.* **LV**:663–678.

Green, E.J., B.L. McNaughton, and C.A. Barnes. 1990. Exploration-dependent modulation of evoked responses in fascia dentata: Dissociation of motor, EEG and sensory factors, and evidence for a synaptic efficacy change. *J. Neurosci.* **10**:1455–1471.

Hebb, D.O. 1949. The Organization of Behavior. New York: Wiley.

Heeger, D.J. 1992. Normalization of cell responses in cat striate cortex. *Vis. Neurosci.* **9**:181–197.

Hirsch, J.C., and F. Crépel. 1992. Postsynaptic calcium is necessary for the induction of LTP and LTD in prefrontal neurones. An *in vitro* study in the rat. *Synapse* **10**:173–175.

Horel, J., D.E. Pytko-Joiner, M. Vooytko, and K. Salsbury. 1987. The performance of visual tasks while segments of the inferotemporal cortex are suppressed by cold. *Behav. Brain Res.* **23**:29–42.

Ito, M. 1984. The Cerebellum and Neural Control. New York: Raven.

Ito, M. 1989. Long-term depression. *Ann. Rev. Neurosci.* **12**:85–102.

Jeffery, K.J., and R.G.M. Morris. 1993. Cumulative long-term potentiation in the rat dentate gyrus correlates with, but does not modify, performance in the watermaze. *Hippocampus* **3**:133–140.

Kaas, J.H., L.A. Krubitzer, Y.M. Chino, A.L. Langston, E.H. Polley, and N. Blair. 1990. Reorganization of retinotopic cortical maps in adult mammals after lesions of the retina. *Science* **248**:229–230.

Kano, M., K. Iino, and M. Kano. 1991. Functional reorganization of adult cat somatosensory cortex is dependent on NMDA receptors. *NeuroReport* **2**:77–80.

Kerr, D.S., and W.C. Abraham. 1993. A comparison of associative and nonassociative conditioning procedures in the induction of LTD in CA1 of the hippocampus. *Synapse* **14**:305–313.

Kesner, R.P., K. Crutcher, and D.R. Beers. 1988. Serial position curves for item (spatial location information): Role of the dorsal hippocampal formation and medial septum. *Brain Res.* **454**:219–226.

Kim, J.J., and M.S. Fanselow. 1992. Modality-specific retrograde amnesia of fear. *Science* **256**:675–677.

Kimura, F., T. Tsumoto, A. Nishigori, and Y. Yoshimura. 1990. Long-term depression but not potentiation is induced in CA^{2+}-chelated visual cortex neurons. *NeuroReport* **1**:65–68.

Komatsu, Y., Y. Narajima, and K. Toyama. 1991. Induction of long-term potentiation without the participation of N-methyl-D-aspartate receptors in kitten visual cortex. *J. Neurophysiol.* **65**:20–32.

Laroche, S. 1993. Neural mechanisms of associative memory: Role of long-term potentiation. In: Brain and Memory: Modulation and Mediation of Neuroplasticity, ed. J.L. McGaugh. London: Oxford Univ. Press, in press.

Levy, W.B., and O. Steward. 1979. Synapses as associative memory elements in the hippocampal formation. *Brain Res.* **175**:233–245.

Levy, W.B., and O. Steward. 1983. Temporal contiguity requirements for long-term associative potentiation/depression in the hippocampus. *Neurosci.* **8**:791–797.

Lisberger, S.G. 1988. The neural basis for learning of simple motor skills. *Science* **242**:728–735.

Luebke, A.E., and D.A. Robinson. 1992. Climbing fiber intervention blocks plasticity of the vestibulo-ocular reflex. *Ann. NY Acad. Sci.* **656**:428–431.

Lynch, G.S, T. Dunwiddie, and V. Grybkoff. 1977. Heterosynaptic depression: A postsynaptic correlate of long-term potentiation. *Nature* **266**:737–739.

Maffei, L., A. Fiorentini, and S. Bisti. 1973. Neural correlate of perceptual adaptation to gratings. *Science* **182**:1036–1039.

Marder, E., and A.I. Selverston. 1992. Modeling the stomatogastric nervous system. In: Dynamic Biological Networks: The Stomatogastric Nervous System, ed. R.M. Harris-Warrick, E. Marder, A.I. Selverston, and M. Moulins, pp. 161–196. Boston: MIT Press.

Marr, D. 1971. Simple memory: Theory for archicortex. *Phil. Trans. R. Soc. Lond. B* **262**:23–81.

Mazzoni, P., R.A. Andersen, and M.I. Jordan. 1991. A more biologically plausible learning rule for neural networks. *Proc. Natl. Acad. Sci. USA* **88**:4433–4437.

McClelland, J.L., B.L. McNaughton, R. O'Reilly, and L. Nadel. 1992. Complementary roles of hippocampus and neocortex in learning and memory. *Soc. Neurosci. Abstr.* **18**:1216.

McCloskey, M., and N.J. Cohen. 1989. Catastrophic interference in connectionist networks. In: The Psychology of Learning and Motivation, ed. G.H. Bower, vol. 24, pp. 109–164. New York: Academic.

McCollough, C. 1965. Color adaptation of edge detectors in the human visual system. *Science* **149**:1115–1116.

Merzenich, M.M., J.H. Kaas, J.T. Wall, M. Sur, R.J. Nelson, and D.J. Felleman. 1983. Progression of change following median nerve section in the cortical representation of the hand in areas 3b and 1 in adult owl and squirrel monkeys. *Neurosci.* **10**:639–655.

Merzenich, M.M., R.J. Nelson, M.P. Stryker, M.S. Cynader, A. Schoppmann, and J.M. Zook. 1984. Somatosensory cortical map changes following digital amputation in adult monkeys. *J. Comp. Neurol.* **224**:591–605.

Miller, E.K., L. Li, and R. Desimone. 1991. A neural mechanism for working and recognition memory in inferior temporal cortex. *Science* **254**:1377–1379.

Miller, E.K., L. Li, and R. Desimone. 1993. Activity of neurons in anterior inferior temporal cortex during a short-term memory task. *J. Neurosci.* **13**:1460–1478.

Moser, E., I. Mathiesen, and P. Andersen. 1993. Association between brain temperature and dentate field potentials in exploring and swimming rats. *Science* **259**:1324–1326.

Movshon, J.A., and P. Lennie. 1979. Spatially selective adaptation in striate cortical neurones. *Nature* **278**:850–852.

Movshon, J.A., I.D. Thompson, and D.J. Tolhurst. 1978. Spatial summation in the receptive fields of simple cells in the cat's striate cortex. *J. Physiol.* **283**:53–77.

Mulkey, R.M., and R.C. Malenka. 1992. Mechanisms underlying induction of homosynaptic long-term depression in area CA1 of the hippocampus. *Neuron* **9**:967–975.

Murray, E.A. 1992. Medial temporal lobe structures contributing to recognition memory: The amygdaloid complex versus rhinal cortex. In: The Amygdala: Neurobiological Aspects of Emotion, Memory, and Mental Dysfunction, ed. J.P. Aggleton, pp. 453–470. London: Wiley-Liss.

Ohzawa, I., G. Sclar, and R.D. Freeman. 1985. Contrast gain control in the cat's visual system. *J. Neurophysiol.* **54**:651–667.

O'Keefe, J., and L. Nadel. 1978. The Hippocampus as a Cognitive Map. Oxford: Clarendon.

Pastor, A.M., M. Weiser, S. McElligott, and R. Baker. 1990. Velocity step training of the goldfish vestibulo-ocular reflex suggests multiple sites are involved in gain modification. *Soc. Neurosci. Abstr.* **16**:1083.

Paulsen, O., O. Hvalby, and P. Andersen. 1990. Failure to produce long-term depression in hippocampal synapses by an anti-correlation procedure. *Eur. J. Neurosci.* **41**:261.

Pigott, S., and B. Milner. 1993. Memory for different aspects of complex visual scenes after unilateral temporal- or frontal-lobe resection. *Neuropsych.* **31**:1–15.

Pockett, S., N.H. Brookes, and L.J. Bindman. 1990. Long-term depression at synapses in slices of rat hippocampus can be induced by bursts of postsynaptic activity. *Exp. Brain Res.* **80**:196–200.

Recanzone, G.H., M.M. Merzenich, W.M. Jenkins, K.A. Grajski, and H.R. Dinse. 1992. Topographic reorganization of the hand representation in cortical area 3b of owl monkeys trained in a frequency-discrimination task. *J. Neurosci.* **67**:1031–1055.

Reiter, M.O., and M.P. Stryker. 1988. Neural plasticity without postsynaptic action potentials: Less active inputs become dominant when kitten visual cortical cells are pharmacologically inhibited. *Proc. Natl. Acad. Sci. USA* **85**:3623–3627.

Rispal-Padel, L., and E.M. Meftah. 1993. Changes in the motor responses induced by cerebellar stimulation during classical forelimb flexion conditioning in the cat. *J. Neurophysiol.* **68**:908–926.

Robinson, D.A. 1976. Adaptive gain control of vestibulo-ocular reflex by the cerebellum. *J. Neurophysiol.* **39**:954–969.

Sakai, K., and Y. Miyashita. 1991. Neural organization for the long-term memory of paired associates. *Nature* **354**:152–155.

Scharfman, H.E., M.E. Bickford, S.-M. Lu, W. Guido, P.R. Adams, and S.M. Sherman. 1991. Frequency facilitation and long-term potentiation of retinogeniculate and corticogeniculate EPSPs of cat lateral geniculate neurons recorded in thalamic slices. *Soc. Neurosci. Abstr.* **17**:709.

Sejnowski, T. 1977. Storing covariance with non-linearly interacting neurons. *J. Math. Biol.* **4**:303–321.

Sharp, P.E., B.L. McNaughton, and C.A. Barnes. 1989. Exploration-dependent modulation of evoked responses in fascia dentata: Fundamental observations and time course. *Psychobiol.* **17**:257–269.

Singer, W. 1990. Search for coherence: A basic principle of cortical self-organization. *Concepts Neurosci.* **1**:1–26.

Skowbo, D., T. Gentry, B. Timney, and R.B. Morant. 1974. The McCollough effect: Influence of several kinds of visual stimulation on decay rate. *Percep. Psych.* **16**:47–49.

Squire, L.R. 1992. Memory and the hippocampus: A synthesis from findings with rats, monkeys, and humans. *Psychol. Rev.* **99**:195–231.

Stanton, P.K., S. Chattarji, and T.J. Sejnowski. 1991. 2-amino-3-phosphonopropionic acid, an inhibitor of glutamate-stimulated phosphoinositide turnover, blocks induction of homosynaptic long-term depression, but not potentiation, in rat hippocampus. *Neurosci. Lett.* **127**:61–66.

Stanton, P.K., and T.J. Sejnowski. 1989. Associative long-term depression in the hippocampus induced by Hebbian covariance. *Nature* **339**:215–218.

Thompson, P.G., and J.A. Movshon. 1978. Storage of spatially specific threshold elevation. *Perception* **7**:65–73.

Vautin, R.G., and M.A. Berkley. 1977. Responses of single cells in cat visual cortex to prolonged stimulus movement: Neural correlates of visual aftereffects. *J. Neurophysiol.* **40**:1051–1065.

von der Malsburg, C., and W. Singer. 1988. Principles of cortical network organization. In: Neurobiology of Neocortex, ed. P. Rakic and W. Singer, pp. 69–99. Dahlem Workshop Report LS 42. Chichester: Wiley.

Woody, C.D. 1982. Memory, Learning and Higher Function: A Cellular View. New York: Springer.

Woody, C.D., E. Gruen, and D. Birt. 1991. Changes in membrane currents during Pavlovian conditioning of single cortical neurons. *Brain Res.* **539**:76–84.

Wright, A.A., R.G. Cook, J.J. Rivera, M.R. Shyan, J.J. Neiworth, and M. Jitsumori. 1990. Naming, rehearsal, and interstimulus interval effects in memory processing. *J. Exp. Psychol.* **16**:1043–1059.

Yoshimura, Y., T. Tsumoto, and A. Nishigori. 1991. Input-specific induction of long-term depression in CA^{2+}-chelated visual cortex neurons. *NeuroReport* **2**:393–396.

Zola-Morgan, S., L.R. Squire, and D.G. Amaral. 1989a. Lesions of the amygdala that spare adjacent cortical regions do not impair memory or exacerbate the impairment following lesions of the hippocampal formation. *J. Neurosci.* **9**:1922–1936.

Zola-Morgan, S., L.R. Squire, D.G. Amaral, and W. Suzuki. 1989b. Lesions of perirhinal and parahippocampal cortex that spare the amygdala and hippocampal formation produce severe memory impairment. *J. Neurosci.* **9**:4355–4370.

Zola-Morgan, S., L.R. Squire, R.P. Clower, and N.L. Rempel. 1993. Damage to the perirhinal cortex exacerbates memory impairment following lesions to the hippocampal formation. *J. Neurosci.* **13**:251–265.

8

Modulation of Small Neural Networks in the Crustacean Stomatogastric Ganglion

R.M. HARRIS-WARRICK
Section of Neurobiology and Behavior, Seeley G. Mudd Hall,
Cornell University, Ithaca, NY 14853, U.S.A.

ABSTRACT

Recent studies of the neural networks in the stomatogastric nervous system of decapod crustacea have clearly shown that a single, anatomically defined neural network can be modulated to generate a variety of different output patterns. Modulatory inputs can reconfigure a neural network through two major mechanisms: (a) by altering the strength of synaptic connections in the network and (b) by altering the baseline electrophysiological response properties of the component neurons. These same mechanisms can alter interactions between networks, allowing neurons to switch from one network to another and even causing separate networks to fuse together to generate novel motor patterns. Thus, modulatory inputs are essential components in determining what pattern will emerge from an anatomically defined neural network.

INTRODUCTION

The last two decades have seen tremendous advances in our knowledge of the electrophysiological properties of single neurons. However, we are still far from understanding how these neurons interact to generate even the simplest of behaviors. To understand how neurons generate behavior, we need to analyze the neural networks that coordinate behavioral output. This has been very difficult to accomplish in vertebrate nervous systems, due to the large number of neurons in any behavioral network and the difficulty in reproducibly identifying the network's component neurons. In contrast, the invertebrates provide a number of very simple rhythmic behaviors that can be analyzed at the cellular level (Selverston 1985). Due to the numerical simplicity and distributed nature of the invertebrate nervous system, the neural networks in these simple preparations can be thoroughly mapped, and the component neurons identified and studied individually.

Cellular and Molecular Mechanisms Underlying Higher Neural Functions
Edited by A.I. Selverston and P. Ascher

The crustacean stomatogastric ganglion (STG) contains some of the best understood neural networks (Selverston and Moulins 1987; Harris-Warrick, Marder et al. 1992). This ganglion, which has only 30 neurons, drives several motor patterns that control rhythmic movements of the foregut. Among the best understood networks are those controlling the gastric mill rhythm, which drives the internal teeth in the foregut, and the pyloric rhythm, which drives a peristaltic pumping and filtering movement in the posterior foregut, or pylorus. All of the neurons in these networks have been individually identified; a great deal is known about their intrinsic electrophysiological properties, including such properties as conditional bursting, bistability, and variable postinhibitory rebound. The synaptic connections in each network have been thoroughly studied and include both electrical coupling and chemical inhibition mediated by either acetylcholine or glutamate. A number of studies have shown that both the pattern of synaptic connectivity and differences in the intrinsic properties of the component neurons are essential to explain the rhythmic motor patterns generated by each network.

All animals must be able to vary even simple rhythmic movements, to adapt them to the changing demands of the environment. Over the past decade, a number of laboratories have studied the neuronal basis for this behavioral flexibility using the STG as a model system. *In vivo*, the pyloric and gastric mill rhythms are highly variable, with changes in timing, phasing, and intensity during and following feeding (Rezer and Moulins 1983; Heinzel 1988). While this variability could conceivably arise from variable activation of a number of independent networks, a more parsimonious explanation is that the output from a single network is modified by modulatory neurons that are not themselves members of the network. The STG networks are the targets of 60–120 modulatory neurons located in other ganglia or in the periphery (Nagy and Moulins 1987; Katz and Harris-Warrick 1990; Coleman et al. 1992). These modulatory neurons use at least 15 different neurotransmitters, including classical transmitters, monoamines, and a variety of peptides (Harris-Warrick, Nagy et al. 1992). They act to modify the electrophysiological properties of the component neurons and their synapses within the pyloric and gastric mill networks in the STG, thus "sculpting" a variety of different functional circuits from a single anatomically defined network. Several groups have studied how this modulation occurs by stimulating identified modulatory neurons or applying their transmitters and by monitoring their effects on the STG neurons and networks. In this chapter, I will summarize the main findings from this research.

MODULATION WITHIN A NETWORK

An Anatomically Defined Neural Network Can Generate a Variety of Different Motor Patterns Due to the Actions of Different Neuromodulators

When the STG is isolated from all modulatory input by blocking input nerve conduction, the pyloric and gastric mill networks typically slow down or fall silent. Stimulation of single identified modulatory neurons, or bath application of the transmitters they use, can restore rhythmic activity in these networks (Figure 8.1; Harris-Warrick, Nagy

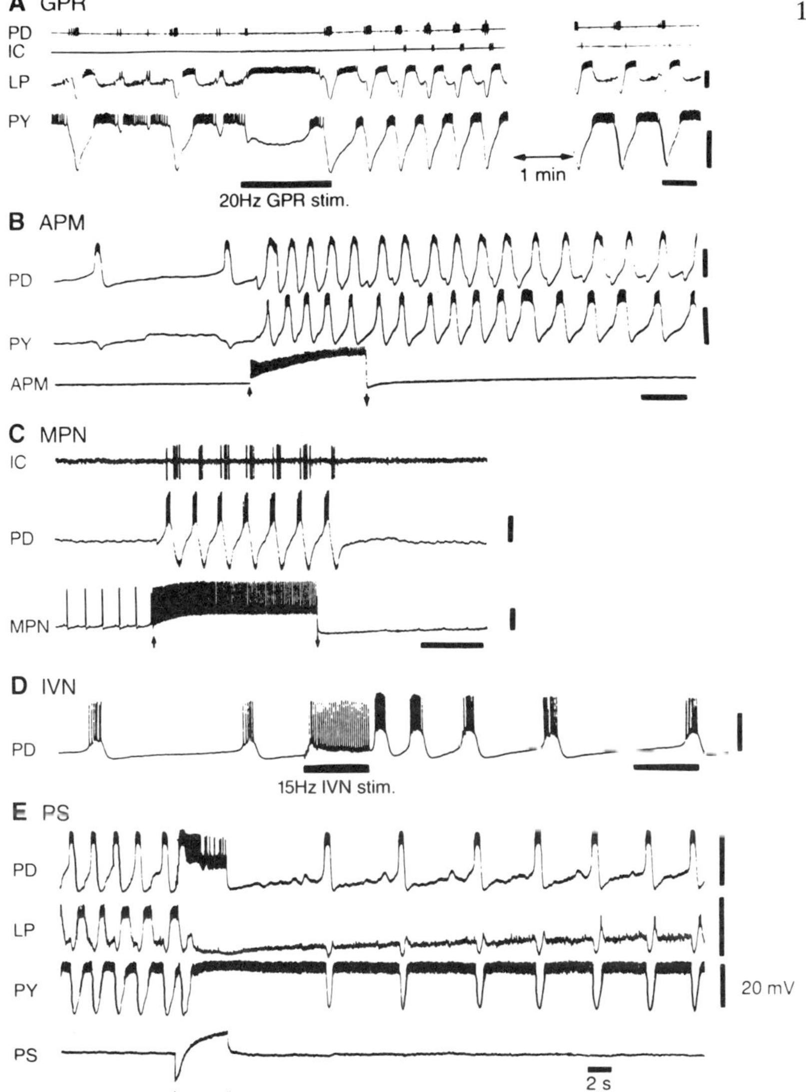

Figure 8.1 Effects of stimulating modulatory cells on the pyloric motor pattern. In each case, the pyloric rhythm is monitored by a mixture of intracellular and extracellular recordings. (A) Stimulation of the serotonergic/cholinergic sensory neuron, the gastropyloric receptor (GPR) evokes an initial disruption of the pyloric pattern followed by an increase in cycle frequency lasting over 1 min. (B) Anterior pyloric modulator (APM) stimulation evokes an immediate and prolonged enhancement of the pyloric rhythm. (C) Stimulation of the modulatory proctolin-containing neuron (MPN) evokes a transient activation of the pyloric rhythm. (D) Inferior ventricular nerve (IVN) stimulation initially disrupts and then enhances pyloric activity. (E) Pyloric suppressor (PS) stimulation evokes a prolonged interruption of pyloric activity. PD: pyloric dilator; IC: inferior cardiac neuron; LP: lateral pyloric; PY; pyloric constrictor. From Katz and Harris-Warrick (1990).

et al. 1992). However, each modulatory neuron and transmitter evokes a unique variant on the basic motor pattern. Figure 8.1 shows the activation of the pyloric rhythm during stimulation of five different identified modulatory neurons. Each modulatory neuron generates a unique variant of the pyloric pattern, which differs in such physiological parameters as which neurons in the network are active, the cycle frequency, the intensity of each neuron's firing, and the phasing of neuronal activity within the cycle; this can best be seen in the phase diagrams of Figure 8.2. There are also important differences in the duration of the modulatory action evoked by different modulatory neurons (Figure 8.1). Thus, modulatory inputs can sculpt a network to generate a whole family of variants on a basic theme. The output from a neural network is not fixed or predetermined by its anatomical connectivity; knowledge of the circuitry is not sufficient to predict the output of the network.

Synaptic Interactions between the Modulatory Neurons and the Neural Network Can be Bidirectional

Typical models of neural network modulation assume that the modulatory input drives the network to change its output without itself being involved in network function. These models may turn out to be oversimplified. Nusbaum and coworkers (1992) have

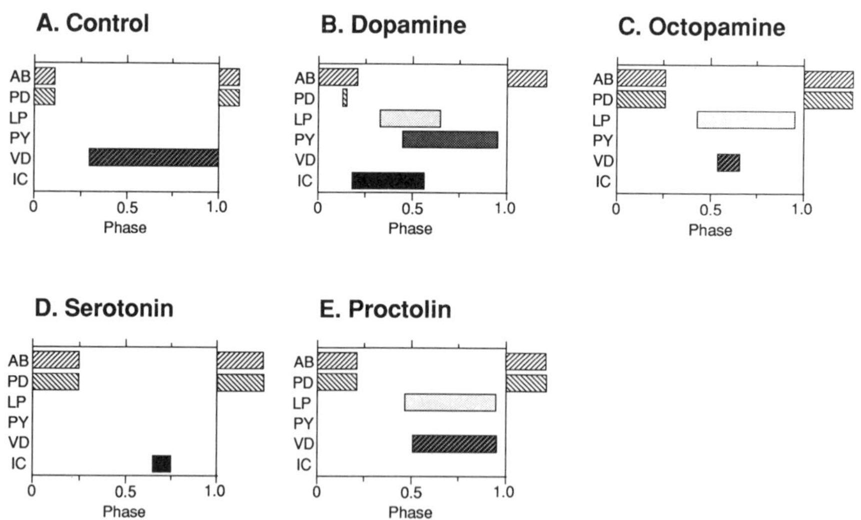

Figure 8.2 Phase diagrams of *Panulirus interruptus* pyloric activity (A) after sucrose block of the *stn*, and in the presence of (B) 10^{-4}M dopamine, (C) 10^{-4}M octopamine, (D) 10^{-5} M serotonin, and (E) 10^{-6}M proctolin. The period of spike activity of each pyloric neuron within a single cycle is shown by bars, with the phase defined by the beginning of the anterior burster (AB) activity. Each transmitter evokes a unique set of neurons to fire with unique phase relations. PD: pyloric dilator; LP: lateral pyloric; PY: pyloric constrictor; VD: ventricular dilator; IC: inferior cardiac neuron. From Harris-Warrick et al. 1992b.

recently begun to record intracellularly from axons of identified modulatory neurons near their terminations in the STG. The somata of these modulatory neurons are in a distant ganglion. Stimulation of either the axon or the soma can evoke rhythmic STG motor patterns. This is seen in Figure 8.3, where stimulation of the axon of the modulatory neuron SNAX1 activates the slow gastric mill rhythm. Recordings, however, from the SNAX1 axon show that its terminals receive direct synaptic feedback from the STG network, which can shape the axonal firing pattern and inhibit axonal spike generation at particular phases of the motor pattern even though the axon is receiving tonic electrical stimulation (Figure 8.3). This inhibition is not observed during recordings from the soma in the distant ganglion (M.P. Nusbaum, pers. comm.). Thus, the terminal and the soma do not necessarily carry the same message. The terminals of these modulatory neurons can apparently function independently of the soma to interact with the STG networks, and under some conditions they may be functional members of the network even when the soma is not involved. In this case, recordings of activity from the soma can give a misleading idea of the activity that is occurring in the terminals.

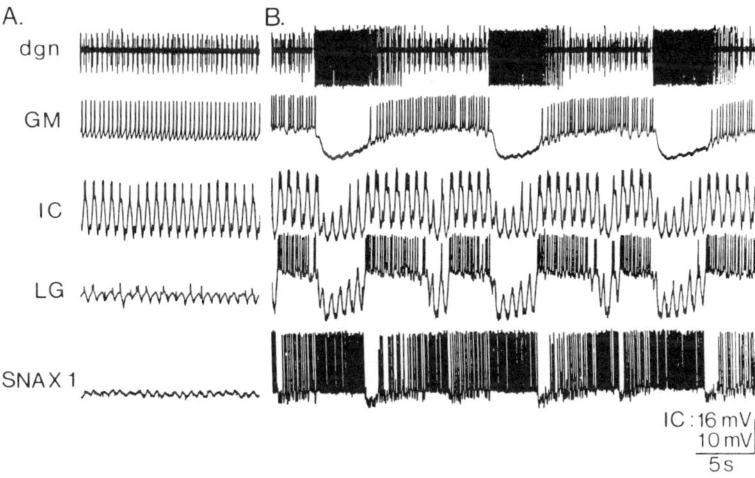

Figure 8.3 Stimulation of a modulatory axon, SNAX1, initiates the gastric mill rhythm and shows activity time-locked to that rhythm. SNAX1 is the axon of an identified modulatory neuron whose soma is in the commissural ganglion. It is recorded near its terminals in the STG. (A) In the absence of SNAX1 stimulation, there is an ongoing pyloric rhythm (monitored by the activity of the inferior cardiac (IC) neuron) but no gastric mill rhythm (seen by silence or tonic activity in the dorsal gastric nerve (dgn), the gastric mill (GM) and lateral gastric (LG) neurons). (B) During tonic current injection (+1 nA) into SNAX1, pyloric activity is strengthened and the gastric mill is activated (seen by rhythmic activity in the dgn and GM and LG neurons). SNAX1 itself shows periodic feedback inhibition from the gastric mill LG neuron, which is sufficient to block spike generation despite the tonic current injection into SNAX1. From Nusbaum et al. (1992).

Modulatory Inputs Alter Network Function by Changing the Synaptic Efficacy and by Altering the Intrinsic Response Properties of the Component Neurons within the Network

What cellular mechanisms are used by neuromodulators to alter the output from an anatomically defined network? One common mechanism involves modulation of the strength of synaptic interactions within the network. This has been studied in a number of different systems. Perhaps the most familiar example is found in *Aplysia*, where serotonin and peptides can enhance the release of transmitter from sensory neurons onto motoneurons, thus enhancing the gill withdrawal reflex (Kandel et al. 1987). As might be expected, in the STG networks, neuromodulatory neurons and transmitters can change the strength of synaptic interactions. In the pyloric network, monoamines such as dopamine, octopamine, and serotonin can enhance, diminish, or completely eliminate synaptic interactions; under some conditions they can even reverse the sign of a mixed inhibitory chemical/electrical synapse (Johnson and Harris-Warrick 1990; Johnson et al. 1993). Bath application of red pigment-concentrating hormone (RPCH) can evoke up to 9-fold enhancements of synaptic interactions among neurons in the cardiac sac and gastric mill networks (Figure 8.4). The cellular mechanisms for this synaptic modulation are not well worked out but probably involve changes in the amount of transmitter released as well as in the postsynaptic responsiveness. This synaptic modulation can quantitatively "rewire" the neural network, resulting in a new motor output (Dickinson et al. 1990).

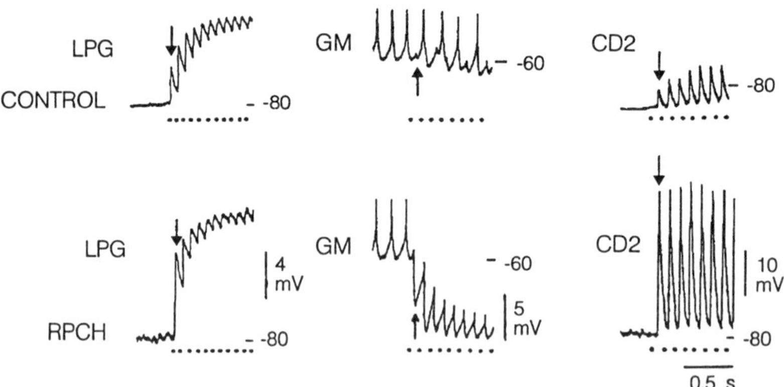

Figure 8.4 Enhancement of synaptic potentials from the inferior ventricular (IV) neurons during bath application of the peptide red pigment-concentrating hormone (RPCH). The inferior ventricular nerve (containing the axons of the IV neurons) was stimulated at 10 Hz in the absence (top) and presence (bottom) of 10^{-6}M RPCH. Excitatory postsynaptic potentials onto the gastric mill lateral posterior gastric (LPG) neuron, the cardiac sac dilator 2 (CD2), and inhibitory postsynaptic potentials in the gastric mill (GM) neurons were potentiated 1.5- to 9-fold. From Dickinson et al. (1990).

Another way for neuromodulators to alter the output from an anatomically defined network is to change fundamentally the baseline activity profiles and intrinsic response properties of the neurons in the network. This qualitative and global change in how a neuron interprets synaptic signals can be more important than the quantitative changes in the synaptic signals themselves. This has been studied by analyzing the effects of bath-applied neuromodulators on neurons that have been isolated from all detectable synaptic input by a combination of pharmacological blockade and photoinactivation (where selected neurons are filled with a fluorescent dye and killed by illumination; Miller and Selverston 1979). As seen in Figure 8.5, a single neuromodulator can have entirely different effects on the different neurons in a single network. For example, dopamine can evoke endogenous oscillatory properties in one of the pyloric network neurons (the anterior burster, or AB neuron), allowing this neuron to become the pacemaker in the pyloric rhythm. Dopamine causes other neurons to depolarize and fire tonically, while still others hyperpolarize and fall silent (Figure 8.5). This change of baseline activity obviously alters the ways these neurons interpret synaptic inputs (Flamm and Harris-Warrick 1986a, b). Dopamine also alters the rate of postinhibitory rebound in some pyloric neurons, leading to a change in the phasing of activity in the motor pattern (Harris-Warrick, Tierney et al. 1992). As another example, the dorsal

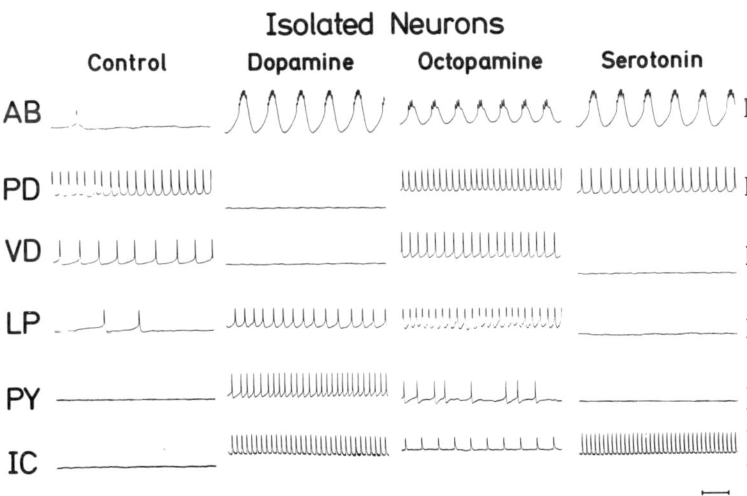

Figure 8.5 Effects of dopamine, octopamine, and serotonin on synaptically isolated pyloric neurons. Each neuron was isolated from all detectable synaptic input by a combination of photoinactivation (done by injecting 5,6-carboxyfluorescein into presynaptic neurons and killing them during illumination) and pharmacological blockade (with 5×10^{-6}M picrotoxin to eliminate glutamatergic transmission; Flamm and Harris-Warrick 1986b). Dopamine (10^{-4}M), octopamine (10^{-4}M) and serotonin (10^{-5}M) were bath applied. All recordings for a single neuron are from a single experiment. AB: anterior burster neuron; PD: pyloric dilator neuron; VD: ventricular dilator neuron; LP: lateral pyloric neuron; PY: pyloric constrictor neuron; IC: inferior cardiac neuron. From Harris-Warrick (1988).

gastric (DG) neuron develops bistable plateau potential capabilities in the presence of a variety of neuromodulators, including serotonin, or during stimulation of a serotonergic modulatory neuron (Katz and Harris-Warrick 1989). When the DG neuron is in this state, a brief synaptic depolarization (which could evoke a few spikes before modulation) now evokes a prolonged burst of action potentials lasting many seconds. This results, at least in part, from a combined conductance decrease of $I_{K(Ca)}$ and a conductance increase of I_h (Kiehn and Harris-Warrick 1992a, b).

These radical changes in intrinsic electrophysiological properties of network neurons have sweeping effects on the STG motor patterns. It would not be possible to generate the diversity of pyloric and gastric mill motor patterns simply by altering the strength of synaptic interactions between the neurons: changes in the intrinsic electrophysiological properties qualitatively change how these networks function. This is an important principle that should be carefully addressed in other systems. In studying how change can occur in the nervous system, are we making a mistake by focusing most of our efforts on modulation of synaptic efficacy?

MODULATION OF INTERACTIONS BETWEEN NETWORKS

In an important review on the neural organization of locomotion in vertebrates, Grillner (1981) proposed that complex movements are generated by coordination of activity of subnetworks, which he termed "unit CPGs." Each unit CPG controls a single aspect of the behavior (e.g., movement around a single joint). These units are then coordinated into larger neuronal aggregates, which eventually generate a complex movement. In the STG, the neural mechanisms underlying this coordination are now being directly studied. The stomatogastric system generates four major motor patterns: the gastric mill, pyloric, cardiac sac, and esophageal rhythms. Previously, each pattern was believed to act more or less independently of the others. Recent work by Moulins, Marder and their coworkers has shown that these networks are in fact not separate CPGs. Rather, they interact with each other in a number of different ways to coordinate complex movements involving different parts of the foregut (Dickinson and Moulins 1992).

Neurons Can Switch Their Activity Pattern from One Network to a Different Network

It is now clear that an identified neuron can participate in more than one network, depending on modulatory inputs that change its properties. For example, Hooper and Moulins (1989) found that stimulation of an identified sensory nerve in the stomatogastric system activates the slow cardiac sac motor rhythm. Simultaneously, one of the neurons in the pyloric network (VD) switches its activity pattern to drop out of the rapid pyloric rhythm and to fire strictly in phase with the slow cardiac sac rhythm (Figure 8.6). Stimulation of the sensory nerve activates a polysynaptic pathway that

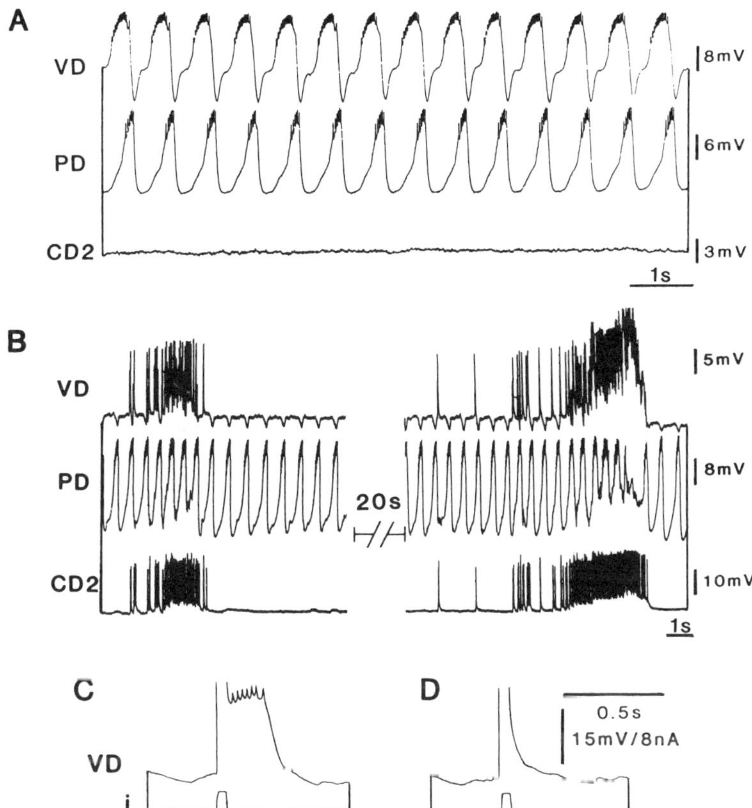

Figure 8.6 The ventricular dilator (VD) neuron can switch from the pyloric to the cardiac sac rhythm. (A) When the cardiac sac is inactive, VD oscillates rhythmically in time with the pyloric rhythm (seen in the pyloric dilator (PD) neuron). (B) When both the pyloric (seen in PD) and cardiac sac (seen in the activity of the cardiac dilator 2 (CD2)) rhythms are active, VD fires exclusively with the cardiac sac rhythm. (C) When firing in time with the pyloric rhythm, VD shows a prolonged regenerative plateau response to brief depolarization. (D) When firing in time with the cardiac sac, VD has lost its regenerative plateau response to depolarization. Modified from Hooper and Moulins 1989.

causes this cell to lose its endogenous oscillatory properties, leading it to stop firing rhythmically with the ongoing pyloric rhythm. A strong synaptic drive from one of the cardiac sac neurons leads it to fire with the new cardiac sac rhythm. Thus, due to a change in its intrinsic electrophysiological properties, this neuron can switch between two neural networks.

In the crab, *Cancer borealis*, the neurons that generate the pyloric and gastric mill patterns form a single large pool, from which varying combinations can be selected (Weimann et al. 1991). Some neurons almost always fire in either the pyloric or gastric mill rhythm, but others switch between pyloric-timed and gastric mill-timed activity. This allows an enormous variety of intermediate motor patterns to be generated from a single gastropyloric pool of neurons.

Networks that Operate Independently of One Another Can be Modulated to Fuse into Novel Conjoint Networks

In the above examples, the basic integrity of the separate pyloric and gastric mill rhythms was maintained, although a varying number of neurons participated in each rhythm. Under the control of neuromodulatory inputs, however, more radical rearrangements of these networks are possible. For example, the RPCH can fuse the gastric mill and cardiac sac networks into a single conjoint network that generates a novel motor pattern which is not seen under any other known conditions (Figure 8.7A; Dickinson et al. 1990). This is partly caused by a dramatic increase in the strength of weak synaptic interactions between the two networks, such that they become functional in coupling the networks (Figure 8.4). Thus, the modulatory actions of the peptide RPCH create a neural network that does not exist in the absence of the peptide.

The most dramatic interactions between the stomatogastric networks occur in the lobster, *Homarus gammarus*, where stimulation of a single neuron, the pyloric suppressor (PS), causes selected neurons from three separate networks to combine to form a new motor pattern for swallowing (Meyrand et al. 1991). When the PS neuron is active, the esophageal, pyloric, and gastric mill motor patterns are completely disrupted, and neurons from all three networks are specified in a new network whose motor pattern is different from any of the previous patterns (Figure 8.7B). PS appears to act primarily by changing the endogenous oscillatory properties of the component neurons, increasing bursting in some cells while decreasing or eliminating bursting in others (Simmers et al. 1991).

Figure 8.7 Network fusion during neuromodulation. (A_1) Spontaneous activity showing relatively independent cycling of the faster gastric mill rhythm (seen in the extracellular recordings of the gastric mill [GM] and lateral gastric neurons [lgn] and intracellular recording from the lateral posterior gastric [LPG] neuron) and the much slower cardiac sac rhythm (seen in the intracellular recording of the cardiac sac 2 (CD2) neuron). (A_2) Fusion of the gastric mill rhythm (LPG) with the cardiac sac rhythm (CD2) during bath application of the peptide red pigment-concentrating hormone (RPCH). The novel rhythm has a different cycle frequency, intensity of firing and phasing than either of the former rhythms. (B_1) Spontaneous and independent activity of the rapid pyloric rhythm (seen with the ventricular dilator [VD] and pyloric dilator [PD] neurons) and the slow gastric mill rhythm (seen with the GM and LPG neurons). (B_2) Fusion of the pyloric rhythm (VD, PD) with the gastric mill rhythm (GM, LPG) after stimulation of the modulatory pyloric suppressor (PS) neuron. The new pattern has markedly different phasing and cycle frequency. Neurons of the esophageal rhythm also participate in this novel rhythm. From Dickinson and Moulins (1992).

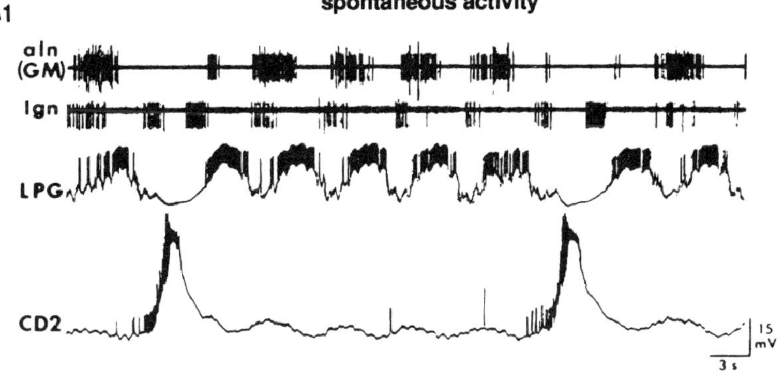
A1
spontaneous activity
aln (GM)
lgn
LPG
CD2
15 mV
3 s

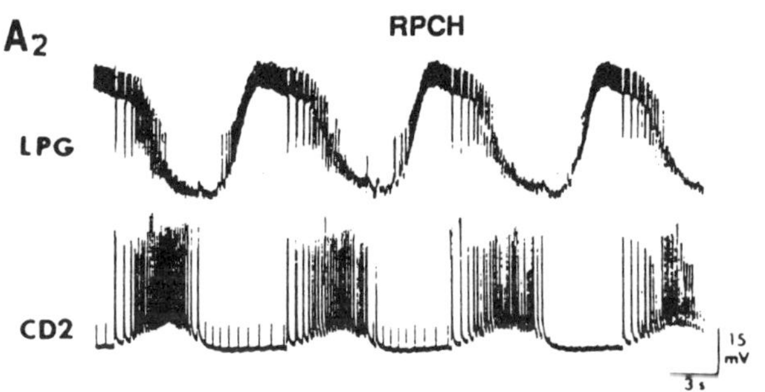
A2
RPCH
LPG
CD2
15 mV
3 s

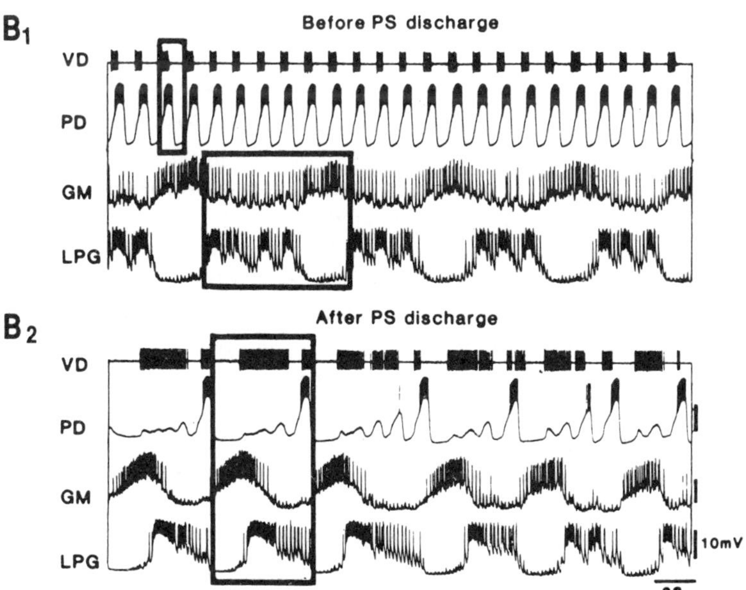
B1
Before PS discharge
VD
PD
GM
LPG
B2
After PS discharge
VD
PD
GM
LPG
10mV
2s

These results show that the neural networks in the stomatogastric system can interact with each other to generate motor patterns that combine aspects of the individual subnetworks in novel ways. The mechanisms underlying this network rearrangement appear to be the same as for modulation within a single network: changes in synaptic strength and alterations in the intrinsic and baseline firing properties of the component neurons.

FUTURE DIRECTIONS

Small neural networks are ideal for linking cellular and molecular-based approaches with system-based analyses. To do so, it will be necessary to develop new approaches to study the molecular mechanisms of neuromodulator action.

The STG has provided excellent examples of modulation of network function, yet the cellular mechanisms underlying this modulation are in most cases not well understood. The neuronal somata are electrically inexcitable, and modulatory responses only arise in the distal neuropil, making it difficult to voltage clamp modulatory currents *in situ*. Recent advances in tissue culturing of STG neurons have made it possible to study modulatory responses in isolated neurons with more favorable geometry (Turrigiano and E. Marder 1993). In addition, synapse formation between identified neurons in culture has now been achieved, making it possible to study synaptic modulation under well controlled circumstances (Panchin et al.1993). It is probable that the slow actions of neuromodulators in the STG will be mediated by G-protein-coupled second messenger mechanisms, similar to those found in other systems. The second messenger mechanisms underlying the actions of neuromodulators have not yet been studied in detail; however, the modulatory actions of octopamine on pyloric neurons are mimicked by a variety of pharmacological manipulations that increase cAMP levels, and octopamine evokes a 5-fold increase in cAMP levels in the isolated STG (Flamm et al. 1987). This is similar to the well-studied actions of serotonin on sensory terminals in *Aplysia* (Kandel et al. 1987) and suggests that common biochemical mechanisms can be shared in different systems to modulate network activity.

Molecular biology is giving us new tools with which to analyze the neurons in the STG. For example, previous work has shown that different STG neurons have characteristically different types and amounts of K^+ channels (Hartline et al. 1990), and these are essential in determining the unique electrophysiological properties that define each neuron's role in generating the motor pattern (Tierney and Harris-Warrick 1992). Molecular probes are being developed to the *Shaker* family of K^+ channels, and a single cell PCR method is being developed which will allow the mapping of different K^+ channel transcripts in individual identified neurons (Baro et al. 1992). These studies should help us define the molecular basis for the different electrophysiological properties of the STG neurons. They will also help us answer why there are so many related K^+ channels by determining their roles in the STG networks.

Neural Network Modulation Will Not be Fully Understood without Mathematical Modeling

When do we finally "understand" a neural network? The networks in the STG have been thoroughly studied, all the component neurons are known, and their transmitters and synaptic connections have been fully mapped. A great deal is known about the variable intrinsic properties of the component neurons, and it is clear that each network is multipotential. We are in danger of being overwhelmed by all the details of this network and thus failing to see the forest for the trees. How can we determine what is really important in generating variants from these networks? Modeling provides a way to determine the relative importance of different variables in the final generation of a particular motor pattern. At present, a variety of different modeling strategies are being used, from detailed conductance-based models to networks of simple neuronal caricatures (Marder and Selverston 1992). Useful models will allow modulation of many variables underlying the changes in synaptic strength and intrinsic properties that have been observed experimentally. It is not adequate to generate a model that successfully reproduces "the" motor pattern; the model should be able to generate the variety of biologically relevant variants on the basic motor theme. The most useful models will be those that yield explicitly testable hypotheses and which can be easily altered as biological data demand.

Control of Modulatory Inputs: Are These Neurons Part of a Modulatory Supernetwork?

In most studies of modulatory inputs to a neural network, the unspoken assumption is that these inputs are parallel paths to the network and do not interact with each other. Recent work in the STG suggests that in some cases, modulatory neurons are interacting to control each other's activity (F. Nagy, pers. comm.). Thus, their actions appear to be coordinated by a higher-level modulatory supernetwork. Understanding how this modulatory network functions and changes will be a fruitful approach to placing the actions of neuromodulators in a behavioral context.

How Will Studies of Small Neural Networks "Scale Up" to Complex Vertebrate Networks?

The studies I have described on the STG show that neuromodulators play essential instructive roles in "sculpting" a variety of functional circuits from a single anatomically defined neural network. These different circuits generate the many variants on a single motor pattern that allow us to adapt our behavior to the demands of the moment. Research on simple spinal cord and thalamocortical preparations (see chapters by Grillner and McCormick, both this volume) suggests that the same basic principles for neuromodulation of neural networks occur in vertebrates as well as invertebrates. These preparations show that modulation of baselineintrinsicelectrophysiological properties and of synaptic strength allow even complex vertebrate networks to generate a variety of related outputs based on a single major theme. The major change that is apparent in the vertebrates is the pronounced duplication of cell numbers, and this may lead to new methods of computation that are not accessible to the numerically impoverished invertebrate networks. Further research will be needed to determine whether new principles of motor network function have coevolved with the increase in numbers of neurons in the networks.

REFERENCES

Baro, D.J., C. Cole, M. Tapia, A. Zarrin, A. Chen, T.R. Podleski, and R.M. Harris-Warrick. 1992. Expression of *Shaker* family K^+ channel mRNA in the spiny lobster, *Panulirus interruptus. Soc. Neurosci. Abst.* **18**:77.

Coleman, M.J., M.P. Nusbaum, I. Cournil, and B.J. Claiborne. 1992. Distribution of modulatory inputs to the stomatogastric ganglion of the crab, *Cancer borealis. J. Comp. Neurol.* **325**:581–594.

Dickinson, P.S., C. Mecsas, and E. Marder. 1990. Neuropeptide fusion of two motor pattern generator circuits. *Nature* **344**:155–158.

Dickinson, P.S., and M. Moulins. 1992. Interactions and combinations between different networks in the stomatogastric nervous system. In: Dynamic Biological Networks: The Stomatogastric Nervous System, ed. R.M. Harris-Warrick, E. Marder, A.I. Selverston, and M. Moulins, pp. 139–160. Boston: MIT Press.

Flamm, R.E., D. Fickbohm, and R.M. Harris-Warrick. 1987. cAMP elevation modulates physiological activity of pyloric neurons in the lobster stomatogastric ganglion. *J. Neurophysiol.* **58**:1370–1386.

Flamm, R.E., and R.M. Harris-Warrick. 1986a. Aminergic modulation in the lobster stomatogastric ganglion. I. Effects on the motor pattern and activity of neurons within the pyloric circuit. *J. Neurophysiol.* **55**:847–865.

Flamm, R.E., and R.M. Harris-Warrick. 1986b. Aminergic modulation in the lobster stomatogastric ganglion. II. Target neurons of dopamine, octopamine and serotonin within the pyloric circuit. *J. Neurophysiol.* **55**:866–881.

Grillner, S. 1981. Control of locomotion in bipeds, tetrapods and fish. In: Handbook of Physiology, Section 1: The Nervous System, vol. II, part 2., ed. V. B. Brooks, pp. 1179–1236. Bethesda: American Physiological Society.

Harris-Warrick, R.M. 1988. Chemical modulation of central pattern generators. In: Neural Control of Rhythmic Movements, ed. A. H. Cohen, S. Rossignol, and S. Grillner, pp. 285–331. New York: Wiley.

Harris-Warrick, R.M., E. Marder, A.I. Selverston, and M. Moulins, eds. 1992. Dynamic Biological Networks: The Stomatogastric Nervous System. Boston: MIT Press.

Harris-Warrick, R.M., F. Nagy, and M.P. Nusbaum. 1992. Neuromodulation of stomatogastric networks by identified neurons and transmitters. In: Dynamic Biological Networks: The Stomatogastric Nervous System, ed. R.M. Harris-Warrick, E. Marder, A.I. Selverston, and M. Moulins, pp. 87–137. Boston: MIT Press.

Harris-Warrick, R.M., A.J. Tierney, and L. Coniglio. 1992. Mechanisms for dopamine-induced phase shifts in the pyloric motor pattern in the lobster stomatogastric ganglion. *Soc. Neurosci. Abst.* **18**:1055.

Hartline, D.K., D.V. Gassie, B.A. Tomiyasu, and B.R. Jones. 1990. Ionic current fingerprints in lobster stomatogastric neurons. *Soc. Neurosci. Abst.* **16**:1131.

Heinzel, H.-G. 1988. Gastric mill activity in the lobster. I. Spontaneous modes of chewing. *J. Neurophysiol.* **59**:528–550.

Hooper, S.L., and M. Moulins. 1989. Switching of a neuron from one network to another by sensory-induced changes in membrane properties. *Science* **244**:1587–1589.

Johnson, B.R., and R.M. Harris-Warrick. 1990. Aminergic modulation of graded synaptic transmission in the lobster stomatogastric ganglion. *J. Neurosci.* **10**:2066–2076.

Johnson, B.R., J. Peck, and R.M. Harris-Warrick. 1993. Dopamine induces sign reversal at mixed chemical-electrical synapses. *Brain Res.* **625:**159–164.

Kandel, E.R., M. Klein, B. Hochner, M. Schuster, S.A. Siegelbaum, R.D. Hawkins, D.L. Glanzman, V. Castelluci, and T.W. Abrams. 1987. Synaptic modulation and learning: New insights into synaptic transmission from the study of behavior. In: Synaptic Function, ed. G.M. Edelman, W.S.E. Gall, and W.M. Cowan, pp. 471–518. New York: Wiley.

Katz, P.S., and R.M. Harris-Warrick. 1989. Serotonergic/cholinergic muscle receptor cells in the crab stomatogastric nervous system. II. Rapid nicotinic and prolonged modulatory effects on neurons in the stomatogastric ganglion. *J. Neurophysiol.* **62**:571–581.

Katz, P.S., and R.M. Harris-Warrick. 1990. Actions of identified neuromodulatory neurons in a simple motor system. *Trends Neurosci.* **13**:367–373.

Kiehn, O., and R.M. Harris-Warrick. 1992a. Serotonergic stretch receptors induce plateau properties in a crustacean motor neuron by a dual-conductance mechanism. *J. Neurophysiol.* **68**:485–495.

Kiehn, O., and R.M. Harris-Warrick. 1992b. 5–HT modulation of hyperpolarization-activated inward current and calcium-dependent outward current in a crustacean motor neuron. *J. Neurophysiol.* **68**:496–508.

Marder, E., and A.I. Selverston. 1992. Modeling the stomatogastric nervous system. In: Dynamic Biological Networks: The Stomatogastric Nervous System, ed. R.M. Harris-Warrick, E. Marder, A.I. Selverston, and M. Moulins, pp. 161–196. Boston: MIT Press.

Meyrand, P., A.J. Simmers, and M. Moulins. 1991. Construction of a pattern-generating circuit with neurons of different networks. *Nature* **351**:60–63.

Miller, J.P., and A.I. Selverston. 1979. Rapid killing of single neurons by irradiation of intracellularly injected dye. *Science* **206**:702–704.

Nagy, F., and M. Moulins. 1987. Extrinsic inputs. In: The Crustacean Stomatogastric System: A Model for the Study of Central Nervous Systems, ed. A.I. Selverston and M. Moulins, pp. 205–242. Berlin: Springer.

Nusbaum, M.P., J.M. Weimann, J. Golowasch, and E. Marder. 1992. Presynaptic control of modulatory fibers by their neural network targets. *J. Neurosci.* **12**:2706–2714.

Panchin, Y.V., Y.I. Arsharsky, A. Selverston, and T.A. Cleland. 1993. Lobster stomatogastric neurons in primary culture. I. Basic characteristics. *J. Neurophysiol.* **69:**1976–1992.

Rezer, E., and M. Moulins. 1983. Expression of the crustacean pyloric pattern generator in the intact animal. *J. Comp. Physiol. A.* **153**:17–28.

Selverston, A.I., ed. 1985. Model Neural Networks and Behavior. New York: Plenum.

Selverston, A.I., and M. Moulins, eds. 1987. The Crustacean Stomatogastric System: A Model for the Study of Central Nervous Systems. Berlin: Springer.

Simmers, A.J., P. Meyrand, and M. Moulins. 1991. Mechanisms subserving construction of a novel motor-pattern generating network by a multiaction interneuron. *Soc. Neurosci. Abstr.* **17**:1489.

Tierney, A.J., and R.M. Harris-Warrick. 1992. Physiological role of the transient potassium current, I_A, in the pyloric circuit of the lobster stomatogastric ganglion. *J. Neurophysiol.* **67**:599–609.

Turrigiano, G.G., and E. Marder. 1993. Regeneration and modulation of identified stomatogastric ganglion neurons in primary cell culture. *J. Neurophysiol.* **69:**1993–2002.

Weimann, J.M., P. Meyrand, and E. Marder. 1991. Neurons that form multiple pattern generators: Identification and multiple activity patterns of gastric/pyloric neurons in the crab stomatogastric system. *J. Neurophysiol.* **65**:111–122.

9

Dynamic Changes in Functional Connectivity in a Lower Vertebrate Model

S. GRILLNER, A. EL MANIRA, J. TEGNÉR, T. WADDEN,
L. VINAY, and J.-Y. BARTHE
Nobel Institute for Neurophysiology, Karolinska Institute, Box 60400,
S–10 401 Stockholm, Sweden

ABSTRACT

A hard-wired network may have many degrees of freedom. In this chapter, a comparatively well-analyzed simple lower vertebrate network controlling locomotion in lamprey is considered. The backbone of this brainstem-spinal cord network is built with excitatory glutamatergic and inhibitory glycinergic neurons. The different neuronal mechanisms contributing to the timing within the network are considered. The phase relations of the network components or muscle groups can be drastically changed or finely tuned by several different neuronal mechanisms. Such effects can be elicited by a system of GABA neurons acting via $GABA_A$ and $GABA_B$ receptors, a serotonin (5-HT) and dopamine system, and other mechanisms controlling the local excitability within parts of the network.

INTRODUCTION

The neuronal networks of the nervous system constitute the basic functional units of the brain. They produce all the patterns of behavior for which we are capable, analyze the sensory signals which reach the nervous system from the sense organs, and process and store information. Some networks are already in operation at birth (e.g., as in respiration), others mature gradually during childhood and are to a varying degree dependent on interactions with the environment (Shik and Orlovsky 1976; Stein 1978; Grillner 1981).

Each pattern-generator network coordinates the motoneurons and muscles that produce a given behavior when activated in the appropriate sequence (Selverston and Moulins 1985; Roberts and Tunstall 1990; Grillner, Wallén et al. 1991; Harris-Warrick

Cellular and Molecular Mechanisms Underlying Higher Neural Functions
Edited by A.I. Selverston and P. Ascher

et al. 1992). Motor patterns such as those of chewing, breathing, or walking have their specific distinguishing features. Each successive movement cycle will differ from the preceding one in small details. Movements are adapted to the instantaneous needs of the animal by subtle or more prominent changes in the pattern of activation of different motoneurons. Complex patterns of behavior, such as locomotion, are coordinated by a family of different control systems, each of which is crucial for successful ambulation (Grillner 1981, 1985). One control system generates the specific synergy that produces the propulsion (Figure 9.1); another takes care of maintaining a certain body position during the movements (cf. Orlovsky 1991; Deliagina et al. 1992a, b); a third controls the accurate foot placement in each movement cycle (Georgopoulos and Grillner 1989); while a fourth produces the appropriate steering of the locomotion towards a particular point in space. Each of these control systems can profoundly modify the motor pattern. This serves to emphasize the need for different neural mechanisms for short- and long-term changes of the pattern of coordination.

In this chapter we focus on the first of these control systems, propulsion. The flexibility within this system alone is formidable. We can walk at different speeds—from slow to very fast—with different step cycle frequency and amplitude of the movement. We can walk forwards, backwards, or sideways in an upright or a crouching posture. As dancers have demonstrated, the possibility for variation is almost unlimited. The pattern-generating system underlying propulsion can be

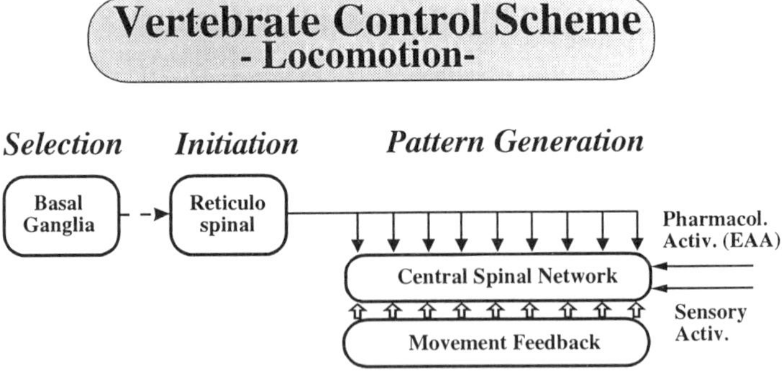

Figure 9.1 Vertebrate scheme of the control of locomotion. The basal ganglia keep a number of neural networks controlling different patterns of behavior under a tonic GABAergic inhibition. As one type of behavior is selected, the inhibitory output neurons directed to that particular network compartment will cease to be active, thereby causing a disinhibition of the selected network (see Hikosaka 1991). The reticulospinal neurons will thus become activated via intermediate mesencephalic centers (Garcia-Rill and Skinner 1986). The reticulospinal cells will, in their turn, control the level of activity in the spinal pattern-generating circuits. The central spinal network interacts with the sensory input, which senses the different phases of the movement. The spinal networks determine the sequences in which different motoneurons become activated.

subdivided into different networks, each controlling one limb, which can be combined in different ways during walking, trotting, or galloping. The coordination between the muscle groups within one limb is changed as we proceed from walking to running or from backwards to forwards locomotion. This can be explained by a further subdivision of the limb network into components controlling only groups of muscles at a single joint. These networks have been referred to as unit pattern generators (Grillner 1981, 1985, 1991). Thus, a recombination of different network components can produce a necessary versatility of the motor pattern. Furthermore, a modulation of certain neurons within a unit pattern generator network can change the output to the particular muscle groups controlled by this subunit but can also modify the overall coordination within a limb.

The neuronal networks underlying locomotion in vertebrates have gradually evolved during more than 500 million years. The essential components of the control system for propulsion have been conserved during evolution (Grillner, Wallén et al. 1991). For instance, the corresponding areas of the brainstem initiate locomotion in species from fish to primates, a spinal organization occurs in all classes of vertebrates, a sensory control of different components occurs, etc. (Figure 9.1). Information on the network level in a lower vertebrate is therefore relevant for the understanding of other vertebrate networks generating locomotion. To analyze the mode of operation of the neuronal networks themselves and the cellular mechanisms for their modulation, we have changed to a simpler experimentally amenable vertebrate preparation: the lamprey (Rovainen 1974, 1979). Due to the large number of neurons and the vast complexity of the mammalian system, it would be difficult to reach any conclusion on a cell-network level in mammals. The brainstem-spinal cord network of the lamprey has, by orders of magnitude, fewer neurons than higher vertebrates, and the motor patterns are produced *in vitro* by the isolated nervous system. This has allowed a characterization of the network underlying locomotion in the lamprey, with its supraspinal, spinal, and sensory components. We will first describe the lamprey neuronal network with its different components and later the different neuronal systems and modulatory mechanisms used to finely tune the system.

THE BACKBONE OF THE LOCOMOTOR NETWORK IS A GLUTAMATERGIC-GLYCINERGIC BRAINSTEM-SPINAL CORD NETWORK THAT INCLUDES A SENSORY FEEDBACK SYSTEM

The lamprey is an eel-like primitive vertebrate, a cyclostome. It swims by alternating contractions on the left and right sides of the body. During forward swimming, the caudal segments are activated progressively later with a phase delay that produces a rostrocaudal mechanical wave that pushes the animal forward through the water. Reticulospinal glutamatergic neurons control the level of activity in the spinal cord circuits (McClellan and Grillner 1984; Ohta and Grillner 1989), which generate the motor pattern in conjunction with the sensory signals that sense the lateral displacement of the body (Grillner et al. 1981a; McClellan and Sigvardt 1988; Viana di Prisco et al. 1990). Each segment can generate the alternating activity if the neuronal excitability is increased. This can be achieved experimentally by adding glutamate agonists to the bath. By combining NMDA receptor agonists and kainate/AMPA receptor agonists, the whole physiological frequency range from 0.2 to 10 Hz can be produced in the isolated spinal cord (Cohen and Wallén 1980; Grillner et al. 1981b; Brodin et al. 1985). The reticulospinal neurons which initiate locomotion (R in Figure 9.2) activate both NMDA and kainate/AMPA receptors on all types of segmental network neurons (Ohta and Grillner 1989; see Figure 9.2). On the level of the motoneurons each cycle consists of a phasic activation from excitatory interneurons followed by an inhibitory half cycle when the contralateral side is contracting.

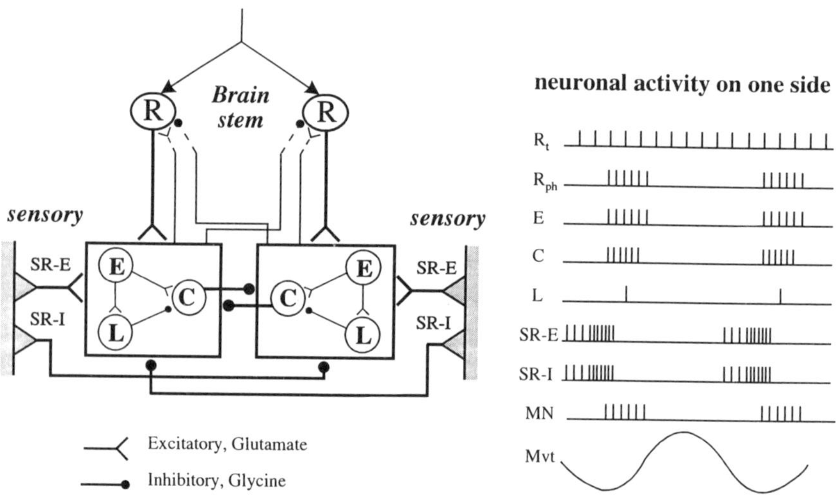

Figure 9.2 The segmental pattern-generating network. To the left is the brainstem reticulospinal neurons (R), which are responsible for initiating locomotion. They monosynaptically excite all types of neurons on the segmental level (inside the rectangular frame). There is one type of excitatory (E) glutamate interneuron, which excites the two segmental inhibitory types of interneurons (L and C) and motoneurons (not indicated). The C interneurons have crossed axons and inhibit all types of interneurons (E, C, L) and motoneurons on the contralateral side. The patterns of activity during two cycles are indicated on the right. The E and C neurons are active together, but the C interneurons tend to terminate earlier, possibly due to an inhibition from L interneurons, which spike only in midcycle. The sensory excitatory (SR-E) and inhibitory (SR-I) stretch receptor neurons become activated as the contralateral side is contracting. The SR-E excites all ipsilateral neurons, and SR-I inhibits all contralateral network neurons. The R neurons control the level of activity, activating both AMPA/kainate and NMDA receptors, but to a varying degree. Reticulospinal neurons can be subdivided into two types (Kasicki et al. 1988): one is predominantly phasic (R_{ph}; Dubuc and Grillner 1989; Vinay and Grillner 1992) while the other predominantly tonic (R_t).

The Segmental Burst-Generating Network

Spinal circuitry (see Figure 9.2) is comprised of spinal excitatory glutamatergic interneurons (E in Figure 9.2), which activate postsynaptic NMDA and AMPA/kainate receptors and have ipsilateral axons with short ascending and descending axons (Dale and Grillner 1986; Buchanan and Grillner 1987). Crossed inhibitory glycinergic interneurons (C in Figure 9.2) with long descending branches inhibit network interneurons on the contralateral side; these interneurons receive inhibition from ipsilateral inhibitory interneurons (L in Figure 9.2; Buchanan 1982). This network can account for the basic alternating pattern (see Grillner, Wallén et al. 1991). Modeling has been used as an analytical tool extensively (Grillner et al. 1988; Wallén et al. 1992; Hellgren et al. 1992). Each type of network neuron has been given its characteristic properties in terms of input impedance, afterhyperpolarization, and firing properties as a response to current injection. Voltage-dependent channels (Na^+, K^+, and Ca^{2+}), Ca^{2+}-dependent K^+ channels, synaptically gated Cl^- channels, and glutamatergic channels with the characteristics of voltage-dependent NMDA receptive channels, and conventional cationic conductance channels of the kainate/AMPA type have been simulated. The interneurons were connected as established experimentally. The sensory control from stretch receptor neurons was also included in the simulations (Grillner, Wallén et al. 1991; Tråvén et al. 1993). With the known connectivity, membrane properties, and types of synaptic transmission, the pattern of activity of the segmental network in its full physiological frequency range has been simulated. This shows that we have sufficient information to account for the motor pattern generation in a segment. However, additional levels of complexity are known to add to this basic circuit (see below), and this circuit should be solely regarded as a backbone of the functional circuit, rather than a final and complete description of the network.

Timing Is Critical — Factors that Determine Burst Termination

In a pattern-generating neural circuit, timing is the critical factor. Let us consider a single segment as stipulated above. It operates in a wide range over a cycle duration from around 5 s to 0.1 s, depending on the excitatory drive. Several complementary neuronal mechanisms are utilized to maintain precision in the control of burst termination and burst onset in motoneurons. These key mechanisms are subject to modulation via several different transmitter systems. One crucial factor in the network is the control of the termination of activity in the inhibitory CC interneurons, which leads to a disinhibition of all contralateral network interneurons (see Figure 9.2). Due to the background excitability and to other factors discussed below, they start firing upon disinhibition. The following mechanisms contribute to a decreased CC interneuron activity during the excitatory half cycle.

Afterhyperpolarization and Spike Frequency Adaptation

Spike frequency adaptation is important in both the CC interneurons and in their excitatory input interneurons. This adaptation is due mainly to a summation of the afterhyperpolarization (AHP), which follows the action potential (Figure 9.3A). AHP is due to an activation of Ca^{2+}-dependent K^+ channels (K^+_{Ca2+}) and is controlled by no less than three different transmitter systems in network neurons (serotonin [5-HT], dopamine [DA], baclofen [$GABA_B$). During a burst of a few hundred ms there is only time for several spikes. Following each spike, the larger the AHP, the more pronounced the decline in spike frequency. AHP can determine whether there will be one or two spikes within the appropriate time window. Compare the control record in Figure 9.3A and the response after a partial blockade of K^+_{Ca2+} with apamin (cf. also Figure 9.3Ab). This factor has been shown to be important in kainate-induced swimming (without NMDA receptor activation), since a partial blockade of K^+_{Ca2+} channels with apamin produces a lengthening of the bursts (Hill et al. 1992; El Manira et al., pers. comm.). The effects of the AHP summation in this network have been simulated with pools of neurons (Hellgren et al. 1992). The smaller the AHP, the smaller the AHP summation, and consequently less spike frequency adaptation will occur. Everything being equal, a given neuron will continue to fire at a higher level for a longer time and will therefore act to make the locomotor neuron burst longer. The AHP summation within a given pool of neurons appears to be an important factor (Hellgren et al. 1992; Hill et al. 1992; Wallén et al. 1989).

NMDA Channels and Calcium-dependent K^+ Channels

Part of the excitatory drive to a pool of neurons in the excitatory half cycle depends on the activation of voltage-dependent NMDA channels. The activation of NMDA channels is of critical importance at low burst rates, with NMDA channels contributing to the ability of the network to maintain long-lasting stable bursting (Brodin and Grillner 1985, 1986; Alford and Grillner 1990; Grillner, Hill et al. 1991) for two reasons. First, when NMDA channels are open, Ca^{2+} ions will pass through the NMDA channels into the cell and gradually activate K^+_{Ca2+} channels, leading to a progressive decline in the depolarization during the excitatory half cycle. Second, voltage-dependent properties of the NMDA channels induce plateau-like depolarizations or pacemaker-like potentials (Sigvardt et al. 1985; Wallén and Grillner 1987). As depolarization reaches a certain level, NMDA channels will open up and further depolarize the cell (Figure 9.3B). This plateau would be maintained as long as the cell remains under an excitatory drive. However, Ca^{2+} ions would gradually accumulate, thereby activating K^+_{Ca2+} channels, which will hyperpolarize the membrane potential to a level that will cause the NMDA channels to close. With pools of interacting neurons, this effect can be markedly amplified. Under these conditions, K^+_{Ca2+} plays a critical role for the burst-plateau termination. This has been confirmed by experiments in which these channels were blocked by apamin (Figure 9.3B); a marked prolongation of the pacemaker-like plateaus was affected and confirmed earlier conclusions. During slow swimming, the addition of apamin will cause a marked prolongation of the bursts and a marked increase in the irregularity of bursting or even a complete breakdown (Hill et al. 1992; El Manira et al., pers. comm.). It is interesting

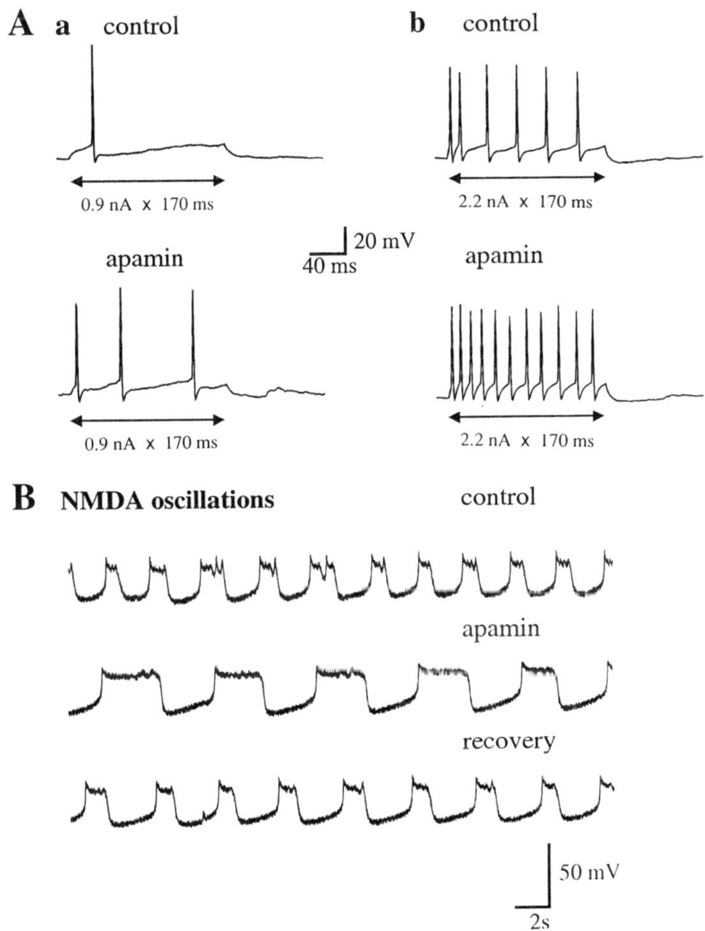

Figure 9.3 Role of calcium-dependent K^+ channels (K^+_{Ca2+}) for frequency adaptation and NMDA-induced pacemaker-like potentials. (A) Near threshold, a DC current passed through the microelectrodes for 170 ms will cause only one spike followed by a large afterhyperpolarization (AHP). After a partial blockade of K^+_{Ca2+} by apamin (2.5 μM), three spikes occur as a response to the same pulse. At 2.2 nA a tonic discharge occurs to a pulse of the same duration, and the level of activity remains much higher after apamin. (B) NMDA induces pacemaker-like potentials in tetrodotoxin (see text). The termination of the plateau is due to Ca^{2+} entering through NMDA channels, which progressively activates more K_{Ca2+} leading to an afterhyperpolarization (see text). As expected, an apamin blockade leads to a plateau prolongation.

to note that the K^+_{Ca2+} blockade varies with the burst rate and is small at a rate around 2 Hz. This level of activation was used in similar experiments by Meer and Buchanan (1992) and accounts for their recent negative results through the administration of apamin during NMDA-induced swimming. Thus the availability of K^+_{Ca2+} channels and their degree of activation by intracellular Ca^{2+} ions plays an important role for the operation of the network.

Circuit Mechanism for Burst Termination

A circuit mechanism exists that may contribute to burst termination. The lateral interneuron (L in Figure 9.2) and smaller cells, which may have a similar function (Buchanan and Grillner 1988), are activated with one or a few spikes in the middle of the burst (Buchanan and Cohen 1982). When they become active they will provide inhibition to the crossed inhibitory CC interneurons. The quantitative importance of this mechanism remains to be determined; however, we predict that it will not play an important role at low burst rates, since the IPSPs will only last for some milliseconds and a burst, under these conditions, can continue for hundreds of milliseconds. At fast burst rates, however, this mechanism could play a role (cf. above). In simulations with pools of interneurons, L interneurons are not needed to achieve network operation in the entire physiological range (Hellgren et al. 1992; see also Wallén et al. 1992).

Sensory Control of Burst Termination and Burst Initiation

In the intact swimming lamprey, sensory stretch receptor neurons play an important role (Grillner et al. 1981a). They become activated as the contralateral side of a segment contracts. One type of stretch receptor neuron is inhibitory (glycine; SR-I in Figure 9.2), inhibiting all types of contralateral network neurons including the CC interneurons. They will therefore contribute to the burst termination of the contralateral side and also to the initiation of a new burst on the other side through the disinhibition, resulting from inhibition of CC neurons. The other type of stretch receptor neuron is excitatory (glutamate) and provides monosynaptic excitation to all ipsilateral network interneurons (SR-E in Figure 9.2). They will further contribute to the activation of the ipsilateral half of the network to the stretch receptors (Viana di Prisco et al. 1990).

Burst Initiation Is Due to Disinhibition, Postinhibitory Rebound, and EAA Activation

In addition to the sensory effects on burst initiation we have just considered, the onset of activity in a hemisegment and a motoneuronal burst will be produced by several different complementary factors. As the reciprocal inhibition from the contralateral receptive C interneurons (Figure 9.2) is terminated, the disinhibition will bring the membrane potential back to a more depolarized level. The deeper the inhibition, the longer the delay to initiate a new burst (Hellgren et al. 1992). In many cells, there is a postinhibitory rebound depolarization due entirely or partially to an activation of low voltage-activated (LVA) Ca^{2+} channels (Figure 9.4C, D), which can bring a cell to threshold (Matsushima et al. 1992, 1993). The LVA Ca^{2+} channels may also contribute to plateau potentials (Hounsgaard et al. 1988). In this case, the plateau termination is also achieved by a gradual K^{+}_{Ca2+} channel activation.

The background excitability in combination with the factors mentioned above can bring the membrane potential up to a level at which excitatory interneurons start firing. At the present, they will further excite other interneurons, motoneurons, and CC interneurons. Activity in the latter will assure that the contralateral side becomes silent. As depolarization in all neurons gets close to the firing threshold, the synaptically gated NMDA channels will open up again, thereby boosting the depolarizing effect already produced by the activation of conventional AMPA/kainate receptors (see Grillner, Wallén et al. 1991).

INTERSEGMENTAL COORDINATION BY A NETWORK WITH DYNAMIC FLEXIBILITY

In a simplified manner, different segments along the spinal cord can be said to form segmental oscillators, each of which produces rhythmic burst activity within the entire frequency range in which locomotion can occur. Normally, forward swimming is characterized by a constant phase coupling (Grillner 1974; Williams et al. 1989; Grillner et al. 1993) in which there is a constant phase lag between each segment (1% of the cycle duration in the lamprey between each segment). Thus, in percentage of the cycle duration, the phase lag will remain the same regardless of whether the cycle duration is 0.1 s or 5 s. Consequently, the shape of the body during a locomotor cycle will essentially have the same configuration regardless of the speed of locomotion. The intersegmental coordination, however, need not be constant under all conditions. It can be made to change from a rostrocaudal delay of 2% between each segment to a converse caudorostral delay, in which the direction of the locomotor wave has been reversed from caudal to rostral, as in backwards swimming (Grillner 1974; Matsushima and Grillner 1990, 1992a, b; Tegnér et al. 1993).

The simplest solution to account for such a varied and yet stereotyped pattern of activity is that the same group of neurons produces these different motor patterns. This could be achieved by a very simple neuronal organization, based on the circuitry already established experimentally (cf. Figure 9.5; Matsushima and Grillner 1990, 1992a, b). Each segmental oscillator circuit could receive mutual excitation not only from its rostral and caudal neighbor, but from its second and third rostral and caudal neighbor (Dale and Grillner 1986; Buchanan et al. 1989). This type of connectivity has been experimentally established. With such a chain of segmental oscillators, all segments would be synchronous if each had the same basic excitability level (cf. Cohen et al. 1982; Matsushima and Grillner 1990, 1992b; Wadden et al. 1993). With

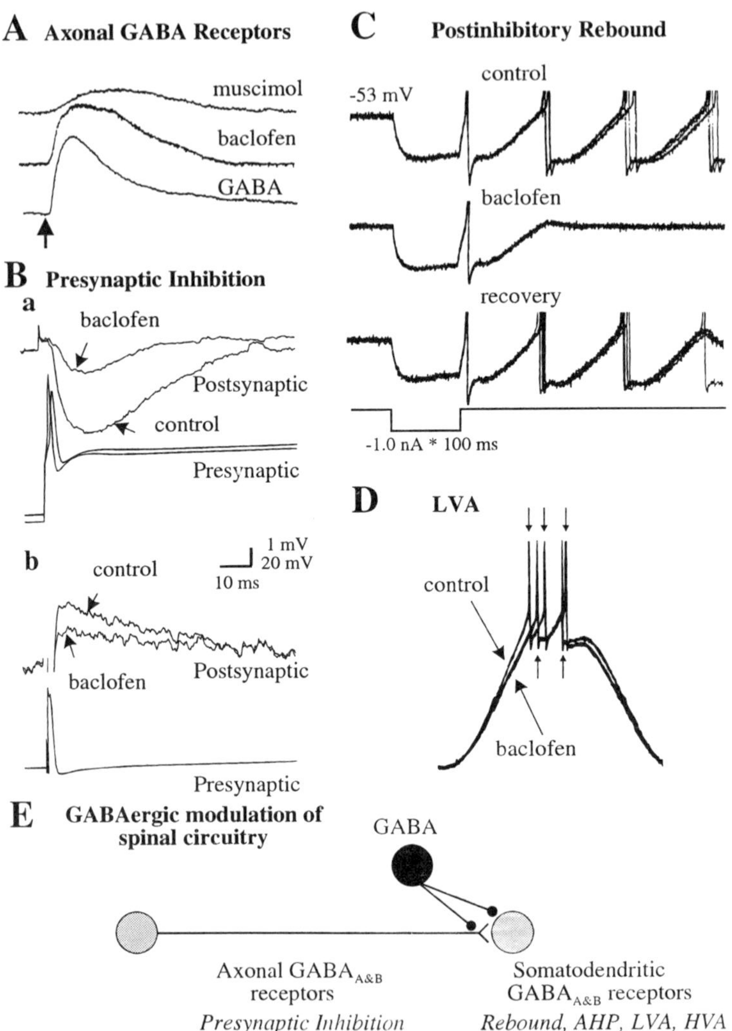

Figure 9.4 Pre- and postsynaptic effects of $GABA_A$ and $GABA_B$ receptors. (A) shows recordings from an axon of a network interneuron, and the response to a selective $GABA_A$ (muscimol) and $GABA_B$ (baclofen) agonist. This axon exhibited locomotor-related membrane potential oscillations. Before administering the GABA agonists, tetrodotoxin had been added to exclude indirect effects from adjacent neurons by the drug application (modified from Alford et al. 1991). (Ba) shows an IPSP (upper trace) elicited from a network interneuron by intracellular stimulation (action potential in lower trace). Upon administration of baclofen, the IPSP is depressed, due to a presynaptic action on $GABA_B$ receptors. (Bb) shows corresponding data on excitatory synaptic transmission from an E interneuron (see Figure 9.2; modified from Alford and Grillner 1991). (C) shows the response of a neuron to a brief hyperpolarizing current pulse. The neuron was held at a membrane potential level close to threshold for eliciting an action potential. The 100 ms pulse elicited a spike on the repolarization at the end of the pulse, and

such a network, a constant phase lag could only occur if there was a difference in excitability. For instance, if the rostral oscillator had a somewhat higher excitability than the remaining oscillators, this rostral oscillator would entrain its caudal neighbor, which in its turn would entrain its caudal neighbor, and so forth, along the entire spinal cord (Matsushima and Grillner 1992b). Correspondingly, if the most caudal segment in a chain was given the role of being the leading segment, its higher frequency would result in a phase lag from this caudal segment to its rostral neighbor, which would, in its turn, entrain its rostral neighbor and so forth. In conclusion, by determining which segment should be given the role of being the leading segment (by elevating the excitability level), one may also determine the direction of swimming. The difference in excitability between a given segment and all remaining segments can thus determine the phase lag between each consecutive segment along the entire spinal cord.

There is, however, an anatomical asymmetry built into the system that can account for the fact that the network normally organizes itself into resting activity with a rostrocaudal lag (Grillner et al. 1993; see Williams et al. 1990). The C interneurons (Figure 9.2) responsible for the reciprocal inhibition have long descending axons, and the amount of reciprocal inhibition is less in the rostral segments (Wallén et al. 1993). This means that the rostral segments will obtain a higher net excitability (that is a higher intrinsic frequency). This condition will automatically make them constitute a leading segment and consequently create a basic configuration with a rostrocaudal lag. By increasing the excitability at any point along the spinal cord, this point can be made the leader from which a phase lag will arise in the rostral or caudal direction (or both). Thus, through a simple type of control, one can even make the locomotor wave change direction, such as providing an extra excitatory drive to a caudal segment, thereby creating a caudorostral drive. Based on modeling, Williams et al. (1990; Kopell 1988; see also Sigvardt 1993 and Williams 1992) emphasized an asymmetric coupling function, rather than the excitability differences discussed above, as a mechanism to obtain a rostrocaudal phase lag. This alternative mechanism can produce a constant stable phase lag but would appear less flexible in terms of changing or reversing the phase coupling.

Figure 9.4 (*cont.*)

several subsequent spikes on the rebound following each post-spike afterhyperpolarization. This powerful "postinhibitory rebound" observed in the control and recovery trace is depressed markedly by $GABA_B$ receptor activation (baclofen). The rebound depolarization is dependent on a low voltage-activated (LVA) Ca^{2+} current. (D) shows another cell subject to sinusoidal current injection simulating the locomotor drive current. The slope of the depolarizing trajectory leading up to the first action potential is steeper in the control record than after baclofen or cobalt (not illustrated). This effect of baclofen is due to a depression of an LVA Ca^{2+} current. C and D is modified from Matsushima et al. 1993. (E) summarizes the effects of GABA on the pre- and postsynaptic level.

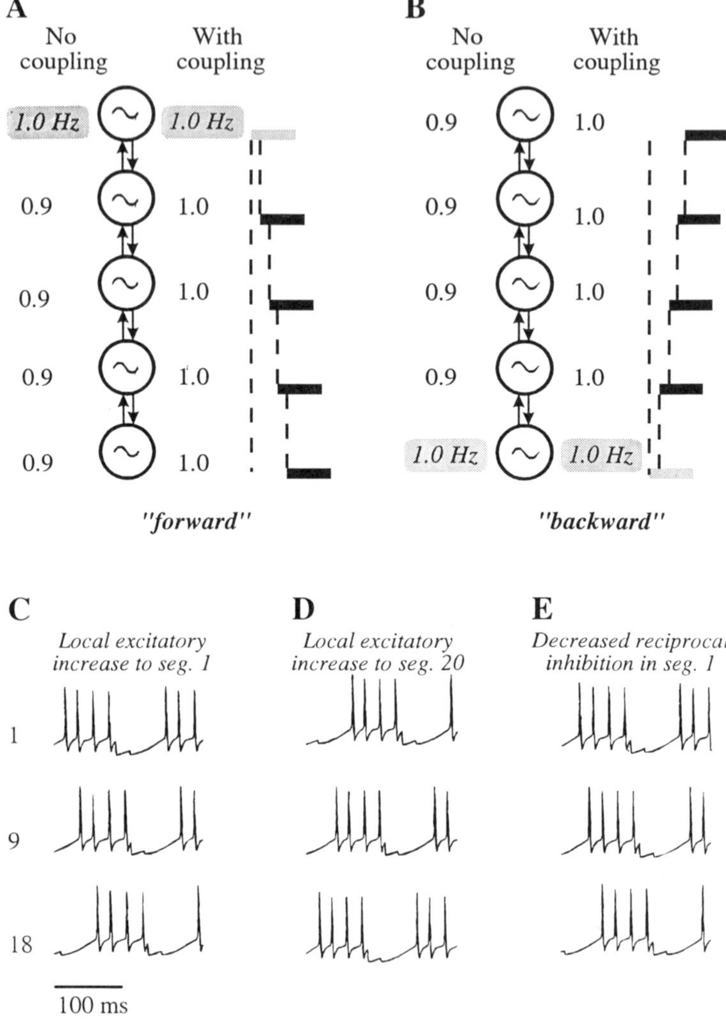

Figure 9.5 "Trailing oscillator hypothesis" for intersegmental coordination. Each segmental network as depicted in Figure 9.2 can, in a simplified manner, be regarded as an oscillator circuit (circles in A and B). The frequency of each oscillator circuit is set by the background excitability. If all such oscillator circuits have the same excitability, they will have the same frequency. If they are coupled together with a symmetric coupling, they will all become active in a synchronous fashion (e.g., 0.9 Hz). If, however, one oscillator has a somewhat higher intrinsic frequency (e.g., 1.0 Hz), when independent than all other oscillators (intrinsic frequency of 0.9 Hz), the latter can become entrained by the fastest oscillator, so that they all become active at 1.0 Hz. In addition, there will be a phase lag (as in A) between each consecutive oscillator network. If the most rostral oscillator is leading, there will be a phase lag between each segment from rostral to caudal. If the most caudal segment is leading as in (B), the lag will instead be

MODULATION OF THE SEGMENTAL CIRCUITRY

The Spinal GABA System(s)

There is a rich GABAergic innervation in the lamprey spinal cord both in the grey matter and dorsal horn and within the fiber tracts of the lateral and ventral tracts (see Brodin et al. 1990; Brodin and Grillner 1990; Christenson, Bongianni et al. 1991). Three types of local segmental GABA neurons have been identified in the lamprey: one small type of neuron, which forms close appositions on the axons of sensory axons; one larger type, which most likely impinges upon the somata and interneuronal axons in the grey matter; and a third type of cell that lines the central canal. GABA neurons exert their effects on both the presynaptic and the somatodendritic level, via $GABA_A$ and $GABA_B$ receptors.

Both $GABA_A$ and $GABA_B$ Receptors Mediate Presynaptic Modulation of Network Interneurons

It has generally been assumed that the presynaptic GABAergic inhibition in the spinal cord is limited to sensory afferents (Rudomin 1990; Nicoll and Alger 1979). This, however, is not the case since the axons of both the excitatory and inhibitory premotor interneurons in the locomotor network are subject to presynaptic modulation, which is mediated by both $GABA_A$ and $GABA_B$ receptors located on the axonal terminals (Alford et al. 1991; Alford and Grillner 1991). In addition, the membrane potential of

---

Figure 9.5 *(cont.)*

from caudal to rostral corresponding to backward locomotion. (C), (D), and (E) show simulations in which the neurons (E, C, and L in Figure 9.2) in each of 20 segments have been simulated; they have been combined with mutual excitation as demonstrated experimentally (see Matsushima and Grillner 1992a; Wadden et al. 1993). In (C), segment 1 has been given extra excitation, resulting in a rostrocaudal phase lag between all consecutive segments. In (D), the caudal-most segment 20 has been made the leader resulting in a caudorostral lag. All segments except the leading one have the same excitability level (inherent frequency). The simulations in (C) and (D) disregard the fact that the most rostral segments, as a rule, have less reciprocal inhibition than more caudal segments, due to the asymmetric anatomical arrangements of the C interneurons (Figure 9.2), which have comparatively long descending axons. In (E) the reciprocal inhibition has been decreased in segment 1, which then produces an intersegmental phase lag similar to that in C. This condition can account for the fact that the isolated spinal cord in most cases exhibits a stable rostrocaudal lag (modified from Grillner et al. 1993). What we have described here is a very simple, basically symmetric organization in which the different segmental oscillators provide mutual excitation to their rostral and caudal neighbors over one or several segments. We have shown that such a network can provide a phase delay from the leading segment, and the larger the excitability difference between the leading segment and the remaining segments, the larger the phase lag will become between each consecutive segment along the spinal cord (Grillner et al. 1993; Wadden et al. 1993).

these axons is modulated in each locomotor cycle, affecting thus the synaptic transmission. This is a modulatory mechanism that is continuously in operation. By decreasing or increasing the level of presynaptic GABAergic modulation, the synaptic transmission in the network can be amplified or reduced (see Figure 9.4A, B). This type of presynaptic mechanism has also been found in the stomatogastric network (Nusbaum et al. 1992) and will most likely turn out to be a general synaptic tuning mechanism. Afferents are also subject to presynaptic modulation in this system as well as in invertebrates and in other vertebrates (El Manira et al. 1991; Clarac et al. 1992; Dubuc et al. 1988).

GABA Effects on Somadendritic Level Include Actions on LVA and HVA Ca^{2+} Channels

Ultrastructurally, GABAergic boutons occur on dendrites of grey matter neurons. They tend to have a more distal location than that of glycinergic boutons (Christenson et al. 1993), which are responsible for the conventional postsynaptic inhibition from network interneurons (Grillner and Wallén 1980; Russell and Wallén 1983; Buchanan 1982; Grillner et al. 1988). Although $GABA_A$ receptors are present on spinal neurons (Homma and Rovainen 1978), conventional $GABA_A$IPSPs have not yet been observed in these neurons.

The G-protein-mediated $GABA_B$ receptors act on HVA Ca^{2+} channels. By reducing the Ca^{2+} inflow during the action potential, Ca^{2+}-activated K^+ channels become less activated, which reduces the AHP following the action potential (Matsushima et al. 1992, 1993). AHP is a main determinant of the frequency regulation in the cell, and this has important consequences (see above). The same cellular mechanism may be effective in the axonal $GABA_B$-induced presynaptic depression of synaptic transmission.

The LVA Ca^{2+} channels referred to above are also modulated by a $GABA_B$ receptor activation. LVA Ca^{2+} channels are responsible for the rebound depolarization following postsynaptic inhibition in several types of neurons, and they play an important role near the firing threshold. The $GABA_B$-induced depression of LVA channels must therefore be expected to play a significant modulatory role.

GABA-induced Modulation on the Network Level

From the above it can be inferred that GABAergic neurons provide a phasic input to spinal neurons in each locomotor cycle (Alford et al. 1991). One way to test the net contribution of this GABA system is to manipulate the GABAergic effect by either increasing the available level of synaptically released GABA, through the administration of GABA uptake blockers, or conversely by blocking the effects of GABA with receptor antagonists. From such experiments it can be concluded that the net effect of the GABA system is to produce a certain reduction of the overall burst rate. Thus, by increasing or decreasing the level of activity in the GABA interneurons, the network activity can be modulated (Tegnér et al. 1993). The GABA-induced reduction of LVA Ca^{2+} channels as well as the AHP reduction (see above) and the presynaptic effects would all be expected to contribute to a burst prolongation. In addition, we note that the presence of a certain level of $GABA_A$ receptor activation will contribute to a maintenance of the regularity of the burst activity.

On the intersegmental level, a potentiation of the GABA system induced effects along a portion of the spinal cord. This leads to an increased intersegmental phase delay in this particular part of the spinal cord, presumably due to the effect of reducing the "net excitability" in the local segmental networks.

GABAergic and Peptidergic Cells Lining the Central Canal May Modulate Intraspinal Stretch Receptor Neurons

Central canal cells have cilia projecting out into the central canal. They also form long processes projecting to the lateral margin of the spinal cord, where a very dense GABAergic plexus is found around the dendrites of the intraspinal stretch receptor neurons (Christenson, Alford et al. 1991). The GABA varicosities originating from the ventrolateral central canal cells also contain somatostatin. The net inhibitory effects of $GABA_A$ and $GABA_B$ receptor activation are similar to those of grey matter neurons (Barthe, pers. comm.), and somatostatin acts via a third type of ionic mechanism causing a hypolarization via K^+ channels (Christenson, Alford et al. 1991; Barthe et al., pers. comm.). The same type of cell can therefore exert an action by using several different postsynaptic ionic mechanisms to provide a net inhibitory effect. The dorsolateral GABAergic central canal cells contain neurotensin instead of somatostatin. Neurotensin produces a net depolarizing effect on stretch receptor neurons, but this remains to be explored further (Barthe, pers. comm.). This type of ciliated central canal cells exists in all vertebrates. A very dense projection to the lateral margin of the spinal cord is characteristic of most species studied (Vigh et al. 1977). The function of these enigmatic cells is as yet unknown; however, the indirect evidence presented here could indicate a modulatory role for movement related feedback. The physiological stimulus that normally activates these central canal cells is as yet unknown.

The 5-HT-DA System Modulates the Network via an Action on Different Ion Channels

In the midline of the spinal cord ventral to the central canal, there is a column of unpaired cells that contain both 5-HT and DA. Together they form a bilateral ventromedial dense plexus of varicosities (van Dongen et al. 1985; Harris-Warrick et al. 1985), in which all network neurons have dendritic ramifications. 5-HT has a powerful action on Ca^{2+}-dependent K^+ channels, which (above) affects both the AHP and NMDA receptor-induced effects (Wallén et al. 1989). DA, on the other hand, acts on HVA Ca^{2+} channels and will therefore indirectly causes a reduction in the activation of Ca^{2+}-dependent K^+ channels (Schotland et al. 1993). The cellular effects of DA and

5-HT are complementary to each other. DA acts via D_2 receptors and 5-HT via 5-HT_{1C} or 5-HT_2 receptors (Wikström et al., pers. comm.).

On the network level, 5-HT causes a burst prolongation and corresponding cycle duration increase. In addition, there is an increased intersegmental phase delay (Harris-Warrick and Cohen 1985; Christenson et al. 1989; Matsushima and Grillner 1992a). These effects are also produced by an increased endogenous release of 5-HT. The network effects of 5-HT would, in principle, be those expected from the 5-HT-induced reduction of K^+_{Ca2+}. A comparison with the effects of a selective apamin blockade of K^+_{Ca2+} on the network would, however, indicate (Hill et al. 1992) that 5-HT may exert additional effects, such as a certain hypolarization in some neurons (Wallén et al. 1989). Application of DA will also cause a net decrease of burst rate (Schotland et al. 1993), but the effects remain to be explored both on the network and the cellular level.

CONCLUSION

As the lamprey swims at a broad range of frequencies, the control of intrinsic neuronal properties and the kinds of synaptic interactions appear to act together so that coordination can be maintained despite the massive changes in local excitability that are required to change frequency. We have illustrated several different cellular mechanisms used at the network level to achieve the dynamic flexibility in pattern generation required for an optimal adaptation to the ever changing demands of the environment.

REFERENCES

Alford, S., J. Christenson, and S. Grillner. 1991. Presynaptic $GABA_A$ and $GABA_B$ receptor-mediated phasic modulation in axons in spinal motor interneurons. *Eur. J. Neurosci.* **3**:107–117.

Alford, S., and S. Grillner. 1990. CNQX and DNQX block non-NMDA synaptic transmission but not NMDA-evoked locomotion in lamprey spinal cord. *Brain Res.* **506**:297–302.

Alford, S., and S. Grillner. 1991. The involvement of $GABA_B$ receptors and coupled G-proteins in spinal GABAergic presynaptic inhibition. *J. Neurosci.* **11**:3718–3728.

Brodin, L., N. Dale, J. Christenson, J. Storm-Mathisen, T. Hökfelt, and S. Grillner. 1990. Three types of GABA-immunoreactive cells in the lamprey spinal cord. *Brain Res.* **508**:172–175.

Brodin, L., and S. Grillner. 1985. The role of putative excitatory amino acid neurotransmission in the initiation of locomotion in the lamprey spinal cord. I. The effects of excitatory amino acid antagonists. *Brain Res.* **360**:139–148.

Brodin, L., and S. Grillner. 1986. Effects of magnesium on fictive locomotion induced by activation of N-methyl-D-aspartate (NMDA) receptors in the lamprey spinal cord *in vitro*. *Brain Res.* **380**:244–252.

Brodin, L., and S. Grillner. 1990. The lamprey CNS *in vitro*, an experimentally amenable model for synaptic transmission and integrative functions. In: Preparations of Vertebrate Central Nervous System *In Vitro*, ed. H. Jahnsen, pp. 103–153. Chichester: Wiley.

Brodin, L., S. Grillner, and C.M. Rovainen. 1985. N-methyl-D-aspartate (NMDA), kainate and quisqualate receptors and the generation of fictive locomotion in the lamprey spinal cord. *Brain Res.* **325**:302–306.

Buchanan, J.T. 1982. Identification of interneurons with collateral caudal axons in the lamprey spinal-cord: Synaptic interactions and morphology. *J. Neurophysiol.* **47**:961–975.

Buchanan, J.T., and A.H. Cohen. 1982. Activities of identified interneurons, motoneurons and muscle fibers during fictive locomotion in the lamprey and effects of reticulospinal and dorsal cells stimulation. *J. Neurophysiol.* **42**:948–960.

Buchanan, J.T., and S. Grillner. 1987. Newly identified "glutamate interneurons" and their role in locomotion in the lamprey spinal cord. *Science* **236**:312–314.

Buchanan, J.T., and S. Grillner. 1988. A new class of small inhibitory interneurons in the lamprey spinal cord. *Brain Res.* **438**:404–407.

Buchanan, J.T., S. Grillner, S. Cullheim, and M. Risling. 1989. Identification of excitatory interneurons contributing to generation of locomotion in lamprey: Structure, pharmacology, and function. *J. Neurophysiol.* **62**:59–69.

Christenson, J., S. Alford, S. Grillner, and T. Hökfelt. 1991. Co-localized GABA and somatostatin use different ionic mechanisms to hyperpolarize target neurons in the lamprey spinal cord. *Neurosci. Lett.* **134**:93–97.

Christenson, J., F. Bongianni, S. Grillner, and T. Hökfelt. 1991. Putative GABAergic input to axons of spinal interneurons and primary sensory neurons in the lamprey spinal cord as shown by intracellular Lucifer Yellow and GABA immunohistochemistry. *Brain Res.* **538**:313–318.

Christenson, J., J. Franck, and S. Grillner. 1989. Increase in endogenous 5-hydroxytryptamine levels modulates the central network underlying locomotion in the lamprey spinal cord. *Neurosci Lett.* **100**:188–192.

Christenson, J., O. Shupliakov, S. Cullheim, and S. Grillner. 1993. Possible morphological substrates for GABA-mediated presynaptic inhibition in the lamprey spinal cord. *J. Comp. Neurol.* **328**:463–472.

Clarac, F., A. El Manira, and D. Cattaert. 1992. Presynaptic control as a mechanism of sensory-motor integration. *Curr. Opin. Neurobiol.* **2**:764–769.

Cohen, A.H., P.J. Holmes, and R.H. Rand. 1982. The nature of the coupling between segmental oscillators of the lamprey spinal generator for locomotion: A mathematical model. *J. Math. Biol.* **13**:345–369.

Cohen, A.H., and P. Wallén. 1980. The neuronal correlate of locomotion in fish. "Fictive swimming" induced in an *in vitro* preparation of the lamprey spinal cord. *Exp. Brain Res.* **41**:11–18.

Dale, N., and S. Grillner. 1986. Dual-component synaptic potentials in the lamprey mediated by excitatory amino acid receptors. *J. Neurosci.* **6**:2653–2661.

Deliagina, T.G., G.N. Orlovsky, S. Grillner, and P. Wallén. 1992a. Vestibular control of swimming in lamprey. 2. Characteristics of spatial sensitivity of reticulospinal neurons. *Exp. Brain Res.* **90**:489–498.

Deliagina, T.G., G.N. Orlovsky, S. Grillner, and P. Wallén. 1992b. Vestibular control of swimming in lamprey. 3. Activity of vestibular afferents. Convergence of vestibular inputs on reticulospinal neurons. *Exp. Brain Res.* **90**:499–507.

Dubuc, R., J.-M. Cabelguen, and S. Rossignol. 1988. Rhythmic fluctuation of dorsal root potentials and antidromic discharges of primary afferents during fictive locomotion in the cat. *J. Neurophysiol.* **60**:2014–2036.

Dubuc, R., and S. Grillner. 1989. The role of spinal cord inputs in modulating the activity of reticulospinal neurons during fictive locomotion in the lamprey. *Brain Res.* **483**:196–200.

El Manira, A., R.A. DiCaprio, D. Cattaert, and F. Clarac. 1991. Monosynaptic interjoint reflexes and their central modulation during fictive locomotion. *Eur. J. Neurosci.* **3**:1219–1231.

Garcia-Rill, E., and R.D. Skinner. 1986. The basal ganglia and the mesencephalic locomotor region. In: Neurobiology of Vertebrate Locomotion, ed. S. Grillner, P.S.G. Stein, D. Stuart, H. Forssberg, and R. Herman, pp. 77–104. New York: Macmillan.

Georgopoulos, A.P., and S. Grillner. 1989. Visuomotor coordination in reaching and locomotion. *Science* **245**:1209–1210.

Grillner, S. 1974. On the generation of locomotion in the spinal dogfish. *Exp. Brain Res.* **20**:459–470.

Grillner, S. 1981. Control of locomotion in bipeds, tetrapods and fish. In: Handbook of Physiology, vol. 11, Motor Control, ed. V. Brooks, pp. 1179–1236. Bethesda: Am. Physiol. Soc.

Grillner, S. 1985. Neurobiological bases of rhythmic motor acts in vertebrates. *Science* **228**:143–149.

Grillner, S. 1991. Recombination of motor pattern generators: Simple neuronal networks combine to produce complex versatile motor patterns. *Curr. Biol.* **1**:231–233.

Grillner, S., J.T. Buchanan, and A. Lansner. 1988. Simulation of the segmental burst generating network for locomotion in lamprey. *Neurosci. Lett.* **89**:31–35.

Grillner, P., R. Hill, and S. Grillner. 1991. 7-chlorokynureic acid blocks NMDA receptor-induced fictive locomotion in lamprey: Evidence for a physiological role of the glycine site. *Acta Physiol. Scand.* **141**:131–132.

Grillner, S., and T. Matsushima. 1991. The neuronal network underlying locomotion in the lamprey: Synaptic and cellular mechanisms. *Neuron* **7**:1–15.

Grillner, S., T. Matsushima, T. Wadden, J. Tegnér, A. El Manira, and P. Wallén. 1993. The neurophysiological basis of undulatory locomotion in vertebrates. *Sem. Neurosci.* **5**:17–27.

Grillner, S., A. McClellan, and C. Perret. 1981a. Entrainment of the spinal pattern generators for swimming by mechanosensitive elements in the lamprey spinal cord *in vitro*. *Brain Res.* **217**:380–386.

Grillner, S., A. McClellan, A. Sigvardt, P. Wallén, and M. Wilén. 1981b. Activation of NMDA receptors elicits "fictive locomotion" in lamprey spinal cord *in vitro*. *Acta Physiol. Scand.* **113**:549–551.

Grillner, S., and P. Wallén. 1980. Does the central pattern generation for locomotion in lamprey depend on glycine inhibition? *Acta Physiol. Scand.* **110**:103–105.

Grillner, S., P. Wallén, L. Brodin, and A. Lansner. 1991. Neuronal network generating locomotor behavior in lamprey circuitry, transmitters, membrane properties and simulation. *Ann. Rev. Neurosci.* **14**:169–199.

Harris-Warrick, R.M., and A.H. Cohen. 1985. Serotonin modulates the central pattern generator for locomotion in the isolated lamprey spinal cord. *J. Exp. Biol.* **116**:27–46.

Harris-Warrick, R.M., E. Marder, A.I. Selverston, and M. Moulins. 1992. Dynamic Biological Networks. Cambridge, MA.: MIT Press.

Harris-Warrick, R.M., J.C. McPhee, and J.A. Filler. 1985. Distribution of serotonergic neurons and processes in the lamprey spinal cord. *Neurosci.* **14**:1127–1140.

Hellgren, J., S. Grillner, and A. Lansner. 1992. Computer simulation of the segmental neuronal network generating locomotion in lamprey by using populations of network interneurons. *Biol. Cybern.* **68**:1–13.

Hikosaka, O. 1991. Basal ganglia—Possible role in motor coordination and learning. *Curr. Opin. Neurobiol.* **1**:638–643.

Hill, R.H., T. Matsushima, J. Schotland, and S. Grillner. 1992. Apamin blocks the slow AHP in the lamprey and delays termination of locomotor bursts. *NeuroReport* **3**:943–945.

Homma, S., and C.M. Rovainen. 1978. Conductance increases produced by glycine and gammma-aminobutyric acid in lamprey interneurons. *J. Physiol. Lond.* **279**:231–252.

Hounsgaard, J., H. Hultborn, B. Jespersen, and O. Kiehn. 1988. Bistability of α-motoneurons in the decerebrate cat and in the acute spinal cat after intravenous 5-hydroxytryptophan. *J. Physiol.* **405**:345–367.

Kasicki, S., S. Grillner, Y. Ohta, R. Dubuc, and L. Brodin. 1988. Phasic modulation of reticulospinal neurons during fictive locomotion and other types of motor activity in lamprey. *Brain Res.* **484**:203–216.

Kopell, N. 1988. Toward a theory of modeling central pattern generators. In: Neural Control of Rhythmic Movements in Vertebrates, ed. A.H. Cohen, S. Rossignol, and S. Grillner, pp. 369–413. New York: Wiley-Interscience.

Matsushima, T., and S. Grillner. 1990. Intersegmental co-ordination of undulatory movements: A "trailing oscillator" hypothesis. *NeuroReport* **1**:97–100.

Matsushima, T., and S. Grillner. 1992a. Local serotonergic modulation of calcium-dependent potassium channels controls intersegmental coordination in the lamprey spinal cord. *J. Neurophysiol.* **67**:1683–1690.

Matsushima, T., and S. Grillner. 1992b. Neuronal mechanisms of intersegmental coordination in lamprey: Local excitability changes modify the phase coupling along the spinal cord. *J. Neurophysiol.* **67**:373–388.

Matsushima, T., J. Tegnér, A. El Manira, J.-Y. Barthe, R. Hill, and S. Grillner. 1992. $GABA_B$-ergic modulation of somatodendritic Ca^{2+}-currents and firing properties of spinal neurons in the lamprey locomotor network. *Pharmacol. Comm.* **2**:155–156.

Matsushima, T., J. Tegnér, R. Hill, and S. Grillner. 1993. $GABA_B$ receptor activation causes a depression of low and high voltage-activated Ca^{2+}-currents, postinhibitory rebound and post spike afterhyperpolarization in lamprey neurons. *J. Neurophysiol.* **70**:2606–2619.

McClellan, A.D., and S. Grillner. 1984. Activation of "fictive swimming" by electrical microstimulation of brainstem locomotor regions in an *in vitro* preparation of the lamprey central nervous system. *Brain Res.* **300**:357–361.

McClellan, A.D., and K.A. Sigvardt. 1988. Features of entrainment of spinal pattern generators for locomotor activity in the lamprey spinal cord. *J. Neurosci.* **8**:133–145.

Meer, D.P., and J.T. Buchanan. 1992. Apamin reduces the late afterhyperpolarization of lamprey spinal neurons, with little effect on fictive swimming. *Neurosci. Lett.* **143**:1–4.

Nicoll, R.A., and B.E. Alger. 1979. Presynaptic inhibition: Transmitter and ionic mechanisms. *Int. Rev. Neurobiol.* **21**:217–258.

Nusbaum, M.P., J.M. Weimann, J. Golowasch, and E. Marder. 1992. Presynaptic control of modulatory fibers by their neural network targets. *J. Neurosci.* **12**:2706–2714.

Ohta, Y., and S. Grillner. 1989. Monosynaptic excitatory amino acid transmission from the posterior rhombencephalic reticular nucleus to spinal neurons involved in the control of locomotion in lamprey. *J. Neurophysiol.* **62**:1079–1089.

Orlovsky, G.N. 1991. Gravistatic postural control in simpler systems. *Curr. Opin. Neurobiol.* **1**:621–627.

Roberts, A., and M.J. Tunstall. 1990. Mutual re-excitation with post-inhibitory rebound: A simulation study on the mechanisms for locomotor rhythm generation in the spinal cord of *Xenopus* embryos. *Eur. J. Neurosci.* **2**:11–23.

Rovainen, C.M. 1974. Synaptic interactions of reticulospinal neurons and nerve cells in the spinal cord of the sea lamprey. *J. Comp. Neurol.* **154**:207–223.

Rovainen, C.M. 1979. Neurobiology of lampreys. *Physiol. Rev.* **59**:1007–1077.

Rudomin, P. 1990. Presynaptic inhibition of muscle spindle and tendon organ afferents in the mammalian spinal cord. *Trends Neurosci.* **13**:499–505.

Russell, D.F., and P. Wallén. 1983. On the control of myotomal motoneurons during "fictive swimming" in the lamprey spinal cord *in vitro*. *Acta Physiol. Scand.* **117**:161–170.

Schotland, J., O. Shupliakov, L. Brodin, T. Hökfelt, and S. Grillner. 1993. Co-localized monoamine transmitters regulate neuronal firing properties via complementary ionic mechanisms. Submitted.

Selverston, A.I., and M. Moulins. 1985. Oscillatory neural networks. *Ann. Rev. Physiol.* **47**:29–48.

Shik, M.L., and G.N. Orlovsky. 1976. Neurophysiology of locomotor automatism. *Physiol. Rev.* **56**:465–501.

Sigvardt, K.A. 1993. Intersegmental coordination in the lamprey central pattern generator for locomotion. *Sem. Neurosci.* **5**:3–15.

Sigvardt, K.A., S. Grillner, P. Wallén, and P.A.M. Van Dongen. 1985. Activation of NMDA receptors elicits fictive locomotion and bistable membrane properties in the lamprey spinal cord. *Brain Res.* **336**:390–395.

Stein, P.S.G. 1978. Motor systems, with special reference to the control of locomotion. *Ann. Rev. Neurosci.* **1**:61–81.

Tegnér, J., T. Matsushima, A. El Manira, and S. Grillner. 1993. The spinal GABA system modulates burst frequency and intersegmental coordination in the lamprey: Differential effects of $GABA_A$ and $GABA_B$ receptors. *J. Neurophysiol.* **69:**647–657.

Tråvén, H.G.C., L. Brodin, A. Lansner, Ö. Ekeberg, P. Wallén, and S. Grillner. 1993. Computer simulations of NMDA and non-NMDA receptor-mediated synaptic drive: Sensory and supraspinal modulation of neurons and small networks. *J. Neurophysiol.*, in press.

Van Dongen, P.A.M., T. Hökfelt, S. Grillner, A.A.J. Verhofstad, and H.W.M. Steinbusch. 1985. Possible target neurons of 5-hydroxytryptamine fibers in the lamprey spinal cord. *J. Comp. Neurol.* **234**:523–535.

Viana Di Prisco, G., P. Wallén, and S. Grillner. 1990. Synaptic effects of intraspinal stretch receptor neurons mediating movement-related feedback during locomotion. *Brain Res.* **530**:161–166.

Vigh, B., I. Vigh-Teichmann, and B. Aros. 1977. Special dendritic and axonal endings formed by the cerebrospinal fluid contacting neurons of the spinal cord. *Cell Tiss. Res.* **183**:541–552.

Vinay, L., and S. Grillner. 1992. Spino-bulbar neurons convey information to the brainstem about different phases of the locomotor cycle in the lamprey. *Brain Res.* **582**:134–138.

Wadden, T., S. Grillner, T. Matsushima, and A. Lansner. 1993. Realistic simulation of undulatory locomotion. In: Computation and Neural Systems, ed. F.M. Eeckman and J.M. Bower. Norwell, MA.: Kluwer Acad., in press.

Wallén, P., J.T. Buchanan, S. Grillner, R.H. Hill, J. Christenson, and T. Hökfelt. 1989. Effects of 5-hydroxytryptamine on the afterhyperpolarization, spike frequency regulation, and oscillatory membrane properties in lamprey spinal cord neurons. *J. Neurophysiol.* **61**:759–768.

Wallén, P., Ö. Ekeberg, A. Lansner, L. Brodin, H. Tråvén, and S. Grillner. 1992. A computer-based model for realistic simulations of neuronal networks. II. The segmental network generating locomotor rhythmicity in the lamprey. *J. Neurophysiol.* **68**:1939–1950.

Wallén, P., and S. Grillner. 1987. N-methyl-D-aspartate receptor induced, inherent oscillatory activity in neurons active during fictive locomotion in the lamprey. *J. Neurosci.* **7**:2745–2755.

Wallén, P., O. Shupliakov, and R.H. Hill. 1993. Origin of phasic synaptic inhibition in motoneurons during fictive locomotion in the lamprey. *Exp. Brain Res.*, in press.

Williams, T.L. 1992. Phase coupling by synaptic spread in chains of coupled neuronal oscillators. *Science* **258**:662–665.

Williams, T.L., S. Grillner, V.V. Smoljaninov, P. Wallén, S. Kashin, and S. Rossignol. 1989. Locomotion in lamprey and trout: The relative timing of activation and movement. *J. Exp. Biol.* **143**:559–566.

Williams, T.L., K.A. Sigvardt, N. Kopell, G.B. Ermentrout, and M.P. Remler. 1990. Forcing of coupled nonlinear oscillators: Studies of intersegmental coordination in the lamprey locomotor central pattern generator. *J. Neurophysiol.* **64**:862–871.

10

Cellular Basis of Generation and Modulation of Thalamocortical Activity

D.A. McCormick
Section of Neurobiology, Yale University School of Medicine,
333 Cedar St., New Haven, CT 06510, U.S.A.

ABSTRACT

Thalamocortical systems display synchronized rhythmic activity both during normal (e.g., slow wave sleep or attentiveness and cognition) and abnormal (e.g., epilepsy) neural function. Synchronized rhythmic activity in the forebrain is generated as an interaction between intrinsic membrane properties and axonal connections between identified subgroups of neurons in the thalamus and cerebral cortex. Ascending and descending neurotransmitter systems control the occurrence and pattern of oscillatory activity through the modulation of specialized K^+ currents in a highly precise manner. Understanding the cellular basis of these oscillatory activities and their control is shedding light on the mechanisms of generation of the EEG during sleep, seizures, and cognition and may help to clarify the role of state-dependent activity in forebrain structures.

INTRODUCTION

Since the earliest recordings of electrical activity on the surface of the cerebral cortex by Richard Caton in the late 1800s (Caton 1887), we have known that the pattern of activity generated by the nervous system varies with the state of arousal, sleep, attentiveness, and anesthesia. During naturally occurring sleep, or under the influence of certain types of anesthesia, oscillatory activity in the electroencephalogram (EEG) appears in two prominent frequency ranges: (a) delta waves appear as 0.5–4 Hz oscillations that are rather irregular in form, and (b) spindle waves appear as 7–14 Hz oscillations that wax and wane over 2- to 4-second periods and which reappear with a remarkable regularity of one every 3–10 seconds (see Figure 10.2; for a review see Steriade and McCarley 1990). Although we do not yet understand the role of these oscillations in neural function, knowledge of the cellular mechanisms of the generation

Cellular and Molecular Mechanisms Underlying Higher Neural Functions
Edited by A.I. Selverston and P. Ascher

and regulation of these two different patterns of activity has gained considerable clinical importance, since they figure prominently in the study of sleep disorders and generalized seizures, and perhaps even in such disparate abnormal functions as motor tremor, chronic deafferented limb pain, and cognitive deficits (e.g., see Buzsaki et al. 1988). Indeed, more recent *in vivo* results suggest that synchronized oscillatory activity may form an important mechanism in sensory/motor processing for the temporary formation of functional units in cortical (and thalamocortical?) systems in the behaving animal (see Gray et al. 1989). *Together, these observations of sensory processing and naturally occurring sleep as well as generalized seizures and other abnormal activities in the forebrain indicate that thalamocortical systems possess specialized cellular properties and axonal connections that allow the temporary formation of coherent oscillatory activity.* The cellular mechanisms by which this oscillatory activity is generated and synchronized is the topic of this chapter.

STATE-DEPENDENT ACTIVITY IN THALAMOCORTICAL NETWORKS

Extracellular and intracellular recording studies, as well as lesion and pharmacological investigations, indicate that delta and spindle waves are associated with barrages of EPSPs and IPSPs in cortical pyramidal cells, with the site of origin of spindle waves being the thalamus and the site of origin of delta waves being undetermined, although generation in both the cerebral cortex and thalamus has been suggested (see Steriade and McCarley 1990). Upon awakening from sleep, or after stimulation of the regions of the brainstem which contain ascending cholinergic and noncholinergic fibers (e.g., the "reticular activating system"), both patterns of slow oscillation disappear and are replaced by higher-frequency components in the EEG. Although the presence of higher-frequency (30–80 Hz) oscillation in the EEG has long been associated with behavioral arousal and attentiveness, a renewed interest in the generation of this activity has recently occurred, due to the finding that these oscillations also occur in the primary visual system during visual stimulation (or the primary somatosensory system during sensory stimulation) and are indicative of synchronized neuronal activity in functionally related groups of cortical neurons (see Gray et al. 1989).

What are the cellular mechanisms of the generation of these three different patterns of activity: delta (0.5–4 Hz); spindle (7–14 Hz), and gamma (30–80 Hz) waves? Although, as mentioned above, the cellular mechanisms of generation of true delta waves in the EEG have not been thoroughly detailed, *in vitro* and *in vivo* studies of the thalamus demonstrate that virtually all thalamic relay neurons possess the intrinsic ability to oscillate rhythmically in the frequency range of delta waves (McCormick and Pape 1990b). The detailed ionic analysis of the currents underlying this oscillation has revealed that it results from the interplay between two main currents: I_h and I_t. The H-current is a cation current (carried by both Na^+ and K^+) that is slowly activated by hyperpolarization of the membrane potential. Activation of I_h depolarizes the cell towards its reversal potential (approximately –40 mV). This I_h-induced depolarization activates the low threshold Ca^{2+} current I_t. Activation and inactivation of I_t results in the generation of a low threshold Ca^{2+} spike, the final form of which is modulated by the activation of various K^+ currents. The depolarization provided by the occurrence of the low threshold Ca^{2+} spike results in deactivation of a portion of the H-current, thereby restarting the cycle once again. In this manner, an interplay between I_h and I_t results in the generation of rhythmic burst discharges in the frequency range of 0.5–4 Hz (Figure 10.1D). How and whether these intrinsic slow oscillations become synchronized in thalamic relay cells to generate delta waves in the EEG is an open question, although *in vivo* recordings indicate that they do contribute (Steriade et al. 1991).

Spindle (7–14 Hz) waves are generated within the thalamus as an interaction between the GABAergic neurons of the nucleus reticularis (nRt) and thalamic relay neurons (Figure 10.2; see Steriade and Deschênes 1984). At present, nearly all of the data collected on this phenomenon can be explained by the following scenario: arrival of a critical level of synchronized activity in the nucleus reticularis, either from the cortex or thalamus, results in the excitation of a critical number of nRt neurons. This excitation of nRt cells results in the generation of pronounced IPSPs in the postsynaptic relay neurons (which may be considerable in number, since nRt cells have a widely divergent axon). In addition, the entry of Ca^{2+} into the nRt cells during the excitation arriving from the cortex or thalamus also results in an afterhyperpolarization owing to the activation of a Ca^{2+}-activated K^+ current. As the membrane potential of the postsynaptic relay cells repolarizes and the IPSPs decay, a few of these cells will generate a rebound, low threshold Ca^{2+} spike and burst of action potentials. Likewise, as the Ca^{2+}-activated afterhyperpolarization in nRt cells lessens, these cells will also be primed to generate a low threshold Ca^{2+} spike. The generation of low threshold Ca^{2+} spikes in the relay neurons will be reflected in the nRt cells as the arrival of a barrage of EPSPs, which will subsequently activate the "primed" low threshold Ca^{2+} spike and burst of action potentials in the nRt cells, thus resulting again in the generation of another IPSP in thalamic relay cells. If, on the other hand, the nRt cell does not receive a barrage of EPSPs from its connected relay cells, it will still burst at the appropriate interval owing to the depolarization of the membrane potential from the lessening of the Ca^{2+}-activated K^+ current (Bal and McCormick 1992). As the spindle wave grows, more and more thalamic cells are recruited into oscillation and synchrony. Interestingly, for unknown reasons, the spindle wave reaches a peak and then "dampens out," with the entire event lasting approximately 2–4 seconds. One possible mechanism of this dampening could involve changes in the voltage dependence or recruitment of more H-current, an effect which is known to dampen thalamic oscillations (McCormick and Pape 1990a). In this manner, spindle waves are generated through an interaction between the synaptic connections of thalamic relay cells and nRt cells and their intrinsic membrane properties. These spindle waves can be initiated from practically anywhere within the thalamus and layer VI of cerebral cortex and may never take exactly the same form twice, indicating the equipotentiality of thalamocortical systems in generating these events.

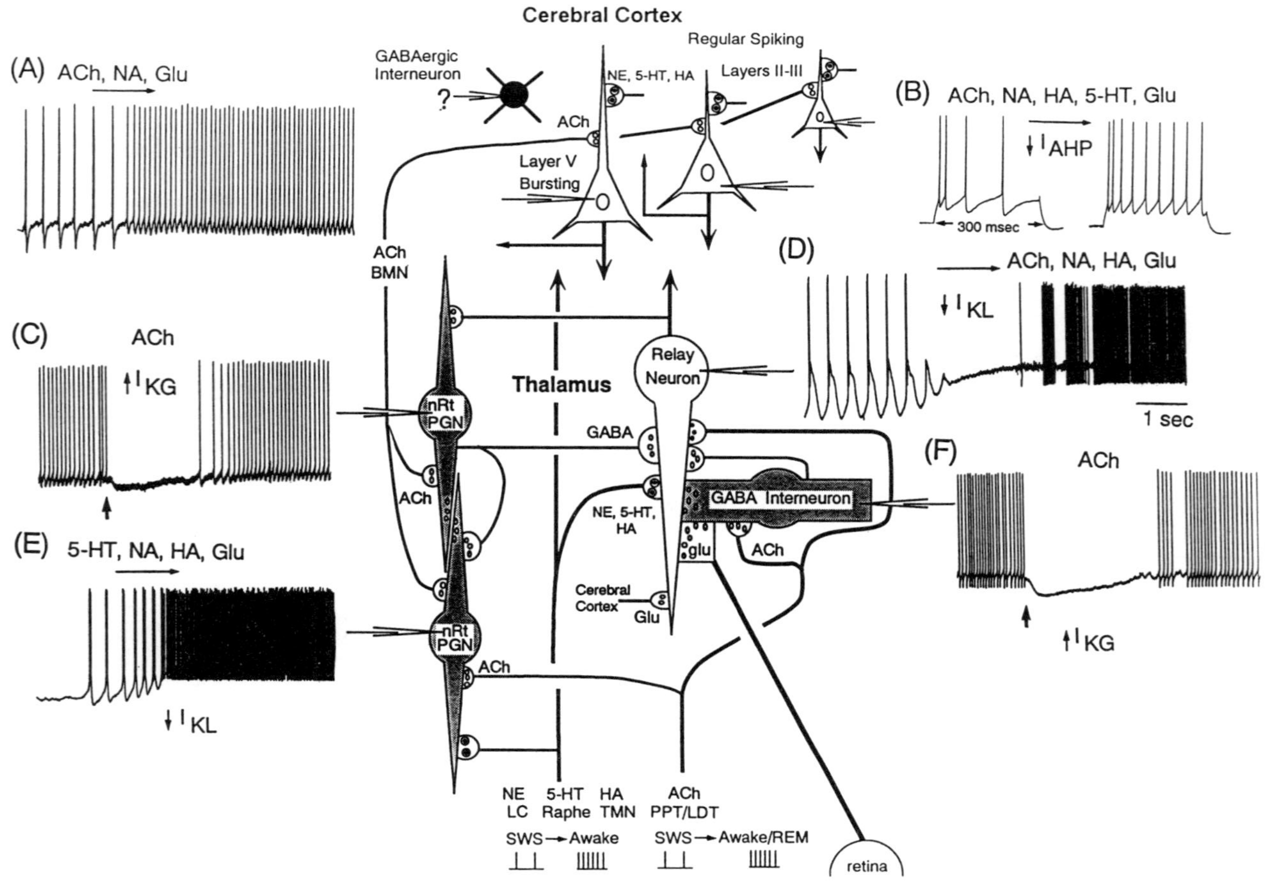

Cerebral Cortex
Regular Spiking
Layers II-III
GABAergic Interneuron
?
NE, 5-HT, HA
ACh
Layer V Bursting
(A) ACh, NA, Glu
(B) ACh, NA, HA, 5-HT, Glu
$\downarrow I_{AHP}$
300 msec
ACh BMN
(C) ACh
$\uparrow I_{KG}$
(D) ACh, NA, HA, Glu
$\downarrow I_{KL}$
1 sec
Relay Neuron
Thalamus
nRt PGN
GABA
ACh
NE, 5-HT, HA
GABA Interneuron
glu
ACh
Cerebral Cortex
Glu
(F) ACh
$\uparrow I_{KG}$
(E) 5-HT, NA, HA, Glu
$\downarrow I_{KL}$
nRt PGN
ACh
NE LC
5-HT Raphe
HA TMN
ACh PPT/LDT
SWS→Awake
SWS→Awake/REM
retina

Figure 10.1 Summary diagram. Thalamic relay cells (D) and nRt cells (E) can generate action potential either as rhythmic bursts or as tonic, single spike activity, depending upon the membrane potential of the cell. Activation of muscarinic, α1-adrenergic, H_1-histaminergic, or glutamate metabotropic receptors results in a depolarization of LGNd relay neurons through reduction of I_{KL}(D). This depolarization subsequently shifts these neurons to the single spike mode of action potential generation. Similarly, activation of α1-adrenoceptors, 5-HT_2 receptors, H_1 receptors, or glutamate metabotropic receptors has similar effects in the nucleus reticularis thalami (E). By contrast, activation of muscarinic receptors in this nucleus (C), or in local GABAergic interneurons (F), results in inhibition of axon output through an increase in a potassium conductance (I_{KG}). In the cerebral cortex, activation of muscarinic, α1-adrenergic or glutamate metabotropic receptors results in the abolition of rhythmic burst firing in layer V burst-generating neurons and a switch to the tonic, single spike mode of action potential generation through the reduction of a voltage-independent resting K^+ conductance (A). In regular spiking cells, by contrast, activation of muscarinic, β-noradrenergic, H_2-histaminergic, serotoninergic, and perhaps glutamate metabotropic receptors results in a decrease in spike frequency adaptation by blocking I_{AHP} (and I_M for ACh and 5-HT; B). Not illustrated are the inhibitory effects of adenosine and serotonin. These responses allow ascending modulatory transmitter systems to prepare thalamocortical systems for sensory transmission, processing, and cognition.

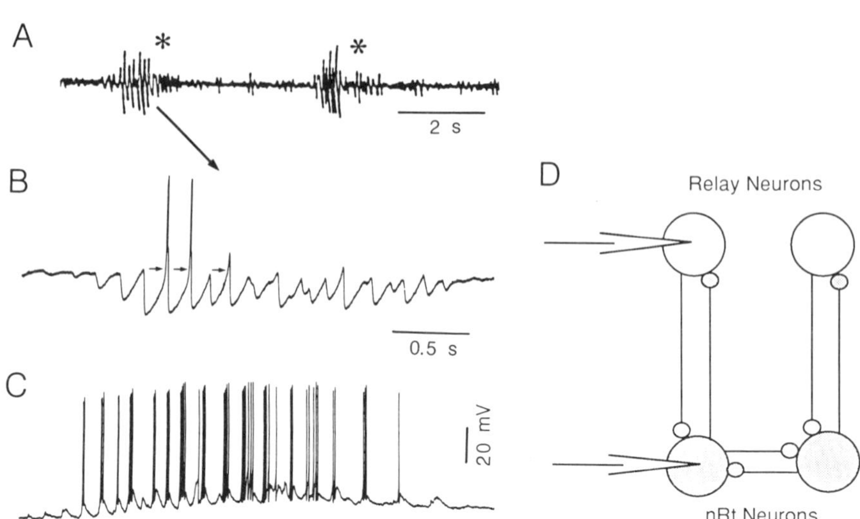

Figure 10.2 Cellular mechanisms of spindle wave generation. (A) Cortical field potential recording during the occurrence of spindles (*: filtered to illustrate these 7–14 Hz oscillations). (B, C) Intracellular recording from thalamocortical relay (B) and nRt (C) neurons during the generation of a spindle sequence. Thalamic relay neurons undergo a series of rhythmic hyperpolarizations (presumably representing IPSPs), the rebound of which can generate a low threshold Ca^{2+} spike (arrows). At the same time nRt neurons generate bursts of action potentials riding upon a slow depolarization. (D) simplified schematic diagram of anatomical interactions between nRt cells and thalamocortical relay cells. The nRt neurons possess recurrent collatorals as well as dendrodendritic synapses. The nRt and other thalamic nuclei are reciprocally connected, although nRt cells are inhibitory and thalamocortical relay cells are excitatory. Modified from Steriade and Llinás (1988).

Recordings from cortical pyramidal cells reveal that spindle waves in the EEG reflect largely the arrival of EPSPs from the thalamus with only a minor response in the form of action potentials from the cortical cells (see Gloor and Fariello 1988). Importantly, in all animal models of absence seizures (which are characterized by immobility, staring, and a pronounced 3–6 Hz spike and wave synchronized discharge throughout the whole EEG), cortical and corticothalamic neurons appear to become abnormally activated by normally occurring spindle waves, thus adding an additional thalamo-cortico-thalamic excitatory loop which results in a slowing and great enhancement of the oscillation (thus a seizure), presumably through additional strong activation of the nRt and relay cells (Buzsaki et al. 1988).

In the transition from sleep to waking, or from drowsiness to attentiveness, these low-frequency oscillations are suppressed and thalamocortical activity is associated with tonic activation and the generation of higher (30–60 Hz) frequency oscillations. How is this achieved? In the visual system, we have known for a long time that this transition takes place even in the absence of the eyes, indicating that it occurs through some extra-retinal influence, of which there are many. Numerically, the largest innervation of thalamic cells derives from layer VI of the cerebral cortex, followed by cholinergic, noradrenergic, and serotoninergic fibers from the brainstem and histaminergic fibers from the hypothalamus. Detailed studies of the postsynaptic actions of these transmitters in thalamic and cortical neurons reveal that they exhibit pronounced "arousing" effects on these cells. For example, activation of muscarinic, α_1-adrenergic, H_1-histaminergic, glutamate metabotropic, and 5-HT_2 receptors on thalamic and some cortical neurons blocks specialized K^+ currents through the activation of nonpertussis-toxin-sensitive G-proteins. This results in a pronounced slow depolarization, which strongly suppresses burst discharges through the inactivation of the low threshold Ca^{2+} current and moves the cells into the tonic mode of action potential generation (Figure 10.1D, E). This change in firing mode greatly increases the ability of thalamic and cortical neurons to follow faithfully and process incoming sensory information (reviewed in McCormick 1992). That this may occur *in vivo* is evidenced by the increased discharge rate of cholinergic, noradrenergic, histaminergic, and serotoninergic neurons in anticipation to increases in arousal and attentiveness and awakening from sleep (see McCormick 1992; Steriade and McCarley 1990). In addition, sedation is a well-known side effect of H_1 antagonists (H_1 antagonists are the active ingredients in over-the-counter sleeping aids in the U.S.A., and sedation is often associated with the use of antihistamines for allergies) or blockage of muscarinic receptors. Blockage of α_1 and 5-HT_2 receptors can also have sedatory side effects; however, all of the ascending transmitter systems do not have equivalent actions in the forebrain. Indeed, if one takes an overview, it is found that each transmitter system modulates the forebrain in a unique manner. For example, while both acetylcholine (ACh) and norepinephrine (NE) depolarize relay cells through reduction of the same potassium current, ACh hyperpolarizes intrathalamic interneurons and nRt cells through an increase in K^+ conductance, while NE depolarizes nRt cells and has no apparent effect on local interneurons (Figure 10.1).

An interesting finding that arose from our investigation of the corticothalamic pathway *in vitro* is that repetitive activation of this pathway may result in a slow depolarization of thalamic relay cells through a reduction in the same K^+ conductance that is reduced by α_1, muscarinic, and H_1 receptors (McCormick and von Krosigk 1992). This slow depolarization appears to result from the activation of glutamate metabotropic receptors by the release of glutamate from cortical afferents. This result has the important implication that arousal may not be something that is generated only in the brainstem and imposed upon the forebrain, but rather may also be a consequence of increased activity in forebrain circuits themselves, with the corticothalamic pathway forming a major "descending activating system." In addition, the point-to-point specificity of the corticothalamic system suggests that corticothalamic activation may be involved in the selective facilitation of particular regions of sensory space, e.g., during the performance of selective attention, a possibility which requires further investigation.

EFFECTS OF STATE-DEPENDENT ACTIVITY ON SENSORY PROCESSING AND LEARNING AND MEMORY

The generation of different patterns of activity in thalamocortical systems during different behavioral states not only has important implications for the understanding of the generation of the EEG, but also for the understanding of the processing of sensory information, the generation of movements, and the formation of memories. It is a well-known feature in animals that their behavioral and neuronal responsiveness to sensory stimuli and ability to form new memories is markedly reduced during slow wave sleep as compared to the waking state (e.g., Livingstone and Hubel 1981). Using different techniques, work from a wide variety of laboratories has revealed that these alterations result from the ability of ascending and descending modulatory neurotransmitter systems to control the electrophysiological and biochemical "state" of every different cell type in the nervous system, thus preparing each cell for the various functional features required to fulfill its particular role in the brain. In thalamocortical sensory systems, this means that the transition from sleep to waking is associated with an increased responsiveness to synaptic inputs that arrive from lower-level sensory structures (e.g., retina for vision and brainstem for audition). How may the increase in release of ACh, NE, 5-HT, and HA, which is known to occur with the transition from sleep to waking, increase the ability of neurons to process sensory information? During periods of slow wave sleep or drowsiness, the membrane potential of thalamic neurons is relatively hyperpolarized (Hirsch et al. 1983). This hyperpolarized state of the membrane results in the generation of rhythmic oscillations in thalamic networks, both intrinsic and in a circuit manner (see above). Together, the hyperpolarized membrane potential and intrathalamic oscillation, result in a reduced responsiveness of thalamic cells to phasic synaptic inputs, such as those associated with activation of sensory receptive fields, and therefore a block of sensory transmission and processing. The appearance of these oscillations during sleep is the cellular correlate of noncognition, while the markedly reduced responsiveness to sensory stimuli is the cellular correlate of "nonsensory processing." Together, these results indicate that when thalamocortical systems are involved in the generation of slow rhythmic oscillations (such as during slow wave sleep or absence seizures), their ability to participate and generate higher cognitive functions, such as sensory perception and cognition, is degraded.

Sleep, however, is more complex than merely a simple block of sensorimotor processing, since rapid eye movement (REM) sleep is associated with depolarization of thalamic and cortical neurons and a block of intrinsic rhythmic oscillations, as during the waking state. During REM sleep, thalamic and cortical neurons discharge as if there is sensory input, even though there is none, perhaps giving rise to dreams (e.g., Hirsch et al. 1983). An interesting and relevant finding for the field of learning and memory is the fact that memories are formed only poorly during REM sleep, even though dreams can be quite vivid. One possible explanation for this lack of memory formation is the inhibition of firing of noradrenergic, serotoninergic, and histaminergic neurons in the hypothalamus and brainstem during REM sleep (see Steriade and McCarley 1990). Indeed, application of at least ACh and NE results in a facilitation of the ability to induce long-term potentiation (LTP) in both the hippocampus and cerebral cortex (Blitzer et al. 1990; Brocher et al. 1992; Hopkins and Johnston 1988), and stimulation in the hypothalamus or brainstem during various learning paradigms increases the rate of acquisition and prolongs the period in which retrieval can be achieved (e.g., Kim et al. 1983).

Taken together with developmental studies on the role of ascending modulatory transmitter systems in facilitating synaptic plasticity (Bear and Singer 1986; Singer 1982), these studies indicate that modulatory neurotransmitter systems control not only the state of neuronal activity in the forebrain but also the ability to analyze synaptic information and to store memories of this information in a behaviorally relevant manner.

CONCLUSION

Thalamocortical systems are ideally built to generate temporary associations, which during sleep are expressed as synchronized oscillations. An important feature of these oscillations is the potential of nearly all parts of the thalamocortical network to initiate them, their ability to cause widespread synchrony, and their variability between occurrences (indicating a nonfixed action pattern and a significant degree of "plasticity"). These oscillations are generated from a mixture of intrinsic membrane properties and axonal connections and their function is still unknown, although they are of considerable clinical importance. Understanding the cellular mechanisms of generation of sleep-associated oscillations as well as those associated with arousal and attentiveness may yield new information on the manner in which forebrain structures process information, direct attention, form temporary, as well as prolonged (memories), associations, and the biological function of sleep.

REFERENCES

Bal, T., and D.A. McCormick. 1993. Mechanisms of rhythmic burst and tonic activity in guinea pig nucleus reticularis thalami *in vitro*: A mammalian pacemaker. *J. Physiol. Lond.* **468:**669–691.

Bear, M.F., and W. Singer. 1986. Modulation of visual cortical plasticity by acetylcholine and noradrenaline. *Nature* **320**:172–176.

Blitzer, R.D., O. Gil, and E.M. Landau. 1990. Cholinergic stimulation enhances long-term potentiation in the CA1 region of rat hippocampus. *Neurosci. Lett.* **119**:207–210.

Brocher, S., A. Artola, and W. Singer. 1992. Agonists of cholinergic and noradrenergic receptors facilitate synergistically the induction of long-term potentiation in slices of rat visual cortex. *Brain Res.* **573**:27–36.

Buzsaki, G., A. Smith, S. Berger, L.J. Fisher, and F.H. Gage. 1988. Petit mal epilepsy and Parkinsonian tremor: Hypothesis of a common pacemaker. *Neurosci.* **36**:1–14.

Caton, R. 1887. Researches on electrical phenomena of cerebral grey matter. *IX Int. Cong. Med.* **3**:246.

Gloor, P., and R.G. Fariello. 1988. Generalized epilepsy: Some of its cellular mechanisms differ from those of focal epilepsy. *Trends Neurosci.* **11**:63–68.

Gray, C.M., P. Konig, A.K. Engel, and W. Singer. 1989. Oscillatory responises in cat visual cortex exhibit inter-columnar synchronizatioin which reflects global stimulus properties. *Nature* **338**:334–337.

Hirsch, J.C., A. Vourment, and M.E. Marc. 1983. Sleep-related variations of membrane potential in the lateral geniculate body relay neurons of the cat. *Brain Res.* **259**:308–312.

Hopkins, W.F., and D. Johnston. 1988. Noradrenergic enhancement of long-term potentiation at mossy fiber synapses in the hippocampus. *J. Neurophysiol.* **59**:667–687.

Kim, E.H., C.D. Woody, and N.E. Berthier. 1983. Rapid acquisition of conditioned eye blink responses in cats following pairing of an auditory CS with glabella tap US and hypothalamic stimulation. *J. Neurophysiol.* **49**:767–779.

Livingstone, M.S., and D.H. Hubel. 1981. Effects of sleep and arousal on the processing of visual information in the cat. *Nature* **291**:554–561.

McCormick, D.A. 1992. Neurotransmitter actions in the thalamus and cerebral cortex and their role in neuromodulation of thalamocortical activity. *Prog. Neurobiol.* **39**:337–388.

McCormick, D.A., and H.R. Feeser. 1990. Functional implications of burst firing and single spike activity in lateral geniculate relay neurons. *Neurosci.* **39**:103–113.

McCormick, D.A., and H.-C. Pape. 1990a. Noradrenergic and serotoninergic modulation of a hyperpolarization-activated cation current in thalamic relay neurones. *J. Physiol. Lond.* **431**:319–342.

McCormick, D.A., and H.-C. Pape. 1990b. Properties of a hyperpolarization-activated cation current and its role in rhythmic oscillation in thalamic relay neurones. *J. Physiol. Lond.* **431**:291–318.

McCormick, D.A., and M. von Krosigk. 1992. Corticothalamic activation modulates thalamic firing through activation of glutamate metabotropic receptors. *Proc. Natl. Acad. Sci. USA* **89**:2774–2778.

Singer, W. 1982. Central core control of developmental plasticity in the kitten visual cortex: I. Diencephalic lesions. *Exp. Brain Res.* **47**:209–222.

Steriade, M., R. Curro Dossi, and A. Nunez. 1991. Network modulation of a slow intrinsic oscillation of cat thalamocortical neurons implicated in sleep delta waves: Cortical potentiation and brainstem suppression. *J. Neurosci.* **11**:3200–3217.

Steriade, M., and Deschenes, M. 1984. The thalamus as a neuronal oscillator. *Brain Res. Rev.* **8**:1–63.

Steriade, M., and R.R. Llinás. 1988. The functional states of the thalamus and the associated neuronal interplay. *Physiol. Rev.* 68:649–742.

Steriade, M., and R.W. McCarley. 1990. Brainstem Control of Wakefulness and Sleep. New York: Plenum.

11

Modulation of Ion Channels in Functional Circuits

L.K. KACZMAREK[1,2] and T.M. PERNEY[1]
Departments of Pharmacology[1] and Cellular and Molecular Physiology[2],
Yale University School of Medicine, 333 Cedar Street,
New Haven, CT 06510, U.S.A.

ABSTRACT

The genes for a relatively large number of voltage-dependent ion channels have been isolated and are beginning to account for the varied types of electrical behavior found in neurons. For a neuron to function effectively in a circuit, it must express specific subtypes of channels, which allow it to respond appropriately to synaptic stimulation. Moreover, these channels and their genes must be regulated so as to permit changes in the performance of the neuron with changes in the pattern of synaptic inputs. For ion channels present at neurotransmitter release sites, both short-term and long-term regulatory mechanisms can provide for the potentiation or depression of secretion. These topics are illustrated with examples of ion channels expressed in the auditory system of vertebrates and in the bag cell neurons of *Aplysia*.

INTRODUCTION

A key problem in studies of the cellular biology of neurons is to understand the mechanisms by which these cells are able to control prolonged animal behaviors. In response to brief sensory stimuli, the behavior of an animal may be altered for periods of tens of minutes to hours or even days. In the case of learning and memory, permanent changes must occur in the properties of certain neurons. To understand these mechanisms, investigators have turned to several model neuronal preparations. These include several invertebrate systems of neurons, whose biological roles are relatively well understood, as well as discrete systems of neurons in vertebrates, such as the hippocampus or specific sets of neurons in sensory systems.

Work from a number of laboratories has shown that stimulus-evoked changes in the properties of specific ion channels may account for many prolonged changes in animal behavior. A change in the number or the characteristics of ion channels of a neuron may have one of two general effects on the processing of information:

Cellular and Molecular Mechanisms Underlying Higher Neural Functions
Edited by A.I. Selverston and P. Ascher

1. The intrinsic electrical properties of the neurons may be altered. This would change the way in which the neuron responds to a particular synaptic input and, in turn, might influence the behavioral response to particular sensory stimuli. It can be considered a "postsynaptic" effect.
2. The amount of neurotransmitter that is released from the terminals of the neuron may increase or decrease. Such a change in the synaptic strength is a common candidate for a cellular event underlying a change in the behavior of an animal, and may be termed a "presynaptic" effect.

Over the past three or four years, new possibilities for investigating ion channel regulation have opened up. This is due to the fact that the molecular identity of ion channel proteins and related components influencing long-term excitability of a neuron is now being revealed. In this chapter, we describe the regulation of channels that may contribute to the two types of changes in excitability described above. The first example is in neurons of the auditory system while the second is in a group of peptidergic neurons of *Aplysia*.

A NEURON SELECTS THE CHANNELS IT NEEDS TO GET THE JOB DONE: AN EXAMPLE FROM NEURONS OF THE AUDITORY SYSTEM

An important lesson learned from the cloning of the genes for ion channel proteins is that their diversity is much greater than that suggested by electrophysiological analysis. This is especially apparent in the area of potassium channels. For example, a large number of genes for outwardly rectifying, voltage-dependent potassium channels have been cloned. Our laboratory has recently cloned five different voltage-dependent potassium channel genes from rat cDNA and genomic libraries (Pragnell et al. 1990; Swanson et al. 1990; Luneau et al. 1991). Each of these is expressed in different types of cells, as judged by northern analysis and *in situ* hybridization studies. One of these genes, termed Kv3.1 (homologous to the *Drosophila* Shaw gene) can give rise to two different ion channel proteins by alternate splicing of its RNA (Figure 11.1). Both of these are co-expressed only in a subset of neurons, although they are highly expressed in many of the auditory nuclei, including the cochlear nucleus, medial nucleus of the trapezoid body, and the inferior colliculus (Perney et al. 1992).

Upon closer examination of the distribution of the Kv3.1 channel within nuclei of the lower auditory system, we find that the Kv3.1 channel (in both alpha and beta forms) is present in neurons with very specific electrical properties. These properties include the ability to follow precisely the timing of an input stimulus, to fire at frequencies that sometimes reach 500–1000 Hz, and to "phase lock" to sound stimuli of frequencies up to ~2000 Hz (Oertel 1991).

One of the features of the Kv3.1 channel that differentiates it from other potassium channels whose genes have been isolated is that, when expressed in *Xenopus* oocytes or in a mammalian cell line, it is found to encode a delayed rectifier channel that

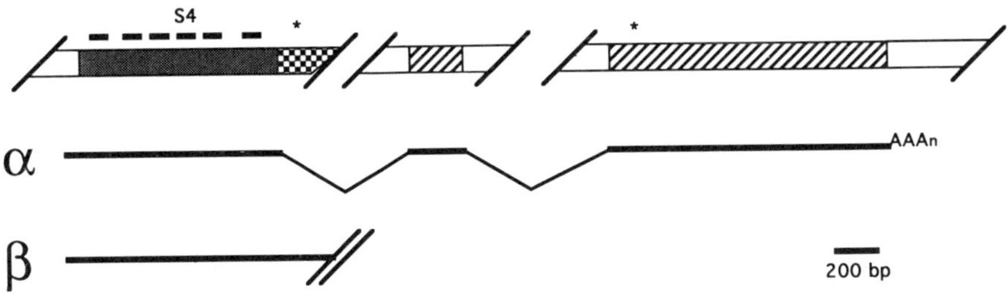

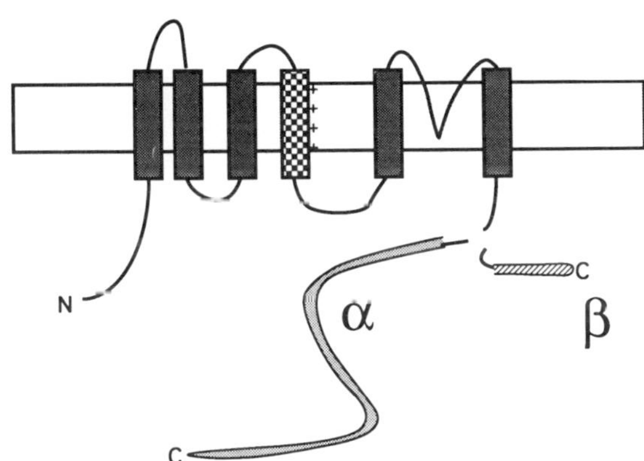

Figure 11.1 Organization of the gene for the Kv3.1 channel (top) and a diagram of the two Kv3.1 channel proteins that arise from this gene (bottom). The central core of the channel protein, which contains all of the putative transmembrane segments (including the S4 region), are encoded on one exon that is common to both the alpha and beta forms of the channel. During transcription, the first exon-intron boundary that is shown may either be read through, generating the beta form of mRNA and protein, or may be spliced to two additional exons to yield the alpha form (Luneau et al. 1991).

activates at relatively positive membrane potentials. Computer simulations of the electrical properties of auditory neurons have demonstrated the specific role that such a channel may play in the responses of these neurons to external stimulation. In particular, its voltage range of activation allows the cells to fire action potentials that have no "undershoot" (Figure 11.2). Because the action potentials are not followed by a relative refractory period, the cells are able to respond to very high rates of synaptic input.

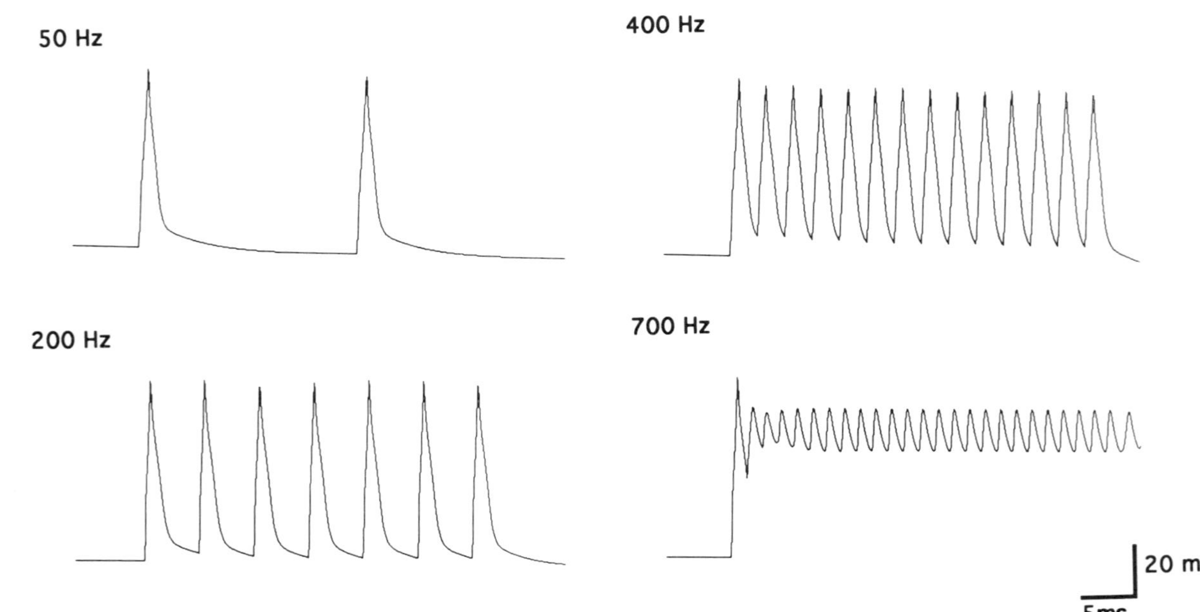

Figure 11.2 Computer simulation of the response of an auditory neuron to stimulation at frequencies up to 700 Hz. Parameters for currents were adopted from the literature for presumed bushy cells of the cochlear nucleus (Manis and Marx 1991) and from expression studies with the Kv3.1 channel. At 700 Hz the cell begins to fail to follow synaptic inputs with full action potentials.

A NEURON CAN DO ITS JOB ONLY IF IT HAS THE RIGHT NUMBER OF CHANNELS

One prominent set of cells in the auditory system that contains high amounts of the Kv3.1 protein, as judged by both immunocytochemical and *in situ* hybridization experiments, are the bushy cells of the ventral cochlear nucleus. Voltage clamp recordings of these cells reveal that different cells may express different amounts of their high threshold potassium current (Manis and Marx 1991), the current that is most likely to correspond to the Kv3.1 channel. Moreover, immunocytochemical staining of neurons in other regions that express this channel indicate that, within some auditory nuclei, there may be a gradient of expression of the Kv3.1 channel. In particular, neurons that respond optimally to sound frequencies up to 1–2 kHz, and can phase lock faithfully to such frequencies, may possess more Kv3.1 protein than those devoted to other frequencies.

Computer simulations of auditory neurons expressing the Kv3.1 channel clearly show that changes in the level of this channel may profoundly influence the ability of the cells to follow specific frequencies of applied inputs. As shown in Figure 11.3, a cell that is able to follow a low frequency of stimulation may fail to follow a train of stimuli applied at a higher frequency. An increase in the number of Kv3.1 channels within the cell, however, allows the cell to follow the high-frequency input faithfully.

HOW DOES A NEURON IMPROVE ITS PERFORMANCE?

Simulations suggest that a neuron may alter the number of its functional channels in order to respond appropriately to a particular pattern of stimulation. This may occur either during development or learning. For example, repeated stimulation of an auditory neuron at a high frequency may alter the level of expression of the channels so as to improve the response of the cell. To understand the mechanisms that ultimately determine both the choice of a particular ion channel species by a neuron and the level at which that channel is expressed requires a thorough characterization of the promoter regions of the channel genes, as well as an understanding of the developmental factors to which the neuron is exposed. Using model systems, such as cell lines, or transgenic animal models, it may be possible, however, to gain some understanding of the long-term regulation of genes for ion channels.

A cell line that has been particularly useful for the study of Kv3.1 gene expression is the AtT20 cell line (Hemmick et al. 1992). Although normal AtT20 cells do not express this channel, Kv3.1 mRNA can be induced by transfection with the *ras* gene, by treatment with B–FGF (a growth factor that may use the *ras* signaling pathway), or by an elevation of intracellular cyclic AMP levels. A particularly interesting finding is that the level of its expression can be altered by depolarizing the cells with high-potassium media. The effects of depolarization can be blocked by calcium channel antagonists and potentiated by calcium channel agonists. This suggests, as

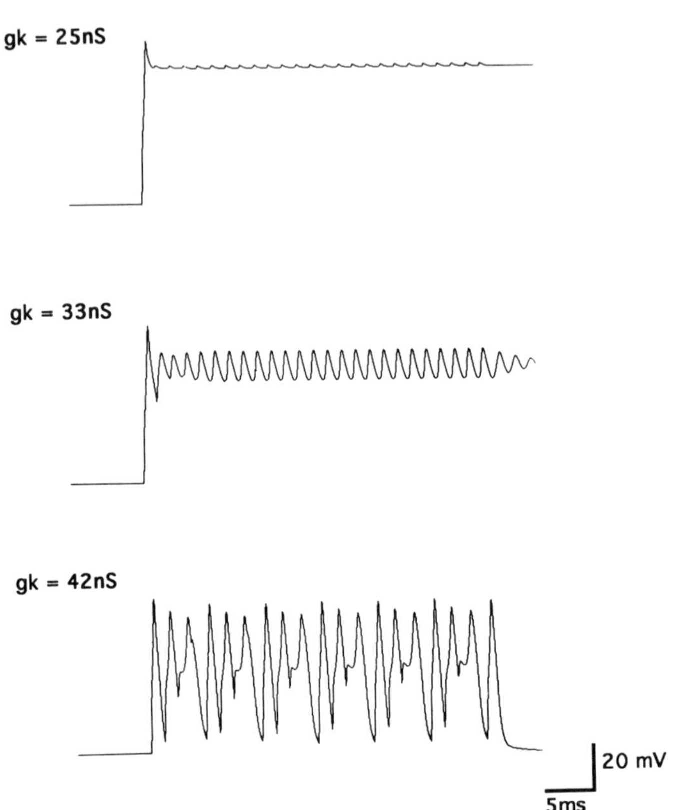

Figure 11.3 Computer simulation of the effect of changes in the level of the Kv3.1 channel in an auditory neuron. Parameters are the same as in Figure 11.2; the cell was stimulated at 700 Hz. An increase in the Kv3.1 channel allows the cell to follow the high-frequency input.

has been shown for several neuropeptide genes, that the promoter region of the Kv3.1 gene may contain a calcium and cyclic AMP response element.

The regulation of Kv3.1 mRNA by depolarization provides a plausible mechanism for changes in the number of Kv3.1 channels in response to repeated stimulation of neurons, such as those in auditory pathways. Experiments that manipulate the pattern of stimulation to which these neurons are exposed in the intact nervous system will be required to test whether changes in the Kv3.1 indeed contribute to long-lasting changes in the ability of the auditory system to respond to or discriminate among particular frequencies.

MODULATION OF ION CHANNELS MAY PRODUCE NEW SITES OF NEUROTRANSMITTER RELEASE: AN EXAMPLE IN THE BAG CELL NEURONS OF *APLYSIA*

It is likely that changes in the response properties of neurons in auditory pathways are accompanied by changes in the strength of synaptic inputs onto these neurons. For example, the very large synapses from primary afferents in the auditory nerve onto the Kv3.1-containing bushy cells in the cochlear nucleus retain growth cones even in adult animals. This suggests that they may be able to undergo changes in structure and size (Jones et al. 1992). As yet, little is known about the regulation of ion channels in such terminals, or of how changes in these growth cone/synaptic structures alter release of neurotransmitter.

An example of neurons well suited to study the regulation of secretion by changes in ion channels is found in the bag cell neurons of *Aplysia*. When isolated in cell culture, these neurons have large growth cone endings (up to 50 μm or more in width) and large neuropeptide-containing secretory granules (200–1000 nm in diameter), which can readily be visualized by video-enhanced microscopy (Knox et al. 1992).

The bag cell neurons control a sequence of reproductive behaviors that lasts for many hours. This is accomplished by a series of transitions in their electrical properties. Although these neurons normally maintain rather negative resting potentials and display no spontaneous electrical activity, brief electrical stimulation of an afferent input causes the cells to depolarize and generate an afterdischarge that lasts for about thirty minutes. During the onset of afterdischarge in the bag cell neurons, there is a marked enhancement of the calcium component of action potentials (Kaczmarek et al. 1982). This change in the shape of the action potentials is associated with a strong potentiation of the release of peptide neurotransmitters from the bag cell neurons (Loechner et al. 1990).

Two types of calcium channels have been detected in these neurons (Strong et al. 1987). In the absence of external stimulation, a voltage-dependent calcium channel with a unitary conductance of 12 pS can be recorded in cell-attached patches. In the presence of activators of protein kinase C, however, an additional channel with a unitary conductance of 24 pS can also be detected. Several lines of evidence suggest that this channel is rapidly unmasked by the activation of protein kinase C during an afterdischarge in the bag cell neurons and that its recruitment contributes to the potentiation of neurotransmitter release (Conn et al. 1989; Loechner et al. 1992).

The unmasking of the protein kinase C-regulated channel is associated with a profound change in the morphology of the growth cone terminals of isolated bag cell neurons and the appearance of new sites of calcium influx during action potentials (Knox et al. 1992). Images of cells injected with the calcium indicator fura-2 reveal that a train of action potentials normally generates an increase in intracellular calcium in the central region of their neurites, with little or no influx

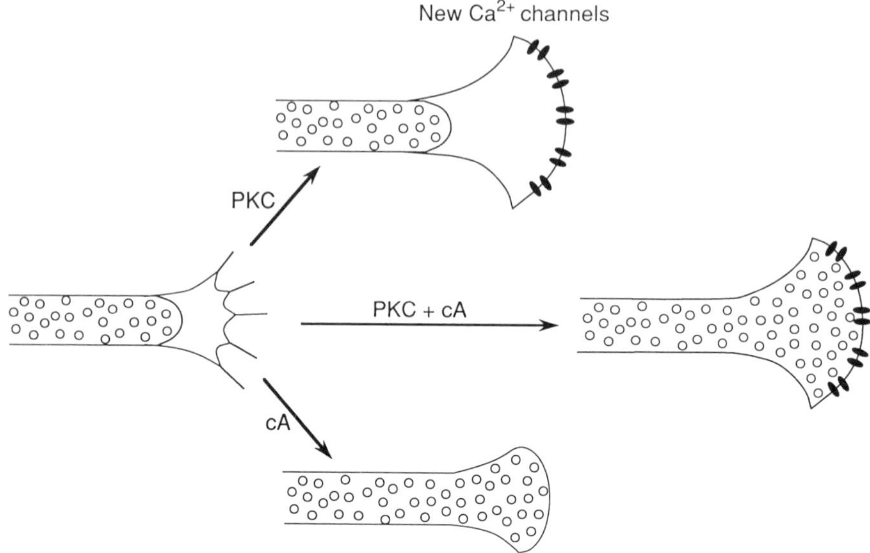

Figure 11.4 An illustration of the effects of activators of protein kinase C (PKC) and cyclic AMP analogs (cA) on the growth cone terminals of isolated bag cell neurons. Circles within the axon represent secretory organelles.

at the very distal edge of the terminal growth cone. Within a few minutes of exposure of the cell to an activator of protein kinase C, however, there is a rapid (~5 min) outgrowth of the lamellipodium. When a train of action potentials is then stimulated, a ring of new calcium entry occurs at the distal edge of the newly extended membrane (Figure 11.4), presumably because of the unmasking of new calcium channels at these sites.

At the onset of an afterdischarge, there is an elevation of cyclic AMP levels, as well as the stimulation of phosphoinositide hydrolysis, in the bag cell neurons. Video images of the movement of individual neuropeptide-containing granules in the isolated cells have shown that an elevation of cyclic AMP levels triggers the movement of these secretory granules towards the new sites of calcium entry (Figure 11.4). Thus, it is likely that the role of the newly recruited calcium channels, and the associated change in the structure of the terminals, is to provide new sites of neuropeptide release, thereby contributing to the strong potentiation of release that occurs during the first few minutes that follow stimulation of the afferent input. Direct confirmation of this hypothesis will require localization and imaging of these channels in the intact nervous system. The cloning of two calcium channel genes expressed in clusters of bag cell neurons (White and Kaczmarek, pers. comm.) may provide tools required for progress in this direction.

CONCLUSION: WHAT FEATURES MUST AN ION CHANNEL HAVE TO ALLOW A NEURON TO PARTICIPATE IN CONTROLLING A LONG-LASTING CHANGE IN BEHAVIOR?

The dedication of specific ion channels to neurons with specific electrical characteristics is clearly one of the reasons for the multiplicity of ion channel genes. This probably accounts for the presence of the Kv3.1 potassium channel in a subset of neurons, including certain auditory neurons. To participate in the adaptive response of a neuron to external inputs, however, an ion channel must have more than just the requisite electrical features. It must have regulatory elements that produce changes in the conductance, kinetics, or localization of the channel in response to external stimuli. These regulatory elements may exist either in the gene for the channel, thus controlling long-term adaptive responses (as we have postulated for the Kv3.1 channel in auditory neurons), or may be part of the channel complex itself, thus producing rapid changes in the behavior of the channels, as occurs in the bag cell neurons.

Recently, there has been much progress in identifying regions of ion channels that confer specific electrical characteristics, such as voltage-sensing, permeation, and inactivation. The investigation of the regulatory regions in the genes and on the channels themselves is less advanced, although significant progress is being made on both fronts for several channels, including the voltage-dependent sodium channel (see Catterall, this volume). The exploration of these areas in cells with well-characterized biological roles is certain to produce insights into the way the nervous system is able to produce long-lasting changes in the behavior of an animal.

REFERENCES

Conn, P.J., J.A. Strong, and L.K. Kaczmarek. 1989. Inhibitors of protein kinase C prevent enhancement of calcium current and action potentials in peptidergic neurons of *Aplysia*. *J. Neurosci.* **9**:480–487.

Hemmick, L.M., T.M. Perney, R.E. Flamm, L.K. Kaczmarek, and N.C. Birnberg. 1992. Expression of the H-*ras* oncogene induces potassium conductance and neuron-specific potassium channel mRNAs in the AtT20 cell line. *J. Neurosci.* **12**:2007–2014.

Jones, D.R., K.A. Hutson, and D.K. Morest. 1992. Growth cones and structural variation of synaptic end-bulbs in the cochlear nucleus of the adult cat brain. *Synapse* **10**:291–309.

Kaczmarek, L.K., K.R. Jennings, and F. Strumwasser. 1982. An early sodium and a late calcium phase in the afterdischarge of peptide secreting neurons of *Aplysia*. *Brain Res.* **283**:105–115.

Knox, R.J., E.A. Quattrocki, J.A. Connor, and L.K. Kaczmarek. 1992. Recruitment of calcium channels during rapid formation of putative neuropeptide release sites in isolated *Aplysia* neurons. *Neuron* **8**:883–889.

Loechner, K.J., E.M. Azhderian, R. Dreyer, and L.K. Kaczmarek. 1990. Progressive potentiation of peptide release during a neuronal discharge. *J. Neurophysiol.* **63**:738–744.

Loechner, K.J., J. Mattessich-Arrandale, E.M. Azdherian, and L.K. Kaczmarek. 1992. Inhibition of peptide release from invertebrate neurons by the protein kinase inhibitor H–7. *Brain Res.* **581**:315–318.

Luneau, C.J., J.B. Williams, J. Marshall, E.S. Levitan, C. Oliva, J.S. Smith, J. Antanavage, K. Folander, R.B. Stein, R. Swanson, L.K. Kaczmarek, and S.A. Buhrow. 1991. Alternative splicing contributes to K^+ channel diversity in the mammalian central nervous system. *Proc. Natl. Acad. Sci. USA* **88**:3932–3936.

Manis, P.B., and S.O. Marx. 1991. Outward currents in isolated ventral cochlear nucleus neurons. *J. Neurosci.* **11**:2865–2880.

Oertel, D. 1991. The role on intrinsic neuronal properties in the encoding of auditory information in the cochlear nuclei. *Curr. Opin. Neurobiol.* **1**:221–228.

Perney, T.M., J. Marshall, K.A. Martin, S. Hockfield, and L.K. Kaczmarek. 1992. Expression of the mRNAS for the Kv3.1 potassium channel gene in the adult and developing rat brain. *J. Neurophysiol.* **68**:756–766.

Pragnell, M., K.J. Snay, K.S. Trimmer, N.J. McCluskey, F. Naftolin, L.K. Kaczmarek, and M.B. Boyle. 1990. Estrogen induction of a small putative K channel mRNA in rat uterus. *Neuron* **4**:807–812.

Strong, J.A., A.P. Fox, R.W. Tsien, and L.K. Kaczmarek. 1987. Stimulation of protein kinase C recruits covert calcium channels in *Aplysia* bag cell neurons. *Nature* **325**:714–717.

Swanson, R., J. Marshall, J.S. Smith, J.B. Williams, M.B. Boyle, K. Folander, C.J. Luneau, J. Antanavage, C. Oliva, S.A. Buhrow, C. Bennett, R.B. Stein, and L.K. Kaczmarek. 1990. Cloning and expression of cDNA and genomic clones encoding three delayed rectifier potassium channels in rat brain. *Neuron* **4**:929–939.

Standing left to right:
Uwe Frey, Hans Hultborn, Menahem Segal, Leonard Kaczmarek, Jennifer Altman, David McCormick
Seated, left to right:
Sten Grillner, Paul Benjamin, Scott Hooper, Irwin Levitan, Eve Marder

12

Group Report: What Are the Mechanisms for State-dependent Changes?

S.L. HOOPER, Rapporteur

J.S. ALTMAN, P.R. BENJAMIN, U. FREY,
S. GRILLNER, H.R. HULTBORN,
L.K. KACZMAREK, I. LEVITAN, E. MARDER,
D.A. MCCORMICK, M. SEGAL

INTRODUCTION

The principal theme of our discussion group was to examine the cellular mechanisms underlying state-dependent changes in neural networks. In order to examine this problem, five specific sets of questions were formulated:

1. What constitutes a "state" in neurobiology? What is a "state-dependent" change? Is all change state dependent?
2. What mechanisms underlie state changes in neurobiology? What relationship exists between the time scales of state changes and the mechanisms underlying those changes?
3. What are the different roles or consequences of changes in synaptic strength as compared to changes in intrinsic membrane properties?
4. When and why are computational methods necessary to understand network properties and plasticity? What are the limits of reductionism?
5. To what extent can lessons learned from one experimental system be extrapolated to other systems? Are there generalizable rules?

Fundamental to a discussion of how changes in cellular and synaptic properties can alter the output properties of a neural circuit is the concept of "state." The word is used to describe processes that are characterized by both continuous and discontinuous

Cellular and Molecular Mechanisms Underlying Higher Neural Functions
Edited by A.I. Selverston and P. Ascher © 1994 John Wiley & Sons Ltd

changes in response to graded changes in parameters. Consequently, we found that the concept of state was a source of considerable disagreement, and therefore we examined it in some detail.

WHAT IS A STATE?

A system can be characterized in many ways, e.g., by a description of its constituent elements and their interactions, or by a description of the system's output in time, by a description of the response of the system to external inputs. A state of the system refers to each unique description, and changes in state can either be continuous or discontinuous. For instance, if we characterize a volume of gas by its temperature, each temperature defines a different state of the system (continuous). Alternatively, if we characterize the gas by the number of individual molecules in it, the state of the system changes with every addition or subtraction of an individual molecule (discontinuous). An important consideration is that apparent discontinuity can be imposed by limitations of observational technique or by experimental design, e.g., by taking readings at only two or three discrete points along a change continuum.

Many systems, including nervous systems, have dynamic properties such that only particular values of certain of their defining characteristics are stable with time; if these characteristics are set to some other value, the system evolves through time to restore the value of this characteristic to one of these stable points. For example, a seesaw has only three stable positions: balanced, side A down, or side B down. An important characteristic of these stable points is their response to external perturbation. For the seesaw, side A or B down are stable to small external perturbations; if the down side is lifted slightly, the system returns to that position. A balanced seesaw is not perturbation stable; any motion will result in the system driving to a one-side down state. Another important point is that, just because certain of the defining characteristics of a system can exist only in a few stable values, the other defining characteristics of the system are not similarly constrained. For example, the color of a seesaw is an unconstrained system characteristic. An unfortunate corollary is that if one chooses the wrong defining characteristic to study, one may miss stable states that are present in the system.

The response of many neural systems to external stimuli depends upon the state of the system. The response of the NMDA receptor to glutamate, for example, depends upon the neuron's membrane potential (Nowak et al. 1984). This is a tremendous problem because it is necessary to characterize the response of the system in each of its states. If the input-output relationship varies nonlinearly with change in state, and the system can assume a great many states, it can be extremely difficult experimentally to describe the input-output relationship of the system, since large numbers of system states must be observed. Linear systems and systems with only a few dynamically stable states (like a seesaw) are attractive to the experimentalist because it is necessary to characterize the response in only a few imposed system states or in the system's inherent stable states.

WHAT CONSTITUTES A "STATE" IN NEUROBIOLOGY? WHAT IS A "STATE-DEPENDENT" CHANGE? IS ALL CHANGE STATE DEPENDENT?

In considering the concept of state of the nervous system, two other issues arise. The first is that of level. Clearly, if one defines the nervous system on the level of its individual molecules, functionally identical states of the nervous system will be characterized as different, which is counterproductive from a biological point of view. The second is that of time. Few of the modifications of neurons or the nervous system that neurobiologists consider different states (e.g., the refractory period following an action potential, the action of amphetamine) are maintained if enough time is allowed to elapse. Thus, whether a state is dynamically stable depends upon the relative durations of the state and the test being applied (the refractory period is stable with respect to testing the effect of EPSPs on neuronal response, the action of amphetamine is stable with respect to testing the ability to learn tasks). *Thus, neurobiologically, a state can be usefully defined as a set of system-defining characteristics (e.g., intracellular messenger levels, membrane currents, and voltage on the neuronal level; neuronal interconnectivity and activity pattern at the network level), a change in which results in an observable change in the system's activity and one that is long lasting relative to experimental perturbations and relevant physiological inputs.*

Since the nervous system is generally highly nonlinear, neural systems that seem to exist only in a few states have most often been selected for study. A classic example of state-dependent effects has been the study of acquisition and retrieval of tasks learned under amphetamine administration, where it was found that tasks learned under amphetamine could be retrieved only under amphetamine. More recently, it has been observed that the response of the nervous system to inputs, or the ability of the nervous system to perform certain tasks, covaries with other defining characteristics of the nervous system, and this has been used to infer the existence of nervous system states and state dependence in the nervous system. From a behavioral point of view, the most global of these state differences is sleep/waking; within a global state many different substates can be expressed (e.g., REM vs. NREM sleep, hunger, thirst, sexual arousal; see McCormick, this volume). Each of these states is characterized by a different pattern of neuronal activity and behavior; in each state the ability of the animal to perform certain tasks (e.g., learn) and to respond to the same stimuli (e.g., food presentation) is different. Similar state dependence has been observed in defined neural circuits in, for example, the pyloric network of the lobster, where the application of the peptide neurotransmitter proctolin changes the network's cycle frequency only if the cycle frequency before application is less than 1 Hz (Hooper and Marder 1987; Nusbaum and Marder 1989). On the neuronal level, an example is the bag cell neurons of *Aplysia*, which respond to excitatory input to give an after-discharge only if they have not been similarly stimulated within the prior 6 to 18 hours (Kupfermann and Kandel 1970).

An important—and, for many systems, unresolved—general problem is whether seemingly discrete, dynamically stable states actually represent inherent properties of these systems or whether these states have been artificially imposed, either observationally or experimentally. In the case of the bag cell neurons and some other cellular phenomena (e.g., refractory period), it seems clear that the system inherently can exist in a few or several discrete different states. In other cases, it is not so clear. For instance, arousal is a continuum, and the ability to perform tasks or learn has not been well investigated all along this continuum. These arousal-dependent phenomena may vary with arousal level in some complicated fashion that has been overlooked because the observational filter (e.g., sleep/wake) has been too coarse. *In the absence of specific reasons to believe that the underlying system divides inherently into discrete states as a parameter changes, tests must be performed at many intermediate values of the parameter to characterize fully how the test depends upon the state of the system.*

Finally, are the effects of all inputs to a system dependent upon the state of the system? With sufficiently strong stimuli it is often possible to elicit the desired response regardless of the system state (e.g., action potentials can be elicited in the relative refractory period if enough current is injected). Yet the stimulus strength needed to drive the system to yield a desired response depends upon the system's state, so even the effects of saturating inputs are, in a sense, state dependent. Alternatively, it is possible for specific inputs to not interact with the specific system states one is studying (e.g., gene expression is probably not affected generally by the refractory period), but in a way, this is also a trivial example. Upon some very fine observational level, almost all inputs are probably state dependent; thus it is very important to be aware of the possible confounding influences of system state when designing experiments and interpreting data.

WHAT MECHANISMS UNDERLIE STATE CHANGES IN NEUROBIOLOGY?

There are two conceptually distinct ways in which system state changes can occur. The first is state changes that occur because the system can assume two or more stable configurations without any changes occurring in the fundamental properties of the individual units of the system. The second is state changes that are due to changes in the basic properties of the constituent units, e.g., by various neuromodulatory systems.

Plateau neurons illustrate the first possibility on a cellular level. These neurons can remain semistably at either a depolarized firing level or a hyperpolarized level; they can be switched between these two states as a result of either short synaptic excitation (or depolarizing current injection) or inhibition (or hyperpolarizing current injection). These neurons are present both in invertebrate (Harris-Warrick, this volume; Elliot and Benjamin 1985; Ramirez and Pearson 1991; Russell and Hartline 1982) and vertebrate (Grillner et al. 1987; Hounsgaard and Kjaerulff 1992; Kiehn 1991) nervous systems. A similar example of a "bistable state" on the network level would be reverberatory activity in neuronal circuits with recurrent excitatory connections, in which sustained network activity could result from the brief excitation of a few neuronal elements (Forbes 1929). This type of mechanism has been hypothesized to be involved in various phenomena, ranging from "integration" in the vestibulo-ocular reflex (Robinson 1971) to maintenance of initial memory (Hebb 1949). Experimental evidence for such network-based reverberatory activity is largely lacking (see, however, Tsukahara 1972), and many of these phenomena could be equally well explained through bistable cellular mechanisms, such as plateau properties.

The second type of mechanism, i.e., the change of fundamental properties of individual elements, has been studied in a wide variety of systems (see McCormick, Grillner et al., Kaczamarek and Perney, and Harris-Warrick, all this volume). An example that shows particularly well the difference between, and interdependence of, this and the first type of mechanism is the ability to express the plateau properties. Plateau potentials depend upon the neuron possessing a specific complement of voltage-dependent conductances such that, both at the depolarized and hyperpolarized membrane potentials, net membrane current is zero (otherwise the membrane potential would, of course, change). However, whether these voltage-dependent conductances are capable of opening often in turn depends upon the activity of modulatory inputs to the neuron (Harris-Warrick, this volume; Dickinson and Nagy 1983; Kiehn 1991). Thus the ability to elicit plateau potentials and neuronal bistability (the first mechanism) is often contingent upon the neuromodulatory inputs that alter the fundamental properties of the neuron (the second mechanism).

A particularly well-understood example of the second type of mechanism is the bag cell neurons of *Aplysia*. These neurosecretory neurons are generally silent but can be induced by a brief excitatory stimulus to fire a long (up to 30 minutes) train of spikes, after which further stimulation fails to trigger another long-lasting discharge for periods of up to 18 hours (Figure 12.1) (Kupfermann and Kandel 1970). During the period of intense activity, they release a mixture of neuromodulatory peptides that induce egg-laying behavior in the animal (Chiu et al. 1979; Dudek et al. 1979). The state change of the bag cell neurons with respect to excitatory input (excitable before input stimulation, inexcitable after their subsequent period of activity) results from the activation of a series of intracellular second messenger systems. Immediately after the excitatory input, there is an initial increase in intracellular Ca^{2+} levels for 5 to 15 seconds. This increase in Ca^{2+} levels results, among other early changes, in the activation of a nonspecific cation channel that depolarizes the neurons and drives their high-frequency firing (Wilson and Kaczmarek, pers. comm.; Kaczmarek, this volume; Wilson and Kaczmarek 1992). The initial stimulus also results in an increase in IP3 and cAMP levels and the activation of protein kinases A and C (Kaczmarek and Perney, this volume; Conn et al. 1989; Loechner et al. 1992). Over the next 30 minutes, these pathways result in many cellular changes including changes in secretion, increases in release site area, and increased processing and synthesis of the peptides released by the bag cell neurons (Connard and Kaczmarek 1989). Finally, it is believed that

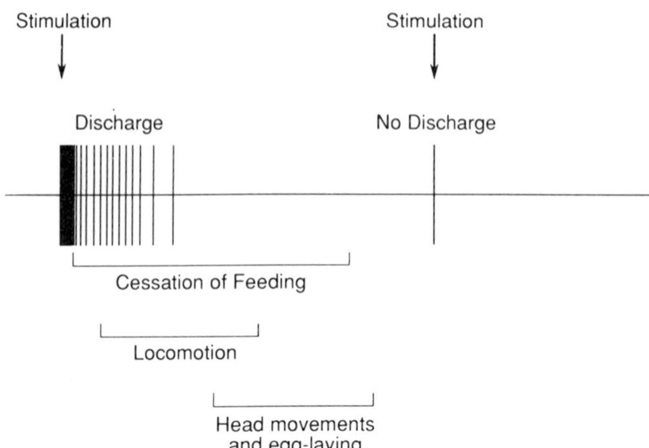

Figure 12.1 Changes in the state of the bag cell neurons after a brief stimulus to an afferent pathway. Immediately after stimulation, the bag cell neurons generate a long-lasting discharge that triggers a stereotyped sequence of behaviors in the animal. After the discharge, the neurons enter a prolonged (approx. 18 hr) inhibited state, during which stimulation of the afferent pathway fails to trigger discharges.

multiple changes in the phosphorylation state of the cation channel close the channel and that the neurons therefore become nonresponsive to further input. This example illustrates a common theme in second messenger system activation, namely, that a cascade of responses is often activated in response to modulatory input.

When more than one second messenger system is activated, there is the opportunity for interactions, either among the systems themselves (i.e., one second messenger system modifying the receptors or enzymes of other systems) or by multiple modification of common final targets. In the case of the bag cell neurons, this interaction is observed on the level of the cation channel. Single-channel recordings reveal that this channel can exist in multiple states, including a "bursty," a "high-activity," and a "silent" state. Interconversion among the three states can be brought about by the combined activity of at least three protein kinases. Particularly important is the observation that application of the catalytic subunit of the cAMP-dependent protein kinase can produce either a decrease or an increase in the opening of the channel, depending upon the prior activity of the other kinases. It is believed that these different responses to the cAMP-dependent kinase may underlie the different responses of the bag cell neurons to stimulation in the excitable and inexcitable states (Wilson and Kaczmarek, pers. comm.). Similar examples of interactions among multiple second messenger systems are seen in the modulation of many other ion channels. In cloned and expressed rat brain Na^+ channels, for example, channel activity can be altered by PKA phosphorylation only if the channel has first been phosphorylated by protein kinase C (Catterall 1992 and this volume), and a brain Ca^{2+}-dependent K channel's affinity for Ca^{2+} is increased by protein kinase C and decreased by PKA (although in this case neither kinase requires prior phosphorylation by the other to exert its effect) (Reinhart et al. 1991; Chung et al. 1991).

These observations show that modification of channel function depends upon the state of the individual channels, and presumably direct interactions among different second messenger systems will also depend upon the state of the second messenger systems themselves. Thus all the issues concerning stable states mentioned above are likely to apply to intracellular messenger systems as well, and network modeling studies will likely be required to achieve a full understanding of these systems (Kennedy, this volume). We felt that too little is known in this area to come to any particular conclusion; however, as seen from Catterall's example, we find it interesting to note that the functional effect of the multiple phosphorylation pathways is initially to increase Na^+ channel activity, and then to provide a damping mechanism that would act as a negative feedback system to prevent excessive Na^+ channel activation. Other examples of similar feedback-type interactions are (for Ca^{2+} channels) Ca^{2+}-dependent inactivation of Ca^{2+} channels and Ca^{2+}-dependent K channels (by limiting "excessive" neuron depolarization). *The potential combinatorial explosion predicted by interactions among the many different second messengers present in neurons thus may not after all be so difficult to comprehend. These set point interactions among messengers may result in the combined second messenger system actually assuming only a limited number of stable states. At the network level, this may mean that despite the overwhelming list of different modulatory inputs to such systems as the crustacean stomatogastric system (Harris-Warrick, this volume; Marder et al. 1987), there may be in fact only a limited number of possible configurations that can be induced.*

WHAT RELATIONSHIP EXISTS BETWEEN THE TIME SCALES OF STATE CHANGES AND THE MECHANISMS UNDERLYING THOSE CHANGES?

Initiation and maintenance of the neurobiological state span time periods ranging from milliseconds to days. *A basic question is whether these different kinetics reflect the kinetics of the fundamental mechanisms underlying the state change.* For systems where the state change is not caused by changes of basic properties in individual units, the transition time between states only depends upon how long the system takes to "settle" in its new configuration and so is highly dependent upon the exact kinetics of the individual units and their interconnections. In cases in which no mechanism intrinsic to the system exists that changes the system back to its original state, these systems will remain in a given state indefinitely until another extrinsic influence is received that induces a state change.

The transition time in systems in which the state change is due to underlying changes in the individual units of the system is obviously a function of both how long it takes to change the individual unit and the settling time of the system. In most of the well-understood systems, the "settling" time of the system is rapid, and the transition time between states is thus determined largely by the kinetics of the underlying unit modification. A wide range of transition times is observed, consistent with the wide range of modulatory mechanisms that are known in neurons. If we consider the example of the bag cell neurons given above, we can define four states of the system physiologically: prestimulation, initial firing, long firing, and refractory period. The kinetics of each of these physiologically defined state transitions is well reflected by the kinetics of the underlying mechanisms that produce them: initial firing is due to rapid Ca^{2+} entry, prolonged firing is related to cAMP activation and initial protein kinase activity, the inhibited period may be due to eventual phosphorylation of a critical number of cation channels by these kinases. Finally, the ultimate transition back to a prestimulation state may perhaps reflect the kinetics of the activity of phosphatases or other enzymes that remove the cation channel inactivation.

Similar matches between underlying mechanism kinetics and the kinetics of physiologically observed state changes are seen (a) in processes that depend upon protein synthesis, such as some forms of learning (hours), (b) in processes that depend upon gene expression, such as c-*fos* induction (hours to days), and (c) in the induction of oscillatory properties in crustacean stomatogastric neurons after the removal of endogenous modulatory inputs (days). These examples demonstrate particularly well how underlying mechanism kinetics and behavioral expression are linked when the state change occurs via a chain of reactions, of which only the final step results in behaviorally observable consequences. For instance, ongoing protein synthesis is necessary during the acquisition time in learning experiments (Rainbow 1979); however, the effect of inhibiting protein synthesis can be observed only after a delay of about four hours. The changes induced by the learning paradigm are presumably initiated during the learning paradigm itself; the delay noted above reflects presumably the time it takes for the triggered sequence of intracellular reactions necessary for new molecules—perhaps receptor or channel proteins—to be synthesized and incorporated into the appropriate neurons. It thus seems clear that the transition time between states in these systems is determined largely by the kinetics of the modification of the underlying units.

Finally, in systems where the sequence of state changes ultimately returns the system to its original state (e.g., the bag cell neurons), it is important to note that this series of state changes proceeds inevitably from the initial triggering stimulus by the action of several intracellular processes that are either activated sequentially in a cascade or are coactivated and have different kinetics. In systems lacking such "return" mechanisms (e.g., learning, cell transformation), state changes induced by changes in individual units last until some other externally derived state change signal is received or the changes are permanent.

WHAT ARE THE DIFFERENT ROLES/CONSEQUENCES OF CHANGES IN SYNAPTIC STRENGTH AS COMPARED TO CHANGES IN INTRINSIC MEMBRANE PROPERTIES?

Networks that change state as a result of modulation can be altered by modifying synaptic strength and/or modifying intrinsic cellular properties (e.g., passive membrane properties, activation parameters of ionic conductances). It is commonly believed that changes in synaptic strength underlie long-term plasticity, whereas changes in intrinsic properties are responsible for adjusting the responsiveness of the nervous system, i.e., its "internal state" (e.g., arousal level, hunger vs. satiation, motivation). This belief, however, was a source of considerable disagreement among our group. One faction held that, although invertebrate learning and plasticity have often been associated with changes in intrinsic properties (Kandel and Schwartz 1982), such changes have never been seen in vertebrate learning, and thus vertebrate learning was almost certainly due to changes in synaptic strength alone. The other faction noted that various technical difficulties limit our ability to observe changes in intrinsic properties in vertebrate preparations, particularly if the changes were limited to only parts of the neuron, and that in all probability changes in intrinsic properties will eventually be implicated in plasticity in vertebrates as well.

As a result of this discussion, we explicitly considered the different effects of modifying synaptic versus intrinsic cellular properties. Classical rapid synapses have several inherent properties that are important to understanding the possible effects of modifying them. First, they are good at transiently driving or inhibiting their follower neurons, and for resetting oscillators and triggering follower neurons that generate plateaus to switch states. Second, the location of synaptic inputs is extremely important because spatial and temporal summation determine the strength of the synapse. Third, individual synapses can be individually strengthened or weakened. Finally, because synaptically activated conductances have reversal potentials and because of the way in which changes in synaptic conductance couple to changes in membrane potential, changing synaptic strength is most effective for synapses that are originally weak; as synapses become increasingly stronger the incremental effect on the postsynaptic membrane potential of increasing synaptic conductance decreases.

On the other hand, modification of intrinsic cellular properties may change the effective time constants in a neuron, e.g., by changing its frequency response characteristics or transforming a neuron into an endogenous oscillator. Comparing the effects of inducing classic ligand-gated conductance changes vs. modification of intrinsic cellular properties suggests that only changes in the latter can separately modify amplitude and oscillation frequency of endogenous oscillators, since a simple conductance change inevitably alters both the oscillator's baseline membrane potential and its frequency (Figure 12.2) (Marder and Meyrand 1989).

To a first approximation, this list of properties supports the dogma of synapses for learning, inherent cellular properties for internal state. There are, however, at least three cases in which changes in cellular properties could be involved in learning. First,

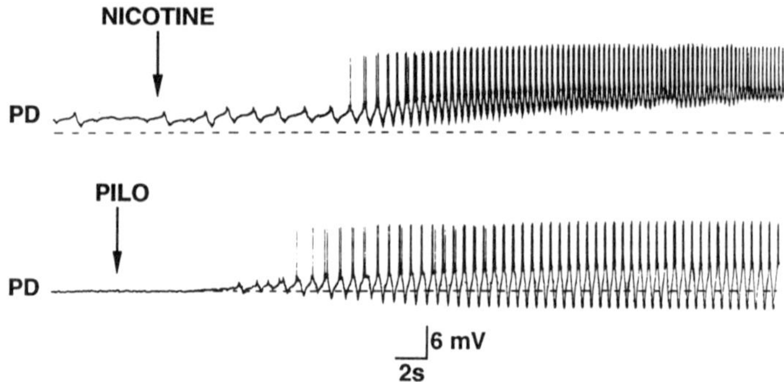

Figure 12.2 Comparison of the effects of voltage-independent (nicotine) and voltage-dependent (pilocarpine, a muscarinic acetylcholine agonist) excitatory conductance increases on the activity of oscillatory neurons. Both nicotine and pilocarpine (PILO), when applied to quiescent preparations of the crustacean pyloric network, result in rhythmic pyloric dilator (PD) neuron oscillations. Since the effect of nicotine is voltage independent, it induces a depolarization (compare to dotted line) at all phases of PD neuron oscillation, and thus results in small amplitude oscillations. Pilocarpine, alternatively, opens a voltage-dependent excitatory conductance, and thus induces oscillations without causing a depolarization (compare to dotted line) of the neuron's baseline membrane potential. Thus pilocarpine, but not nicotine, is able to alter oscillation frequency without changing oscillation amplitude (see text). When these agonists are applied to spontaneously rhythmic preparations, similar effects to those shown here are seen.

as noted earlier, reverberating circuits could be a substrate for the retention of short-term memories (Forbes 1929). This long-lasting neuronal firing classically has been believed to result from an excitatory feedback loop; however, it could just as easily result from the induction of a long-lasting plateau in these neurons. Second, work in invertebrate preparations has shown that changing the effective time constants of a neuron can result in it "switching" between neural networks that operate at different frequencies (Hooper and Moulins 1989). Thus, changing a neuron's intrinsic cellular properties could be a viable mechanism for learning that occurs on the cellular level through switching neurons to another network. Third, work in vertebrate motor neurons has shown that plateau potential induction in these neurons by monoamine application amplifies the response of these neurons to excitatory inputs (Kiehn 1991). Thus, by analogy, inputs that induce long-lasting induction or alteration of the plateau properties of a neuron could be a mechanism that alters effective strength of the neuron's synaptic inputs.

From invertebrate work, it is clear that changes in intrinsic cellular properties within a network of fixed synaptic connectivity results in the effective formation of a new neural network (Marder et al. 1987). The use of such networks to store memories would provide a multiplexing mechanism that could have two possible advantages. First, it could significantly increase the total memory storage capacity of the nervous system by creating overlapping ensembles of neurons, each activated by a specific set of inputs. Second, if these global rearrangements were associated with specific behavioral states (e.g., emotional state, amphetamine application, arousal), it could provide an internal state-dependent mapping between memory storage and retrieval, where memories established during a particular state might be most easily retrievable when that state recurred. Finally, it should be noted that it may be possible for these modulatory changes in membrane properties to occur only in limited areas of neurons (e.g., parts of the dendritic tree or even individual spines), which would considerably increase their potential power to sculpt neuronal activity and responses to inputs.

WHEN AND WHY ARE COMPUTATIONAL METHODS NECESSARY TO UNDERSTAND NETWORK PROPERTIES AND PLASTICITY? WHAT ARE THE LIMITS OF REDUCTIONISM?

It is relatively easy, both by simulation and intuition, to understand neurobiological systems that consist either of only two interacting units or of chains of serially connected units. However, the analysis of distributed systems in which large numbers of units are highly interconnected with multiple-embedded feedback and feedforward loops, is computationally demanding and extremely nonintuitive, particularly when the individual units are inherently nonlinear. The recent availability of inexpensive computer power has allowed complex systems to be simulated, and a burst of inquiry into distributed systems and nonlinear phenomena, in general, has resulted. In their recent theoretical work, Wang and Rinzel (1992) provide us with an example of the extraordinary nonintuitiveness of these systems. They show that two reciprocally inhibitory, nonlinear model neurons can, depending upon their membrane properties and the dynamics of the coupling, fire synchronously (as well as out of phase).

Similar results have been obtained by studying the effect of electrical coupling on oscillator frequency in the pyloric network of the lobster stomatogastric system. This work was originally triggered by the observation that removing neurons that were electrically coupled to the oscillator neuron resulted in an increase in the oscillator frequency; this seemed reasonable because removing neurons "reduced the drag on the oscillator" (Hooper and Marder 1987). However, when this system was simulated (Kepler et al. 1990), it was found that oscillator neurons can respond in two ways to injected current (which is similar to the current flow between electrically coupled neurons). Briefly, the injection of hyperpolarizing current can either primarily lengthen the hyperpolarized phase of the neuronal oscillation (hence decreasing oscillation frequency) or shorten the burst duration (hence increasing frequency), depending upon the exact parameters used in the model oscillator. Thus, the effect of electrical coupling or current injection into an oscillator cannot be predicted without a detailed understanding of the properties of the oscillator. Perhaps even more surprisingly, the change in "state" between these two oscillator types can be produced by modest changes in one of the model's currents (Epstein and Marder 1990; Kepler et al. 1990).

These and similar combinations of experimental and theoretical investigations of nonlinear highly connected systems have shown that (a) small changes in such systems may induce large changes in system output, (b) large changes in the systems may induce only small or no changes in system output, and (c) it is essential that the full range of the system's various parameters be systematically searched in order to understand the system as fully as possible. The question then naturally arises: "If our intuition is poor, and the activity of these systems is so critically parameter dependent, when is it appropriate to model, and how can we judge the validity of a given model?" The answer to this question falls into two distinct but complementary approaches.

The first uses a completely abstract model containing no physiological parameters (conductances, currents, time constants, etc.). Many back propagation and attractor neural network models are of this type. Essentially, such models are analogies, and their value is that they provide new ways of thinking about the organization and operation of complex systems. For example, attractor networks are dynamic systems that settle into particular states (attractors) according to the total activity in the network, which includes inputs and feedback loops. This suggests that the selection of a particular motor output could simply emerge from the current state of the nervous system; there is no theoretical need for command neurons or centers to select particular outputs or system states. Certain requirements for the network architecture have been identified that are essential to produce an attractor network displaying behavior similar to biological motor systems, e.g., stable maintenance of a selected output and the ability to change rapidly to a new output (Altman, pers. comm.). These include highly diluted, asymmetrical connections and heterogeneous synaptic delays. Experiments can now be designed to explore biological motor systems to see whether such features are implemented.

Two notes of caution are necessary here. First, it is essential to explore the full range of network parameters to ensure that the model is generalizable to all systems states and thus to avoid anecdotal or chance similarities to the biological system. Second, just because these models may have activity similar to that of biological systems, it does not necessarily follow that the biological system has a similar form or underlying logic—several architectures can produce nearly identical activity patterns. In the attractor network model for motor output selection, the network requirements are sufficiently plausible biologically to be worth exploring. In contrast, back propagation models can point to solutions for a problem without reference to underlying mechanisms; an example is the connectivity of interneurons involved in the local bending reflex in the leech (Lockery et al. 1989).

Another variation on the analog model is the work of Mead and colleagues (see Mead 1989), which uses solid-state silicon technology to build replicas of parts of the nervous system, such as the retina. This approach provides insights into circuit design.

Rather than treating neurons individually, as is the tendency with information gained from single-cell recordings, the behavior of each element is seen in the context of the circuit and its interactions with its neighbors. For example, experience with the silicon retina suggests that the voltage-sensitive calcium channel in cone photoreceptors is involved in inter-receptor calibration, through the horizontal cells, rather than in the adaptation of single photoreceptors (Mahowald 1993).

The second approach is to model systems on the basis of empirical observation. The main problems with this approach are knowing when one has "enough" data and, given the parameter sensitivity of many models, whether the data are accurate enough. Ultimately, whether these difficulties have been overcome is revealed by whether the model's activity matches that of the real system. An important feature of this matching is that the model must be compared to as many of the real system's states as possible. This avoids selection of a model that may, by chance, perform correctly under some conditions. Varying the "experimental" conditions (e.g., changing the calcium concentration of the saline), and examining several system states will, as a rule, rapidly narrow the number of competing models.

Under ideal conditions (particularly when modeling and experiments are performed by the same person, or at least in the same lab), modeling can lead to novel insights. A combination of modeling and experiment in the lamprey (Grillner, this volume) revealed that (a) even though serotonin reduces the afterhyperpolarization following an action potential and thus might be expected to increase cycle frequency, it actually decreases cycle frequency because it leads to longer burst durations, and (b) a primary functional role of the NMDA receptor in the lamprey locomotor network is to support slow cycle-frequency swimming. Combining modeling and experiment may also be useful in investigating the real roles of apparently "redundant" connections or units in a system, since it is possible in a model to manipulate the system and to observe membrane and synaptic currents on a level of detail that is often impossible in real networks. Similarly, building models in silicon, because of the emphasis on circuit design, can point to functions of components that were previously obscure.

The value of modeling, particularly in complex systems in which relatively little biological data were available, was also somewhat controversial. M. Segal noted that while the examples given above illustrate the possible predictive value of a model in proposing experiments and leading to discovery of basic biological principles, it is unfortunate that current models of plasticity and higher brain functions have failed to do so. Thus far, most models of hippocampal or cortical networks, in relation to plasticity, have failed to predict a single novel neuronal property or mechanism that could not be predicted on the basis of biological information. This failure might be due to the complexity of the networks involved, and to the fact that many of the parameters are approximated. This is in contrast to the invertebrate models, where the number of participating elements is discrete and known, and where modeling has had clear predictive value (Kepler et al. 1990; Wang and Rinzel 1992).

TO WHAT EXTENT CAN LESSONS LEARNED FROM ONE EXPERIMENTAL SYSTEM BE EXTRAPOLATED TO OTHER SYSTEMS? ARE THERE GENERALIZABLE RULES?

A review across many levels of organization in nervous systems suggests that evolution is often surprisingly conservative, and thus observations made in one experimental system often apply to others. For instance, gene structure, second messenger systems, ion channel structure, and synaptic transmitters and junctions seem to be conserved in all multicellular animals. Organizations of networks that subserve a similar function (e.g., the vestibulo-ocular reflex), and gross anatomy (e.g., the presence of descending systems in the spinal cord) seem to be largely conserved across all vertebrates. On the level of synaptic connectivity within networks, there is much less conservation, even within phyla and in networks that produce similar outputs. There is, however, a clear conservation of functional design principles across phyla. For instance, neuromodulation induces state changes; slow regenerative processes, such as postinhibitory rebound and plateau potentials, transform and amplify input signals and provide substrates for dynamic regulation of network output; endogenously oscillatory neurons provide sources of rhythmic drive; mutual inhibition and recurrent inhibition regulate the relative timing of neuronal activity; and changes in synaptic strength provide a mechanism for learning. It is thus likely that there is a family of general mechanisms appropriate for endowing a given network with a specific property, and that any of these mechanisms can be used within a given network. It follows that the study of these mechanisms in various organisms will lead to generally applicable descriptions of network function, just as the Hodgkin/Huxley description of the squid axon led to a general understanding of the electrical activity of all neurons.

These observations suggest that a primary determinant in choosing an experimental preparation should be its appropriateness to the problem being studied, not its phylogenetic position. Small invertebrate systems are ideal for studying how the activity of a neuronal network arises from specific interconnectivity patterns and cellular properties, and for relating network design to behavior. The insights gained from this work are likely to apply to the activity of similar small, local circuits in other organisms. Thus, for instance, recent studies of fully described neural networks in invertebrate preparations have shown that (a) single small neuronal networks can assume many different functional configurations (Marder et al. 1987), (b) neurons can switch between different neuronal networks (Hooper and Moulins 1989), and (c) different networks can be fused and melded to create novel networks (Dickinson et al. 1990; Meyrand et al. 1991; Weimann et al. 1991). These concepts may well be applicable to the activity of local circuits in vertebrates, as studies in vertebrate motor pattern generation (Grillner 1981) and visual scene segmentation (Engel et al. 1991) have suggested. In general, neuromodulation is likely to be as important in vertebrates as it is in invertebrates. An illustration of this is the reduction in memory ability in mammals when cholinergic forebrain neurons are destroyed; although such lesions do not directly affect the complex mechanisms for acquisition and storage of memories, the removal of state-setting acetylcholine renders them ineffective (Dunnett et al. 1991). A similar example is provided by the effect on motor performance of losing dopamine neurons in the substantia nigra (e.g., in Parkinson's disease) (Robbins and Everitt 1992).

A completely unresolved question is how the rules governing neural network function change as the size of the network increases from small (less than 100) to intermediate (100 to 1000s) to large (1000s to millions) numbers of neurons. Intermediate-sized networks can be profitably studied in invertebrates (Skingsley et al. 1993), but obviously large networks can only be studied in vertebrates. It is possible that the rules governing such large distributed networks may be different from those of small to intermediate invertebrate neural networks. This last point brought forward the question of whether the mechanisms underlying neural network function in invertebrates and vertebrates may be fundamentally different, as opposed to the networks differing only in size. The majority felt that similar general mechanisms were likely to be present in both phyla; however, an argument was made for there existing two profoundly different organizational principles, with invertebrates resembling analog devices and vertebrates digital devices.

This last point specifically raises an issue that was a persistent theme in our discussion: we understand so little of the how network structure leads to network activity. All of the systems we have discussed, from second messengers to neural circuits, are highly interconnected systems composed of nonlinear individual elements. We now have a tremendous *amount* of information about how individual units work at all of these levels, but we *understand* very poorly how the systems constructed from these units actually function. Second messenger systems often seem to operate in cascades and in concert, memories are presumably encoded by alteration of synapses that function as a part of a neural network, and behavior results from the interaction of thousands or hundreds of thousands of individual neural networks. Fundamentally, we need precise descriptions of the organization of these systems, e.g., of the interactions among the different second messenger systems or of the synaptic connectivity of vertebrate brain structures, such as cortical "columns" and the hippocampus. Without these data, building models or designing functional experiments to investigate the design principles of these systems is extremely difficult. Nonetheless, these complex systems *are* governed by organizational principles that connect the internal architecture of the systems to their activity. The description of these rules will clearly be difficult and will require a great deal of interdisciplinary experimental and theoretical work in a multitude of different systems. However, it is very unlikely that we will ever be able to understand behavior on the cellular level until we describe these rules. As I was told when I began to write this report, "Sooner begun, sooner done."

REFERENCES

Catterall, W.A. 1992. Cellular and molecular biology of voltage-gated sodium channels. *Physiol. Rev.* **72**:S15–S48.

Chiu, A.Y., M.W. Hunkapiller, E. Heller, D.K. Stuart, L.E. Hood, and F. Strumwasser. 1979. Purification and primary structure of the neuropeptide egg-laying hormone of *Aplysia californica. Proc. Natl. Acad. Sci. USA* **76**:6656–6660.

Chung, S., P.H. Reinhart, B.L. Vartin, D. Brautigan, and I.B. Levitan. 1991. Protein kinase activity closely associated with a reconstituted calcium-activated potassium channel. *Science* **253**:560–562.

Conn, P.J., J.A. Strong, and L.K. Kaczmarek. 1989. Inhibitors of protein kinase C prevent enhancement of calcium current and action potentials in peptidergic neurons of *Aplysia. J. Neurosci.* **9**:480–487.

Connard, P.G., and L.K. Kaczmarek. 1989. The bag cell neurons of *Aplysia*: A model for the study of the molecular mechanisms involved in the control of prolonged animal behaviors. *Mol. Neurobiol.* **3**:237–273.

Dickinson, P.S., C. Mecsas, and E. Marder. 1990. Neuropeptide fusion of two motor-pattern generator circuits. *Nature* **344**:155–158.

Dickinson, P.S., and R. Nagy. 1983. Control of a central pattern generator by an identified modulatory interneurone in *Crustacea*. II. Induction and modification of plateau properties in pyloric neurons. *J. Exp. Biol.* **105**:59–82.

Dudek, R., J.S. Cobbs, and H. Pinsker. 1979. Bag cell electrical activity underlying spontaneous egg laying in freely behaving *Aplysia brasiliana. J. Neurophysiol.* **42**:804–817.

Dunnett, S.B., B.J. Everitt, and T.W. Robbins. 1991. The basal forebrain-cortical cholinergic system: Interpreting the functional consequences of excitotoxic lesions. *Trends Neurosci.* **14**:494–501.

Elliot, C.J.H., and P.R. Benjamin. 1985. Interactions of pattern-generating interneurons controlling feeding in *Lymnaea stagnalis. J. Neurophysiol.* **54**:1396–1411.

Engel, A.K., P. König, and W. Singer. 1991. Direct physiological evidence for scene segmentation by temporal coding. *Proc. Natl. Acad. Sci. USA* **88**:9236–9140.

Epstein, I.R., and E. Marder. 1990. Multiple modes of a conditional neural oscillator. *Biol. Cybern.* **63**:25–34.

Forbes, A. 1929. The Foundations of Experimental Psychology. Worchester: Clark Univ. Press.

Grillner, S. 1981. Control of locomotion in bipeds, tetrapods, and fish. In: Handbook of Physiology, section 1, The Nervous System, Motor Control, ed. V.B. Brooks, vol. 4, pp. 1179–1236. Bethesda: Am. Physiological Soc.

Grillner, S., P. Wallén, N. Dale, L. Brodin, J. Buchanan, and R. Hill. 1987. Transmitters, membrane properties, and network circuitry in the control of locomotion in lamprey. *Trends Neurosci.* **10**:34–41.

Hebb, D.O. 1949. The Organization of Behavior. A Neuropsychological Theory. London: Chapman and Hall; New York: Wiley.

Hooper, S.L., and E. Marder. 1987. Modulation of the lobster pyloric rhythm by the peptide proctolin. *J. Neurosci.* **7**:2097–2112.

Hooper, S.L., and M. Moulins. 1989. Switching of a neuron from one network to another by sensory-induced changes in membrane properties. *Science* **244**:1587–1589.

Hounsgaard, J., and O. Kjaerulff. 1992. Ca^{2+}-mediated plateau potentials in a subpopulation of interneurons in the ventral horn of the turtle spinal cord. *Eur. J. Neurosci.* **4**:183–188.

Kandel, E.R., and J.H. Schwartz. 1982. Molecular biology of learning: Modulation of transmitter release. *Science* **218**:433–443.

Kepler, T.B., E. Marder, and L.F. Abbott. 1990. The effect of electrical coupling on the frequency of model neuronal oscillators. *Science* **248**:83–85.

Kiehn, O. 1991. Plateau potentials and active integration in the "final common pathway" for motor behaviour. *Trends Neurosci.* **14**:68–73.

Kupfermann, I., and E.R. Kandel. 1970. Electrophysiological properties and functional interconnections of two symmetrical neurosecretory clusters (bag cells) in abdominal ganglion of *Aplysia*. *J. Neurophysiol.* **33**:865–876.

Lockery, S.R., G. Wittenberg, W.B. Kristan, Jr., and G. Cottrell. 1989. Function of identified interneurons in the leech elucidated using neural networks trained by back-propagation. *Nature* **340**:648–671.

Loechner, K.J., J. Nattessich-Arrandale, E.M. Azdherian, and L.K. Kaczmarek. 1992. Inhibition of peptide release from invertebrate neurons by the protein kinase inhibitor H-7. *Brain Res.* **581**:315–318.

Mahowald, M. 1993. Analog VLSI systems for stereo vision. Norwell, MA.: Klewer Academic.

Marder, E., S.L. Hooper, and J.S. Eisen. 1987. Multiple neurotransmitters provide a mechanism for the production of multiple outputs from a single neuronal circuit. In: Synaptic Function, ed. G.M. Edelman, W.E. Gall, and M.W. Cowan, pp. 305–327. New York: Wiley.

Marder, E., and P.M Meyrand. 1989. Chemical modulation of oscillatory neural circuit. In: Neuronal and Cellular Oscillators, ed. J. Jacklet, pp. 317–338. New York: Marcel Dekker, Inc.

Mead, C. 1989. Analog VLSI and Neural Systems. Reading, MA: Addison-Wesley Publ. Co.

Meyrand, P., J. Simmers, and M. Moulins. 1991. Construction of a pattern-generating circuit with neurons of different networks. *Nature* **351**:60–63.

Nowak, L., P. Bregetowski, P. Ascher, A. Hervet, and A. Prochiantz. 1984. Magnesium gates glutamate-activated channels in mouse central neurones. *Nature* **307**:462–465.

Nusbaum, M.P., and E. Marder. 1989. A modulatory proctolin-containing neuron (MPN). II. State-dependent modulation of rhythmic motor activity. *J. Neurosci.* **9**:1600–1607.

Rainbow, T.C. 1979. Role of RNA and protein synthesis in memory formation. *Neurochem. Res.* **4**:297–312.

Ramirez, J.-M., and K.G. Pearson. 1991. Octopamine induces bursting and plateau potentials in insect neurones. *Brain Res.* **549**:332–337.

Reinhart, P.H., S.K. Chung, B.L. Martin, D.L. Brautigan, and I.B. Levitan. 1991. Modulation of calcium-activated potassium channels from rat brain by protein kinase A and phosphatase 2A. *J. Neurosci.* **11**:1627–1635.

Robbins, T.W., and B.J. Everitt. 1992. Functions of dopamine in the dorsal and ventral striatum. *Sem. Neurosci.* **4**:119–127.

Robinson, D.A. 1971. Models of oculomotor neural organization. In: The Control of Eye Movements, ed. P. Bach-y-Rita, C.C. Colins, and J. E. Hyde, pp. 519–538. New York: Academic.

Russell, D.F., and D.K. Hartline. 1982. Slow active potentials and bursting motor patterns in pyloric network of the lobster, *Panulirus interruptus*. *J. Neurophysiol.* **48**:914–937.

Skingsley, D.R., R. Bright, N. Santama, J. Van Minnen, M.J. Brierley, J.F. Burke, and P.R. Benjamin. 1993. A molecularly defined cardiorespiratory interneuron expressing SDPFLRFamide/GDPFLRFamide in the snail *Lymnaea*: Monosynaptic connections and physiology. *J. Neurophysiol.* **69**:915–927.

Tsukahara, N. 1972. The properties of the cerebello-pontine reverberating circuit. *Brain Res.* **40**:67–71.

Wang, X.-J., and J. Rinzel. 1992. Alternating and synchronous rhythms in reciprocally inhibitory model neurons. *Neural Comp.* **4**:84–97.

Weimann, J.M., P. Meyrand, and E. Marder. 1991. Neurons that form multiple pattern generators: Identification and multiple activity patterns of gastric/pyloric neurons in the crab stomatogastric system. *J. Neurophysiol.* **65**:111–122.

Wilson, G.F., and L.K. Kaczmarek. 1992. Modulation of an *Aplysia* divalent-permeable cation channel by endogenous kinase and the catalytic subunit of protein kinase A. *Soc. Neurosci. Abstr.* **18**:586.

13

Current Physiological Models for Long-term Potentiation in the CA1 Region of the Hippocampus

R.A. NICOLL, D.J.A. WYLLIE, T. MANABE, and D.J. PERKEL
Departments of Pharmacology and Physiology, University of California,
San Francisco, CA 94143–0450, U.S.A.

ABSTRACT

Long-term potentiation (LTP) is perhaps the best cellular model for learning and memory in the mammalian brain. In the CA1 region of the hippocampus its induction requires a rise in postsynaptic Ca^{2+}. This rise occurs as a consequence of Ca^{2+} entry via the NMDA receptor channel when common stimulus patterns are used to induce LTP. It has recently been demonstrated, however, that NMDA receptor-independent increases in intracellular Ca^{2+} can, in some instances, also potentiate synaptic transmission. It is unclear whether Ca^{2+} alone is sufficient to trigger sustained potentiation or whether synaptic activity provides some additional factor.

The site of LTP expression remains controversial. Studies involving the analysis of paired-pulse facilitation, dual component EPSCs, miniature EPSC amplitudes, separation of quantal peaks and postsynaptic sensitivity to AMPA favor a postsynaptic component to LTP. On the other hand, studies involving analyses of synaptic variability, failures of evoked release, and miniature EPSC frequency favor a presynaptic mechanism. Taken together, these data suggest that both pre- and postsynaptic mechanisms are involved. If the expression of LTP is entirely dependent upon a postsynaptic induction, a presynaptic mechanism must involve a retrograde signal. Evidence has recently been presented suggesting that nitric oxide may fulfill this role.

Much remains to be learned about the induction and expression of LTP, which will require further understanding of the basic mechanisms involved in synaptic transmission.

Cellular and Molecular Mechanisms Underlying Higher Neural Functions
Edited by A.I. Selverston and P. Ascher

INTRODUCTION

It is generally accepted that the synapse is a likely site for changes that accompany learning and memory. In addition, it is assumed that these changes are long lasting. The discovery of long-term potentiation (LTP) provided a phenomenon that incorporates most of the features expected for a form of synaptic modification appropriate for learning and memory. In particular, LTP exhibits an associative property that was first predicted by Hebb in the late 1940s. Specifically, the induction of LTP requires the near simultaneous coincidence of synaptic activity and adequate postsynaptic depolarization. We now know that the NMDA receptor provides the molecular basis for this coincidence detection. Under normal conditions for the NMDA receptor channel to conduct, glutamate must bind to the receptor and the postsynaptic membrane must be depolarized. The basis for this voltage dependence is a voltage-dependent block of the ion channel by extracellular Mg^{2+}. The NMDA receptor channel is known to be highly permeable to Ca^{2+} as well as to monovalent cations, and therefore activation of this channel will lead to an influx of Ca^{2+} into the postsynaptic spine. It has been proposed that the rise in Ca^{2+} serves as the trigger for LTP. The events that are initiated by Ca^{2+} and ultimately lead to an increased synaptic strength are not, as yet, clearly resolved. These events, however, must all occur within the time scale of a few seconds (Gustafsson et al. 1989).

LTP has been the subject of numerous reviews (Bliss and Lynch 1988; Collingridge and Singer 1990; Gustafsson and Wigström 1988; Madison et al. 1991). The purpose of this chapter is not to provide a comprehensive review of the LTP field but rather to focus on a few specific outstanding problems with LTP in the CA1 region of the hippocampus and to determine how adequately these problems have been addressed.

INDUCTION OF LTP

Is NMDA Receptor Activation Necessary for LTP?

One of the key early observations was that the NMDA receptor antagonist APV blocked the induction of LTP (Collingridge et al. 1983); this finding has been confirmed in numerous subsequent studies. Under certain conditions, however, long-lasting potentiation can be induced in the absence of NMDA-receptor activity in the CA1 region. Application of high extracellular Ca^{2+} has been reported to cause a lasting potentiation (Reymann et al. 1986; Turner et al. 1982). Tetanic stimulation of presynaptic fibers at 200 Hz, which is a higher frequency than normally used to induce LTP, can evoke a Ca^{2+}-dependent, NMDA receptor-independent potentiation (Grover and Teyler 1990) that is specific to the tetanized pathway (Grover and Teyler 1992). A similar potentiation can be induced by blocking potassium channels with a brief application of tetraethylammonium (TEA) (Aniksztejn and Ben-Ari 1991). Finally, activation of metabotropic glutamate receptors by the selective agonist 1S,3R–ACPD can cause a long-lasting potentiation that is independent of NMDA receptor activation (Bortolotto and Collingridge 1992), although previous studies using ACPD failed to see a potentiation (Aniksztejn et al. 1992; Baskys and Malenka 1991; McGuinness et al. 1991). Whether these NMDA receptor-independent forms of potentiation are equivalent to LTP has not been entirely established, but a recent study has reported some degree of occlusion of the TEA-induced potentiation with tetanus-induced LTP (Huang and Malenka 1993). These findings suggest that, although NMDA receptor activation is definitely necessary for LTP when it is induced by the usual protocol, this requirement can be bypassed when conditions favor entry of Ca^{2+} via voltage-sensitive Ca^{2+} channels (see below) or presumably when Ca^{2+} is released from intracellular stores in the case of ACPD-induced potentiation.

Is NMDA Receptor Activation Sufficient for LTP?

This has been a long-standing question and is still not completely resolved. Typically, application of NMDA results in a transient potentiation lasting for approximately 30 min (Collingridge et al. 1983; Kauer et al. 1988a), suggesting that activation of NMDA receptors alone is not sufficient for sustained potentiation. While initial studies found that NMDA-induced potentiation did occlude with tetanus-induced LTP early but not late (Kauer et al. 1988a), a recent study found some degree of occlusion up to two hours after the induction of LTP (Asztely et al. 1991). With elevated extracellular Ca^{2+} a longer-lasting potentiation can be observed with NMDA application (Malenka 1991; Manabe et al. 1992; Thibault et al. 1989); however, the time course of this potentiation has not been rigorously examined. Moreover, it has not, as yet, been tested whether this potentiation occludes with LTP

Is a Rise in Postsynaptic Ca^{2+} Necessary for LTP?

The finding that injection of Ca^{2+} chelators into the postsynaptic cell blocks LTP (Lynch et al. 1983; Malenka et al. 1988) strongly supports a role for Ca^{2+} in LTP induction. However, whether intracellular Ca^{2+} plays a permissive or instructive role is unclear. For example, the presence of high concentrations of chelator could substantially lower resting Ca^{2+} levels, blocking some constitutive Ca^{2+}-dependent processes that are required for LTP. Two lines of evidence argue that postsynaptic Ca^{2+} plays an instructive role.

First, if Ca^{2+} entry through the NMDA receptor channel is required for LTP one should be able to demonstrate a suppression potential at which no net Ca^{2+} enters the cell (Katz and Miledi 1967). It should be possible to depolarize the postsynaptic cell to such an extent that, although the NMDA receptor channel is unblocked, no net Ca^{2+} influx will occur because the driving force is reduced. Such a finding was reported using microelectrode recording (Malenka et al. 1988), although the actual membrane potential achieved during these experiments could not be accurately determined. We have repeated these experiments using whole-cell voltage clamp techniques, which provide better control over membrane potential (Perkel and Nicoll 1993), and have confirmed that strong depolarization of cells (to approximately +70 mV) during synaptic stimulation blocks LTP. Pairing synaptic stimulation with depolarization to approximately +20 to +30 mV, which was verified to be beyond the EPSC reversal potential, was as effective as pairing at –30 to –20 mV. This is somewhat surprising, because the Ca^{2+} entry, in theory, should be considerably reduced at potentials beyond the reversal potential. However, an NMDA receptor-dependent rise in Ca^{2+} at these potentials can be detected using optical imaging techniques (Perkel et al. 1993). These findings, in general, support the proposed rise in Ca^{2+} as the trigger for LTP.

Second, recent experiments involving the photo-release of a Ca^{2+} chelator (Malenka et al. 1992) have shown that to block LTP, the chelator need only be active during the tetanus and not before. Furthermore, if the chelator is released 2 sec after the tetanus, normal LTP ensues. These findings support the notion that LTP is induced by a brief rise in Ca^{2+} .

While the above data indicate that Ca^{2+} entry through NMDA channels is required for LTP, there are data which suggest that an additional source of Ca^{2+} may be required. Thapsigargin, which blocks Ca^{2+}-induced Ca^{2+} release from intracellular stores, has been reported to block LTP (Harvey and Collingridge 1992), although in earlier studies the use of dantrolene, which has a similar action, gave mixed results (Obenaus et al. 1989; Xu and Krnjevic 1990).

Is a Rise in Postsynaptic Ca^{2+} Sufficient for LTP?

This issue is similar to the issue of whether NMDA receptor activation is sufficient for LTP. A number of studies have addressed this by raising Ca^{2+} in a manner independent of NMDA receptors. This has involved activating voltage-sensitive Ca^{2+} channels (Aniksztejn and Ben-Ari 1991; Field et al. 1992; Grover and Teyler 1990; Kullmann et al. 1992) and releasing Ca^{2+} from the caged compound Nitr-5 (Malenka et al. 1988). In only one study was synaptic stimulation stopped during the time when Ca^{2+} was presumably elevated, and although large potentiation was observed, synaptic responses decayed to baseline levels within about 30 min (Kullmann et al. 1992). By contrast, in the other studies, the potentiation was long lasting, suggesting that synaptic stimulation provides something in addition to raising Ca^{2+}. Indeed, when synaptic stimulation is paired with a rise in Ca^{2+} induced by activating voltage-sensitive Ca^{2+} channels, the transient potentiation can be converted to a stable potentiation (Kullmann et al. 1992). A number of possible mechanisms might be invoked to explain the effect of synaptic stimulation, including sodium entry via non-NMDA receptors (or additionally NMDA receptors under normal conditions) or protein kinase C activation by metabotropic glutamate receptors, analogous to cerebellar long-term depression (Linden and Connor 1991). Many studies have implicated the activation of protein kinase C in LTP (Anwyl 1989; Linden and Routtenberg 1989; Malenka et al. 1986; Malinow et al. 1989; Wang and Feng 1992). It has recently been reported that activating metabotropic glutamate receptors can cause a long-lasting potentiation in the dorsolateral septal nucleus (Zheng and Gallagher 1992) and the hippocampus

(Bortolotto and Collingridge, 1992). The inability of glutamate application to evoke long-lasting potentiation (Kauer et al. 1988a) may have resulted from an inability to reach adequate concentrations in the synaptic cleft because of strong uptake mechanisms. Another possibility is that some synaptic process, in addition to the release of glutamate, is responsible for sustained potentiation. A cotransmitter released with glutamate from the same synapses is one possibility. In considering a cotransmitter mechanism, it is important to realize that it must be released with low-frequency stimulation, since pairing low-frequency synaptic activation with depolarization evokes sustained LTP (Gustafsson et al. 1987; Kauer et al. 1988b), thus apparently ruling out most peptide transmitters. Finally, some aspect of presynaptic activity that is independent of neurotransmitter release may prime these synapses so that they are receptive to some retrograde factor. The studies reviewed in this section strongly suggest that a rise in postsynaptic Ca^{2+} is sufficient to potentiate synaptic transmission transiently, but that sustained potentiation may require some additional component provided by synaptic stimulation.

What Is the Relationship Between $[Ca^{2+}]_i$ and LTP?

This relationship appears to be complex and is still poorly understood. Clearly it is possible to reduce slightly the Mg^{2+} block of the NMDA receptor channel and not induce LTP, suggesting that the level of Ca^{2+} must rise above a threshold before LTP is induced. Indeed, it has been proposed that at intermediate levels of Ca^{2+}, a transient potentiation occurs and that only when Ca^{2+} rises above this level does sustained potentiation occur (Hanse and Gustafsson 1992; Malenka 1991). Once the threshold for stable potentiation is passed, it is unclear whether the magnitude of the potentiation at individual synapses is dependent on the level of Ca^{2+} or whether it is all-or-none.

Recent experiments add further complexity to this topic. It has been proposed that intermediate levels of NMDA receptor activation can actually inhibit the subsequent induction of LTP (Coan et al. 1989; Huang et al. 1992; Izumi et al. 1992). Indeed, even more surprising is the finding (Dudek and Bear 1992; Mulkey and Malenka 1992) that low-frequency stimulation (e.g., 1 Hz for 10 min) can actually induce a long-lasting depression that is dependent upon NMDA receptor activation and intracellular Ca^{2+}. This depression has not been reported when brief tetani of varying stimulus strength are delivered. In such cases, as the stimulus strength is increased, one sees posttetanic potentiation, short-term potentiation, and LTP (Malenka 1991). Thus, to obtain depression, the Ca^{2+} rise must apparently occur for a period of time.

SITE OF LTP EXPRESSION

While it is universally agreed that the induction of LTP requires the postsynaptic cell, the site at which the persistent change takes place has been extremely contentious. A number of approaches have been used to address the issue of whether the expression of LTP occurs pre- or postsynaptically. These include the measurement of glutamate overflow, paired-pulse facilitation, the relative change in NMDA and non-NMDA components of the EPSP, analysis of synaptic variability, quantal analysis, miniature EPSCs, and postsynaptic sensitivity to exogenous agonist. It is fair to conclude that each one of these approaches has resulted in seemingly conflicting data. We will limit our discussion to a few issues.

Paired-pulse Facilitation (PPF)

PPF is generally agreed to be of presynaptic origin and is modified by a large number of manipulations that alter transmitter release (e.g., posttetanic potentiation, changed Ca^{2+}/Mg^{2+} ratio, adenosine, phorbol esters, baclofen, 4–AP, theophylline). There is also general agreement that PPF is not altered during LTP (Gustafsson et al. 1988; McNaughton 1982; Muller and Lynch 1989; Manabe et al. 1993). This suggests that if LTP is presynaptic, then its mechanism must differ from that involved in all of the known presynaptic manipulations examined to date.

Relative Change in NMDA and Non-NMDA Component of the EPSP(C)

There has been much controversy on this topic. Two recent studies have reexamined this issue by designing experiments in which both components could be monitored simultaneously: one using field potentials and reduced extracellular Mg^{2+} (Asztely et al. 1992); the other using whole-cell recording at positive membrane potentials (Perkel and Nicoll 1993). While the results differ to some extent, the major conclusions were quite similar. When transmitter release is altered, the amplitude of the two components changes to the same extent. It is well established that there is an approximate 100-fold difference in the apparent K_D's for glutamate binding to NMDA and non-NMDA receptors, and it is generally thought that a single synaptic response results in near saturation of the NMDA receptors (Clements et al. 1992). The scaling of the two components with large changes in transmitter release supports the proposal that transmitter release at individual boutons is all-or-none, since changes in synaptic cleft concentration would be expected to affect primarily the non-NMDA synaptic component. On the other hand, with LTP the potentiation of the non-NMDA component is considerably greater than the NMDA component. These results, similar to the results with PPF, highlight the difference between LTP and manipulations known to change transmitter release. A presynaptic mechanism for LTP that could account for these data would involve an increase in glutamate release at a single bouton, as would be expected with increased vesicle filling.

Analysis of Synaptic Variability

Statistical analysis of synaptic variability can be useful in determining whether a change in synaptic strength is pre- or postsynaptic. Data have been presented to indicate that the mean^2/variance, a parameter related to quantal content, increases during LTP; this is consistent with a presynaptic mechanism (Bekkers and Stevens, 1990; Malinow and Tsien 1990). A number of known pre- and postsynaptic manipulations, which uniformly affects all synapses also cause the appropriate change in this value (Lupica et al. 1992; Malinow and Tsien 1990; Manabe et al. 1993). However, it has been argued that if LTP involved a nonuniform change in postsynaptic sensitivity, a reasonable possibility, the analysis of mean^2/variance could lead erroneously to a presynaptic interpretation (Faber and Korn 1991).

Quantal Release

There are now a number of studies that have used minimal extracellular stimulation (Foster and McNaughton 1991; Kullmann and Nicoll 1992; Larkman et al. 1992; Liao et al. 1992; Malinow and Tsien 1990) or paired recordings (Malinow 1991) to examine the effect of LTP on failures and separation of quantal peaks. The easiest parameter to measure with this approach is the incidence of failures, and there is unanimous agreement that the failure rate can decrease during LTP. This is classically interpreted as being due to an increase in release. In three recent studies (Kullmann and Nicoll 1992; Larkman et al. 1992; Liao et al. 1992), equally spaced peaks in the amplitude histogram were obtained in a subset of cells. The separation between the peaks often increased during LTP, a finding consistent with a postsynaptic change. All three studies suggested that both changes in quantal content and quantal size can occur during LTP, the relative contribution depending upon the initial probability of release.

One of the major problems associated with studies involving quantal analysis is the limited knowledge of the variability associated with each quantum. Recording of miniature EPSCs indicates a wide range in sizes that cannot be accounted for by electrotonic filtering (Bekkers et al. 1990; Manabe et al. 1992; Wyllie et al. 1994). A key issue is to understand the basis for this variability. A significant part of the variability could be due to different synapses having different numbers of non-NMDA receptors. In addition, there are at least two sources of variability that could arise at a single synapse. First, each quantum could contain different amounts of glutamate. For this mechanism to work, the concentration of released glutamate would have to be well below saturation for the non-NMDA receptor. Second, since it is estimated that only about 10–20 channels contribute to a quantum, one would expect considerable fluctuation based simply on the probability of channel opening to a constant concentration of glutamate (Hestrin 1992). An understanding of these basic properties of synaptic transmission (see Edwards 1991) is essential before a thorough quantal analysis can be achieved.

Another limitation to these studies is that a large number of responses are required to generate adequate amplitude histograms and yet stimulus rates above about 1 Hz cannot be used because responses run down. Furthermore, one is limited to at most 20 min of baseline recording, since the ability to generate LTP is lost due to "wash out" associated with whole-cell recording. Many more responses can be obtained after LTP;

however, the interpretation of the analysis highly depends upon the stationarity of the responses. This is particularly true for quantal size. If quantal size should vary at different times during LTP, this will tend to obscure any peaks that might otherwise exist. Thus, if the locus of expression were to shift during LTP, this would be difficult to detect with current approaches.

Miniature EPSCs

A number of the technical and interpretative problems with quantal analysis can be bypassed through recording miniature EPSCs. The classical interpretation is that a change in miniature EPSC (mEPSC) size reflects a postsynaptic change whereas a change in frequency reflects a presynaptic change. This approach, too, has limitations. Pyramidal cells receive thousands of excitatory synapses that will all release quanta spontaneously, and only a small percentage of synapses can be electrically stimulated to induce LTP. While a significant increase in the incidence of large mEPSCs occurs following the induction of LTP through electrical stimulation (Manabe et al. 1992), investigators have resorted to application of glutamate or NMDA to expose all synapses to the stimulus. Two studies involving agonist-induced potentiation have been carried out—one in cultured hippocampal neurons (Malgaroli and Tsien 1992), the other in hippocampal slices (Manabe et al. 1992)—and essentially opposite results were obtained. In the slice preparation, NMDA application caused a dramatic increase in the size of mEPSCs with only minimal changes in recorded frequency. In culture, glutamate application caused a marked increase in mEPSC frequency, and in only 2 out of 19 cases was there an increase in size of the mEPSCs. The only obvious difference in these two studies is the preparation. Perhaps cultured pyramidal cells are less likely to express the machinery required for the increase in mEPSC amplitude seen in the slice. The results with NMDA application in the slice preparation have been repeated by activating voltage-sensitive Ca^{2+} channels (Wyllie et al. 1994). The potentiation following this manipulation is also associated with a large increase in mEPSC amplitude. As discussed earlier, the relationship between these manipulations and LTP is still unresolved, and it is quite possible that synaptic stimulation does more than simply activate NMDA receptors.

Postsynaptic Sensitivity to Exogenous Agonist

If one were to demonstrate unambiguously that following LTP, the response to exogenously applied non-NMDA receptor agonist increased, only one explanation is possible: a postsynaptic modification has occurred. There are, however, a number of reasons why such a change might go undetected. As discussed above, only a portion of the synapses in a region will undergo tetanus-induced LTP. Therefore, much of the response to exogenous agonist would result from synapses that did not undergo LTP. An additional complication is the presence of extrasynaptic receptors, which are known to exist on pyramidal cells and would also not undergo LTP. Despite these limitations, it has been reported that responses to AMPA are increased following tetanus-induced LTP (Davies et al. 1989). This increase developed slowly after about 20 min. Since the investigators were able to detect a change late but not early, they concluded that LTP is initially expressed presynaptically and then postsynaptically. We have been unable to detect any change in AMPA sensitivity up to 60 min following a tetanus, despite the fact that synapses in the vicinity have undergone LTP (P. Renner and R.A. Nicoll, unpublished observations). In an attempt to maximize the number of receptors involved we have examined responses to AMPA application following the application of NMDA and voltage pulses (Wyllie et al. 1994). In this situation, a clear increase in sensitivity can be recorded, which develops within a few minutes after the application of NMDA. The same caution discussed in the section on mEPSCs also applies here, i.e., it is not entirely clear whether the potentiation evoked by NMDA is identical to LTP. These studies, as well as many others, would benefit immensely from the discovery of a manipulation that would induce LTP in all excitatory synapses in the slice.

In reviewing the data on the site of expression of LTP, it is extremely difficult to reach a satisfactory consensus. Studies involving PPF and the differential modulation of the dual component EPSP(C) indicate that any presynaptic mechanism for LTP must differ from other well-characterized presynaptic mechanisms. The increase in mEPSC amplitudes and in AMPA responses clearly favor a postsynaptic component. On the other hand, quantal analysis (especially analysis of failures), measurement of mEPSC frequency, and analysis of synaptic variability each have pointed to presynaptic mechanisms. All of these studies have technical and/or interpretative constraints and therefore do not provide conclusive proof for one mechanism over the other. Perhaps the most compelling evidence for a presynaptic change associated with LTP, and therefore the existence of a retrograde factor, would be the demonstration that a protein that is present exclusively in the presynaptic terminal is modified in an APV-sensitive manner following a tetanus. Such is apparently the case for GAP–43, a presynaptic protein that shows an APV-sensitive increase in phosphorylation following tetanus-induced LTP (Gianotti et al. 1992; Nelson et al. 1989).

MECHANISM OF LTP EXPRESSION

Maintaining the Enhancement

Much discussion has gone into possible molecular processes that could account for a relatively persistent change in function. It is generally agreed that kinases, including protein kinase C, Ca^{2+}/calmodulin-dependent kinase II (CAM kinase II), and tyrosine kinase may be required for LTP. Transient activation of a kinase would not necessarily produce a sustained potentiation. Various proposals have been made to provide sustained kinase activity. First, it has been well established that proteolytic cleavage of protein kinase C in some systems can create a constitutively active molecule. Second, the enzyme CAM kinase II, which is present in high concentrations in the postsynaptic density, undergoes a Ca^{2+}-dependent autophosphorylation, which then converts the enzyme into a constitutively active Ca^{2+}-independent kinase. Whether, in fact, LTP expression is dependent upon the continued action of a protein kinase is very controversial. Another possible mechanism involves proteolytic cleavage of nonkinase proteins. For instance, proteolytic cleavage of a protein might cause a persistent change in ion channel function. Finally, relatively long-lasting changes can be produced by ADP ribosylations. In many of these situations, the duration of the change will ultimately be limited by the turnover of the protein unless a multimolecular structure is created in which subunits can be replaced without overall loss of function by the structure. CAM kinase II, which is multimeric, could well function in such a manner (see Kennedy, this volume).

Retrograde Factors

It has been repeatedly stressed that if the expression of LTP is presynaptic, then there must be some retrograde signal from the postsynaptic spine to the presynaptic terminal. While it has been assumed that such a factor would be diffusible, it could, in theory, be mechanical. The linkage of the pre- and postsynaptic membranes is, in fact, very tight and survives homogenization, and it is possible that a postsynaptic change could be relayed mechanically to the presynaptic membrane (J. Lisman, pers. comm.). In terms of diffusible messengers, nitric oxide (NO) is close to the ideal molecule, in that it freely crosses cell membranes and has a very short half life. Four laboratories independently reported that inhibitors of NO synthase could block LTP (Böhme et al. 1991; Bon et al. 1992; Haley et al. 1992; O'Dell et al. 1991; Schuman and Madison 1991). While these studies are in general agreement, there are a number of discrepancies. The degree of the blockade varied greatly in the different studies. In addition, the effectiveness of the L–N^G nitro arginine inhibition ranged over three orders of magnitude. Finally, L–N^G-monomethylarginine had little effect in one study (Bon et al. 1992) but was effective in another (Schuman and Madison 1991). The possibility that NO is the messenger that relays the LTP signal from the postsynaptic cell is of fundamental importance in studying the expression of LTP. If LTP is entirely dependent on NO, then all of the machinery in the postsynaptic spine is simply involved in converting a Ca^{2+} rise into an NO rise. Thus, NO would be the key to pursuing the trail of LTP expression. The question "What is the mechanism underlying LTP expression?" becomes equivalent to the question "What is the mechanism underlying the action of NO on these synapses?" Two signaling pathways are known to be involved in the action of NO. The most studied pathway is the activation of guanylyl cyclase with formation of cGMP and the other is an ADP-ribosylation. Some controversy exists over which of these pathways may be involved.

CONCLUSION

In reviewing the field of LTP, one is struck by the enormous amount of controversy that exists. Why is this the case? A combination of factors may well be responsible.

First, LTP is undoubtedly a very complex phenomenon and will not be adequately explained until the fundamental properties of synaptic transmission are understood. Second, the magnitude and ability to generate LTP is variable from experiment to experiment. This variability becomes very important when comparisons must be made between groups of slices. Third, since LTP is widely recognized as an extremely valuable model for one of the most important functions of the brain, it has attracted a very large number of investigators. While this has the disadvantage that some confusion may arise in the short run, advantages also exist. Ideally, key experiments should be repeated with little delay by others in order for consensus to develop more rapidly.

REFERENCES

Aniksztejn, L., and Y. Ben-Ari. 1991. Novel form of long-term potentiation produced by a K^+ channel blocker in the hippocampus. *Nature* **349**:67–69.

Aniksztejn, L., S. Otani, and Y. Ben-Ari. 1992. Quisqualate metabotropic receptors modulate NMDA currents and facilitate induction of long-term potentiation through protein kinase C. *Eur. J. Neurosci.* **4**:500–505.

Anwyl, R. 1989. Protein kinase C and long-term potentiation in the hippocampus. *Trends Pharmacol. Sci.* **10**:236–239.

Asztely, F., E. Hanse, H. Wigstrom, and G. Gustafsson. 1991. Synaptic potentiation in the hippocampal CA1 region induced by application of N-methyl-D-aspartate. *Brain Res.* **558**:153–156.

Asztely, F., H. Wigström, and B. Gustafsson. 1992. The relative contribution of NMDA receptor channels in the expression of long-term potentiation in the hippocampal CA1 region. *Eur. J. Neurosci.* **4**:681–690.

Baskys, A., and R.C. Malenka. 1991. Agonists at metabotropic glutamate receptors presynaptically inhibit EPSCs in neonatal rat hippocampus. *J. Physiol.* **444**:687–701.

Bekkers, J.M., G.B. Richerson, and C.F. Stevens. 1990. Origin of variability in quantal size in cultured hippocampal neurons and hippocampal slices. *Proc. Natl. Acad. Sci. USA* **87**:5359–5362.

Bekkers, J.M., and C.F. Stevens. 1990. Presynaptic mechanism for long-term potentiation in the hippocampus. *Nature* **346**:724–729.

Bliss, T.V.P., and M.A. Lynch. 1988. Long-term potentiation of synaptic transmission in the hippocampus: Properties and mechanisms. In: Long-Term Potentiation: From Biophysics to Behavior, ed. P.W. Landfield and S.A. Deadwyler, pp. 3–72. New York: Alan R. Liss.

Böhme, G.A., C. Bon, J.-M. Stutzmann, A. Doble, and J.C. Blanchard. 1991. Possible involvement of nitric oxide in long-term potentiation. *Eur. J. Pharmacol.* **199**:379–381.

Bon, C., G.A. Böhme, A. Doble, J.-M. Stutzmann, and J.-C. Blanchard. 1992. A role for nitric oxide in long-term potentiation. *Eur. J. Neurosci.* **4**:420–424.

Bortolotto, Z.A., and G.L. Collingridge. 1992. Activation of glutamate metabotropic receptors induces long-term potentiation. *Eur. J. Pharmacol.* **214**:297–298.

Clements, J.D., R.A.J. Lester, G. Tong, C.E. Jahr, and G.L. Westbrook. 1992. The time course of glutamate in the synaptic cleft. *Science*: **258**:1498–1501.

Coan, E.J., A.J. Irving, and G.L. Collingridge. 1989. Low-frequency activation of the NMDA receptor system can prevent the induction of LTP. *Neurosci. Lett.* **105**:205–210.

Collingridge, G.L., S.J. Kehl, and H. McLennan. 1983. Excitatory amino acids in synaptic transmission in the Schaeffer collateral-commissural pathway of the rat hippocampus. *J. Physiol.* **334**:33–46.

Collingridge, G.L., and W. Singer. 1990. Excitatory amino acid receptors and synaptic plasticity. *Trends Pharmacol. Sci.* **11**:290–296.

Davies, S.N., R.A.J. Lester, K.G. Reymann, and G.L. Collingridge. 1989. Temporally distinct pre- and postsynaptic mechanisms maintain long-term potentiation. *Nature* **338**:500–503.

Dudek, S.M., and M.F. Bear. 1992. Homosynaptic long-term depression in area CA1 of the hippocampus and effects of N-methyl-D-aspartate receptor blockade. *Proc. Natl. Acad. Sci. USA* **89**:4363–4367.

Edwards, F. 1991. LTP is a long term problem. *Nature* **350**:271–272.

Faber, D.S., and H. Korn. 1991. Applicability of the coefficient of variation method for analyzing synaptic plasticity. *Biophys. J.* **60**:1288–1294.

Field, A.C., S.J. Redman, and C. Stricker. 1992. NMDA receptor activation at synapses on CA1 neurons is not necessary for the induction of LTP. *Soc. Neurosci. Abstr.* **18**:1347.

Foster, T.C., and B.L. McNaughton. 1991. Long-term enhancement of CA1 synaptic transmission is due to increased quantal size, not quantal content. *Hippocampus* **1**:79–91 .

Gianotti, C., M.G. Nunzi, W.H. Gispen, and R. Corradetti. 1992. Phosphorylation of the presynaptic protein B–50 (GAP–43) is increased during electrically induced long-term potentiation. *Neuron* **8**:843–848.

Grover, L.M., and T.J. Teyler. 1990. Two components of long-term potentiation induced by different patterns of afferent activation. *Nature* **347**:477–479.

Grover, L.M., and T.J. Teyler. 1992. N-methyl-D-aspartate receptor independent long-term potentiation in area CA1 of rat hippocampus: Input specific induction and preclusion in a nontetanized pathway. *Neurosci.* **49**:7–11.

Gustafsson, B., F. Asztely, E. Hanse, and H. Wigström. 1989. Onset characteristics of long-term potentiation in the guinea-pig hippocampal CA1 region *in vitro*. *Eur. J. Neurosci.* **1**:382–394.

Gustafsson, B., Y.-Y. Huang, and H. Wigström. 1988. Phorbol ester-induced synaptic potentiation differs from long-term potentiation in the guinea pig hippocampus *in vitro*. *Neurosci. Lett.* **85**:77–81.

Gustafsson, B., and H. Wigström. 1988. Physiological mechanisms underlying long-term potentiation. *Trends Neurosci.* **11**:156–162.

Gustafsson, B., H. Wigström, W.C. Abraham, and Y.-Y. Huang. 1987. Long-term potentiation in the hippocampus using depolarizing current pulses as the conditioning stimulus to single volley synaptic potentials. *J. Neurosci.* **7**:774–780.

Haley, J.E., G.L. Wilcox, and P.F. Chapman. 1992. The role of nitric oxide in hippocampal long-term potentiation. *Neuron* **8**:211–216.

Hanse, E., and B. Gustafsson. 1992. Postsynaptic, but not presynaptic, activity controls the early time course of long-term potentiation in the dentate gyrus. *J. Neurosci.* **12**:3226–3240.

Harvey, J., and G.L. Collingridge. 1992. Thapsigargin blocks the induction of long-term potentiation in rat hippocampal slices. *Neurosci. Lett.* **139**:197–200.

Hestrin, S. 1992. Activation and desensitization of glutamate-activated channels mediating fast excitatory synaptic currents in the visual cortex. *Neuron* **9**:991–999.

Huang, Y.-Y., A. Colino, D.K. Selig, and R.C. Malenka. 1992. The influence of prior synaptic activity on the induction of long-term potentiation. *Science* **255**:730–733.

Huang, Y.-Y., and R.C. Malenka. 1993. Examination of TEA-induced synaptic enhancement in area CA1 of the hippocampus: The role of voltage-dependent Ca^{2+} channels in the induction of LTP. *J. Neurosci.* **13**:568–576.

Izumi, Y., D.B. Clifford, and C.F. Zorumski. 1992. Inhibition of long-term potentiation by NMDA-mediated nitric oxide release. *Science* **257**:1273–1276.

Katz, B., and R. Miledi. 1967. A study of synaptic transmission in the absence of nerve impulses. *J. Physiol.* **192**:407–436.

Kauer, J.A., R.C. Malenka, and R.A. Nicoll. 1988a. NMDA application potentiates synaptic transmission in the hippocampus. *Nature* **334**:250–252.

Kauer, J.A., R.C. Malenka, and R.A. Nicoll. 1988b. A persistent postsynaptic modification mediates long-term potentiation in the hippocampus. *Neuron* **1**:911–917.

Kullmann, D.M., and R.A. Nicoll. 1992. Long-term potentiation is associated with increases in both quantal content and quantal amplitude. *Nature* **357**:240–244.

Kullmann, D.M., D.J. Perkel, T. Manabe, and R.A. Nicoll. 1992. Calcium entry via postsynaptic voltage-sensitive calcium channels can transiently potentiate excitatory synaptic transmission in the hippocampus. *Neuron* **9**:1175–1183.

Larkman, A., T. Hannay, K. Stratford, and J. Jack. 1992. Presynaptic release probability influences the locus of long-term potentiation. *Nature* **360**:70–73.

Liao, D., A. Jones, and R. Malinow. 1992. Direct measurement of quantal changes underlying long-term potentiation in CA1 hippocampus. *Neuron* **9**:1089–1097.

Linden, D.J., and J.A. Connor. 1991. Participation of postsynaptic PKC in cerebellar long-term depression in culture. *Science* **254**:1656–1659.

Linden, D.J., and A. Routtenberg. 1989. Role of protein kinase C in long-term potentiation: A testable model. *Brain Res. Rev.* **14**:279–296.

Lupica, C.R., W.R. Proctor, and T.V. Dunwiddie. 1992. Presynaptic inhibition of excitatory synaptic transmission by adenosine in rat hippocampus: Analysis of unitary EPSP. Variance measured by whole-cell recording. *J. Neurosci.* **12**:3753–3764.

Lynch, G., J. Larson, S. Kelso, G. Barrionuevo, and F. Schottler. 1983. Intracellular injections of EGTA block induction of hippocampal long-term potentiation. *Nature* **305**:719–721.

Madison, D.V., R.C. Malenka, and R.A. Nicoll. 1991. Mechanisms underlying long-term potentiation of synaptic transmission. *Ann. Rev. Neurosci.* **14**:379–397.

Malenka, R.C. 1991. Postsynaptic factors control the duration of synaptic enhancement in area CA1 of the hippocampus. *Neuron* **6**:53–60.

Malenka, R.C., J.A. Kauer, R.J. Zucker, and R.A. Nicoll. 1988. Postsynaptic calcium is sufficient for potentiation of hippocampal synaptic transmission. *Science* **242**:81–84.

Malenka, R.C., B. Lancaster, and R.S. Zucker. 1992. Temporal limits on the rise in postsynaptic calcium required for long-term potentiation. *Neuron* **9**:121–128.

Malenka, R.C., D.V. Madison, and R.A. Nicoll. 1986. Potentiation of synaptic transmission in the hippocampus by phorbol esters. *Nature* **321**:695–697.

Malgaroli, A., and R.W. Tsien. 1992. Glutamate-induced long-term potentiation of the frequency of miniature synaptic currents in cultured hippocampal neurons. *Nature* **357**:134–139.

Malinow, R. 1991. Transmission between pairs of hippocampal slice neurons: Quantal levels, oscillations and LTP. *Science* **252**:722–724.

Malinow, R., H. Schulman, and R.W. Tsien. 1989. Inhibition of postsynaptic PKC or CaMKII blocks induction but not expression of LTP. *Science* **245**:862–866.

Malinow, R., and R.W. Tsien. 1990. Presynaptic enhancement shown by whole-cell recordings of long-term potentiation in hippocampal slices. *Nature* **346**:177–180.

Manabe, T., D.J.A. Wyllie, D.J. Perkel, and R.A. Nicoll. 1993. Modulation of synaptic transmission and long-term potentiation: Effects on paired-pulse facilitation and EPSC variance in the CA1 region of the hippocampus. *J. Neurophysiol.* **70:**1451–1459.

Manabe, T., P. Renner, and R.A. Nicoll. 1992. Postsynaptic contribution to long-term potentiation revealed by the analysis of miniature synaptic currents. *Nature* **355**:50–55.

McGuinness, N., R. Anwyl, and M. Rowan. 1991. The effects of trans-ACPD on long-term potentiation in the rat hippocampal slice. *NeuroReport* **2**:688–690.

McNaughton, B.L. 1982. Long-term synaptic enhancement and short-term potentiation in rat fascia dentata act through different mechanisms. *J. Physiol.* **324**:249–262.

Mulkey, R.M., and R.C. Malenka. 1992. Mechanisms underlying induction of homosynaptic long-term depression in area CA1 of the hippocampus. *Neuron* **9**:967–975.

Muller, D., and G. Lynch. 1989. Evidence that changes in presynaptic calcium currents are not responsible for long-term potentiation in hippocampus. *Brain Res.* **479**:290–299.

Nelson, R.B., D.J. Linden, and A. Routtenberg. 1989. Phospho-proteins localized to presynaptic terminal linked to persistence of long-term potentiation (LTP): Quantitative analysis of two-dimensional gels. *Brain Res.* **497**:30–42.

Obenaus, A., I. Mody, and K.G. Bainbridge. 1989. Dantrolene-Na (Dantrium) blocks induction of long-term potentiation in hippocampal slices. *Neurosci. Lett.* **98**:172–178.

O'Dell, T.J., R.D. Hawkins, E.R. Kandel, and O. Arancio. 1991. Tests of the roles of two diffusible substances in long-term potentiation: Evidence for nitric oxide as a possible early retrograde messenger. *Proc. Natl. Acad. Sci. USA* **88**:11285–11289.

Perkel, D.J., and R.A. Nicoll. 1993. Evidence for all-or-none regulation of neurotransmitter release: Implications for long-term potentiation. *J. Physiol.* **471:**481–500.

Perkel, D.J., J.J. Petrozzino, R.A. Nicoll, and J.A. Connor. 1993. The role of Ca^{2+} entry via synaptically activated NMDA receptors in the induction of long-term potentiation. *Neuron* **11:**817–823.

Reymann, K.G., H.K. Matthies, V. Frey, V.S. Vorobyev, and H. Matthies. 1986. Calcium-induced long-term potentiation in the hippocampal slice: Characterization of the time course and conditions. *Brain Res. Bull.* **17**:291–296.

Schuman, E.M., and D.V. Madison. 1991. A requirement for the intercellular messenger nitric oxide in long-term potentiation. *Science* **254**:1503–1506.

Thibault, O., M. Joly, D. Muller, F. Schottler, S. Dudek, and G. Lynch. 1989. Long-lasting physiological effects of bath applied N-methyl-D-aspartate. *Brain Res.* **476**:170–173.

Turner, R.W., K.G. Bainbridge, and J.J. Miller. 1982. Calcium-induced long-term potentiation in the hippocampus. *Neurosci.* **7**:1411–1416.

Wang, J.-H., and D.-P. Feng. 1992. Postsynaptic protein kinase C essential to induction and maintenance of long-term potentiation in the hippocampal CA1 region. *Proc. Natl. Acad. Sci. USA* **89**:2576–2580.

Wyllie, J.A., T. Manabe, and R.A. Nicoll. 1994. A rise in postsynaptic Ca^{2+} potentiates miniature excitatory postsynaptic currents and AMPA responses in hippocampal neurons. *Neuron* **12:**127–138.

Xu, Y.Z., and K. Krnjevic. 1990. Induction of long-term potentiation in isolated slices of Sprague-Dawley rat hippocampus is not blocked by dantrolene sodium. *J. Physiol.* **426**:50.

Zheng, F., and J.P. Gallagher. 1992. Metabotropic glutamate receptors are required for the induction of long-term potentiation. *Neuron* **9**:163–172.

14

Current Molecular Models for Long-term Synaptic Plasticity

M.B. KENNEDY
Division of Biology 216–76, California Institute of Technology,
Pasadena, CA 91125, U.S.A.

ABSTRACT

In this chapter, I discuss molecular mechanisms for induction and maintenance of long-term potentiation at synapses of the Schaeffer collateral pathway in area CA1 of the hippocampus, focusing first on general theoretical issues. Next I discuss a few recently proposed molecular models that I believe are still consistent with the abundance of physiological and biochemical data concerning regulation of this class of synapses.

DEFINITIONS

Associative long-term potentiation in area CA1 of the hippocampus (hereafter LTP) is defined as a long-lasting increase in the size of postsynaptic potentials (currents) at excitatory synapses produced by simultaneous brief strong depolarization of the postsynaptic dendrite and release of glutamate from presynaptic terminals (Madison et al. 1991). In discussions about molecular mechanisms underlying LTP, conceptual difficulties sometimes arise from the ambiguity inherent in the phrase "long-lasting." Over the last few years, most investigators have agreed to define LTP as a synaptic enhancement that lasts longer than 20 to 30 minutes after the inducing stimulus. However, it seems increasingly likely that several distinct molecular events, all triggered by the same stimulus, may produce changes in synaptic transmission that persist for varying lengths of time. Thus LTP, as measured by physiologists, may consist of a set of related molecular events, each with its own distinct kinetics of onset and decay. We may eventually need more precise terms and definitions of LTP that take into account different parallel mechanisms. More precise terms could include, for example, phase 1 LTP (mechanisms functioning after the first 30 minutes), stabilized LTP (mechanisms functioning after the first few hours), structural LTP (mechanisms

Cellular and Molecular Mechanisms Underlying Higher Neural Functions
Edited by A.I. Selverston and P. Ascher

functioning after several days of reinforcement in the animal), etc. It is already clear that phase 1 LTP does not require protein synthesis or new gene expression, and may itself result from a composite of several posttranslational modifications occurring both pre- and postsynaptically. Stabilized LTP may require new protein synthesis (cf., however, Role et al., this volume). Structural LTP seems almost certain to require both protein synthesis and new gene expression; however, the newly expressed and synthesized proteins may simply replenish precursor proteins that have been used to assemble new or larger synaptic structures. In this chapter, I am primarily concerned with phase 1 LTP.

LINEAR REGULATORY PATHWAYS VS. NETWORKS

As the molecular mechanisms of complex biological control systems, including the cell cycle, developmental morphogenesis, and synaptic transmission, are studied in greater detail, our thinking about regulatory pathways is undergoing a subtle paradigm shift. One previous idealized linear paradigm includes the following sequence. Activation of a metabotropic receptor catalyzes exchange of GTP for GDP on a G-protein. The activated G-protein dissociates and its α subunit binds to and activates adenylate cyclase. The cyclase produces cAMP, which diffuses away and activates a protein kinase. The protein kinase phosphorylates one or maybe two nearby molecules, producing a physiologically measurable change in the behavior of the cell. In this paradigm, the occurrence of the measurable physiological change depends upon the integrity of the linear sequence from receptor to phosphorylated protein. The rate constant of the physiological change is determined by the limiting rate in the linear regulatory sequence. Finally, in the basal state the regulatory pathway is thought of as off or "silent" until it is activated by the presence of a hormone at the beginning of the linear sequence.

Several years ago, it was recognized that modulatory biochemical interactions occur at various points between the elements of the three major idealized linear regulatory pathways: the cAMP pathway, the phosphatidylinositol trisphosphate pathway, and the Ca^{2+} pathway. For example, some adenylate cyclase isozymes can be activated by Ca^{2+}/calmodulin as well as by G-proteins (Rosenberg and Storm 1987). These interactions have been referred to as cross-talk and have usually been conceptualized as superimpositions upon still essentially linear pathways (Nishizuka 1992). The presence of cross-talk implies that the system will sometimes behave nonlinearly; the effect of two transmitters or hormones activating distinct regulatory pathways will not necessarily be the sum of the effects of each acting alone.

More recently, a variety of experimental findings have begun to alter fundamentally our thinking about regulatory paradigms. It seems likely that paradigms involving networks in which the state of any one element is always determined by the states of several other interacting elements will be more accurate for describing the workings of regulatory machinery. This appears to be true for regulation of the cell cycle. A large number of external agents and internal protein kinases can influence the onset of mitosis (O'Farrell 1992). The complexity of interactions among these agents suggests that there are many routes by which a cell can be triggered into mitosis, and the regulatory apparatus appears to respond continually to a wide variety of factors in the external environment. Similarly, many different regulatory molecules have been implicated in the induction of LTP, as I will discuss later.

Several distinctive features of network paradigms can have profound effects upon the design and interpretation of experiments. For example, the existence of a network of constantly interacting regulatory molecules necessitates a different conception of the basal state. Second messenger synthesizing enzymes and protein kinases must exist in a partially activated steady state that continually adjusts to changing influences from various parts of the network. Two examples from the literature on synaptic regulation suggest that this is the case in neurons. In sensory presynaptic terminals of the mollusc, *Aplysia*, the cAMP-dependent protein kinase phosphorylates and regulates a K^+ channel that indirectly controls the amount of transmitter release (Shuster et al. 1985). Short-term facilitation of transmitter release from these synapses produces behavioral sensitization. Repeated sensitizing stimuli produce a long-lasting facilitation of release. The long-lasting facilitation results from a persistent reduction in the number of inhibitory regulatory subunits for the cAMP-dependent protein kinase; the effect is a higher steady-state level of cAMP-dependent protein kinase activity (Greenberg et al. 1987). This shift can be thought of as a long-lasting adjustment in the equilibrium steady state of the regulatory network controlling the cAMP-dependent protein kinase. In hippocampal neurons, type II CaM kinase is maintained in a partially activated steady state. Ten to thirty percent of the kinase is activated at basal Ca^{2+} concentration by autophosphorylation of a regulatory threonine residue (Kennedy et al. 1990; Molloy and Kennedy 1991; Ocorr and Schulman 1991; Patton et al. 1993). The steady-state level of autophosphorylation is maintained by a balance between autophosphorylation and dephosphorylation; however, the mode of regulation of the equilibrium level is not yet known. Since it has generally been assumed in the past that protein kinases are off most of the time, and are turned on by relevant physiological stimuli, investigators have designed experiments to determine which stimuli produce large increases in kinase activity. However, network paradigms imply, instead, that rather subtle changes in steady-state levels of kinase activity may be physiologically important, because they result in adjustments of steady-state activities of other proteins throughout the network.

Network models also complicate the interpretation of genetic knockout experiments. Because complex regulatory networks can include parallel, redundant pathways, removal of one element may produce only variable or incomplete loss of regulation. Upon removal of a single element, regulation may occur normally under some conditions but be less "robust"; instabilities may appear in the face of experimental conditions that exceed narrow laboratory limits. Furthermore, sequential ordering of regulatory reactions through classical genetic techniques may not be possible.

Finally, the behavior of highly nonlinear regulatory networks will not be easily predicted by intuition. We will increasingly find ourselves turning to appropriate mathematical simulations of interacting biochemical reactions to aid in the design and interpretation of experiments.

MOLECULAR MODELS FOR INDUCTION OF LTP

Several specific molecular models have been proposed for induction of LTP, some of which are supported by experiments. Most investigators now agree that a first, critical step in the induction of LTP is activation of postsynaptic NMDA-type glutamate receptors (see Nicoll, this volume). The properties of the NMDA receptor fully explain the need for simultaneous postsynaptic depolarization and presynaptic release of glutamate during induction. Activation of the NMDA receptor allows influx of Ca^{2+} ion into the postsynaptic compartment and this influx has been shown to be a critical event for induction (cf. Nicoll, this volume).

The steps following Ca^{2+} influx are far less clear. Pharmacological inhibition of at least four different second messenger pathways has been reported to attenuate LTP induction severely. Perfusion of postsynaptic neurons with specific peptide inhibitors of the C kinase and of CaM kinase II prior to tetanic stimulation eliminates LTP, whereas perfusion with similar control peptides does not interfere with induction (Malinow et al. 1989). This experiment suggests that both C kinase and CaM kinase II must be active for induction to occur. An involvement of CaM kinase II in induction of LTP is also supported by a report of seriously compromised LTP in the hippocampi of mice bearing a homozygous null mutation in the neuron-specific α subunit of CaM kinase II (Silva et al. 1992; for a review, see Morris and Kennedy 1992). Four different groups have reported that application of inhibitors of the enzyme nitric oxide synthase to hippocampal slices severely attenuates induction of LTP (Böhme et al. 1991; Haley et al. 1992; O'Dell et al. 1991a; Schuman and Madison 1991). Two of these groups showed that postsynaptic application was sufficient to inhibit induction, implicating NO as a diffusible retrograde messenger (O'Dell et al. 1991a; Schuman and Madison 1991). Finally, inhibitors of tyrosine kinases, as well as genetic knockout of the *fyn* tyrosine kinase, have been reported to interfere with induction (O'Dell et al. 1991b; Grant et al. 1992). This multiplicity of inhibitory effects suggests that induction of LTP depends upon the integrity of a network of highly interdependent regulatory systems.

Although there is agreement that the initial induction of LTP occurs postsynaptically, physiological experiments have not yet identified, with reasonable certainty, whether the molecular changes that underlie maintenance of LTP occur presynaptically, postsynaptically, or in both places (see Nicoll, this volume). Below I divide the discussion of current models into those that deal with postsynaptic expression of LTP and those that deal with presynaptic expression.

Postsynaptic Mechanisms

Two groups of investigators have measured an increase in the size of postsynaptic EPSPs after induction of LTP (Kauer et al. 1988; Muller et al. 1988; Davies et al. 1989). In their experiments, two of the groups showed via pharmacological methods that the increase was confined to EPSPs carried by quisqualate/AMPA-type glutamate receptors (Q/K receptors); whereas EPSPs carried by NMDA-receptors were not increased (Kauer et al. 1988; Muller et al. 1988). Thus, they postulated that LTP reflects a specific increase in the response of postsynaptic Q/K receptors without a change in transmitter release. The increase in the size of the EPSP could be produced either by an increase in the number or sensitivity of the Q/K receptors, or by an increase in the size of the current flowing through each receptor. One simple possibility is that glutamate receptor function can be altered by phosphorylation of receptor subunits. Because inhibition of either C kinase or CaM kinase II inhibits induction, a logical hypothesis is that one or both of these protein kinases phosphorylates Q/K receptors, thereby enhancing the response to glutamate. However, no one has yet reported regulation of glutamate receptor function by C kinase or CaM kinase II. Surprisingly, two groups have shown that phosphorylation by the cAMP-dependent protein kinase can upregulate Q/K receptor function (Greengard et al. 1991; Wang et al. 1991) by increasing the frequency and duration of channel open times (Greengard et al. 1991). This finding is particularly curious because only one glutamate receptor subunit termed GluR6 (or β2) contains a clear cAMP-kinase consensus substrate sequence (RRQSV) in a region expected to be cytoplasmic. In contrast, subunits GluR1–7 (α1–α4 and β1–β3) all contain one or more potential consensus phosphorylation sites for CaM kinase II (R–X–X–S/T). Thus, the relevance for LTP of the regulation of glutamate receptor function by the cAMP system is not yet clear.

An alternative mechanism for controlling glutamate receptor function has emerged from the work of the Heinemann and Seeburg laboratories and collaborators (reviewed by Seeburg, this volume). Introduction of new combinations of receptor subunits as well as alternatively spliced or RNA-edited variants of particular subunits could alter glutamate receptor kinetics and selectivity. This process seems likely to require at least new protein synthesis, if not gene expression, and so may be involved in the later phases of LTP.

Presynaptic Mechanisms

Recent quantal analyses of potentiated Schaeffer collateral synapses in area CA1 have suggested that most, if not all, of the persistent synaptic enhancement following induction of LTP is accounted for by an increased release of transmitter, although the interpretation of these experiments has been questioned (Edwards 1991). (For a discussion of the physiological issues, see Nicoll, this volume, as well as Edwards et al., this volume.) The possibility of a presynaptic mechanism for expression and maintenance of LTP implies that a retrograde messenger generated postsynaptically by a calcium-dependent process must carry information to the presynaptic terminal during induction.

The small molecule nitric oxide (NO), identified as the "endothelial-derived relaxing factor" in 1987 (Palmer et al. 1987), has emerged as a strong candidate for a retrograde messenger. NO is released from arginine by a calcium-dependent enzyme. Two research groups have found that extracellular application or intracellular injection into postsynaptic neurons of two arginine derivatives that are specific inhibitors of NO synthase inhibit the induction of LTP (O'Dell, et al. 1991a; Schuman and Madison 1991). The inhibition is reversed by addition of excess L-arginine to compete with the inhibitors (Böhme et al. 1991; Haley et al. 1992; O'Dell et al. 1991a; Schuman and Madison 1991). Application of an inactive arginine derivative has no effect. Furthermore, bath-applied hemoglobin, which binds NO in the extracellular space, also blocks induction of LTP, implying that NO may travel from the postsynaptic site to presynaptic terminals during induction of LTP. The effects of these pharmacological agents appeared potent and specific in all four published articles; nevertheless, other research groups have not been able to repeat the results, suggesting that undetermined factors might influence the importance of the NO pathway versus other possible pathways of induction (see Edwards et al., this volume). Another remaining question is whether C kinase, CaM kinase II (Malinow et al. 1989), or the *fyn* tyrosine kinase (Grant et al. 1992) affect LTP induction through the NO induction pathway or through entirely different mechanisms. Both C kinase and CaM kinase II can phosphorylate the brain form of NO synthase; however, no regulatory effect of phosphorylation by either kinase has yet been reported (Bredt et al. 1992).

To alter transmitter release, the retrograde messenger must interact with a regulatory component of the release apparatus (see Südhof, this volume). Haley et al. (1992) reported that application of dibutyryl cGMP to hippocampal slices together with inhibitors of NO synthase partially reversed the effects of the inhibitors, suggesting that a target of NO in neurons may be guanylate cyclase as it is in endothelial cells. In contrast, Schuman et al. (1992) have proposed that ADP ribosyl transferase, a target of NO in platelets, might also be the NO target in the hippocampus. Three different inhibitors of ADP ribosyl transferase are all effective inhibitors of LTP induction. When one of the inhibitors was applied intracellularly through an electrode into a postsynaptic neuron, it did not block LTP induction in synapses on that neuron. Thus the externally applied inhibitors may be acting on an ADP ribosyl transferase in the presynaptic terminal.

THE FUTURE

Many molecular components involved in induction and maintenance of LTP have been identified; however, the remaining inability to construct a coherent molecular model for LTP implies that more characters await discovery. As in the past, progress seems likely to come from both pharmacological and physiological experiments designed to pinpoint key processes as well as from structural work on the major organelles of CNS synapses. In addition, mathematical simulations of interacting biochemical regulatory networks will play an increasingly important role in organizing our thinking about molecular processes underlying LTP.

REFERENCES

Böhme, G.A., C. Bon, J.-M. Stutzman, A. Doble, and J.C. Blanchard. 1991. Possible involvement of nitric oxide in long-term potentiation. *Eur. J. Pharmacol.* **199**:379–381.

Bredt, D.S., C.D. Ferris, and S.H. Snyder. 1992. Nitric-oxide synthase regulatory sites; Phosphorylation by cyclic AMP-dependent protein-kinase, protein-kinase-C, and calcium calmodulin protein-kinase—Identification of flavin and calmodulin binding sites. *J. Biol. Chem.* **267**:976–981.

Davies, S.N., R.A. Lester, K.G. Reymann, and G.L. Collingridge. 1989. Temporally distinct pre- and postsynaptic mechanisms maintain long-term potentiation. *Nature* **338**:500–503.

Edwards, F. 1991. LTP is a long-term problem. *Nature* **350**:271–272.

Grant, S.G.M., T.J. O'Dell, K. Karl, P. Stein, P. Soriano, and E.R. Kandel. 1992. Impaired long-term potentiation, spatial-learning, and hippocampal development in *fyn* mutant mice. *Science* **258**:1903–1910.

Greenberg, S.M., V.F. Castellucci, H. Bailey, and J.H. Schwartz. 1987. A molecular mechanism for long-term sensitization in *Aplysia*. *Nature* **329**:62–64.

Greengard, P., J. Jen, A.C. Nairn, and C.F. Stevens. 1991. Enhancement of the glutamate response by cAMP-dependent protein kinase in hippocampal neurons. *Science* **253**:1135–1138.

Haley, J.E., G.L. Wilcox, and P.F. Chapman. 1992. The role of nitric oxide in hippocampal long-term potentiation. *Neuron* **8**:211–216.

Kauer, J.A., R.C. Malenka, and R.A. Nicoll. 1988. A persistent postsynaptic modification mediates long-term potentiation in the hippocampus. *Neuron* **1**: 911–917.

Kennedy, M.B., M.K. Bennett, R.F. Bulleit, N.E. Erondu, V.R. Jennings, S.G. Miller, S.S. Molloy, B.L. Patton, and L.J. Schenker. 1990. Structure and regulation of type II calcium/calmodulin-dependent protein kinase in central nervous system neurons. *Cold Spring Harbor Symp. Quant. Biol.* **55**:101–110.

Madison, D.V., R.C. Malenka, and R.A. Nicoll. 1991. Mechanisms underlying long-term potentiation of synaptic transmission. *Ann. Rev. Neurosci.* **14**:379–397.

Malinow, R., H. Schulman, and R.W. Tsien. 1989. Inhibition of postsynaptic PKC or CaMKII blocks induction but not expression of LTP. *Science* **245**:862–866.

Molloy, S.S., and M.B. Kennedy. 1991. Autophosphorylation of type II Ca^{2+}/calmodulin-dependent protein kinase in cultures of postnatal rat hippocampal slices. *Proc. Natl. Acad. Sci. USA* **88**:4756–4760.

Morris, R.G.M., and M.B. Kennedy. 1992. The Pierian Spring. *Curr. Biol.* **2**:511–514.

Muller, D., M. Joly, and G. Lynch. 1988. Contributions of quisqualate and NMDA receptors to the induction and expression of LTP. *Science* **242**:1694–1697.

Nishizuka, Y. 1992. Signal transduction: Crosstalk. *Trends Biochem. Sci.* **17**:367.

Ocorr, K.A., and H. Schulman. 1991. Activation of multifunctional Ca^{2+}/calmodulin-dependent kinase in intact hippocampal slices. *Neuron* **6**:907–914.

O'Dell, T.J., R.D. Hawkins, E.R. Kandel, and O. Arancio. 1991a. Tests of the roles of two diffusible substances in long-term potentiation: Evidence for nitric oxide as a possible early retrograde messenger. *Proc. Natl. Acad. Sci. USA* **88**:11285–11289.

O'Dell, T.J., E.R. Kandel, and S.G.N. Grant. 1991b. Long-term potentiation in the hippocampus is blocked by tyrosine kinase inhibitors. *Nature* **353**:558–560.

O'Farrell, P.H. 1992. Cell cycle control: Many ways to skin a cat. *Trends Cell Biol.* **2**:159–162.

Palmer, R.M.J., A.G. Ferridge, and S. Moncada. 1987. Nitric-oxide release accounts for the biological activity of endothelium-derived relaxing factor. *Nature* **327**:524–526.

Patton, B.L., S.S. Molloy, and M.B. Kennedy. 1993. Autophosphorylation of type II CaM-kinase in hippocampal neurons: Localization of phospho- and dephospho-kinase with complementary phosphorylation site-specific antibodies. *Mol. Biol. Cell.* **3**:159–172.

Rosenberg, G.B., and D.R. Storm. 1987. Immunological distinction between calmodulin-sensitive and calmodulin-insensitive adenylate cyclases. *J. Biol. Chem.* **262**:7623–7628.

Schuman, E.M., and D.V. Madison. 1991. A requirement for the intercellular messenger nitric oxide in long-term potentiation. *Science* **254**:1503–1506.

Schuman, E.M., M.K. Meffert, H. Schulman, and D.V. Madison. 1992. A potential role for an ADP-ribosyl transferase (ADPRT) in hippocampal long-term potentiation (LTP). *Soc. Neurosci. Abstr.* **18**:761.

Shuster, M.J., J.S. Camardo, S.A. Siegelbaum, and E.R. Kandel. 1985. Cyclic AMP-dependent protein kinase closes the serotonin-sensitive K^+ channels of *Aplysia* sensory neurones in cell-free membrane patches. *Nature* **313**:392–395.

Silva, A.J., C.F. Stevens, S. Tonegawa, and Y. Wang. 1992. Deficient hippocampal long-term potentiation in α-calcium-calmodulin kinase II mutant mice. *Science* **257**:201–206.

Wang, L.-Y., M.W. Slater, and J.F. MacDonald. 1991. Regulation of kainate receptors by cAMP-dependent protein kinase and phosphatases. *Science* **253**:1132–1135.

15

Plasticity-related Changes in Synapse Morphology

W.T. GREENOUGH, K.E. ARMSTRONG, T.A. COMERY, N. HAWRYLAK, A.G. HUMPHREYS, J. KLEIM, R.A. SWAIN, and X. WANG
Departments of Psychology and Cell and Structural Biology,
Beckman Institute, University of Illinois at Urbana-Champaign,
405 N. Mathews, Urbana, IL 61801, U.S.A.

ABSTRACT

In this chapter, we present a summary of the research findings in morphological synaptic plasticity: (a) *synapse number* changes are found consistently across developmental and adult as well as behavioral and electrophysiological plasticity paradigms; (b) *synapse size* changes tend to be restricted to developmental and invertebrate paradigms; (c) *postsynaptic density shape* variations, particularly those involving perforated synapses, have been reported in both developmental and adult paradigms and in dentate gyrus LTP; (d) *vesicle position effects* have been reported with increasing frequency across paradigms; and (e) morphological indications of *synapse-associated protein synthesis* suggest mechanisms whereby some of these phenomena may be locally mediated.

INTRODUCTION

In this chapter, we separately discuss two general categories of morphological plasticity: (a) alteration of preexisting synapse structure and (b) formation of new synapses. While formation of new synapses of particular morphologies could be misinterpreted as a morphological alteration of existing synapses, if the added synapses altered the relative frequency of particular classes of synapses, we treat apparent morphological alterations as real here. More detailed reviews include Greenough and Chang (1988) and Wallace et al. (1991). Space limitations prevent citing many primary sources.

A cautionary note must be expressed with regard to the quantification of numerical change. In addition to the obvious need for proper stereological assessment of parameters, e.g., synapse density using individual tools such as the disector, the

Cellular and Molecular Mechanisms Underlying Higher Neural Functions
Edited by A.I. Selverston and P. Ascher

characteristics of the tissue as a whole must be considered. Mere quantification of synaptic density, for example, without quantification of either (a) the volume of the structure or region of interest or (b) the density of neurons (or some other stable reference) can be misleading. The density of synapses reflects both synaptic number and the density of other tissue components, such as vasculature and glia, both of which are also sensitive to manipulations that affect synaptic measures (e.g., Black et al. 1990). This can "dilute" the components that do not change, thereby lowering their density. Figure 15.1 shows that synapse density in the cerebellar cortex remains relatively constant across groups that differ substantially in the number of synapses and in the density of blood vessels. Geinisman et al. (1991) present a near-textbook example of dealing properly with these issues.

ALTERATIONS OF PREEXISTING SYNAPSES

Various alterations in the shape and size of preexisting synapses, schematized in Figure 15.2, have been proposed as indications of altered synaptic efficacy. Changes in various aspects of synaptic size have been reported in a number of experimental paradigms, including rats housed in complex environments, long-term potentiation, monocular deprivation in cats, acquisition of birdsong following testosterone administration in canaries, and avoidance training in domestic chicks (e.g., DeVoogd et al. 1985; Tieman 1991; reviewed in Rose 1991; Wallace et al. 1991).

Postsynaptic changes include increases in the diameter of the spine head and a decrease in the length of the spine neck with or without alteration in overall spine length or in neck width (reviewed in Wallace et al. 1991). Recently, an increase in the length and cross-section of spine necks has been reported with LTP (Trommald et al. 1990). Postsynaptic spine swelling is often associated with an enlarged area of apposition between the pre- and postsynaptic components of the synapse (Bailey and Chen 1991; reviewed in Greenough and Chang 1988). Studies in *Aplysia* have demonstrated that both presynaptic and postsynaptic components of the active zone increase in size following sensitization and decrease following habituation (Bailey and Chen 1991).

Changes in spine shape and active zone size may alter the characteristics of synaptic transmission. It has been widely suggested that the overall shape and size of the postsynaptic process may affect the propagation of the EPSP into the dendrite and soma. The area and shape of the apposition zone may play a role in regulating the release, sequestering and diffusing of neurotransmitters across the synaptic cleft, and in increasing the number of receptor complexes available on the postsynaptic surface.

The postsynaptic density (PSD), the primary demarcator of the active zone of the synapse, appears as a heavily stained region inside the postsynaptic membrane. Nonperforated synapses are characterized by a uniform PSD across the active zone, whereas perforated synapses have at least one discontinuity in the PSD that, in three

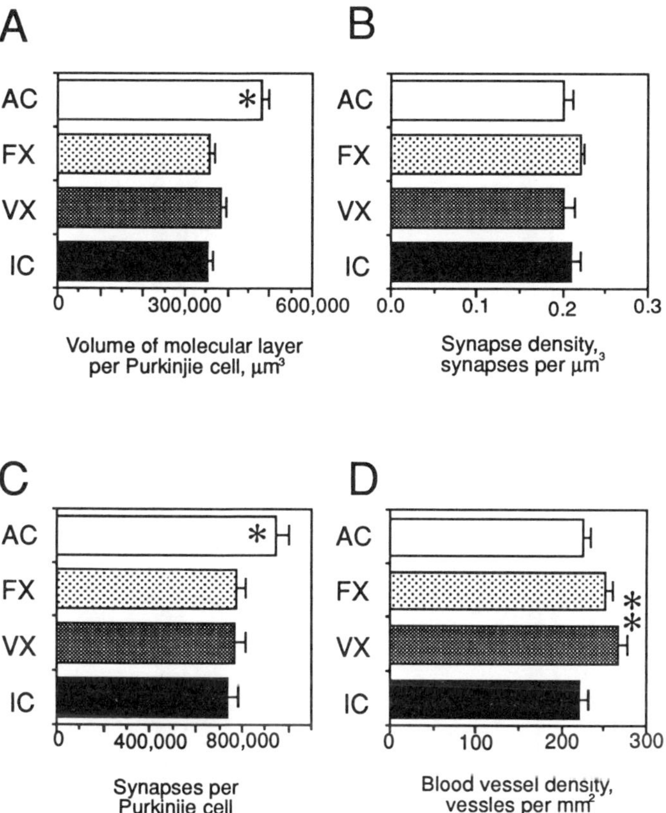

Figure 15.1 Morphological measures of paramedian lobule of cerebellar cortex in mature adult rats following 30 days of acrobatic (learning) conditions (AC), forced exercise on a treadmill (FX), voluntary exercise in activity wheels (VX), or inactivity (IC). (A) The relative volume of the molecular layer is increased in the AC rats while (B) synapse density remains constant across groups. Thus (C) the absolute number of synapses per Purkinje neuron is increased in the learning group but does not change in the neuronal activity control exercise groups. By contrast (D) the density of blood vessels increases in the exercise groups. This indicates that different components of the tissue may vary independently according to behavioral demands placed upon the organism and that new synapse formation tends to be associated with learning. (Reprinted by permission from Black et al. 1990)

dimensions, may appear as a perforation in the disc constituting the PSD, as a gap between separate PSD segments, or as an irregularity in the external boundary of the PSD (reviewed in Calverly and Jones 1990). The PSD is thought to contain many different proteins, including cytoskeletal and signal transduction proteins, which have been implicated in both learning and ultrastructural modification. The size (diameter) of the PSD has been reported to be altered by a number of manipulations, including

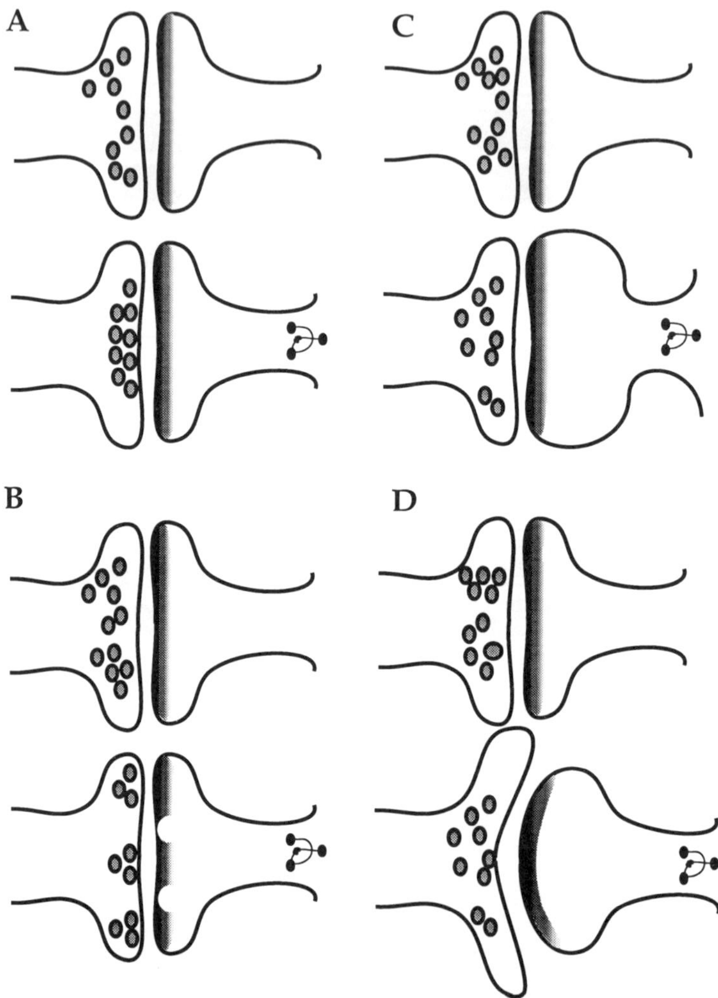

Figure 15.2 Schematic representations of activity induced plasticity of ultrastructure and morphology of the synaptic complex. (A) Vesicular aggregation at the presynaptic membrane and expression of polyribosomal aggregates at the base of the postsynaptic spine. (B) Perforated postsynaptic densities and associated vesicle aggregation. (C) Alteration in postsynaptic shape and size, including: increased spine head volume, neck and head diameter and neck shortening (note lack of change in total spine length). (D) Changes in pre- and postsynaptic morphology from a postsynaptically concave (or flat) orientation to a convex postsynaptic process.

postweaning complex environment exposure and visual deprivation (Tieman 1991; reviewed in Greenough and Chang 1988).

Two hypotheses have been presented concerning the functions of perforated synapses. One proposes that they are an intermediate stage between nonperforated synapses and synaptogenesis (synapse splitting) (Nieto-Sampedro et al. 1982). The other suggests that they are a discrete subpopulation of synapses (Calverly and Jones 1990). Whatever their role, alterations in the frequency of perforated synapses have been correlated with normal cortical development (Calverly and Jones 1990), as well as behavioral (Greenough et al. 1978) and LTP synaptic plasticity (Geinisman et al. 1991).

In addition to size changes correlated or uncorrelated with changes in PSD size, several studies have revealed presynaptic alterations in the number or distribution of vesicles as a result of stimulation. Rose (1991) reviews a reported increase in vesicle number in the chick brain following a single trial passive avoidance task. A similar result was found in the rat hippocampus following long-term potentiation (Meshul and Hopkins 1990). Stimulation also appears to alter vesicle location in the synapse; for example, Bailey and Chen (1991) found an increase in the number of vesicles near the active zone in the sensitized synapses of Aplysia, and similar findings have been reported with LTP (reviewed in Wallace et al. 1991). Although recent work by Betz et al. (1992) questions the functional significance of increased vesicle number and aggregation at the active zone, the fact that vesicle position can be altered by experience and LTP induction leaves open the possibility that these changes reflect alterations of synaptic strength via neurotransmitter availability.

POTENTIAL ROLE OF LOCAL PROTEIN SYNTHESIS

There is evidence for the association of local protein synthesis with either synapse alteration or synaptogenesis. Protein synthesis inhibitors can prevent some of the structural changes seen following a learning task in the chick (reviewed in Rose 1991). Steward (1983) described polyribosomal aggregates in and near dendritic spines, and several findings indicate that more spines contain aggregates during periods of developmental and regenerative plasticity (reviewed in Wallace et al. 1991). Weiler and Greenough (1991) demonstrated that the stimulation of synaptoneurosomes via potassium depolarization causes the rapid formation of these polyribosomal aggregates. Animals reared in an enriched environment have a greater proportion of spines containing polyribosomes than their individually housed littermate controls (Greenough et al. 1985). A mechanism by which neuronal activation translates into aggregation appears to involve metabotropic glutamate receptor activation and phosphatidyl inositol hydrolysis (Weiler and Greenough, in prep.). A possible role for this local synthesis is to initiate synapse modification or formation processes that are subsequently completed by constitutively available agents or by agents induced as an aspect of plastic change. The role of immediate early gene activation in orchestrating such a cascade has been reviewed by Rose (1991), among others. It is important to point out that these morphological changes may well be accomplished through the redistribution of existing proteins, the production of new proteins through enhanced gene expression, or some combination of both mechanisms depending upon the magnitude of the cellular response (for further discussion, see Role et al., this volume).

FORMATION OF NEW SYNAPSES

Development

In the developing PNS and CNS, the overproduction of synapses is followed by a selective loss that is coupled to neuronal activity driven, in many cases, by sensory experience (reviewed in Greenough and Chang 1988). Altering activity in the PNS can accelerate or slow the elimination process as well as selectively preserve an increased number of synapses or supernumerary connections. Manipulations of the sensory experience of neonatal animals that alter the amount or pattern of neural activity have been most extensively studied with regard to synaptic structure in the sensory cortices. A change in the number of synapses is a consistent feature of sensory manipulations during development and with storage of information from the environment in the adult. Studies of synaptic development in the visual cortex following visual deprivation provide a basis for understanding how neural activity might modify cortical circuitry through the production and elimination of synapses. The extent of overproduction and loss is probably greatly underestimated. Greenough and Chang (reviewed in 1988) found that in the adult rat, somatosensory whisker barrel neurons extend dendrites predominantly towards the barrel hollow, where thalamic afferents are concentrated. During development, these neurons began with radial dendritic fields, and the polarity arose through simultaneous loss of inappropriately oriented dendrites and growth of appropriately oriented ones. Such selective growth and loss may be common but would not be detected with traditional measures of numbers of synapses per neuron or dendritic field size.

In the mammalian visual cortex the most pronounced effects of visual deprivation have been shown to occur in layer IV; however, they have also been reported in layers II–III and superficial layer V. In visually deprived rat pups and kittens, overall development of synaptic density was not disrupted, but marked reductions in the number of type I asymmetric and type II symmetric synapses were found (Fifkova 1970; Gabbott and Stewart 1987; reviewed in Tieman 1991). The effects on the synaptic types are differential: activity block by intraocular tetrodotoxin injection of rats during the period P0–P21 reduced type I synapses between P9–P21, while no reductions in type II synapses were found until P21 (Riccio and Matthews 1985).

These studies do not permit reliable inferences about the afferent cell type(s) associated with the postsynaptic alterations. Two studies, both using monocular deprivation, have addressed this issue. Deprived eye (D) geniculocortical afferents appeared to branch less frequently and formed fewer and smaller synaptic terminals (Tieman 1991). Analysis of functionally defined Y-type geniculocortical (GC) axons has demonstrated that D axons have a reduced arbor size but higher bouton density compared to nondeprived (ND) axons. ND axons, however, form more synapses per bouton ("ectopic" shaft synapses) than D axons or GC axons from ND animals. The induction of ectopic synapses may represent an additional component of synaptic rearrangement that is not related to direct competition for postsynaptic sites (Friedlander et al. 1991).

Age-related effects on synaptic performance and plasticity also occur in crustacean motor systems. Atwood (1992) reported that in crustacean motor neurons, new branches and synapses form to keep up with the growth of innervated muscle cells. In the American lobster, innervation of abdominal extensor muscles by common excitatory and inhibitory neurons is more widespread in the embryo and early postembryonic stages than in later postembryonic stages and adults; retraction of axonal branches and synaptic elimination is inferred. Subsequently, growth predominates in decapod crustaceans, where the number of terminals and individual synapses for a single neuron may increase by 1 or 2 orders of magnitude.

Synapse Formation During Vertebrate and Invertebrate Learning

Substantial evidence indicates that changes in the number (either increases or decreases) of synapses may underlie behavioral learning. This evidence includes alterations of dendritic field size, spine density counts, synapse number, and density counts or brain structure volume and has been reported following tasks as diverse as avian vocal learning (Nottebohm and Arnold 1976), environmental enrichment of rats and cats (reviewed in Greenough and Chang 1988), Pavlovian eyeblink conditioning in rabbits (Anderson et al., in prep.; Woodruff-Pak et al. 1990), and acrobatic motor skill training (Black et al. 1990), reach training, and maze learning in rats (reviewed in Wallace et al. 1991). Studies that have actually calculated changes in the number of synapses per neuron have largely done so in the context of environmental complexity or acrobatic training paradigms. Exposure to the environmental complexity condition for as little as four days has been reported to increase significantly the weight of specific tissue samples within occipital cortex and to increase significantly dendritic length; longer exposures increased dendritic length by as much as 20–25% compared to rats in socially caged or individually caged conditions (reviewed in Greenough and Chang 1988). In similar studies, calculation of the number of synapses per neuron in occipital cortex yielded a 20–25% increase in environmental complexity rats compared to their individually caged controls.

Beaulieu and Colonnier (1987) performed similar experiments using cats. In visual cortical area 17, environmental complexity cats exhibited an 18% increase in (excitatory) asymmetrical synapses with round vesicles and a 34% reduction of (inhibitory) flat vesicle, symmetrical synapses as compared to individually caged cats. The overall number of flat-vesicle boutons remained unchanged.

Changes in the number of synapses per neuron have also been observed in rats trained to perform a series of acrobatic tasks (e.g., walk a tightrope, climb a ladder) involving a considerable degree of motor learning (Black et al. 1990). As Figure 15.1 indicates, the number of synapses in the molecular layer of the cerebellum increased following this motor learning but was not affected by exercise. Rats from two exercise groups showed significant increases in blood capillary density but no synapse number change. These results are important because they clearly dissociate changes in brain morphology induced by neural activity from those resulting from learning.

Bailey and Chen (reviewed in 1991), studying the gill withdrawal reflex of *Aplysia*, found that long-term sensitized animals had twice as many sensory neuron presynaptic varicosities as did untrained animals, while long-term habituated animals had fewer varicosities than controls. Moreover, in untrained animals only 40% of the synaptic terminals had active zones and seemed capable of releasing transmitter. The percentage of varicosities with active zones was significantly reduced in long-term habituated animals (to 10%) and was significantly increased in long-term sensitized animals (to 65%). Schacher et al. (1990) also observed new varicosities in the sensory neurons of sensitized *Aplysia* and argued that the learning-related growth is associated with reorganization of cell adhesion molecules present during early embryogenesis, i.e., synapse formation during development and learning-related growth changes may share certain common molecular regulatory mechanisms. Unlike the *Aplysia*, classical conditioning of the mollusc *Hermissenda* seems to produce structural changes characterized by reduction of dendritic volume in the type B photoreceptor cells (Ledehendler et al. 1990). These changes in dendritic morphology were correlated with increased resistance across the cell membrane caused by learning-induced reduction of outward somatic K^+ currents. Finally, in an instrumental learning paradigm, as early as one day following learning, plated cultured cells from pupal honeybee brains involved in proboscis extension learning started to sprout new processes. Many neuritic branches grew simultaneously, but other growth patterns were also observed (Kreissl and Bicker 1992).

Synaptogenesis During LTP

Synaptogenesis has been described in association with LTP induction in the CA1 region of the hippocampus, where the numbers of synapses onto dendritic shafts and onto stubby "sessile" spines, but not onto mature "mushroom" spines, is increased. In the dentate gyrus, both increases in synapse number (per unit dendrite length) and no numerical change (per neuron) have been reported, in addition to increases in bifurcating spines (reviewed in Wallace et al. 1991; Trommald et al. 1990). Morphological studies of behaviorally induced electrophysiological change in hippocampus are not available. However, in the visual cortex of rats reared in enriched housing, where dendritic and synaptic increases have been reported, there is also dramatic "behavioral LTP" in response to white matter stimulation (Wang and Greenough, in prep.).

REFERENCES

Atwood, H.L. 1992. Age-dependent alterations of synaptic performance and plasticity in crustacean motor systems. *Exp. Gerontol.* **27**:51–61.

Bailey, C.H., and M. Chen. 1991. Morphological aspects of synaptic plasticity in *Aplysia*. An anatomical substrate for long-term memory. *Ann. NY Acad. Sci.* **627**:181–196.

Beaulieu, C., and M. Colonnier. 1987. Effect of the richness of the environment on the cat visual cortex. *J. Comp. Neurol.* **266**:478–494.

Betz, W.J., G.S. Bewick, and R.M. Ridge. 1992. Intracellular movements of fluorescently labeled synaptic vesicles in frog motor nerve terminals during nerve stiumlation. *Neuron* **9**:805–813.

Black, J.E., K.R. Isaacs, B.J. Anderson, A.A. Alcantara, and W.T. Greenough. 1990. Learning causes synaptogenesis, whereas motor activity causes angiogenesis, in cerebellar cortex of adult rats. *Proc. Natl. Acad. Sci. USA* **87**:5568–5572.

Calverly, R.K., and D.G. Jones. 1990. Contributions of dendritic spines and perforated synapses to synaptic plasticity. *Brain Res. Rev.* **15**:215–249.

DeVoogd, T.J., B. Nixdorf, and F. Nottebohm. 1985. Synaptogenesis and changes in synaptic morphology related to acquisition of a new behavior. *Brain Res.* **329**:304–308.

Fifkova, E. 1970. The effect of monocular deprivation on the synaptic contacts of the visual cortex. *J. Neurobiol.* **1**:285–294.

Friedlander, M.J., K.A.C. Martin, and D. Wassenhove-McCarthy. 1991. Effects of monocular visual deprivation on geniculocortical innervation of area 18 in cat. *J. Neurosci.* **11**:3268–3288.

Gabbott, P.L.A., and M.G. Stewart. 1987. Quantitative morphological effects of dark-rearing and light exposure on the synaptic connectivity of layer 4 in the rat visual cortex (area 17). *Exp. Brain Res.* **68**:103–114.

Geinisman, Y., L. deToledo-Morrell, and F. Morrell. 1991. Induction of long-term potentiation is associated with an increase in the number of axospinous synapses with segmented postsynaptic densities. *Brain Res.* **566**:77–88.

Greenough, W.T., and F.-L. Chang. 1988. Plasticity of synapse structure and pattern in cerebral cortex. In: Cerebral Cortex: Development and Maturation of the Cerebral Cortex, ed. A. Peters and E.G. Jones, vol. 7, pp. 391–439. New York: Plenum.

Greenough, W.T., H.M. Hwang, and C. Gorman. 1985. Evidence for active synapse formation, or altered postsynaptic metabolism in visual cortex of rats reared in complex environments. *Proc. Natl. Acad. Sci. USA* **82**:4459–4452.

Greenough, W.T., R.W. West, and T.J. DeVoogd. 1978. Subsynaptic plate perforations: Changes with age and experience in the rat. *Science* **202**:1096–1098.

Kreissl, S., and G. Bicker. 1992. Dissociated neurons of the pupal honeybee brain in cell culture. *J. Neurocytol.* **21**:545–56.

Lederhendler, I.I., R. Etcjeberrigaray, E.N. Yamoah, L.D. Matzel, and D.L. Alkon. 1990. Outgrowths from *Hermissenda* photoreceptor somata are associated with activation of protein kinase C. *Brain Res.* **534**:195–200.

Meshul, C.K., and W.F. Hopkins. 1990. Presynaptic ultrastructural correlates of long-term potentiation in the CA1 subfield of the hippocampus. *Brain Res.* **514**:310–319.

Nieto-Sampedro, M., S.F. Hoff, and C.W. Cotman. 1982. Perforated postsynaptic densities: Probable intermediates in synapse turnover. *Proc. Natl. Acad. Sci. USA* **79**:5718–5722.

Nottebohm, F., and A.P. Arnold. 1976. Sexual dimorphism in vocal control areas of the song bird brain. *Science* **194**:211–213.

Riccio, R.V., and M.A. Matthews. 1985. The postnatal development of the rat primary visual cortex during optic nerve impulse blockade by intraocular tetrodotoxin: A quantitative electron microscopic analysis. *Devel. Brain Res.* **20**:55–68.

Rose, S. 1991. How chicks make memories: The cellular cascade from c-*fos* to dendritic remodelling. *Trends Neurosci.* **14**:390–397.

Schacher, S., D. Glanzman, A. Barzilai, P. Dash, S.G.N. Grant, F. Keller, M. Mayford, and E.R. Kandel. 1990. Long-term facilitation in *Aplysia*: Persistent phosphorylation and structural changes. *Cold Spring Harbor Symp. Quant. Biol.* **55**:187–201.

Steward, O. 1983. Polyribosomes at the base of dendritic spines of CNS neurons, their possible role in synapse construction and modification. *Cold Spring Harbor Symp. Quant. Biol.* **48**:745–759.

Tieman, S.B. 1991. Morphological changes in the geniculocortical pathway associated with monocular deprivation. *Ann. NY Acad. Sci.* **627**:212–230.

Trommald, M., J. Line Vaaland, T.W. Blackstad, and P. Andersen. 1990. Dendritic spine changes in rat dentate granule cells associated with long-term potentiation. In: Neurotoxicity of Excitatory Amino Acids, ed. A. Guidotti, pp. 163–174. New York: Raven.

Wallace, C.S., N. Hawrylak, and W.T. Greenough. 1991. Studies of synaptic structural modification after long-term potentiation and kindling: Context for a molecular morphology. In: Long-Term Potentiation: A Debate of Current Issues, ed. M. Baudry and J.L. Davis, pp. 189–232. Cambridge, MA: MIT Press.

Weiler, I.J., and W.T. Greenough. 1991. Potassium ion stimulation triggers protein translation in synaptoneurosomal polyribosomes. *Mol. Cell. Neurosci.* **2**:305–314.

Woodruff-Pak, D.S., J.F. Cronholm, and J.B. Sheffield. 1990. Purkinje cell number related to rate of classical conditioning. *NeuroReport* 1:165–168.

Standing, left to right:
Per Andersen, Alain Artola, Tobias Bonhoeffer, Chuck Stevens, Mary Kennedy, Graham Collingridge
Seated, left to right:
Robert Malenka, Fran Edwards, Roger Nicoll, Joël Bockaert, Bruce McNaughton
Not present:
Hannah Monyer

16

Group Report: How Adequate Are Current Explanations of Long-term Potentiation/Depression?

F.A. EDWARDS, Rapporteur

P. ANDERSEN, A. ARTOLA, J. BOCKAERT, T. BONHOEFFER, G.L. COLLINGRIDGE, M.B. KENNEDY, R.C. MALENKA, B.L. MCNAUGHTON, H. MONYER, R.A. NICOLL, C.F. STEVENS

INTRODUCTION

The group gathered for this discussion consisted of scientists from a variety of fields: electrophysiology, pharmacology, biochemistry, molecular biology, and anatomy. The majority of people work on synaptic phenomena in the hippocampus and thus the discussions centered around these areas. The questions formulated for discussion were:

1. Are there different types of long-term potentiation/depression (LTP/LTD)?
2. Induction of LTP/LTD: are activation of NMDA receptors and consequent Ca^{2+} influx essential and sufficient?
3. Is it necessary to propose a different model for synaptic transmission in the CNS from that proposed for transmission at the neuromuscular junction?
4. What is the locus for LTP expression?
5. What happens after Ca^{2+} influx?
6. What do we know about LTP maintenance?

These questions were addressed and despite the apparently contentious nature of the field, certain difficult points were clarified. Where an overall consensus or near

Cellular and Molecular Mechanisms Underlying Higher Neural Functions
Edited by A.I. Selverston and P. Ascher

consensus was reached on an important point, it is listed in the text below under the heading CONSENSUS.

Some points, however, were unresolvable, and wherever possible suggested experimental approaches to these problems have been included under the heading EXPERIMENT.

The most important or illuminating results of our group discussions are listed in the conclusions sections. Please note that this report is not a review of the literature, and although some references are included, in most cases the background papers in this volume will be more detailed in this sense.

ARE THERE DIFFERENT TYPES OF LTP/LTD?

Defining the Terms and Width of Discussion

Although we appreciated that there are many forms of plasticity, we decided that, considering the constraints of time and the expertise of the participants, it would be necessary to restrict our discussion to LTP and, where appropriate, LTD. Most of the discussion inevitably revolved around the extensive, though sometimes controversial, work using hippocampal preparations (most commonly brain slices) on potentiation of the Schaffer collateral/CA1 synapse. Where it is not mentioned, this will be the synapse referred to.

If There Are Different Types of LTP, How Can They Be Defined?

The first question which arose in this context concerned the definition and significance of short-term potentiation. Short-term potentiation (STP) will be defined for the purpose of this discussion as a postsynaptically induced potentiation that decays back to control levels within about the first hour of recording.

Are Short- and Long-term Potentiation Part of the Same Process?

Three possibilities exist:

1. STP and LTP may be part of the same process such that STP is a case that does not last long, due to insufficient activation of important intracellular mechanisms (i.e., LTP that did not quite happen).
2. STP and LTP may be sequential processes such that it is necessary to induce STP before LTP can be expressed.
3. STP and LTP may be totally independent processes with similar triggering requirements.

So far, sufficient data is not available to distinguish between these possibilities. Some evidence, which has been put forward to suggest that STP and LTP are independent processes, comes from experiments in which it was demonstrated that LTP can be blocked without affecting the expression of STP (application of many kinases; mouse gene knockout experiments). Neither of the other possibilities can, however, be discounted using such data. For example, if the processes are sequential, kinases could be involved in the switch from STP to LTP. On the other hand, if they are versions of the same process, there may be a certain threshold of kinase activity or another factor necessary for continued maintenance.

> EXPERIMENT: The definitive demonstration that STP and LTP were independent processes would come if a manipulation were found that blocked STP while leaving LTP intact.

An alternative approach that has been used to address this issue is to test whether saturating LTP prevents the development of STP. There is unfortunately a discrepancy between the groups that have used this approach. Kauer et al. (1988a) found that STP could not be generated after saturating LTP while Gustafsson et al. (1989) showed no occlusion. Such an experiment always presents difficulties, however, as it is difficult to be sure that LTP in a certain path is saturated.

Other Ways of Defining "Types" of LTP

> CONSENSUS: Mechanisms rather than protocols should be used to define "types of LTP." Two types of stimulation-induced LTP can be defined on the basis of induction mechanisms:

1. LTP dependent upon postsynaptic calcium influx (usually triggered via the NMDA receptor, e.g., CA1, associative CA3, dentate gyrus, cortex.)
2. LTP not dependent upon NMDA-R activation and perhaps no postsynaptic calcium influx necessary, (e.g., mossy fiber-CA3, cerebellar Purkinje cells).

So far it is unclear how many types of LTP will appear on the basis of expression mechanisms. It has been suggested that definitions of temporal phases could be used, but there was largely agreement that our present lack of knowledge of expression processes limits this approach.

In the future, however, further types of LTP could possibly be defined in terms of such factors as long-term synapse formation or evidence for induction of protein synthesis.

Types of LTD

STD and LTD

In the neocortex and hippocampus, both homosynaptic LTD and STD have been described with time courses very similar to those of LTP and STP in the hippocampus. Similarly to potentiation, LTD can be blocked by a variety of methods without affecting STD.

Other Types of LTD

Again, the definition should be mechanistic, and while processes that trigger LTD and LTP are similar in some ways, unlike LTP, all types of LTD known are dependent upon postsynaptic Ca^{2+} influx. It does, however, seem sensible to divide LTD into two operationally defined groups, according to requirement for NMDA receptor activation:

1. NMDA receptor-dependent LTD (CA1; can be induced with 1 Hz stimulation).
2. NMDA receptor-independent LTD (cerebellum, hippocampus, neocortex; requires high-frequency presynaptic stimulation and independent of postsynaptic depolarization).

HOW IS ASSOCIATIVE LTP/LTD INDUCED?

Is Stimulation of the Postsynaptic NMDA Receptor Necessary/Sufficient for LTP Induction in the CA1?

CONSENSUS: Although other nonphysiological methods could be found to bypass the NMDA receptor, its stimulation is necessary under normal conditions. In most cases, however, exogenous application of NMDA causes only a brief potentiation, similar to STP. In those cases where potentiation is longer lasting, synaptic stimulation during the applications might be involved. Thus it seems likely that activation of the NMDA receptor is not sufficient for induction of LTP.

Is Postsynaptic Calcium Influx Necessary/Sufficient for LTP Induction in the CA1?

CONSENSUS: Calcium influx was agreed to be necessary in the induction of associative LTP, since LTP does not occur if calcium chelators are present in the postsynaptic cell (for a review, see Nicoll, this volume).

The question of whether calcium influx is sufficient presents some difficulties, because most laboratories that have tried to induce LTP by raising the postsynaptic concentration of intracellular calcium have also had a slow “test” stimulus running concurrently (e.g., Malenka et al. 1988). Even where this has not been the case, effects of spontaneous glutamate release cannot be excluded. It became clear both in this context and later, that members of the group imagined very different levels of free glutamate likely to be in the slice. This important issue remains unresolved and could vary greatly depending upon the precise experimental conditions.

EXPERIMENT: Test the free glutamate concentration in the slice under different conditions.

There is, however, evidence that depolarization causing enough calcium influx to result in up to a fourfold potentiation, over the short term, did not result in a long-term potentiation. In both cases, however, we should note that it cannot be definitely shown that an adequate level of calcium reached the spine.

CONSENSUS: A factor additional to Ca^{2+} influx is probably necessary for induction of LTP.

Candidates for the Necessary Additional Factor

We generally agreed that, although NMDA application in the absence of concurrent stimulation may not be sufficient to induce LTP, application of glutamate can probably be sufficient under certain circumstances (Cormier et al. 1993). This suggests that another factor delivered by stimulation of either AMPA receptors or metatropic glutamate receptors (mGlu Rs) is required.

There are two lines of evidence indicating that mGluRs may provide a second essential trigger for the induction of LTP (but not STP). First, activation of mGluRs by (1S, 3R)-1-aminocyclopentane-1,3-dicarboxylic acid (1S, 3RA2PD) can induce a slow onset of potentiation, which occludes with tetanus-induced LTP (Bortolotto and Collingridge 1993). Second, a specific mGluR antagonist blocks the induction of LTP without interfering with STP or synaptic transmission (Bashir et al. 1993).

EXPERIMENT: It may be instructive to determine whether the effects of mGluR stimulation interact with norepinephrine receptor stimulation, as the two receptors stimulate similar intracellular processes. A negative result would, however, be inconclusive since the localization of the receptors on the cells may be different.

Is Postsynaptic Calcium Influx Necessary/Sufficient for LTD Induction in the Neocortex and Hippocampus?

CONSENSUS: A change in the calcium level of the postsynaptic cell is necessary, as evidenced by the observation that induction of LTD is blocked by intracellular injection of calcium chelators (Bröcher et al. 1992; Hirsch and Crépel 1992; Mulkey and Malenka 1992; but see Kimura et al. 1990).

This calcium dependence is most likely due to a calcium influx, resulting in an increase of calcium concentration in the postsynaptic cell. This hypothesis is supported by the observation that raising the extracellular calcium concentration from 2–4 mM for 10 minutes can result in the induction of LTD in neocortical neurons (Artola et al. 1992). Moreover, in the hippocampus, it has been shown that strong depolarization of CA1 pyramidal cells results in LTD (Pockett and Lippold 1986; Pockett et al. 1990), but only if the extracellular calcium concentration is sufficiently high (Christofi et al.

1993). During our discussions, however, both Knöpfel and Ascher pointed out that raising extracellular calcium concentration could cause a reduction in leak currents, resulting in a decrease in intracellular calcium concentration. Thus, although considered less likely, it cannot be completely ruled out that the change in intracellular calcium level necessary to induce LTD is a decrease rather than an increase.

EXPERIMENT: Establish effects on intracellular calcium level of changing extracellular calcium from 2 mM to 4 mM.

Relation between LTD and LTP

Both phenomena are probably dependent upon an increase in the calcium concentration in the postsynaptic cell. Whether the synapse is potentiated or depressed is probably a threshold effect. Crossing an initial low threshold of calcium influx probably leads to LTD, while at higher concentrations, a second threshold must be crossed to result in LTP induction. Discussion ensued over possible mechanisms by which different calcium levels could have opposite effects. One possibility could depend upon a difference in the localization of enzymes. Alternatively, two or three enzymes with different thresholds for calcium could be involved (Lisman 1989). Such a mechanism could result in competition of LTD and LTP as the high threshold enzyme becomes activated or, alternatively, one enzyme may act to switch another off.

An example of the diversity of intra or intercellular messengers, activated through agents that all increase intracellular Ca^{2+} is seen in cultured neurons. NMDA receptors stimulate both arachidonic acid as well as superoxide ion production, whereas AMPA and K^{+} (50–100 mm) do not, despite their ability to trigger comparable increases in intracellular Ca^{2+}. At least two explanations are possible:

1. An active factor other than Na^{+} or Ca^{2+} is entering through the NMDA receptor channel.
2. The NMDA receptor channels are localized differently from AMPA-R and voltage-sensitive Ca^{2+} channels.

Other examples in the literature were quoted in which different concentrations of calcium had opposing effects. A particularly apt example is the effect of calcium concentration on growth cones (Guthrie et al. 1991). Low calcium is required for the growth of growth cones, while higher levels result in retraction.

Specificity

Within Cells

One of the features of LTP is that it is more or less input specific. In the extreme case, this would mean that potentiation of a single input would not cause potentiation in the neighboring spines. However, it is currently not possible to define specificity to this extent. Andersen suggested that it can be demonstrated that potentiation induced via a few incoming fibers does not spread to spines more than 75 μm away.

> EXPERIMENT: It would be extremely useful if an experiment could be designed to test whether input specificity is absolute (i.e., whether it holds for single spines). Sparse cell cultures could perhaps be used to approach this question.

Between Cells

Experiments first performed in slice cultures of the hippocampus (Bonhoeffer et al. 1989) and slices of the visual cortex (Kossel et al. 1990), and subsequently repeated in slices of hippocampus (Madison, pers. comm.), suggest that enhancement may not be completely specific with regard to the postsynaptic cells. Bonhoeffer explained that the spread of enhancement between cells has been observed over more than 50 μm but less than 1 mm. These results are controversial since it has been difficult to explain why synaptic potentiation could be blocked by hyperpolarization (Malinow and Miller 1986) or injection of calcium chelators (e.g., Lynch et al. 1983). Bonhoeffer suggested that a possible explanation of the blocking experiments is that in the hyperpolarized cell, rather than LTP being blocked, LTD (caused by lower calcium levels, see above) could be superimposed upon LTP. In this context, it is interesting to note that in some of the "blocking" experiments (e.g., Malinow and Miller 1986), a decrease in synaptic efficacy was seen rather than a perfect block.

Several possible mechanisms may be proposed to explain "presynaptic spread of enhancement," including retrograde messengers that may spread beyond the synaptic cleft. For example, Collingridge proposed a mechanism by which K^+ may act as a second messenger: during procedures which induce LTP, K^+ will be rapidly released into the synaptic cleft, largely by permeating through NMDA channels. This local change in extracellular K^+ concentration would be more or less proportional to NMDA receptor activation and could thus almost instantaneously signal the degree of activation to the presynaptic terminal. Such an effect would be fairly well localized by restricted diffusion and uptake into surrounding glia, and this localization could be further refined by, for example, an extra requirement for synaptically released glutamate. Such localization would not necessarily be strictly synapse specific, and the resulting effects of changes in extracellular K^+ concentration could have not only direct effects on the presynaptic terminal but other far-reaching effects, such as changes in fiber excitability.

EXPRESSION OF LTP

Glutamate Overflow

Bliss and Dolphin were the first to demonstrate an AP5-sensitive increase in the concentration of glutamate in the dentate gyrus after induction of LTP (Dolphin et al.

1982, but see Aniksztejn et al. 1989). They interpreted this result as evidence for increased glutamate release from the presynaptic cell. The method used (push-pull cannula) makes the localization of the source of glutamate difficult. It would clearly be advantageous to use a smaller probe that could be placed in the immediate vicinity of the synapse. Nicoll reported having attempted to use NMDA receptors on an outside out-patch as a probe, but had failed to see glutamate release.

> CONSENSUS: It is clear that glutamate levels increase in the extracellular space in parallel with LTP induction. This effect is of interest, but it was considered that several different loci (e.g., glia) could be proposed for the source of the transmitter.

Quantal Analysis

Introduction to the Problem

There has been considerable discussion over recent years concerning the use of quantal analysis in reference to central synapses. Several studies have used this approach to attempt to determine whether maintained LTP is a purely postsynaptic phenomenon or whether a presynaptic component is involved. This section of the discussion was outlined beforehand by F. Edwards and the group asked that a resume be included here. Thus this introductory section represents Edwards' view of the problem rather than the result of group discussion (see also Edwards 1991).

The neuromuscular junction. From the elegant work of del Castillo and Katz, Boyd and Martin, and others a great deal is known about the neuromuscular junction, and its function is now considered to be well understood (for a detailed description, see Katz 1966). The generally accepted description of the synapse consists of a series of release sites on the presynaptic terminal, each of which has an equal probability of releasing a vesicle of transmitter in response to the arrival of an action potential. Each vesicle contains a very similar quantity of transmitter, and if a vesicle fuses to the presynaptic membrane, it releases the transmitter molecules, which diffuse across the synaptic cleft where they bind to some of a virtually unlimited supply of receptors on the postsynaptic membrane. If several vesicles are released simultaneously, the response will be a multiple of the response to a single vesicle. Thus the amplitude distribution of miniature currents (being due to random release of individual vesicles) is Gaussian, having a mean "q" and a variance "V." Note that the measurement of these variables was possible because the size of the currents is so large, due to the opening of thousands of acetylcholine receptor/channels. The amplitude distribution of evoked currents is thus the sum of several Gaussian distributions, each being the multiple of the miniature distribution. Using this model and recording enough currents or potentials to construct amplitude distributions, it is possible to measure "q" and "V" and to estimate other parameters from the shape of the distribution. These calculated parameters, "n" and "p" are thought to reflect the total number of release sites and the probability of release from any one of those sites, respectively. Thus if either or both of these parameters is seen to change in response to a stimulus, a presynaptic change is said to have occurred. The interpretation of these latter parameters is highly dependent upon the description of synaptic transmission. Any model which suggests that release probabilities or response can vary at different release sites makes the interpretation much more difficult. For the neuromuscular junction, however, these assumptions seem to hold.

Synapses in the central nervous system. From a study of GABA-mediated synaptic currents in rat hippocampal granule cells (Edwards et al. 1990), four features emerged important to considerations of mechanisms of synaptic transmission in the central nervous system:

1. Amplitude distributions of evoked currents fall into multiple equidistant peaks with small separation, constituting about 10 channels opening per peak. This is consistent with data from excitatory synapses.
2. The coefficient of variation of the peaks in the amplitude distribution is about 15% (i.e., about 1–2 channels per peak). Again, this is consistent with, but not clearly demonstrated for, data from excitatory synapses.
3. Both evoked and miniature synaptic currents have very fast rise times, (often < 0.5 ms, even without any compensation for the series resistance or filtering properties of the system). This is also true for all excitatory synapses that are electrically close to the soma, from which currents have been recorded.
4. The amplitude distribution of miniature currents, rather than being a single Gaussian, is skewed and probably falls into equidistant peaks equivalent to about the first three peaks of the evoked distribution. This last feature, common to all synapses so far studied in the brain, means that the term "quantal size" becomes ambiguous in this context and has caused some confusion in the literature. For example, some studies have noted the wide variety of miniatures and referred to this as representing a high coefficient of variation of the "quantal size" as defined by mean miniature amplitude (e.g., Bekkers and Stevens 1990). Although not incorrect, this definition could be rather misleading if the miniatures really show multiple peaks in their amplitude distribution and depending upon the model used for the synapse. To avoid this problem I will refer to "peak separation" rather than "quantal size."

The four considerations above must be taken into account when comparing central synapses with the neuromuscular junction. Just taking the first point alone requires some variation from the neuromuscular junction model. The small peak separation of the amplitude distribution (representing opening of about 10 channels) is very different from that of the neuromuscular junction, where the peak separation represents the opening of thousands of subsynaptic channels. This implies that central synapses are in some way different from the neuromuscular junction.

The neuromuscular junction model could be altered in various ways to allow the small peak separation. Three of the simplest possibilities are listed below:

1. A mechanism could be proposed by which each vesicle could be filled with only a small and exact number of molecules of transmitter (e.g., 10). This idea is, however, unlikely due to the fast rise time of the currents, which implies a high concentration of transmitter in the cleft. Moreover, to allow the small coefficient of variation of the evoked distribution (about 1 channel), virtually no transmitter molecule could be lost by diffusion out of the cleft, and the probability of a transmitter molecule opening a channel would have to be very close to 1.
2. Another possibility would be to propose a high concentration of transmitter but a very low, open probability of the channels, or an uptake and breakdown rate for transmitter that was much faster than the binding rate of the ligand to its receptor. Under these conditions, very few of the molecules released would result in the opening of a channel. Although this variation of the model would allow for the fast rise time, it would be difficult to propose realistic parameters under these conditions which would result in a sufficiently low coefficient of variation.
3. The third possibility (that we proposed and which would best explain our data and that reported for other synapses) involves a high concentration of transmitter being released (similar to the neuromuscular junction), but few receptors being available on the postsynaptic membrane. Thus in this variation of the model, the peak separation would be determined not by the amount of transmitter released but by the number of receptors available on the postsynaptic membrane. In order for the coefficient of variation to be low, this would imply that the open probability of the channels was very high and that the channels were inserted or otherwise congregated in the membrane in "quantal clumps" of, for example, 10 receptors.

For all these possible variations, it is necessary to propose an explanation for the probable multipeaked distribution of miniature currents. So far there is no evidence that the rise time of miniatures is correlated with their amplitude, and in our study (Edwards et al. 1990), any currents with inflections on the rise were excluded from the analysis. This suggests that the explanation is not that release of independent vesicles occurs simultaneously, as some jitter in the release time would be expected. For the first variation (described above), it could be suggested that vesicles could be released in some nonindependent manner such as, e.g., in the fusion of two vesicles before release. Note that this would have further implications for the assumptions underlying classic quantal analysis. For the second variation, the same explanation of nonindependent release may be possible, but it would put severe limitations on the parameters proposed for uptake, breakdown, and open probability in order for a linear relation to be maintained between the amount of transmitter released and the final number of channels opening. For the third variation, the amount of transmitter released will not affect the number of channels opening, and thus a postsynaptic explanation must be proposed for the skewed miniature distribution. We proposed that opposite any one release site, the number of quantal groups might vary from zero to about three. Thus at any one release site, the size of the miniature would be constant but between release sites, the amplitude would vary from an apparent failure to a miniature with three times the amplitude of the peak separation.

Thus in the light of the small separation between peaks of the amplitude distribution of evoked currents collected at central synapses, the accepted model for neuromuscular transmission cannot be transferred to central nervous system synapses without alteration. All the obvious mechanisms that would allow the small quantal size imply that some of the assumptions which underlie quantal analysis at the neuromuscular junction do not apply. For the first two variations described above, independence of release is put in doubt. For the last variation, the interpretation of the changes in the parameters "n" and "p" (or "mean^2/variance") derived from traditional quantal analysis could be due to pre- or postsynaptic changes. In fact, if some release sites lost a "quantal cluster" of receptors facing them, and thus release from these sites resulted in no postsynaptic response, even changes in apparent failure rate could have a postsynaptic origin.

Is Quantal Analysis Useful in Studies of the Locus of Maintenance of LTP?

Some discussion ensued that centered particularly on the reason for the skewed miniature distribution. Stevens pointed out that if it could be shown that a particular synapse had only one release site, and miniatures from that synapse still resulted in a multipeaked or skewed miniature distribution, then the distribution could not be explained by different numbers of postsynaptic receptor clusters.

> EXPERIMENT: It would be very valuable to do a detailed anatomy on synapses in culture, such as those described in Bekkers and Stevens (1990), with the aim of establishing the dimensions of different boutons and the maximum number of possible release sites. Localized sucrose stimulation could then be used to study miniature distributions from individual synapses in detail.

Overall, from the discussion, it was clear that much still needs to be clarified about the function of a central synapse, and this would be very helpful in any further analysis of plastic changes. There was some difference of opinion as to the most likely of the three variations listed above. There was, however, agreement that the concentration of transmitter in the cleft must be high, and thus it was unlikely that the small quantal size was due to packaging of very few transmitter molecules per vesicle. Detailed computer modeling may be useful in distinguishing between the remaining possibilities.

CONSENSUS: (except Stevens) Use of classical quantal analysis for determining the locus of maintenance of LTP was considered of limited use until basic mechanisms of central synaptic transmission are better understood. McNaughton pointed out, however, that all presynaptic changes known would result in a change in mean^2/variance in all the descriptions put forward. Thus, although a change in mean^2/variance may be ambiguous, if this parameter were demonstrated *not* to change a postsynaptic locus would be fairly sure.

Minimal Stimulation/Failures

When very few fibers are stimulated, the low probability of release results in a significant rate of failure to respond to presynaptic stimuli. In almost all studies in which failures have been counted (except Foster and McNaughton 1991), the failure rate decreases after induction of LTP. Although it is possible to apply a postsynaptic explanation to these findings (see *Introduction to the Problem* above), the presynaptic explanation of increased release probability is perhaps more likely in the light of the magnitude of the change.

McNaughton pointed out, however, that at least under certain conditions, electrical stimulation can cause increases in presynaptic axon excitability, which could account for the findings. At 22°C, weak, repetitive stimulation of Schaffer collaterals led to a robust lowering of the antidromic activation threshold of CA3 cells that lasted for more than 30 minutes. The effect was blocked by both AP5 and the inhibitor of nitric oxide synthase, L-nitroarginine-methyl-ester. These results have important implications for the interpretation of experiments concerning quantal analysis, using the so-called minimal stimulation method at reduced temperatures; however, they also provide further evidence that, under some conditions, lasting, NMDA receptor-dependent presynaptic changes can result from repetitive activation of hippocampal axons.

CONSENSUS: Everyone agreed that while such observations must be taken into account, a decrease in failure rate would most likely point to a presynaptic component to LTP, under some conditions.

Minis

Both changes in amplitude (Manabe et al. 1992) and frequency (Malgaroli and Tsien 1992; see section on **Possible Retrograde Messengers**, below) have been observed after stimuli that would be expected to result in potentiation. It was agreed that the classical interpretation of minis, in terms of pre- or postsynaptic sites, was likely to be applicable. Thus, change in miniature amplitude would be most likely a postsynaptic change, while a change in frequency would most be likely to be a presynaptic change. However, the skewed multiquantal nature of the minis distribution does cause some difficulties of interpretation (see *Introduction to the Problem* above).

Paired Pulse Facilitation (PPF)

Several studies have shown that PPF is not affected by induction of LTP. Everyone except Stevens agreed that given our current understanding of PPF, this phenomenon was of some value in addressing the site of LTP expression. Thus if LTP is expressed presynaptically, the mechanism is likely to be fundamentally different from all tested manipulations that affect PPF. These manipulations, including increasing the Ca^{2+}/Mg^{2+} ratio, blockade of adenosine receptors, blockade of presynaptic potassium channels and posttetanic potentiation, are all likely to affect calcium levels in the presynaptic terminal, at least to some degree.

Stevens argued that the lack of effect on PPF may be a detection problem, such that if LTP were restricted to a small subset of synapses with very low release probability, one might not see a change in PPF.

> EXPERIMENT: It would be useful, in terms of Stevens' comments, to test—both in cultures and slice preparation—whether known presynaptically mediated manipulations (e.g., change in extracellular Ca^{2+}) would result in measurable change in PPF when the same path was stimulated as that used for LTP induction.

NMDA vs. Non-NMDA Receptor Enhancement

While there was general agreement that a change in the NMDA component after LTP can occur, under certain conditions, when both components are simultaneously monitored, a differential sensitivity has been reported in the hippocampus (Muller et al. 1988; Wigström and Gustafsson 1988; Kauer et al. 1988b) and neocortex (Bindman and Murphy 1987; Artola and Singer 1990). This differs from manipulations that change transmitter release, in which there is a parallel increase in both components. The strength of the conclusion, that differential modulation of the two components is consistent with a postsynaptic change, depends upon the magnitude of the change in NMDA component. This issue could not be entirely agreed upon.

Postsynaptic Sensitivity to Exogenous Agonists

It was generally agreed that, if one could detect a change in sensitivity of the subsynaptic receptors, this would be very strong evidence for a postsynaptic locus of potentiation. A problem arises, however, as extrasynaptic receptors are generally more accessible to applied agonists and, as they would not be expected to be potentiated, they would be likely to swamp any synaptic change.

Aniracetam

Squire mentioned the results of Tang et al. (1991), who reported that the postsynaptic enhancement of AMPA receptors by aniracetam is less on pathways expressing LTP than on control pathways (Tang et al. 1991). This would be consistent with a postsynaptic expression mechanism. Two labs have had difficulty replicating these results (Asztely et al. 1992; Isaacson and Nicoll 1991).

WHAT HAPPENS AFTER CALCIUM?

Induction and/or expression of LTP have been shown to be prevented by manipulation of a wide variety of intracellular biochemical processes. At face value, this suggests many different possible pathways for LTP or an extremely complicated pathway to its expression. However, this interpretation ignores the complexity of interactions that occur between biochemical pathways, such that activation or inactivation of any one enzyme may influence most other pathways in the cell. There was a general consensus that it is, at this stage, difficult to interpret which of these processes is involved in the direct line of induction of LTP and which affects LTP via interacting pathways. In other words, we may be seeing an illustration of the complexity of interactions of intracellular processes rather than a profile of processes directly relevant to LTP. Thus it would not be surprising if disturbing cellular equilibrium by blocking or activating one or more enzyme prevented development of LTP.

Kinases in the Postsynaptic Cell

Several different approaches have been used to study the role of protein kinases in the postsynaptic cell. The two most common approaches have been to inject kinase blockers into the postsynaptic cell (Malenka et al. 1989) or to apply them to the slice (Malinow et al. 1988). The latter approach has the added complication of uncertainty as to whether a pre- or postsynaptic locus is involved and moreover the specificity of the blocking agents is yet to be established. A few groups have also used gene knockout experiments and presented evidence for the importance of kinases. These experiments must be treated with some caution, as other mechanisms may fall in to compensate for missing enzymes, thus causing false negative results. Alternately, side effects due to other effects of the missing enzyme could cause false positives. It is difficult to perform suitable controls for such experiments.

EXPERIMENT: Establish the specificity of the kinase blocking agents.

Enzymes have been studied by several groups using both pharmacological and gene knockout experiments: CaM kinase II (Malenka et al. 1989), tyrosine kinase (O'Dell, Kandel et al. 1991). In all cases there are several isozymes of each enzyme, and there is a possibility that other isozymes could compensate for the deleted enzyme. Thus there is some problem with the interpretation of both positive and negative effects. Some of the participants felt that these problems were particularly relevant to the observed tyrosine kinase effects. (It should be noted that in these mice anatomical changes were visible in Nissl stained sections.)

Possible Retrograde Messengers: Is Proposal of a Retrograde Messenger Necessary?

CONSENSUS: There was agreement that the work of Malgaroli and Tsien (1992), which showed an increased frequency of miniature excitatory postsynaptic currents (EPSCs) after postsynaptic activation of NMDA receptors, was a clear demonstration that a retrograde message existed. (Note that the postsynaptic localization of the induction process was established by demonstrating that potentiation was blocked by chelating Ca^{2+} in the postsynaptic cell or through hyperpolarization of the postsynaptic cell.) The fact that increased miniature frequency may not be directly related to LTP does not detract from the fact that this study clearly demonstrates that the messenger exists and thus whether or not it is essential to LTP induction, it is useful to pursue this line.

EXPERIMENT: The importance and pivotal nature of the experiment would make it very valuable for it to be repeated in other preparations, such as slices.

Currently the main candidates for the retrograde messenger are nitric oxide, carbon monoxide, and arachidonic acid. Other possibilities include mechanical effects, K^+, PAF gene activation, and released protein. Time did not allow for discussion of these latter possibilities in this context.

Nitric Oxide

Perhaps the most controversial findings discussed by our group during the whole period were the involvement of nitric oxide (NO) in the expression of LTP. Several groups, working in the CA1 region of the hippocampus, have now reported that application of NO synthetase inhibitors and/or hemoglobin (preventing rises in extra-cellular NO) block the development of LTP in the slice (Böhme et al. 1991; Bon et al. 1992; Haley et al. 1992; O'Dell, Hawkins et al. 1991; Schumann and Madison 1991; also cf. negative findings of Bliss and Collingridge 1993). From the discussion, it became apparent that, despite the apparent consensus, several groups represented at the workshop had also attempted similar experiments but had not observed effects on LTP, (in CA1, Andersen, Nicoll, Malenka, Collingridge; in dentate gyrus, McNaughton). Unfortunately none of the people who had reported positive results in the hippocampus were at the meeting, and thus possible unknown details of differences in their methods could not be brought forward. It would be very useful to compare any small differences in methodology or experimental conditions between the groups with different results, as this could not only resolve the discrepancy but might also point to factors essential to the LTP process. It was agreed that this apparent discrepancy was important, especially in view of the amount of work now being devoted to NO by labs using a wide variety of techniques. It is also of interest to note that several NO donors (including S-nitroso-glutathione, S-nitroso-acetyl penicillamine, and the photoactivable donor, Roissin's Black Salt) do not induce LTP (Errington et al. 1991).

Resolution of this issue is important. As Nicoll (this volume) states:

> If LTP is entirely dependent upon NO, it means that all of the machinery in the postsynaptic spine is simply involved in converting a Ca^{2+} rise into an NO rise. Thus, NO would be the key to pursuing the trail of LTP expression. The question "What is the mechanism underlying LTP expression?" becomes equivalent to the question "What is the mechanism underlying the action of NO on these synapses?

To resolve this question, we feel that a detailed comparison of all the methods and conditions of the different laboratories must be undertaken. It was suggested that the most effective method would be for members of laboratories with conflicting results to perform experiments together. A few suggestions were made as to possible differences in conditions. Variables may include such factors as age, species and temperature; however, in view of the methods sections in the different background papers, none of these would provide a simple correlation with the findings. Bockaert pointed out that the effective concentration of the inhibitors must be taken into account. Various effects have been reported in other systems, e.g., (a) NO has been reported to inhibit NMDA receptor activity (Manzoni et al. 1992) such that a strong decrease in NO production can increase NMDA receptor activation; (b) low concentrations of NO inhibitors have been shown to protect the brain from ischemia whereas high concentrations of inhibitors reverse this protection (Nowicky, Christofi, and Bindman, pers. comm.). It is interesting to note that Nowicky and Bindman (1993) have recently described a block of an LTP-like phenomenon in slices of rat medial frontal cortex in the presence of an NO synthetase inhibitor.

Carbon Monoxide

Evidence was reported from the labs of Stevens and of Kandel, that CO might serve as a retrograde messenger. Application of gaseous CO together with weak synaptic stimulation can lead to long-term synaptic enhancement. Moreover, application of zincprotoporphyrin IX, a blocker of the CO-producing enzyme, blocks the induction of LTP. Most interestingly, Stevens reported that zincprotoporphyrin IX does not only block induction of LTP but also reverses already established LTP. Whether or not further results show that CO has an important role as a retrograde messenger, the LTP-reversing effect of zincprotoporphyrin is interesting as it is the first agent that has been suggested to have this effect and it could thus be a very useful tool in the behavioral analysis of the significance of LTP.

> EXPERIMENT: What are the behavioral effects of zincprotoporphyrin IX *in vivo*? Does it affect memory or learning tasks?

Arachidonic Acid

The fact that the membrane permeable molecule, arachidonic acid, is released in response to NMDA receptor activation makes it a tempting candidate for a retrograde messenger.

Two labs (Williams et al. 1989; O'Dell, Hawkins et al. 1991) have demonstrated that application of arachidonic acid to hippocampal slices in conjunction with a weak tetanus imitates the potentiation effects of tetanus. Interestingly, the onset of the effect shows a similar time course to the border (if definable) between STP and LTP, to the time course of effectiveness of protein kinase inhibitors and to potentiation induced by IS,3R-ACPD. There is disagreement, however, between the groups as to whether this potentiation is blocked by AP5.

Although the effects of arachidonic acid are inconclusive in terms of LTP, the molecule is interesting in terms of the wide range of pre and postsynaptic processes it affects. Some examples include:

1. increased activation of the g-isoenzyme of protein kinase C,
2. increased phosphoinositol turnover in isolated synaptosomes,
3. increase in current response to NMDA application (Miller et al. 1992; cerebellar granule cells),
4. increased glutamate release from synaptosomes (Freeman et al. 1990).
5. increased glutamate uptake by glial cells (Barbour et al. 1989).

WHAT DO WE KNOW ABOUT LONG-TERM MAINTENANCE?

There are basically three theories about how LTP/LTD could be maintained in the longer term:

1. gene activation (discussed for most of the session),
2. structural changes (touched on at the end of the discussion),
3. persistent activation of a kinase system (not further discussed in the group; see, however, Nicoll, this volume).

The general consensus was that we know very little about maintenance so far but that certain cautions were important. Perhaps the most general of these was that application of a tetanus or other strong inputs to a neuronal system will cause many effects which may or may not be related to LTP. Thus, after tetanus, increase of a gene product that correlates with LTP may only be coincident due to pushing the system, thus causing activation of genes in order to refill stores of proteins.

For these reasons, it was clear that it is extremely difficult and perhaps not useful to dissociate maintenance from induction/expression, at least in the temporal sense. Mechanisms that could underlie changes, which would last beyond the half life of proteins in the cell, could be referred to as maintenance.

Gene Activation/Protein Synthesis

It was pointed out in this and other groups that LTP is a local phenomenon, such that any change occurring must be able to be targeted to one or a few spines. It was considered rather unlikely that this would involve sending a message back to the nucleus of the cell, turning on or upregulating a gene and then sending a few molecules of protein back targeted to arrive at a few spines out of perhaps 10,000–30,000 on the pyramidal cell. However, it was also noted that it was not necessary to activate synthesis to increase the density of a particular protein in the membrane. As many proteins are at all times moving up and down the dendrites and being inserted at a particular rate in the membrane, decreasing the removal rate would increase the density.

There is, however, evidence that protein synthesis inhibitors prevent the maintenance of LTP (Otani and Abraham 1989), even if applied up to a few hours after application of an LTP-inducing stimulus. Moreover, increasing protein synthesis can stabilize LTP so that it lasts >30 days rather than decaying over about two weeks. Other postinduction manipulators can also prolong LTP, e.g., repeated tetanization (Barnes 1979).

> EXPERIMENT: Establishment of an exact time window for protein synthesis effects would be useful.

A brief discussion of the significance of observed turn-on of immediate early genes (e.g., Curran, this volume) resulted in the conclusion that it was difficult at present to assess their significance.

Structure

Although there is convincing documentation that environmental factors correlate with structural alterations of the relevant areas of the nervous system (Greenough, this volume), there is less information on possible structural changes associated with LTP. So far, only correlative changes are available.

In LTP experiments, three types of anatomical changes have been observed (Chang and Greenough 1984; Greenough and Bailey 1988): the first type includes changes at individual synapses that may influence the transmitter release probability. These are changes of the shape of presynaptic boutons, of the vesicle number and distribution, and of the size and detailed form of the postsynaptic densities. Given the likely low release probability, the reported changes remain of uncertain significance. These results are in contrast to the much clearer changes seen in *Aplysia*, where the much greater changes fit the increased release probability in synapses subserving long-lasting sensitization and conditioned reflexes (Bailey and Chen 1983, 1988).

The second type of change is an altered number of synapses per target neuron from a pathway showing LTP, as compared with an untetanized control pathway to the same neuron. No definitive experimental evidence exists to support this type. Several correlative studies suggest an increase in synapse number in areas showing LTP as compared to nontetanized regions of equivalent cells. Our group agreed that new methods are needed to answer whether morphologically measurable synapse number can be associated with LTP.

The third candidate for neuronal change that could explain a LTP alteration would be real change in connectivity. Again, new techniques are needed to secure credible results. In such studies, both pre- and postsynaptic elements have to be marked to allow precise counts. Suggestive evidence on dentate granule cells was mentioned by Andersen and concerned an increased number of simple spines per unit dendritic length after medial perforant path-induced LTP compared to control material from the unstimulated contralateral side. Further, such LTP material contains a fourfold increase in bifurcating spines with at least two boutons at each of the two spine heads. The findings suggest spine growth and increased number of sites served by the afferent fibers (Trommald et al. 1990).

> CONSENSUS: There is a major problem with this approach in that a stimulation of a large number of pathways, such as is used for LTP induction could have many effects other than induction of LTP, including turn-on of various genes. We agreed that if such a line were to be pursued further, the very minimum requirements should be that the effect be prevented by AP5 infusion at the time of tetanus. Nevertheless, the results would still be difficult to interpret.

CONCLUSIONS

This brief section is not designed to list all the points of consensus that were reached by the group, but rather to stress a few points which the rapporteur found particularly helpful in understanding the problems involved and determining useful future directions for investigation.

1. *Quantal variability*: Establishing the source of the skewed nature of the central miniature distribution and investigating whether it is truly multipeaked (and, if so, the origins of the peaks) would be a very valuable step towards understanding the structure and function of central synapses, which is really the essential information needed to allow interpretation of much of the LTP literature.
2. *Nitric oxide as a retrograde messenger:* The theory that nitric oxide is a retrograde messenger involved in the induction of LTP is still open to considerable debate. Unfortunately none of the laboratories which have reported blockage of LTP with NO synthetase inhibitors were represented at the meeting.

The workshop was, however, particularly useful in highlighting the tendency for negative results to remain unpublished. Once these are taken into account, the balance of the case against NO being an essential retrograde messenger, except under very specific conditions, grows considerably. Perhaps one of the most important conclusions made in both our group and group 4 (see Role et al., this volume) was that it would be valuable for scientists from both groups to come together to compare the details of their experimental conditions and, if possible, to spend time repeating experiments together. It is possible that the NO debate, and that concerning whether the locus of LTP expression is pre- or postsynaptic, revolves around subtle differences in experimental technique. Perhaps when we uncover these differences, a major clue in the advancement of understanding of this phenomenon will be provided.

3. *Paired pulse facilitation*: Another important issue was the doubt expressed over the meaning of PPF. It was agreed that this issue should be addressed experimentally. This is particularly important as PPF has been used in a large number of experiments and has generally been considered a very reliable and readily interpretable parameter.
4. *Protein synthesis*: Much discussion ensued around this topic. Here it was particularly useful to have the contributions of different fields. Two important points emerged which, though perhaps clear to protein chemists, were useful to other members of the group:
   a) It is not necessary to turn on genes in order to increase the density of a particular protein in a piece of membrane. This can be achieved by specific local changes in protein removal or insertion rates.
   b) It is probably impractical to use specific gene upregulation at the nucleus in order to insert proteins in one or a few spines out of the thousands of spines in the dendritic field.
5. *Interpretation of results*: One point, repeatedly stressed, was the complex interconnections of intracellular processes. Thus blocking any one enzyme would be likely to change the balance of metabolic processes and therefore affect many other enzymes in the system. Similarly, blockage of protein synthesis or genetic deletion of certain enzymes might have far-reaching effects on all intracellular processes. Moreover, it was suggested that in conditions of extreme activation, such as the tetanus often applied for LTP induction, cellular stores could be depleted, resulting in protein synthesis which would correlate with, but not necessarily be causal in, LTP induction. This left the discussion in a rather difficult position, more or less concluding that it was impossible to interpret most of the results concerning what happens in LTP induction or expression after calcium influx. In fact, this uncertainty could be pressed further to include calcium influx, as calcium buffers will also undoubtedly affect many cellular processes. However, the fact that NMDA channels must open to induce LTP makes the calcium hypothesis very attractive.

REFERENCES

Aniksztejn, L., M.P. Roisin, R. Amsellem, and Y. Ben-Ari. 1989. Long-term potentiation in the hippocampus is not associated with a sustained enhanced release of endogenous excitatory amino acids. *Neurosci.* **28**:387–392.

Artola, A., T. Hensch, and W. Singer. 1992. A rise of [Ca^{2+}] in the postsynaptic cell is necessary and sufficient for induction of long-term depression (LTD) in neocortex. *Soc. Neurosci. Abstr.* **18**:567.30.

Artola, A., and W. Singer. 1990. The involvement of N-methyl-D-aspartate receptors in induction and maintenance of long-term potentiation in rat visual cortex. *Eur. J. Neurosci.* **2**:254–269.

Asztely, F., E. Hanse, H. Wigström, and B. Gustafsson. 1992. Aniracetam-evoked potentiation does not interact with long-term potentiation in the CA1 region of the hippocampus. *Synapse* **11**:342–345.

Bailey, C.H., and M. Chen. 1983. Morphological basis of long-term habituation and sensitization in *Aplysia*. *Science* **220**:91–93.

Bailey, C.H., and M. Chen. 1988. Long-term memory in *Aplysia* modulates the total number of varicosities of single identified sensory neurons. *Proc. Natl. Acad. Sci.* **85**:2373–2377.

Barbour, B., M. Szatkowski, N. Ingledew, and D. Attwell. 1989. Arachidonic acid induces a prolonged inhibition of glutamate uptake into glial cells. *Nature* **342**:918–920.

Barnes, C.A. 1979. Memory deficits associated with senescence: A neurophysiological and behavioural study in the rat. *J. Comp. Physiol. Psychol.* **931**:74–104.

Bashir, Z.I., Z.A. Bortolotto, C.H. Davies, N. Berretta, A.J. Irving, A.J. Seal, J.M. Henley, D.E. Jane, J.C. Watkins, and G.L. Collingridge. 1993. Induction of LTP in the hippocampus needs synaptic activation of glutamate metabotropic receptors. *Nature* **363**:347–350.

Bekkers, J.M., and C.F. Stevens. 1990. Presynaptic mechanism for long-term potentiation in the hippocampus. *Nature* **346**:724–729.

Bindman, L.J., and K.P.S.J. Murphy. 1988. NMDA-receptors participate in the maintenance of long-term potentiation of synaptic transmission in slices of neocortex *in vitro*. *J.Physiol.* **406**:176P.

Bliss, T.V.P., and G.L. Collingridge. 1993. A synaptic model of memory: Long-term potentiation in the hippocampus. *Nature* **361**:31.

Böhme, G.A., C. Bon, J.M. Stutzman, A. Doble, and J.C. Blanchard. 1991. Possible involvement of nitric oxide in long-term potentiation. *Eur. J. Pharmacol.* **199**:379–381.

Bon, C., G.A. Böhme, A. Doble, J.M. Stutzman, and J.C. Blanchard. 1992. A role for nitric oxide in long-term potentiation. *Eur. J. Neurosci.* **4**:420–424.

Bonhoeffer, T., V. Staiger, and A. Aertsen. 1989. Synaptic plasticity in rat hippocampal slice cultures: Local "Hebbian" conjunction of pre- and postsynaptic stimulation leads to synaptic enhancement. *Proc. Natl. Acad. Sci. USA* **86**:8113–8117.

Bortolotto, Z.A., and G.L. Collingridge. 1992. Activation of glutamate metatropic receptors induces long-term potentiation. *Eur. J. Pharmacol.* **214**:297–298.

Bröcher, S., A. Artola, and W. Singer. 1992. Intracellular injection of Ca^{2+} chelators blocks induction of long-term depression in rat visual cortex. *Proc. Natl. Acad. Sci. USA* **89**:123–127.

Chang, F.-L.F., and W.T. Greenough. 1984. Transient and enduring morphological correlates of synaptic activity and efficacy change in the rat hippocampal slice. *Brain Res.* **309**:35–46.

Christofi, G., A.V. Nowicky, S.R. Bolsover, and L.J. Bindman. 1993. The postsynaptic induction of non-associative long-term depression of excitatory synaptic transmission in rat hippocampal slices. *J. Neurophysiol.* **69**:219–229.

Cormier, R.J., M.D. Mark, and P.T. Kelly. 1993. Glutamate iontophoresis induces long-term potentiation in the absence of evoked presynaptic activity. *Neuron* **10**:907–919.

Dolphin, A.C., M.L. Errington, and T.V.P. Bliss. 1982. Long-term potentiation of the perforant path *in vivo* is associated with increased glutamate release. *Nature* **297**:496–498.

Edwards, F.A. 1991. LTP is a long-term problem. *Nature* **350**:271–272.

Edwards, F.A., A. Konnerth, and B. Sakmann. 1990. Quantal analysis of inhibitory synaptic transmission in the dentate gyrus of rat hippocampal slices: A patch clamp study. *J. Physiol.* **430**:213–249.

Errington, M.L., Y.-G. Li, H. Matthies, J.H. Williams, and T.V.P. Bliss. 1991. The nitric oxide synthetase inhibitor N-nitro-L-arginine reduces magnitude of long-term potentiation in the dentate gyrus but not in area CA1 of the hippocampus *in vitro*. *Soc. Neurosci. Abst.* **17**:951.

Foster, T.C., and B.L. McNaughton. 1991. Long-term enhancement of CA1 synaptic transmission is due to increased quantal size, not quantal content. *Hippocampus* **1**:79–91.

Freeman, E.J., D.M. Terrian, and R.V. Dorman. 1990. Presynaptic facilitation of glutamate release from isolated hippocampal mossy fiber nerve endings by arachadonic acid. *Neurochem. Res.* **15**:743–750.

Greenough, W.T., and C.H. Bailey. 1988. The anatomy of a memory: Convergence of results across a diversity of tests. *Trends Neurosci.* **11**:142–147.

Gustafsson, B.F., E. Asztely, and H. Wigström. 1989. Onset characteristics of long-term potentiation in the guinea-pig hippocampal CA1 region *in vitro*. *Eur. J. Neurosci.* **1**:382–394.

Guthrie, P.B., M. Segal, and S.B. Kater. 1991. Independent regulation of calcium revealed by imaging dendritic spines. *Nature* **354**:76–80.

Haley, J.E., G.L. Wilcox, and P.F. Chapman. 1992. The role of nitric-oxide in hippocampal long-term potentiation. *Neuron* **8**:211–216.

Hirsch, J.C., and F. Crépel. 1992. Postsynaptic calcium is necessary for induction of LTP and LTD of monosynaptic EPSPs in prefrontal neurons. An *in vitro* study in the rat. *Synapse* **10**:173–175.

Isaacson, J.S., and R.A. Nicoll. 1991. Aniracetam reduces receptor desensitization and slows the decay of fast excitatory synaptic currents in the hippocampus. *Proc. Nat. Acad. Sci. USA* **88**:10936–10940.

Katz, B. 1966. Nerve, Muscle, and Synapse. New York: McGraw-Hill.

Kauer, J.A., R.C. Malenka, and R.A. Nicoll. 1988a. NMDA application potentiates synaptic transmission in the hippocampus. *Nature* **334**:250–252.

Kauer, J.A., R.C. Malenka, and R.A. Nicoll. 1988b. A persistent postsynaptic modification mediates long-term potentiation in the hippcampus. *Neuron* **1**:911–917.

Kimura, F., T. Tsumoto, A. Nishigori, and Y. Yoshimura. 1990. Long-term depression but not potentiation is induced in Ca^{2+} chelated visual cortex neurons. *NeuroReport* **1**:65–68.

Kossel, A., T. Bonhoeffer, and J. Boltz. 1990. Non-Hebbian synapses in rat visual cortex. *NeuroReport* **1**:115–118.

Lisman, J.E., and M.A. Goldring. 1988. Feasibility of long-term storage of graded information by the Ca^{2+}/calmodulin-dependent protein kinase molecules of the postsynaptic density. *Proc. Natl. Acad. Sci. USA* **85**:5320–5324.

Lynch, G., J. Larson, S. Kelso, G. Barrionuevo, and F. Schottler. 1983. Intracellular injections of EGTA block induction of hippocampal long-term potentiation. *Nature* **305**:719–721.

Malenka, R.C., J.A. Kauer, D.J. Perkel, M.D. Mauk, P.T. Kelly, R.A. Nicoll, and M.N. Waxham. 1989. An essential role for postsynaptic calmodulin and protein kinase activity in long-term potentiation. *Nature* **340**:554–557.

Malenka, R.C., J.A. Kauer, R.S. Zucker, and R.A. Nicoll. 1988. Postsynaptic calcium is sufficient for potentiation of hippocampal synaptic transmission. *Science* **242**:81–84.

Malgaroli, A., and R.W. Tsien. 1992. Glutamate-induced long-term potentiation of the frequency of miniature synaptic currents in cultured hippocampal neurons. *Nature* **357**:134–139.

Malinow, R., D.V. Madison, and R.W. Tsien. 1988. Persistent protein kinase activity underlying long-term potentiation. *Nature* **335**:820–824.

Malinow, R., and J.P. Miller. 1986. Postsynaptic hyperpolarization during conditioning reversibly blocks induction of long-term potentiation. *Nature* **320**:529–530.

Manabe, T., P. Renner, and R.A. Nicoll. 1992. Postsynaptic contribution to long-term potentiation revealed by analysis of miniature synaptic currents. *Nature* **355**:50–55.

Manzoni, O., L. Prezeau, P. Marin, S. Desagher, J. Bockaert, and L. Fagni. 1992. Nitric oxide-induced blockade of NMDA receptors. *Neuron* **8**:653–662.

Miller, B., M. Sarantis, S.F. Traynelis, and D. Attwell. 1992. Potentiation of NMDA receptor currents by arachidonic acid. *Nature* **355**:722–725.

Mulkey, R.M., and R.C. Malenka. 1992. Mechanism underlying induction of homosynaptic long-term depression in area CA1 of the hippocampus. *Neuron* **9**:967–975.

Muller, D., M. Joly, and G. Lynch. 1988. Contributions of quisqualate and NMDA receptors to the induction and expression of LTP. *Science* **242**:1694–1697.

Nowicky, A.V., and L. Bindman. 1993. The nitric oxide synthesis inhibitor, N-monomethyl-L-arginine blocks the induction of a long-term potentiation like phenomenon in rat medial frontal cortical neurons *in vitro*. *J. Neurophysiol.*, in press.

O'Dell, T.J., R.D. Hawkins, E.R. Kandel, and O. Arancio. 1991. Tests of the roles of two diffusible substances in long-term potentiation: Evidence for nitric oxide as a possible early retrograde messenger. *Proc. Natl. Acad. Sci. USA* **88**:11285–11289.

O'Dell, T.J., E.R. Kandel, and S.G.N. Grant. 1991. Long-term potentiation in the hippocampus is blocked by tyrosine kinase inhibitors. *Nature* **353**:558–560.

Otani, S., and W.C. Abraham. 1989. Inhibition of protein synthesis in the dentate gyrus but not the entorhinal cortex blocks maintenance of long-term potentiation in rats. *Neurosci. Lett.* **106**:175–180.

Pockett, S., N.H. Brookes, and L.J. Bindman. 1990. Long-term depression at synapses in slices of rat hippocampus can be induced by bursts of postsynaptic activity. *Exp. Brain Res.* **80**:196–200.

Pockett, S., and O.C.J. Lippold. 1986. Long-term potentiation and depression in hippocampal slices. *Exp. Neurol.* **91**:481–487.

Schumann, E.M., and D.V. Madison. 1991. A requirement for the intercellular messenger nitric oxide in long-term potentiation. *Science* **254**:1503–1506.

Tang, C.-M., Q.-Y. Shi, A. Katchman, and G. Lynch. 1991. Modulation of the time course of fast EPSCs and glutamate channel kinetics by aniracetam. *Science* **254**:288–290.

Trommald, M., J. Line Vaaland, T.W. Blackstad, and P. Andersen. 1990. Dendritic spine changes in rat dentate granule cells associated with long-term potentiation. In: Neurotoxicity of Excitatory Amino Acids, ed. A. Guidotti, pp. 163–174. New York: Raven.

Wigström, H., and B. Gustafsson. 1988. Presynaptic and postsynaptic interactions in the control of hippocampal long-term potentiation. In: Long-Term Potentiation: From Biophysics to Behaviour, ed. P.W. Landfield and S.A. Deadwyler, pp. 73–107. New York: Alan R. Liss.

Williams, J.H., M.L. Errington, M.A. Lynch, and T.V.P. Bliss. 1989. Arachidonic acid induces a long-term activity dependent enhancement of synaptic transmission in the hippocampus. *Nature* **341**:739–742.

17

Functional Diversity of Glutamate Receptor Channels

P.H. SEEBURG
ZMBH, University of Heidelberg, Im Neuenheimer Feld 282,
D–69120 Heidelberg, F.R. Germany

ABSTRACT

Glutamate receptor (GluR) channels are classified by pharmacological criteria and designated as AMPA receptors, kainate receptors, and NMDA receptors. At AMPA receptors, glutamate activates channels with rapid kinetics (on and offset time courses approximately 1 msec) and, generally, low permeability to divalent cations. Commensurate with these properties, AMPA receptor channels mediate the fast synaptic excitatory neurotransmission. At NMDA receptor channels, glutamate evokes currents with relatively slow rise and offset time courses. Current responses are subject to voltage-dependent Mg^{2+} block and channels are highly permeable to Ca^{2+} ions. NMDA channels have a role in fast signal transmission but their main function may involve activity-dependent synaptic modifications. Kainate receptors possess high-affinity binding of the neurotoxins kainate and domoate and these compounds activate desensitizing current responses in kainate receptor channels, as does glutamate. The synaptic location/physiological role of this class of GluR channels is not clear.

Biophysical and molecular biological analyses of GluR channels in the mammalian central nervous system provide an increasingly complex picture of functional channel diversity. Significant advances in the detailed characterization of the various GluR channels have emerged from biophysical analyses of pure receptor populations expressed by recombinant technology. GluR channels assemble from sequence-related subunits and, thus, one way to form channels with different properties is to select subunit assembly from sets of suitable subunit partners. This strategy is operative in the CNS, where readout of GluR subunit genes is subject to spatial and developmental regulation. Additional diversification is achieved through posttranscriptional processes (alternative splicing, RNA editing), resulting in microheterogeneity of particular subunits. Functional consequences include altered divalent ion permeability and gating properties of GluR channels.

SUBUNIT CONSTITUENTS OF GluR CHANNELS

Extensive molecular studies following the expression cloning of two GluR channel subunits (Hollmann et al. 1989; Moriyoshi et al. 1991) have demonstrated that the

Cellular and Molecular Mechanisms Underlying Higher Neural Functions
Edited by A.I. Selverston and P. Ascher

mammalian (rodent) brain expresses more than 14 genes that encode distinct subunits (reviewed in Nakanishi 1992; Sommer and Seeburg 1992). These subunits are approximately 1,000 amino acids in length and share sequence elements that characterize all subunits as belonging to the same structural family. Subunits can be grouped according to primary sequences and sequence relationships can be represented in the form of an evolutionary tree where vicinity often indicates similar functional properties (Figure 17.1).

It has been commonly held—possibly incorrectly—that GluR subunits and constituents of other ligand-gated ion channels have the same transmembrane topology. Topology has been established for the nicotinic acetylcholine receptor (nAChR) whose subunits cross the cell membrane four times, and thus in these subunits the N- and C-termini face the synaptic cleft (Chavez and Hall 1992; Unwin 1989). Furthermore, a large body of evidence points to the second transmembrane segment (TM2) as lining the ion channel in nAChRs (e.g., Imoto et al. 1988; reviewed in Unwin 1989). It should be stressed that the situation is unresolved for GluR channels whose subunits may belong to a topologically distinct protein family.

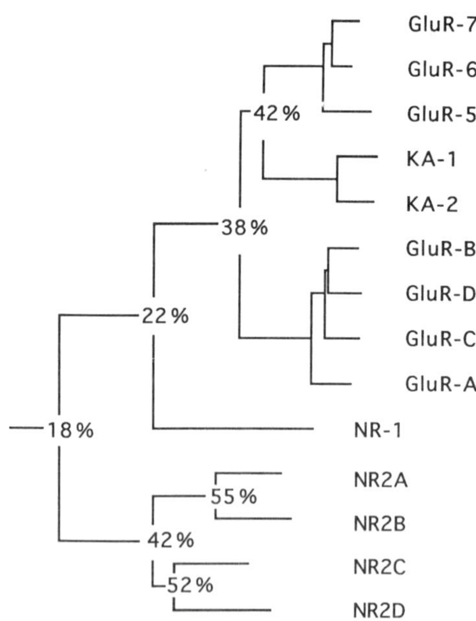

Figure 17.1 Sequence relationships of ionotropic glutamate receptor subunits. GluR-5, -6, -7 and KA-1, KA-2 are constituents of high-affinity kainate receptors, GluR-A to -D (also termed GluR-1 to -4) are AMPA receptor subunits and NR1, NR2A to NR2D are NMDA receptor subunits (reviewed in Nakanishi 1992; Sommer and Seeburg 1992). The percent identities in primary sequence between "sequence branches" or (sometimes) subunits are indicated.

Functional GluR channels are composed of an unknown number of subunits. Most subunits form homo-oligomeric (homomeric) GluR channels *in vitro*. The emergent functional aspects of subunits co-expressed *in vitro* indicate that native channels constitute heteromeric assemblies (Figure 17.2). Subunits with high sequence similarity do not necessarily form heteromeric channels. Such a simple relationship only applies to the AMPA receptor whose constituents are closely sequence related. In NMDA receptors, channels with properties comparable to those of native receptor channels configure from subunits with little sequence identity (Monyer et al. 1992). Similarly, high-affinity kainate receptors can assemble from structurally distant partners. Hence, GluR subunits carry structural signals for preferred subunit assembly. These signals, unidentified in GluR subunits, may reside in interfaces of subunit partners, as has been demonstrated for voltage-activated K^+ channels (Li et al. 1992) and nAChRs (Verall and Hall 1992).

MICROHETEROGENEITY OF GluR SUBUNITS

Analysis of cDNA has revealed that GluR subunits can occur in different molecular forms generated by alternative splicing (Bettler et al. 1990; Gallo et al. 1992; Nakanishi 1992; Sommer and Seeburg 1992; Sugihara et al. 1992). Several subunits are further spot-changed by RNA editing (Sommer et al. 1991). As depicted in a generalized diagram (Figure 17.3), microheterogeneity occurs in the N-terminal domain, the putative channel region, which is an area preceding the C-terminal-most transmembrane segment and sequences beyond (C-terminal heterogeneity). The functional consequences have been determined in several instances.

Each AMPA receptor subunit exists in two forms (flip and flop) with respect to a 38 amino acid residue sequence preceding the predicted TM4 segment. These forms, which incorporate alternative exons, show CNS developmental and area-specific expression patterns and affect desensitization time course and the ratio of peak to steady-state components of glutamate-evoked currents in AMPA receptor channels.

For AMPA receptor subunit GluR-B and kainate receptor subunits GluR-5 and -6, RNA editing targets a residue within the putative channel, forming segment TM2. The genomic DNA sequence of these subunits predicts that a glutamine residue occupies the glutamine/arginine (Q/R) position of TM2, whereas an arginine codon is (GluR-B), or can be (GluR-5, GluR-6), found instead in the respective cDNAs. This residue exchange affects the divalent ion permeability of GluR channels (reviewed in Sommer and Seeburg 1992). In GluR-6, two additional amino acid residues, located in the putative TM1 region, can also be altered by RNA editing (Köhler et al. 1993). Thus, for this subunit, eight distinct molecular forms (seven are edited and one form carries the genomically encoded sequence) occur in CNS at different levels in the CNS. TM1 editing in GluR-6 also affects the divalent ion permeability of GluR-6 channels.

Some subunits are expressed with or without small insertion sequences in their N-terminal domains (i.e., NR1 and GluR-5) and show C-terminal heterogeneity (i.e.,

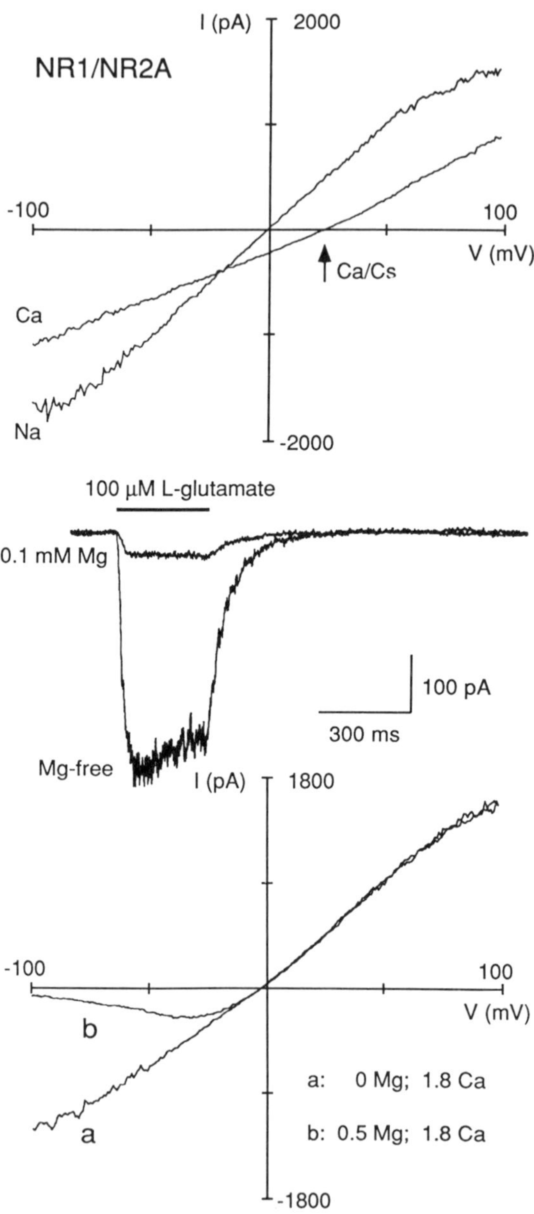

Figure 17.2 Properties of heteromeric NMDA receptors (NR1/NR2A). The upper panel shows current-voltage relationships recorded in high Na^{2+} and high Ca^{2+} extracellular solution. Note high Ca^{2+} permeability (positive reversal potential). Middle panel shows blockade of whole-cell current traces by 0.1 mM Mg^{2+} [compare whole-cell current traces (Na^{+} currents) in the presence and absence of 0.1 mM Mg^{2+}]. Bottom panel demonstrates voltage dependence of Mg^{2+} block (trace a, recorded in 0 Mg^{2+}, 1.8 mM Ca^{2+}; trace b, recorded in 0.5 mM Mg^{2+}, 1.8 mM Ca^{2+}). Courtesy of N. Burnashev.

GluR channel subunit

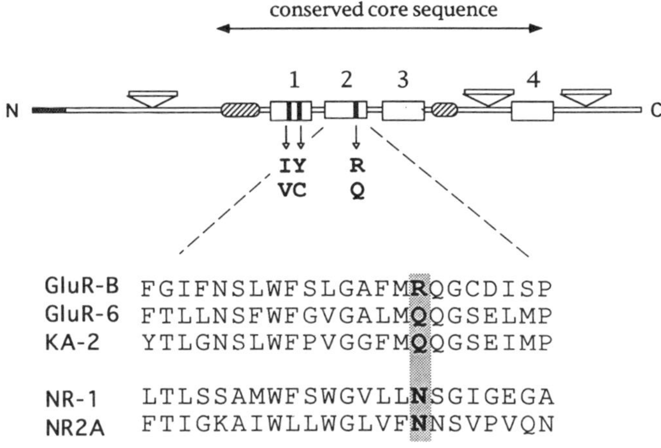

Figure 17.3 Diagram of GluR channel subunit. GluR subunits are approximately between 900 and 1,400 amino acid residues in length, with differences mainly in the C-terminal region. The immature N-terminus carries a signal sequence for vectorial cotranslational transfer. Open boxes 1 to 4 represent predicted transmembrane segments TM1 to TM4. (Please note that topology is unknown). The hatched ovals correspond to regions with sequence similarities to a bacterial glutamine binding protein. Regions affected by alternative splicing are indicated by triangles. RNA editing targets residues in TM1 and TM2. A region (TM2) with molecular determinants for ion conductance and permeability properties of glutamate-activated ion channels is shown in detail for several key subunits (reviewed in Nakanishi 1992; Sommer and Seeburg 1992). The extent of a conserved core sequence for all subunits is indicated.

NR1, GluR-D, GluR-5). These sequence variants generated by alternative exon selection are cell specific when analyzed by *in situ* hybridization. Physiological consequences might include differential phosphorylation (Chen and Huang 1992; Greengard et al. 1991), provided that C-termini are intracellularly located.

DETERMINANTS OF Ca^{2+} PERMEABILITY IN GluR CHANNELS

Perhaps the best understood feature of GluR channels is their selective permeability/impermeability to Ca^{2+} ions. As a rule, the NMDA receptor channel is designed for high Ca^{2+} permeability (Ascher and Nowak 1988) whereas the AMPA receptor possesses low Ca^{2+} permeability. Since both channel types are built from sequence-related subunits, distinct molecular determinants should underlie these selective functional properties in both channel subtypes. The consensus from several laboratories is that major determinants lie in a region that is termed TM2; Heinemann and his colleagues, however, do not assign a membrane-spanning character to this region. In this segment (here designated TM2 for convenience, although this should not prejudice for or against a particular topology), a certain position (homologous in all sequenced GluR subunits) is occupied by either glutamine, arginine, or asparagine. The particular residue occupying this position largely determines the Ca^{2+} permeability of the glutamate-gated channel (Sommer and Seeburg 1992).

Most AMPA receptors contain the GluR-B subunit, which carries an arginine in this TM2 position. The positively charged residue determines the low Ca^{2+} permeability of heteromeric AMPA receptor channels. AMPA receptors built without participation of GluR-B show a much increased Ca^{2+} (and Mg^{2+}) permeability. Indeed, as shown in at least one neural cell—namely the Bergmann glia cell of the cerebellum—AMPA receptor channels do not contain GluR-B occur *in vivo* (Burnashev, Khodorova et al. 1992; Müller et al. 1992). This demonstrates that control over GluR-B gene expression is critical for setting the level of glutamate-activated Ca^{2+} influx into cells through AMPA receptors. The example further indicates that the level of GluR-B subunit expression relative to that of other AMPA receptor subunits is important. If the level is low, AMPA receptor channel mosaics may form; they would be composed of channels with low divalent ion permeability containing the GluR-B subunit and of those without GluR-B, which are Ca^{2+} permeable (see Sommer and Seeburg 1992).

In the NMDA receptor NR1 and NR2 subunits, the critical TM2 position is occupied by an asparagine residue (Nakanishi 1992). The TM2 asparagine in NMDA receptor subunits determines both: the high Ca^{2+} permeability of NMDA receptor channels and the voltage-dependent block by extracellular Mg^{2+} ions (Figure 17.2). However, in heteromeric NMDA receptors, the TM2 asparagine of the NR1 subunit (the subunit common to all NMDA receptor subtypes) is essential for high Ca^{2+} permeability; the asparagine of the NR2 subunits contributes more towards the Mg^{2+} block (Burnashev, Schoepfer et al. 1992).

FUNCTIONAL DIVERSITY OF GluR CHANNELS IN NEURAL CELLS

Functional diversity of GluR channels is evident when measuring glutamate-activated currents in diverse membrane preparations (reviewed in Nicoll et al. 1990). In general, current properties correspond to those measured from recombinantly expressed AMPA, kainate, and NMDA receptor channels. Here I list observations regarding different channel properties within a given GluR channel type (AMPA, kainate, NMDA receptor) in native cells/membranes, which may be linked to molecular differences.

The first observation concerns Ca^{2+} permeability of AMPA receptor channels in neural cells. Iino et al. (1990) and Ogura et al. (1992), when analyzing primary hippocampal cells, observed that a certain percentage of these cells showed glutamate-activated Ca^{2+} influx into cells via non-NMDA receptors. The I-V relation of glutamate-evoked whole-cell currents in such cells was inwardly rectifying. In the majority of cells, currents had a linear I-V relation and cells showed low Ca^{2+} permeability in response to glutamate. These differences in Ca^{2+} permeability and ion conductance properties of AMPA receptor channels can be mimicked with recombinantly expressed channels, and these reflect whether or not the GluR-B subunit participates in channel formation. Indeed, as exemplified by cultured and native cerebellar Bergmann glial cells, neural cells can lack expression of the GluR-B gene (Burnashev, Khodorova et al. 1992; Müller et al. 1992). Hence, regulation of GluR-B gene expression might serve to set the level of Ca^{2+} influx through glutamate-activated channels of the AMPA receptor subtype. Whether this type of regulation is used by neurons in normal physiology or can occur in pathological situations is currently under intense investigations, which so far have provided conflicting results (Pellegrini-Giampietro et al. 1992; Gall, as well as Monyer and Wieloch, pers. comm.). A second mechanism controlling the Ca^{2+} permeability through AMPA receptor channels is that of RNA editing, which targets the codon of a critical determinant (TM2 R/Q site) in the GluR-B subunit (Sommer et al. 1991). Our knowledge of this mechanism is rudimentary. RNA editing may be regulated because in the developing brain, more unedited (Ca^{2+} permeable) GluR-B-containing mRNA seem to be expressed than in the adult brain. In summary, Ca^{2+}-permeable AMPA receptors in CNS contain no GluR-B subunit or may incorporate an unedited GluR-B subunit.

AMPA receptor channels have distinctive rapid on and off kinetics, commensurate with their primary function of fast excitatory neurotransmission. Measurements in native membranes using the natural agonist glutamate, or using kainate as the agonist, suggest that AMPA receptor channels may differ with respect to onset, offset (termination) and desensitization kinetics (Colquhoun et al. 1992; Trussel and Fischbach 1989). Structural determinants for rapid desensitization are located within the alternatively spliced modules flip and flop which reside in the vicinity of TM4. In certain heteromeric subunit configurations, the flop module, which contains subunit variants, shows faster desensitization than the corresponding flip homologs. Particularly fast desensitization is seen with GluR-D flop in homo- and heteromeric assemblies, suggesting that GluR-D flop dominates the desensitization behavior of some native AMPA channel populations (J.P. Ruppersberg et al., pers. comm.). In fact, GluR-D flop might participate in AMPA channels in cochlear neurons where glutamate activates currents with very fast desensitization time courses (Ramon and Trussell 1992). The developmental expression profiles of alternatively spliced AMPA receptor subunits predict that early AMPA receptor channels (mostly flip configurations) should be characterized by slower desensitization kinetics than developmentally later channels (both flip and flop modules). Also affected by the flip-flop expression switch is the ratio of peak to steady-state current evoked by glutamate through AMPA receptor channels. This ratio should decrease during postnatal development time, reflecting the higher incidence of flop modules in AMPA channels of late versus early postnatal brain. The physiological significance of steady-state currents mediated by AMPA receptor channels is unclear but might be of relevance with respect to ambient glutamate levels in brain, which are estimated to be in the micromolar range. Such low glutamate levels may affect the steady-state population of desensitized AMPA receptor channels. These phenomena, coupled with the Ca^{2+} permeability of some AMPA receptors, might allow developmental cues to be transmitted by glutamate through non-NMDA receptor channels.

Several studies have suggested that NMDA receptors change properties in the developing brain (Ben-Ari et al. 1988; Carmignoto and Vicini 1992; Hestrin 1992). The observed property changes involve the strength of the Mg^{2+} block and the time course of NMDA currents following removal of glutamate (offset kinetics). Changes in these parameters can be mimicked *in vitro* by substituting different NR2 subunits in heteromeric NR1/NR2 receptor channels (Monyer et al. 1992). Such a model of heteromeric substitution would predict subunit switches during development, reminiscent of the g to e switch in nAChRs of muscle endplate (Mishina et al. 1986). The latter switch is triggered by innervation, i.e., electrical signals (Witzemann et al. 1991). It is likely that, in the case of NMDA receptor channels, such a subunit switch might also be triggered by synaptic activity. Differences in offset kinetics would alter the Ca^{2+} influx following removal of glutamate from the synaptic cleft (for synaptic receptors) and may correlate with the extent of architectural changes in synapses and the resetting of synaptic efficacies. Developmentally, earlier NMDA receptor subtypes appear to have slower offset kinetics, which is consistent with glutamate triggering; Ca^{2+}-mediated changes (developmental cues) are also more efficient via earlier NMDA receptors, which is consistent with the high plasticity of the early postnatal brain, at least as far as the involvement of NMDA receptors is concerned.

The role of high-affinity kainate receptors in the CNS remains puzzling. Currents desensitizing in the presence of kainate (a characteristic of these channels) have not been reported for central neurons but have been observed in afferent sensory neurons (e.g., Huettner 1990). It is highly likely that CNS kainate receptors are localized presynaptically or on dendrites.

REFERENCES

Ascher, P., and L. Nowak. 1988. The role of divalent cations in the N-methyl-D-aspartate responses of mouse central neurones in culture. *J. Physiol. Lond.* **399**:247–266.

Ben-Ari, Y., E. Cherubini, and K. Krnjevic. 1988. Changes in voltage dependence of NMDA currents during development. *Neurosci. Lett.* **94**:88–92.

Bettler, B., J. Boulter, I. Hermans-Borgmeyer, A. O'Shea-Greenfield, E.S. Deneris, C. Moll, U. Hollmann, M. Borgmeyer, and S. Heinemann. 1990. Cloning of a novel glutamate receptor subunit, GluR5: Expression in the nervous system during development. *Neuron* **5**:583–595.

Burnashev, N., A. Khodorova, P. Jonas, W. Wisden, H. Monyer, P.H. Seeburg, and B. Sakmann. 1992. Calcium-permeable AMPA-kainate receptors in fusiform cerebellar glial cells. *Science* **256**:1566–1570.

Burnashev, N., R. Schoepfer, H. Monyer, J.P. Ruppersberg, W. Günther, P.H. Seeburg, and B. Sakmann. 1992. Control by asparagine residues of calcium permeability and magnesium blockade in the NMDA receptor. *Science* **257**:1415–1419.

Carmignoto, G., and S. Vicini. 1992. Activity-dependent decrease in NMDA receptor responses during development of the visual cortex. *Science* **258**:1007–1011.

Chavez, R.A., and Z.W. Hall. 1992. Expression of fusion proteins of the nicotinic acetylcholine receptor from mammalian muscle identifies the membrane-spanning regions in the a and d subunits. *J. Cell Biol.* **116**:385–393.

Chen, L., and L.-Y. Huang. 1992. Protein kinase C reduces Mg^{2+} block of NMDA receptor channels as a mechanism of modulation. *Nature* **356**:521–523.

Colquhoun, D., P. Jonas, and B. Sakmann. 1992. Onset and offset of glutamate action on AMPA/KA receptors measured by brief concentration jumps on patches from different hippocampal neurones in rat brain slices. *J. Physiol.*, in press.

Gallo, V., L.M. Upson, W.P. Hayes, L. Vyklicky, Jr., C.A. Winters, and A. Buonanno. 1992. Molecular cloning and developmental analysis of a new glutamate receptor subunit isoform in cerebellum. *J. Neurosci.* **12**:1010–1023.

Greengard, P., J. Jen, A.C. Nairn, and C.F. Stevens. 1991. Enhancement of the glutamate response by cAMP-dependent protein kinase in hippocampal neurons. *Science* **253**:1135–1138.

Hestrin, S. 1992. Developmental regulation of NMDA receptor-mediated synaptic currents at a central synapse. *Nature* **357**:686–689.

Hollmann, M., A. O'Shea-Greenfield, S.W. Rogers, and S. Heinemann. 1989. Cloning by functional expression of a member of the glutamate receptor family. *Nature* **342**:643–648.

Huettner, J.A. 1990. Glutamate receptor channels in rat DRG neurons: Activation by kainate and quisqualate and blockade of desensitization by Con A. *Neuron* **3**:255–268.

Iino, M., S. Ozawa, and T.K. Tsuzuki. 1990. Permeation of calcium through excitatory amino acid receptor channels in cultured rat hippocampal neurones. *J. Physiol. Lond.* **424**:151–165.

Imoto, K., C. Busch, B. Sakmann, M. Mishina, T. Konno, J. Nakai, H. Bujo, Y. Mori, K. Fukuda, and S. Numa. 1988. Rings of negatively charged amino acids determine the acetylcholine receptor channel conductance. *Nature* **335**:645–648.

Köhler, M., N. Burnashev, B. Sakmann, and P.H. Seeburg. 1993. Determinants of Ca^{2+} permeability in both TM1 and TM2 high-affinity kainate receptor channels: Diversity by RNA editing. *Neuron* **10**:491–500.

Li, M., Y.N. Jan, and L.Y. Jan. 1992. Specification of subunit assembly by the hydrophilic amino-terminal domain of the shaker potassium channel. *Science* **257**:1225–1230.

Mishina, M., T. Takai, K. Imoto, M. Noda, T. Takahashi, S. Numa, C. Methfessel, and B. Sakmann. 1986. Molecular distinction between fetal and adult forms of muscle acetylcholine receptors. *Nature* **321**:406–411.

Monyer, H., R. Sprengel, R. Schoepfer, A. Herb, M. Higuchi, H. Lomeli, N. Burnashev, B. Sakmann, and P.H. Seeburg. 1992. Heteromeric NMDA receptors: Molecular and functional distinction of subtypes. *Science* **256**:1217–1221.

Moriyoshi, K., M. Masu, T. Ishii, R. Shigemoto, N. Mizuno, and S. Nakanishi. 1991. Molecular cloning and characterization of the rat NMDA receptor. *Nature* **354**:31–37.

Müller, T., T. Möller, T. Berger, J. Schnitzer, and H. Kettenmann. 1992. Calcium entry through kainate receptors and resulting potassium-channel blockade in Bergmann glia cells. *Science* **256**:1563–1566.

Nakanishi, S. 1992. Molecular diversity of glutamate receptors and implications for brain function. *Science* **258**:597–603.

Nicoll, R.A., R.C. Malenka, and J.A. Kauer. 1990. Functional comparison of neurotransmitter receptor subtypes in mammalian central nervous system. *Physiol. Rev.* **70**:513–565.

Ogura, A., M. Nakazawa, and Y. Kudo. 1992. Further evidence for calcium permeability of non-NMDA receptor channels in hippocampal neurons. *Neurosci. Res.* **12**:606–616.

Pellegrini-Giampietro, D.E., R.S. Zukin, M.V.L. Bennett, S. Cho, and W.A. Pulsinelli. 1992. Switch in glutamate receptor subunit gene expression in CA1 subfield of hippocampus following global ischemia in rats. *Proc. Natl. Acad. Sci. USA* **89**:10499–10503.

Raman, I., and L.O. Trussell. 1992. The kinetics of the response to glutamate and kainate in neurons of the avian cochlear nucleus. *Neuron* **9**:173–186.

Sommer, B., M. Köhler, R. Sprengel, and P.H. Seeburg. 1991. RNA editing in brain controls a determinant of ion flow in glutamate-gated channels. *Cell* **67**:11–19.

Sommer, B., and P.H. Seeburg. 1992. Glutamate receptor channels: Novel properties and new clones. *Trends Pharmacol. Sci.* **13**:291–296.

Sugihara, H., K. Moriyoshi, T. Ishii, M. Masu, and S. Nakanishi. 1992. Structures and properties of seven isoforms of the NMDA receptor generated by alternative splicing. *Biochem. Biophys. Res. Comm.* **185**:826–832.

Trussel, L.O., and G.D. Fischbach. 1989. Glutamate receptor desensitization and its role in synaptic transmission. *Neuron* **3**:209–218.

Unwin, N. 1989. The structure of ion channels in membranes of excitable cells. *Neuron* **3**:665–676.

Verall, S., and T.W. Hall. 1992. The N-terminal domain of acetylcholine receptor subunits contains recognition signals for the initial steps of receptor assembly. *Cell* **68**:23–31.

Witzemann, V., H.-R. Brenner, and B. Sakmann. 1991. Neural factors regulate AChR subunit mRNAs at rat neuromuscular synapses. *J. Cell Biol.* **114**:125–141.

18

Protein Targeting and Synaptic Plasticity

R.B. KELLY
Department of Biochemistry and Biophysics, University of California,
San Francisco, CA 94143–0534, U.S.A.

ABSTRACT

A neuron may respond to electrical activity through a local change in the synapses that are activated. Whereas global changes could result from controlling gene expression in the nucleus, local changes require selective modifications of some synapses while others are unaffected.

The preexisting proteins of the activated synapses could be changed by local phosphorylation and proteolysis. It is also possible to alter the protein composition of the activated synapse without changing gene transcription in the nucleus. Local changes could occur postsynaptically through local control of RNA translation, perhaps using the polyribosomes located under the dendritic spines. Proteins could also accumulate in the synapse by selective targeting from an intracellular pool of the proteins. Alternatively, the rate of protein turnover could be regulated. Although there is no direct evidence in hippocampal neurons for selective targeting or protein turnover regulation, both processes are well-established in other types of intracellular contact, particularly between epithelial cells.

INTRODUCTION

Many of the changes that occur during long-term potentiation (LTP) in the hippocampus can be explained by short-lived events such as phosphorylation (for review see Bliss and Collingridge 1993). Longer-term changes appear to involve structural alterations in the synapse, such as increases in synaptic vesicle number (Meshul and Hopkins 1990), increases in the fraction of postsynaptic densities that are segmented (Geinisman et al. 1991), or decreases in multisynaptic contacts and spine-associated polyribosomes (Desmond and Levy 1990) (for a review, see Greenough, this volume). Long lasting synaptic changes in the hippocampus, particularly changes in synaptic morphology, are expected to require changes in the protein composition of the synapse. The protein composition of synapses can be altered by changing the rates of protein

Cellular and Molecular Mechanisms Underlying Higher Neural Functions
Edited by A.I. Selverston and P. Ascher

synthesis, or degradation, or by redistributing the protein within a cell. The pattern of protein synthesis does change during LTP. In addition to the induction of immediate early genes (Curran and Morgan, this volume) there is evidence for elevated mRNAs for regulating enzymes, receptors, and neurotrophins (Patterson et al. 1992; Mackler et al. 1992). The significance of changes in gene transcription to LTP is, however, not obvious. It is well established that LTP can be a local event, affecting only a small number of synapses, whereas switching on genes can only affect global properties of neurons. Given our current knowledge of protein sorting it is highly unlikely that a newly synthesized protein could be sent selectively to only those synapses undergoing LTP. It is perhaps not surprising, therefore, that LTP can be established even in the presence of transcriptional inhibitors.

There are other potential mechanisms for producing local changes in synaptic protein composition. One possibility is local protein synthesis. The presence of polyribosomes under dendritic spines (Desmond and Levy 1990) suggests that local protein synthesis is occurring. Synthesis of dendritic spine proteins could be regulated at the translational level by synaptic activity. Encouraging this speculation is the finding that although RNA transcription is not required to establish LTP, RNA translation is essential (for a review, see Bliss and Collingridge 1993). Since ribosomes are absent from axons, local translational control allows only postsynaptic modifications.

Alternatively, long-term changes in protein composition could be effected by proteolysis. Involvement of proteases in LTP is suggested by the inhibition of LTP by the thiol protease inhibitor leupeptin (Oliver et al. 1989) and by the secretion of a protease from the dentate gyrus during production of LTP (Fazeli et al. 1990). If a protease were locally activated (e.g., by calcium) during LTP, then changes in protein composition might occur. Spectrin, an actin-binding protein that is a major component of the postsynaptic density, is proteolytically cleaved when NMDA receptors are stimulated (Seubert et al. 1988). A difficulty, however, with proteolytic mechanisms is their relative lack of substrate specificity.

A third possibility is that activity induces a local change in protein targeting, thereby mobilizing membrane and cytoskeletal proteins from intracellular pools to a synaptic site. No data for or against changes in protein targeting are currently available. Comparisons of neurons with nonneuronal cells, however, show us that protein targeting is a feasible control mechanism and, with these as a background, experiments can be found to look for its occurrence. Because long-term synaptic plasticity and synaptic development are likely to use similar mechanisms, I consider both areas in this chapter.

PROTEINS HAVE SPECIFIC TARGETING DOMAINS

A newly synthesized protein can contain sequence information that instructs it to be targeted to a specific location within a cell. In an epithelial cell, for example, basolateral proteins and apical proteins have basolateral and apical targeting sequence, respectively. A basolateral protein that also has a sequence specifying endocytosis will also be directed to basolateral endosomes. The intracellular location of a protein can be specified, therefore, by more than one targeting domain (for a review, see Mostov et al. 1992).

We can see examples of selective targeting in hippocampal neurons grown in culture (for a review, see Kelly and Grote 1993). When such neurons mature sufficiently (stage III), they have one process that has the characteristic morphology of an axon. The axon has a protein composition different from that of the dendrites and cell body. For example, the synaptic vesicle membrane protein, synaptophysin, is targeted to the endosomes and plasma membrane of the axonal domain. Other proteins that have endosomal targeting information, such as the transferrin receptor, are excluded from axonal endosomes (Mundigl et al. 1993). Synaptophysin, therefore, has sorting information specifying that it should be targeted to a specialized class of endosomes, a class that is capable of being transported down the axon. Synaptophysin cannot diffuse down the axonal plasma membrane selectively, since there is a barrier to lateral diffusion of membrane components in the vicinity of the axon hillock (Dotti et al. 1991).

Since one endosomal protein, synaptophysin, is transported to axons and another, the transferrin receptor, is not, we know there is selective targeting. In many cases in which very immature neurons or cells in culture extend processes, membrane proteins accumulate at the growing tips. The accumulation of membrane proteins may be because microtubules end at the growing tips. Membrane vesicles moving down the microtubules, therefore, will accumulate at the terminus, awaiting insertion in the plasma membrane or retrograde transport. In many cases, however, it appears as if this transport is nonselective, since no membrane protein is excluded from the tip (Matsuuchi et al. 1988).

Two types of selective targeting can therefore be distinguished. Vesicles carrying one class of membrane proteins may be selectively transported in carrier vesicles along axonal microtubules in neurons. A second is the selective insertion of one class of carrier vesicle in different subdomains of the epithelial cell plasma membrane. A growing body of information suggests that the targeting of axonal membrane proteins in neurons may resemble targeting of apical membrane proteins in epithelial cells (Dotti and Simons 1990; Dotti et al. 1991). In liver cells, apical membrane proteins are sorted away from basolateral membrane proteins, such as the transferrin receptor, into a subclass of carrier vesicles (Sztul et al. 1993). These vesicles appear to be selectively transported to the apical surface along microtubules. After transport they selectively dock and fuse with apical plasma membranes. It is likely that the sorting of synaptophysin to the axon also requires selective transport and selective insertion.

A conceptual difficulty bedevils these explanations of membrane protein sorting. They only work because some sorting has already taken place. In some way, axonal microtubules must be different from dendritic ones, and apical or axonal membranes must have recognition elements that also select insertion of apical carrier vesicles. The specialization of axonal microtubules seems to be associated with expression of the *tau* microtubule associated proteins (for a review, see Kelly and Grote 1993). It is obviously impossible to explain the initial localization of apical docking sites by invoking selective insertion mechanisms. A more satisfying model invokes the concept of selective stabilization (see below).

MEMBRANE PROTEINS CAN BE LOCALIZED IN PLASMA MEMBRANE DOMAINS BY SELECTIVE STABILIZATION

The parallel between neurons and epithelial cells encourages us to believe that mechanisms of protein stabilization found when epithelial cells contact each other will also be pertinent to what happens during neuronal contact.

The sodium pump accumulates in the lateral membranes in monolayers of Madin-Darby Canine Kidney (MDCK) cells. This is not due to selective targeting but to selective stabilization of the sodium pumps by interacting with the actin-based cytoskeleton that lies under the lateral plasma membranes (Nelson et al. 1990). Selective stabilization of this type occurs when cell to cell contact occurs. The monolayer of MDCK cells is held together by E-cadherin, also called uvomorulin or L-CAM. E-cadherins bind homotypically to each other, where the lateral membranes of one cell apposes the lateral membranes of another. Cell-to-cell contact will, therefore, accumulate E-cadherins in the junctional zone, a sorting mechanism we shall call selective retention.

Adhesion requires more than binding of one cadherin to another. The association between E-cadherins in adjacent cells triggers the formation of an interaction between the cytoplasmic tails of the E-cadherin molecules and the actin-fodrin based cytoskeleton. Adhesion requires the assembly of this cortical cytoskeleton behind the lateral membranes; if the cytoplasmic tails of E-cadherin are removed, the proteins can still bind with each other but cannot trigger adhesion.

When epithelial cells form a confluent monolayer, there is a dramatic increase in the amounts of actin, the spectrin-like actin-binding protein, fodrin and the sodium pump. The rate of synthesis of these proteins is unaffected, however (Nelson et al. 1990). They increase in amount because the formation of the lateral cortical cytoskeleton stabilizes both its protein components and the membrane proteins with which it interacts, against proteolytic degradation. Some membrane proteins, therefore, are not selectively targeted to lateral membranes. They are inserted promiscuously but are rapidly degraded unless they are adhesion proteins that bind to a surface protein in an adjacent cell, or unless they interact with the cytoskeleton that is anchored to the adhesion proteins.

Selective stabilization also gives us one plausible mechanism whereby selective targeting might arise. If the membrane proteins required for selective docking on the lateral membranes were concentrated there by selective stabilization, then we have at least one explanation of how selective sorting might be set up *de novo*.

SYNAPSE FORMATION MAY REQUIRE SELECTIVE TARGETING, SELECTIVE RETENTION AND SELECTIVE STABILIZATION

The subdivision of axonal and dendritic domains of the neuronal plasma membrane probably involves selective movement of carrier vesicles along axonal microtubules and selective insertion. In addition to this global specification of domains that can occur in an individual neuron in culture, making no contacts with other cells, there is the much finer microtargeting of proteins that occurs when cell-to-cell contact induces synapses. The sites where synapses are made are not specified by complex endogenous targeting mechanisms within the neuron; they are induced at sites of cell-to-cell contact. Although we lack direct evidence, it is highly likely that some postsynaptic membrane proteins localize to the site of contact by interacting with some presynaptic membrane proteins, in analogy to the selective retention of E-cadherin at points of epithelial cell contact. Some candidates for adhesion molecules are the neurexins (Ushkaryov et al. 1992) and the agrin receptors (Nastuk et al. 1991). We also expect cytoskeletal rearrangements on both sides of the synapse. Candidates for cyoskeletal proteins, beside actin and spectrin, are the dystrophins, 43 kd protein, and synapsin (for reviews, see Kelly and Grote 1993; Hall and Sanes 1993). Indeed, the synapse may be looked at as one large macromolecular aggregate. The synaptic vesicles are anchored by cytoskeletal elements in the vicinity of the presynaptic release sites, which are in turn held in register with the postsynaptic receptor assembly. Given the example of the epithelial cell, we would be surprised if the elements of the synapse were not made less susceptible to protein degradation by assembly into a synapse.

LOCAL MODIFICATION OF NEURONS IS UNLIKELY TO INVOLVE SELECTIVE TARGETING

The mechanisms that allow axonal targeting could be used to modify all the nerve terminals of an axon. It is difficult to imagine how changing axonal protein synthesis or targeting could affect a specific synapse, or subgroups of synapses. On the other hand, it is not difficult to imagine how activity might insert more membrane proteins in a synapse, facilitating selective retention, or modify the synaptic cytoskeleton, changing stabilization. It is even possible, as we have seen, that selective retention or stabilization could lead to selective insertion of carrier vesicles.

There is some evidence for protein stabilization at the synapse. When a neuroblastoma cell line is transfected with DNA-encoding synapsin IIb, a synaptic vesicle-associated cytoskeletal protein (Han et al. 1991), synapse formation is induced. As I have pointed out (Kelly 1991), this remarkable result is consistent with models of selective stabilization of the type proposed here, particularly since elevated expression of synapsin IIb also elevated the levels of other synapsins. Unfortunately, we still do not know if the increased level of other synaptic proteins was due to enhanced synthesis or reduced degradation. A second familiar example of stabilization is the increase in acetylcholine receptor turnover time that occurs when the neuromuscular junction forms (for a review, see Hall and Sanes 1993).

It is also possible to account for local changes in synaptic membrane protein composition by invoking changes in turnover and insertion rates. The plasma membrane composition of fat or muscle cells is regulated by insulin (Jhun et al. 1992). When a fat or muscle cell is exposed to insulin, intracellular vesicles containing the GLUT4 class of glucose transporter are mobilized to the plasma membrane, where they increase transiently the rate of glucose uptake. The protein composition of the apical surface of epithelial cells can also be modified from an intracellular pool. In kidney cells, antidiuretic hormone induces the translocation of water channels from an intracellular vesicle pool selectively to the apical plasma membrane (Brown 1991). Local electrical activity could similarly facilitate selective membrane addition to, or removal from, the pre- or postsynaptic plasma membranes. Alternatively, adhesion molecules could be locally activated. Adhesion molecules of the cadherin type require the proteolytic removal of an NH_2-terminal pro region before they can bind. If local modifications allow new membrane or cytoskeletal elements to add to the synaptic structure, reduction in the rates of their degradation can lead to accumulation in the modified synapse.

Modifications of protein stability could be readily detected experimentally. As mentioned earlier, the two-dimensional gel patterns of hippocampal proteins are changed during LTP. If these changes can be detected in the absence of protein synthesis, then it is likely they are due to alterations in turnover rate. Mobilization models predict an intracellular pool of synaptic components.

SUMMARY AND LONG-TERM PROSPECTS

The targeting of proteins to synapses probably requires a series of sorting steps. Axonal plasma membrane proteins and dendritic ones are segregated from each other in the cell body into separate carrier vesicles. Axonal carrier vesicles are transported selectively along axonal microtubules. Carrier vesicles will accumulate at the ends of axons, where they fall off the microtubules; they may also dissociate from the axonal microtubules at other points of membrane insertion, such as the nodes of Ranvier. Clustering of synaptic membrane proteins at synapses is triggered by cell-to-cell contact. Interactions between the synaptic adhesion proteins and cytoskeletal elements are likely to stabilize the components of the synapse. Finally, local stabilization of the membrane insertion apparatus could ensure that future membrane addition is selective at synaptic sites.

How might these postulates be tested? One encouraging strategy is exemplified by the experiment of Han in which overexpressing one synaptic vesicle component led to synapse formation. Experiments of this type could help to identify components that are rate-limiting for synapse formation. Then we would be able to predict that synaptic modification will cause an increase (or decrease) in some essential component of the synapse. If such a change can be detected by quantitative immunofluorescence, then the synapses of the hippocampal neurons will be unequally stained and the number of heavily labeled synapses will change as a result of LTP. Perhaps such an experiment can be done even now, using antibodies to synapsin IIb. Such experiments will be much more tractable using dissociated hippocampal neurons in culture.

REFERENCES

Bliss, T.V.P., and G.L. Collingridge. 1993. A synaptic model of memory: Long-term potentiation in the hippocampus. *Nature* **361**:31–39.

Brown, D. 1991. Structural-functional features of antidiuretic hormone-induced water transport in the collecting duct. *Sem. Nephrol.* **11**:478–501.

Desmond, N.L., and W.B. Levy. 1990. Morphological correlates of long-term potentiation imply the modification of existing synapses, not synaptogenesis, in the hippocampal dentate gyrus. *Synapse* **5**:139–143.

Dotti, C., R. Parton, and K. Simons. 1991. Polarized sorting of glypiated proteins in hippocampal neurons. *Nature* **349**:158.

Dotti, C., and K. Simons. 1990. Polarized sorting of viral glycoproteins to the axon and dendrites of hippocampal neurons in culture. *Cell* **62**:63–72.

Fazeli, M.S., M.L. Errington, A.C. Dolphin, and T.V.P. Bliss. 1990. Increased efflux of a haemoglobin-like protein and an 80 kDa protease into push-pull perfusates following the induction of long-term potentiation in the dentate gyrus. *Brain Res.* **521**:247–253.

Geinisman, Y., L. deToledo-Morrell, and F. Morrell. 1991. Induction of long-term potentiation is associated with an increase in the number of axospinous synapses with segmented postsynaptic densities. *Brain Res.* **566**:77–88.

Hall, Z.W., and J.R. Sanes. 1993. Synaptic structure and development: The neuromuscular junction. *Cell* **72**/*Neuron* **10** *(Suppl)*:99–121.

Han, H.-Q., R.A. Nichols, M.R. Rubin, M. Bahler, and P. Greengard. 1991. Induction of formation of presynaptic terminals in neuroblastoma cells by synapsin IIb. *Nature* **349**:697–699.

Jhun, B.H., A.L. Rampal, H. Liu, M. Lachaal, and C.Y. Jung. 1992. Effects of insulin on steady state kinetics of GLUT4 subcellular distribution in rat adipocytes. *J. Biol. Chem.* **267**:17710–17715.

Kelly, R.B. 1991. Neurobiology: A system for synapse control. *Nature* **349**:650–651.

Kelly, R.B., and E. Grote. 1993. Protein targeting in the neuron. *Ann. Rev. Neurosci.* **16**:95–127.

Mackler, S.A., B.P. Brooks, and J.H. Eberwine. 1992. Stimulus-induced coordinate changes in mRNA abundance in single postsynaptic hippocampal CA1 neurons. *Neuron* **9**:539–548.

Matsuuchi, L., K. Buckley, A. Lowe, and R.B. Kelly. 1988. Targeting of secretory vesicles to cytoplasmic domains in AtT-20 and PC-12 cells. *J. Cell Biol.* **106**:239–251.

Meshul, C.K., and W.F. Hopkins. 1990. Presynaptic ultrastructural correlates of long-term potentiation in the CA1 subfield of the hippocampus. *Brain Res.* **514**:310–319.

Mostov, K., G. Apodaca, B. Aroeti, and C. Okamoto. 1992. Plasma membrane protein sorting in polarized epithelial cells. *J. Cell Biol.* **116**:577–583.

Mundigl, O., M. Matteoli, L. Daniell, A. Thomas-Reetz, A. Metcalf, R. Jahn, and P. De Camilli. 1993. Synaptic vesicle proteins and early endosomes in cultured hippocampal neurons: Differential effects of Brefeldin A in axon and dendrites. *J. Cell Biol.* **122(6):**1207–1221.

Nastuk, M.A., E. Lieth, J. Ma, C.A. Cardasis, E.B. Moynihan, B.A. McKechnie, and J.R. Fallon. 1991. The putative agrin receptor binds ligand in a calcium-dependent manner and aggregates during agrin-induced acetylcholine receptor clustering. *Neuron* **7**:807–818.

Nelson, W., R. Hammerton, A. Wang, and E. Shore. 1990. Involvement of the membrane-cytoskeleton in development of epithelial cell polarity. *Sem. Cell Biol.* **1**:359–371.

Oliver, M.W., M. Baudry, and G. Lynch. 1989. The protease inhibitor leupeptin interferes with the development of LTP in hippocampal slices. *Brain Res.* **505**:233–238.

Patterson, S.L., L.M. Grover, P.A. Schwartzkroin, and M. Bothwell. 1992. Neurotrophin expression in rat hippocampal slices: A stimulus paradigm inducing LTP in CA1 evokes increases in BDNF and NT–3 mRNAs. *Neuron* **9**:1061–1088.

Seubert, P., J. Larson, M. Oliver, M.W. Jung, M. Baudry, and G. Lynch. 1988. Stimulation of NMDA receptors induces proteolysis of spectrin in hippocampus. *Brain Res.* **460**:189–194.

Sztul, E., M. Colombo, P. Stahl, and R. Samanta. 1993. Control of protein traffic between distinct plasma membrane domains. *J. Biol. Chem.* **268**:1876–1885.

Ushkaryov, Y.A., A.G. Petrenko, M. Geppert, and T.C. Sudhof. 1992. Neurexins: Synaptic cell surface proteins related to the α-latrotoxin receptor and laminin. *Science* **257**:50–56.

19

Immediate-Early Genes: Function and Expression

T. CURRAN and J.I. MORGAN
Roche Institute of Molecular Biology, Roche Research Center,
Nutley, NJ 07110, U.S.A.

ABSTRACT

Increased neuronal activity, resulting from the application of a wide range of pharmacological and physiological stimuli, elicit a dramatic, but transient, elevation in the levels of a large number of cellular immediate-early (cIE) gene products. Several cIE genes, such as the *fos* proto-oncogene, encode transcription factors that are believed to regulate expression of target genes that contribute to activity-dependent alterations in cell phenotype. Some of the major questions now facing the field are: (a) how specific is the cIE gene response, (b) what are the target genes of cIE transcription factors, and (c) do alterations in cIE gene expression contribute to neuronal plasticity? Recent findings indicate that the cIE response is extremely complex and that it has several regulatory components that could, in concert, provide a high degree of cell type- and stimulus-dependent specificity.

INTRODUCTION

It has long been speculated that activity-driven alterations in gene expression would contribute to phenotypic changes in neurons. Indeed, several lines of evidence have suggested that transcriptional alterations may accompany and/or be necessary for some forms of neuronal plasticity. First, administration of the protein synthesis inhibitors, anisomycin and cycloheximide, to mammals can block memory acquisition (Barondes 1970) and attenuate induction of LTP (Bliss and Collingridge 1993) and kindling (reviewed in Morgan and Curran 1991a). In *Aplysia*, similar agents can impair heterosynaptic facilitation (Bailey et al. 1992; Montarolo et al. 1987). Second, several forms of neuronal stimulation can lead to long-term growth responses in the CNS, typically involving axonal sprouting (Greenough and Bailey 1988; Sutula et al. 1988). It has been presumed that this new growth requires the concerted, stimulus-dependent synthesis of additional synaptic components. Third, alterations in neuronal gene

Cellular and Molecular Mechanisms Underlying Higher Neural Functions
Edited by A.I. Selverston and P. Ascher

expression have been observed in hippocampal pyramidal neurons following induction of LTP (Mackler et al. 1992). A class of inducible genes, known as cellular immediate-early (cIE) genes, has been suggested to provide a molecular link that couples cellular stimuli to the alterations in gene expression that are required for these phenotypic responses (Curran and Morgan 1987; Goelet et al. 1986).

CELLULAR IMMEDIATE-EARLY GENES

Cellular immediate-early genes were first defined as genes that were induced immediately after treatment of cells with mitogenic polypeptide growth factors, serum, or phorbol esters. They are expressed rapidly but transiently after cell stimulation, and they are transcribed even in the presence of protein synthesis inhibitors. Many, but not all, of these genes were found to encode transcription factors such as the archetypes, the *myc* and *fos* proto-oncogenes. With time it has become clear that the cIE response is not restricted to mitogenic situations. Currently, the cIE response is viewed as a general signal transduction mechanism that operates in many different contexts. Immediate-early transcription factors are viewed as providing a nuclear "third messenger" function in most cell types, including neurons. A model depicting this scheme is illustrated in Figure 19.1.

The evidence that cIE gene products are involved in plasticity is currently circumstantial. The following lists some of the major observations that have linked cIE genes to activity-dependent alterations in neurons.

1. Many cIE genes encode transcription factors that could provide a biochemical link to the regulation of target gene expression.
2. Expression of several cIE genes is induced in the appropriate neuronal populations by stimuli that induce LTP, neuronal sprouting, and behavioral changes (Morgan and Curran 1991a, b).
3. The time course of induction of immediate-early genes precedes sprouting.
4. The dose-responsiveness for the two phenomena is similar.
5. Agents that block either sprouting or LTP also block induction of the immediate-early gene response.
6. Microinjection of DNA sequences corresponding to cyclic AMP response elements can block long-term facilitation in *Aplysia* neurons (Dash et al. 1990).

Unfortunately, experiments that might prove a causal relationship between the two events have been difficult to design. However, as we will discuss, the advent of transgenic mouse technology and gene knock-outs using homologous recombination may provide a route to establish this link.

It is not the purpose of this chapter to review the many and varied conditions in which altered gene expression involving cIE genes occurs. Rather, this review will focus on the properties of cIE transcription factors and the mechanisms responsible

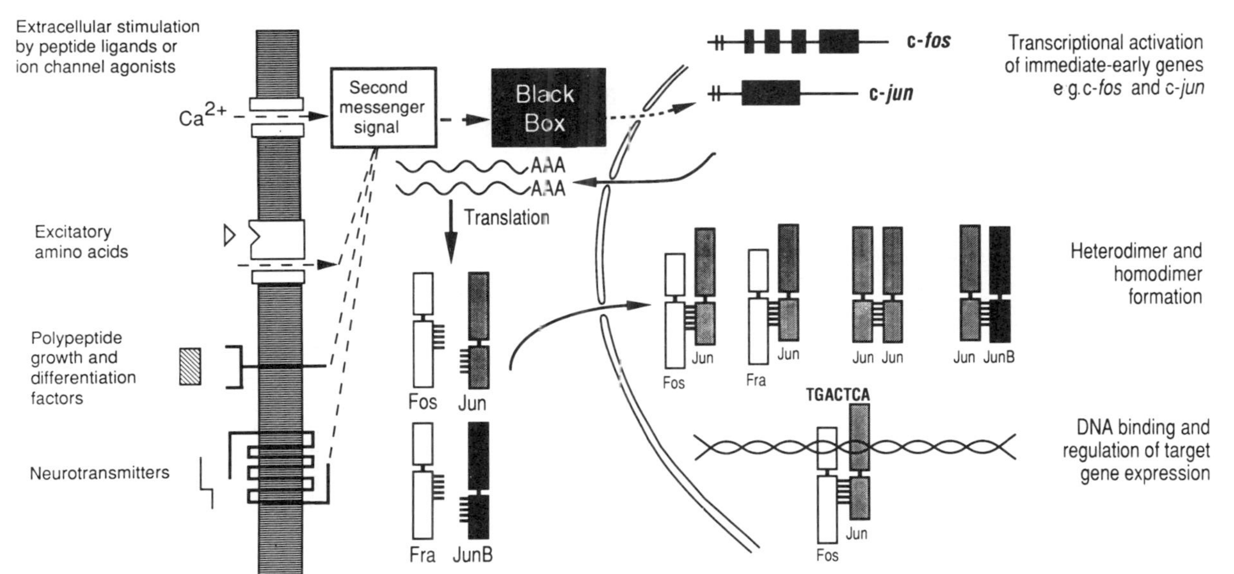

Figure 19.1 A schematic illustration of the activation of *c-fos* and *c-jun* expression in response to extracellular stimuli. Several different stimuli—including polypeptide growth factors, neurotransmitters, excitatory amino acids, and voltage-gated calcium fluxes—elicit the transient induction of cIE gene transcription. The "black box" indicates that the exact second messenger coupling systems are complex and are not yet completely understood.

for the activation of gene expression in response to extracellular signals. A complex picture of transcription factor function is emerging: it provides a flexible, yet cell- and stimulus-specific, transcriptional response mechanism.

c-*fos* AND c-*jun*

The most intensely studied cIE transcription factors are the *fos* and *jun* proto-oncogenes. In addition to their intrinsic interest, they illustrate several important general features of this class of genes. The *fos* and *jun* genes were identified independently as retroviral oncogenes (Curran and Teich 1982; Maki et al. 1987). Like other retroviral oncogenes, they were derived from normal cellular genes (c-*fos* and c-*jun*, respectively) termed proto-oncogenes. Analysis of the properties of the *fos* and *jun* proteins revealed that they were DNA-binding proteins that formed a dimeric complex through a leucine zipper structure and regulated gene transcription (Curran and Franza 1988). In fact, *fos* and *jun* are members of a family of genes, many of which are cIE genes, that form mixed heterodimeric complexes. These complexes are components of the mammalian transcription factors, AP-1 (activator protein-1) and CREB (cyclic AMP response element-binding protein) (Figure 19.1). Thus, a relatively large number of transcription factor complexes can be generated from a small number of subunits. Each protein dimer may have different properties, such as its specificity and affinity for DNA and its transcriptional activity. This mechanism for generating complexity, by mixing and matching subunits, is seen with several other transcription factor families, and it is quite common among cell-surface receptors. In the case of cIE genes, it can result in a high degree of cell-type and stimulus-specific heterogeneity because only a limited subset of these proteins is present at a given time, in individual cells or in response to certain stimuli.

REGULATION OF GENE EXPRESSION

For many years, the mechanisms responsible for the selective regulation of gene expression have been studied intensely. The field has progressed primarily by taking a reductionist approach to a rather complicated question. Basic principles were uncovered as a result of analyzing simple systems such as the regulation of bacteriophage genes and cell-type specific genes that are expressed at very high levels. However, in considering the regulation of gene expression by *fos* and *jun* in neurons in response to physiological signals, we must be prepared to deal with a much higher order of complexity. It is now clear that a substantial integration of signals and processing of information occurs at the transcription factor-genome interface. It is likely that many processes will contribute to the identification of specific AP-1 DNA sequences by *fos* and *jun* and that other signaling events will influence the outcome of the protein-DNA interaction, in terms of target gene transcription.

fos AND *jun*

Like many other transcription factors, *fos* and *jun* have been shown to contain specific domains that are primarily responsible for their dimerization (leucine zipper), DNA-binding (basic region), and transcriptional (activator domain) properties. Transcription factors are thought to associate with DNA through one protein surface and present another surface (activation domain) that contacts either the basal transcriptional machinery or putative bridging proteins, referred to as TFIID-associated factors (TAFs) (Figure 19.2). There are approximately 50 individual proteins involved in the polymerase/TATA box transcription machinery, which means that this complex is of the same size and complexity as the ribosome. At present, the mechanisms whereby enhancer-binding proteins initiate gene transcription are unclear. Several different types of activator domains have been defined based on their amino acid content (e.g., acidic, proline-rich, etc.). However, the relevance and function of the prevalent amino acids in these regions are not known. The activator regions in *fos* and *jun* are not as highly conserved as the leucine zipper/basic region among members of the gene

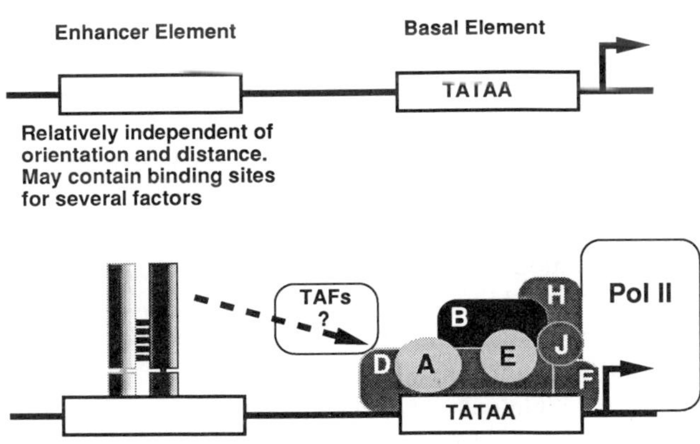

Figure 19.2 Outline of transcriptional regulation. RNA polymerase II (Pol II) consists of a multiprotein complex that synthesizes mRNA from a DNA template. It interacts with DNA at sequences (TATA box) that are occupied by a complex of TATA-binding proteins (A-H). A set of proteins termed TFIID-associated factors (TAFs) are required for activation of transcription by enhancer elements. Enhancer-binding proteins such as *fos* and *jun* are believed to initiate transcription by contacting TAFs or basal factors such as TFIID directly.

families. Furthermore, some of these proteins have different activities in co-transfection assays. This suggests that transcriptional specificity may be determined in part by the constellation of such regions present in any particular dimeric complex.

A further level of complexity is encountered when we consider the fact that AP-1 DNA sequences are usually located within elements containing recognition sequences for many transcription factors. *fos* and *jun* have been suggested to interact with several other transcription factors, including the glucocorticoid receptor, the retinoic acid receptor, and MyoD. Thus, a picture of transcriptional regulation is evolving in which multiple low-affinity protein-protein interactions—involving basal factors, polymerase, accessory proteins, and sequence-specific DNA-binding transcription factors—are integrated to create a highly specific multicomponent complex. It is likely that DNA topology, in particular protein-induced DNA bends, also contributes to this three-dimension puzzle. In this scenario, many proteins could influence the rate of initiation of any particular target gene. In each cell type, the array of transcriptional components would be determined by a combination of differentiated state and exposure to environmental stimuli (experience). This is unlikely to lead to a simple on/off decision; however, it would be a highly dynamic situation with perhaps several possible stable states. Switching from one state to another could occur after transient elevation of a small number of components. During the cIE response, dramatic increases occur in the levels of several classes of transcription factors for a brief period of time. Thus, cIE proteins may provide the impetus for such a change of state.

In addition to changes in their abundance, the activity of many proteins may be altered by posttranslational modification such as phosphorylation. For example, both *fos* and *jun* are phosphorylated in a stimulus-dependent manner, and it has been suggested that specific phosphorylation events affect their activity. Similarly, phosphorylation can influence both the DNA-binding and transcriptional activity of the CREB factor (Sheng et al. 1991). Activation of protein kinase cascades is triggered during the cIE gene response, so it is not easy to dissect out the exact signaling pathway or to determine which kinase is responsible for a particular phosphorylation event. Other posttranslational modification events are also likely to influence transcription factor function. The DNA-binding activity of *fos* and *jun* is highly sensitive to reduction/oxidation conditions. A highly conserved *cys* residue located in the DNA-binding domain readily becomes modified to a presumed oxidized state (not a disulfide bond) that is not compatible with DNA binding (Abate et al. 1990). Thus, there are several biochemical processes that, in concert, confer a very high degree of specificity on single transcription factors.

TRANSCRIPTION FACTOR NETWORKS

It is a mistake to consider a single transcription factor protein as a functional unit. In the case of *fos*, this is obvious because it cannot bind to AP-1 sites without a partner (e.g., one of the *jun* or ATF/CREB proteins). However, the high degree of cross-talk among transcription factor families implies that they function as components of a network. In free solution, in the absence of DNA, there is a rapid exchange of *fos-jun* subunits. Therefore, it is possible that, inside the cell, compatible leucine zipper proteins are in equilibrium prior to the synthesis of further components during the cIE response. Thus, altering the levels of only a few proteins could change the properties of a large number of dimeric complexes.

Both *fos* and *jun* exhibit autoregulatory properties in cotransfection assays: negative in the case of *fos* and positive in the case of *jun*. In fact, it appears that several members of the *fos* family share this property, which is encoded in a conserved C-terminal domain. Therefore, changing the levels of expression of one of these proteins could result in alterations in the levels of other family members or, conceivably, the levels of unrelated transcription factors. There are likely to be several mechanisms that affect the relative levels of these transcription factors. Clearly, the cIE gene response has a feedback control system. Once the response is triggered, it enters a refractory phase that can persist for several hours (Morgan et al. 1987). This process is stimulus-specific. For example, prior exposure of mice to kainic acid blocks induction of cIE genes by a subsequent challenge of kainic acid but does not affect induction by Metrazole. Thus, the interpretation of overexpression or ablation experiments must take into account this complexity.

REGULATION OF c-*fos* EXPRESSION

The c-*fos* gene contains several control elements that are required for basal and stimulated levels of transcription. The best characterized of these, the serum-response element (SRE) (Treisman 1990), the calcium/cAMP responsive element (Ca/CRE) (Sheng et al. 1990), and the *sis*-conditioned medium responsive element (SCM) (Wagner et al. 1990), are located in the 5′ nontranscribed region. Pharmacological and genetic studies in cell culture have revealed that each of these DNA elements can respond to specific stimuli. For example, the Ca/CRE element is at the distal end of a signaling pathway mediated by voltage-gated calcium flux, calmodulin (CaM) kinase activation, and phosphorylation of CREB. However, recent results indicate that the situation may be more complicated. It appears that CREB can be phosphorylated after nerve growth factor treatment in the absence of a Ca/CaM kinase signal (Greenberg, pers. comm.). Furthermore, *in vivo* studies using transgenic mice suggest that all of these elements are required in concert for both basal and stimulated levels of c-*fos* expression.

GENE EXPRESSION ASSAYS

It is important to evaluate *in vitro* gene expression studies critically before addressing the regulation of gene expression *in vivo* in response to physiological signals. Both cotransfection assays and *in vitro* transcription experiments utilize artificial reporter constructs to monitor levels of gene expression. Generally, such constructs use simple factor-binding sites that are reiterated and placed proximal (usually within 50 base pairs) to a promoter element. This is artificial for two reasons: generally transcription factor-binding sites are not reiterated and they are usually located further away from the promoter than 50 base pairs. The reason for these manipulations is simple. The constructs do not work otherwise. These types of experiments have been extremely useful in defining elements that can respond to certain stimuli and for studying the molecular and genetic properties of the proteins that interact with them. However, they do not address the physiological basis of gene regulation *in vivo*. The mechanisms responsible for action at a distance through DNA looping and the molecular basis of transcription factor and second messenger cooperativity are not yet known. Currently, several investigators are addressing these processes by using natural promoters as targets for gene regulation. Furthermore, transcription factor cooperativity and cross-talk among signal transduction pathways are now viewed as important features of gene regulation rather than unfortunate experimental artifacts. Progress is now being made to unravel the complex interactions that occur among transcription control elements using transgenic animals (flies and mice). Hopefully, in the future, better *in vitro* systems will be developed that will allow biochemical analysis of inducible gene expression using natural enhancer/promoter elements.

TARGETS OF cIE GENES

It is rather difficult to answer the question, "Which genes does *fos*, or any other cIE transcription factor, regulate in neurons?" Several good candidate genes have been suggested, such as preproenkephalin, nerve growth factor, receptors, ion channels, etc. However, the real answer is that all of these genes are regulated by multiple transcription factors, directly and indirectly. Any one of these may not be essential, but together they strike a critical balance. An indication of this "flexible complexity" has been obtained from gene knock-out experiments, using the technique of homologous recombination. Several transcription factors that had been viewed as playing a critical role in development or in the control of cellular proliferation (e.g., homeobox proteins, retinoic acid receptor, MyoD and *fos*) have been deleted from the genome with relatively modest consequences. These results do not mean that these proteins have no function, rather that there is the possibility that compensation mechanisms exist. In fact, it is likely that such mechanisms are necessary for normal development. Despite certain drawbacks, these genetic approaches offer great hope for investigating the role of specific gene products in adaptive phenomena. Indeed, the studies on mice lacking CaM kinase or certain tyrosine kinases have already yielded interesting insights. Furthermore, mice lacking the c-*fos* gene also appear to have some behavioral deficiencies, although the most obvious phenotype in these animals is defective bone development. Thus, the hope for the future is that current models for cIE function can be tested in whole animals using transgenic or homologous recombination technologies. Furthermore, as we learn more about the molecular basis of transcriptional control, more incisive approaches may be developed to address the role of activity-dependent changes in gene expression in plasticity. However, it is likely that alterations in gene expression will be tightly linked to the many other changes that occur in neurons in response to excitation.

REFERENCES

Abate, C., L. Patel, F.J. Rauscher, III, and T. Curran. 1990. Redox regulation of *fos* and *jun* DNA-binding activity *in vitro*. *Science* **249**:1157–1161.

Bailey, C.H., P. Montarolo, M. Chen, E.R. Kandel, and S. Schacher. 1992. Inhibitors of protein and RNA synthesis block structural changes that accompany long-term heterosynaptic plasticity in *Aplysia*. *Neuron* **9**:749–758.

Barondes, S.H. 1970. Cerebral protein synthesis inhibitors block long-term memory. *Int. Rev. Neurobiol.* **13**:177–205.

Bliss, T.V.P., and G.L. Collingridge. 1993. A synaptic model of memory: Long-term potentiation in the hippocampus. *Nature* **361**:31–39.

Curran, T., and B.R. Franza, Jr. 1988. *fos* and *jun*: The AP-1 connection. *Cell* **55**:395–397.

Curran, T., and J.I. Morgan. 1987. Memories of *fos*. *BioEssays* **7**:255–258.

Curran, T., and N.M. Teich. 1982. Candidate product of the FBJ murine osteosarcoma virus oncogene: Characterization of a 55,000-Dalton phosphoprotein. *J. Virol.* **42**:114–122.

Dash, P.K., B. Hochner, and E.R. Kandel. 1990. Injection of the cAMP-responsive element into the nucleus of *Aplysia* sensory neurons blocks long-term facilitation. *Nature* **345**:718–721.

Goelet, P., V.F. Castellucci, S. Schacher, and E.R. Kandel. 1986. The long and short of long-term memory: A molecular framework. *Nature* **322**:419–422.

Greenough, W.T., and C.H. Bailey. 1988. The anatomy of a memory: Convergence of results across a diversity of tests. *Trends Neurosci.* **11**:142–147.

Mackler, S.A., B.P. Brooks, and J.H. Eberwine. 1992. Stimulus-induced coordinate changes in mRNA abundance in single postsynaptic hippocampal CA1 neurons. *Neuron* **9**:539–548.

Maki, Y., T.J. Bos, C. Davis, M. Starbuck, and P.K. Vogt. 1987. Avian sarcoma virus 17 carries a new oncogene, *jun*. *Proc. Natl. Acad. Sci. USA* **84**:2848–2852.

Montarolo, P.G., P. Goelet, V.F. Castellucci, J. Morgan, E.R. Kandel, and S. Schacher. 1987. A critical period of macromolecular synthesis in long-term heterosynaptic facilitation in *Aplysia*. *Science* **239**:1249–1255.

Morgan, J.I., D.R. Cohen, J.L. Hempstead, and T. Curran. 1987. Mapping patterns of c-*fos* expression in the central nervous system after seizure. *Science* **237**:192–197.

Morgan, J.I., and T. Curran. 1991a. Proto-oncogene transcription factors and epilepsy. *Trends Pharmacol. Sci.* **12**:343–349.

Morgan, J.I., and T. Curran. 1991b. Stimulus-transcription coupling in the nervous system: Involvement of the inducible proto-oncogenes *fos* and *jun*. *Ann. Rev. Neurosci.* **14**:421–451.

Sheng, M., G. McFadden, and M.E. Greenberg. 1990. Membrane depolarization and calcium induce c-*fos* transcription via phosphorylation of transcription factor CREB. *Neuron* **4**:451–587.

Sheng, M., M.A. Thompson, and M.E. Greenberg. 1991. CREB: A Ca^{2+}-regulated transcription factor phosphorylated by calmodulin-dependent kinases. *Science* **252**:1427–1430.

Sutula, T., X.-X. He, J. Cavazos, and S. Grayson. 1988. Synaptic reorganization in the hippocampus induced by abnormal functional activity. *Science* **239**:1147–1150.

Treisman, R. 1990. The SRE: A growth factor responsive transcriptional regulator. In: Seminars in Cancer Biology: Transcription Factors, Differentiation, and Cancer, ed. N.C. Jones, pp. 47–58. London: Saunders.

Wagner, B.J., T.E. Hayes, C.J. Hoban, and B.H. Cochran. 1990. The SIF binding element confers *sis*/PDGF inducibly onto the c-*fos* promoter. *EMBO J.* **9**:4477–4484.

20

Modulation of Ion Channels by Protein Phosphorylation

W.A. CATTERALL
Department of Pharmacology, SJ–30, University of Washington,
Seattle, WA 98195, U.S.A.

ABSTRACT

Modulation of ion channel activity is a flexible mechanism of regulating neuronal function. Two main pathways of ion channel modulation are recognized: an indirect pathway in which neurotransmitters and hormones act through G-protein-coupled receptors, second messengers, and protein phosphorylation, and a membrane-delimited pathway in which G-proteins can modulate ion channels without the participation of soluble second messengers. Multiple regulatory pathways involving distinct G-proteins can impinge upon a single ion channel. Modulation often involves change in the mode of channel gating, imposing a new pattern of channel opening and closing in response to depolarization. For voltage-gated ion channels and nicotinic acetylcholine receptors, the mechanism of modulation involves direct phosphorylation of one or more ion channel subunits. In the case of the sodium channel, a functional gating component of the protein, the inactivation gate, is phosphorylated to modify its function. Identification of the sites and elucidation of the mechanisms of modulation of ion channels will be an important step toward understanding the regulation of neural function.

INTRODUCTION

Ion channel modulation is the long-term regulation of ion channel function by neurotransmitters and hormones. The initial example of ion channel modulation was provided by Reuter, Tsien, and their colleagues (Reuter 1983; Tsien et al. 1986); they described the regulation of the cardiac calcium channel by β-adrenergic agents acting through cAMP and cAMP-dependent protein kinase. Activation of the β receptors and the cAMP regulatory pathway greatly enhances the activation of calcium channels and increases the beat rate and force of contraction of the heart. Concurrent work on potassium channels in snail neurons by Levitan, Kaczmarek, Kandel, and their colleagues first demonstrated modulation of ion channels in neurons (Levitan 1985; Kaczmarek 1987; Kandel and Schwarz 1982). In their background paper, Kaczmarek

Cellular and Molecular Mechanisms Underlying Higher Neural Functions
Edited by A.I. Selverston and P. Ascher

and Perney (this volume) focus on the role of ion channel modulation in regulating the function of neural circuits. This chapter focuses on the cellular and molecular mechanisms through which ion channels are modulated and emphasizes modulation through protein phosphorylation.

PATHWAYS OF ION CHANNEL MODULATION

The functional activity of ion channels is modulated through two parallel pathways, each of which is activated by the actions of neurotransmitters and hormones on G-protein-coupled receptors. In the classical pathway, neurotransmitters or hormones activate G-protein-coupled receptors which, in turn, activate the cAMP, calcium/diacylglycerol, or arachidonic acid/lipoxygenase second messenger pathways. Cyclic AMP or diacylglycerol/calcium then activate protein phosphorylation by cAMP-dependent protein kinase, protein kinase C, or calcium/calmodulin kinase II, which phosphorylate ion channel subunits directly (reviewed in Hille 1992). Modulations of calcium, sodium, and potassium channels and GABA, glycine, glutamate, and nicotinic acetylcholine receptors via phosphorylation pathways have been demonstrated through activation of cellular protein kinases, by direct application of activated kinases to the intracellular surface of ion channels in the whole cell or excised inside-out patch clamp recording configurations, or in reconstituted preparations.

The scope of ion channel modulation has been dramatically expanded, due to the discovery of a membrane-delimited pathway of regulation, which evidently does not require diffusible second messengers (Hille 1992). Neuronal calcium and potassium channels are modulated through this pathway. The molecular mechanism of this modulation remains unknown; however, it has been best studied in cardiac potassium channels where direct binding of G-protein subunits to ion channels is proposed to modify their gating behavior.

Recent extensive studies of the multiple pathways of calcium channel modulation in the superior cervical ganglion neuron have revealed a surprising complexity and flexibility in channel activity regulation. At least three parallel pathways modulate the N-type calcium channels which are responsible for neurotransmitter release in these cells (Hille 1992). These pathways are used in different combinations by acetylcholine acting through muscarinic receptors, norepinephrine acting through $\alpha 2$ receptors, somatostatin, adenosine, substance P, and dopamine. The first pathway acts rapidly (< 400 ms) through a pertussis toxin-sensitive G-protein to slow channel activation and shift it to more positive membrane voltages. It persists when the intracellular calcium is buffered to a low level and appears to be a membrane-delimited pathway that does not require diffusible intermediates. Some neurotransmitters also activate a pertussis toxin-insensitive, membrane-delimited regulatory pathway, which reduces calcium channel activity without changes in time course or voltage dependence. If intracellular calcium is not buffered to a low level, a third, slower pathway of modulation can be discerned. It is insensitive to pertussis toxin and can modulate both

N-type and L-type calcium channels through an unknown intracellular second messenger. Together with previously established pathways of ion channel modulation through protein phosphorylation, these novel pathways provide remarkably flexible and diverse mechanisms of regulation of neuronal excitability.

FUNCTIONAL MECHANISMS OF ION CHANNEL MODULATION

Modes of Ion Channel Gating

An important mechanism of modulation of ion channel function is through shifting gating modes. Gating modes, first described for cardiac calcium channels (Hess et al. 1984), govern the relative values of the complete set of rate constants defining the transitions among the closed, open, and inactivated states. Changes in gating mode cause simultaneous, characteristic changes in the values of the entire set of rate constants to impose a new pattern of channel gating. Such a change in gating mode may result from a single molecular event, such as protein phosphorylation or an interaction with a G-protein that alters the energetic relationship among the distinct functional states of the channel. In the case of the cardiac calcium channel, activation of β-adrenergic receptors acts through phosphorylation by cAMP-dependent protein kinase to cause a shift of gating pattern from a mode with a low probability of opening in response to depolarization to a mode with a much higher probability (Yue et al. 1990). Among neuronal channels, the most complete analysis of modulation by shift of gating mode is for the N-type calcium channels in sympathetic neurons (Delcour et al. 1993). Three distinct gating modes, characterized by different probabilities of channel opening and different single channel conductances, are observed. The lifetime of a single gating mode is about 10 sec, far longer than a single gating transition in a calcium channel. All three gating modes can be observed without adding any agonist to the cells; however, norepinephrine and other agonists modify the fraction of time that individual calcium channels spend in each gating mode.

Modal gating transitions are observed for sodium channels and potassium channels as well. For sodium channels in the skeletal muscle, a small fraction of depolarizations elicits a mode of gating in which the channels open repetitively throughout a depolarization instead of opening once or twice and inactivating (Patlak and Ortiz 1986). A similar effect is caused by phosphorylation of the skeletal muscle or brain sodium channels by protein kinase C (Numann et al. 1991, 1992). Moreover, phosphorylation by cAMP-dependent protein kinase causes the brain sodium channel to enter a null gating mode in which it fails to open during a fraction of the depolarizations (Li et al. 1992). Serotonin, acting through cAMP and cAMP-dependent protein kinase, causes an all-or-none closure of a continuously active potassium channel in *Aplysia* neurons (Shuster et al. 1985). This all-or-none closure may also result from transition to a null gating mode due to cAMP-dependent protein phosphorylation.

Inactivation and Desensitization

Protein phosphorylation often regulates the duration of cellular signals. For many G-protein-coupled receptors, phosphorylation by receptor-specific protein kinases or second messenger-activated protein kinases uncouples the receptor from its intracellular signaling pathway (reviewed in Huganir and Greengard 1990). The processes of inactivation and desensitization serve to terminate the cellular signal produced by the voltage- and ligand-gated ion channels, respectively. These processes are also regulated by protein phosphorylation. Phosphorylation by cAMP-dependent protein kinase accelerates the desensitization of the nicotinic acetylcholine receptor (Huganir and Greengard 1990) and may modulate desensitization of GABA receptors as well (Browning and Rogers 1994). Phosphorylation by protein kinase C slows the inactivation of sodium channels, induces repetitive reopening at moderate levels of activation, and reduces peak sodium currents at high levels of kinase activation (Numann et al. 1991).

MOLECULAR MECHANISMS OF MODULATION BY PROTEIN PHOSPHORYLATION

While modulation of ion channels by the membrane-delimited G-protein pathway is observed in many neurons and other cell types, its molecular mechanism has not been established in any case. By contrast, considerable information is available on the sites and mechanisms of ion channel modulation by protein phosphorylation.

Potassium Channels

Calcium-activated potassium channels provide clear examples of differential channel modulation by protein phosphorylation in neurons (Levitan 1988). Different members of this family of channels can be either activated or inhibited by protein phosphorylation. For one high-conductance, calcium-activated potassium channel present in the brain, two modulations—one due to phosphorylation by an unidentified endogenous protein kinase, the other to dephosphorylation through added phosphoprotein phosphatases—are retained after single channels are incorporated into planar bilayer membranes (Chung et al. 1991). Since single channels are nearly infinitely diluted into the bilayer lipid upon incorporation, the retention of modulation by an endogenous protein kinase indicates that the channel and kinase are stably associated. Specific association of kinases with channels may provide a novel molecular mechanism for differential regulation of channel properties in response to particular cellular signals.

It has not yet been possible to determine the peptide substrates or the sites of phosphorylation responsible for modulating voltage-gated potassium channels in neurons. However, an atypical, slowly activated potassium channel formed by a protein of 130 amino acid residues with a single transmembrane segment is inhibited by phosphorylation of a single serine residue in the 60 residue intracellular domain by protein kinase C (Busch et al. 1992). The inhibition was caused by a shift in the voltage dependence of activation toward more positive membrane potentials. This "min K" channel, which is expressed primarily in nonneuronal cells, may be a valuable model for the regulation of more complex voltage-gated potassium channels of neurons and other excitable cells.

Calcium Channels

L-type calcium channels in the skeletal muscle mediate long-lasting calcium currents and are localized in the transverse tubule membrane. Because of the high density of L-type calcium channels in T-tubules, this preparation has been the major molecular model for analyzing the structure and function of calcium channels. As in cardiac calcium channels, the activation of skeletal muscle L-type calcium channels is enhanced through phosphorylation by cAMP-dependent protein kinase (Arreola et al. 1987). In cultured muscle cells, strong repetitive depolarization causes a dramatic potentiation of calcium currents (Sculptoreanu et al. 1993). This enhancement can increase calcium currents tenfold in the critical membrane potential range near –20 mV, in response to tetanic stimulation of muscle cells (Figure 20.1A). Potentiation, which is strongly voltage dependent, requires the activity of cAMP-dependent protein kinase, and most likely results from a voltage-dependent phosphorylation of the calcium channel itself. This novel regulatory mechanism greatly increases the calcium channel activity during tetanic stimulation of skeletal muscle cells. It may play a critical role in the regulation of contractile force of skeletal muscle, in response to the frequency of motor nerve stimulation, analogous to the regulation of contractile force of cardiac muscle through regulation of the cardiac calcium channel.

The most abundant form of the rabbit skeletal muscle L-type calcium channel is a complex of five subunits (Catterall 1991). The $\alpha 1$ subunit alone, however, can function as a voltage-gated ion channel when expressed in mammalian cells. The $\alpha 1$ subunit has four internally homologous domains, each of which contains six transmembrane helices, S1–S6 (Figure 20.1B). Calcium flux through the purified skeletal muscle calcium channel is regulated by phosphorylation (Flockerzi et al. 1986; Hymel et al. 1988; Nunoki et al. 1989). Both full-length and C-terminal truncated forms of the $\alpha 1$ subunit are present in purified preparations, T-tubule membranes, and intact skeletal muscle cells in culture (De Jongh et al. 1989, 1991; Lai et al. 1990). cDNAs, encoding either form of the $\alpha 1$ subunit, can restore excitation-contraction coupling and ion conductance in calcium-channel-deficient *mdg* muscle cells (Beam et al. 1992). Both forms are phosphorylated in response to physiological stimuli which activate cAMP-dependent protein phosphorylation in intact muscle cells (Lai et al. 1990). The full-length form of the $\alpha 1$ subunit contains three cAMP-dependent phosphorylation sites in its C-terminus that are missing in $\alpha 1_{190}$ (Figure 20.1B). The most rapidly phosphorylated site in the truncated form is serine 687 located in the intracellular loop between domains II and III (Figure 20.1B; Röhrkasten et al. 1988). By contrast, serine

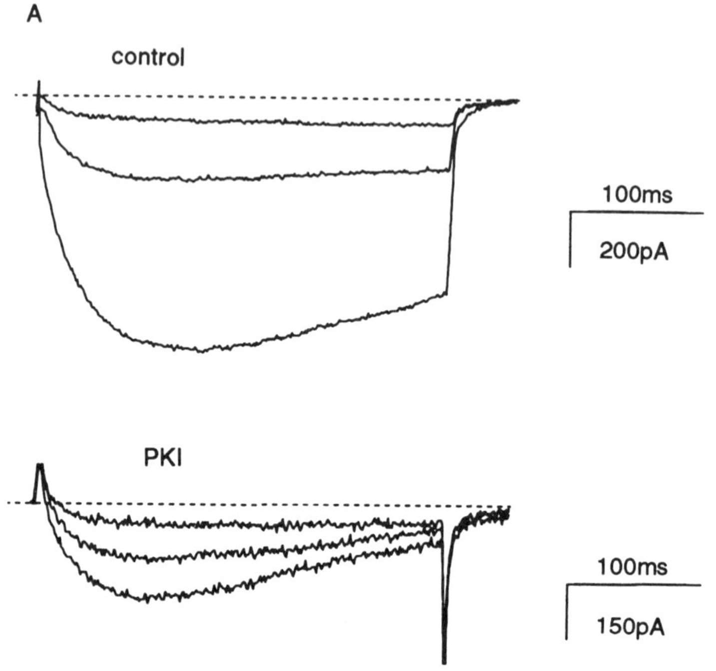
A
control
100ms
200pA
PKI
100ms
150pA

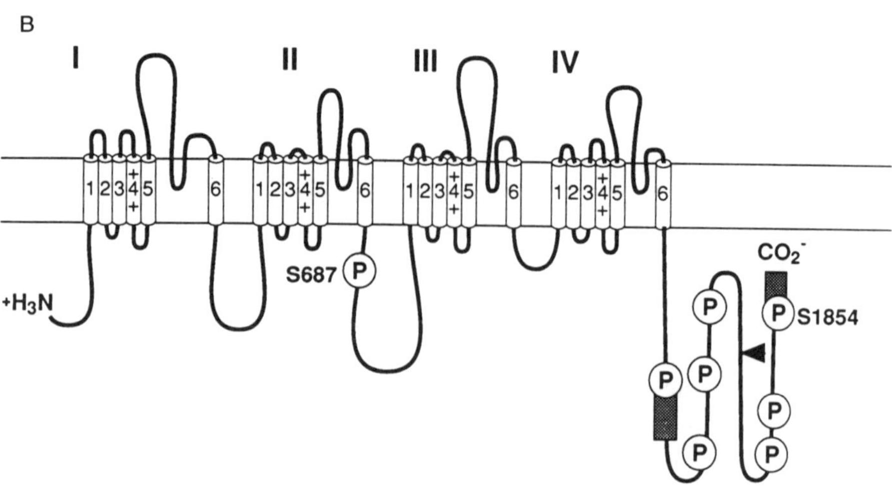
B
I
II
III
IV
+H3N
S687
P
CO2-
S1854

1854, which is located at the extreme carboxyl terminal of the full-length α1 subunit, is phosphorylated about 100-fold more rapidly than serine 687 (Rotman et al. 1992). If phosphorylation of this residue is required for some aspect of calcium channel regulation, the function of calcium channels containing the two size forms of the α1 subunit would be differentially affected.

Like the α1 subunit of the skeletal muscle calcium channel, the intracellularly associated β subunit is stoichiometrically phosphorylated by cAMP-dependent protein kinase in reconstituted calcium channels that are modulated by cAMP-dependent protein kinase (Flockerzi et al. 1986; Nunoki et al. 1989). Both serine 182 and threonine 205 have been shown to be phosphorylated *in vitro* (De Jongh et al. 1989; Ruth et al. 1989), but only the phosphorylation site at serine 205 is conserved in different β subunits. Since phosphorylation of both α1 and β subunits is correlated with regulation of the ion conductance activity of skeletal muscle calcium channels, both are candidates for sites of channel modulation by phosphorylation.

The activity of the neuron-specific N-type calcium channels is enhanced through phosphorylation by protein kinase C (Yang and Tsien 1992), and the α1 subunit of N-type calcium channels is phosphorylated by both protein kinase C and cAMP-dependent protein kinase (Ahlijanian et al. 1991). Thus, the α1 subunit of this calcium channel may also be a target for regulation by phosphorylation.

At present, it has not been possible to restore regulation by protein phosphorylation to calcium channels expressed from cloned DNA. This is a critical step toward analyzing the molecular basis for modulation of calcium channel function by protein phosphorylation in more detail and confirming that direct phosphorylation of the calcium channel subunits is the underlying mechanism of regulation. By contrast, for sodium channels and nicotinic acetylcholine receptors, the sites of phosphorylation that are responsible for ion channel regulation have been defined as described below.

Figure 20.1 Regulation of skeletal muscle calcium channels by cAMP-dependent protein phosphorylation. (A) Myoballs prepared by colchicine treatment of rat skeletal muscle myotubes in cell culture were studied by the whole cell voltage clamp technique (Sculptoreanu et al. 1993). With a control intracellular solution, strong positive prepulses of 200 msec duration to +47 mV or +114 mV greatly potentiated the calcium current activated by a test pulse of –19 mV in comparison to a control prepulse to –19 mV. In contrast, with the peptide inhibitor of cAMP-dependent protein kinase (PKI) in the intracellular solution, the potentiation by prepulses was nearly completely blocked. (B) Phosphorylation sites of the α1 subunit of the rabbit skeletal muscle L-type calcium channel predicted from the amino acid sequence. The recognition sites of antibodies directed against residues 1505–1522 (anti-CP–1505–1522) and 1856–1873 (anti-CP–1856–1873) are shown. The arrowhead indicates the region in which the C-terminus of $\alpha 1_{190}$ occurs. P circled indicates cAMP-dependent phosphorylation sites in the C-terminal region, with * indicating the mostly rapidly phosphorylated site (serine 1854).

Sodium Channels

The sodium channel from the rat brain is a complex of α (260 kDa), β1 (36 kDa), and β2 (33 kDa) subunits (Catterall 1992). The α subunit is rapidly phosphorylated by cAMP-dependent protein kinase on at least three sites *in vitro* and in intact neurons. Substantial phosphorylation is observed at the basal level of cAMP in the cultured neurons, and a twofold increase is observed upon stimulation.

The physiological effect of cAMP-dependent phosphorylation of sodium channels is revealed most clearly through an analysis of the effect of direct phosphorylation, by purified cAMP-dependent protein kinase, of sodium channels on excised membrane patches from transfected cells (Li et al. 1992). Phosphorylation of the inside-out membrane patches from rat brain neurons or transfected Chinese hamster ovary (CHO) cells reduces sodium currents by approximately 50% with no change in the time course or the voltage dependence of activation or inactivation (Figure 20.2A, right). The modulation is due to a change in gating mode; phosphorylation causes an increase in the number of null responses to depolarization. If the basal activity of cAMP-dependent protein kinase in transfected cells is blocked by co-expression of a dominant-negative mutant form of the regulatory subunit, the level of sodium current per expressed sodium channel is increased, indicating that the level of channel activity is subject to tonic modulation at the basal level of activity of cAMP-dependent protein kinase in CHO cells. Phosphorylation of sodium channels in excised membrane patches from these kinase-negative

---

Figure 20.2 Differential modulation of sodium currents by protein phosphorylation. (A, left) Sodium currents were recorded in the cell-attached patch configuration in Chinese hamster ovary cells expressing Type IIA sodium channel α subunits during depolarizations from a holding potential of –110 mV to a test potential of 0 mV. Ensemble average currents were recorded from macropatches containing up to 30 active sodium channels. Current traces are illustrated under control conditions and after activation of protein kinase C with the synthetic diacylglycerol oleylacetylglycerol (OAF). (A, right) Sodium currents were recorded from the same cells in the excised patch clamp configuration during depolarization from a holding potential of –130 mV to a test potential of –20 mV. Current traces are illustrated under control conditions, after addition of 1 mM ATP, and after addition of 1 mM ATP and 2 μM cAMP-dependent protein kinase. Ensemble average currents were recorded from macropatches containing approximately 15 or more active sodium channels (Li et al. 1992; Numann et al. 1991; Catterall 1992). (B) Primary structures of α- and β1-subunits of sodium channel illustrated as transmembrane folding diagrams. Bold line: polypeptide chains of α- and β1-subunits with length of each segment approximately proportional to its true length in rat brain sodium channel. Cylinders represent probable transmembrane α-helices; additional membrane-associated segments are drawn as loops in extended conformation like remainder of sequence. Sites of experimentally demonstrated glycosylation (Ψ), cAMP-dependent phosphorylation (P in a circle), protein kinase C phosphorylation (P in a diamond), amino acid residues required for tetrodotoxin binding (small circles with +, —, or open field depict positively charged [Lys^{1422}], negatively charged, or neutral [Ala^{1714}] residues, respectively), and amino acid residues that form the inactivation particle (h in a circle) (Catterall 1992).

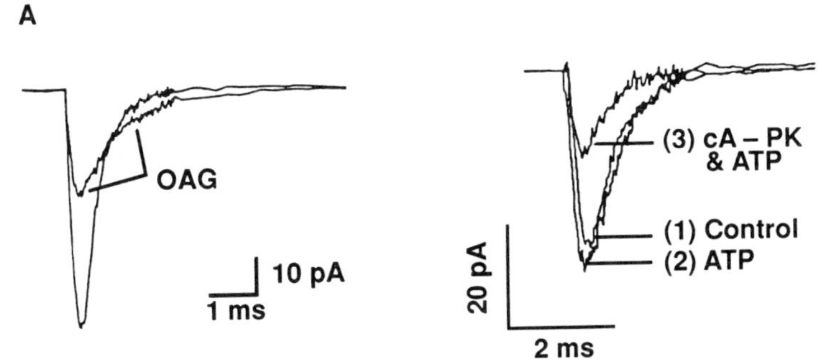

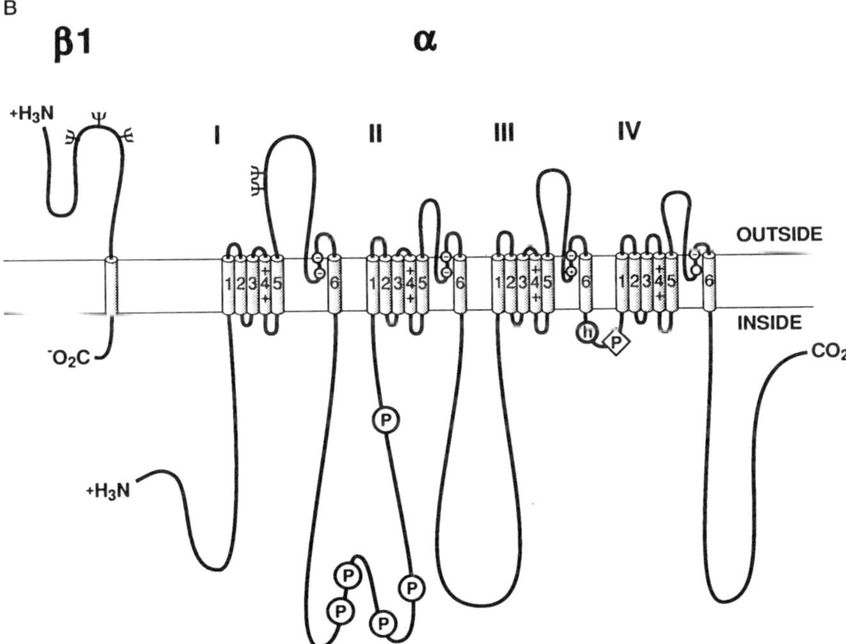

cells by purified cAMP-dependent protein kinase causes up to 80% reduction of sodium current. Thus, the dynamic range over which sodium channel activity can be modulated by cAMP-dependent phosphorylation is substantial.

The modulation of sodium channel function in intact neuronal preparations such as brain slices has not yet been studied. However, sodium currents in acutely dissociated neurons from the striatum are reduced by agonists acting at D1 dopamine receptors, which activate adenylate cyclase, and are increased by agonists acting at

D2 dopamine receptors, which inhibit adenylate cyclase (Surmeier et al. 1992). Neither the time course nor the voltage dependence of the sodium current is altered. These results show that neuronal sodium channels can be modulated by neurotransmitters acting through cAMP as a second messenger. This dynamic modulation of sodium channel function by the wide range of neurotransmitters and neuromodulators that alter cAMP levels is expected to have profound effects on the excitability of central neurons.

The sites of phosphorylation of the sodium channel by cAMP-dependent protein kinase have been identified by a combination of two-dimensional peptide mapping, immunoprecipitation of phosphopeptides with site-directed anti-peptide antibodies, and microsequence determination (reviewed in Catterall 1992). Five sites of *in vitro* phosphorylation are clustered in the large intracellular loop connecting homologous domains I and II (Figure 20.2B). These sites are all phosphorylated in intact neurons; however, their different rates of phosphorylation *in vitro* suggest that a subset of the sites may play a predominant role in channel regulation. Mutation of individual serine residues followed by expression and functional analysis will be required to define the role of each site in regulation by cAMP-dependent phosphorylation.

α subunits of purified sodium channels from rat brain are also phosphorylated by protein kinase C (reviewed in Catterall 1992). This suggests that they may be modulated by the calcium/diacylglycerol signaling pathway. Activation of protein kinase C in rat brain neurons, or in CHO cells transfected with cDNA encoding the type IIA sodium channel α subunit, by treatment with diacylglycerols causes two functional effects: slowing of inactivation and reduction of peak current (Figure 20.2A, left; Numann et al. 1991).

The intracellular loop connecting domains III and IV has been implicated in sodium channel inactivation. This segment has a consensus sequence for phosphorylation by protein kinase C centered at serine 1506 (Figure 20.2B). Mutagenesis of this serine residue to alanine blocks both of the modulatory effects of protein kinase C (West et al. 1991). Evidently, phosphorylation of this site is required for both slowing of sodium channel inactivation and a reduction of peak sodium current by protein kinase C. Treatment of neurons or transfected cells with increasing concentrations of diacylglycerol reveals a biphasic modulation; low concentrations slow sodium channel inactivation while higher concentrations are required to cause reduction of peak sodium currents. These results suggest that a second site of phosphorylation is required for reduction of peak sodium currents. Because cAMP-dependent phosphorylation of sites in the intracellular loop between domains I and II causes reduction of peak sodium currents, mutant sodium channels with alterations in consensus sequences for protein kinase C phosphorylation in that region of the channel were examined for modulation by protein kinase C. Mutation of serine 554 located in a protein kinase consensus sequence toward the amino terminal end of this intracellular loop (Figure 20.2B) prevented the reduction in sodium current by protein kinase C (Catterall 1992). These results implicate phosphorylation of this residue in the reduction of peak sodium current caused by protein kinase C and suggest that this effect of protein kinase C phosphorylation has the same underlying molecular mechanism as reduction of peak sodium current by cAMP-dependent protein phosphorylation.

Nicotinic Acetylcholine Receptors

Nicotinic acetylcholine receptors in sympathetic neurons are modulated by both cAMP-dependent protein kinase and protein kinase C. Activation of cAMP-dependent protein kinase increases the acetylcholine-induced current, while activation of protein kinase C by substance P accelerates the desensitization of the receptor (Role 1992). Stimulation of cAMP-dependent phosphorylation in skeletal muscle cells with adenylate cyclase activators, cAMP derivatives, or CGRP also leads to acceleration of desensitization of the receptor (Figure 20.3; Middleton et al. 1988; Mulle et al. 1988). Nicotinic acetylcholine receptors, like the other members of the neurotransmitter-gated ion channel family, are pentamers of five homologous or identical subunits (Huganir and Greengard 1990). Analysis of the hydrophobicity of the amino acid sequence indicates that these subunits all have a large N-terminal extracellular domain followed by three transmembrane segments, a large intracellular domain, and a fourth transmembrane segment (Numa 1989). Typically, the large intracellular domains between transmembrane segments 3 and 4 of these proteins contain multiple consensus sequences for phosphorylation by protein kinases (Figure 20.3B). Purified skeletal muscle nicotinic acetylcholine receptor is phosphorylated on sites in this intracellular domain on the β, γ, and δ subunits of the receptor by tyrosine kinases, on the γ and δ subunits by cAMP-dependent protein kinase, and on the δ subunit by protein kinase C (Huganir and Greengard 1990). Analysis of the functional effects on purified receptors reconstituted in phospholipid vesicles by ion flux or patch clamp methods showed that the rapid phase of receptor desensitization was accelerated by phosphorylation of either the γ or δ subunit of the receptor by cAMP-dependent protein kinase. No effects on the affinity of the receptor for agonists or on the rate of activation of the receptor were observed. These experiments demonstrate that phosphorylation of specific serine residues in these two subunits is sufficient for receptor modulation.

The δ subunit of the nicotinic acetylcholine receptor is phosphorylated skeletal muscle cells in cell culture after activation of adenylate cyclase by calcitonin gene-related peptide (CGRP) or after treatment with cAMP analogs. Phosphorylation of the γ subunit was not detected in intact cells but could have been missed due to proteolysis of the subunit (Huganir and Greengard 1990).

Other Neurotransmitter-Gated Ion Channels

There is growing evidence that the receptors for GABA, glycine, and glutamate are also modulated by protein phosphorylation (reviewed in Browning and Rogers 1994; Raymond et al. 1993). Purified GABA receptors are phosphorylated *in vitro* by cAMP-dependent protein kinase. Although there is considerable debate about the functional effects of phosphorylation, the most direct experiments involve injection

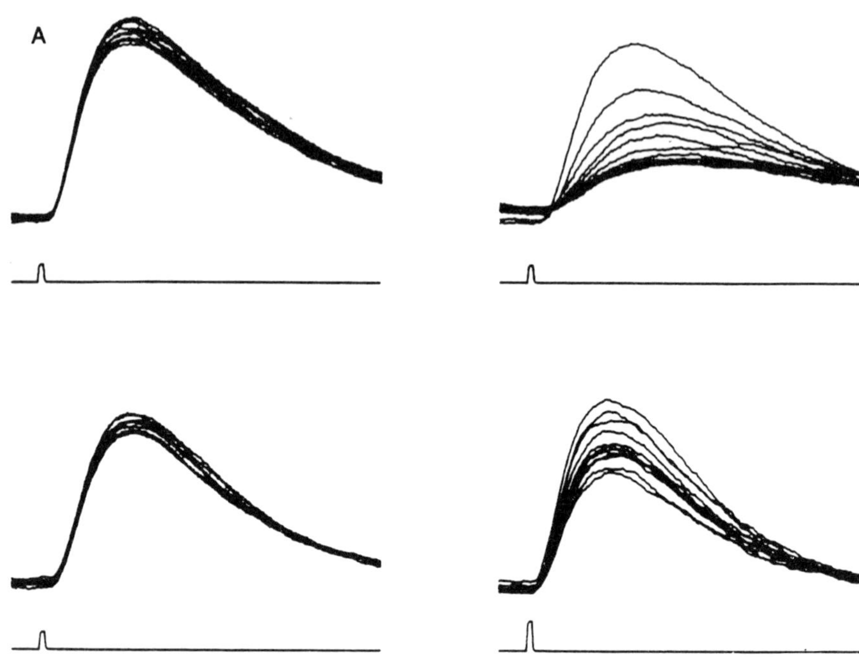
A

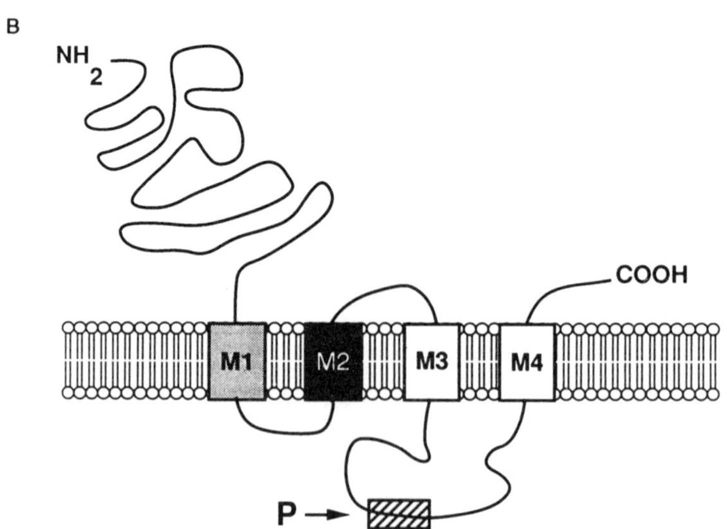
B
NH
2
COOH
M1
M2
M3
M4
P

of the catalytic subunit of the kinase directly into spinal cord neurons under voltage clamp control. These experiments show that phosphorylation greatly reduces GABA receptor currents by stabilizing a long, closed state that is possibly a normal desensitized state of the receptor. In contrast to GABA receptors, both the inhibitory strychnine-sensitive glycine receptors of spinal neurons and the excitatory ionotropic glutamate receptors of the brain are potentiated by phosphorylation through the cAMP and protein kinase C second messenger pathways.

REFERENCES

Ahlijanian, M.K., J. Striessnig, and W.A. Catterall. 1991. Phosphorylation of an α1-like subunit of an ω-conotoxin-sensitive brain calcium channel by cAMP-dependent protein kinase and protein kinase C. *J. Biol. Chem.* **266**:20192–20197.

Arreola, J., J. Calvo, M.C. Garcia, and J.A. Sánchez. 1987. Modulation of calcium channels of twitch skeletal muscle fibres of the frog by adrenaline and cyclic adenosine monophosphate. *J. Physiol.* **393**:307–330.

Beam, K.G., B.A. Adams, T. Niidome, S. Numa, and T. Tanabe. 1992. Function of a truncated dihydropyridine receptor as both voltage sensor and calcium channel. *Nature* **360**:169–171.

Browning, M.D., and S.W. Rogers. 1994. Ligand-gated ion channels: Molecular structure and functional regulation by phosphorylation. In: Regulation of Cellular Signal Transduction by Desensitization and Amplification, ed. D.R. Sibley. Chichester: Wiley.

Busch, A.E., M.D. Varnum, R.A. North, and J.P. Adelman. 1992. An amino acid mutation in a potassium channel that prevents inhibition by protein kinase C. *Science* **255**:1705–1707.

Catterall, W.A. 1991. Functional subunit structure of voltage-gated calcium channels. *Science* **253**:1499–1500.

Catterall, W.A. 1992. Cellular and molecular biology of voltage gated sodium channels. *Physiol. Rev.* **72**:S15–S48.

Chung, S., P.H. Reinhart, B.L. Martin, D. Brautigan, and I.B. Levitan. 1991. Protein kinase activity closely associated with a reconstituted calcium-activated potassium channel. *Science* **253**:560–562.

Figure 20.3 Cyclic AMP-dependent protein phosphorylation enhances AChR desensitization. (A) Myotubes were stimulated with a train of 2 msec ACh pulses delivered at 7 Hz. In each panel the responses are shown superimposed. Top left: Ten consecutive responses recorded from a myotube in control medium. Top right: Twelve responses recorded from the same cell after 45 min in 10 μM forskolin and 35 μM RO 20–1724. Bottom left: Eleven responses recorded from the same cell 30 min after the drugs were removed. Bottom right: Eleven responses recorded from a different myotube after 4 min in 30 μM 8–(4–chlorophenylthio)-cAMP. Resting membrane potentials in this and other experiments ranged from –50 to –70 mV and were unaffected by the drugs. Calibration bars: 4 mV (*upper traces*), 20 nA (*lower traces*); 20 msec (Middleton et al. 1988). (B) Transmembrane folding model of the subunits of the nicotinic acetylcholine receptor. The locations of the proposed phosphorylation sites for cAMP-dependent protein kinase, protein kinase C, and tyrosine kinases are indicated (Huganir and Greengard 1990).

De Jongh, K.S., D.K. Merrick, and W.A. Catterall. 1989. Subunits of purified calcium channels: A 212-kDa form of $\alpha 1$ and partial amino acid sequence of a phosphorylation site of an independent beta subunit. *Proc. Natl. Acad. Sci. USA* **86**:8585–8589.

De Jongh, K.S., C. Warner, A.A. Colvin, and W.A. Catterall. 1991. Characterization of the two size forms of the $\alpha 1$ subunit of skeletal muscle L-type calcium channels. *Proc. Natl. Acad. Sci. USA* **88**:10778–10782.

Delcour, A.H., D. Lipscombe, and R.W. Tsien. 1993. Multiple modes of N-type calcium channel activity distinguished by differences in gating kinetics. *J. Neurosci.* **13:**181–194.

Flockerzi, V., H.-J. Oeken, F. Hofmann, D. Pelzer, A. Cavalie, and W. Trautwein. 1986. Purified dihydropyridine-binding site from skeletal muscle T-tubules is a functional calcium channel. *Nature* **323**:66–68.

Hess, P., J.B. Lansman, and R.W. Tsien. 1984. Differential modes of Ca channel gating behaviour favoured by dihydropyridine Ca agonists and antagonists. *Nature* **311**:538–544.

Hille, B. 1992. G-protein-coupled mechanisms and nervous signaling. *Neuron* **9**:187–195.

Huganir, R.L., and P. Greengard. 1990. Regulation of neurotransmitter receptor desensitization by protein phosphorylation. *Neuron* **5**:555–567.

Hymel, L., J. Striessnig, H. Glossmann, and H. Schindler. 1988. Purified skeletal muscle 1,4-dihydropyridine receptor forms phosphorylation-dependent oligomeric calcium channels in planar bilayers. *Proc. Natl. Acad. Sci. USA* **85**:4290–4294.

Kaczmarek, L.K. 1987. The role of protein kinase C in the regulation of ion channels and neurotransmitter release. *Trends Neurosci.* **10**:30–34.

Kandel, E.R., and J.H. Schwarz. 1982. Molecular biology of learning: Modulation of transmitter release. *Science* **218**:433–443.

Lai, Y., M.J. Seagar, M. Takahashi, and W.A. Catterall. 1990. Cyclic AMP-dependent phosphorylation of two size forms of $\alpha 1$ subunits of L-type calcium channels in rat skeletal muscle cells. *J. Biol. Chem.* **265**:20839–20848.

Levitan, I.B. 1985. Phosphorylation of ion channels. *J. Membr. Biol.* **87**:177–190.

Levitan, I.B. 1988. Modulation of ion channels in neurons and other cells. *Ann. Rev. Neurosci.* **11**:119–136.

Li, M., J.W. West, Y. Lai, T. Scheuer, and W.A. Catterall. 1992. Functional modulation of brain sodium channels by cAMP-dependent phosphorylation. *Neuron* **8**:1151–1159.

Middleton, P., L.L. Rubin, and S.M. Schuetze. 1988. Desensitization of acetylcholine receptors in rat myotubes is enhanced by agents that elevate intracellular cAMP. *J. Neurosci.* **8**:3405–3412.

Mulle, C., P. Benoit, C. Pinset, M. Roa, and J.-P. Changeux. 1988. Calcitonin gene-related peptide enhances the rate of desensitization of the nicotinic acetylcholine receptor in cultured mouse muscle cells. *Proc. Natl. Acad. Sci. USA* **85**:5728–5732.

Numa, S. 1989. A molecular view of neurotransmitter receptors and ionic channels. *Harvey Lectures* **83**:121–165.

Numann, R., W.A. Catterall, and T. Scheuer. 1991. Functional modulation of brain sodium channels by protein kinase C phosphorylation. *Science* **254**:115–118.

Numann, R., J.W. West, M. Li, R.D. Smith, A.L. Goldin, T. Scheuer, and W.A. Catterall. 1992. Biphasic modulation of sodium channels by phosphorylation at two different sites. *Soc. Neurosci. Abstr.* **18:**1133.

Nunoki, K., V. Florio, and W.A. Catterall. 1989. Activation of purified calcium channels by stoichiometric protein phosphorylation. *Proc. Natl. Acad. Sci. USA* **86**:6816–6820.

Patlak, J.B., and M. Ortiz. 1986. Two modes of gating during late Na^+ channel currents in frog sartorius muscle. *J. Gen. Physiol.* **87**:305–326.

Raymond, L.A., C.D. Blackstone, and R.L. Huganir. 1993. Phosphorylation of amino acid neurotransmitter receptors in synaptic plasticity. *Trends Neurosci.* **16**:147–152.

Reuter, H. 1983. Calcium channel modulation by neurotransmitters, enzymes, and drugs. *Nature* **301**:569–574.

Röhrkasten, A., H.E. Meyer, W. Nastainczyk, M. Sieber, and F. Hofmann. 1988. cAMP-dependent protein kinase rapidly phosphorylates serine-687 of the skeletal muscle receptor for calcium channel blockers. *J. Biol. Chem.* **263**:15325–15329.

Role, L.W. 1992. Diversity in primary structure and function of neuronal nicotinic acetylcholine receptor channels. *Curr. Opin. Neurobiol.* **2**:254–262.

Rotman, E.I., K.S. Jongh, V. Florio, Y. Lai, and W.A. Catterall. 1992. Specific phosporylation of a COOH-terminal site on the full-length form of the $\alpha 1$ subunit of the skeletal muscle calcium channel by cAMP-dependent protein kinase. *J. Biol. Chem.* **267**:16100–16105.

Ruth, P., A. Röhrkasten, M. Biel, E. Bosse, S. Regulla, H.E. Meyer, V. Flockerzi, and F. Hofmann. 1989. Primary structure of the beta subunit of the DHP-sensitive calcium channel from skeletal muscle. *Science* **245**:1115–1118.

Sculptoreanu, A., T. Scheuer, and W.A. Catterall. 1993. Voltage-dependent potentiation of L-type Ca^{2+} channels due to phosphorylation by cAMP-dependent protein kinase. *Nature* **364:**240–243.

Shuster, M.J., J.S. Camardo, S.A. Siegelbaum, and E.R. Kandel. 1985. Cyclic AMP-dependent protein kinase closes the serotonin-sensitive K^+ channels of *Aplysia* sensory neurones in cell-free membrane patches. *Nature* **313**:392–395.

Surmeier, D.J., J. Eberwine, C.J. Wilson, Y. Cao, A. Stefani, and S.T. Kitai. 1992. Dopamine receptor subtypes colocalize in rat striatonigral neurons. *Proc. Natl. Acad. Sci. USA* **89**:10178–10182.

Tsien, R.W., B.P. Bean, P. Hess, J.B. Lansman, B. Nilius, and M.C. Nowycky. 1986. Mechanisms of calcium channel modulation by beta-adrenergic agents and dihydropyridine calcium agonists. *J. Mol. Cell. Cardiol.* **18**:691–710.

West, J.W., R. Numann, B.J. Murphy, T. Scheuer, and W.A. Catterall. 1991. A phosphorylation site in a conserved intracellular loop that is required for modulation of sodium channels by protein kinase C. *Science* **254**:866–868.

Yang, J., and R.W. Tsien. 1992. Enhancement of neuronal N- and L-type Ca^{2+} channel currents by protein kinase C in frog sympathetic neurons. *Neuron* **10:**127–136.

Yue, D.T., S. Herzig, and E. Marban. 1990. β-adrenergic stimulation of calcium channels occurs by potentiation of high-activity gating modes. *Proc. Natl. Acad. Sci. USA* **87**:753–757.

21

The Presynaptic Machinery for Neurotransmitter Release: Possible Modulatory Targets

T.C. SÜDHOF[1] and R. JAHN[2]
[1]Department of Molecular Genetics, Howard Hughes Medical Institute, University of Texas Southwestern Medical School, Dallas, TX 75235, U.S.A.
[2]Departments of Pharmacology and Cell Biology, Howard Hughes Medical Institute, Yale University School of Medicine, New Haven, CT 06536, U.S.A.

ABSTRACT

Neurotransmitters are released from presynaptic nerve terminals after depolarization by action potentials. Neurotransmitter release occurs over a short time period in a highly localized area of the presynaptic plasma membrane. The extent of neurotransmitter release as a function of the action potential is subject to modulation. Neurotransmitter release requires the targeted translocation of synaptic vesicles to the synaptic active zone, their exocytosis, and their endocytotic recycling. Great progress has been made in recent years in the characterization of proteins with putative functions in these processes. Although definitive evidence is missing, candidate proteins are now known for many central functions in neurotransmitter release, such as those of the Ca^{2+} sensor in exocytosis, of synaptic vesicle docking and fusion proteins, and of potential transsynaptic cell-cell interaction molecules. It is likely, however, that the concerted activities of a large number of trafficking proteins, and not the isolated actions of single proteins, will form the basis for the synaptic vesicle cycle in the nerve terminal. With the proteins now being studied, only a fraction of the presynaptic apparatus has been grasped, and the fundamental mechanisms of basic steps such as membrane fusion or Ca^{2+} triggering are still obscure. In this chapter, we address the functionally most important, recent results regarding presynaptic proteins and discuss major questions that have emerged as a consequence.

THE PRESYNAPTIC NERVE TERMINAL: CURRENT MODEL OF ITS FUNCTIONING

The presynaptic nerve terminal secretes neurotransmitters in a regulated manner. In the prevailing model, neurotransmitters are actively accumulated by synaptic vesicles

Cellular and Molecular Mechanisms Underlying Higher Neural Functions
Edited by A.I. Selverston and P. Ascher

and secreted by exocytosis. According to this model, membrane trafficking events form the basis for neurotransmitter release. An understanding of the molecular mechanisms and the modulation of neurotransmitter release depends upon an understanding of the underlying membrane trafficking events.

It is possible to distinguish two classes of regulated exocytosis that differ in the mechanisms of vesicle recycling. Pathways of the first class require recycling of the membranes after exocytosis and re-endocytosis via the trans-Golgi network. These pathways secrete polypeptides that are synthesized in the endoplasmic reticulum and the Golgi complex. Most pathways of regulated exocytosis that are currently studied belong to this class, including exocrine secretion as well as polypeptide hormone and neuropeptide secretions.

In pathways of the second class, vesicles recycle locally after exocytosis instead of passing through the trans-Golgi network. The most representative of these pathways is the synaptic vesicle pathway in the nerve terminal. Synaptic vesicles recycle efficiently without transport to the cell body that contains the Golgi complex. Other examples of these pathways include the regulated insertion of transporter proteins into the plasma membrane, such as glucose transporters in insulin-sensitive tissues or proton pumps in osteoclasts.

Compared to other forms of regulated secretion, neurotransmitter release has unusual characteristics. First, exocytosis is confined to a small section of the plasma membrane that is part of the synapse and is referred to as the active zone. The exquisite targeting of synaptic vesicle exocytosis has a morphological correlate in the presynaptic density, a thickening in the presynaptic plasma membrane at the active zone. Second, synaptic vesicle exocytosis is very rapid. The delay between Ca^{2+} influx in the presynaptic nerve terminal and neurotransmitter release has been shown to be on the order of 200 μsec (for a review, see Almers and Tse 1990).

Morphological observations suggest that synaptic vesicles are already docked at the active zone in resting nerve terminals (Peters et al. 1991). Because of the speed of synaptic vesicle exocytosis, neurotransmitter release probably only involves synaptic vesicles already docked at the active zone. A specific Ca^{2+}-binding protein associated with the docked vesicles may sense the Ca^{2+} influx after membrane depolarization and trigger exocytosis via a conformational change. Exocytosis would then proceed via a fusion pore. However, despite these hypothetical intermediates in synaptic vesicle exocytosis, its molecular basis has not yet been elucidated.

COMPONENTS OF THE NERVE TERMINAL: SYNAPTIC VESICLES

Synaptic vesicles are relatively easy to isolate. They are uniformly small organelles (25 to 30 nm in radius) with a highly specialized function. Only a limited number of proteins fit into the membrane of such a small vesicle (estimates range from 30 to 50 intrinsic membrane proteins [see Jahn and Südhof 1993]), and it is likely that the composition of synaptic vesicles is comparatively simple. Over the last five years, more than ten synaptic vesicle proteins have been purified and cloned, often in multiple isoforms, which account for close to one-half of the mass of the synaptic vesicle protein (for references, see Südhof and Jahn 1991).

The first synaptic vesicle proteins that were intensely studied were synapsins Ia and Ib. Three major results, which proved typical for most synaptic vesicle proteins, emerged from these studies. *First*, synapsins Ia and Ib were revealed to be part of a synaptic vesicle-specific protein gene family that includes the highly related synapsins IIa and IIb. This has become a general pattern for synaptic vesicle proteins, most of which are members of families of isoforms. *Second*, the sequences of the synapsins were disappointingly uninformative because they were novel, i.e., not homologous to any known proteins. This result (which has also been obtained for other vesicle proteins) suggests that the newly discovered proteins are related to functions not previously investigated at the molecular level. Interestingly, homologues of some of the vesicle proteins have recently been discovered in nonsecretory tissues, where they apparently reside on organelles of nonregulated pathways. *Third*, the synapsins were shown to be specific for small synaptic vesicles to the extent that they are excluded from other intracellular organelles or the plasma membrane. Again, similar results were obtained for other vesicle proteins, such as synaptophysins and synaptobrevins. These results indicate that the synaptic vesicle pathway is indeed separate from other neuronal pathways and contains a distinct set of proteins (which may nevertheless be related to proteins in other trafficking pathways with similar functions).

In addition to the synapsins, the most abundant synaptic vesicle proteins are the synaptotagmins, synaptophysins, and synaptobrevins. Together, these four protein families are estimated to account for one-third of the total vesicle protein. Other important components of synaptic vesicles include proteins with probable functions in neurotransmitter uptake: the vacuolar proton pump, neurotransmitter transporters, a chloride channel, and the recently described interesting structure of *SV2* which suggests a transport protein (Bajjalieh et al. 1992; Feany et al. 1992). Finally, synaptic vesicles contain an array of low molecular weight GTP-binding proteins, most notably *rab3a*, and a series of immunologically identified proteins that have not yet been purified or cloned.

Functionally, synapsins are thought to mediate interactions of synaptic vesicles with the cytoskeleton. Interactions of synapsins Ia and Ib with actin, tubulin, spectrin, and neurofilaments have been described. Some of these interactions may be modulated by phosphorylation and could potentially play a role in synaptic vesicle dynamics *in vivo*. Considering the abundance and stoichiometric phosphorylation of synapsins, it seems likely that synapsins have additional important roles (see below).

Synaptophysins are the major component of synaptic vesicles of unknown function. Based on transfection experiments, a possible function of synaptophysin I consists of synaptic vesicle biogenesis. Another hypothesis suggests that synaptophysins may have a role in the fusion pore. This hypothesis is based on the observation that synaptophysins are part of high molecular weight complexes; however, the nature and composition of these complexes are controversial.

Synaptotagmins are intrinsic membrane proteins in synaptic vesicles that bind Ca^{2+} and phospholipids (Brose et al. 1992). Synaptotagmins form homo-oligomers and exhibit cooperation in their Ca^{2+} binding. With these properties, they are candidate proteins for the Ca^{2+} sensor in synaptic vesicle exocytosis or in other Ca^{2+}-dependent segments of the synaptic vesicle pathway. Interestingly, synaptotagmins are also found on peptidergic secretory vesicles, suggesting a general role for these proteins in Ca^{2+}-regulated membrane trafficking events (Walch-Solimena et al. 1993).

Synaptobrevins are short, evolutionarily highly conserved proteins. Two groups recently discovered that clostridial neurotoxins irreversibly inhibit neurotransmitter release by acting as site-specific proteases for synaptobrevin II (Link et al. 1992; Schiavo et al. 1992). Clostridial intoxication of nerve terminals leads to no detectable morphological change, in particular no change in the number of docked vesicles. Clostridial toxins, therefore, probably inhibit synaptic vesicle fusion but not synaptic vesicle docking. The fact that they act via synaptobrevin breakdown indicates that synaptobrevin may be part of the fusion protein involved in synaptic vesicle exocytosis.

Rab3A is an abundant low molecular weight GTP-binding protein that is specific for synaptic vesicles in the brain. *Rab3A* is probably only one of several GTP-binding proteins associated with synaptic vesicles. Low molecular weight GTP-binding proteins are thought to have essential roles in most membrane trafficking steps, possibly by mediating protein-protein interactions. *Rab3A* dissociates from synaptic vesicles after synaptic vesicle exocytosis, which suggests a role for *rab3A* in synaptic vesicle exocytosis. However, the precise functions of the low molecular weight GTP-binding proteins on synaptic vesicles are still unclear.

COMPONENTS OF THE NERVE TERMINAL: THE PRESYNAPTIC ACTIVE ZONE

The presynaptic plasma membrane is thought to have three major functions: (a) as a docking or fusion site for synaptic vesicles; (b) as a high-density site for voltage-activated Ca^{2+} channels, so that the Ca^{2+} influx occurs close to the site of Ca^{2+} action; and (c) as the location for cell-cell interaction molecules that contact ligands on the postsynaptic plasma membrane, making them responsible for the alignment of pre- and postsynaptic specializations.

Unfortunately, no component of the presynaptic active zone has been unequivocally identified at this point. Based on the functions outlined above and on biochemical experiments, members of four protein families have been suggested to reside in the active zone.

Ca^{2+} Channels

It is likely that Ca^{2+} channels are concentrated at the active zone, close to the site of synaptic vesicle exocytosis (Almers and Tse 1990); however, it is unclear which type of Ca^{2+} channel is involved. In the frog neuromuscular junction, ω-conotoxin-sensitive Ca^{2+} channels seem to be responsible for neurotransmitter release whereas in the rat brain, ω-conotoxin has no effect on neurotransmitter release. Neurotransmitter release from rat synaptosomes is blocked by ω-agatoxin IVA, a neurotoxin that acts on a different class of Ca^{2+} channels (Mintz et al. 1992). This suggests that in the rat brain, the majority of ω-conotoxin-sensitive Ca^{2+} channels are not at the active zone. Perhaps in different species, and maybe at different synapses in the same species, different types of Ca^{2+} channels are used for neurotransmitter release.

Neurexins/α-Latrotoxin Receptor

α-Latrotoxin is a presynaptic neurotoxin that causes massive neurotransmitter release. Although it is unclear how α-latrotoxin triggers exocytosis, it appears to act via specific receptors that are enriched at the active zone of the neuromuscular junction. Cloning the high molecular weight subunit of a receptor for α-latrotoxin led to the discovery of a new family of neuronal cell surface proteins called neurexins (Ushkaryov et al. 1992). There are three neurexin genes, each of which contains alternative promoters generating two classes of transcripts encoding α- and β-neurexins. All neurexins are extensively spliced alternatively, resulting in the presence of hundreds of different neurexin transcripts. The neurexins have structures resembling cell surface receptors and are homologous to extracellular matrix proteins involved in cell-cell interactions, such as laminin A, agrin, and slit. The neurexins are brain-specific, and at least neurexin I is highly enriched at synapses, although not necessarily at the active zone.

Presently, the functions of the neurexins are unclear. One potential function of the neurexins involves their intracellular actions via their short cytoplasmic tail. Initial purification of the α-latrotoxin receptor demonstrated that synaptotagmin, a major synaptic vesicle protein that binds Ca^{2+}, co-purified with the receptor by binding to the receptor (Petrenko et al. 1991). More recent studies demonstrated that the short intracellular domains of all three neurexins directly interacts with synaptotagmin *in vitro* in a sequence-specific manner (Hata et al. 1993). This interaction is dependent on a 40 amino acid sequence in the tail of the neurexins and is abolished if only the last three amino acids are deleted from the tail. Together, these findings suggest that the cytoplasmic domains of the neurexins could serve as docking or targeting proteins for synaptic vesicles in the nerve terminal.

Another potential function of the neurexins is proposed and is based on their receptor-like structure and polymorphic expression. These properties suggest that the neurexins may represent polymorphic cell surface proteins that could contribute to synaptic specificity by mediating cell-cell interactions at the nerve terminal (Ushkaryov et al. 1992). Although such a function would be extremely attractive, it would imply that there should be equivalent numbers of transsynaptic ligands which have not yet been defined. Together, the hypotheses regarding the extra- and intracellular functions of neurexins postulate that these proteins might represent major components of the mechanism, whereby synaptic vesicle release sites are aligned with postsynaptic specializations.

HPC-1/Syntaxins/Epimorphins

Recently, a protein named syntaxin was shown to co-immunoprecipitate with synaptotagmin and ω-conotoxin binding sites (Bennett et al. 1992). Cloning of syntaxin demonstrated it to be identical with HPC-1, a previously characterized protein discovered by a monoclonal antibody against retinal cells (Inoue et al. 1992). In addition, syntaxin turned out to be highly related to a mesenchymal protein called epimorphin, with a putative function in morphogenesis (Hirai et al. 1992). Immunocytochemistry of the neuromuscular junction with syntaxin antibodies demonstrated enrichment at the synapse cleft. However, HPC-1 immunocytochemistry shows no enrichment at synapses in the retina (Barnstable et al. 1985), and HPC-1/syntaxin and its close relative epimorphin are not brain-specific, suggesting that they also have functions outside of synapses.

It is possible that HPC-1/syntaxins/epimorphins have similar functions in neuronal and nonneuronal cells and represent general trafficking proteins. In this case, the function of these proteins in the active zone would be similar to trafficking functions the protein may have in nonneuronal cells. This possibility would be very exciting in view of the possible similarities between constitutive and regulated membrane trafficking pathways in eukaryotic cells.

Physophilin

Physophilin is a 36 kD integral membrane protein derived from the synaptic plasma membrane and seems to be part of a high molecular weight complex. Through affinity chromatography on immobilized synaptic vesicles, the protein was identified as a binding protein for synaptophysin and might represent a synaptic vesicle docking protein (Thomas and Betz 1990). Physophilin, however, has not yet been purified or cloned, making it necessary for future studies to establish its properties and localization.

UNEXPECTED NEW RESULTS DIFFICULT TO INTERPRET WITHIN THE CURRENT FRAMEWORK

In the preceding discussion, we have portrayed the synapse as a specialized secretory system that requires a number of specific proteins to function. Although evidence has accumulated, indicating that the synaptic vesicle pathway may represent a specialization of more basic trafficking pathways, it is generally believed that synapses are distinguished from all other secretory systems by an intricate set of unique elements required for function. In addition, a large number of studies have demonstrated that discrete external stimuli are required to induce the formation of presynaptic specializations. Below we discuss a set of recently published papers that are difficult to interpret using this conceptual framework.

A series of three papers reported that brain RNA injected into oocytes resulted in quantal neurotransmitter release from the injected oocytes and that injection of acetylcholine into myocytes also resulted in quantal release of acetylcholine (Cavalli et al. 1991; Alder et al. 1992; Dan and Poo 1992). The mechanisms of neurotransmitter release were interpreted very differently in these studies, although the experimental designs were very similar. Independent of the interpretations, these results imply that very little is needed to achieve quantal, synaptic-like neurotransmitter release. In particular, a synapse does not seem necessary.

None of these papers report morphological or controlled electrophysiological data, which makes an exact evaluation impossible. Nevertheless, the ability to study synaptic neurotransmitter release in the absence of synapses would provide us with a great technological advance that would, in turn, simplify future studies. Furthermore, it would necessitate a revision of the idea that synapses require a unique apparatus with a separate set of specific proteins for neurotransmitter release.

Using a different approach, recent studies have suggested that synapsins, the most abundant synaptic vesicle protein, may have important unanticipated regulatory functions. The major finding was that synapsins IIa and IIb (and presumably also synapsins Ia and Ib, because of the great degree of homology between the synapsins) induce gene expression of secretory vesicle proteins after transfection into cells (Han et al. 1991). The results suggest that synapsins may directly or indirectly regulate transcription factors for neuronal proteins. In an ingenuous "News and Views" article in *Nature*, Regis Kelly offered an alternative explanation, suggesting that the transfected synapsins may stabilize the vesicles without a direct effect on gene expression (Kelly 1991). This hypothesis, however, does not explain the induction of dense core proteins, which do not interact with synapsins, that was observed by Han et al. (1991). If confirmed in subsequent studies, the induction of gene expression by synapsins, through whatever mechanism, would imply a major function for synapsins in regulating synapses at a level not currently envisioned.

In a second study conducted recently (Benfenati et al. 1992), synapsins Ia and Ib were shown to bind to synaptic vesicles through a specific interaction of their carboxyl termini with Ca^{2+}/calmodulin-dependent protein kinase II. This is surprising for two reasons. First, the kinase is an abundant protein with ubiquitous localization, with major pools being postsynaptic. If the kinase is indeed the binding protein of synapsin I, then it is unclear why synapsins are not associated with the kinase in the other subcellular pools. Second, synapsin II is also found on synaptic vesicles but does not share sequence homology with synapsin I in the region of its proposed interaction with

Ca^{2+}/calmodulin-dependent protein kinase II. One wonders how synapsin II is targeted. A possible explanation is that synapsin I may function to regulate the activity of Ca^{2+}/calmodulin-dependent protein kinase II instead of being targeted by it. As long as the functions of synapsins are unknown, this issue cannot be resolved.

MECHANISTIC MODELS OF NEUROTRANSMITTER RELEASE: POTENTIAL TARGETS FOR MODULATION

Modulation of neurotransmitter release may have a function in processes of neural plasticity and is therefore of considerable interest. In the following, we would like to speculate on three principal possibilities to regulate release.

1. The rise in intracellular Ca^{2+} as a function of the action potential is probably subject to regulation. The rise in intracellular Ca^{2+} could be modulated by either changes in the action potential duration or the voltage-gated Ca^{2+} channels. Many examples have been observed for the functional modulation of channels by phosphorylations, which could easily change the effective Ca^{2+} concentration achieved in the nerve terminal. In *Aplysia,* for example, changes in a K^+ conductance are thought to be instrumental for short- and long-term memory (for a review, see Kandel and Schwartz 1982).
2. The size of the released neurotransmitter quanta could be modulated (for a review, see Van der Kloot 1991). This could be achieved by regulating the loading of synaptic vesicles with neurotransmitters. It is conceivable that either the synaptic vesicle proton pump, their chloride channels, or neurotransmitter transporters are regulated.
3. Neurotransmitter release could be modulated by changing the release probability of synaptic vesicles. Several mechanisms could be envisioned for this effect:
   a. The availability of synaptic vesicles for exocytosis could be regulated. It has been hypothesized that this could be achieved by anchoring the synaptic vesicles onto the nerve terminal cytoskeleton via synapsins (Valtorta et al. 1992). Synapsin phosphorylation is then thought to regulate synaptic vesicle availability. However, synapsins appear to be quantitatively phosphorylated under conditions of regular neuronal activity, suggesting that their phosphorylation is part of the synaptic vesicle recycling pathway and not a regulatory mechanism. It is still possible that other mechanisms serve to anchor vesicles to the cytoskeleton in a manner that is regulated independently of nerve terminal depolarization.
   b. The docking of synaptic vesicles at the active zone could be subject to modulatory control. Possible regulatory targets include *rab3A*, which may be necessary for synaptic vesicle targeting and could be modulated by GDP-GTP exchange proteins in analogy to *ras*. Synaptotagmin has also

been implicated in synaptic vesicle docking, either via the neurexins or via HPC-1/syntaxins (see above). Synaptotagmin is an excellent substrate for casein kinase II and is phosphorylated in synaptosomes, independently of nerve terminal depolarization (Davletov et al. 1993). Although the functional consequences of this phosphorylation are unknown, casein kinase II activation has been reported during induction of long-term potentiation and could conceivably work via synaptotagmin.

c. Another potential mechanism to modulate release is a change in the Ca^{2+} sensitivity of the Ca^{2+}-binding protein that is the trigger for exocytosis. If synaptotagmin indeed represents this protein, then its phosphorylation might also change its Ca^{2+} affinity. Synaptobrevins, which are now known to be involved in the fusion reaction, might also be modulated.

This description demonstrates that there are many possibilities to regulate release. It seems certain that regulation of release via modulation of ion channels will occur. There is also indirect evidence that the presynaptic machinery for release can be directly modulated; however, the mechanisms and the extent of this regulation are unclear. Future experiments will need to address these questions as soon as more about the actual release process is known.

ACKNOWLEDGEMENTS

Research in our laboratories was supported by the National Institutes of Health and the Perot Family Foundation. We are grateful to our colleagues and co-workers for their advice and contributions, in particular Dr. Harvey McMahon, who critically read the manuscript.

REFERENCES

Alder, J., B. Lu, F. Valtorta, P. Greengard, and M. Poo. 1992. Calcium-dependent transmitter secretion reconstituted in *Xenopus* oocytes: Requirement for synaptosin. *Science* **257**:657–661.

Almers, W., and F.W. Tse. 1990. Transmitter release from synapses: Does a preassembled fusion pore initiate exocytosis? *Neuron* **4**:813–818.

Bajjalieh, S.M., K. Peterson, R. Shinghal, and R.H. Scheller. 1992. SV2, a brain synaptic vesicle protein homologous to bacterial transporters. *Science* **257**:1271–1273.

Barnstable, C.J., R. Hofstein, and K. Akagawa. 1985. A marker of early amacrine cell development in rat retina. *Devel. Brain Res.* **20**:286–290.

Benfenati, F., F. Valtorta, J.L. Rubenstein, F.S. Gorelick, P. Greengard, and A.J. Czernik. 1992. Synaptic vesicle-associated Ca^{2+}/calmodulin-dependent protein kinase II is a binding protein for synapsin I. *Nature* **359**:417–420.

Bennett, M.K., N. Calakos, and R.H. Scheller. 1992. Syntaxin: A synaptic protein implicated in docking of synaptic vesicles at presynaptic active zones. *Science* **257**:255–259.

Brose, N., A.G. Petrenko, T.C. Südhof, and R. Jahn. 1992. Synaptotagmin: A calcium sensor on the synaptic vesicle surface. *Science* **256**:1021–1025.

Cavalli, A., L. Eder-Colli, Y. Dunant, F. Loctin, and N. Morel. 1991. Release of acetylcholine by *Xenopus* oocytes injected with mRNAs from cholinergic neurons. *EMBO J.* **10**:1671–1675.

Dan, Y., and M. Poo. 1992. Quantal transmitter secretion from myocytes loaded with acetylcholine. *Nature* **359**:733–741.

Davletov, B., J.M. Sontag, Y. Hata, A.G. Petrenko, E.M. Fykse, R. Jahn, and T.C. Südhof. 1993. Phosphorylation of synaptotagmin I by casein kinase II. *J. Biol. Chem.* **268**:6816–6822.

Feany, M.B., S. Lee, R.H. Edwards, and K.M. Buckley. 1992. The synaptic vesicle protein SV2 is a novel type of transporter. *Cell* **70**:861–867.

Han, H.-Q., R.A. Nichols, M.R. Rubin, M. Bähler, and P. Greengard. 1991. Induction of formation of presynaptic terminals in neuroblastoma cells by synapsin IIb. *Nature* **349**:697–700.

Hata, Y., B. Davletov, A.G. Petrenko, R. Jahn, and T.C. Südhof. 1993. Interaction of synaptotagmin with the cytoplasmic domains of neurexins. *Neuron* **10**:307–315.

Hirai, Y., K. Takebe, M. Takashina, S. Kobayashi, and M. Takeichi. 1992. Epimorphin: A mesenchymal protein essential for epithelial morphogenesis. *Cell* **69**:471–481.

Inoue, I., K. Obata, and K. Akagawa. 1992. Cloning and sequence analysis of cDNA for a neuronal cell membrane antigen, HPC-1. *J. Biol. Chem.* **267**:10613–10619.

Jahn, R., and T.C. Südhof. 1993. Synaptic vesicles and exocytosis. *Ann. Rev. Neurosci.*, submitted.

Kandel, E.R., and J.H. Schwartz. 1982. Molecular biology of learning: Modulation of neurotransmitter release. *Science* **218**:433–442.

Kelly, R.G. 1991. A system for synapse control. *Nature* **349**:650–651.

Link, E., L. Edelman, J. Chow, T. Binz, U. Eisel, M. Baumert, T.C. Südhof, N. Niemann, and R. Jahn. 1992. Inhibition of neurotransmission by tetanus toxin is associated with a degradation of the synaptic vesicle protein synaptobrevin. *Biochem. Biophys. Res. Comm.* **189**:1017–1023.

Mintz, I.M., V.J.U. Venema, K. Swiderek, T. Lee, B.P. Bean, and M.E. Adams. 1992. P-type Ca^{2+} channels blocked by the spider toxin ω-aga-IVA. *Nature* **355**:827–829.

Peters, A., S.L. Palay, and H.D. Webster. 1991. The Fine Structure of the Nervous System. Neurons and Their Supporting Cells, 3rd ed. Oxford: Oxford Univ. Press.

Petrenko, A.B., M.S. Perin, A.D. Bazbek, Y.A. Ushkaryov, M. Geppert, and T.C. Südhof. 1991. Binding of synaptotagmin to the α-latrotoxin receptor implicates both in synaptic vesicle exocytosis. *Nature* **353**:65–68.

Schiavo, G., F. Benfenati, B. Poulain, O. Rosetto, P.P. de Laureto, B.R. Das Gupta, and C. Montecucco. 1992. Tetanus and botulinum-B neurotoxins block neurotransmitter release by proteolytic cleavage of synaptobrevin. *Nature* **359**:832–835.

Südhof, T.C., and R. Jahn. 1991. Proteins of synaptic vesicles involved in exocytosis and membrane recycling. *Neuron* **6**:665–677.

Thomas, L., and H. Betz. 1990. Synaptophysin binds to physophilin, a putative synaptic plasma membrane protein. *J. Cell Biol.* **111**:2041–2052.

Ushkaryov, Y.A., A.G. Petrenko, M. Geppert, and T.C. Südhof. 1992. Neurexins: Synaptic cell surface proteins related to the α-latrotoxin receptor and laminin. *Science* **257**:50–56.

Valtorta, F., F. Benfenati, and P. Greengard. 1992. Structure and function of synapsins. *J. Biol. Chem.* **267**:7195–7198.

Van der Kloot, W. 1991. The regulation of quantal size. *Prog. Neurobiol.* **36**:93–130.

Walch-Solimena, C., K. Takei, K. Marek, K. Midyett, T.C. Südhof, P. DeCamilli, and R. Jahn. 1993. Synaptotagmin: A membrane constituent of neuropeptide-containing large dense-core vesicles. *J. Neurosci.* **13**:3895–3903.

Standing, left to right:
Philippe Ascher, Peter Jonas, Tom Südhof, Al Selverston, Steve Heinemann, Peter Seeburg, Bill Catterall
Seated, left to right:
Tom Curran, Lorna Role, Regis Kelly, Wolfgang Müller

22

Group Report: What Molecular Mechanisms Are Likely to Be Central for Plasticity in the Operation of the Nervous System?

L.W. ROLE, Rapporteur

P. ASCHER, W.A. CATTERALL, T. CURRAN,
S. HEINEMANN, P. JONAS, R.B. KELLY,
W. MÜLLER, P.H. SEEBURG, A.I. SELVERSTON,
T.C. SÜDHOF

INTRODUCTION

Implementation of long-lasting changes in neural function involves the fundamental alteration of cellular properties. To dissect the molecular bases of these changes requires an integrated approach, combining biochemical, cell biological, molecular biological, and biophysical techniques. Our goal was to attempt such a dissection of plasticity by identifying the most likely targets and mechanisms of molecular modification. This dissection of molecular mechanisms of plasticity draws heavily from recent work and is firmly based on our collective (and divergent) personal biases. In this regard, the group considered the following questions in pursuit of the molecular mechanisms most likely to underlie neural plasticity:

1. Are the molecular mechanisms that underlie topologically restricted vs. global changes in plasticity fundamentally different?
2. What are the molecular mechanisms that could contribute to pre- and postsynaptic aspects of plasticity?
3. Is changing gene expression required for long-term plasticity?
4. What is the role of microtargeting in synaptic plasticity?

Cellular and Molecular Mechanisms Underlying Higher Neural Functions
Edited by A.I. Selverston and P. Ascher

5. Is there a role for morphological changes in long-term synaptic plasticity?
6. How adequate are current tools and approaches to dissecting basic mechanisms of synaptic plasticity?
7. Can we propose new perspectives and models to pursue mechanisms of plasticity?

TOPOLOGICALLY RESTRICTED VS. GLOBAL MECHANISMS OF NEURONAL PLASTICITY

Neuronal plasticity may be roughly divided into topologically restricted (i.e., synapse-specific) mechanisms (such as long-term potentiation [LTP] and long-term depression [LTD]) and more global mechanisms that modulate the physiological properties of groups of synapses or an entire cell. Topologically restricted mechanisms of plasticity would alter synaptic strength of only a small fraction of established synapses. By contrast, global mechanisms of neuronal plasticity affect multiple synapses or the input-output relationships of a neuron as a whole by altering critical membrane properties. Synapse-specific plasticity may be required for learning, memory, and cognitive function in vertebrates. Global mechanisms of plasticity can change the functional states that control the tone of networks and may underlie attentiveness, mood, etc. These two complementary forms of neuronal plasticity interact to create and control vertebrate behavior.

We first considered whether global mechanisms of plasticity might have features that distinguish them from mechanisms of topologically restricted plasticity. Neuromodulatory peptides and amines, acting through G-protein-coupled pathways to regulate the function of voltage-gated ion channels, often initiate global forms of plasticity. The global actions of these agents depend upon their relatively broad diffusion from sites of release and the high affinity of their receptors, allowing low concentrations to be effective. Several examples of modulation of voltage-gated ion channels have been described in detail and two general modulatory pathways are recognized: a direct, membrane-delimited regulation of ion channels by G-proteins, and an indirect modulation via cellular second messengers and protein phosphorylation (Catterall, this volume; for reviews see Levitan 1988 and Hille 1992). Modulation of voltage-gated Na^+, K^+, and Ca^{2+} channels by protein phosphorylation is well-studied, and specific subunits and sites of phosphorylation have been identified in some cases. There is also considerable evidence that modulation of voltage-gated channels can alter transmitter release. Thus, these modulatory processes could serve as good molecular models for ion channel modifications that contribute to synaptic plasticity. However, in contrast to the important role of modulation of voltage-gated channels in global forms of plasticity, there is no evidence (in vertebrates) that this type of modulation is important in topologically restricted plasticity. On the other hand, there are numerous examples of modifications of the properties of neurotransmitter-gated ion channels and some evidence for changes in postsynaptic receptors during synapse-specific plasticity (Nicoll, this volume). Thus it seems likely that some molecular mechanisms of the triggering and/or expression of plasticity may be common to both topologically restricted *and* global neuronal changes while others are uniquely suited to synapse-specific events. Topological restriction of transmitter release and receptor localization can serve to confine modulation to single synapses.

Despite potential similarities between some aspects of global and synapse-specific plasticity, our consensus was that, in view of both the constraints of time and the attendant expertise, we should focus our discussion on synapse-specific plasticity. We also agreed to focus further on a particularly interesting form of synaptic plasticity that seemed to be the best understood: LTP. Results from studies of global plasticity will be considered, however, when these findings might suggest likely molecular mechanisms for LTP. The focus of our deliberations on LTP was not meant to suggest that LTP is equivalent to learning. Since there are clearly a multitude of learning processes and many forms of synaptic plasticity, our decision to focus on LTP was intended as a useful, *albeit* oversimplified, artifice for further discussion.

MOLECULAR MECHANISMS THAT COULD CONTRIBUTE TO PRESYNAPTIC ASPECTS OF SYNAPSE-SPECIFIC PLASTICITY

In view of the general perception that induction, expression, and maintenance of long-term synaptic plasticity could involve both pre- and postsynaptic changes (Edwards et al., this volume), we continued our discussion by outlining potential targets for modification on both sides of the synapse. In addition, we sought to outline possible/probable molecular mechanisms that might regulate each step.

We first considered several stages in the control of transmitter release that could be targets for regulation. (We did manage to agree that transmitter release is a presynaptic phenomenon!) These steps were outlined as: (a) activation of transmitter release, (b) release per se, and (c) inactivation of released transmitter. There was general agreement that the first type of regulatory mechanism probably operates in the nerve terminal, although there is little direct evidence for this. The second type of mechanism has been demonstrated in several systems, although its molecular basis is unclear. The third mechanism has yet to be examined in detail.

The activation or initiation of transmitter release would include phenomena that alter Ca^{2+} influx to the presynaptic terminal, thereby enhancing Ca^{2+}-dependent release. An example of such an event would be changes in the function of presynaptic channels, such as the modulation of voltage-dependent Ca^{2+}, K^+, or Na^+ channels (see Catterall, this volume). One major problem considered at this point was the comparative lack of knowledge of the properties of central synapses as opposed to the neuromuscular junction. Exact description of the functional parameters and range of variation of central synapses would facilitate designing experiments to test regulatory targets. Examples of the modulation of presynaptic ion channels controlling transmitter release by second messenger mechanisms are not abundant in the CNS. However, effects of PKA and PKC on transmitter release from central neurons have been demonstrated and the mini frequency can be altered via a G-protein-mediated, membrane-delimited action of adenosine (Lupica et al. 1992; for reviews see Hawkins et al. 1993, Levitan 1988, Thompson et al. 1993). In view of the numerous examples of modulation of voltage-gated ion channels and transmitter release from peripheral neurons this seems a likely target of presynaptic modulation.

A role for second messenger-mediated modulation of presynaptic voltage-dependent ion channels in sustained plasticity of hippocampal synapses is not supported by studies to date, although it must be admitted that experiments testing this hypothesis are also a bit sparse. In particular, while there is evidence for modulation of voltage-dependent Ca^{2+} channels in central neurons, a contribution of this type of modulation to LTP in CA1 neurons seems unlikely. In this regard, changes in external Ca^{2+} do not differentially affect release at control vs. potentiated synapses in hippocampus (Nicoll, this volume). In addition, there is no evidence for long-lasting changes in either basal Ca or in Ca transients in presynaptic terminals after expression of LTP as deduced from Ca imaging experiments on hippocampal terminals in areas CA3 and CA1 (e.g., Regehr and Tank 1991). Finally, long-term facilitation of *Aplysia* sensorimotor synapses, although accompanied by changes in the voltage-dependent Ca^{2+} current and in transmitter release, is apparently mediated by a voltage-insensitive K channel closed by cAMP-dependent kinase-mediated phosphorylation (for a review, see Hawkins et al. 1993).

Examination of some interneuronal synapses also suggests that presynaptic ligand-gated channels might be considered as a possible locus in the control of transmitter release (e.g., see Lena et al. 1993). Profound changes in synaptic current frequency (without changes in mini amplitude) are evoked through application of nicotinic agonists at several central synapses. The presynaptic facilitatory effects of nicotine may be due to direct Ca^{2+} entry through αBGT sensitive nicotinic receptors (D. McGehee and L. Role, unpublished observations) which are abundant in hippocampus (e.g., Freedman et al. 1993).

Our discussion moved on to consider possible aspects of regulation of release after initial "activation" (i.e., the second stage mentioned above). Regulation of transmitter release would include phenomena that change the probability of Ca^{2+}-dependent vesicular fusion with the plasma membrane, hence changing the probability of transmitter release. This sort of mechanism could involve posttranslational modification of expressed synaptic vesicle proteins or switches between synaptic vesicle protein isoforms (see Südhof and Jahn, this volume).

The first possibility discussed regarding potential regulatory modifications of the secretory apparatus was that release could be controlled by regulating the equilibrium between vesicles dwelling in two distinct pools: a " rapidly releasable" vs. a "reserve" pool. Is this distinction real? Is regulation of the flux between these pools an important control point for presynaptic plasticity?

Neither biochemical nor physiological studies provide evidence for functionally distinct vesicular pools, rather they indicate that vesicles are lined up in a continuum for release. Vesicles docked and ready to go are closely followed by the next releasable pool of vesicles operating like a conveyor belt. Furthermore, low numbers of vesicles exocytose per action potential, arguing against regulatory mechanisms regarding vesicle numbers. Data from Betz (1992) as well as from Koenig and Ikeda (1989) suggest that the distinction between a "readily releasable" and "reserve" pool might be spurious. At *Drosophila* neuromuscular junctions, the EPP amplitude is proportional to the number of synaptic vesicles in the entire terminal (as opposed to a subset within a "priority pool"). More recent work, again from neuromuscular junctions, demonstrates that okadaic acid disperses vesicles throughout the presynaptic terminal (unpublished work cited by Kelly). Under these circumstances, all vesicles would presumably have an equal chance to dock, fuse, and exocytose and, hence, if there are normally separate pools, one would predict that release from such a "vesicle-diffused" terminal should look very different. Since this is not so, it seems likely that vesicles are in a continuum rather than in distinct releasable vs. reserve pools. If a continuum of vesicles is available for release without appreciable delay, there is no need to postulate regulation of this step in the activation of release. However, the rate of vesicle docking might still serve as a mechanism for enhanced release.

Another possible control point for vesicular release would be through posttranslational modification or isotype switching of particular synaptic vesicle proteins. One might propose an increasing probability of vesicular fusion following phosphorylation of proteins such as the synapsins. Some skepticism was expressed about the possible role of synapsin I phosphorylation in specialized forms of long-term plasticity, since the extent of phosphorylation appears to be stoichiometric with the degree of activation and occurs equally in all synapses (Nestler and Greengard 1982).

This interpretation of the results was softened a bit since it was pointed out that the stimuli used in these experiments were not graded electrical stimuli but, rather, elevated K^+-induced depolarization. The phosphorylation of synapsins at the N terminus, rather than at the carboxyl end, is mediated by activation of either calcium/calmodulin kinase or PKA. This N-terminal site may be an excellent candidate for important regulation of synapsin by phosphorylation since it is present in both synapsin I and II and therefore may relate more generally to synapsin function. Another potential phosphorylation event, suggested by Südhof as a regulatory mechanism in neurotransmitter release, was the phosphorylation of synaptotagmin by casein kinase. Apparently, synaptotagmin is a major casein kinase II substrate in the brain. The drawback of this hypothesis is the absence of known physiological activators of casein kinase. From this discussion, it was apparent that there is no strong evidence to indicate that phosphorylation of any of the synaptic vesicle proteins examined to date provides a mechanism for regulation of release with long-term plasticity. It was agreed that even if phosphorylation of a particular synaptic vesicle protein could be shown to be induced by stimulation, one still would not know how this was related to LTP. Simply neutralizing the action of a particular synaptic vesicle protein by antibody treatment is interesting because it documents that the protein is important, but reveals neither the locus of action nor provides any insights into regulatory mechanisms. Nonetheless, regulation of vesicular fusion by altering the function of one or more of the known synaptic vesicle proteins still seems to be an attractive mechanism for controlling presynaptic plasticity (see Südhof and Jahn, this volume). Experiments that could be pursued to further test this idea could include:

- *in vitro* reconstitution of a synapse with and without specific synaptic vesicle proteins,
- selective deletion of specific synaptic vesicle proteins and examination of functional consequences,
- functional modifications of synaptic vesicle proteins that might occur in LTP (e.g., phosphorylation),
- knockout of normal synaptic vesicle proteins and replacement with specific forms (e.g., minus potential phosphorylation sites, etc.)

The group conceded to a (brief) consideration of possible presynaptic targets of a retrograde messenger, such as nitric oxide. Since NO can potentially interact with any iron-containing protein or enzyme, as well as bind to cysteine residues within any protein, there are more than enough presynaptic targets for NO interaction. One known target of NO is the soluble isoform of guanylate cyclase, which is activated by NO. Downstream substrates for the soluble guanylate cyclase, including but not limited to cGMP kinase, need to be tested further for possible effects on transmitter release.

Another known effect of NO is to enhance the ADP ribosylation of several proteins including GPH, which can lead to an enhancement of RNA transfer from the nucleus to the cytoplasm. The interaction with *cys* residues is potentially important to NO action, both in the stabilization and buffering of the bound NO. In addition, the *cys*-NO interaction is sensitive to the redox state of the cell. Curran reminded us that a feature of several transcription factors is redox sensitivity, e.g., the activation of the transcription factor NFkB by oxidants and the effect of *cys* reduction in specific sequences of *Fos* and *Jun* (*lys-cys-arg*) that block DNA binding activity. Clearly this blocking of DNA binding could lead to transcriptional activation or repression, depending on the target *cis* element. In addition to transcription factors, a voltage-gated K channel has been shown to be modulated by oxidation/reduction of a –SH/–S–S bond in the intracellular domain. This redox mechanism could also be a target for NO, since presynaptic modulation of K channel function would also modulate transmitter release. Thus, NO effects on RNA or *cys* residues might alter presynaptic function by changing gene expression, protein synthesis, and/or ion channel function. The consensus was that although potential regulatory targets for NO are in abundance, there is little evidence to help us whittle down the options to those that are most likely.

A final possible locus of regulation pertaining to transmitter release would be to alter the rate of inactivation of the transmitter following its release into the synaptic cleft. This phenomenon, which could involve changes in transmitter uptake mechanisms or changes in the activity of degradative enzymes has not been explored extensively. Again, studies of peripheral synapses have demonstrated activity-dependent changes in transmitter re-uptake into nerve terminals, suggesting that this mechanism is worth considering.

MOLECULAR MECHANISMS THAT COULD CONTRIBUTE TO POSTSYNAPTIC ASPECTS OF PLASTICITY

Before evaluating changes in postsynaptic function that might underlie LTP, we first reconsidered some of the basic mechanisms of synaptic transmission (for reviews see Madison et al. 1991 and Stevens 1993). The size of a unitary EPSC is determined by $I_{quant} \times N_{release}$ (quantal currents × number of active release sites). $N_{release}$ might be modified by presynaptic mechanisms, as considered in detail above. The size of a quantal current depends on three factors:

$$I_{quant} = N_{channels} \times P_{open} \times i,$$

where N is the number of available channels in a postsynaptic density, P_{open} is the maximal open probability of the channels, and i is the single-channel current.

Quantal analysis reveals that the quantal conductance, and hence $N_{channels} \times P_{open}$, is relatively small. At the mossy fiber CA3 synapse, $N_{channels} \times P_{open}$ was estimated between 15 and 65. There was agreement that similar numbers apply to other central and peripheral synapses.

Examination of quantal current variability is important because it provides information about the open probability of the channels at the peak. If P_{open} is low, there is considerable variation due to stochastic opening and closing of channels. There are at least quantitative differences in the variability of a single quantal event in different synapses reported by different groups: 15% (IPSCs dentate gyrus; Edwards et al. 1990), 22% (EPSCs MF-CA3; Jonas and Sakmann 1992), and "small variability" (Nicoll, this volume; Madison et al. 1991; Larkman et al. 1992) but higher values reported by others (50% CA1; C. Stevens, P. Andersen, and their colleagues). There is evidence that the glutamate concentration in the synaptic cleft is about 1 mM, which would be close to saturation. For example, Jonas has developed rapid application techniques (rise time: 100 µsec) to estimate synaptic glutamate by comparing the rise time of currents evoked by fast application with that of synaptic currents. In addition, studies with GluR channel antagonists and the low quantal current variability for some synapses also suggest a high P_{open} and, therefore, a high glutamate concentration (e.g., Clements et al. 1992). At saturating concentrations, the P_{open} of GluR channels is 0.7–0.8 (with fast application of glutamate to extrasynaptic GluR channels), resulting in a CV of 5–15% due to channel gating. The critical assumptions for this comparison are that the extrasynaptic glutamate receptors (GluR) are identical in functional properties to the GluRs at the synapse. It was agreed that *if* the concentration of glutamate in the cleft is close to saturating, it is difficult to evaluate how changes other than in the number of available channels could influence the size of the synaptic current.

The final determinant of I_{quant} considered was i, the single channel current. The conductance of extrasynaptic AMPA/kainate type GluR channels is also small (< 10 pS), and there is evidence for multiple conductance states, which makes the analysis of i difficult.

We moved on to consider which of the factors that contribute to I_{quant} might change with LTP, a difficult task in view of the paucity of data. First, morphological evidence does not suggest that LTP results in changes in vesicle size. However, other mechanisms, such as the variable filling of vesicles, are still possible presynaptic mechanisms for quantal variability.

Increases in the total number of surface GluR channels or changes in the distribution of particular channel subtypes could, in principle, provide a mechanism for postsynaptic changes. Although attempts at NMDA-R localization by immunocytochemical techniques have been initiated (Heinemann, pers. comm.), determination of the number and distribution of surface receptors awaits development of ecto domain antibodies. Current probes, directed against the putative TM3–4 cytoplasmic domain (which require permeabilization prior to staining), have revealed an extensive intracellular pool of NMDA-Rs subunits, as seen for other neuronal ligand-gated receptors. Since previous studies indicate spatial segregation of distinct channel subtypes on peripheral neurons following the establishment of synaptic input (Moss and Role 1993), it would not be surprising to see similar changes in NMDA-Rs with long-lasting changes in synaptic function.

The number of available channels might be modified by posttranslational mechanisms, such as phosphorylation. Such modifications might increase receptor insertion from the large internal receptor pools (see above) or might unmask functionally "silent" receptors already on the cell surface. It is clear that GluR channels can be functionally regulated by cAMP-dependent phosphorylation (Greengard et al. 1991). In view of recent data that both assembly and insertion of other ligand-gated channels can be enhanced by cAMP-dependent kinase (Green et al. 1991), this mechanism might be worth examining for NMDA-Rs.

Finally, in addition to changes in channel number, GluR desensitization might be regulated during LTP (e.g., Trussell and Fischbach 1989). Desensitization can affect the amplitude of synaptic currents due to desensitization occurring with repeated brief pulses or by desensitization at equilibrium (after fast application of glutamate to somatic GluRs). It is not clear, however, if either the rate or extent of desensitization is affected during LTP.

IS CHANGING GENE EXPRESSION REQUIRED FOR LONG-TERM PLASTICITY?

Initially, two extreme positions were summarized. First, changes in gene expression in response to the extracellular environment can be considered to be an integral component of normal cellular physiology. Therefore, at some level, they must contribute to plastic changes. Second, modification of single synapses can be accounted for by protein redistribution or stabilization mechanisms. Therefore, it is not necessary to propose additional regulation at the level of gene expression. Furthermore, it is difficult to envisage a coupling mechanism that activates gene expression and targets protein products to single synapses. It is likely that the actual mechanism lies somewhere between these two extremes.

The question of the role of gene expression has been addressed by two different experimental strategies: activation of gene expression has been correlated with plastic change and protein synthesis inhibitors (and other types of inhibitors) have been used to block alterations in gene expression and acquisition of learned responses (see Curran, this volume).

In the discussion, drawbacks of both approaches were pointed out. The regulation of gene expression is complex and there is no simple relationship to learning. However, particularly in the case of the cellular immediate-early response, rapid and transient alterations in mRNA and protein levels have been demonstrated to accompany plastic change in a great many circumstances. The use of protein synthesis inhibitors to block learning is now more sophisticated than in previous years. Ongoing protein synthesis is clearly required for certain kinds of learning such as long-term heterosynaptic facilitation in *Aplysia* and in the rat gustatory learning paradigm (for a review, see Hawkins et al. 1993). Examples of learning blocked by very brief (1 hour) and precise application of protein synthesis inhibitors were also presented. These inhibitors, however, cannot distinguish between a need for ongoing gene expression as opposed to an alteration in the levels of gene expression. However, to postulate that protein synthesis inhibitors block learning by inhibiting the ongoing expression of a small set of "LTP-specific" proteins, the turnover rate of such proteins must be unusually rapid. It seems more likely that protein synthesis inhibitors block increased expression of a set of genes whose expression is required for structural/functional alterations that accompany learning.

The consensus was that there is no need to postulate "magical" memory proteins that are expressed as a result of stimulating a single synapse, whose protein products are then specifically targeted to the activated synapse by some novel mechanism. The local protein targeting processes are sufficient to explain the structural/functional synaptic modifications that occur in response to activation. A single synaptic alteration is not likely to deplete significantly preexisting protein pools, so there may be no need to synthesize more. In the case of LTP, ongoing protein synthesis is required for maintenance beyond the first few hours. In this situation, a large number of synapses are modified simultaneously. Therefore, the structural/functional alterations accompanying LTP may well deplete protein pools significantly. Thus, an increase in gene expression would be required to balance this loss. This can be viewed as a general (global) physiological response to activity. The genes involved could encode synaptic proteins; however, there will also be a requirement for other proteins, such as those involved in transport, energy metabolism, etc. In each stimulated neuron, there will have to be a coordination between protein turnover rates, proteins utilized for new structures, precursor pool sizes, and the level of change in gene expression. While it is acknowledged that LTP may represent a special situation associated with overstimulation, there will also be a similar requirement for new gene expression in more physiological circumstances, depending on the load on the individual cell. There may also be additional global changes in the properties of neurons in a network that will require more dramatic alterations in the levels of specific gene products.

One can view the requirement for *de novo* gene expression in maintenance of synaptic plasticity as part of a homeostatic mechanism that balances neuronal activity with structural alterations. This would necessitate a highly complex regulatory network in individual neurons capable of responding rapidly and precisely to changes in protein pool levels and composition. It was the general feeling of the group that the complexity of protein kinase and second messenger signaling cascades, existing protein microtargeting mechanisms, and the diversity of interactions among immediate-early transcription factors provides such a complex response mechanism. Thus, a significant feature of the molecular basis of synaptic plasticity is the complexity of the signaling mechanisms that may be involved in the process. Indeed, the problems encountered in trying to dissect the molecular basis of plasticity provides evidence for the existence of such biochemical complexity.

There was no final resolution of the question; no formal proof exists for the role of gene regulation in plasticity. However, Tom Curran submits that the preponderance of circumstantial evidence argues that "if it looks like a goat, sounds like a goat, and smells like a goat..."

POTENTIAL ROLE AND MECHANISMS OF MICROTARGETING IN SYNAPTIC PLASTICITY

Topologically restricted forms of synaptic plasticity require the selective modification of a small subset of synapses made by a neuron. In these circumstances, how might the cell regulate the proteins at these selectively activated synapses? Three potential mechanisms were proposed: instructive mechanisms, selective mechanisms, and stabilization mechanisms (for a review, s[illegible]lly, this volume, and Kelly 1993).

The assembly of new synaptic sites would not necessarily imply a need for new protein synthesis. In epithelia, for example, tight junctions can be assembled from preexisting pools of proteins by a nucleation and assembly process, involving the attachment of cytoskeletal proteins to cytoplasmic domains of cell surface proteins.

The targeting mechanisms utilized during neural development and synaptogenesis might suggest the mechanisms employed for later changes in synaptic function. In developing neurons, several equivalent neurites are first extended. These neurites end in growth cones, into which virtually all components of the cell are transported by microtubule-based motors. Later, a single neurite becomes an axon and the other neurites become dendrites. This is characterized by a selective targeting of synaptic proteins to the axonal growth cone and by a conversion of the dendritic microtubule organization from a unipolar to a bipolar type. When synapses are formed, synaptic proteins (e.g., P38) become completely localized to the axon terminal, while endocytic receptors, such as the transferrin receptor, are specifically excluded from the axons. These observations suggest that proteins contain specific targeting information, which directs them to their respective locations (an "address system"). A neuron contains several functional and structural subcompartments, each of which is characterized by different sets of proteins, including dendritic spines, dendritic shafts, proximal dendrites, axon hillocks, myelinated axons, nodes of Ranvier, presynaptic nerve terminals, postsynaptic densities. However, the molecular nature of a specific "address system" to these structures is not known.

Discussion centered on the role of cell-cell interactions in determining the sites to which proteins would be targeted. There is considerable evidence for cell interactions directing protein targeting in other neural and nonneural systems. Perhaps the most obvious and relevant example is the role of cell contact in the organization of both pre- and postsynaptic components during synaptogenesis. Targeting specific for long-term synaptic changes in mature animals might combine molecular mechanisms used by nonneural cells with those specifically designed to target molecules within neurons. The more general mechanism may involve inclusion of specific membrane binding sites (like "hooks") to act as a sink for proteins that would otherwise be transported up or down the process, past the selected site. Additional levels of mechanistic complexity might be superimposed on the general mechanisms to enhance specific targeting to the small numbers of activated synaptic structures.

What mechanisms might be utilized to transduce the selective activation of a synapse into a specific "instruction" to the cell nucleus to activate transcription of specific genes and return their gene products to the synapse? One novel idea suggested was an activity-dependent proteolytic cleavage of a synaptic protein to create simultaneously a signaling protein that can be transported to the nucleus and a receptor site in the synapse that can specifically bind a new protein product. The newly synthesized gene product would then be transported along the dendrite and bind to receptors in only appropriately activated synapses. The mechanism of activation of the thrombin receptor, in which there is proteolytic cleavage of an amino-terminal at the receptor, may suggest a model for this kind of mechanism.

WHAT ARE THE MECHANISMS OF MORPHOLOGICAL CHANGES IN SYNAPTIC PLASTICITY?

There is considerable evidence for extensive morphological changes with synaptic plasticity (see Greenough, this volume; Edwards et al., this volume; for reviews see Greenough and Bailey 1988, Bailey and Chen 1991, and Calverly and Jones 1990). In LTP experiments, the anatomical changes observed include changes of (a) the shape of the presynaptic boutons, (b) the vesicle number and distribution, (c) the size and form of the postsynaptic densities, (d) the number of synapses per target neuron, and (e) apparent changes in net connectivity. In the latter case, only suggestive evidence is available and is based on an increased number of spines per unit dendritic length and a fourfold increase of the number of bifurcating spines.

The molecular mechanisms supporting these sorts of changes over the short term (i.e., hours) may not require protein synthesis. Temporary structures, modified in both form and function, can evolve from existent structures and rearrangements of existent proteins. Activation of both intracellular and extracellular proteases might be involved in mobilization, extension, and structural changes. It is unlikely that the mechanisms employed are specifically devoted to LTP; the structural changes are frankly reminiscent of alterations seen with injury and early development. Combination of protein stabilization, microtargeting (see above), and enzyme activation is likely to be followed by synaptic replenishment supported in part by local changes in protein synthesis and by alterations in expression of genes encoding synaptic components. If one assumes that most proteins required for synaptic changes are expressed in excess, the only change may be to increase the "trapping" of these needed proteins at specific synapses (see above and Kelly, this volume).

HOW ADEQUATE ARE CURRENT TOOLS AND APPROACHES TO DISSECTING BASIC MECHANISMS OF SYNAPTIC PLASTICITY?

There was an overwhelming consensus that current tools of physiology, imaging, pharmacology, and genetics are too blunt for the task at hand. Although at this time a prediction of future methods is not possible—by definition—a wish list was drawn up.

Our current hopes rest heavily on optimism for the further development of molecular genetic techniques. Genes playing a role in plasticity can be ablated by stem cell technology. The homozygous null mutants fall in three categories: the first shows no easily identifiable phenotype; the second is lethal; and the third does present a phenotype. It can be argued that problems regarding a phenotype may stem from developmental plasticity and/or redundancy of genes. Problems with developmental compensation for deleted genes may be avoided by engineering genes that can be specifically controlled at a designated time later in development. This would allow switching genes off at particular times during development or at adult stages. This sort of control over the timing of mutation might be less likely to produce lethal mutants or might get around the activation of other genes that compensate for the loss. However, rapid compensatory mechanisms—equivalent in timing to the rate of turnover of the targeted proteins—have been observed with antisense-mediated deletion of ionic channels (Listerud et al. 1991). Although regulatory engineering of genes will be cumbersome, work might be facilitated by crossing animals carrying the newly engineered genes into a genetic background containing the regulatory components. A related tool for precise genetic engineering will involve the characterization of DNA segments that allow for the cell-specific expression of transgenes in brain. Currently, one of the only specific DNAs for this purpose is derived from the L7 gene, which is expressed selectively in Purkinje cells (Oberdick et al. 1990) and in retinal ganglion cells. Further dissection of the regulatory region of the L7 gene reveals a substructure in terms of expression in subsets of Purkinje cells.

It will be increasingly important to engineer point mutations into genes of interest. Such point mutations might generate [subtle?] changes in functional properties of proteins believed to play a role in neural plasticity. One way to construct animals homozygous for a mutated site is by the "hit and run" variant of homologous recombination (Hasty et al. 1991). Another way would be to cross animals having the gene of interest deleted through stem cell technology with animals carrying as transgene the point mutated gene.

We also need higher resolution in biophysical experiments to ensure quantitative descriptions of the behavior of synaptic currents and synaptic channels. Improvements should come with preparations other than those from the soma of neurons. At this time, patches can be pulled perisynaptically from dendrites (Stuart and Sakmann 1993) and, with some initial success, from large boutons (Stanley 1991).

Regarding optical imaging, dyes need to be developed for visualization of second messengers in addition to ions (Na, Ca^{2+}). High-resolution imaging in real time might reveal compartmentalized synchronous changes in second messengers important for plasticity (T. Knöpfel and W. Müller, unpublished). The use of flash photolysis and the need for further caged compounds to analyze synaptic function was emphasized. Such a signal then would not require the use of ion-specific dyes, and thus the system under analysis would be more physiological.

Although synaptic plasticity is undeniably complex, we continue to hope for pharmacological "silver bullets" to knock out key enzymes and receptors. There is a great need for specific compounds (inhibitors, competitive, and noncompetitive antagonists), which has arisen from the fact that a multitude of receptors and channels are now characterized where before we naively believed that there were only a few (see Seeburg, this volume). It is now clear that the brain expresses many subtypes of each receptor class and myriad enzymes (phosphates, kinases, synthases) that differ slightly in structure and function within a class. Hope was expressed that the development of these tools would be accelerated by the pharmaceutical industry.

Last but not least, some of us felt that an old-fashioned, straightforward bucket biochemistry of synaptic plasticity is needed. If an approach that yielded concurrent activation of most of the synapses could be identified, the biochemical tools are already in place. In this manner, the enzymatic cascades involved in synaptic plasticity could be identified and their relative order established. It is not at all clear whether the multiple pathways potentially involved in LTP might operate in parallel, in series, or both.

Available evidence, in fact, points to the involvement of multiple signaling pathways in the induction of LTP in the CA1 hippocampal cell. For example, calcium/calmodulin kinase, protein kinase C, and the *fyn* tyrosine kinase have all been implicated in the induction of LTP, and arachidonic acid, NO, and CO have been suggested as potential retrograde messengers (Edwards et al. and Kennedy, both this volume). While this apparent complexity may seem daunting or unnecessary, the lessons from other second messenger systems argue that such complexity is the rule rather than the exception. Regulation of a single enzyme, glycogen synthase, involves several protein kinases whose phosphorylation of the enzyme is interdependent and whose regulatory effects are convergent and interconnected. Regulation of cell growth involves dozens of protein kinases and many convergent phosphorylations. One aspect of modulation of voltage-gated sodium channels in brain neurons requires convergent phosphorylation at two distinct sites by protein kinases A and C (Catterall, this volume).

These examples from less intricate biological processes argue that LTP and other forms of plasticity underlying higher neural function may also require convergent phosphorylation by multiple protein kinases or convergent regulation by multiple second messenger pathways. Such convergent mechanisms increase the fidelity and flexibility of regulation, two characteristics that would be valuable in neuronal plasticity.

NOVEL PERSPECTIVES AND NEW APPROACHES TO SOLVING THE MOLECULAR BASIS OF SYNAPTIC PLASTICITY: WHERE DO WE GO FROM HERE?

Early studies of LTP were global. The presynaptic stimulation involved multiple presynaptic afferents; the event recorded concerned a population of postsynaptic neurons; no effort was made to eliminate the activation of interneurons, etc. With time, a continuous effort has been made to reduce the system to a two-cell system by attempting to restrict the presynaptic stimulation to a single presynaptic fiber, by recording the postsynaptic response in a single neuron, and by using pharmacological antagonists to eliminate GABAergic inhibitory synapses from the circuit.

Despite this effort, one may wonder if LTP (and LTD for that matter) does not actually require more than two cells. Stimulating a single presynaptic fiber does not exclude the activation of more than one postsynaptic neuron, and postsynaptic neurons can interact (Bonhoeffer et al. 1989); glial contributions have not been excluded; the participation of non-GABAergic interneurons could be considered. The complexities of the intact system are substantial. Is this complexity to "blame" for the inability of numerous excellent laboratories to replicate reliably one anothers' results? One possibility is that although investigators think they are conducting identical experiments, subtle differences in techniques introduce vagaries into the system. In view of this possibility, we agreed that a welcome event would be an experimental congress, where multiple laboratories could work alongside one another, hopefully resolving the sources of conflict. An alternative is that the system, despite its virtues, is too complex for it to be possible for investigators to do the same experiment.

A clear-cut answer could be provided if there existed a well-documented example in which LTP had been observed between two cells in culture under conditions rigorously excluding other influences. The autaptic synapses described by Bekkers and Stevens do not show LTP, but LTP has been seen in primary hippocampal cultures at nonautaptic sites (C.F. Stevens, pers. comm.). However, even these "simplified systems" do not exclude the activity of interneurons. Hirano has reported the presence of LTD in a two- and three-cell system, but the process he described does not resemble that observed in slices or in the whole brain (REF). This could mean that cultured neurons lack some key properties required for LTD (and LTP), or that simply a two-cell system cannot express LTD (LTP). If so, what are the missing components?

The group felt that, despite obvious experimental difficulties, it would be worthwhile to continue the search for a two-cell system producing synaptic plasticity. The use of slices and the attempt to identify visually (and record from) a single presynaptic and a postsynaptic neuron are among the possible directions of such a search. Another direction consists of searching for such pairs in cultured neurons (recognizing that culturing neurons at low density is not an easy task). Finally, the group discussed the possible use of genetically engineered cell lines. Unfortunately, at present there does not exist any cell line having either the required properties for a glutamatergic presynaptic element or bearing an adequate set of postsynaptic receptors.

In desperation, we reductionists called for the two oocyte-synapse model. One oocyte would be compelled to express the appropriate array of presynaptic genes encoding the ion channels, transporters, all the enzymes of the messenger cascades, and synaptic vesicles complete with modifiable synaptic vesicle proteins, and (of course) containing glutamate. The other oocyte would express the perfect complement of postsynaptic genes—encoding NMDA and non-NMDA receptors, second messenger cascades, and the appropriate array of ion channels. And, oh yes, if the oocytes could be cuboidal, it would greatly facilitate pushing them together to form the perfect, plastic CA1-pseudo synapse which would be suitable for study.

REFERENCES

Bailey, C.H., and M. Chen. 1991. Morphological aspects of synaptic plasticity in *Aplysia*. An anatomical substrate for long-term memory. *Ann. NY Acad. Sci.* **627**:181–196.

Betz, W.J., G.S. Bewick, and R.M. Ridge. 1992. Intracellular movements of fluorescently labeled synaptic vesicles in frog motor nerve terminals during nerve stiumlation. *Neuron* **9**:805–813.

Bonhoeffer, T., V. Staiger, and A. Aertsen. 1989. Synaptic plasticity in rat hippocampal slice cultures: Local "Hebbian" conjunction of pre- and postsynaptic stimulation leads to synaptic enhancement. *Proc. Natl. Acad. Sci. USA* **86**:8113–8117.

Calverly, R.K., and D.G. Jones. 1990. Contributions of dendritic spines and perforated synapses to synaptic plasticity. *Brain Res. Rev.* **15**:215–249.

Clements, J.D., R.A.J. Lester, G. Tong, C.E. Jahr, and G.L. Westbrook. 1992. The time course of glutamate in the synaptic cleft. *Science* **258**:1498–1501.

Edwards, F.A., A. Konnerth, and B. Sakmann. 1990. Quantal analysis of inhibitory synaptic transmission in the dentate gyrus of rat hippocampal slices: A patch-clamp study. *J. Physiol.* **430**:213–249.

Freedman, R., C. Wetmore, I. Stromberg, S. Leonard, and L. Olson. 1993. α-bungarotoxin binding to hippocampal interneurons: Immunocytochemical characterization and effects on growth factor expression. *J. Neurosci.* **13**:1965–1975.

Green, W.N., A.F. Ross, and T. Claudio. 1991. Acetylcholine receptor assembly is stimulated by phosphorylation of its gamma subunit. *Neuron* **7**:659–666.

Greengard, P., J. Jen, A.C. Nairn, and C.F. Stevens. 1991. Enhancement of the glutamate response by cAMP-dependent protein kinase in hippocampal neurons. *Science* **253**:1135–1138.

Greenough, W.T., and C.H. Bailey. 1988. The anatomy of a memory: Convergence of results across a diversity of tests. *Trends Neurosci.* **11**:142–147.

Hasty, P., R. Ramirez-Solis, R. Krumlauf, and A. Bradley. 1991. Induction of a subtle mutation into the Hox-2.6 locus in embryonic stem cells. *Nature* **350:**243–246.

Hawkins, R.D., E.R. Kandel, and S.A. Siegelbaum. 1993. Learning to modulate transmitter release: Themes and variations in synaptic plasticity. *Ann. Rev. Neurosci.* **16**:625–665.

Hille, B. 1992. G-protein-coupled mechanisms and nervous signaling. *Neuron* **9**:187–195.

Jonas, P., and B. Sakmann. 1992. Glutamate receptor channels in isolated patches from CA1 and CA3 pyramidal cells of rat hippocampal slices. *J. Physiol.* **455**:143–171.

Kelly, R.B. 1993. Storage and release of neurotransmitters. *Rev. Supp. Cell* 72/*Neuron* 10:43–53.

Koenig, J.H., and K. Ikeda. 1989. Disappearance and reformation of synaptic vesicle membrane retrieval. *J. Neurosci.* **9**:3844–3860.

Larkman, A., T. Hannay, K. Stratford, and J. Jack. 1992. Presynaptic release probability influences the locus of long-term potentiation. *Nature* **360**:70–73.

Lena, C., J.-P. Changeux, and C. Mulle. 1993. Evidence for "preterminal" nicotinic receptors on GABAergic axons in the rat interpeduncular nucleus. *J. Neurosci.* **13**:2680–2688.

Levitan, I. 1988. Modulation of ion channels in neurons and other cells. *Ann. Rev. Neurosci.* **11**:119–136.

Listerud, M., A.B. Brussaard, P. Devay, D.R. Colman, and L.W. Role. 1991. Functional contribution of neuronal AChR subunits revealed by antisense oligonucleotides. *Science* **254**:1518–1521.

Lupica, C.R., W.R. Proctor, and T.V. Dunwiddie. 1992. Presynaptic inhibition of excitatory synaptic transmission by adenosine in rat hippocampus: Analysis of unitary EPSP. Variance measured by whole-cell recording. *J. Neurosci.* **12**:3753–3764.

Madison, D.V., R.C. Malenka, and R.A. Nicoll. 1991. Mechanisms underlying long-term potentiation of synaptic transmission. *Ann. Rev. Neurosci.* **14**:379–397.

Moss, B.L., and L.W. Role. 1993. Enhanced ACh sensitivity is accompanied by changes in ACh receptor channel properties and segregation of ACh receptor subtypes on sympathetic neurons during innervation *in vivo*. *J. Neurosci.* **13:** 13–28.

Nestler, E.J., and P. Greengard. 1982. Nerve impulses increase the phosphorylation state of protein I in rabbit superior cervical ganglion. *Nature* **296**:452–454.

Oberdick, J., R.J. Smeyne, J.R. Mann, S. Zackson, and J.L. Morgan. 1990. A promoter that drives transgene expression in cerebellar Purkinje and retinal bipolar neurons. *Science* **248**:223–226.

Regehr, W.G., and D.W. Tank. 1991. The maintenance of LTP at hippocampal mossy fiber synapses is independent of sustained presynaptic calcium. *Neuron* **7**:451–459.

Stanley, E.F. 1991. Single calcium channels on a cholinergic presynaptic nerve terminal. *Neuron* **7**:585–591.

Stevens, C.F. 1993. Quantal release of neurotransmitter and long-term potentiation. *Rev. Supp. Cell* 72/*Neuron* **10**:55–63.

Thompson, S.M., M. Capogna, and M. Scanziani. 1993. Presynaptic inhibition in the hippocampus. *Trends Neurosci.* **16**:222–227.

Trussell, L.O., and G.D. Fischbach. 1989. Glutamate receptor desensitization and its role in synaptic transmission. *Neuron* **3**:209–218.

Author Index

Subject Index

Notes: Page references in *italics* refer to figures; those in **bold** refer to Tables; LTD = long-term depression; LTP = long-term potentiation

Index compiled by Annette Musker